S0-AVD-225

THE WELLNESS NUTRITION COUNTER

BY SHELDON MARGEN, M.D.

and the Editors of the
University of California at Berkeley
WELLNESS LETTER

REBUS
NEW YORK

University of California at Berkeley

The Wellness Nutrition Counter

The Essential Guide to
Complete Nutritional Information
For Over 6,000 Foods & Products

THE UNIVERSITY OF CALIFORNIA AT BERKELEY WELLNESS LETTER

The *Wellness Letter* is a monthly eight-page newsletter that delivers brisk, useful coverage on health, nutrition and exercise topics in language that is clear, engaging and nontechnical. It's a unique resource that covers fundamental ways to prevent illness. For information on how to order this award-winning newsletter from the world-famous School of Public Health at the University of California at Berkeley, write to Health Letter Associates, Department 1108, 632 Broadway, New York, NY 10012.

This book was created and produced by
Rebus, Inc.
New York, NY

For information about permission to reproduce selections from this book, write to Permissions, Health Letter Associates,
632 Broadway,New York, NY 10012

Library of Congress Cataloging-in-Publication Data

Margen, Sheldon.
The Wellness nutrition counter : the essential guide to complete nutritional information on over 6,000 foods & products / by Sheldon Margen and the editors of the University of California at Berkeley wellness letter.
p. cm.
Includes index.
ISBN 0-929661-38-9
1. Food—Composition—Tables. 2. Nutrition—Tables.
I. University of California, Berkeley, wellness letter. II. Title.
TX551.M23 1997 97-17959
613.2'8—dc21 CIP

Printed in the United States of America
00 10 9 8 7 6 5 4 3 2 1

This book is not intended as a substitute for medical advice. Readers who suspect they may have specific medical problems should consult a physician about any suggestions made in this book.

The nutritional information listed in the Brand Name Foods section of this book was provided by the food manufacturers. The publisher would like to thank these companies for supplying this data and for giving us permission to use it in this book.

THE UNIVERSITY OF CALIFORNIA
LET THERE BE LIGHT
1868

CONTENTS

FOODS, BRAND NAME 224

INDEX 430

BASICS OF A HEALTHY DIET

The ideal diet supplies the right balance of nutrients to meet your daily needs and promote good health. It is low in fat, rich in complex carbohydrates and fiber, and contains just enough calories to meet your energy needs. It provides enough of each vitamin and mineral to perform essential functions and a bit extra to add to reserves, but not enough of any nutrient to cause side effects or interfere with the absorption of other nutrients.

Unfortunately, few people's diets meet these ideals. A reliance on processed foods, combined with a national preference for high-fat, high-sugar foods and simple confusion over what makes up a healthy diet leaves many people falling short on several of the dietary recommendations. *The Wellness Nutrition Counter* can help you "shape up" an unbalanced diet.

This introduction provides an overview of nutrition and presents guidelines for you to follow in order to maintain a healthy diet. Once you understand what you should be eating and why, the rest of this book can help you determine where various foods fit into your daily meals. The first section, *Vitamins and Minerals,* discusses the functions of the vitamins and minerals, how much of each one you need, and which foods supply them. The next two sections, *Foods, General* and *Foods, Brand Name* will help you evaluate the nutritional content of more than 6,000 foods by supplying detailed information on calories, fat, protein, vitamins, minerals, and more.

The building blocks of nutrition

Foods are made of macronutrients, micronutrients, water, and non-nutrients, such as fiber. The macronutrients—carbohydrates, fats, and protein—are so named because they are present in foods and needed by the body in large amounts. Most foods contain a combination of at least two macronutrients—and sometimes all three—but one macronutrient tends to predominate. Take dried beans and ground beef, for example. Both supply about the same amount of protein per serving; but the beans contain about twice as much carbohydrates as protein, whereas ground beef typically contains about equal amounts of protein and fat.

Vitamins and minerals are classified as micronutrients because the body needs only very small amounts—so small, in fact that the requirements for some vitamins are given in micrograms, one-millionth of a gram (there are approximately 28 grams to an ounce).

Water makes up 85 to 96 percent of the weight in foods. Even foods that you might not think

How nutrients are measured

- The energy in foods is measured in *calories,* or more accurately *kilocalories* or *kcalories.* The caloric content of a food is determined by measuring the amount of heat produced when the food is burned in a laboratory device called a calorimeter. The heat that is generated is analogous to the energy produced in the human body.
- Protein, fat, carbohydrates, and fiber are measured in *grams* (g). These units are so small that it takes 28.33 grams to make up one ounce. These nutrients (with the exception of fiber) provide energy (calories). A gram of protein or carbohydrate contains 4 calories; a gram of fat contains 9 calories.
- Calcium, iron, thiamin, niacin, riboflavin, vitamin C , vitamin E, and cholesterol are measured in *milligrams* (mg), or thousandths of a gram: 1,000 milligrams equals 1 gram. Other vitamins and minerals are measured in *micrograms* (mcg), or millionths of a gram.
- Vitamin A and Vitamin D are measured in *international units* (IU), which is a measure of the activity of fat-soluble vitamins. (Vitamin E is also sometimes measured in IU.) Vitamin A may also be measured in *retinol equivalents* (RE), which is a more accurate measurement since it is based on weight. One IU of vitamin A is equal to 0.3 RE. We use RE in this book, but be aware that some food tables still use IU.

of as being predominately water, such as meats, in fact contain significant amounts. The body requires considerable quantities of water for good health. All cell processes and organ functions depend on it.

The macronutrients provide you with energy and help maintain and repair the body. Vitamins regulate chemical processes. Minerals assist in this, and play a role in body maintenance as well, notably in the formation of new tissue, including bones, teeth, and blood. Water provides a fluid medium for all chemical reactions in the body, and for the circulation of blood and the removal of waste. Below are descriptions of each macronutrient, and of vitamins and minerals in general. Starting on page 28, you will find descriptions of the individual vitamins and minerals.

Carbohydrates

Starches and sugars, collectively known as carbohydrates, are the body's primary fuel. The carbohydrates we eat are broken down mainly into glucose, a simple sugar, or into other simple sugars. Glucose is released into the bloodstream, where it is picked up by the cells to use for energy. Excess glucose is either converted to glycogen and stored in limited amounts by the liver and muscles, or is turned into body fat. Glycogen in the liver can be changed back to glucose when the need arises.

Carbohydrates are often referred to as simple or complex. Sugars—such as glucose, sucrose (table sugar), lactose, and fructose—are called simple carbohydrates because they are made up of short chains of chemical units called saccharides. (See page 10 for more on sugar.) Complex carbohydrates—or starches—are simply longer chains of saccharide units. Fiber (see page 10) is also considered a complex carbohydrate, although it has no energy value (calories).

Nutritionists recommend that complex carbohydrates predominate in your diet. Grains, legumes, and vegetables are rich in complex carbohydrates, and also provide dietary fiber, vitamins, and minerals. Experts generally recommend that 60 to 70 percent of your daily calories come from carbohydrates.

FIBER

Fiber, the indigestible parts of plants, is not one substance, but a variety of compounds. There are two general types of fiber: insoluble and soluble. Insoluble fiber helps prevent constipation (when consumed with adequate fluid intake) by adding bulk to the stool. In addition, this type of fiber may play a role in preventing colon cancer, either by speeding food through the intestinal tract (thus reducing the time potential carcinogens come into contact with the colon wall) or by diluting or inactivating the carcinogens in some way.

Soluble fiber helps lower blood cholesterol levels and therefore reduces the risk of heart disease. It also helps keep blood glucose (sugar) levels in check, and so is beneficial in the treatment of diabetes. Both types of fiber can help promote weight loss because high-fiber foods are filling (so you eat less of them) and tend to be low in fat.

Experts recommend that you get 20 to 30 grams of fiber a day from a variety of foods. Insoluble fiber is found primarily in wheat, especially in wheat bran, and in other whole grains. Soluble fiber is found primarily in vegetables, fruits, legumes, barley, brown rice, oats, and oat bran.

SUGAR

Like other carbohydrates, sugar is used by the body for fuel. When most people talk about sugar, however, they are usually referring to table sugar (sucrose). In fact, there are many other forms of sugar, including fructose (found in fruit) and lactose (found in milk). Honey, corn syrup, molasses, and maple syrup are other sugar sources. Some people claim that these sugars behave differently in the body than pure sucrose, but no scientific studies have shown this to be the case. No sugar has a nutritional advantage over the others, and they all have the same amount of calories, four per gram (like all other carbohydrates).

If all sugars are the same, then why is an orange considered better for you than a candy bar? Simply because the orange provides nutritional benefits in the form of vitamins, minerals, and dietary fiber. The candy bar contains few nutrients and is packed with fat that can clog the arteries and expand the waistline. Still, there is no reason to ban sugar from your diet. As long as most of your carbohydrate intake is in the form of complex carbohydrates (starches and dietary fiber), sugar can be part of a healthy diet.

FATS

Fats are essential to the proper functioning of the human body. Technically fats belong to a class of substances called lipids. Unlike carbohydrates, fats are insoluble in water. Most of the fats in foods are triglycerides, which consist of three fatty acids attached to a glycerol molecule. Some of

Leading Sources of Fiber

Food	Calories	Fiber (g)	Fiber per oz
Wheat bran, crude —*½ cup*	63	12.4	12.1
Apricots, dried, sulfured —*1 cup*	309	11.7	2.6
Pears, asian —*1 medium*	116	9.9	1.0
Avocados, california —*1 medium*	306	8.5	1.4
Raspberries, fresh —*1 cup*	60	8.4	1.9
Bulgur, ckd —*1 cup*	151	8.2	1.3
Kidney beans, ckd —*½ cup*	109	8.2	2.6
Split peas, ckd —*½ cup*	116	8.1	2.4
Lentils, ckd —*½ cup*	115	7.8	2.2
Blackberries, fresh —*1 cup*	75	7.6	1.5
Rye wafers —*3 crackers*	110	7.6	6.5
Sunflower seed kernels, dried —*½ cup*	410	7.6	3.0
Wheat germ, crude —*½ cup*	207	7.6	3.7
Apples, dried, sulfured —*1 cup*	209	7.5	2.5
Black beans, ckd —*½ cup*	114	7.5	2.5
Pinto beans, ckd —*½ cup*	117	7.4	2.4
Lima beans, baby, ckd —*½ cup*	115	7.0	2.2
Corn pasta, ckd —*1 cup*	176	6.7	1.4
Navy beans, canned —*½ cup*	148	6.7	1.5
Artichoke, fresh, boiled —*1 medium*	60	6.5	1.5
Baked beans, vegetarian, canned —*½ cup*	118	6.4	1.4
Spaghetti, whole-wheat, ckd —*1 cup*	174	6.3	1.3
White beans, canned —*½ cup*	153	6.3	1.4
Barley, pearled, ckd —*1 cup*	193	6	1
Oat bran, ckd —*1 cup*	88	6	0.7
Chickpeas (garbanzo beans), canned —*½ cup*	143	5.3	1.3
Potatoes, fresh, baked, w/skin —*1 potato*	220	4.9	0.7
Pita bread, whole-wheat —*1 large*	170	4.7	2.1
Figs, dried —*¼ cup*	127	4.6	2.6
Buckwheat, groats, roasted, ckd —*1 cup*	155	4.5	0.8
Lima beans, fresh, boiled —*½ cup*	105	4.5	1.5
Squash, winter, acorn, fresh, baked, cubes —*½ cup*	57	4.5	1.3
Tangerines —*1 medium*	86	4.5	0.7
Peas, green, fresh, boiled —*½ cup*	67	4.4	1.6
Oatmeal, reg/quick/instant, ckd —*1 cup*	145	4	0.5
Pears, fresh —*1 medium*	98	4	0.7
Almonds, dry roasted, unblanched —*1 oz*	166	3.9	3.9
Blueberries, fresh —*1 cup*	81	3.9	0.8
Whole-wheat hot natural cereal, ckd —*1 cup*	150	3.9	0.5
Apples, fresh, whole —*1 medium*	81	3.7	0.8
Carrots, fresh, raw, slices —*1 cup*	52	3.7	0.9
Pumpkin, canned —*½ cup*	42	3.6	0.8
Rice, brown, ckd —*1 cup*	216	3.5	0.5
Strawberries, fresh, halves —*1 cup*	46	3.5	0.7
Cauliflower, green, fresh, boiled —*3 ½ oz*	100	3.4	0.9
Oranges, navel —*1 orange*	64	3.4	0.7
Sweet potato, fresh, baked —*1 medium*	117	3.4	0.9
Cherries, sweet, fresh —*1 cup*	32	3.3	0.6
Matzo, whole-wheat —*1 cracker*	104	3.3	3.3
Peaches, dried, halves —*¼ cup*	96	3.3	2.3

How much fat?

Use the chart below to determine the maximum number of grams of fat you should consume per day to maintain a 20% or a 30% fat diet.

Calorie intake	Grams of fat per day	
	20% calories	*30% calories*
1200	27	40
1500	33	50
1800	40	60
2000	44	66
2500	56	83

the fatty acids are called "essential" fatty acids, so named because the body cannot make them and must get them from foods. Fatty acids are the raw materials for several hormonelike compounds, including prostaglandins, that help control blood pressure, blood clotting, inflammation, and other bodily functions. Fats perform many other important functions. They serve as the storage substance for the body's excess calories, filling the balloonlike adipose cells that insulate the body. Extra calories from carbohydrates and proteins, as well as from fats, are stored as body fat. The body begins to rely more on fats and less on carbohydrates for energy after about 20 to 30 minutes of continual activity (such as brisk walking or cycling). In addition, fats help maintain healthy skin and hair, transport the fat-soluble vitamins (A, D, E, and K) through the gastrointestinal tract and bloodstream, and regulate blood cholesterol levels.

All fats are combinations of saturated and unsaturated fatty acids, and depending on their proportions, may be highly saturated or highly unsaturated. These fatty acids vary in length of the molecular chain and degree of saturation by hydrogen atoms, and it is these variations that determine the properties of different fats.

Saturated fatty acids are loaded with all the hydrogen atoms they can carry. Fats that are largely saturated are usually solid at room temperature. Such fats come chiefly from animal sources—meats, poultry, and whole-milk dairy products. Three vegetable oils—coconut, palm, and palm kernel—are also highly saturated.

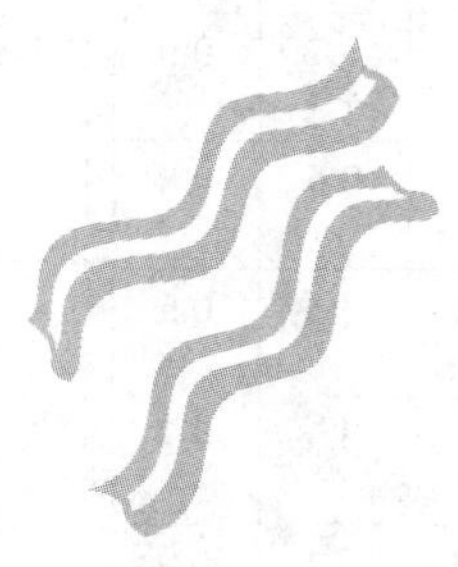

Unsaturated fatty acids do not have all the hydrogen atoms they can carry. Depending on the number of missing hydrogen atoms, these fatty acids are called either monounsaturated (olive, canola, peanut, and avocado oils are largely monounsaturated) or polyunsaturated (corn, safflower, and sesame oils are primarily polyunsaturated). These important dietary fats come from plants and fish. They are generally liquid at room temperature.

A diet high in saturated fat can raise blood cholesterol levels, which increases the risk of heart disease. This does not mean, however, that it is healthy to have a diet high in unsaturated fats: since all fats contain 9 calories per gram (versus 4 calories per gram in carbohydrates and protein), too much of any kind of fat increases your chance of becoming overweight or obese, which is another risk factor for cardiovascular disease. Therefore, experts recommend that you get no more than 30 percent of your daily calories from fat, and that no more than one-third of those fat calories should come from saturated fat. Some doctors believe that a 30 percent fat diet is still too much fat, and suggest that you lower your fat intake to 20 percent of calories. Your decision as to whether to go that low should depend on several things: your weight, your personal and family risk for heart disease, and your blood cholesterol level.

Cholesterol

Although cholesterol performs many essential functions in the body, the cholesterol from foods is not an essential nutrient. The human body can make all the cholesterol it needs from the dietary fats. Too much cholesterol in the bloodstream increases the risk of developing atherosclerosis—clogged arteries that can lead to heart attack or stroke. Surprisingly, there does not seem to be a simple relationship between dietary cholesterol and blood cholesterol levels. Researchers theorize that only about 20 to 30 percent of the population is genetically hypersensitive to dietary cholesterol—that is, their blood cholesterol levels increase when they eat high-cholesterol foods. There is no simple test for cholesterol hypersensitivity, but experts still recommend that healthy people consume no more than 300 milligrams of cholesterol per day. Cholesterol is found only in animal products. The richest sources are organ meats (such as liver), egg yolk, and shrimp.

Protein

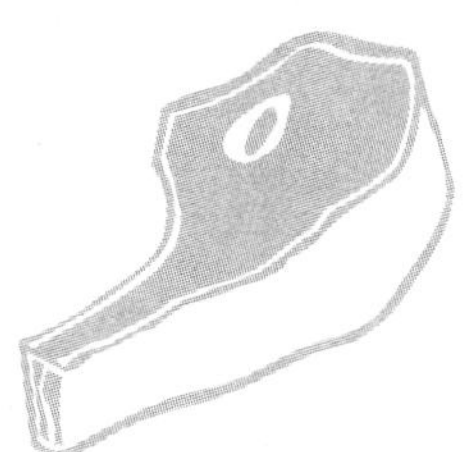

Muscles, organs, antibodies, some hormones, and all enzymes (the compounds that direct cell chemical reactions) are largely composed of protein. Yet protein is not a single, simple substance, but a multitude of chemical combinations. The basic units of proteins are amino acids. Just 22 amino acids are combined in a variety of ways to create the thousands of different types of proteins that the body uses to build muscles, organs, hormones, and enzymes. The body can manufacture the majority of amino acids on its own; these are called "nonessential" amino acids.

The other nine amino acids are called "essential" because they must come from foods. Foods that contain all of the essential amino acids in sufficient amounts are called complete; those that are missing one or more amino acid are called incomplete. All animal proteins—meats, poultry, fish, dairy products, and eggs—are complete proteins.

Plant proteins are incomplete proteins, with the exception of soy beans and soy products like tofu, which are complete. Foods that provide incomplete proteins can be made complete by eating (either at the same meal or within the same day) a complementary protein that provides the amino acids that the other food lacks. Rice and beans, peanut butter and bread, and macaroni and cheese are traditional combinations that provide complementary proteins.

In general, experts recommend that everyone get 12 to 15 percent of their calories from protein. Most Americans consume more protein than that. Some sports physiologists believe that athletes and body builders need more protein because their bodies break down and rebuild body tissue at a higher rate, and because they have more muscle mass. However, simply by eating more food, athletes will get more protein without increasing the percentage of protein in their diet.

Water

We can live for several weeks without the nutrients in foods, but without water we would die in a few days. More than half the weight of the human body is water, which is the basis of all body fluids, including digestive juices, blood, urine, lymph, and perspiration. It is essential as a lubricant, and it is the major component of saliva, mucous secretions throughout the body, and the fluids that bathe the joints. Water helps move food through the digestive system. It also helps regulate body temperature by distributing heat and cooling the body via perspiration.

The body loses two to three quarts of water a day. If you exercise or do heavy physical work, especially in the heat, the loss is greater. It is essential to replace this water. Some of our water needs are met through the liquids in the foods we eat, but most people need an additional six to eight glasses of water or other liquid per day—juice, milk, or soup. Alcoholic and caffeinated beverages (coffee, tea, and cola) are not ideal for this purpose because they have a diuretic effect, that is, they increase urine production, which leads to a greater loss of water.

To replace the fluids you lose during prolonged intense exercise, drink four to eight ounces of fluid, preferably water, every 10 to 20 minutes during your workout, and drink about eight ounces after you've finished. In hot weather, you should also drink 16 to 20 ounces of fluid two hours before exercising, and another eight ounces 15 to 20 minutes before you start to work out.

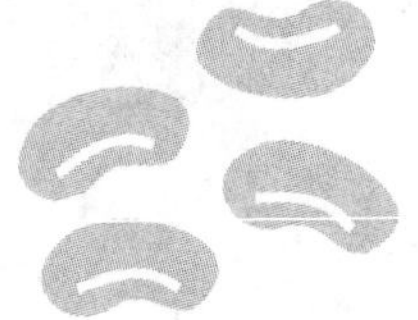

VITAMINS

A vitamin is an organic substance (meaning it contains carbon) that your body requires in order to help regulate functions within cells. For the most part, vitamins must be obtained from food. Exceptions are vitamin D, which the body can synthesize, and to some extent vitamin K, which the body can produce from bacteria that normally inhabit the intestines. Vitamins affect all functions in the body. Only very small amounts are needed, but these tiny amounts are absolutely essential.

Vitamins can be categorized as either fat-soluble (A, D, E, and K) or water-soluble (the B vitamins—biotin, folic acid, pantothenic acid, niacin, thiamin, riboflavin, B_6 and B_{12}—and vitamin C). The distinction is important because the body stores fat-soluble vitamins for relatively long periods (usually in the liver and body fat tissue), whereas water-soluble vitamins, which are stored in various tissues, remain in the body for only a relatively short time and so need to be replenished frequently (except for vitamin B_{12}). Otherwise, symptoms associated with deficiencies of water-soluble vitamins can occur within weeks or months.

MINERALS

Minerals are basic elements of the earth's crust. In contrast to vitamins, they are inorganic—they contain no carbon. Minerals are involved in a host of vital processes in the body, from bone formation to the functioning of the heart and digestive system. Many are necessary for the activity of enzymes (proteins that serve as catalysts in the body's chemical reactions). There are more than 60 minerals in the body (making up about 4 percent of its weight), but only about 22 are considered essential. Of these, seven—calcium, chlorine, magnesium, phosphorus, potassium, sodium, and sulfur—are called macro-minerals because they are present in the body in relatively large quantities. The other essential minerals are termed trace or even ultratrace nutrients because they are present in such minute quantities.

Preparation and Cooking
Preserving Nutrients in Fruits and Vegetables

If you are careless in your preparation and cooking of fruits and vegetables, you can significantly reduce the nutritional value of your meal. Nutrient loss occurs when produce is exposed to heat, light and air, or is soaked or cooked in large amounts of water. The water-soluble vitamins—B vitamins and vitamin C—are more susceptible to destruction. Fat-soluble vitamins are more stable. Minerals are virtually indestructible, but they may leech into cooking or soaking water, so if the water is discarded the minerals are lost. To preserve vitamins and minerals, follow the guidelines below:

- *Don't wash, chop, or slice fruits or vegetables until you are ready to use them.*
- *Don't soak produce in water to clean it; this may leech out water-soluble vitamins. Instead, quickly but thoroughly rinse fruits and vegetables under cold running water. Use a soft brush to remove dirt that clings.*
- *Many nutrients are concentrated just beneath the skin of many fruits and vegetables. Cook vegetables such as potatoes and beets in their skins and peel them after cooking, when their thick skins will slip off. Even if you do not eat the skin, leaving it intact during cooking helps preserve nutrients. Peel other vegetables, such as carrots, thinly—or simply scrub them with a soft brush under cold running water.*
- *Cook vegetables whole, or in large pieces rather than diced or finely sliced or chopped.*
- *Steam or microwave vegetables till just crisp-tender. These methods preserve the most nutrients. Long boiling of vegetables will cause most of the vitamin C and other water-soluble vitamins to leech into the cooking liquid. Plus, vitamin C and thiamin are easily destroyed by heat. If you prefer to boil, do so in a small amount of water, and be sure not to overcook.*

Antioxidants

Antioxidants are chemical substances that help protect the body from the adverse effects of oxygen. Oxygen is necessary for energy generation, and cells will die within minutes without it. But the chemical changes that take place when the body uses oxygen create unstable oxygen molecules called free radicals, which can damage cells and structures within the cells, including genetic material. Free radicals may be formed in response to external factors such as: heat; radiation (such as ultraviolet light and X-rays); alcohol; cigarette smoke; and certain pollutants. In addition, the cells themselves, without any aggravating environmental factors, produce their own free radicals. If the genetic material is damaged by free radicals and is not totally repaired, the damaged DNA is replicated in new cells. This can lead to the development of tumors and other health problems.

However, just as our cells have methods of fighting infectious agents, they also have orderly systems for battling free radicals and repairing molecular damage—systems that quench or inactivate dangerous molecular by-products and mend the molecular defects. The free-radical fighters are called antioxidants. Some antioxidants are enzymes and other compounds manufactured by the cells themselves, Others are nutrients that we eat—namely vitamin C, vitamin E, and beta carotene. Other carotenoids (the yellow/orange/red pigments in fruits and vegetables) may also have antioxidant activity, as may other substances in foods.

By neutralizing free radicals, antioxidants can protect against cancer, heart disease, and cataracts. Antioxidants may play a protective role against other diseases, such as diabetic retinopathy (which can lead to blindness), AIDS, arthritis, and Parkinson's disease, but research is still preliminary.

PHYTOCHEMICALS

During the past few years, researchers have uncovered many chemicals in foods that have no nutritional value in the traditional sense, but can affect the body in various ways. These compounds are referred to by some scientists as "phytochemicals" (from the Latin *phyto,* referring to plant life) and include carotenoids, isoflavones, and indoles. Many of these substances are now being investigated for potential anti-cancer and heart-protective effects. These are being studied in such foods as broccoli, citrus fruits, soybeans, and strawberries. The chart below lists some of the phytochemicals discovered and the foods in which they are found.

FOOD SOURCES OF PHYTOCHEMICALS

Phytochemicals are found in many foods, and work singly and together to lower the risk of disease. The chart below lists the phytochemicals that currently show the most disease-protective promise and the foods that contain them.

Phytochemical	Possible Action	Food Sources
Allylic sulfides	May protect against heart disease, and cancer. May boost immune function.	Garlic and onions
Flavonoids	May protect against heart disease and cancer.	Citrus fruits, apples, tomatoes, onions, green tea, and wine
Genistein	May block the formation of new blood vessels, which are necessary for tumor growth.	Soybeans and soy products (tofu, soy milk)
Indoles	Stimulate production of anticarcinogenic enzymes and may help protect against breast cancer by converting the active form of estrogen, which possibly trigger the growth of breast tumors, to a safer, inactive form.	Broccoli, cabbage, Brussels sprouts, and other members of the cabbage family.
Isoflavones	May inhibit estrogen production	Soybeans and soy products (tofu, soy milk)
Polyphenols	May have an antioxidant effect. May inhibit nitrosamine production, which helps protect against stomach and esophageal cancers.	Green tea
Sulforaphane	Stimulate production of enzymes that may neutralize carcinogens and help remove them from the body.	Broccoli, cabbage, Brussels sprouts, kale, carrots, and scallions.

Nutrient needs

In the United States, recommendations for the amounts of vitamins and minerals you need to maintain good health are set by the Food and Nutrition Board of the National Research Council, a committee funded in part by the federal government. This group, made up of scientists from many specialties, evaluates the current research on nutrition to establish estimates of nutrient needs for protein, carbohydrates, fats, energy (calories), eleven vitamins, and seven minerals. These recommendations are called the Recommended Dietary Allowances, or RDAs. In addition, the committee has established a range of "safe and adequate intakes" for some vitamins and mineral for which insufficient scientific evidence exists to establish an RDA.

The RDAs are designed to apply to healthy individuals; different levels are given for men, women, and children, and for different age groups, as well as for pregnant and lactating women. The RDAs are revised periodically to include any new information about human nutrient needs. Each entry in this book's section on vitamins and minerals gives the RDA or the estimated safe and adequate dietary intake for adult men and women. A complete list of the RDAs and the estimated safe and adequate dietary intakes for all groups can be found in the charts on pages 18–19.

On food labels, the nutrient content of foods is expressed by the percentage of the Daily Value (DV) for a particular nutrient supplied by a serving of the food. The DV recommendations for vitamins and minerals are based on Reference Daily Intakes (RDIs). These values, which are basically the highest end of the RDA or estimated safe and adequate dietary intake values for adults, represent the nutrient needs of an average healthy person. The RDIs are listed in the chart at right.

It is important to remember that the RDAs and the RDIs are recommendations, not requirements. Individual dietary needs vary, and these values are set at a level assumed to cover the nutrient needs of most people, plus a generous margin of safety. Over a period of time, an intake well below the RDA may leave some people deficient in a particular nutrient; in some cases, a regular intake far in excess of the RDA may have unpleasant side effects or may even be toxic. On the other hand, many experts think the RDAs for some nutrients are too low. For example, the adult RDA for calcium is 800 milligrams, but leading researchers recommend consuming 1,000 milligrams or more, especially for women. Other nutrients for which the RDA may be set too low include vitamin C, vitamin E, and folic acid. The entries in the vitamin and mineral section point out discrepancies where they exist.

Reference Daily Intakes (RDIs)

The Reference Daily Intakes (RDIs) are the values that are the basis for the nutritional requirements listed on food labels. In most cases, they are the high end of the adult RDAs. However, the RDIs also take other guidelines into account. On food labels, values are given as a percentage of the RDI.

Biotin	200 mcg
Folic acid	400 mcg
Niacin	20 mg
Pantothenic acid	10 mg
Riboflavin	1.7 mg
Thiamin	1.5 mg
Vitamin A	5000 IU
Vitamin B_{12}	6 mg
Vitamin B_6	2 mg
Vitamin C	60 mg
Vitamin D	400 IU
Vitamin E	30 IU
Vitamin K	80 mcg
Calcium	1000 mg
Chloride	3400 mg
Copper	2 mg
Iodine	150 mcg
Iron	18 mg
Magnesium	400 mg
Manganese	2 mg
Molybdenum	75 mcg
Phosphorus	2000 mg
Selenium	70 mcg
Zinc	15 mg

RECOMMENDED DIETARY ALLOWANCES[a]

Category	Age	Weight[b] (lb)	Height[b] (in)	Protein (g)	Vitamin A (mcg RE)[c]	Vitamin D (mcg)[d]	Vitamin E (mg a-TE)[e]	Vitamin K (mcg)	Vitamin C (mg)	Thiamine (mg)
Infants	0-6 months	13	24	13	375	7.5	3	5	30	0.3
	6-12 months	20	28	14	375	10	4	10	35	0.4
Children	1-3	29	35	16	400	10	6	15	40	0.7
	4-6	44	44	24	500	10	7	20	45	0.9
	7-10	62	52	28	700	10	7	30	45	1.0
Males	11-14	99	62	45	1000	10	10	45	50	1.3
	15-18	145	69	59	1000	10	10	65	60	1.5
	19-24	160	70	58	1000	10	10	70	60	1.5
	25-50	174	70	63	1000	5	10	80	60	1.5
	51 plus	170	68	63	1000	5	10	80	60	1.2
Females	11-14	101	62	46	800	10	8	45	50	1.1
	15-18	120	64	44	800	10	8	55	60	1.1
	19-24	128	65	46	800	10	8	60	60	1.1
	25-50	138	64	50	800	5	8	65	60	1.1
	51 plus	143	63	50	800	5	8	65	60	1.0
Pregnant women				60	800	10	10	65	70	1.5
Lactating women	1st 6 months			65	1,300	10	12	65	95	1.6
	2nd 6 months			62	1,200	10	11	65	90	1.6

[a] *The allowances, expressed as average daily intakes over time, are intended to provide for individual variations among most normal persons as they live in the United States under usual environmental stresses. Diets should be based on a variety of common foods in order to provide other nutrients for which human requirements have been less well defined.*

[b] *Weights and heights of Reference Adults are actual medians for the U.S. population of the designated age. The use of these figures does not imply that the height-to-weight ratios are ideal.*

[c] *Retinol equivalents. 1 retinol equivalent= 1 mcg retinol or 6 mcg beta carotene. To calculate IU value: for fruits and vegetables, multiply the RE value by ten; for animal-source foods, multiply the RE value by 3.3.*

OTHER RECOMMENDED INTAKES

The following nutrients have no RDA or Estimated Safe and Adequate Daily Dietary Intake. Instead the daily recommendations listed below are based on guidelines established by various health organizations and experts.

Beta Carotene	5 to 6 milligrams
Cholesterol	no more than 300 milligrams
Dietary Fiber	20 to 30 grams
Potassium	3000 milligrams
Sodium	no more than 2400 milligrams

Riboflavin (mg)	Niacin (mg NE)[f]	Vitamin B_6 (mg)	Folate[g] (mcg)	Vitamin B_{12} (mcg)	Calcium (mg)	Phosphorus (mg)	Magnesium (mg)	Iron (mg)	Zinc (mg)	Iodine (mcg)	Selenium (mcg)
0.4	5	0.3	25	0.3	400	300	40	6	5	40	10
0.5	6	0.6	35	0.5	600	500	60	10	5	50	15
0.8	9	1.0	50	0.7	800	800	80	10	10	70	20
1.1	12	1.1	75	1.0	800	800	120	10	10	90	20
1.2	13	1.4	100	1.4	800	800	170	10	10	120	30
1.5	17	1.7	150	2.0	1200	1200	270	12	15	150	40
1.8	20	2.0	200	2.0	1200	1200	400	12	15	150	50
1.7	19	2.0	200	2.0	1200	1200	350	10	15	150	70
1.7	19	2.0	200	2.0	800	800	350	10	15	150	70
1.4	15	2.0	200	2.0	800	800	350	10	15	150	70
1.3	15	1.4	150	2.0	1200	1200	280	15	12	150	45
1.3	15	1.5	180	2.0	1200	1200	300	15	12	150	50
1.3	15	1.6	180	2.0	1200	1200	280	15	12	150	55
1.3	15	1.6	180	2.0	800	800	280	15	12	150	55
1.2	13	1.6	180	2.0	800	800	280	10	12	150	55
1.6	17	2.2	400	2.2	1200	1200	320	30	15	175	65
1.8	20	2.1	280	2.6	1200	1200	355	15	19	200	75
1.7	20	2.1	260	2.6	1200	1200	340	15	16	200	75

[d] *As cholecalciferol. 10 mcg cholecalciferol=400 IU of vitamin D.*

[e] *a-tocopherol equivalents. 1 mg d-a tocopherol=1 a-TE.*

[f] *1 NE (niacin equivalent) is equal to 1 mg of niacin or 60 mg of dietary tryptophan.*

[g] *Folacin/Folic Acid*

Estimated Safe and Adequate Daily Dietary Intakes of Selected Vitamins and Minerals[a]

		Vitamins		Trace Minerals[b]				
Category	Age	Biotin (mcg)	Pantothenic acid (mg)	Copper (mg)	Manganese (mg)	Fluoride (mg)	Chromium (mcg)	Molybdenum (mcg)
Infants	0-6 months	10	2	0.4-0.6	0.3-0.6	0.1-0.5	10-40	15-30
	6-12 months	15	3	0.6-0.7	0.6-1.0	0.2-1.0	20-60	20-40
Children and adolescents	1-3	20	3	0.7-1.0	1.0-1.5	0.5-1.5	20-80	25-50
	4-6	25	3-4	1.0-1.5	1.5-2.0	1.0-2.5	30-120	30-75
	7-10	30	4-5	1.0-2.0	2.0-3.0	1.5-2.5	50-200	50-150
	11 plus	30-100	4-7	1.5-2.5	2.0-5.0	1.5-2.5	50-200	75-250
Adults		30-100	4-7	1.5-3.0	2.0-5.0	1.5-4.0	50-200	75-250

[a] *Because there is less information on which to base allowances, these figures are not given in the main table of RDAs and are provided here in the form of ranges of recommended intakes.*

[b] *Since the toxic levels for many trace elements may be only several times usual intakes, the upper levels for the trace elements given in this table should not be habitually exceeded.*

15 keys to a healthy diet

How do you use this basic nutrition information to create into a healthful diet? It is not as difficult as it might seem. We've developed a straightforward set of guidelines for you to use as a blueprint for constructing a healthy diet. Alternatively, you could simply follow the recommendations of the United States Department of Agriculture (USDA) for planning daily menus. These recommendations are listed on page 21.

1. **Limit your total fat intake so that it supplies less than 30 percent of your total daily calories.** Choose only lean meats, light-meat poultry without the skin, fish, and low-fat dairy products. In addition, cut back on vegetable oils, margarine, and butter—or foods made with these—as well as on mayonnaise, salad dressings, and fried foods.
2. **Limit your intake of saturated fat to less than one-third of the calories derived from fat (10 percent of total calories).** A diet high in saturated fat contributes to high blood cholesterol levels. The richest sources of saturated fat are animal products and tropical vegetable oils, such as coconut or palm.
3. **Keep your cholesterol intake below 300 milligrams per day.** Cholesterol is found only in animal products—meats, poultry, dairy products, and egg yolks.
4. **Eat foods rich in complex carbohydrates.** Carbohydrates should supply at least 55 percent of your total daily calories. To meet this requirement, eat plenty of fruits and vegetables and six or more servings of grains (preferably whole grains) or legumes daily. This will help you obtain the 20 to 30 grams of dietary fiber you need each day.
5. **Be sure to include green, orange, and yellow fruit, and vegetables**—such as broccoli, carrots, cantaloupe, and citrus fruits. The nutrients and phytochemicals in these foods are regarded as increasingly important in helping protect against certain types of cancer and other diseases. Eat five to nine servings of fruits and vegetables a day.
6. **Avoid excessive amounts of sugar.** Besides contributing to tooth decay, sugar is a source of "empty" calories, and many foods that are high in sugar are also high in fat.
7. **Maintain a moderate protein intake.** Protein should make up 12 to 15 percent of your total daily calories. Choose low-fat sources, such as legumes and skinless light-meat poultry, rather than red meat.
8. **Eat a variety of foods.** Don't try to fill your nutrient requirements by eating the same foods day in, day out. Eating a wide assortment of foods helps ensure that you will get all the necessary nutrients. In addition, this will limit your exposure to any pesticides or toxic substances that may be present in one particular food.
9. **Limit your sodium intake to no more than 2,400 milligrams per day.** This is equivalent to the amount of sodium in a little more than a teaspoon of salt. Cut back on your use of salt in cooking and at the table and eat fewer salty foods, such as cheese, chips, olives, tomato juice, luncheon meats, and pickles. Be sure to check sodium levels on the nutrition labels of processed foods.

Daily Food Guide

Nutrient and calorie needs vary from person to person, depending on age, sex, body size, and level of physical activity. The chart here presents recommendations from the USDA for planning daily menus. Adults of all ages should consume at least the lower number of servings from each food group. However, most adults will need more calories than this, depending on body size and degree of physical activity. Most men, for example, should aim for the high end of the ranges shown below.

The needs of children vary widely, but they, too, should eat at least the lower number of servings from each group. Teenagers need at least three servings of milk, cheese, or yogurt each day to meet their calcium needs. Adolescent boys can eat the higher number of servings from each food group, while girls usually can eat a middle range of servings, and more if they are quite active. Very young children, pregnant or lactating women, and other people with special dietary needs may have higher nutritional requirements.

Food Group	**Suggested Daily Servings**	**What Counts as a Serving?**
Breads, Cereals, and Other Grain Products *(whole-grain or enriched)*	6 to 11 servings *Include several servings of whole-grain products daily.*	1 slice of bread; ½ hamburger bun or English muffin; a small roll, biscuit, or muffin; 3 to 4 small, or 2 large crackers; ½ cup cooked cereal, rice, or pasta; 1 ounce of ready-to-eat breakfast cereal
Fruits *(citrus; melons; berries; other fruits)*	2 to 4 servings	A whole fruit such as a medium apple, banana, or orange; a grapefruit half; a melon wedge; ¾ cup of juice; ½ cup of berries; ½ cup of cooked or canned fruit; ¼ cup of dried fruit
Vegetables *(dark green leafy; deep yellow; dry beans and peas; starchy vegetables; other vegetables)*	3 to 5 servings *Include all types regularly; use dark green leafy vegetables and dry beans and peas several times a week.*	½ cup of cooked vegetables; ½ cup of chopped raw vegetables; 1 cup of leafy raw vegetables, such as lettuce or spinach
Meat, Poultry, Fish and Alternates *(eggs; dry beans and peas; nuts; seeds)*	2 to 3 servings	Amounts should total 5 to 7 ounces of cooked lean meat, poultry, or fish a day. Count 1 egg, ½ cup cooked beans, or 2 tablespoons of peanut butter as 1 ounce of meat.
Milk, Cheese, and Yogurt *(low- or nonfat types)*	2 servings *3 servings for women who are pregnant or breastfeeding, and for teens; 4 servings for teens who are pregnant or breastfeeding*	1 cup of milk; 8 ounces of yogurt; 1½ ounces of natural cheese; 2 ounces of process cheese
Fats, Sweets, and Alcoholic Beverages	Avoid too many fats and sweets. If you drink alcoholic beverages, do so in moderation.	One drink equals: one 12-ounce beer, 4 to 5 ounces of wine, or 1½ fluid ounces of 80-proof spirits.

10. **Maintain an adequate calcium intake.** Calcium is essential for strong bones and teeth. Get your calcium from low-fat sources, such as skim milk and low-fat yogurt. If you can't get the optimal amount from foods, take supplements.
11. **Consider taking antioxidant supplements—vitamins C and E, and beta carotene.** If you eat lots of fruits and vegetables, you may be getting enough beta carotene and vitamin C, but your diet cannot supply enough vitamin E. (Smokers should not take beta carotene supplements, however.)
12. **Get enough folic acid.** Folic acid has been linked to a reduced risk of neural tube defects and cervical cancer, and may also help protect against heart disease. It is especially important for women of childbearing age to eat a folic acid-rich diet, or to take supplements if necessary.

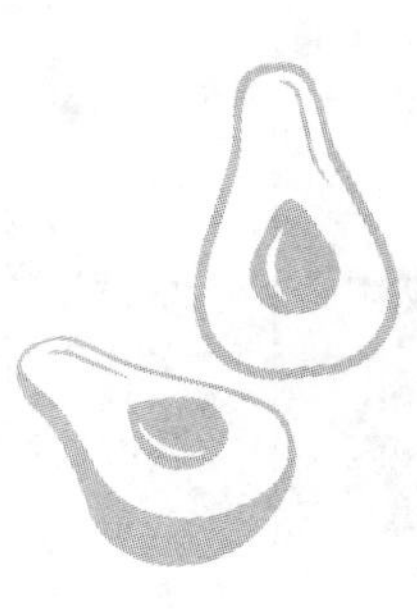

13. **Don't rely on supplements to make up for poor eating habits.** Supplements cannot substitute for a healthy diet, which supplies nutrients and other compounds besides vitamins and minerals. Foods also provide the "synergy" that many nutrients require to be efficiently used in the body—for example, vitamin C helps you utilize iron.
14. **Maintain a desirable weight.** Balance energy (calorie) intake with energy output. Eating a low-fat diet will help you maintain—or lower—your weight, as will regular exercise.
15. **If you drink alcohol, do so in moderation.** A moderate intake is no more than two drinks per day for men, one drink per day for women. A drink is one 12-ounce beer, 4 to 5 ounces of wine, or 1 ½ fluid ounces of 80-proof spirits. Excess alcohol consumption can lead to a variety of serious health problems.

How to read a food label

Food labels are a valuable source of nutrition information. In 1994, the Food and Drug Administration (FDA) revamped the food label, and mandated that nutritional information be carried on practically all packaged foods. Manufacturers must provide nutritional data for specific nutrients, but have the option of providing even more information. While today's food label is a significant improvement over the old food label, consumers may still need some guidance to navigate the information. The label on page 23 lists all of the nutrients a manufacturer is required to cover. The information below will help you put this information into perspective.

Serving size and servings per container. Serving sizes are standardized by product type and reflect the amounts people actually eat. (Previously, the serving size was up to the manufacturer.) What qualifies as a serving depends on the type of food. For example, for cookies, the reference serving is 30 grams (a little more than one ounce) and the serving is for the number of cookies that comes closest to weighing 30 grams. Keep in mind, though, that the reference serving may not be the serving size of the food that you typically eat.

The number of servings per container depends on the size of the package. However, if an individual package is less than 200 percent of the reference serving, the item qualifies as one serving. For example, the reference serving for carbonated beverages is 8 fluid ounces, but a 12 fluid ounce can of soda is less than 200 percent of reference serving, and so qualifies as one serving.

Calories. Caloric content per serving must be shown to the nearest 5-calorie increment for products that supply up to 50 calories per serving and 10-calorie increments for those that supply more than 50 calories. Amounts less than 5 calories can be expressed as zero.

Calories from fat. This section tells you the number of calories that come from fat. (One gram of fat has 9 calories.) The food label does not supply the percentage of calories that come from fat. If you want to determine this percentage, divide the number of fat calories by the number of total calories and multiply by 100. In the label below, you would divide 120 by 260 to get 0.461 and multiply by 100 to get 46.1 percent.

Total fat and saturated fat. Total fat is defined as the sum of all fatty acids (saturated, polyunsaturated, and monounsaturated) plus triglycerides. Fat content is rounded to the nearest 0.5 gram increment if a serving supplies less than 5 grams of fat and rounded to the nearest 1 gram increment if a food supplies more than 5 grams. If a serving of a food supplies less than 0.5 grams of total fat, the manufacturer may express the fat content as zero. The manufacturer is also required to provide the number of grams of saturated fat per serving (the same rounding rules apply), and has the option of also listing polyunsaturated and monounsaturated fats.

Cholesterol. The cholesterol value is rounded to the nearest 5 milligram increment. If a product supplies less than 2 milligrams of cholesterol per serving, the value can be expressed as zero. If the cholesterol content is between 2 and 5 milligrams per serving, it can be expressed as "less than 5 milligrams."

Sodium. If a serving supplies less than 5 milligrams of sodium, the sodium content can be expressed as zero. From 5 to 140 milligrams, sodium is rounded to the nearest 5 milligram increment; above 140 milligrams, the amount per serving is rounded to the nearest 10 milligram increment.

Percent daily value. This column shows how the food fits into your overall daily diet. They are based on a 2,000 calorie diet. In addition to giving the actual rounded amounts per serving of total fat, saturated fat, cholesterol, sodium, total carbohydrate, dietary fiber, sugars, and protein, the FDA mandates the manufacturer to give the Percent Daily Value of these nutrients.

Vitamins and minerals. Manufacturers are required to list the percentage of the daily value of vitamin A, vitamin C, calcium, and iron supplied by a serving of a food. (The percent daily value is based on the reference daily intake, see page 17.) Listing of other vitamins and minerals is voluntary, unless a claim has been made about the nutrient, or they are added to supplement the food (as in breakfast cereals that supply 100 percent of your daily need of various vitamins and minerals). These percentages may be rounded to the nearest 2 percent increment if the food supplies between 2 and 10 percent of the daily value; to the nearest 5 percent increment if the food supplies 11 to 50 percent of the daily value; and to the nearest 10 per-

Nutrition Facts
Serving Size: 1/2 cup
Servings Per Container: 4

Amount Per Serving

Calories 260	Calories from Fat 120
	% Daily Value*
Total Fat 13g	**20%**
Saturated Fat 5g	**25%**
Cholesterol 30mg	**10%**
Sodium 660mg	**28%**
Total Carbohydrate 31g	**11%**
Dietary Fiber 0g	**0%**
Sugars 5g	
Protein 5g	

Vitamin A 4% • Vitamin C 2% • Calcium 15% • Iron 4%

* Percents (%) of a Daily Value are based on a 2,000 calorie diet. Your Daily Values may vary higher or lower depending on your calorie needs:

Nutrient		2,000 Calories	2,500 Calories
Total Fat	Less than	65g	80g
Sat. Fat	Less than	20g	25g
Cholesterol	Less than	300mg	300mg
Sodium	Less than	2,400mg	2,400mg
Total Carbohydrate		300g	375g
Fiber		25g	30g

1g Fat = 9 calories
1g Carbohydrate = 4 calories
1g Protein = 4 calories

cent increment if the food supplies 50 percent or more of the daily value for that nutrient. If a food supplies less than 2 percent of the daily value for the required four nutrients, the value does not have to be listed on the label.

Daily value. These values are given for reference purposes only. Some, such as fat, are maximums, while others, such as carbohydrates are minimums. The values given are for people who eat 2000 and 2500 calories per day. You should adjust the values accordingly, based on your own calorie intake.

How to Use This Book

This book has been designed so that you can open it at any point and find the information you need. There are three main sections: *Vitamins and Minerals*; *Foods, General*; and *Foods, Brand Name.*

Section 1: Vitamins and Minerals

The first section, *Vitamins and Minerals,* describes the individual nutrients and provides a list of the leading sources. The vitamins are presented in alphabetical order, followed by the minerals. Consult this section if you have a question about what a particular nutrient does, how much you need, what the consequences are of getting too little or too much, or if you are interested in finding out which foods provide the highest concentration of the nutrient: For example, which has more vitamin C, a half-cup of broccoli or a half-cup of strawberries?

In this chart, foods are listed by common serving sizes—one cup milk, one tablespoon peanut butter, or one large apple, for example—and are arranged in descending order according to the amount of the nutrient provided. Comparing the nutritional content of foods by common household servings is practical, but comparing foods by volume or per piece does not give an exact picture of the nutrient value of a food because the weight or volume measurements vary by from food to food. Also per piece servings—one large apple, for example—are inexact: what one person might consider large would be medium to another person. Therefore we also provide the nutrient value per ounce of each food listed. These values will allow you to make more precise comparisons.

Section 2: Foods, General

The second section of the book, *Foods, General,* supplies the nutritional values for whole, fresh, and non-branded foods. In this section, you'll find information on whole-wheat bread, pork loin, apricots, cheddar cheese, and carrots, for example.

As in the Leading Sources charts in the *Vitamins and Minerals* section, nutrient values for foods are given per serving. The weight of the food in grams is the first value listed in the chart so you can compare foods on a per weight basis if you wish. (The chart on page 25 tells you how many grams are in an ounce, as well as other equivalent measurements.)

The nutritional values presented in this section are based on the United States Department of Agriculture (USDA) Handbook 8, the standard reference used by nutrition professionals. In each entry, you will find values for the following nutrients: calories, carbohydrates, cholesterol, dietary fiber, total fat, saturated fat, monounsaturated fat, polyunsaturated fat, protein, calcium, iron, potassium, sodium, zinc, vitamin A, vitamin B_{12}, vitamin B_6, vitamin C, folic acid, niacin, riboflavin, and thiamin. It is important to remember that these data represent averages for a particular food.

The nutritional information in this section can be used in many ways. First, it gives you a complete nutritional picture of the foods that make up the majority of most people's diets. You can also use this section to fill in information missing from the nutrition labels on packaged foods. For example, the bag of frozen peas you buy in the store probably does not list folic acid on its nutrition label, but peas are a good source of folic acid. The information in this section can also help you plan a healthful diet, allowing you to choose foods that provide more of nutrients you need—such as fiber or vitamin C—and less of those you should cut back on, such as saturated fat or sodium.

Section 3: Foods, Brand Name

The third section, *Foods, Brand Name,* is a collection of nutritional data on a variety of brand-name products. This information comes from food manufacturers. It is the same information that you find on food labels: calories, total fat, saturated fat, cholesterol, sodium, carbohydrates, dietary fiber, sugars, protein, vitamin A, vitamin C, iron, and calcium. For the vitamins and minerals, the values are listed by the percent of the RDI supplied by a serving of the food. (The RDI amounts are listed on the chart on page 17. For information on how to read a food label, see pages 22-23.) Bringing the information together here allows you to compare different brands more easily. The information we include in this section was up-to-date at the time we went to press, but keep in mind that food manufacturers sometimes reformulate the recipes for their products, and this may alter the nutritional value.

Of course, it would be impossible to include all of the hundreds of thousands of brand name products available in the United States. We have concentrated here on products available nationally, but even there we cannot claim to be comprehensive. (Note, too, that we have included only products available in the United States. The same product sold in other countries may have a different nutritional profile.) If you do not find a particular brand you're looking for in the listings, you can review the nutritional values for a similar product. Another

Common Measurements

Volume equivalents

(fluid ounces/milliliters and liters)

U.S.	Metric
1 tsp	5 ml
1 Tbsp (½ fl oz)	15 ml
¼ cup (2 fl oz)	60 ml
⅓ cup	80 ml
½ cup (4 fl oz)	120 ml
⅔ cup	160 ml
¾ cup (6 fl oz)	180 ml
1 cup (8 fl oz)	240 ml
1 qt (32 fl oz)	950 ml
1 qt plus 3 Tbsp	1 L
1 gal (128 fl oz)	3.785 L

Weight equivalents

(ounces and pounds/grams and kilograms)

U.S.	Metric
¼ oz	7 g
½ oz	15 g
¾ oz	20 g
1 oz	28.33 g
8 oz (½ lb)	225 g
12 oz (¾ lb)	340 g
16 oz (1 lb)	455 g
5 oz (2.2 lb)	1 kg

alternative is to consult the *Foods, General* section for the generic version of the food. The values for these generic whole foods also give you information on the nutrients that are not listed on food labels. Because the nutritional content of whole, generic foods varies little from brand to brand, in most cases we have not listed brand names for these types of foods, such as whole grains, meats, milk, nuts and nut butters, pasta, vegetable oils, and vegetables.

Wherever possible, we have given the nutritional values for packaged foods prepared according to basic package instructions. For example, values for cakes listed in the section on cake mixes are for a portion of the prepared cake, not for the mix alone. The same applies to such products as powdered beverage mixes, muffin mixes, rice products, and pasta products. If the prepared values were unavailable, values for unprepared values are given and identified as such.

The gram weight of a serving of a food is listed whenever we were able to obtain it from the manufacturer's information. If the gram weight was unavailable, we have inserted "n/a" (not available) in the weight column. This is typically the case with packaged products that require preparation before you eat them, such as some desserts, pasta products, or rice mixes.

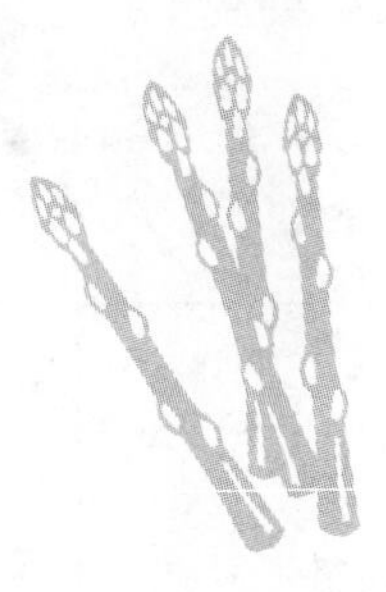

Organizing Principals

In both the *Foods, General* and *Foods, Brand Name* sections, we have organized the foods alphabetically and categorized them in a way that will make sense to a consumer, rather than a strict classification of foods that might be more useful to a nutritionist. For example, you'll find chicken under "C" and turkey under "T," rather than both under "P" for poultry. If you have any questions about where a food might be, you can consult the table of contents or the cross-referenced index, which begins on page 430.

The serving sizes listed for the foods are those provided by the USDA or manufacturer. In some cases, this may not be the same serving size listed on the food label for packaged products. In addition, keep in mind that it also may not be the serving size you typically eat. For example, a typical bowl of dry cereal usually contains more than the one ounce listed as a serving size.

We have listed the foods in the form in which they are most commonly eaten. For example, canned vegetables are typically drained of their liquid before they are used, whereas canned fruits are usually eaten with their juice or syrup. Therefore the values given for canned vegetables are drained, and those for canned fruits are for fruit and liquid. Values for meats, fish, poultry, and fish are given for cooked portions, unless a cooked value was unavailable. Keep in mind that meats and poultry shrink during cooking, so a 4-ounce raw chicken breast, for example, will weigh about 3 ounces when cooked.

Most of the nutritional values have been rounded to the nearest whole number or nearest tenth decimal place. The exceptions are those nutrients needed in such small amounts that rounding even to the nearest tenth decimal place would inaccurately represent the content for that food: thiamin, riboflavin, vitamin B_6 and vitamin B_{12}. These are rounded to the nearest one-hundredth decimal place.

Vitamins & Minerals

VITAMIN A

VITAMIN A was the first fat-soluble vitamin to be discovered. It is present as the preformed vitamin only in some animal products. The majority of the vitamin A in our diets is supplied by beta carotene and other carotenoids from plants (see page 30), a portion of which is converted to vitamin A in the intestines. The various forms of vitamin A are called retinoids because of their importance to the health of the retina of the eye.

WHAT IT DOES

The most commonly known function of vitamin A is its role in maintaining vision, especially night vision. The vitamin is needed in order for the eye to adapt from bright light to darkness—for example, when you encounter headlights from an oncoming car while driving at night.

Vitamin A helps to maintain epithelial tissues—those that make up the skin surface and the linings of systems like the respiratory and gastrointestinal tracts. These tissues are rich in immune cells and are the body's first line of defense against disease. Therefore, vitamin A is important in maintaining immunity. Vitamin A is also important in the development of immune cells, and in the growth of bone. In addition, it is needed for normal reproduction.

HOW MUCH YOU NEED

AGE	RDA/MALE	RDA/FEMALE
19 to 24	1,000 RE	800 RE
25 to 50	1,000 RE	800 RE
51 and over	1,000 RE	800 RE

For recommendations for infants, children, adolescents, and pregnant or lactating women, see pages 18-19.

IF YOU GET TOO LITTLE

A deficiency of vitamin A is a problem only in less-industrialized areas of the world. It can cause night blindness, total blindness, and reduced resistance to infection, which can lead to death.

IF YOU GET TOO MUCH

An excessive intake of preformed vitamin A can be quite toxic. A single dose of 132,000 RE in adults or 44,000 RE in children can cause nausea, vomiting, fatigue, and weakness. Lower doses—10,000 RE in adults, 4,000 RE in children—over time can still be harmful, resulting in headaches, hair loss, drying of mucous membranes, itchy, scaly skin, and liver damage. As little as 10,000 RE of vitamin A can also cause birth defects in pregnant women.

These toxic effects do not result from a high intake of carotenoids, however, since the body carefully controls their conversion to vitamin A. If you eat a lot of carotenoid-rich foods, the palms of your hands and the soles of your feet may take on a yellow-orange tinge; this is harmless and will slowly disappear if you cut back on your carotenoid intake.

Unless you eat a lot of liver or fish oil, it is practically impossible to get too much vitamin A from your diet. Vitamin A supplements, on the other hand, can easily be toxic, and generally should be avoided.

TIPS AND FACTS

- The Egyptians made eye drops from liver to correct night blindness; the effective substance in liver, of course, was vitamin A.
- Only 50 of the more than 600 carotenoids can be converted to vitamin A.
- Vitamin A is measured in either International Units (IU) or Retinol Equivalents (RE): one IU equals 0.3 RE. RE is the preferred measure, since it is more precise, but IU is still used in some food tables.
- It's true that some acne drugs are derivatives of vitamin A. But vitamin A supplements found in health food stores will not cure acne, and may be toxic.

WHERE YOU CAN FIND IT

Preformed vitamin A is found in organ meats, fish, and egg yolks. Milk is often fortified with the vitamin. Dark green, orange, and red fruits and vegetables are good sources of carotenoids, which are converted to vitamin A.

Leading Sources of Vitamin A

	Calories	Vitamin A (RE)	Vitamin A per oz
Beef liver, pan-fried —*2 oz*	123	6083	3040
Carrot juice, canned —*1 cup*	94	6077	730
Chicken liver, simmered —*3 ½ oz*	157	4913	1392
Carrots, fresh, raw, slices —*1 cup*	52	3432	797
Sweet potato, fresh, boiled, mashed —*½ cup*	172	2796	483
Pumpkin, canned —*½ cup*	42	2702	625
Chicken giblets, simmered —*3 ½ oz*	157	2229	632
Apricots, dried, sulfured —*1 cup*	309	941	205
Peppers, sweet, red, fresh, raw, chopped —*1 cup*	40	849	162
Tuna, bluefin, ckd, dry heat —*3 ½ oz*	184	756	214
Spinach, fresh, boiled —*½ cup*	21	737	232
Butternut squash, fresh, baked, cubes —*½ cup*	41	718	198
Mangos, fresh, slices —*1 cup*	107	642	110
Collards, frozen, boiled, chopped —*½ cup*	31	508	169
Cantaloupe, diced —*1 cup*	55	502	91
Kale, fresh, boiled, chopped —*½ cup*	21	481	210
Peppers, hot chili, red, fresh, raw, chopped —*¼ cup*	15	403	305
Turnip greens, fresh, boiled, chopped —*½ cup*	14	396	156
Beet greens, fresh, boiled, chopped —*½ cup*	19	367	145
Persimmons, japanese, fresh —*1 persimmon*	118	365	62
Apricot nectar, canned —*1 cup*	141	331	37
Vegetable juice cocktail, canned —*1 cup*	46	283	33
Swiss chard, fresh, boiled, chopped —*½ cup*	18	275	89
Apricots, fresh —*3 apricots*	50	274	74
Sardines, pacific, canned in tomato sauce, w/ bones, drained —*1 can*	659	259	20
Mackerel, king, ckd, dry heat —*3 ½ oz*	134	252	71
Cabbage, chinese (pak-choi), fresh, boiled, shredded —*½ cup*	10	219	73
Mustard greens, fresh, boiled, chopped —*½ cup*	11	212	86
Cuttlefish, ckd, moist heat —*3 ½ oz*	158	203	58
Avocados, florida —*1 medium*	340	185	17
Tangerines, fresh —*1 medium*	86	179	26
Broccoli, frozen, boiled, chopped —*½ cup*	26	174	54
Clams, ckd, moist heat —*3 ½ oz*	148	171	49
Peaches, dehydrated, sulfured —*1 cup*	377	165	40
Tomato purée —*½ cup*	50	160	36
Skim milk —*1 cup*	86	150	17
Salmon, chinook, ckd —*3 ½ oz*	231	149	42
Oysters, pacific, ckd —*3 ½ oz*	163	146	41
Romaine or cos lettuce, fresh, raw, shredded —*1 cup*	9	146	74
Ricotta cheese, part-skim —*½ cup*	171	140	32
Bluefish, ckd, dry heat —*3 ½ oz*	159	138	39
Egg substitute, liquid —*¼ cup*	53	136	61
Goat cheese, hard —*1 oz*	128	135	135
Mackerel, jack, canned, drained —*3 ½ oz*	156	130	37
Paprika —*1 tsp*	6	127	1717
Egg, whole, scrambled —*1 large*	101	119	55
Tomatoes, fresh, raw —*1 large*	38	113	18
Margarine, stick or soft —*1 Tbsp*	101	113	226

CAROTENOIDS

CAROTENOIDS are the yellow-orange pigments in fruits and vegetables. There are more than 600 carotenoids in foods, of which about 400 have been identified and named; these include beta carotene, lycopene, beta cryptoxanthin, and lutein. Some 50 carotenoids are converted to vitamin A in the intestine, and until recently scientists thought that the others were simply pigments that played no role in health. In recent years, however, research has shown that many of the carotenoids may have disease-preventing potential.

WHAT THEY DO

The conversion of certain carotenoids into vitamin A takes place in the intestine, and is regulated by the body, with more of less of the carotenoids being converted as the body requires. After the conversion, the carotenoids perform all of the functions of vitamin A—so there is no need to consume foods rich in preformed vitamin A to meet the RDA for that vitamin. (See vitamin A, page 28.)

On their own, carotenoids are thought to protect against heart disease and certain forms of cancer. A high intake of beta carotene may reverse certain precancerous conditions. Lycopene may prevent prostate cancer in men. Some studies suggest that lutein and zeoxanthin may protect against macular degeneration, a vision disorder that sometimes occurs with age. Some of the benefits from carotenoids come from their antioxidant potential (see page 15), but they probably work in other, as yet unidentified ways as well.

HOW MUCH YOU NEED

There is no RDA for carotenoids. You can meet the RDA for vitamin A by consuming 6 milligrams of beta carotene a day. Experts vary in their recommendations for the amount needed to get the disease-protective potential. The truth is, no one really knows how much beta carotene, or any of the other carotenoids, is needed, since it is still unclear how they work individually or in combination with each other and with other nutrients, such as vitamin C. For now, consume 6 to 15 milligrams of beta carotene a day, an amount easily obtained from foods. In addition, make an effort to include foods that supply other carotenoids in your diet (see the charts on the following pages).

IF YOU GET TOO LITTLE

Even if you do not consume carotenoid-rich foods, you can still meet your vitamin A needs by eating foods that contain preformed vitamin A (eggs or fortified milk, for example), and this will prevent a vitamin A deficiency. However, preformed vitamin A does not act in body in the same way as the carotenoids. If you do not eat many yellow, orange, or dark green vegetables and fruits, you are not getting enough carotenoids, and you may be increasing your risk of developing cancer or heart disease.

IF YOU GET TOO MUCH

There are no adverse effects of consuming too much beta carotene or other carotenoids from foods. If you consume a lot of certain carotenoids, your skin may turn yellowish—especially on the palms of your hands and the soles of your feet. This discoloration is harmless, and will gradually disappear if you cut back on carotenoids.

Beta carotene in supplement form was also thought to be harmless, but some studies have found that it may *increase* the risk of lung cancer in people at high risk for the disease (smokers and asbestos workers, for example). Exactly why the supplements would have this effect is unclear. One theory is that smokers have low blood levels of vitamin C, and under such circumstances beta carotene enhances free radical formation. For now, experts recommend that smokers not take beta carotene supplements. For nonsmokers, there is no harm—but also no proven benefit—to beta carotene supplements. If you choose to take them, take no more than 6 to 15 milligrams per day.

Tips and Facts

• Spinach and other dark leafy greens are good sources of beta carotene and other carotenoids. The darker the green color of the vegetable, the more beta carotene it contains. For example, romaine lettuce has 10 times more beta carotene than iceburg lettuce, and arugula has three times more than romaine.

• Broccoli that is dark green, purple, or purplish-blue is highest in carotenoids.

• One study found that men who consumed four to seven servings of tomato products—such as tomato sauce or tomato juice—a week reduced their risk of prostate cancer by 22 percent. Tomatoes are one of the richest sources of lycopene, and although the connection is not yet proven, researchers theorize that lycopene may protect against this type of cancer.

• The beta carotene in carrots is more available if the vegetable is cooked slightly, since raw carrots have tough cellular walls that the body cannot easily break down.

Where You Can Find Them

Yellow, orange, and red fruits and vegetables supply carotenoids. Dark green vegetables are also good sources; the yellow/orange color of the carotenoids that are present in these vegetables is masked by the presence of chlorophyll, the green pigment produced by photosynthesis.

Leading Sources of Beta Carotene

	Calories	Beta Carotene (mg)	Beta Carotene per oz
Apricots, dried, sulfured—*1 cup*	309	23	5
Sweet potato, fresh, raw—*1 medium*	137	11.57	2.49
Chicory leaf, fresh, raw, chopped—*1 cup*	41	6.17	0.96
Asparagus, fresh, raw, slices—*1 cup*	31	5	1.04
Carrots, fresh, raw—*1 medium*	26	4.82	2.21
Cantaloupe, diced—*1 cup*	55	4.7	0.84
Apricots, fresh—*3 apricots*	50	3.7	0.99
Peaches, dried, sulfured—*¼ cup*	96	3.7	2.6
Pumpkin, fresh, raw—*1 cup*	30	3.6	0.87
Kale, fresh, raw, chopped—*1 cup*	28	3.15	1.32
Squash, winter, fresh, ckd—*½ cup*	41	2.47	0.67
Mangos, fresh, sliced—*1 cup*	107	2.15	0.36
Collard greens, fresh, raw, chopped—*1 cup*	11	1.94	1.51
Beet greens, fresh, ckd—*½ cup*	19	1.9	0.7
Watercress, fresh, raw, chopped—*1 cup*	4	1.41	1.16
Swiss chard, fresh, raw, chopped—*1 cup*	7	1.31	1.02
Spinach, fresh, raw, chopped—*1 cup*	7	1.23	1.15
Romaine or cos lettuce, fresh, raw, shredded—*1 cup*	9	1.06	0.53
Broccoli, fresh, ckd—*½ cup*	22	1.01	0.36
Parsley, fresh, raw—*¼ cup*	5	0.8	1.5
Beans, snap, green, fresh, ckd—*½ cup*	22	0.4	0.2
Dill, fresh—*5 sprigs*	0	0.05	1.4

Leading Sources of Lycopene

	Calories	Lycopene (mg)	Lycopene per oz
Tomato juice, canned —*1 cup*	41	20.85	2.4
Tomato paste, canned —*½ cup*	107	8.52	1.82
Tomato sauce, canned —*½ cup*	37	7.75	1.76
Watermelon, fresh, diced —*1 cup*	49	6.23	1.15
Tomato, fresh, raw —*1 large*	38	5.64	0.87
Guava, fresh, raw —*1 medium*	46	4.86	1.51
Grapefruit, pink, fresh, raw —*½ grapefruit*	37	4.14	0.94
Apricots, dried, sulfured —*1 cup*	309	1.12	0.24

Leading Sources of Beta Cryptoxanthin

	Calories	Crypto-xanthin (mg)	Crypto-xanthin per oz
Tangerines, fresh —*1 medium*	86	2.07	0.31
Papaya, fresh —*1 cup*	55	0.66	0.13
Tangerine juice —*1 cup*	106	0.53	0.06
Orange, navel, fresh —*1 orange*	64	0.21	0.04
Peaches, dried, sulfured —*¼ cup*	96	0.1	0.07
Mangos, fresh, slices —*1 cup*	107	0.09	0.02
Orange juice —*1 cup*	112	0.06	0.01
Nectarines, fresh —*1 nectarine*	67	0.06	0.02
Peaches, fresh —*1 medium*	42	0.04	0.01

Leading Sources of Alpha Carotene

	Calories	Alpha Carotene (mg)	Alpha Carotene per oz
Pumpkin, fresh, raw —*1 cup*	30	4.4	1.06
Carrots, fresh, raw —*1 medium*	26	2.2	1.01
Peppers, sweet, yellow, fresh, raw —*½ pepper*	25	0.14	0.04
Squash, winter, fresh, ckd —*½ cup*	41	0.11	0.03
Peppers, sweet, red, fresh, raw, chopped —*1 cup*	40	0.09	0.02
Corn, yellow, fresh, raw —*1 cup*	132	0.08	0.01
Guava, fresh —*1 medium*	46	0.06	0.02
Green beans, fresh, raw —*1 cup*	34	0.05	0.01
Cantaloupe, fresh, diced —*1 cup*	55	0.03	0.01
Snow peas, fresh, raw —*1 cup*	26	0.03	0.01
Okra, fresh, raw —*1 cup*	38	0.03	0.01
Swiss chard, fresh, raw —*1 cup*	7	0.02	0.02

Leading Sources of Lutein

	Calories	Lutein (mg)	Lutein per oz
Kale, fresh, raw, chopped—*1 cup*	34	14.67	6.13
Peppers, sweet, red, fresh, raw chopped—*1 cup*	40	10.13	1.9
Collard greens, fresh, raw, chopped—*1 cup*	11	5.87	4.57
Beet greens, fresh, raw, chopped—*½ cup*	19	5.54	2.15
Mustard greens, fresh, raw, chopped—*1 cup*	15	5.54	2.77
Watercress, fresh, raw, chopped—*1 cup*	4	4.3	3.5
Swiss chard, fresh, raw, chopped—*1 cup*	7	4	3.1
Romaine or cos lettuce, fresh, raw, shredded—*1 cup*	9	3.2	1.6
Spinach, fresh, raw, chopped—*1 cup*	7	3.06	2.86

	Calories	Lutein (mg)	Lutein per oz
Endive, fresh, raw, chopped—*1 cup*	9	2	1.12
Pumpkin, canned—*½ cup*	42	1.85	0.42
Parsley, fresh, raw—*¼ cup*	5	1.53	2.9
Broccoli, fresh, boiled, chopped—*½ cup*	22	1.4	0.5
Squash, winter, fresh, ckd—*½ cup*	41	1.34	0.36
Brussels sprouts, fresh, ckd—*½ cup*	30	1.01	0.36
Leaf lettuce, fresh, raw, shredded—*1 cup*	10	1.01	0.5
Coriander (cilantro), raw—*¼ cup*	1	0.24	0.24
Dill, fresh—*5 sprigs*	0	0.07	1.96

VITAMIN B_6

is a collective term used to describe three B vitamins: pyridoxine, pyridoxal, and pyridoxamine. These three substances are involved in over 100 chemical reactions in the body. Probably because of the varied nature of this vitamin, claims have been made for its role in the prevention or treatment of a wide variety of diseases. Adequate intakes may help prevent heart disease and may improve immune system functioning, but the role vitamin B_6 plays in other disorders is either unclear or unproven.

WHAT IT DOES

The 13 nonessential amino acids (the building blocks of protein the body can produce on its own) could not be manufactured without vitamin B_6. In addition, vitamin B_6 helps each cell to assemble the protein it needs by facilitating the breakdown and recombination of all the amino acids.

Vitamin B_6 is needed to produce the chemical changes that must take place to convert amino acids to glucose in the event that the body needs to rely on protein, rather than carbohydrates, for energy. When blood glucose levels are low, B_6 helps convert glycogen stored in the liver into glucose. In addition, it is important in maintaining a healthy immune system, facilitates the conversion of the amino acid tryptophan to niacin (see page 50), and helps produce serotonin, dopamine, and other neurotransmitters (chemical messengers in the brain and nervous system). Recently, vitamin B_6 was found to be a possible protector against heart disease. It works with folic acid and vitamin B_{12} to prevent the excess buildup of the amino acid homocysteine, which can lead to atherosclerosis (see folic acid, page 46).

HOW MUCH YOU NEED

The amount of vitamin B_6 you need depends on your level of protein intake, since protein metabolism is the vitamin's primary role. On average, adults need 0.016 milligrams of vitamin B_6 per gram of protein consumed. To ensure a margin of safety, the RDA for vitamin B_6 is based on a protein intake of about 3 ½ ounces per day, which is twice the recommended amount of protein. (A 3 ½ ounce serving of beef contains about one ounce of protein; a 3 ½ ounce serving of kidney beans contains less than ½ ounce of protein.)

AGE	RDA/MALE	RDA/FEMALE
19 to 24	2.0 mg	1.6 mg
25 to 50	2.0 mg	1.6 mg
51 and over	2.0 mg	1.6 mg

For recommendations for infants, children, adolescents, and pregnant or lactating women, see pages 18-19.

IF YOU GET TOO LITTLE

Marginal deficiencies of vitamin B_6 can contribute to the buildup of homocysteine in the body. Severe vitamin B_6 deficiency is rare, except in connection with a deficiency of other water-soluble vitamins. It can cause weakness, irritability, nervousness, insomnia, and dermatitis. In infants, a deficiency can cause convulsions.

IF YOU GET TOO MUCH

Very high doses of vitamin B_6 can cause nerve damage if taken for months or years. Symptoms of vitamin B_6 toxicity include: muscle soreness and weakness, difficulty walking, loss of sensation in hands and feet, and irritability. Single high doses may impair milk production in breastfeeding women. Doses of less than 250 milligrams per day are generally safe.

TIPS AND FACTS

• According to the Second National Health and Nutrition Examination Survey (NHANES II), 71 percent of men and 90 percent of women consumed less than the RDA for vitamin B_6. People who are especially prone to a low B_6 intake are: the elderly, pregnant or lactating women, and smokers.

• Women taking oral contraceptives also need to pay special attention to their vitamin B_6 intake. About 15 to

20 percent of these women have low levels of vitamin B_6, probably because birth control pills increase the body's production of enzymes that use up the vitamin.

- Megadoses of vitamin B_6 are not necessary to keep homocysteine levels low. Meeting the RDA for the vitamin is all that is needed.
- Vitamin B_6 supplements—50 to 200 milligrams daily—have been reported to help ease the symptoms of premenstrual syndrome (PMS), although the results from well-controlled studies have been inconclusive.
- Supplements of vitamin B_6 have also been reported to alleviate morning sickness in some pregnant women. However, if you are pregnant, do not take supplements without discussing it with your doctor first.
- Vitamin B_6 is easily destroyed by heat and other food-processing methods. For example, in the 1950s, infants fed a particular brand of formula suffered irritability, involuntary muscle contractions, and convulsions. It was discovered that their symptoms were caused by a vitamin B_6 deficiency; much of the vitamin B_6 in the formula was destroyed by heat sterilization.
- Whole-wheat products contain vitamin B_6, but refined grain products (white flour or products made with it) do not. Much of the vitamin is removed during milling of the grains (when the bran and germ are removed) and it is not required to be replaced. Some breakfast cereals are fortified with vitamin B_6, however.

Where You Can Find It

Fish, poultry, meats, organ meats, bananas, and avocados are all good sources of vitamin B_6.

Leading Sources of Vitamin B_6

	Calories	Vitamin B_6 (mg)	Vitamin B_6 per oz
Tuna, yellowfin, ckd —*3 ½ oz*	139	1.04	0.29
Avocados, florida —*1 medium*	340	0.85	0.08
Beef liver, pan-fried —*2 oz*	123	0.81	0.41
Potatoes, fresh, baked, w/skin —*1 potato*	220	0.7	0.1
Bananas, whole —*1 medium*	109	0.68	0.16
Salmon, atlantic, ckd —*3 ½ oz*	206	0.65	0.18
Chicken light meat, no skin, roasted —*3 ½ oz*	173	0.6	0.17
Chicken liver, simmered —*3 ½ oz*	157	0.58	0.16
Chickpeas (garbanzo beans), canned —*½ cup*	143	0.57	0.13
Turkey breast, no skin, roasted —*3 ½ oz*	135	0.56	0.16
Prune juice, canned —*1 cup*	182	0.56	0.06
Pork loin, roasted, trimmed —*3 ½ oz*	209	0.55	0.16
Sunflower seed kernels —*½ cup*	410	0.55	0.22
Herring, pacific, ckd —*3 ½ oz*	250	0.52	0.15
Carrot juice, canned —*1 cup*	94	0.51	0.06
Mackerel, king, ckd —*3 ½ oz*	134	0.51	0.14
Veal leg (top round), ckd —*3 ½ oz*	183	0.51	0.14
Avocados, california —*1 medium*	306	0.48	0.08
Sardines, pacific, canned in tomato sauce, w/ bones, drained —*1 can*	659	0.46	0.04
Snapper, ckd —*3 ½ oz*	128	0.46	0.13
Beef, top sirloin, trimmed —*3 ½ oz*	180	0.45	0.13
Waterchestnuts, chinese, fresh, raw, slices —*1 cup*	131	0.41	0.09
Sweet potato, fresh, boiled, mashed —*½ cup*	172	0.4	0.07
Halibut, atlantic & pacific, ckd, —*3 ½ oz*	140	0.4	0.11
Swordfish, ckd, —*3 ½ oz*	155	0.38	0.11
Tuna, canned, light, in water, drained —*3 ½ oz*	131	0.38	0.11
Chicken leg, roasted —*3 ½ oz*	191	0.37	0.11
Peppers, sweet, green or red, fresh, raw, chopped —*1 cup*	40	0.37	0.07

VITAMIN B_{12}, the last vitamin to be discovered, is unique among the water-soluble vitamins. In general, water-soluble vitamins are found in a wide variety of foods (especially plant foods); are well absorbed by the body; and are not stored in large quantities. Vitamin B_{12}, by contrast, is found only in animal products. The absorption of vitamin B_{12} is complicated: In order for B_{12} to be used, it must bind with a protein secreted by cells in the lining of the stomach. Some people—either because of a genetic defect, age, or some forms of gastric surgery—produce this protein in small amounts or not at all. And, while the body stores other water-soluble vitamins for only a short period of time, large amounts of vitamin B_{12} are held in reserve in the liver, so it can take three to thirty years to become deficient in this vitamin.

WHAT IT DOES

Vitamin B_{12} works closely with folic acid and is involved in many of the same metabolic functions, such as the development of healthy red blood cells, the production of DNA, and the conversion of the amino acid homocysteine to other amino acids the body can use. Vitamin B_{12} is also essential for transforming stored folic acid into a metabolically active form and for the formation of myelin, the fatty sheath that surrounds nerves.

HOW MUCH YOU NEED

AGE	RDA/MALE	RDA/FEMALE
19 to 24	2.0 mcg	2.0 mcg
25 to 50	2.0 mcg	2.0 mcg
51 and over	2.0 mcg	2.0 mcg

For recommendations for infants, children, adolescents, and pregnant or lactating women, see pages 18-19.

IF YOU GET TOO LITTLE

Because of the body's ability to store this vitamin, B_{12} deficiencies are rare. However, they do occur often in people over the age of 60, since the body's production of the protein needed to absorb the vitamin declines with age. Strict vegetarians may also become deficient, but it is rare that they do, since people who become vegetarians as adults usually have adequate vitamin B_{12} stores. (Children who are strict vegans, however, may not have enough stored vitamin B_{12}.) In any case, many foods marketed to vegetarians are fortified with vitamin B_{12}, and supplements are also available.

Vitamin B_{12} deficiency can cause pernicious anemia, a condition where red blood cells fail to reproduce normally. This condition can lead to weakness, extreme fatigue, and eventually death.

Vitamin B_{12} deficiency also has neurological consequences. A lack of the vitamin can cause the deterioration of myelin and can lead to nerve damage. Signs of such nerve damage include: numbness and tingling in hands and feet, poor muscular coordination, moodiness, depression, and confusion. Low levels of vitamin B_{12} in the body may be sometimes responsible for memory loss and senility in older people, and this may be mistaken for Alzheimer's disease. A mild deficiency of this vitamin, as well as of folic acid and vitamin B_6, can contribute to elevated levels of homocysteine in the blood, which increases the risk of heart disease (see folic acid, page 46).

IF YOU GET TOO MUCH

There appear to be no toxic effects of high doses of vitamin B_{12}.

TIPS AND FACTS

• It has been claimed that vitamin B_{12} shots help increase energy and cure a wide array of ills. But the only legitimate use of vitamin B_{12} shots is to correct a vitamin B_{12} deficiency. Injections of the vitamin are preferred over supplements because in most cases the deficiency results from an inability to absorb the vitamin, not because of a lack of B_{12} in the diet. For those who are able to absorb vitamin B_{12}, there is no reason to get vitamin B_{12} shots and indeed no benefit to them.

- Breast-fed babies of strict vegetarian women may suffer vitamin B_{12} deficiency (infants do not have reserves of the vitamin). Lactating women who eat no animal products should be sure to take a vitamin supplement that supplies the RDA for vitamin B_{12}.
- About 4 percent of vitamin B_{12} by weight is actually the mineral cobalt. Thus vitamin B_{12} is also known as cobalamin.
- A high intake of folic acid can mask a vitamin B_{12} deficiency. Because these vitamins work in tandem to maintain healthy red blood cells, adequate folic acid can correct the blood-related consequences of a lack of vitamin B_{12}. However, the neurological damage can continue, and often goes unnoticed until it is too late to correct it.

WHERE YOU CAN FIND IT

Eggs, meats, poultry, fish, shellfish, and dairy products are all reliable sources of vitamin B_{12}.

Leading Sources of Vitamin B12

	Calories	Vitamin B12 (mcg)	Vitamin B12 per oz
Clams, ckd, moist heat—*3 ½ oz*	148	98.89	28.02
Beef liver, pan-fried—*2 oz*	123	63.39	31.68
Oysters, eastern, ckd, moist heat—*3 ½ oz*	137	35	9.92
Sardines, pacific, canned in tomato sauce, w/ bones, drained—*1 can*	659	33.3	2.55
Turkey giblets, simmered—*3 ½ oz*	167	24	6.81
Chicken liver, simmered—*3 ½ oz*	157	19.39	5.49
Mackerel, atlantic, ckd, dry heat—*3 ½ oz*	262	19	5.38
Crab, alaska king, ckd, moist heat—*3 ½ oz*	97	11.5	3.26
Tuna, bluefin, ckd, dry heat—*3 ½ oz*	184	10.88	3.08
Chicken giblets, simmered—*3 ½ oz*	157	10.14	2.87
Sardines, atlantic, canned in oil, w/ bones, drained—*1 can*	191	8.22	2.53
Trout, mixed species, ckd, dry heat—*3 ½ oz*	190	7.49	2.12
Bluefish, ckd, dry heat—*3 ½ oz*	159	6.22	1.76
Salmon, sockeye, ckd, dry heat—*3 ½ oz*	216	5.8	1.64
Bass, striped, ckd, dry heat—*3 ½ oz*	124	4.41	1.25
Salmon, canned, pink, w/o salt, undrained, w/ bones—*3 ½ oz*	139	4.4	1.25
Lamb, shoulder, New Zealand, trimmed—*3 ½ oz*	285	3.71	1.05
Snapper, ckd, dry heat—*3 ½ oz*	128	3.5	0.99
Lamb, shoulder, domestic, choice, broiled, trimmed—*3 ½ oz*	210	3.11	0.88
Tuna, canned, light, in water, drained—*3 ½ oz*	116	2.99	0.85
Beef, tip round, select, roasted, trimmed—*3 ½ oz*	170	2.89	0.82
Yogurt, nonfat, plain—*8 oz container*	127	1.39	0.17
Haddock, ckd, dry heat—*3 ½ oz*	112	1.39	0.39
Veal, loin, braised, trimmed—*3 ½ oz*	226	1.32	0.37
Yellowtail, ckd, dry heat—*3 ½ oz*	187	1.25	0.35
Tuna, white, canned in water, drained—*3 ½ oz*	128	1.17	0.33
Pork, tenderloin, broiled, trimmed—*3 ½ oz*	187	1	0.28
Skim milk—*1 cup*	86	0.93	0.11
Cottage cheese, 1% fat—*½ cup*	82	0.72	0.18
Egg, whole, hard-boiled—*1 large*	78	0.56	0.31
Swiss cheese—*1 oz*	99	0.54	0.06
Turkey, dark meat, roasted—*3 ½ oz*	157	0.37	0.11
Turkey, light meat, roasted—*3 ½ oz*	100	0.37	0.11
Cheddar cheese—*1 oz*	114	0.23	0.23

VITAMIN C

VITAMIN C is touted as a virtual cure-all for what ails you. Many people take vitamin C regularly because they believe it keeps them healthy; others take megadoses in the winter in hopes of preventing a cold; and still others believe it can help prevent cancer. Vitamin C is one of the most versatile vitamins, performing a wide range of functions in the body. And of course, vitamin C prevents scurvy, a debilitating disease that until this century killed many people. (Vitamin C is also called ascorbic acid because of its anti-scorbutic—or anti-scurvy—properties.) Recent research has found that while vitamin C is a powerful immune protector, many of the claims for its healing properties have been overblown.

WHAT IT DOES

Vitamin C provides structure to capillary and cell walls, and is crucial to the production of collagen, the connective tissue that stabilizes bone, muscle, and other tissues in the body. In addition, it helps form hemoglobin, the protein in red blood cells, and enhances iron absorption. It is important for wound healing and helps prevent bruising. And it is involved in the production of the neurotransmitters serotonin and norepinephrine.

The proper functioning of the immune system is also dependant on vitamin C. The vitamin plays a role in defending against disease, and helps fight infection when disease does occur. It is an antioxidant (see page 15), and in this capacity can help prevent and reverse cell damage. Several studies have shown that foods high in vitamin C may prevent cancer and cardiovascular disease, but there is no evidence that supplements do. Vitamin C may also help prevent cataracts.

As for vitamin C and colds: In a recent review of studies investigating the effect of vitamin C on colds, researchers concluded that doses of 1,000 to 6,000 milligrams a day reduced the severity of cold symptoms by about 21 percent, and shortened the duration of the cold by one day, on average. Since there is no evidence that vitamin C prevents colds, such high doses cannot be recommended on a daily basis, but if you feel a cold coming on, it can't hurt to increase your intake for a few days.

HOW MUCH YOU NEED

The adult RDA for vitamin C is 60 milligrams. This is enough to prevent scurvy and other deficiency diseases and establish a reserve of the vitamin in the body's tissues, but is probably not enough to produce its optimal effect. As a result, several experts recommend a daily intake of 250 to 500 milligrams of vitamin C. But if you eat five servings of fruit and vegetables a day, you'll probably have no trouble getting the low end of this recommendation without supplements.

AGE	RDA/MALE	RDA/FEMALE
19 to 24	60 mg	60 mg
25 to 50	60 mg	60 mg
51 and over	60 mg	60 mg

For recommendations for infants, children, adolescents, and pregnant or lactating women, see pages 18-19.

IF YOU GET TOO LITTLE

Although scurvy can occur from a severe vitamin C deficiency, it is extremely rare today. Just a very small amount of vitamin C (about 10 milligrams a day) is needed to prevent scurvy. Consequences of a moderate deficiency include: fatigue, poor healing of wounds, bleeding gums, bruising, and reduced immune function.

IF YOU GET TOO MUCH

Most people can take high doses of vitamin C (as much as 3,000 milligrams a day) with no ill effects—but possibly no benefit, either (see below). Since the vitamin is water soluble, any excess is excreted in urine and feces. However, in some people excess vitamin C causes diarrhea. High doses may also mask blood in the stool (a warning sign of colon cancer), causing a false negative result in a stool sample test even if blood is present. In people with diabetes, high doses may cause a false positive result for glucose in the urine. For people who have hemochromatosis, a disease that causes them to develop excessive iron stores, high doses of vitamin C can be dangerous because the vitamin enhances the absorption of iron. It is possible, but not proven, that a high intake of vitamin C leads to kidney stones.

TIPS AND FACTS

• If you take vitamin C supplements, divide your dose and take half in the morning and half in the evening. The body eliminates vitamin C in about 12 hours, so doing this will keep blood levels high throughout the day and also reduce the risk of diarrhea from too high a dose.

• Vitamin C turnover is greater in people who smoke. Therefore the RDA for smokers is 100 milligrams a day.

• A recent study found that the optimal daily dose of vitamin C may be 200 milligrams. This seems to be the maximum amount the body's tissues can absorb at one time, and intakes above this are almost always excreted.

• Generally, the darker green a vegetable is, the more vitamin C it contains. Therefore romaine lettuce has more of the vitamin than iceberg, and broccoli that is bluish-green has more than green broccoli.

WHERE YOU CAN FIND IT

Vitamin C is present in many fruits and vegetables. Some foods, especially fruit drinks and juices, are fortified with vitamin C.

Leading Sources of Vitamin C

	Calories	Vitamin C (mg)	Vitamin C per oz
Acerola (west indian cherry) —*1 cup*	31	1644	475
Peppers, sweet, red, fresh, raw, chopped —*1 cup*	40	283	54
Peppers, sweet, yellow, fresh, raw —*½ large*	25	171	52
Guavas, common —*1 medium*	46	165	52
Peppers, sweet, green, fresh, raw, chopped —*1 cup*	40	133	25
Orange juice, fresh —*1 cup*	112	124	14
Taro, tahitian, fresh, raw, slices —*1 cup*	50	120	27
Apple juice, w/ vitamin C —*1 cup*	117	103	12
Cassava, fresh, raw —*1 cup*	247	99	14
Orange juice, from frozen concentrate, unsweetened —*1 cup*	112	97	11
Grapefruit juice, pink or white —*1 cup*	96	94	11
Peppers, hot chili, fresh, raw, green or red, chopped —*¼ cup*	15	91	69
Cranberry juice cocktail w/ vitamin C —*1 cup*	144	90	10
Papayas, fresh, cubed —*1 cup*	55	87	18
Strawberries, fresh, halves —*1 cup*	46	86	16
Kohlrabi, fresh, raw —*1 cup*	36	84	18
Broccoli, fresh, raw, chopped —*1 cup*	25	82	26
Pimento, canned —*½ cup*	22	82	24
Kale, fresh, raw, chopped —*1 cup*	34	80	34
Oranges, navel —*1 orange*	64	80	16
Cranberry-apple juice drink, w/ vitamin C —*1 cup*	164	78	9
Brussels sprouts, fresh, raw —*1 cup*	38	75	24
Kiwi fruit, skinned —*1 medium*	46	75	28
Radishes, oriental, fresh, raw —*1 radish*	61	74	6
Cauliflower, green, fresh, boiled —*3 ½ oz*	32	73	21
Vegetable juice cocktail, canned —*1 cup*	46	67	8
Cantaloupe, diced —*1 cup*	55	66	12
Tangerines —*1 medium*	86	60	9
Oranges, valencia —*1 orange*	59	59	14
Broccoli, fresh, boiled, chopped —*½ cup*	22	58	21

Leading Sources of Vitamin C

	Calories	Vitamin C (mg)	Vitamin C per oz
Peas, green, fresh, raw —*1 cup*	117	58	11
Cauliflower, green, fresh, raw —*1 cup*	20	56	25
Lemon juice, fresh —*½ cup*	31	56	13
Cherimoya —*1 medium*	514	49	3
Feijoa, puréed —*1 cup*	119	49	6
Brussels sprouts, fresh, boiled —*½ cup*	30	48	18
Grapefruit, fresh —*½ grapefruit*	37	47	11
Cauliflower, fresh, raw —*1 cup*	25	46	13
Currants, red & white, fresh —*1 cup*	63	46	12
Mangos, fresh, slices —*1 cup*	107	46	8
Kohlrabi, fresh, boiled, slilces —*½ cup*	24	45	15
Tomato juice —*1 cup*	41	45	5
Chicory greens, fresh, raw, chopped — *1 cup*	41	43	7
Honeydew melon, diced —*1 cup*	60	42	7
Cabbage, red, fresh, raw, shredded — *1 cup*	19	40	16
Peas, edible-podded, fresh, boiled — *½ cup*	34	38	14
Peas, edible-podded, fresh, raw — *1 cup*	26	38	17
Lima beans, fresh, raw —*1 cup*	176	37	7
Kumquats —*5 kumquats*	60	36	11
Lime juice, fresh —*½ cup*	33	36	8
Tomatoes, fresh, raw —*1 large*	38	35	5
Cabbage, chinese (pak-choi), fresh, raw, shredded —*1 cup*	9	32	13
Potatoes, fresh, microwaved, w/ skin —*1 potato*	212	31	4
Raspberries, fresh —*1 cup*	60	31	7

	Calories	Vitamin C (mg)	Vitamin C per oz
Blackberries, fresh —*1 cup*	75	30	6
Cabbage, fresh, raw, chopped —*1 cup*	22	29	9
Radishes, white icicle, fresh, raw, slices —*1 cup*	14	29	8
Breadfruit —*¼ small fruit*	99	28	8
Cauliflower, fresh, boiled —*½ cup*	14	28	13
Sweet potato, fresh, baked — *1 medium*	117	28	7
Tomatoes, sun-dried, packed in oil, drained —*¼ cup*	59	28	29
Casaba melon, cubed —*1 cup*	44	27	5
Kale, fresh, boiled, chopped —*½ cup*	21	27	12
Radishes, fresh, raw, slices —*1 cup*	20	27	7
Applesauce, unsweetened, w/ vitamin C —*½ cup*	52	26	6
Cabbage, red, fresh, boiled, shredded —*½ cup*	16	26	10
Potatoes, fresh, baked, w/skin — *1 potato*	220	26	4
Salsa —*½ cup*	29	26	6
Tomato sauce, w/ tomato tidbits, canned —*½ cup*	39	26	6
Taro, tahitian, fresh, ckd, slices —*½ cup*	30	26	11
Avocados, florida —*1 medium*	340	24	2
Pineapple, fresh, diced —*1 cup*	76	24	4
Parsnips, fresh, raw, slices —*1 cup*	100	23	5
Rutabagas, fresh, boiled, mashed — *½ cup*	47	23	5
Squash, summer, scallop, fresh, raw, slices —*1 cup*	23	23	5
Cabbage, chinese (pak-choi), fresh, boiled, shredded —*½ cup*	10	22	7
Cabbage, savoy, fresh, raw, shredded —*1 cup*	19	22	9
Pigeonpeas, fresh, boiled —*½ cup*	85	22	8

Leading Sources of Vitamin C

	Calories	Vitamin C (mg)	Vitamin C per oz
Cabbage, chinese (pe-tsai), fresh, raw, shredded —*1 cup*	12	21	8
Okra, fresh, raw —*1 cup*	38	21	6
Carrot juice, canned —*1 cup*	94	20	2
Parsley, fresh —*¼ cup*	5	20	38
Turnip greens, fresh, boiled, chopped —*½ cup*	14	20	8
Blueberries, fresh —*1 cup*	81	19	4
Carambola (starfruit) —*1 medium*	30	19	6
Onions, spring, tops & bulbs, fresh, raw, chopped —*1 cup*	32	19	5
Tomatoes, canned —*½ cup*	34	19	4
Asparagus, fresh, raw, slices —*1 cup*	31	18	4
Beans, snap, green, fresh, raw —*1 cup*	34	18	7
Beans, snap, yellow, fresh, raw —*1 cup*	34	18	5
Beet greens, fresh, boiled, chopped —*½ cup*	19	18	7
Sprouts, kidney bean, raw —*¼ cup*	13	18	11
Garden cress, fresh, boiled —*½ cup*	16	16	7
Squash, winter, butternut, fresh, baked, cubes —*½ cup*	41	16	4
Swiss chard, fresh, boiled, chopped —*½ cup*	18	16	5
Tomato sauce, canned —*½ cup*	37	16	4
Cabbage, fresh, boiled, shredded —*½ cup*	17	15	6
Chayote, fresh, raw —*1 cup*	32	15	3
Squash, summer, zucchini baby, fresh raw —*4 medium*	9	15	10
Tomatillos, fresh, raw, chopped —*1 cup*	42	15	3
Tomatoes, stewed, canned —*½ cup*	36	15	3
Watercress, fresh, raw, chopped —*1 cup*	4	15	12
Watermelon, fresh, diced —*1 cup*	49	15	3
Avocados, california —*1 medium*	306	14	2
Lima beans, baby, frozen —*1 cup*	216	14	2
Quinces, fresh —*1 quince*	52	14	4
Cranberries, fresh —*1 cup*	47	13	4
Okra, fresh, boiled, slices —*½ cup*	26	13	5
Persimmons, japanese, fresh —*1 persimmon*	118	13	2
Romaine or cos lettuce, fresh, raw, shredded —*1 cup*	9	13	7
Tomato purée, canned —*½ cup*	50	13	3
Artichoke, fresh, boiled —*1 medium*	60	12	3
Cabbage, savoy, fresh, boiled, shredded —*½ cup*	17	12	5
Collards, fresh, raw, chopped —*½ cup*	26	12	3
Cranberry-orange relish, canned —*¼ cup*	122	12	5
Nopales, fresh, raw, slices —*1 cup*	14	12	4
Potatoes, fresh, microwaved, w/o skin —*½ cup*	78	12	4
Beet greens, fresh, raw, chopped —*1 cup*	7	11	9
Carrots, fresh, raw, slices —*1 cup*	52	11	3
Chestnuts, european, raw —*1 oz*	56	11	11
Peas, green, fresh, boiled —*½ cup*	67	11	4
Swiss chard, fresh, raw, chopped—*1 cup*	7	11	9
Fennel, bulb, fresh —*1 cup*	27	10	3
Looseleaf lettuce, fresh, raw, shredded —*1 cup*	10	10	5
Parsnips, fresh, boiled, slices —*½ cup*	63	10	4
Sauerkraut, canned —*½ cup*	13	10	4

VITAMIN E

was discovered at the University of California at Berkeley about 75 years ago and has been a star among nutrients since the late 1980s. There is now good evidence that doses many times greater than the RDA may protect against heart disease, and perhaps other chronic diseases as well. Since vitamin E is found in few foods—and many high in fat, such as vegetable oils and nuts—supplements are needed to obtain the amount needed for a protective effect.

What it does

The disease-preventive potential of vitamin E is due to its action as an antioxidant. Antioxidants inactivate free radicals, which can damage genetic material within cells, cell membranes, and other cell structures. Vitamin E also helps the body use selenium and vitamin K.

Studies have suggested that vitamin E may delay the development of cataracts; bolster the immune system; reduce the risk of cancer and heart disease; prevent angina; combat toxins from cigarette smoke and other pollutants; treat Parkinson's disease; slow the progression of Alzheimer's disease; and even postpone the effects of aging. The final word on many of these claims is not yet in. The most promising evidence is for the role vitamin E plays in the prevention of heart disease. The vitamin appears to prevent an initial step in the atherosclerotic process—the oxidation of LDL (bad) cholesterol. Findings from two large studies suggest that vitamin E supplements may reduce the risk of heart disease by one-quarter to one-half.

If you get too little

Vitamin E intakes below the RDA can lead to neurological damage. But if you are eating a well-balanced diet that contains even a little polyunsaturated fat (from vegetables, vegetable oils, or nuts, for example) it is practically impossible not to meet the RDA for vitamin E.

If you get too much

Even very large doses of vitamin E appear to produce few serious side effects, though diarrhea and headaches have occasionally been reported. At high doses, vitamin E may interfere with the clotting ability of the blood. This is a problem only for those who take blood-thinning medications (anticoagulants), and such people should consult with their doctors before taking vitamin E supplements.

How Much You Need

While the RDA for vitamin E is enough to prevent deficiency, it is not enough to provide the full antioxidant benefits of this vitamin. For that reason, the editors of the *University of California at Berkeley Wellness Letter* recommend consuming 200 to 800 IU (equal to 133 to 533 milligrams) of vitamin E per day. It is impossible to get that amount by diet alone, so supplements are needed.

AGE	RDA/MALE	RDA/FEMALE
19 to 24	10 mg	8 mg
25 to 50	10 mg	8 mg
51 and over	10 mg	8 mg

For recommendations for infants, children, adolescents, and pregnant or lactating women, see pages 18-19.

Tips and facts

• Vitamin E is a generic term for a group of related compounds. It occurs naturally in four major forms—alpha, beta, gamma, and delta tocopherols. Alpha tocopherol is by far the main type in the body, as well as in supplements, but the other tocopherols are also important. Any form of vitamin E supplement is worth taking, though if you have a choice, buy mixed tocopherols.

• Olive oil is one vegetable oil that is not high in vitamin E. While vitamin E is abundant in polyunsaturated fats—the predominant fat in corn, safflower, and sunflower oils—olive oil is predominantly monounsaturated.

Where you can find it

Vegetable oils, margarine, nuts, green leafy vegetables, and whole grains contain significant amounts of vitamin E.

Leading Sources of Vitamin E

	Calories	Vitamin E (mg)	Vitamin E per oz
Wheat germ oil —*1 Tbsp*	120	26.17	54.52
Sunflower seed kernels, dry-roasted —*1 oz*	165	14.25	14.24
Sardines, pacific, canned in tomato sauce, w/ bones, drained —*1 can*	659	13.69	1.05
Sunflower oil, linoleic (60% & over) —*1 Tbsp*	120	6.88	14.33
Almonds, dried, unblanched —*1 oz*	167	6.81	6.8
Filberts (hazelnuts), dried, unblanched —*1 oz*	179	6.78	6.78
Safflower oil, linoleic (over 70%) —*1 Tbsp*	120	5.86	12.2
Almond oil —*1 Tbsp*	120	5.34	11.12
Safflower oil, oleic (over 70%) —*1 Tbsp*	120	4.68	9.75
Almond butter —*1 Tbsp*	101	3.25	5.75
Peanut butter, smooth-style —*2 Tbsp*	190	3.2	2.83
Tomato puree —*½ cup*	50	3.15	0.71
Canola oil —*1 Tbsp*	124	2.93	5.94
Corn oil —*1 Tbsp*	120	2.87	5.98
Peanuts, raw —*1 oz*	161	2.59	2.59
Avocados, california —*1 medium*	306	2.32	0.38
Tomato juice —*1 cup*	41	2.21	0.26
Margarine, stick —*1 Tbsp*	101	2.19	4.39
Peaches, canned, halves or slices, water-pack —*1 cup*	59	2.17	0.25
Brazil nuts, dried, unblanched —*1 oz*	186	2.15	2.15
Apricots, dried, sulfured —*1 cup*	309	1.95	0.43
Flatfish (flounder & sole), ckd, dry heat —*3 ½ oz*	117	1.89	0.54
Mangos, fresh, slices —*1 cup*	107	1.85	0.32
Pistachios, dry-roasted, w/ salt —*1 oz*	172	1.83	1.83
Goose, meat & skin, roasted —*3 ½ oz*	305	1.74	0.49
Olive oil —*1 Tbsp*	119	1.67	3.51
Swiss chard, fresh, boiled, chopped —*½ cup*	18	1.65	0.54
Mayonnaise, soybean oil —*1 Tbsp*	99	1.63	3.34
Salmon, canned, sockeye, drained, w/ bones —*3 ½ oz*	153	1.6	0.45
Tuna, canned, white, in water, drained —*3 ½ oz*	128	1.59	0.45
Papayas, fresh, cubed —*1 cup*	55	1.57	0.32
Broccoli, frozen, boiled, chopped —*½ cup*	26	1.52	0.47
Salad dressing, italian —*1 Tbsp*	69	1.52	2.94
Waterchestnuts, chinese, fresh, raw, slices —*1 cup*	131	1.49	0.34
Pistachios, dried —*1 oz*	164	1.48	1.48
Blueberries, fresh —*1 cup*	81	1.45	0.28
Chicken liver, simmered —*3 ½ oz*	157	1.44	0.41
Mustard greens, fresh, boiled, chopped —*½ cup*	11	1.41	0.57
Rice, brown, ckd —*1 cup*	216	1.4	0.2
Pears, asian —*1 medium*	116	1.38	0.14
Herring, atlantic, ckd, dry heat —*3 ½ oz*	203	1.34	0.38
Dandelion greens, fresh, boiled, chopped —*½ cup*	17	1.31	0.71
Pumpkin, fresh or canned —*½ cup*	25	1.3	0.3
Vegetable oil spread, tub —*1 Tbsp*	78	1.3	2.55
Olives, ripe, canned, jumbo-super colossal —*5 jumbo*	34	1.25	0.85
Turnip greens, fresh, boiled, chopped —*½ cup*	14	1.24	0.49
Nectarines, fresh —*1 nectarine*	67	1.21	0.25
Halibut, atlantic & pacific, ckd, dry heat —*3 ½ oz*	140	1.09	0.31

VITAMIN K is synthesized by bacteria that normally inhabit the intestinal tract. Indeed, about 80 percent of our vitamin K needs are met through this process. It is fortunate that we have the ability to produce vitamin K, since unlike other fat-soluble vitamins, it is not stored by the body in appreciable amounts.

WHAT IT DOES

Without vitamin K, the blood would not clot. Most of the factors involved in blood clotting are present in a "precursor" form in the bloodstream to prevent clot formation within the blood vessels. Vitamin K is the catalyst that changes these precursor proteins into their active form when there is a cut or wound. At the early stages of blood clotting, vitamin K transforms prothrombin into the clotting protein thrombin. Later in the process, it helps change fibrinogen into fibrin.

IF YOU GET TOO LITTLE

Deficiencies of vitamin K are practically unheard of in healthy people. However, deficiencies can occur in people who have malabsorption syndromes or liver disease or who are on long-term or broad-spectrum antibiotic therapy. In addition, deficiencies may occur in infants, who may not have the intestinal bacteria that manufacture the vitamin, and in people who have been on long courses of antibiotics. Some drugs used to reduce blood clotting in people with circulatory or cardiovascular diseases interfere with the body's production of vitamin K. These people must be carefully monitored by a physician, since they could bleed to death in the event of serious injury.

IF YOU GET TOO MUCH

It is difficult to get megadoses of vitamin K, since the body manufactures most of what it needs and the vitamin is not overly abundant in any one food (except leafy greens). In any event, high doses of vitamin K are not toxic.

TIPS AND FACTS

• High doses of vitamin E may impair vitamin K function and increase the risk of hemorrhage. People who are taking vitamin E supplements and anticoagulant drugs are especially at risk.

HOW MUCH YOU NEED

AGE	RDA/MALE	RDA/FEMALE
19 to 24	70 mcg	60 mcg
25 to 50	80 mcg	65 mcg
51 and over	80 mcg	65 mcg

For recommendations for infants, children, adolescents, and pregnant or lactating women, see pages 18-19.

• Vitamin K was discovered in the 1930s when scientists in Copenhagen found that chicks fed a fat-free diet suffered from bleeding disorders. They subsequently determined that the condition could be cured with a substance found in alfalfa. They named the substance vitamin K, for Koagulation.

WHERE YOU CAN FIND IT

Leafy green vegetables are good sources of vitamin K, as are broccoli and Brussels sprouts. Vegetable oils also contain some vitamin K. The vitamin is difficult to measure in foods; the chart on the next page gives provisional values from the United States Department of Agriculture.

Leading Sources of Vitamin K

	Calories	Vitamin K (mcg)	Vitamin K per oz		Calories	Vitamin K (mcg)	Vitamin K per oz
Kale, fresh, raw, chopped —*1 cup*	34	547	231	**Pickles, dill** —*1 medium*	12	16.9	7.4
Swiss chard, fresh, raw —*1 cup*	7	299	235	**Carrots, fresh, boiled, slices** —*½ cup*	35	14	5.1
Broccoli, fresh, boiled, chopped — *½ cup*	22	211	76.5	**Coriander, fresh (cilantro)** —*¼ cup*	1	12.4	87.8
Onions, spring, tops & bulbs, fresh, raw, chopped —*1 cup*	32	207	58.6	**Mayonnaise** —*1 Tbsp*	99	11.2	22.9
Brussels sprouts, fresh, raw —*1 cup*	38	156	50.2	**Miso** —*3 ½ oz*	207	11	3.1
Turnip greens, fresh, raw, chopped — *1 cup*	15	138	71.1	**Tomatoes, fresh, raw** —*1 large*	38	10.9	1.7
Cabbage, fresh, raw, chopped —*1 cup*	22	129	41.1	**Tomato juice** —*1 cup*	41	9.7	1.1
Spinach, fresh, raw —*1 cup*	7	120	113.3	**Tomato sauce, canned** —*½ cup*	37	8.6	2
Lettuce, looseleaf, shredded, fresh, raw —*1 cup*	10	118	59.5	**Potatoes, fresh, baked, w/skin** — *1 potato*	220	8.1	1.1
Endive, fresh, raw, chopped —*1 cup*	9	116	65.5	**Plums, fresh** —*1 fruit*	36	7.9	3.4
Mustard greens, fresh, raw, chopped —*1 cup*	15	95.2	48.2	**Margarine, stick** —*1 Tbsp*	101	7.2	14.5
Watercress, fresh, raw, chopped — *1 cup*	4	85	70.8	**Olive oil** —*1 Tbsp*	119	6.6	13.9
Parsley, fresh —*¼ cup*	5	81	153	**Cauliflower, fresh, boiled** —*½ cup*	14	6.2	2.8
Lettuce, butterhead/boston/bibb, shredded, fresh, raw —*1 cup*	7	67.1	34.6	**Carrots, fresh, raw, slices** —*1 cup*	52	6.1	1.4
Beans, snap, green, fresh, raw —*1 cup*	34	51.7	13.3	**Grapes, european-type (adherent skin), seedless** —*1 cup*	114	4.8	0.9
Cabbage, red, fresh, raw, shredded — *1 cup*	19	30.8	12.5	**Onions, fresh, raw, chopped** —*1 cup*	61	3.2	0.6
Peppers, sweet, green, fresh, raw, chopped —*1 cup*	40	25.3	4.8	**Peanut butter, smooth-style** —*2 Tbsp*	190	3.2	2.8
Pistachios, dried —*1 oz*	164	19.9	19.8	**Peaches, fresh** —*1 medium*	42	2.9	0.9
Cucumber, fresh, raw, sliced —*1 cup*	14	19.8	5.4	**Tofu, raw, regular** — *3 ½ oz*	76	2	0.6
Canola oil —*1 Tbsp*	124	19.7	40	**Yogurt, low-fat, fruit** —*8 oz container*	231	1.6	0.2
Pumpkin, canned —*½ cup*	42	19.6	4.5	**Prune juice, canned** —*1 cup*	182	1.5	0.2
Celery, fresh, raw, stalks —*4 medium*	26	19.2	3.4	**Butter** —*1 Tbsp*	102	1	2
Kiwi fruit, skinned —*1 medium*	46	19	7.1	**Cheddar cheese**—*1 oz*	114	0.85	0.85
Peas, green, fresh, boiled —*½ cup*	67	18.4	6.5	**Sesame seeds, whole, dried** —*1 Tbsp*	52	0.7	2.3

FOLIC ACID, also called folate or folacin, is not a household word, but it should be. While it has not yet achieved the celebrity status of vitamin C, folic acid has recently been found to have a powerful preventive effect against a variety of disorders, from birth defects to heart disease.

WHAT IT DOES

Folic acid is involved in the production of coenzymes used to form DNA and RNA, the genetic material of cells, and so is important for cell reproduction. It is also essential for the formation of hemoglobin, the oxygen-carrying component of red blood cells.

Aside from these basic metabolic functions, folic acid helps prevent spina bifida, a potentially crippling birth defect in which the spinal cord is not completely encased in bone, and anencephaly, a fatal defect in which a major part of the brain never develops. It also helps prevent oral and facial birth defects such as cleft palate.

Folic acid may prevent cervical cancer, and preliminary evidence shows that it may also help protect against other cancers, such as colorectal cancer or lung cancer.

An adequate blood level of folic acid can lower levels of homocysteine in the blood. High levels of this amino acid have been linked to an increased risk of heart attack and stroke. It has long been known that people with homocystinuria—a rare genetic disorder that results in extremely high levels of homocysteine—often develop atherosclerosis at a early age. More recently it was discovered that people who do not get enough folic acid, vitamin B_6, and vitamin B_{12} in their diets also have elevated homocysteine levels, and therefore an increased risk of cardiovascular disease. In normal metabolic processes, these B vitamins help convert homocysteine into amino acids that the body can use, and thus homocysteine does not rise to potentially harmful levels.

IF YOU GET TOO LITTLE

Without folic acid, cell reproduction is severely impaired. In addition, a lack of folic acid can cause a form of anemia called megoblastic anemia, which prohibits red blood cells from reproducing normally. Other results of folic acid deficiency include glossitis (inflammation and soreness of the tongue), poor growth, and gastrointestinal disturbances.

HOW MUCH YOU NEED

The RDA for folic acid is listed below. However, most experts recommed that adults consume 400 micrograms of folic acid per day. (The adult RDA used to be 400 micrograms; it was changed in 1989.) This is especially important for women who are capable of becoming pregnant because of the role folic acid plays in preventing birth defects. An estimated 50 percent of all pregnancies are unplanned, hence the recommendation to keep intakes high at all times.

AGE	RDA/MALE	RDA/FEMALE
19 to 24	200 mcg	180 mcg
25 to 50	200 mcg	180 mcg
51 and over	200 mcg	180 mcg

For recommendations for infants, children, adolescents, and pregnant or lactating women, see pages 18-19.

If a woman who becomes pregnant has a low level of folic acid at the time of conception, there is an increased risk that the baby will be born with birth defects. *Because spina bifida and similar birth defects occur in the first two weeks of pregnancy—before most women know they are pregnant—women must build up folic acid stores at least 28 days before conceiving.*

IF YOU GET TOO MUCH

High doses of folic acid can mask the symptoms of a vitamin B_{12} deficiency. Because folic acid and vitamin B_{12} work in a similar fashion to maintain healthy red blood cells, a high intake of folic acid will correct the blood-related aspects of a lack of vitamin B_{12}. However, in the absence of adequate vitamin B_{12}, the neurological consequences of the deficiency can be aggravated, resulting in paralysis, loss of balance, numbness and tingling in the extremeties, and dementia. (See vitamin B_{12}, page 36).

TIPS AND FACTS

• As of 1996, it was estimated that 88 percent of the U.S. adult population consumed too little folic acid, making it the most common nutritional deficiency.

• After studying 1,160 elderly adults, researchers from the USDA Human Nutrition Research Center on Aging at Tufts University concluded that elevated levels of homocysteine in the elderly could be attributed to their poor intake of folic acid, vitamin B_6, and vitamin B_{12}.

• Grain products are now being fortified with folic acid. Manufacturers of enriched breads, flour, pasta, and cereals have until January 1998 to begin fortification. But this does not necessarily mean that people will be consuming enough of this vitamin. For example, fortification will add 100 to 200 micrograms of folic acid—one-fourth to one-half the recommended amount—to the daily diet of the average woman of childbearing age, depending on how many grain products she eats.

• The level of fortification approved by the FDA (140 micrograms per 3 ½ ounces of grain product) is estimated to reduce the risk of heart disease by 5 percent and of severe blockage of the carotid artery by 3 percent, according to a recent study.

• There is some question as to whether folic acid from foods is 100 percent available to the body. Therefore some experts recommend that all women of childbearing age take a folic acid supplement containing 400 micrograms.

WHERE YOU CAN FIND IT

Good sources of folic acid include: dried beans and peas, green vegetables, oranges, whole grains, and fortified grain products.

Leading Sources of Folic Acid

Food	Calories	Folic Acid (mcg)	Folic Acid per oz
Chicken liver, simmered—*3 ½ oz*	157	770	218
Chicken giblets, simmered—*3 ½ oz*	157	376	107
Turkey giblets, simmered—*3 ½ oz*	167	345	98
Seaweed, agar, dried—*2 oz*	174	329	164
Veal liver, pan-fried—*3 ½ oz*	245	320	91
Oatmeal, instant, fortified, plain, ckd—*1 cup*	138	199	24
Chicory greens, fresh, raw, chopped—*1 cup*	41	197	31
Cranberry beans, ckd—*½ cup*	120	183	59
Cowpeas (black-eyed peas), ckd—*½ cup*	100	179	59
Lentils, ckd—*½ cup*	115	179	51
Asparagus, fresh, raw, slices—*1 cup*	31	172	36
Sunflower seed kernels, dried—*½ cup*	410	164	64
Avocados, florida—*1 medium*	340	162	15
Wheat germ, crude—*½ cup*	207	162	80
Pinto beans, ckd—*½ cup*	117	147	49
Pink beans, cooked—*½ cup*	126	142	48
Chickpeas (garbanzo beans), ckd—*½ cup*	134	141	49
Adzuki beans, ckd—*½ cup*	147	139	34
Lima beans, baby, ckd—*½ cup*	115	136	42
Asparagus, fresh, boiled, slices—*½ cup*	22	131	41
Spinach, fresh, boiled—*½ cup*	21	131	41
Black beans, ckd—*½ cup*	114	128	42
Navy beans, ckd—*½ cup*	129	127	40
Yardlong beans, ckd—*½ cup*	101	125	41
Small white beans, ckd—*½ cup*	127	123	39
Kidney beans, red, ckd—*½ cup*	112	115	37
Avocados, california—*1 medium*	306	113	19
Orange juice, from frozen concentrate, unsweetened—*1 cup*	112	109	12

Leading Sources of Folic Acid

Food	Calories	Folic Acid (mcg)	Folic Acid per oz
Great northern beans, canned —*½ cup*	149	107	23
Turnip greens, fresh, raw, chopped —*1 cup*	15	107	55
Soybeans, fresh, boiled —*½ cup*	127	100	32
Radishes, oriental, fresh, raw —*1 radish*	61	95.3	8
Peas, green, fresh, raw —*1 cup*	117	94.2	18
Pigeon peas, cooked —*½ cup*	102	93	31.4
Great northern beans, ckd —*½ cup*	104	90.5	29
Sardines, pacific, canned in tomato sauce, w/ bones, drained —*1 can*	659	89.9	6.9
Parsnips, fresh, raw, slices —*1 cup*	100	88.8	18.9
Fava beans (broad beans), ckd —*½ cup*	94	88.5	29.5
White beans, canned —*½ cup*	153	85.8	18.5
Turnip greens, fresh, boiled, chopped —*½ cup*	14	85.3	33.6
Navy beans, canned —*½ cup*	148	81.6	17.7
Chickpeas (garbanzo beans), canned —*½ cup*	143	80.2	18.9
Black turtle soup beans, cooked —*½ cup*	120	79	24.2
Brussels sprouts, frozen, boiled —*½ cup*	33	78.4	28.7
Lima beans, large, boiled —*½ cup*	108	78.1	23.6
Wild rice, raw —*½ cup*	286	76	26.9
Romaine or cos lettuce, fresh, raw, shredded —*1 cup*	9	75.9	38.5
Mussel, blue, ckd, moist heat —*3 ½ oz*	172	75.6	21.4
Orange juice, fresh —*1 cup*	112	75.1	8.6
Black turtle soup beans, canned —*½ cup*	109	73	17.23
Humus, raw —*½ cup*	210	73	16.8
Pinto beans, canned —*½ cup*	103	72.2	17
White beans, ckd —*½ cup*	124	72.2	22.9
Endive, fresh, raw, chopped —*1 cup*	9	71	40.2
Corn, sweet, white or yellow, fresh, raw, kernels —*1 cup*	132	70.5	13
Beets, fresh, boiled, slices —*½ cup*	37	68	22.7
Peanuts, raw —*1 oz*	161	68	67.9
Sunflower seed kernels, dry-roasted —*1 oz*	165	67.3	67.3
Kidney beans, royal red, ckd —*½ cup*	109	65.2	20.9
Kidney beans, red, canned —*½ cup*	109	64.8	14.3
Collards, frozen, boiled, chopped —*½ cup*	31	64.7	21.6
Onions, spring, tops & bulbs, fresh, raw, chopped —*1 cup*	32	64	18.1
Split peas, ckd —*½ cup*	116	63.6	18.4
Broccoli, fresh, raw, chopped —*1 cup*	25	62.5	20.1
Artichoke, fresh, boiled —*1 medium*	60	61.2	14.5
Lima beans, large, canned —*½ cup*	95	60.7	14.3
Cabbage, chinese (pe-tsai), fresh, raw, shredded —*1 cup*	12	59.8	22.3
Spinach, fresh, raw —*1 cup*	7	58.3	55
Peas, edible-podded, frozen —*1 cup*	60	57.9	11.4
Broad-beans, fresh, boiled —*3 ½ oz*	56	57.8	16.3
Pineapple juice, canned, unsweetened —*1 cup*	140	57.8	6.6
Corn, sweet, white or yellow, canned, cream style, kernels —*½ cup*	92	57.3	12.7
Cauliflower, fresh, raw —*1 cup*	25	57	16.2
Leeks (bulb & lower leaf-portion), fresh, raw —*1 medium*	54	57	18.2
Cabbage, savoy, fresh, raw, shredded —*1 cup*	19	56.1	22.7
Brussels sprouts, fresh, raw —*1 cup*	38	53.4	17.3

Leading Sources of Folic Acid

Food	Calories	Folic Acid (mcg)	Folic Acid per oz
Papayas, fresh, cubed —*1 cup*	55	53	11
Broccoli, frozen, boiled, chopped —*½ cup*	26	52	16
Corn, white or yellow, canned vacuum-pack, kernels —*½ cup*	83	51.8	14
Tempeh —*3 ½ oz*	198	51.8	15
Mustard greens, fresh, boiled, chopped —*½ cup*	11	51.4	20.8
Crab, alaska king, ckd, moist heat —*3 ½ oz*	97	51	14.5
Vegetable juice cocktail, canned —*1 cup*	46	51	6
Crab, blue, ckd, moist heat —*3 ½ oz*	102	50.8	14.4
Peas, green, fresh, boiled —*½ cup*	67	50.6	18
Blackberries, fresh —*1 cup*	75	49	9.6
Tomato juice —*1 cup*	41	48.4	5.6
Amaranth, dry —*½ cup*	365	47.8	13.9
Pumpkin pie mix, canned —*½ cup*	140	47.3	9.9
Oranges, navel —*1 orange*	64	47.2	9.6
Peas, green, frozen, boiled —*½ cup*	62	46.9	16.6
Brussels sprouts, fresh, boiled —*½ cup*	30	46.8	17
Oranges, valencia —*1 orange*	59	46.7	10.9
Soybeans, cooked —*½ cup*	149	46.3	15.2
Cabbage, chinese (pak-choi), fresh, raw, shredded —*1 cup*	9	46	18.6

Food	Calories	Folic Acid (mcg)	Folic Acid per oz
Millet, ckd —*1 cup*	286	45.6	5.38
Parsnips, fresh, boiled, slices —*½ cup*	63	45.4	16.5
Celery, fresh, raw, stalks —*4 medium*	26	44.8	7.9
Sprouts, pea, raw —*¼ cup*	38	43.2	40.8
Wild rice, ckd —*1 cup*	166	42.6	7.4
Quinoa, dry —*½ cup*	318	41.7	13.9
Peanuts, dry-roasted —*1 oz*	166	41.2	41.2
Cauliflower, green, fresh, boiled —*3 ½ oz*	32	41	11.6
Lettuce, fresh, raw, butterhead/boston/bibb, shredded —*1 cup*	7	40.3	20.8
Plantains, sliced, ckd —*1 cup*	179	40	7.4
Tangerines, fresh —*1 medium*	86	39.8	5.8
Raspberries, fresh —*1 cup*	60	32	7.4
Casaba melon, cubed —*1 cup*	44	29	4.9
Kiwi fruit, skinned —*1 medium*	46	28.9	10.8
Strawberries, fresh, halves —*1 cup*	46	26.9	5
Cantaloupe, diced —*1 cup*	55	26.5	4.8
Grapefruit juice, canned, unsweetened —*1 cup*	94	25.7	3
Mangos, fresh, slices —*1 cup*	107	23.1	4
Bananas, whole —*1 medium*	109	22.5	5.4

NIACIN

NIACIN is unusual in that the human body can not only get it preformed in foods, but can also synthesize the vitamin from tryptophan, an amino acid (protein component). This means that you don't have to eat foods high in niacin to meet the niacin requirement. Most people, in fact, get about half of the niacin they need from foods containing tryptophan. For example, milk and eggs contain very little preformed niacin, but they end up being ample niacin sources because they are rich in tryptophan.

What it does

Niacin aids in the release of energy from foods. It helps to synthesize glycogen (a form of carbohydrate stored in muscles and the liver). At the cellular level, niacin is an essential part of coenzymes involved in processes such as metabolizing fatty acids and mobilizing calcium stored in cells. By contributing to these functions, niacin also maintains the health of the skin, nerves, and digestive system.

Niacin supplements are sometimes prescribed to control blood cholesterol levels. At high doses—usually 1.5 to 6 grams per day—the vitamin acts as a drug, not a dietary supplement, and should be used only under medical supervision. Niacin is considered one of the safest and most effective drugs for lowering cholesterol. Studies have shown that it reduces both heart attacks and heart attack deaths—in part because raises levels of HDL ("good") cholesterol.

How Much You Need

AGE	RDA/MALE	RDA/FEMALE
19 to 24	19 mg	15 mg
25 to 50	19 mg	15 mg
51 and over	15 mg	13 mg

For recommendations for infants, children, adolescents, and pregnant or lactating women, see pages 18-19.

If you get too little

The principal consequence of niacin deficiency is pellagra, a disease characterized by dry, scaly skin at any areas exposed to sunlight. Other symptoms include diarrhea, inflamed mucous membranes, and, in severe cases, depression, headache, memory loss, and dementia. The disease was common in the southern United States and parts of Europe in the early 1900s, mainly in areas where diets were based on cornmeal. Cornmeal is low in tryptohpan and the niacin it contains is in a form unavailable to the body. Pellagra is no longer a problem in industrialized countries—it disappeared as more varied protein sources became part of the diet—but it still occurs in parts of Asia and Africa.

If you get too much

It is virtually impossible to consume too much dietary niacin. Megadoses of niacin supplements can be dangerous, however, causing rashes, liver damage, ulcers, and other side effects. Some people taking megadoses of niacin to control blood cholesterol levels experience side effects, most notably extreme flushing of the skin and stomach distress, which can be uncomfortable for some people and injurious to those with asthma or peptic ulcers.

Tips and facts

- Although corn contains niacin, most of it is unavailable to the body. However, when corn is mixed with an alkaline substance—for example, when it is ground with lime to make corn tortillas—much of the niacin becomes available.
- Grains are ordinarily poor sources of niacin, but enrichment makes them good sources. In fact, much of the niacin in the American diet comes from grain products to which niacin has been added.

Where you can find it

Good sources of protein are generally good sources of niacin. Enriched cereals and breads are also good sources. Meats, poultry, and fish are rich in both preformed niacin and tryptophan. Milk and eggs are excellent sources of tryptophan. Niacin and tryptophan also occur in smaller amounts in peas and other legumes.

Leading Sources of Niacin

	Calories	Niacin (mg)	Niacin per oz
Tuna, skipjack, ckd, dry heat —*3 ½ oz*	132	18.8	5.3
Sardines, pacific, canned in tomato sauce, w/ bones, drained —*1 can*	659	15.5	1.2
Chicken breast, roasted —*3 ½ oz*	165	13.7	3.9
Tuna, canned, light, in water, drained —*3 ½ oz*	116	13.3	3.8
Tuna, yellowfin, ckd, dry heat — *3 ½ oz*	139	11.9	3.4
Swordfish, ckd, dry heat —*3 ½ oz*	155	11.8	3.3
Mackerel, pacific & jack, ckd, dry heat —*3 ½ oz*	201	10.7	3
Tuna, bluefin, ckd, dry heat —*3 ½ oz*	184	10.5	3
Veal, loin, roasted, trimmed —*3 ½ oz*	175	9.5	2.7
Beef liver, pan-fried —*2 oz*	123	8.2	4.1
Lamb, leg, whole, New Zealand, roasted, trimmed —*3 ½ oz*	181	7.5	2.1
Turkey, breast meat, no skin, roasted —*3 ½ oz*	135	7.5	2.1
Oatmeal, instant, fortified, ckd — *1 cup*	138	7.2	0.9
Chicken, dark meat, roasted —*3 ½ oz*	205	6.6	1.9
Lamb, leg, whole, domestic, choice, roasted, trimmed —*3 ½ oz*	191	6.3	1.8
Beef, top loin, select, broiled, trimmed —*3 ½ oz*	184	5.3	1.5
Wheat bran, crude —*½ cup*	63	3.9	3.8
Wheat germ, crude —*½ cup*	207	3.9	1.9
Dark meat, roasted —*3 ½ oz*	187	3.7	1
Mushrooms, fresh, boiled, slices — *½ cup*	21	3.5	1.3
Rice, white, ckd —*1 cup*	242	3.4	0.5
Potatoes, fresh, baked, w/skin — *1 potato*	220	3.3	0.5
Bagels —*1 bagel*	195	3.2	1.3
Barley, pearled, ckd —*1 cup*	193	3.2	0.6
Millet, ckd —*1 cup*	286	3.2	0.4
Rice, brown, ckd —*1 cup*	216	3	0.4
Pita bread, white —*1 large*	165	2.8	1.3
Rice, white, ckd —*1 cup*	242	2.8	0.4
Spaghetti, protein-fortified, ckd —*1 cup*	230	2.6	0.5
Egg noodles, ckd —*1 cup*	213	2.4	0.4
Rolls, hard (including kaiser) —*1 roll*	167	2.4	1.2
Spaghetti, ckd —*1 cup*	197	2.3	0.5
Whole-wheat hot natural cereal, ckd —*1 cup*	150	2.2	0.3
Spaghetti, spinach, ckd —*1 cup*	182	2.1	0.4
Tomato purée, canned —*½ cup*	50	2.1	0.5
Wild rice, ckd —*1 cup*	166	2.1	0.4
Jerusalem artichokes, fresh, raw, slices —*1 cup*	114	2	0.4
Bulgur, ckd —*1 cup*	151	1.8	0.3
Pita bread, whole-wheat —*1 large*	170	1.8	0.8
Buckwheat, groats, roasted, ckd —*1 cup*	155	1.6	0.3
Peas, green, fresh, boiled —*½ cup*	67	1.6	0.6
Couscous, ckd —*1 cup*	176	1.5	0.3
Cream of wheat, ckd —*1 cup*	133	1.5	0.2
Pretzels —*1 oz*	108	1.5	1.5
Nectarines, fresh —*1 nectarine*	67	1.4	0.3
Tomato sauce —*½ cup*	39	1.4	0.3
Corn, sweet, white or yellow, boiled, kernels —*½ cup*	89	1.3	0.5
Farina, ckd —*1 cup*	117	1.3	0.2

PANTOTHENIC ACID

PANTOTHENIC ACID is a B vitamin that is found in a wide variety of foods and involved in many of the body's processes. In fact, its name comes from the Greek word *pantos,* which means "everywhere." It does not participate in biological reactions on its own; instead, it combines with other substances in the body to form two coenzymes: coenzyme A (CoA) and phosphopantetheine attached to a protein known as acyl carrier protein (ACP).

WHAT IT DOES

As part of CoA, pantothenic acid stimulates the release of energy from carbohydrates, fats, and protein. It also provides the basis for the formation of acetylcholine, which is used in the transmission of nerve impulses. As part of ACP, it is involved in the synthesis of fatty acids, cholesterol, and the lipids (fats) that are part of cell membranes.

IF YOU GET TOO LITTLE

A diet lacking in this vitamin produces headaches, fatigue, tingling and numbness in the hands and feet, and intestinal problems. Because pantothenic acid is found in so many foods, deficiencies are extremely rare except in severe malnutrition.

IF YOU GET TOO MUCH

There appear to be no toxic effects of pantothenic acid even in very high doses. However, some people may experience diarrhea.

TIPS AND FACTS

• Some vitamin supplements supply pantothenic acid in the form of calcium pantothenate. Despite its name, this compound actually contains little calcium, and therefore makes no contribution to daily calcium needs.

• There's no truth to the claim that pantothenic acid supplements can prevent gray hair. The myth probably arose from animal studies that showed that a deficiency of the vitamin caused gray hair in rats. However, studies exploring the possiblity that pantothenic acid could prevent gray hair or restore hair color in people showed no effect.

WHERE YOU CAN FIND IT

The richest sources of pantothenic acid are organ meats, fish, poultry, whole grains, yogurt, and legumes.

HOW MUCH YOU NEED

There is no RDA for pantothenic acid, but there are recommendations for an estimated safe and adequate daily dietary intake.

AGE	MALE	FEMALE
19 to 24	4 to 7 mg	4 to 7 mg
25 to 50	4 to 7 mg	4 to 7 mg
51 and over	4 to 7 mg	4 to 7 mg

For recommendations for infants, children, adolescents, and pregnant or lactating women, *see pages 18-19.*

Leading Sources of Pantothenic Acid

Food	Calories	Pantothenic Acid (mg)	Pantothenic Acid per oz
Chicken liver, simmered —*3 ½ oz*	157	5.41	1.53
Beef liver, pan-fried —*2 oz*	123	3.36	1.68
Chicken giblets, simmered —*3 ½ oz*	157	2.96	0.84
Avocados, florida —*1 medium*	340	2.95	0.28
Sardines, pacific, canned in tomato sauce, w/ bones, drained —*1 can*	659	2.7	0.21
Mushrooms, shiitake, ckd —*4 mushrooms*	40	2.59	1.02
Trout, mixed species, ckd —*3 ½ oz*	190	2.24	0.63
Sunflower seed kernels, dry roasted —*1 oz*	165	2	2
Egg substitute, liquid —*¼ cup*	53	1.69	0.77
Avocados, california —*1 medium*	306	1.68	0.28
Veal, shoulder, whole, braised, trimmed —*3 ½ oz*	199	1.61	0.46
Mushrooms, fresh, raw sliced —*1 cup*	18	1.54	0.62
Pumpkin pie mix, canned —*½ cup*	140	1.53	0.32
Duck, meat only, roasted —*3 ½ oz*	201	1.5	0.43
Salmon, atlantic, ckd —*3 ½ oz*	206	1.48	0.42
Yogurt, nonfat, plain —*8 oz container*	127	1.46	0.18
Tuna, bluefin, ckd —*3 ½ oz*	184	1.37	0.39
Yogurt, low-fat, plain —*8 oz container*	144	1.34	0.17
Turkey leg, roasted —*3 ½ oz*	159	1.32	0.38
Wheat germ, crude —*½ cup*	207	1.3	0.64
Dark meat, roasted —*3 ½ oz*	187	1.29	0.36
Salmon, coho, ckd —*3 ½ oz*	178	1.27	0.36
Yogurt, low-fat, vanilla —*8 oz container*	194	1.25	0.16
Chicken leg, roasted —*3 ½ oz*	191	1.24	0.35
Herring, pacific, ckd, dry heat —*3 ½ oz*	250	1.15	0.33
Potatoes, fresh, baked, w/ skin —*1 potato*	220	1.12	0.16
Trout, rainbow, ckd —*3 ½ oz*	150	1.07	0.3
Yogurt, low-fat, fruit — *8 oz container*	225	1.01	0.13
Apricots, dried, sulfured —*1 cup*	309	0.98	0.21
Chicken, light meat, roasted —*3 ½ oz*	173	0.97	0.28
Mackerel, king, ckd, dry heat —*3 ½ oz*	134	0.97	0.27
Mussel, blue, ckd, moist heat —*3 ½ oz*	172	0.95	0.27
Skim milk, protein-fortified —*1 cup*	100	0.92	0.11
Pork, tenderloin, broiled —*3 ½ oz*	187	0.92	0.26
Sweet potato, fresh, boiled, mashed —*½ cup*	172	0.87	0.15
Snapper, ckd, dry heat —*3 ½ oz*	128	0.87	0.25

RIBOFLAVIN, also known as vitamin B_2, might be described as a helper vitamin. Although it has no direct function on its own, riboflavin is used to produce coenzymes that are needed to initiate many chemical reactions throughout the body. Riboflavin was first observed in 1879 as a yellow fluorescent pigment in milk, but it was not identified as a vitamin until 1933. (The word riboflavin is a combination of *ribose,* a sugar found in the vitamin, and *flavin,* the Latin word for yellow.)

WHAT IT DOES

The primary role of riboflavin is as a precursor to two coenzymes that are needed to catalyze a variety of enzymes in the body. (Enzymes initiate and accelerate chemical reactions that must take place within the cells in order for life to continue.) In this way, riboflavin is involved in energy production. It also helps the body distribute and use medications and clear them from the body. Riboflavin is essential for the proper use of vitamin B_6, niacin, folic acid, and vitamin K.

Riboflavin also has an antioxidant effect. It is needed to produce a co-enzyme that catalyizes glutathione reductase, an enzyme that is important in preventing the oxidation of the lipid (fat) in cell membranes. This helps to keep cells healthy. Some evidence suggests that an adequate intake of riboflavin may help prevent esophageal cancer in malnourished populations.

IF YOU GET TOO LITTLE

It would be difficult not to get enough riboflavin, since it is present in a wide variety of foods. Deficiency of riboflavin is rarely seen by itself, but usually occurs in a diet also lacking in other B vitamins (such as niacin and vitamin B_6); some of the signs of deficiency are actually due to an imbalance in these vitamins. However, recent research has shown that some thyroid or adrenal abnormalities can interfere with riboflavin use, as can some drugs used in the treatment of depression and other psychological disorders and in chemotherapy. Large amounts of alcohol inhibit the absorption of the vitamin, so alcoholics are susceptible to riboflavin deficiency.

Signs and symptoms of riboflavin deficiency include: mouth soreness, eye irritation, fatigue, and skin irritation, particularly in the scrotum (in men) or in the vulva (in women).

HOW MUCH YOU NEED

AGE	RDA/MALE	RDA/FEMALE
19 to 24	1.7 mg	1.3 mg
25 to 50	1.7 mg	1.3 mg
51 and over	1.4 mg	1.2 mg

For recommendations for infants, children, adolescents, and pregnant or lactating women, see pages 18-19.

IF YOU GET TOO MUCH

The maximum amount of riboflavin that can be absorbed daily is approximately 20 milligrams—12 to 16 times the RDA. Any excess is promptly excreted in urine, and this does not appear to put any undue stress on the body. Therefore, any adverse effect of a high riboflavin intake is unlikely under normal circumstances.

TIPS AND FACTS

- A high intake of riboflavin can turn urine bright fluorescent yellow, since any excess of the vitamin is excreted in urine.
- Milk and dairy products provide about half the riboflavin intake in the United States.
- Riboflavin is not as easily destroyed by heat as other B vitamins, but it is extremely sensitive to light. This is one reason why milk is packaged in opaque bottles or cardboard cartons—milk sold in clear glass bottles loses a significant amount of riboflavin.

WHERE YOU CAN FIND IT

Riboflavin is found in liver, milk and other dairy products, poultry, fish, and eggs. In the United States, grain products are ususally enriched or fortified with riboflavin.

Leading Sources of Riboflavin

	Calories	Riboflavin (mg)	Riboflavin per oz
Beef liver, pan-fried —*2 oz*	123	2.35	1.17
Chicken liver, simmered —*3 ½ oz*	157	1.75	0.5
Cuttlefish, ckd, moist heat —*3 ½ oz*	158	1.73	0.49
Chicken giblets, simmered —*3 ½ oz*	157	0.95	0.27
Sardines, pacific, canned in tomato sauce, w/ bones, drained —*1 can*	659	0.86	0.07
Mackerel, king, ckd, dry heat —*3 ½ oz*	134	0.58	0.16
Yogurt, nonfat, plain —*8 oz container*	127	0.53	0.07
Lamb, leg, whole, New Zealand, roasted, trimmed —*3 ½ oz*	181	0.5	0.14
Yogurt, low-fat, plain —*8 oz container*	144	0.49	0.06
Skim milk, protein-fortified —*1 cup*	100	0.48	0.06
Duck, meat only, roasted —*3 ½ oz*	201	0.47	0.13
Yogurt, low-fat, vanilla —*8 oz container*	194	0.46	0.06
Pork, boston blade, broiled, trimmed —*3 ½ oz*	227	0.44	0.13
Clams, ckd, moist heat —*3 ½ oz*	148	0.43	0.12
Mussel, blue, ckd, moist heat —*3 ½ oz*	172	0.42	0.12
Trout, mixed species, ckd, dry heat —*3 ½ oz*	190	0.42	0.12

	Calories	Riboflavin (mg)	Riboflavin per oz
Mackerel, atlantic, ckd, dry heat —*3 ½ oz*	262	0.41	0.12
Milk, 1% fat —*1 cup*	102	0.41	0.05
Evaporated milk, skim, canned —*½ cup*	100	0.4	0.09
Milk, 2% or whole —*1 cup*	150	0.4	0.05
Buttermilk, cultured —*1 cup*	99	0.38	0.04
Veal, sirloin, braised, trimmed —*3 ½ oz*	204	0.38	0.11
Avocados, florida —*1 medium*	340	0.37	0.04
Oatmeal, instant, fortified, plain, ckd —*1 cup*	138	0.37	0.05
Goat cheese, hard —*1 oz*	128	0.34	0.34
Quinoa, dry —*½ cup*	318	0.34	0.11
Skim milk, regular —*1 cup*	86	0.34	0.04
Mushrooms, fresh, raw, sliced —*1 cup*	18	0.31	0.13
Tuna, bluefin, ckd, dry heat —*3 ½ oz*	184	0.31	0.09
Tenderloin, broiled, trimmed —*3 ½ oz*	212	0.3	0.09
Egg, whole —*1 extra large*	86	0.29	0.14
Top sirloin, broiled, trimmed —*3 ½ oz*	200	0.29	0.08

THIAMIN

THIAMIN, also known as vitamin B_1, is not a vitamin that has miraculous claims attached to it, so chances are you've never wondered whether or not you're getting enough thiamin in your diet. But a lack of thiamin can cause beriberi—a disease that leads to mental impairment, muscle paralysis, nerve damage, and eventually death. Beriberi was rampant in Japan (as well as in other countries) among sailors in the early 1880s. Many ships returned from their voyages with two-thirds or more of their crew dead. When the sailors' diets—which consisted mostly of white rice—were changed, the problem was eliminated. By 1890 no Japanese sailors died from beriberi. However, it was not until the 1930s that the absence of thiamin—found in the bran and germ of rice (and other grains) that is removed during milling—was identified as the culprit.

What it does

Thiamin is necessary for the release of energy from food. It helps the body convert glucose and other sugars to compounds that can then be broken down to yield energy. It is also essential for the proper functioning of the nervous system.

If you get too little

Moderate deficiencies of thiamin can lead to depression, irritability, poor concentration, and fatigue. At the extreme, a lack of thiamin can lead to the development of beriberi.

If you get too much

There are no known adverse effects of high doses of thiamin.

Tips and facts

• Thiamin is one vitamin that you should make sure you get enough of every day, since the body's stores can be depleted in only a week.

• The importance of thiamin in the diet, combined with the fact that it is plentiful in few foods, led to the requirement that food processors enrich refined grain products, such as white flour and white rice, with thiamin.

• Make sure your thiamin intake is adequate if you drink a lot of tea or coffee. These beverages contain a substance that can deplete the body's stores of this vitamin.

• Raw fish, shellfish, beets, Brussles sprouts, and red cabbage contain an anti-thiamin factor that destroys the vitamin. Cooking inactivates this substance.

How Much You Need

Since the primary function of thiamin is to extract energy from food, the amount you need depends on your overall calorie intake. The adult RDA is 0.5 milligrams per 1,000 calories, with a minimum of 1.0 milligrams per day. Athletes and others who consume large amounts of calories may need more thiamin, but the extra food they consume should also cover their extra thiamin needs.

AGE	RDA/MALE	RDA/FEMALE
19 to 24	1.5 mg	1.1 mg
25 to 50	1.5 mg	1.1 mg
51 and over	1.2 mg	1.0 mg

For recommendations for infants, children, adolescents, and pregnant or lactating women, see pages 18-19.

• Thiamin is best absorbed in an acid medium. If you regularly take antacids or medications to reduce stomach acid production, ask your doctor how this might affect your thiamin absorption.

Where you can find it

Few foods contain abundant amounts of thiamin. Lean pork is one of the best sources. Whole grains, dried beans, nuts, fish, and enriched breads and cereals are also good sources.

Leading Sources of Thiamin

	Calories	Thiamin (mg)	Thiamin per oz
Sausage, meatless —*3 links*	192	1.76	0.66
Sunflower seed kernels, dried —*½ cup*	410	1.65	0.65
Wheat germ, crude —*½ cup*	207	1.08	0.53
Pork loin, roasted —*3 ½ oz*	209	1.02	0.29
Oatmeal, instant, fortified —*1 cup*	138	0.7	0.09
Pompano, florida, ckd, dry heat —*3 ½ oz*	211	0.68	0.19
Tuna, yellowfin, ckd, dry heat —*3 ½ oz*	139	0.5	0.14
Rice, white, long-grain, parboiled, enriched, ckd —*1 cup*	200	0.44	0.07
Spaghetti, protein-fortified, ckd —*1 cup*	230	0.42	0.08
Pasta, fresh, plain, uncooked —*2 oz*	164	0.4	0.2
Egg noodles, spinach, ckd —*1 cup*	211	0.39	0.07
Bagels, plain, onion, poppy, or sesame —*1 bagel*	195	0.38	0.15
Pita bread, white —*1 large*	165	0.36	0.17
Oat bran, ckd —*1 cup*	88	0.35	0.05
Pasta, fresh, spinach, uncooked —*2 oz*	165	0.35	0.17
Salmon, atlantic, ckd, dry heat —*3 ½ oz*	206	0.34	0.1
Avocados, florida —*1 medium*	340	0.33	0.03
Pike, walleye, ckd, dry heat —*3 ½ oz*	119	0.31	0.09
Rice, white, short-grain, ckd —*1 cup*	242	0.31	0.05
Jerusalem-artichokes, fresh, raw, slices —*1 cup*	114	0.3	0.06
Mussel, blue, ckd, moist heat —*3 ½ oz*	172	0.3	0.09
Spaghetti, ckd —*1 cup*	197	0.29	0.06

	Calories	Thiamin (mg)	Thiamin per oz
Brazil nuts, dried, unblanched —*1 oz*	186	0.28	0.28
Spaghetti, whole-wheat, dry —*2 oz*	198	0.28	0.14
Rolls, hard (including kaiser) —*1 roll*	167	0.27	0.14
Oatmeal, reg/quick/instant, ckd —*1 cup*	145	0.26	0.03
Cream of wheat, ckd —*1 cup*	133	0.25	0.03
English muffins, wheat —*1 muffin*	127	0.25	0.12
Potatoes, fresh, microwaved, w/ skin —*1 potato*	212	0.24	0.03
Pineapple, canned, crushed, slices, or chunks, water pack —*1 cup*	79	0.23	0.03
Pine nuts, pignolia, dried —*1 oz*	160	0.23	0.23
Pistachios, dried —*1 oz*	164	0.23	0.23
Carrot juice, canned —*1 cup*	94	0.22	0.03
Orange juice, fresh —*1 cup*	112	0.22	0.03
Pink beans, ckd —*½ cup*	126	0.22	0.07
Pita bread, whole-wheat —*1 large*	170	0.22	0.1
Potatoes, fresh, baked, w/ skin —*1 potato*	220	0.22	0.03
Salmon, sockeye, ckd, dry heat —*3 ½ oz*	216	0.22	0.06
Tahini (sesame butter), from unroasted seeds —*1 Tbsp*	85	0.22	0.45
Black beans, ckd —*½ cup*	114	0.21	0.07
Black turtle soup beans, ckd —*½ cup*	120	0.21	0.06
Peas, green, fresh, boiled —*½ cup*	67	0.21	0.07
Rolls, hamburger or hotdog —*1 roll*	123	0.21	0.14
Small white beans, ckd —*½ cup*	127	0.21	0.07

BIOTIN

BIOTIN, a B vitamin, is essential to animal growth and development. In fact, its name comes from from the Greek word *bios* meaning "life." Despite its importance, biotin is of little dietary concern to most people because deficiences are pracitally unheard of (unless created deliberately for research purposes).

WHAT IT DOES

Biotin is necessary for the transfer of carbon dioxide from one compound to another in a variety of metabolic functions. It is important for the formation and oxidation of fatty acids and helps metabolize amino acids (the building blocks of protein) and carbohydrates.

This vitamin is also in involved in the production of digestive enzymes and in antibody formation. It also helps the body use niacin, another B vitamin.

HOW MUCH YOU NEED

The estimated safe and adequate daily dietary intake for biotin is given in the chart below.

AGE	MALE	FEMALE
19 to 24	30 to 100 mcg	30 to 100 mcg
25 to 50	30 to 100 mcg	30 to 100 mcg
51 and over	30 to 100 mcg	30 to 100 mcg

For recommendations for infants, children, adolescents, and pregnant or lactating women, *see pages 18-19.*

IF YOU GET TOO LITTLE

Weight loss, nausea, vomiting, depression, dermatitis (skin inflammation and itching), hair loss, and an elevated cholesterol level can all occur as the result of a biotin deficiency. In infants, biotin deficiency can cause seborrheic dermatitis. However, there have been no reports of biotin deficiency in people eating normal diets.

IF YOU GET TOO MUCH

There are no known toxic effects of high doses of biotin.

TIPS AND FACTS

- Some biotin is synthesized by bacteria in the intestines, but it is unclear whether this biotin is in a form that contributes much to the body's needs. However, large doses of antibiotics can decrease biotin levels, especially in older people.
- A protein in raw egg binds biotin and makes it unavailable to the body. However, raw egg whites would have to supply 30 percent of your daily calories before absorption would be impaired, so an occasional raw egg in the diet is not going to have any adverse effect in terms of biotin absorption. Cooking eggs inactivates the protein. (However, eating raw eggs or egg whites can lead to food poisoning from samonella bacteria.)
- People who take anticonvulsant medications, such as phenytoin and carbamazepine, may be at risk for biotin deficiency because the drugs interfere with the absorption of the vitamin.
- Although one of the symptoms of biotin deficiency is hair loss, it is a myth that biotin supplements or lotions containing biotin can prevent or reverse baldness.
- Wheat has a high biotin content, but most of the vitamin in this grain is bound and unavailable to the body.

WHERE YOU CAN FIND IT

Small amounts of biotin are found in a number of foods. Yeast, corn, soybeans, egg yolks, liver, cauliflower, peanut butter, and mushrooms are among the best sources.

VITAMIN D

VITAMIN D is produced by the body in response to sunlight, and indeed is the only vitamin the body can manufacture on its own. Technically, vitamin D is a hormone. For many people, sunlight is the primary source of vitamin D, since it is found naturally in only a few foods. Fortunately, as little as 10 to 15 minutes of midday sun exposure two to three times per week is enough to satisfy vitamin D requirements in the summertime. In winter, people in northern climes may need supplements if they do not often eat foods that supply the vitamin.

WHAT IT DOES

Without vitamin D, the body could not use calcium or phosphorus. Vitamin D stimulates the absorption of these minerals from the intestine and limits their excretion from the kidneys. This ensures that blood levels of calcium and phosphorus are high enough to support the constant turnover of bone, and to supply cells with the calcium they need to perform other essential functions.

Recent research has suggested some other possible roles for this vitamin. It is possible that vitamin D affects immune system functioning, reproductive health, and insulin secretion. It may also help prevent cancer—especially colon cancer—by thwarting the growth of cancerous tumors. One study found that intakes greater than the adult RDA of vitamin D (about 400 IU per day) slowed the progression of osteoarthritis in the knees, although it did not prevent the disease from occurring in the first place.

IF YOU GET TOO LITTLE

A lack of vitamin D can cause rickets in children, a condition in which the bones fail to knit together properly. These weakened bones cannot support the weight as the child grows, and this results in bone deformitites such as bowlegs and knock-knees. In adults, a vitamin D deficiency can contribute to osteoporosis and, more rarely, osteomalacia (softening of the bones).

IF YOU GET TOO MUCH

An excessive intake of vitamin D can cause hypercalcemia, a high level of calcium in the blood, resulting in loss of appetite, nausea, weight loss, and slow growth. Excess calcium is deposited in the soft tissues and organs of the body, causing irreversible damage to the heart and kidneys. It is difficult to get toxic levels of vitamin D unless supplements are used. Children are particularly susceptible to vitamin D overload.

HOW MUCH YOU NEED

AGE	RDA/MALE	RDA/FEMALE
19 to 24	400 IU	400 IU
25 to 50	200 IU	200 IU
51 and over	200 IU	200 IU

For recommendations for infants, children, adolescents, and pregnant or lactating women, see page 18–19.

TIPS AND FACTS

• Older people may be at risk for vitamin D deficiency. The ability of the body to produce the vitamin in response to sunlight declines with age, and many older people spend little time outdoors, especially in winter. In addition, most of the dietary sources of the vitamin are not usually included in an older person's diet. Older people should consider taking multivitamins, which typically supply 400 IU of vitamin D per pill.

• Sunscreen use does not appear to inhibit the body's natural production of vitamin D, since enought UV light gets through to synthesize the vitamin.

• If you live in a northern area (such as New England or the pacific Northwest) you may need to be sure your diet contains enough vitamin D in the winter. The combination of weak winter sun, spending less time outdoors, and wearing lots of clothes when outdoors may inhibit the natural production of vitamin D.

WHERE YOU CAN FIND IT

Vitamin D is found naturally in fatty fish, such as salmon. Milk is fortified with vitamin D in the United States and Canada; in the United States, one cup of milk contains 100 IU of vitamin D. Some cereals, breads, and flours are also fortified with vitamin D.

CALCIUM

CALCIUM is essential at every stage of life. An adequate calcium intake during childhood, adolescence, and early adulthood ensures that maximum bone mass (which depends on several factors besides calcium intake, such as genetics and exercise) is achieved. In addition to producing strong bones, achieving maximum bone mass ensures that enough calcium will be available to the body to perform other essential functions. Although the buildup of bone mass slows with age, and eventually calcium depletion will outpace calcium accumulation, the amount of bone lost can be significantly reduced if calcium intake remains adequate throughout life.

WHAT IT DOES

Most of the calcium in the body is used in the formation and maintainence of bone. In fact, bones and teeth contain 99 percent of the body's calcium. The one percent remaining is found in the cells and in the fluid that surrounds them. This amount, though small, is involved in several vital functions. Calcium helps regulate muscle contraction (and so helps control heartbeat). It is needed for the transmission of nerve impulses, signaling the release of messages from one nerve cell to another. It controls cell membrane permeability, so that substances can flow in and out of cells as needed. Calcium is also involved in several enzymatic reactions, especially those that release energy for use by cells, and it is an important factor in blood clotting.

IF YOU GET TOO LITTLE

The primary consequence of a poor calcium intake is an increased risk of developing osteoporosis. This disease weakens bones, especially the vertebrae that make up the spine and, in older people, bones in the hip—so that a fall, or even a jarring movement, a sneeze, or an effort to lift something can cause a fracture.

Some studies suggest that consuming too little calcium may result in high blood pressure. The link is a weak one, however, and no long-term effect has been proven as yet. There is certainly no evidence that calcium intakes above the RDA will lower high blood pressure.

IF YOU GET TOO MUCH

No toxic effects of calcium have been noted at intakes up to 2,500 milligrams a day (an amount usually attainable only with supplements). However, a high calcium intake may cause constipation and could possibly interfere with the absorption of zinc and iron. As a result, a National Institutes of Health consensus panel recommends that daily calcium intake not exceed 2,000 milligrams a day.

A high calcium intake may contribute to the development of kidney stones in individuals prone to them. However, one study found that a calcium-rich diet *reduced* the risk of developing kidney stones by 50 percent over four years. This study looked only at men who previously were free of kidney stones, so the findings may or may not apply to men with a history of stones, or to women. Those prone to kidney stones should discuss dietary measures with their doctor.

HOW MUCH YOU NEED

The RDA for calcium for adults is shown in the chart below. However, a National Institutes of Health consensus panel that studied calcium intake among Americans concluded that the RDA was inadequate to meet the calcium needs for certain groups of people. According to the panel, adolescents should consume between 1,200 and 1,500 milligrams per day; women between the ages of 25 and 50 should get 1,000 milligrams; women over 50 should consume 1,000 milligrams a day if they take estrogen and 1,500 milligrams if they do not. Men 51 to 65 years old should get 1,000 milligrams, and men over 65 should get 1,500 milligrams.

AGE	RDA/MALE	RDA/FEMALE
19 to 24	1,200 mg	1,200 mg
25 to 50	800 mg	800 mg
51 and over	800 mg	800 mg

For recommendations for infants, children, adolescents, and pregnant or lactating women, see pages 18-19.

TIPS AND FACTS

• Compared to other cheeses, cottage cheese is a minor source of calcium, and cream cheese has virtually none.

• Skim and low-fat milk are slightly higher in calcium than whole milk.

• Although caffeine may enhance calcium excretion, you can compensate for this by adding a tablespoon of milk to your coffee.

• Specialty coffee drinks, such as cafe latte or cappuccino, can significantly contribute to your calcium intake. A 12-ounce cafe latte supplies 400 milligrams of calcium, for example. (Opt for skim or low-fat milk.)

• Antacid pills made from calcium carbonate (such as Tums) can serve as inexpensive calcium supplements. Each tablet contains 500 milligrams of calcium carbonate, which supplies 200 milligrams of pure calcium.

• If you take any type of calcium supplement, divide the dose in half and take it at different times of the day, preferably with meals. This will help increase the absorption of calcium.

WHERE YOU CAN FIND IT

Milk, yogurt, and cheese are all excellent sources of calcium. Kale, swiss chard, broccoli, almonds, sardines or salmon eaten with their soft bones, and firm tofu are all good non-dairy sources, as is calcium-fortified orange juice.

Leading Sources of Calcium

	Calories	Calcium (mg)	Calcium per oz
Sardines, pacific, canned in tomato sauce, w/ bones, drained —*1 can*	659	888	68
Yogurt, nonfat, plain —*8 oz container*	127	452	56
Yogurt, low-fat, plain —*8 oz container*	144	415	52
Yogurt, low-fat, vanilla — *8 oz container*	194	389	49
Dry milk, skim, regular, w/ nonfat solids —*¼ cup*	109	377	356
Evaporated milk, skim, canned —*½ cup*	100	371	82
Seaweed, agar, dried —*2 oz*	174	354	177
Sardines, atlantic, canned in oil, w/ bones, drained —*1 can*	191	351	108
Ricotta cheese, part skim —*½ cup*	171	337	77
Parmesan cheese, hard —*1 oz*	111	336	335
Milk, skim, w/ added nonfat milk solids —*1 cup*	90	316	37
Yogurt, low-fat, fruit — *8 oz container*	225	314	39
Milk, 2% fat milk, w/ added nonfat milk solids —*1 cup*	125	313	36
Milk 1% fat, w/ added nonfat milk solids —*1 cup*	104	313	36
Milk, skim, regular —*1 cup*	86	302	35
Romano cheese —*1 oz*	110	302	301
Milk, 1% fat, regular —*1 cup*	102	300	35
Milk, 2%, regular —*1 cup*	121	297	35
Milk, whole, regular —*1 cup*	150	291	34
Buttermilk —*1 cup*	99	285	33
Sesame seeds, toasted —*1 oz*	160	280	280
Yogurt, whole milk, plain —*8 oz container*	139	274	34
Swiss cheese —*1 oz*	107	272	272
Goat cheese, hard —*1 oz*	128	254	254
Nopales, fresh, ckd —*1 cup*	22	244	47
Mackerel, jack, canned, drained —*3 ½ oz*	156	241	68
Salmon, canned, sockeye, drained, w/ bones —*3 ½ oz*	153	239	68
Natto —*3 ½ oz*	211	217	62
Oatmeal, instant, fortified, plain, ckd —*1 cup*	138	215	26
Provolone —*1 oz*	100	214	214

Leading Sources of Calcium

	Calories	Calcium (mg)	Calcium per oz		Calories	Calcium (mg)	Calcium per oz
Salmon, canned, pink, w/o salt, undrained, w/ bones —*3 ½ oz*	139	213	60	**Turnip greens, fresh, boiled, chopped** —*½ cup*	14	99	39
Mozzarella cheese, part-skim, low moisture —*1 oz*	79	207	207	**White beans, canned** —*½ cup*	153	96	21
Cheddar cheese —*1 oz*	114	205	204	**Clams, ckd, moist heat** —*3 ½ oz*	148	92	26
Tofu, raw, firm —*3 ½ oz*	144	204	58	**Radishes, oriental, fresh, raw** —*1 radish*	61	91	8
Gouda —*1 oz*	101	198	198	**Kale, frozen, boiled, chopped** —*½ cup*	20	90	39
Roquefort —*1 oz*	105	188	188	**Okra, frozen, boiled, slices** —*½ cup*	34	88	27
Collards, frozen, boiled, chopped —*½ cup*	31	179	60	**Soybeans, ckd** —*½ cup*	149	88	29
English muffins, whole-wheat —*1 muffin*	134	175	75	**Trout, rainbow, ckd, dry heat** —*3 ½ oz*	150	86	24
American cheese, processed —*1 oz*	106	174	174	**Beet greens, fresh, boiled, chopped** —*½ cup*	19	82	32
Fontina cheese —*1 oz*	110	156	156	**Okra, fresh, raw** —*1 cup*	38	81	23
Blue cheese —*1 oz*	100	150	149	**White beans, ckd** —*½ cup*	124	81	26
Amaranth, dry —*½ cup*	365	149	43	**Almonds, toasted, unblanched** —*1 oz*	167	80	80
Mozzarella cheese, whole-milk —*1 oz*	80	147	147	**Salsify, fresh, raw, slices** —*1 cup*	109	80	17
Mustard spinach (tendergreen), fresh, boiled, chopped —*½ cup*	14	142	45	**Cabbage, chinese (pak-choi), fresh, boiled, shredded** —*½ cup*	10	79	26
Pike, walleye, ckd, dry heat —*3 ½ oz*	119	141	40	**Ice cream, strawberry** —*½ cup*	127	79	34
Ice milk, vanilla, soft serve —*½ cup*	111	138	45	**Cottage cheese, 2% fat** —*½ cup*	101	77	19
Ocean perch, atlantic, ckd, dry heat —*3 ½ oz*	121	137	39	**Pollock, atlantic, ckd, dry heat** —*3 ½ oz*	118	77	22
Soybeans, fresh, boiled —*½ cup*	127	131	41	**Mustard greens, frozen, boiled, chopped** —*½ cup*	14	76	29
Cherimoya —*1 medium*	514	126	7	**Cabbage, chinese (pak-choi), fresh, raw, shredded** —*1 cup*	9	74	30
Sour cream, half & half, cultured —*½ cup*	163	126	30	**Dandelion greens, fresh, boiled, chopped** —*½ cup*	17	74	40
Turnip greens, frozen, boiled —*½ cup*	25	125	43	**Onions, spring, tops & bulbs, fresh, raw, chopped** —*1 cup*	32	72	20
Cheddar cheese, low-fat —*1 oz*	49	118	118	**Peas, edible-podded, frozen** —*1 cup*	60	72	14
Tofu, raw, regular — *3 ½ oz*	76	105	30	**Figs, dried** —*¼ cup*	127	72	41
Perch, ckd, dry heat —*3 ½ oz*	117	102	29	**Cottage cheese, 1% fat** —*½ cup*	82	69	17

Leading Sources of Calcium

	Calories	Calcium (mg)	Calcium per oz
Great northern beans, canned — *½ cup*	149	69	15
Parmesan, grated — *1 Tbsp*	23	69	390
Miso — *3 ½ oz*	207	66	19
Small white beans, ckd — *½ cup*	127	65	21
Celery, fresh, raw, stalks — *4 medium*	26	64	11
Navy beans, ckd — *½ cup*	129	64	20
Tahini (sesame butter) — *1 Tbsp*	86	63	119
Currants, european black, fresh — *1 cup*	71	62	16
Humus, raw — *½ cup*	210	62	14
Lobster, northern, ckd, moist heat — *3 ½ oz*	98	61	17
Great northern beans, ckd — *½ cup*	104	60	19
Apricots, dried, sulfured — *1 cup*	309	59	13
Cabbage, chinese (pe-tsai), fresh, raw, shredded — *1 cup*	12	59	22

	Calories	Calcium (mg)	Calcium per oz
Crab, alaska king, ckd, moist heat — *3 ½ oz*	97	59	17
Rutabagas, fresh, boiled, mashed — *½ cup*	47	58	14
Oranges, navel — *1 orange*	64	56	11
Filberts (hazelnuts), dry-roasted, unblanched — *1 oz*	188	55	55
Artichoke, fresh, boiled — *1 medium artichoke*	60	54	13
Mustard greens, fresh, boiled, chopped — *½ cup*	11	52	21
Pinto beans, canned — *½ cup*	103	52	12
Quinoa, dry — *½ cup*	318	51	17
Swiss chard, fresh, boiled, chopped — *½ cup*	18	51	16
Broccoli, frozen, boiled, chopped — *½ cup*	26	47	15
Kale, fresh, boiled, chopped — *½ cup*	21	47	20
Peas, edible-podded, frozen, boiled — *½ cup*	42	47	17
Almond butter — *1 Tbsp*	101	43	77

COPPER

COPPER is part of at least 15 proteins in the body, including many enzymes, yet the human body contains only about 1⁄250 ounce of copper. That tiny amount makes possible a number of essential functions in the body.

WHAT IT DOES

Copper is part of several reactions in the body that utilize oxygen. For example, copper oxidizes stored forms of iron so that it can be transported to sites in the body where it is needed. It is also used to construct healthy blood vessels and connective tissue, such as collagen. Copper is needed to produce hair and skin pigments and several neurotransmitters (chemicals that carry nerve signals throughout the body). Copper is also involved in fertility and immunity.

IF YOU GET TOO LITTLE

Severe copper deficiency is rare. When it does occur, it causes anemia and a decrease in white blood cell production. Low intakes of copper are common in diets in the United States, but the consequences of this are unknown. Despite claims of supplement manufacturers, there is no evidence that a low copper intake can contribute to arthritis or high blood cholesterol levels.

IF YOU GET TOO MUCH

Excess copper intake can be harmful, causing vomiting and diarrhea, and possibly coma, liver damage, and even death. However, most of the toxic effects of copper have been noted in people who have been working with pesticides containing copper; it appears that the risk of copper toxicity from oral copper intake is low. No toxic effects of oral intake have been noted in humans, even at intakes as high as 35 milligrams per day in a 150-pound person (or 0.5 milligrams per 2.2 pounds of body weight). Some people suffer from a rare genetic disorder called Wilson's disease that causes them to store excessive amounts of copper, which accumulates over the years and can lead to liver failure if left untreated.

TIPS AND FACTS

- Megadoses of zinc supplements can interfere with copper absorption.

HOW MUCH YOU NEED

There is no RDA for copper. Instead, there is a recommendation for an estimated safe and adequate daily intake.

AGE	MALE	FEMALE
19 to 24	1.5 to 3 mg	1.5 to 3 mg
25 to 50	1.5 to 3 mg	1.5 to 3 mg
51 and over	1.5 to 3 mg	1.5 to 3 mg

For recommendations for infants, children, adolescents, and pregnant or lactating women, see pages 18-19.

WHERE YOU CAN FIND IT

Shellfish, organ meats (such as liver), legumes, nuts, and seeds are good sources of copper.

Leading Sources of Copper

	Calories	Copper (mg)	Copper per oz
Veal liver, pan-fried —*3 ½ oz*	245	9.9	2.8
Oysters, eastern, ckd —*3 ½ oz*	137	7.6	2.2
Oysters, pacific, ckd —*3 ½ oz*	163	2.7	0.8
Beef liver, pan-fried —*2 oz*	123	2.5	1.3
Lobster, northern, ckd, moist heat —*3 ½ oz*	98	1.9	0.6
Sunflower seed kernels, dried —*½ cup*	410	1.3	0.5
Crab, alaska king , ckd moist heat — *3 ½ oz*	97	1.2	0.3
Sardines, pacific, canned in tomato sauce, w/ bones, drained —*1 can*	659	1	0.1
Amaranth, dry —*½ cup*	365	0.8	0.2
Avocados, florida —*1 medium*	340	0.8	0.1
Clams, ckd, moist heat —*3 ½ oz*	148	0.7	0.2
Mushrooms, shiitake, ckd — *4 mushrooms*	40	0.7	0.3
Natto —*3 ½ oz*	211	0.7	0.2
Tempeh —*3 ½ oz*	198	0.7	0.2
Cashews, dry roasted —*1 oz*	163	0.6	0.6
Chocolate, semisweet chips —*½ cup*	402	0.6	0.2
Potatoes, fresh, baked, w/skin — *1 potato*	220	0.6	0.1
Avocados, california —*1 medium*	306	0.5	0.1
Brazil nuts, dried, unblanched —*1 oz*	186	0.5	0.5
Prunes, dried, stewed —*1 cup*	265	0.5	0.1
Vegetable juice cocktail, canned —*1 cup*	46	0.5	0.1
Wheat germ, crude —*½ cup*	207	0.5	0.2
Almonds, dry roasted, unblanched —*1 oz*	166	0.4	0.4
Filberts (hazelnuts), dried, unblanched —*1 oz*	179	0.4	0.4

	Calories	Copper (mg)	Copper per oz
Millet, ckd —*1 cup*	286	0.4	0.2
Sesame seeds, whole, dried —*1 Tbsp*	52	0.4	1.2
Tofu, raw, firm —*3 ½ oz*	144	0.4	0.1
Wild rice, raw —*½ cup*	286	0.4	0.1
Pistachios —*1 oz*	172	0.3	0.3
White beans, canned —*½ cup*	153	0.3	0.1
Artichoke, fresh, boiled —*1 medium*	60	0.3	0.1
Baked beans, vegetarian, canned — *½ cup*	118	0.3	0.1
Buckwheat, groats, roasted, ckd — *1 cup*	155	0.3	0
Chicken giblets, simmered —*3 ½ oz*	157	0.3	0.1
Chickpeas (garbanzo beans), ckd —*½ cup*	134	0.3	0.1
Humus, raw —*½ cup*	210	0.3	0.1
Lentils, ckd —*½ cup*	115	0.3	0.1
Lima beans, fresh, boiled —*½ cup*	105	0.3	0.1
Navy beans, ckd —*½ cup*	129	0.3	0.1
Peas, green, fresh, raw —*1 cup*	117	0.3	0.1
Pineapple, canned, crushed, slices, or chunks, water pack —*1 cup*	79	0.3	0
Pine nuts —*1 oz*	160	0.3	0.3
Spaghetti, spinach, ckd —*1 cup*	182	0.3	0.1
Sweet potato, fresh, boiled, mashed —*½ cup*	172	0.3	0
Tomato juice —*1 cup*	41	0.3	0
White beans, ckd —*½ cup*	124	0.3	0.1
Turkey leg, roasted —*3 ½ oz*	159	0.2	0.1
Tomato sauce —*½ cup*	37	0.2	0.1

IRON deficiency is one of the most common nutritional problems in the United States, yet there are only a few stages of life during which people are likely to experience such a deficiency. Periods of rapid growth—infancy, adolescence, and pregnancy—increase the body's demand for iron, as does menstruation, because the monthly blood loss depletes iron stores.

WHAT IT DOES

About 70 percent of the iron in the body is found in red blood cells. Iron is an essential component of hemoglobin. This protein, which gives blood its red color, carries oxygen to all the cells. Iron is also part of myoglobin, which stores oxygen in muscles to provide energy for muscle contraction.

HOW MUCH YOU NEED

AGE	RDA/MALE	RDA/FEMALE
19 to 24	10 mg	15 mg
25 to 50	10 mg	15 mg
51 and over	10 mg	10 mg

For recommendations for infants, children, adolescents, and pregnant or lactating women, see pages 18-19.

IF YOU GET TOO LITTLE

The body carefully monitors its iron status, absorbing more iron when stores of the mineral are low and less iron when stores are adequate. The iron contained in red blood cells is reutilized as those blood cells are broken down by the body. Very little iron is excreted; the only way significant amounts of iron leave the body is through blood loss or blood transfer to a fetus. This means that it can take a long time before a deficiency develops. However, the body's controls cannot override an iron-poor diet in the long term.

The initial stage of iron deficiency usually produces no symptoms. However, even mild iron deficiency can cause irritability in infants, and hinder learning and problem-solving capacity in children.

Anemia, with its accompanying fatigue and weakness, is the ultimate consequence of iron deficiency. In this disorder, there is a decrease in the number of red blood cells circulating in the body, or a below normal hemoglobin content. Either condition reduces the amount of oxygen delivered to the cells.

IF YOU GET TOO MUCH

Because the body reduces absorption when iron stores are high, in most cases even large amounts of iron are not toxic for adults. There are some exceptions, however. It is estimated that one million or more Americans have hemochromatosis, a genetic disorder in which the body does not properly regulate iron absorption, placing them at risk for iron overload. Children are especially susceptible to ill effects from excessive doses of iron. Iron-containing supplements are the leading cause of childhood poisoning death. As few as five high-potency over-the-counter pills could be fatal for a child.

A 1992 Finnish study suggested that even normal iron stores increased risk for heart disease for men. However, the study left several questions unanswered, and at this point there is not enough evidence supporting the link between iron and heart disease.

TIPS AND FACTS

- Heme iron, which is found in animal tissues, is much better absorbed than nonheme iron, which makes up the rest of the iron in animal tissues and all the iron in dairy products, eggs, vegetables, fruits, and grains, and in the supplemental iron used to fortify flour and cereals.
- Vitamin C helps the body absorb nonheme iron. For example, you could triple the amount of iron absorbed from a vegetarian meal of navy beans, rice, corn bread and an apple by adding 75 milligrams of vitamin C—the amount in a cup of steamed broccoli or five ounces of orange juice. Including a small amount of meat in the meal would also boost absorption.
- Cook acidic foods—such as tomato sauce—in cast-iron pots. The iron leaches into the food, boosting its iron content.
- According to the National Health and Nutrition Examination Survey III, 9 percent of toddlers age 1 to 2

years, 9 percent of adolescent girls, and 11 percent of women between the ages of 20 and 49 are deficient in iron. Of those, 3 percent of toddlers, 2 percent of girls, and 5 percent of women have anemia.

• Runners and other endurance athletes tend to have a higher incidence of iron depletion. This has been attributed to a variety of factors, including the increased elimination of iron during prolonged exercise.

• Even if you think you might be deficient in iron, consult a doctor before you take iron supplements. Fatigue and other symptoms of anemia have many causes, and anemia can result from other dietary deficiencies, such as a lack of folic acid, or from some form of internal bleeding.

Where You Can Find It

Liver, beef, and lamb are excellent sources of iron. Pork, poultry, and fish have less. (Dark-meat poultry is higher in iron than white meat.) Dried beans and peas, green leafy vegetables, and nuts and seeds are also good sources.

Leading Sources of Iron

	Calories	Iron (mg)	Iron per oz
Clams, ckd, moist heat—*3 ½ oz*	148	28	7.9
Oysters, eastern, ckd, moist heat—*3 ½ oz*	137	12	3.4
Tofu, raw, firm—*3 ½ oz*	144	10.4	3
Cream of wheat, ckd—*1 cup*	133	10.3	1.2
Oysters, pacific, ckd, moist heat—*3 ½ oz*	163	9.2	2.6
Chicken liver, simmered—*3 ½ oz*	157	8.5	2.4
Sardines, pacific, canned in tomato sauce, w/ bones, drained—*1 can*	659	8.5	0.7
Oatmeal, instant, fortified, plain, ckd—*1 cup*	138	8.3	1
Quinoa, dry—*½ cup*	318	7.9	2.6
Amaranth, dry—*½ cup*	365	7.4	2.2
Mussels, blue, ckd, moist heat—*3 ½ oz*	172	6.7	1.9
Turkey giblets, simmered—*3 ½ oz*	167	6.7	1.9
Apricots, dried, sulfured—*1 cup*	309	6.1	1.3
Jerusalem artichokes, fresh, raw, slices—*1 cup*	114	5.1	1
Soybeans, ckd—*½ cup*	149	4.4	1.5
Tomato sauce, spanish-style—*½ cup*	40	4.3	1
Pumpkin & squash seeds, roasted, hulled—*1 oz*	148	4.2	4.2

	Calories	Iron (mg)	Iron per oz
White beans, canned—*½ cup*	153	3.9	0.8
Beef, tenderloin, select, broiled, trimmed—*3 ½ oz*	200	3.6	1
Lentils, ckd—*½ cup*	115	3.3	0.9
Tuna, canned, in water, light, drained—*3 ½ oz*	131	3.2	0.9
Shrimp, ckd, moist heat—*3 ½ oz*	99	3.1	0.9
Wheat bran, crude—*½ cup*	63	3.1	3
Prune juice, canned—*1 cup*	182	3	0.3
Crab, queen, ckd, moist heat—*3 ½ oz*	115	2.9	0.8
Goose, meat only, roasted—*3 ½ oz*	238	2.9	0.8
Bagels—*1 bagel*	197	2.8	1.1
Miso—*3 ½ oz*	207	2.8	0.8
Potatoes, fresh, baked, w/skin—*1 potato*	220	2.8	0.4
Prunes, dried, stewed—*1 cup*	265	2.8	0.3
Rice, white, ckd—*1 cup*	242	2.8	0.4
Sausage, meatless—*3 links*	192	2.8	1.1
Duck, meat only, roasted—*3 ½ oz*	201	2.7	0.8
Lamb, shoulder, arm, domestic, choice, braised, trimmed—*3 ½ oz*	279	2.7	0.8

Leading Sources of Iron

	Calories	Iron (mg)	Iron per oz
Sardines, atlantic, canned in oil, w/ bones, drained —*1 can*	191	2.7	0.8
Turkey, leg, roasted —*3 ½ oz*	159	2.7	0.8
Black turtle soup beans, ckd —*½ cup*	120	2.6	0.8
Chocolate, semisweet chips —*½ cup*	402	2.6	0.9
Kidney beans, red, ckd —*½ cup*	112	2.6	0.8
Pine nuts, pignolia, dried —*1 oz*	160	2.6	2.6
Egg noodles, ckd —*1 cup*	213	2.5	0.5
Kidney beans, royal red, ckd —*½ cup*	109	2.5	0.8
Small white beans, ckd —*½ cup*	127	2.5	0.8
Chickpeas (garbanzo beans), ckd —*½ cup*	134	2.4	0.8
Navy beans, ckd —*½ cup*	148	2.4	0.5
Adzuki beans, ckd —*½ cup*	147	2.3	0.6
Lamb loin, New Zealand, broiled, trimmed —*3 ½ oz*	199	2.3	0.7
Navy beans, ckd —*½ cup*	129	2.3	0.7
Tempeh —*3 ½ oz*	198	2.3	0.6
Turkey, dark meat, roasted —*3 ½ oz*	187	2.3	0.7
Baked beans, w/ franks, canned —*½ cup*	184	2.2	0.5
Cowpeas (black-eyed peas), ckd —*½ cup*	100	2.2	0.7
Lima beans, baby, ckd —*½ cup*	115	2.2	0.7
Lima beans, large, canned —*½ cup*	95	2.2	0.5
Pinto beans, ckd —*½ cup*	117	2.2	0.7
Sesame seeds, kernels, toasted —*1 oz*	161	2.2	2.2
Barley, pearled, ckd —*1 cup*	193	2.1	0.4
Lima beans, fresh, boiled —*½ cup*	105	2.1	0.7
Great northern beans, canned —*½ cup*	149	2.1	0.4
Avocados, california —*1 medium*	306	2	0.3
English muffins, mixed grain —*1 muffin*	155	2	0.9
Spaghetti, ckd —*1 cup*	197	2	0.4
Swiss chard, fresh, boiled, chopped —*½ cup*	18	2	0.6
Great northern beans, ckd —*½ cup*	104	1.9	0.6
Humus, raw —*½ cup*	210	1.9	0.4
Oat bran, ckd —*1 cup*	88	1.9	0.2
Pasta, fresh, plain, uncooked —*2 oz*	164	1.9	0.9
Peas, edible-podded, frozen, boiled —*½ cup*	42	1.9	0.7
Pink beans, ckd —*½ cup*	126	1.9	0.7
Pistachio nuts, dried —*1 oz*	164	1.9	1.9
Pita bread, whole-wheat —*1 large*	170	1.9	0.8
Rolls, hard (including kaiser) —*1 roll*	167	1.9	0.9
Sunflower seed kernels, toasted —*1 oz*	175	1.9	1.9
Trout, mixed species, ckd, dry heat —*3 ½ oz*	190	1.9	0.5
Black beans, ckd —*½ cup*	114	1.8	0.6
Bulgur, ckd —*1 cup*	151	1.8	0.3
Lima beans, baby, frozen, boiled —*½ cup*	95	1.8	0.6
Pinto beans, canned —*½ cup*	103	1.8	0.4
Currants, european black, fresh —*1 cup*	71	1.7	0.4
Pumpkin, canned —*½ cup*	42	1.7	0.4
Sweet potato, canned, mashed —*½ cup*	129	1.7	0.4
Artichoke, fresh, boiled —*1 medium*	60	1.6	0.4

Leading Sources of Iron

	Calories	Iron (mg)	Iron per oz
Avocados, florida —*1 medium*	340	1.6	0.2
Beets, canned, slices —*½ cup*	26	1.6	0.5
Chickpeas (garbanzo beans), canned —*½ cup*	143	1.6	0.4
Oatmeal, reg/quick/instant, ckd —*1 cup*	145	1.6	0.2
Peaches, dried, halves, sulfured —*¼ cup*	96	1.6	1.2
Peas, edible-podded, fresh, boiled —*½ cup*	34	1.6	0.6
Pita bread, white —*1 large*	165	1.6	0.7
Tomato purée, canned —*½ cup*	50	1.6	0.4
Wild rice, raw —*½ cup*	286	1.6	0.6
Millet, ckd —*1 cup*	286	1.5	0.2
Onions, spring, tops & bulbs, fresh, raw, chopped —*1 cup*	32	1.5	0.4
Pork, tenderloin, roasted, trimmed —*3 ½ oz*	164	1.5	0.4
Spaghetti, whole-wheat, ckd —*1 cup*	174	1.5	0.3
Turkey, breast meat, no skin, roasted —*3 ½ oz*	135	1.5	0.4
Veal, shoulder, whole, braised, trimmed —*3 ½ oz*	199	1.5	0.4
Almonds, toasted, unblanched —*1 oz*	167	1.4	1.4
Beet greens, fresh, boiled, chopped —*½ cup*	19	1.4	0.5
Leeks (bulb & lower leaf-portion), fresh, boiled —*1 medium*	38	1.4	0.3
Mushrooms, fresh, boiled, slices —*½ cup*	21	1.4	0.5
Olives, ripe, canned, jumbo-super colossal —*5 jumbo*	34	1.4	0.9
Pumpkin pie mix, canned —*½ cup*	140	1.4	0.3
Radishes, oriental, fresh, raw —*1 radish*	61	1.4	0.1
Tomato juice, canned —*1 cup*	41	1.4	0.2
Chicken, drumstick, roasted —*3 ½ oz*	172	1.3	0.4
Jute, potherb, fresh, raw —*1 cup*	10	1.3	1.3
Peanuts, raw —*1 oz*	161	1.3	1.3
Tomatoes, crushed, canned —*3 ½ oz*	32	1.3	0.4
Apples, dried, sulfured —*1 cup*	209	1.2	0.4
Currants, zante, fresh —*¼ cup*	102	1.2	0.9
Peas, green, fresh, boiled —*½ cup*	67	1.2	0.4
Tomatoes, sun-dried, regular —*¼ cup*	35	1.2	2.6
Figs, dried —*¼ cup*	127	1.1	0.6
Prunes, dried —*¼ cup*	102	1.1	0.7
Collards, frozen, boiled, chopped —*½ cup*	31	1	0.3
Pears, dried, sulfured, halves —*¼ cup*	118	1	0.6
Pineapple, canned, crushed, slices, or chunks, water-pack —*1 cup*	79	1	0.1
Raisins —*¼ cup*	124	0.9	0.6
Blackberries, fresh —*1 cup*	75	0.8	0.2

MAGNESIUM

MAGNESIUM qualifies as a major mineral, but the body contains far less magnesium than it does of the other major minerals. On average, a 150-pound body contains about an ounce of magnesium—compared to nearly three pounds of calcium, for example. About 60 percent of the body's magnesium is stored in the bones; the rest is found in the cells. Though magnesium has received little attention in the past, recent research has uncovered more information on magnesium's role in health.

WHAT IT DOES

Magnesium is used in over 300 enzymatic reactions in the body, including those that help convert carbohydrates, fats, and protein into energy. It is a major component of bones and teeth and works closely with calcium. It is also involved in the proper functioning of nerves and muscles—for example, magnesium is needed to relax muscles after contraction—and helps regulate heart rhythm.

Some studies suggest that an adequate magnesium intake may help prevent coronary heart disease (CHD). The strongest evidence comes from studies showing that people who live in areas with hard water—which is high in magnesium—have a lower risk of CHD. In one Swedish study, men who lived in areas with the highest levels of magnesium in their drinking water had a 35 percent reduced risk of dying from a heart attack compared with men who lived in areas with the lowest levels. But other studies have shown no connection.

IF YOU GET TOO LITTLE

Weakness, irritability, muscle tremors, irregular heartbeat, and mental derangement are signs of a severe lack of magnesium in the diet. Alcoholics are especially prone to magnesium deficiency.

IF YOU GET TOO MUCH

Excessive magnesium can cause diarrhea, nausea, abdominal cramping, muscle weakness, drowsiness, confusion, heart abnormalities, and eventually, respiratory arrest. But the kidneys are very efficient at maintaining magnesium balance, excreting less of the mineral through urine when intake is low and more of it when intake is high. Thus people with healthy kidneys rarely have to worry about overloading on magnesium. Those with kidney disease, however, should be careful to monitor their magnesium intake.

HOW MUCH YOU NEED

AGE	RDA/MALE	RDA/FEMALE
19 to 24	350 mg	280 mg
25 to 50	350 mg	280 mg
51 and over	350 mg	280 mg

For recommendations for infants, children, adolescents, and pregnant or lactating women, see pages 18-19.

TIPS AND FACTS

- Thiazide diuretics prescribed for hypertension or congestive heart failure may cause magnesium deficiency, since these drugs increase urine output. If you take these drugs, be sure to eat foods high in magnesium, and ask your doctor if you need supplements.
- When used in high doses over long periods, over-the-counter magnesium-containing antacids (such as Mylanta, Maalox, and Di-Gel) or laxatives (milk of magnesia) can cause magnesium poisoning. This can seriously depress the cardiac and central nervous systems. When using these products, do not exceed the maximum dose listed on the label. If gastrointestinal symptoms persist, see your doctor.
- About 80 percent of the magnesium in grains is found in the bran and germ, which are removed in the milling of white rice and white flour. The mineral is not replaced when these grains are enriched. Therefore enriched grain products—white bread, pasta, and white rice, for example—are not good sources of magnesium.

WHERE YOU CAN FIND IT

Whole grains, nuts, seeds, legumes, cocoa, and green leafy vegetables are high in magnesium.

Leading Sources of Magnesium

	Calories	Magnesium (mg)	Magnesium per oz		Calories	Magnesium (mg)	Magnesium per oz
Amaranth, dry — *½ cup*	365	259	75	**Yardlong beans, ckd —** *½ cup*	101	84	28
Sunflower seed kernels, dried — *½ cup*	410	255	100	**Spinach, fresh, boiled —** *½ cup*	21	78	25
Quinoa, dry — *½ cup*	318	179	60	**Swiss chard, fresh, boiled, chopped —** *½ cup*	18	75	24
Wheat bran, crude — *½ cup*	63	177	173	**Cashews, dry-roasted —** *1 oz*	163	74	74
Pumpkin & squash seeds, roasted, hulled — *1 oz*	148	151	151	**Pumpkin & squash seeds, whole, roasted —** *1 oz*	126	74	74
Wild rice, raw — *½ cup*	286	142	50	**Soybeans, ckd —** *3 ½ oz*	149	74	24
Wheat germ, crude — *½ cup*	207	137	68	**Pollock, walleye, ckd —** *3 ½ oz*	113	73	21
Sardines, pacific, canned in tomato sauce, w/ bones, drained — *1 can*	659	126	10	**Artichoke, fresh, boiled —** *1 medium*	60	72	17
Natto — *3 ½ oz*	211	115	33	**Avocados, california —** *1 medium*	306	71	12
Halibut, ckd — *3 ½ oz*	140	107	30	**Sablefish, ckd —** *3 ½ oz*	250	71	20
Millet, ckd — *1 cup*	286	106	13	**Nopales, fresh, ckd —** *1 cup*	22	70	13
Avocados, florida — *1 medium*	340	103	10	**Tempeh —** *3 ½ oz*	198	70	20
Tofu, raw, regular — *3 ½ oz*	76	103	29	**Great northern beans, canned —** *½ cup*	149	67	15
Chocolate, semisweet chips — *½ cup*	402	97	33	**White beans, canned —** *½ cup*	153	67	15
Mackerel, atlantic, ckd — *3 ½ oz*	262	97	28	**Peaches, dehydrated, sulfured —** *1 cup*	377	66	16
Oysters, eastern, ckd — *3 ½ oz*	137	95	27	**Brazil nuts, dried, unblanched —** *1 oz*	186	64	64
Tofu, raw, firm — *3 ½ oz*	144	94	27	**Tuna, bluefin or yellowfin, ckd —** *3 ½ oz*	184	64	18
Oat bran, ckd — *1 cup*	88	88	11	**Crab, alaska king or queen, ckd —** *3 ½ oz*	97	63	18
Spaghetti, spinach, ckd — *1 cup*	182	87	18	**Lima bean, fresh, boiled —** *½ cup*	105	63	21
Almonds, dry-roasted, unblanched — *1 oz*	166	86	86	**Navy beans, canned —** *½ cup*	148	62	13
Buckwheat, groats, roasted, ckd — *1 cup*	155	86	15	**Black beans, ckd —** *½ cup*	114	60	20
Pollock, atlantic, ckd — *3 ½ oz*	118	86	24	**Bulgur, ckd —** *1 cup*	151	58	9
Rice, brown, ckd — *1 cup*	218	86	13	**White beans, ckd —** *½ cup*	124	56	18
Filberts (hazelnuts), dry-roasted, unblanched — *1 oz*	188	84	84	**Oatmeal, reg/quick/instant, ckd —** *1 cup*	145	56	7

MANGANESE

MANGANESE has been recognized as an essential dietary element since 1931, when deficiency of the mineral was found to hinder growth and adversely affect reproductive function in animal studies. However, no case of human deficiency was reported until 1972, when manganese was inadvertently omitted from a nutritional formula fed to a man participating in a study investigating the effects of vitamin K deficiency. Even today, most of our understanding of the functions of manganese comes from animal studies, because researchers have not been able to fully unravel the mechanisms that control its absorption, transport, and storage in the human body.

WHAT IT DOES

Manganese is important for the formation and maintainance of bone and connective tissue, and for proper brain formation. It is involved in a wide variety of enzymatic functions, including those that form urea (a chief component of urine), produce fats and cholesterol, and metabolize carbohydrates for energy. It also is important for the development of superoxide dismutase, an antioxidant enzyme produced by the body.

IF YOU GET TOO LITTLE

Outside of the laboratory, there has never been a report of deficiency of manganese in people. This is probably because this mineral is plentiful in the diets of most cultures, and also because magnesium can substitute for manganese in many functions. Animal studies show that a lack of manganese causes poor growth, skeletal abnormalities, and problems in carbohydrate and fat metabolism.

IF YOU GET TOO MUCH

Manganese toxicity is almost always the result of inhalation of the mineral in an industrial setting. Oral toxicity is possible, but extremely rare. Too much manganese can cause central nervous system complications, iron deficiency, and reproductive problems.

WHERE YOU CAN FIND IT

Nuts, shellfish, and whole grains are good sources of manganese. It is also found in coffee and tea.

HOW MUCH YOU NEED

There is no RDA for manganese, but the estimated safe and adequate daily dietary intake for adults is listed below.

AGE	RDA/MALE	RDA/FEMALE
19 to 24	2 to 5 mg	2 to 5 mg
25 to 50	2 to 5 mg	2 to 5 mg
51 and over	2 to 5 mg	2 to 5 mg

For recommendations for infants, children, adolescents, and pregnant or lactating women, *see pages 18-19.*

Leading Sources of Maganese

	Calories	Maganese (mg)	Maganese per oz
Wheat germ, crude — *½ cup*	207	7.65	3.77
Mussel, blue, ckd — *3 ½ oz*	172	6.8	1.93
Wheat bran, crude — *½ cup*	63	3.34	3.26
Pineapple, canned — *1 cup*	149	2.79	0.32
Pineapple, fresh, diced — *1 cup*	76	2.56	0.47
Amaranth, dry — *½ cup*	365	2.2	0.64
Rice, brown, ckd — *1 cup*	218	2.14	0.31
Oat bran, ckd — *1 cup*	88	2.11	0.27
Spaghetti, spinach, ckd — *1 cup*	182	2.11	0.43
Macaroni, whole-wheat, ckd — *1 cup elbow shaped*	174	1.93	0.39
Quinoa, dry — *½ cup*	318	1.92	0.64
Blackberries, fresh — *1 cup*	75	1.86	0.37
Natto — *3 ½ oz*	211	1.52	0.43
Sunflower seed kernels, dried — *½ cup*	410	1.45	0.57
Whole-wheat hot natural cereal, ckd — *1 cup*	150	1.41	0.17
Oatmeal, reg/quick/instant, ckd — *1 cup*	145	1.37	0.17
Pecans, dry roasted — *1 oz*	187	1.33	1.33
Raspberries, fresh — *1 cup*	60	1.25	0.29
Pine nuts, dried — *1 oz*	178	1.23	1.23
Oysters, pacific, ckd — *3 ½ oz*	163	1.22	0.35
English muffins, whole-wheat — *1 muffin*	134	1.18	0.51
Tofu, raw, firm — *3 ½ oz*	144	1.18	0.34
Bass, freshwater, ckd — *3 ½ oz*	146	1.14	0.32
Bulgur, ckd — *1 cup*	151	1.11	0.17
Pita bread, whole-wheat — *1 large*	170	1.11	0.49
Trout, mixed species, ckd — *3 ½ oz*	190	1.09	0.31
Lima beans, fresh, boiled — *½ cup*	105	1.06	0.36
Clams, ckd, moist heat — *3 ½ oz*	148	1	0.28
Matzo, whole-wheat — *1 matzo*	100	0.99	0.99
Perch, ckd, dry heat — *3 ½ oz*	117	0.9	0.26
Chickpeas (garbanzo beans) — *½ cup*	134	0.84	0.29
Spinach, fresh, boiled — *½ cup*	21	0.84	0.27
Rye wafers — *3 crackers*	110	0.83	0.71
Walnuts — *1 oz*	182	0.82	0.82
Rice, white, long-grain, ckd — *1 cup*	205	0.75	0.13
Okra, fresh, boiled, slices — *½ cup*	26	0.73	0.26
Chickpeas (garbanzo beans), canned — *½ cup*	143	0.72	0.17
Humus, raw — *½ cup*	210	0.7	0.16
Oysters, eastern, ckd, moist heat — *3 ½ oz*	137	0.7	0.2
Rice, white, medium-grain, ckd — *1 cup*	242	0.7	0.11
Buckwheat, groats, roasted, ckd — *1 cup*	155	0.68	0.11
Chocolate, semisweet chips — *½ cup*	402	0.67	0.23
White beans, canned — *½ cup*	153	0.67	0.15
Adzuki beans, ckd — *½ cup*	147	0.66	0.16
Millet, ckd — *1 cup*	286	0.65	0.08
Whole-wheat bread — *1 slice*	69	0.65	0.66
Peanut butter, chunk-style, w/ salt — *2 Tbsp*	188	0.6	0.53
Carrots, fresh, boiled, slices — *½ cup*	35	0.59	0.21

PHOSPHOROUS

PHOSPHOROUS and calcium are often called "twin nutrients," since about 85 percent of the phosphorous in the body is combined with calcium in bones and teeth. Yet nutritionally, phosphorus doesn't command the same attention as calcium, probably because phosphorus is found in such a wide variety of foods that it is difficult not to consume the required intake.

WHAT IT DOES

Phosphorus helps build bone and maintain the integrity of the skeleton. In fact, the bones and teeth will not harden without phosphorus. But phosphorus does much more than that. It also regulates the release of energy. Energy flow in the body is largely controlled by a compound called adenosine triphosphate, or ATP, which requires phosphorus.

Phosphorus is needed to help maintain the pH (the acid-base balance) of the blood. It also helps transport fats—in the form of phospholipids—throughout the bloodstream by making the fat water-soluble. In addition, phosphorus attaches to many nutrients to help transport them into and out of cells, and is needed to produce DNA and RNA.

IF YOU GET TOO LITTLE

A diet lacking in phosphorus can cause fragile bones, fatigue and weakness, loss of appetite, stiff joints, and an increased susceptibility to infection. Premature infants, and people who regularly take large amounts of aluminum-containing antacids, may be susceptible to phosphorus deficiency. The aluminium found in some types of antacids can bind with phosphorus and make it unavailable to the body. Premature infants require more phosphorus than is found in human milk, and without supplementation, are at risk of developing rickets.

IF YOU GET TOO MUCH

Excess phosphorus appears to have no adverse effect on the body. Animal studies have shown that when phosphorus intake far outweighs calcium intake, calcium absorption is inhibited. However, recent research in humans shows that even though excess phosphorus does limit the absorption of calcium, the body reduces calcium excretion in response. Thus, the two effects cancel each other out.

HOW MUCH YOU NEED

AGE	RDA/MALE	RDA/FEMALE
19 to 24	1,200 mg	1,200 mg
25 to 50	800 mg	800 mg
51 and over	800 mg	800 mg

For recommendations for infants, children, adolescents, and pregnant or lactating women, *see pages 18-19.*

WHERE YOU CAN FIND IT

Phosphorus is found in high-protein foods—meat, fish, poultry, and dairy products. It is also found in soft drinks, and it is part of an additive that is used in a wide variety of processed foods. Grains contain some phosphorus, but about 85 percent of it is chemically bound and unavailable to the body.

Leading Sources of Phosphrous

	Calories	Phosphrous (mg)	Phosphrous per oz
Sardines, pacific, canned in tomato sauce, w/ bones, drained —*1 can*	659	1354	104
Carp, ckd —*3 ½ oz*	162	531	151
Sunflower seed kernels, dried —*½ cup*	410	508	200
Wheat germ, crude —*½ cup*	207	484	239
Pollock, walleye, ckd —*3 ½ oz*	113	482	137
Sardines, atlantic, canned in oil, w/ bones, drained —*1 can*	191	451	139
Amaranth, dry —*½ cup*	365	444	129
Salmon, chinook, ckd —*3 ½ oz*	231	371	105
Yogurt, nonfat, plain —*8 oz container*	127	355	44
Quinoa, dry —*½ cup*	318	349	116
Whitefish ckd, dry heat —*3 ½ oz*	172	346	98
Wild rice, dry —*½ cup*	286	346	123
Pompano, florida, ckd, dry heat —*3 ½ oz*	211	341	97
Clams, ckd, moist heat —*3 ½ oz*	148	338	96
Swordfish, ckd, dry heat —*3 ½ oz*	155	337	96
Pumpkin & squash seeds, dried, hulled —*1 oz*	153	333	333
Salmon, coho, ckd, dry heat —*3 ½ oz*	178	332	94
Sunflower seed kernels —*1 oz*	175	328	328
Salmon, canned, sockeye, drained, w/ bones —*3 ½ oz*	153	326	92
Tuna, bluefin, ckd, dry heat —*3 ½ oz*	184	326	92
Yogurt, low-fat, plain —*8 oz container*	144	326	41
Mackerel, king, ckd, dry heat —*3 ½ oz*	134	318	90
Trout, mixed species, ckd, dry heat —*3 ½ oz*	190	314	89

	Calories	Phosphrous (mg)	Phosphrous per oz
Chicken liver, simmered —*3 ½ oz*	157	312	88
Tuna, canned, light, in oil, drained —*3 ½ oz*	198	311	88
Yogurt, low-fat, vanilla —*8 oz container*	194	306	38
Pork, tenderloin, broiled, trimmed —*3 ½ oz*	187	295	84
Salmon, pink, ckd, dry heat —*3 ½ oz*	149	295	84
Wheat bran, crude —*½ cup*	63	294	287
Flatfish (flounder & sole), ckd, dry heat —*3 ½ oz*	117	289	82
Salmon, sockeye, ckd —*3 ½ oz*	216	276	78
Skim milk, protein-fortified —*1 cup*	100	275	32
Bottom round, choice, braised, trimmed —*3 ½ oz*	213	272	77
Trout, rainbow, ckd —*3 ½ oz*	150	269	76
Biscuits, plain or buttermilk, from dry mix, baked —*1 biscuit*	191	268	133
Tuna, canned, white, in oil, drained —*3 ½ oz*	186	267	76
Oat bran, ckd —*1 cup*	88	261	34
Veal, sirloin, braised —*3 ½ oz*	204	259	73
Salmon, atlantic, ckd, dry heat —*3 ½ oz*	206	252	71
Evaporated milk, skim, canned —*½ cup*	100	250	55
Milk, skim —*1 cup*	86	247	29
Capon, meat & skin, roasted —*3 ½ oz*	229	246	70
Milk, 1% fat, w/ added nonfat milk solids —*1 cup*	104	245	28
Tuna, yellowfin, ckd —*3 ½ oz*	139	245	69
Oysters, pacific, ckd —*3 ½ oz*	163	243	69
Millet, ckd —*1 cup*	286	240	28

POTASSIUM, like sodium and chloride, is an electrolyte—a mineral that, when dissolved in body fluids, becomes an electrically charged particle called an ion. Positive and negatively charged ions work together to distribute fluids through the body and to maintain proper fluid balance. They also help to transport electrical impulses, as in nerve transmission or muscle movement.

WHAT IT DOES

Most of the potassium in the body is found in the fluids inside the cells. There, it is part of a number of metabolic actions, especially those that involve the release of energy. It is also needed for muscle growth. Outside the cell, potassium helps to regulate heartbeat and muscle contraction.

Potassium helps to regulate blood pressure. When blood pressure is normal, potassium will not reduce it. In some people with hypertension, however, an adequate potassium intake helps lower blood pressure, thus reducing the risk of stroke and heart disease. One study found that adding one serving of a high-potassium food to the diet every day may reduce the risk of fatal stroke by 40 percent, although this dramatic result has not been confirmed by other studies.

IF YOU GET TOO LITTLE

Potassium is widely found in foods, so true deficiencies are extremely rare. Excessive vomiting or diarrhea may cause a potassium deficiency, as can the use of diuretic drugs (these increase fluid output from the body). When deficiency does occur, it can result in weakness, fatigue, paralysis, abnormalities of heart contractions, and finally cardiac arrest.

IF YOU GET TOO MUCH

A very high level of potassium can cause weakness, paralysis, abdominal distention, and a very rapid heartbeat that can be fatal. But potassium overload is rare. The kidneys carefully control potassium balance, efficiently excreting excess amounts under normal circumstances. If the kidneys aren't functioning properly (as in kidney disease) there is a risk of potassium overload. It is difficult for healthy people to get too much potassium unless they are taking potassium supplements.

HOW MUCH YOU NEED

There is no RDA for potassium, but nutritionists recommend that adults consume 3,000 milligrams of potassium per day.

TIPS AND FACTS

- More potassium is found in lean cuts of meat than in fatty cuts, since potassium is concentrated in muscle tissue.
- Ounce for ounce, avocados and bananas have more potassium than any other fresh fruit.
- Potassium supplements can be dangerous, since they can lead to potassium overdose. The only people who may need supplements are those taking thiazide diuretics for hypertension or congestive heart failure, and then only under the supervision of a doctor. However, other medications prescribed for these conditions, such as ACE inhibitors, may increase potassium levels, so people taking them do not need potassium supplements.
- Endurance exercise can deplete your body of electrolytes but except under the most extreme circumstances, you don't need special sports drinks to replace them—your normal diet should suffice. In any case, sports drinks actually contain only small amounts of potassium.

WHERE YOU CAN FIND IT

Fruits and vegetables are excellent sources of potassium. Meats and some fish are also good sources.

Leading Sources of Potassium

	Calories	Potassium (mg)	Potassium per oz
Apricots, dried, sulfured —*1 cup*	309	1791	390
Peaches, dehydrated, sulfured —*1 cup*	377	1567	383
Avocados, florida —*1 medium*	340	1484	138
Sardines, pacific, canned in tomato sauce, w/ bones, drained —*1 can*	659	1262	97
Avocados, california —*1 medium*	306	1097	180
Potatoes, fresh, baked, w/skin —*1 potato*	220	844	118
Sapotes, fresh —*1 sapote*	302	774	98
Radishes, oriental, fresh, raw —*1 radish*	61	767	64
Natto —*3 ½ oz*	211	727	207
Waterchestnuts, chinese, fresh, raw, slices —*1 cup*	131	724	166
Carrot juice, canned —*1 cup*	94	689	83
Beet greens, fresh, boiled, chopped —*½ cup*	19	655	258
Jerusalem artichokes, fresh, raw, slices —*1 cup*	114	644	122
Pompano, florida, ckd, dry heat —*3 ½ oz*	211	636	180
Quinoa, dry —*½ cup*	318	629	210
Clams, ckd, moist heat —*3 ½ oz*	148	628	178
White beans, canned —*½ cup*	153	595	129
Yogurt nonfat, plain —*8 oz container*	127	579	72
Halibut, atlantic & pacific, ckd, dry heat —*3 ½ oz*	140	576	163
Tuna, yellowfin, ckd, dry heat —*3 ½ oz*	139	569	161
Mackerel, king, ckd, dry heat —*3 ½ oz*	134	558	158

	Calories	Potassium (mg)	Potassium per oz
Yellowtail, ckd, dry heat —*3 ½ oz*	187	538	152
Tomato juice —*1 cup*	41	535	62
Tomato puree, canned —*½ cup*	50	533	121
White beans, ckd —*½ cup*	124	502	159
Orange juice, fresh —*1 cup*	112	496	57
Cantaloupe, diced —*1 cup*	55	482	88
Swiss chard, fresh, boiled, chopped —*½ cup*	18	480	156
Bananas, whole —*1 medium*	109	467	112
Vegetable juice cocktail, canned —*1 cup*	46	467	55
Tomatoes, sun-dried, regular —*¼ cup*	35	463	971
Honeydew melon, diced —*1 cup*	60	461	77
Celery, fresh, raw, stalks —*4 medium*	26	459	81
Tomato sauce —*½ cup*	37	455	105
Pork, tenderloin, broiled, trimmed —*3 ½ oz*	187	451	128
Squash, winter, acorn, baked —*½ cup*	57	448	124
Pink beans, ckd —*½ cup*	126	429	144
Artichoke, fresh, boiled —*1 medium*	60	425	100
Spinach, fresh, boiled —*½ cup*	21	419	132
Skim milk, regular —*1 cup*	86	406	47
Grapefruit juice —*1 cup*	96	400	46
Haddock, ckd, dry heat —*3 ½ oz*	112	399	113

SELENIUM was not demonstrated to be a necessary part of the human diet until 1979, but it soon became a "hot" mineral, with many claims made for its disease-fighting potential. As a result, many people now take it as part of an "antioxidant cocktail" along with vitamins C and E and beta carotene. Though none of selenium's purported benefits have been proven, scientists have been studying its possible protective effects—against cancer and heart disease and perhaps even rheumatoid arthritis and AIDS.

WHAT IT DOES

Scientists are still discovering the exact role of selenium in the body. It is known that the mineral is an integral part of glutathione peroxidase, an antioxidant enzyme present in all cells, and works synergistically with vitamin E. In addition, selenium is needed for the proper functioning of the thyroid gland.

Whether selenium can protect against cancer is unclear. Several studies show that people living in areas of the world where the selenium content of the soil is very low have an increased incidence of cancer, but no study has shown that higher-than-normal intakes of selenium protect people.

A 1996 study showed that selenium supplements (200 micrograms per day) roughly halved the incidence of lung, colorectal, and prostate cancers in men. But several aspects of this study need to be resolved before supplements can be recommended. One important drawback: the subjects were selected because they lived in low-selenium areas, and many Americans get more selenium in their food than these subjects got from the supplements. Further research is needed to determine the cancer-preventive potential of selenium.

IF YOU GET TOO LITTLE

Selenium deficiency is rare, except in regions of the world (notably China) where the selenium content of the soil is five to ten times lower than the lowest levels in the United States, and locally grown foods are the only ones consumed. In China, a lack of selenium is the underlying factor in two health problems—Keshan disease, a condition involving enlargement of the heart, and a form of osteoarthritis that affects children and teenagers. Too little selenium may impair the immune system and reduce the ability of the body to neutralize toxic substances it is exposed to, such as certain drugs or chemicals in the environment.

HOW MUCH YOU NEED

AGE	RDA/MALE	RDA/FEMALE
19 to 24	70 mcg	55 mcg
25 to 50	70 mcg	55 mcg
51 and over	70 mcg	55 mcg

For recommendations for infants, children, adolescents, and pregnant or lactating women, see pages 18-19.

IF YOU GET TOO MUCH

The margin of safety between an adequate intake of selenium and a toxic dose is small compared with other nutrients. Serious side effects have been reported at daily doses of less than 1,000 micrograms.

Excess selenium can cause nausea, diarrhea, fatigue, nerve damage in the hands and feet, and hair and fingernail loss. It also produces a garlic odor on the breath.

TIPS AND FACTS

- If you want to take a selenium supplement, take one that supplies no more than 200 micrograms per day. Your best bet is to choose a multivitamin/mineral supplement that contains selenium; these typically provide 10 to 50 micrograms per pill.

WHERE YOU CAN FIND IT

Selenium is found in Brazil nuts, meats, poultry, seafood, grains, and grain products. The amount of selenium in plant foods depends on the selenium content of the soil. The values in the chart are provisional data from the United States Department of Agriculture.

Leading Sources of Selenium

	Calories	Selenium (mcg)	Selenium per oz
Brazil nuts, dried, unblanched —*1 oz*	186	839	839
Tuna, canned, light, in water, drained —*3 ½ oz*	116	80.4	22.8
Oysters, eastern, ckd, moist heat — *3 ½ oz*	137	71.6	20.3
Tuna, canned, white, in water, drained —*3 ½ oz*	128	65.7	18.6
Flatfish (flounder & sole), ckd, dry heat —*3 ½ oz*	117	58.2	16.5
Mackerel, atlantic, ckd, dry heat — *3 ½ oz*	262	51.6	14.6
Wheat germ, crude —*½ cup*	207	45.5	22.4
Sunflower seed kernels, dried — *½ cup*	410	42.8	16.9
Turkey, dark meat, roasted —*3 ½ oz*	187	40.9	11.6
Haddock, ckd, dry heat —*3 ½ oz*	112	40.5	11.5
Shrimp, ckd, moist heat —*3 ½ oz*	99	39.6	11.2
Turkey, light meat, roasted —*3 ½ oz*	157	32.1	9.1
Chicken breast, roasted —*3 ½ oz*	165	27.6	7.8
Farina, ckd —*1 cup*	117	21.2	2.6
Rice, brown, ckd —*1 cup*	216	19.1	2.8
Oatmeal, reg/quick/instant, ckd — *1 cup*	145	19	2.3
Rice, white, ckd —*1 cup*	242	14	2.1
Egg, whole, scrambled —*1 large*	101	13.7	6.4
Whole-wheat bread —*1 slice*	69	10.3	0.4
Mushrooms, fresh, raw, sliced —*1 cup*	18	8.6	3.5
Rye wafers —*3 crackers*	110	7.9	6.7
Tortillas, flour —*1 medium*	104	7.5	6.6
Yogurt, lowfat, plain —*8 oz container*	144	7.5	0.9
White bread —*1 slice*	67	7.1	8

	Calories	Selenium (mcg)	Selenium per oz
Pinto beans, ckd —*½ cup*	117	6.1	2
Baked beans, vegetarian, canned — *½ cup*	118	6	1.3
Navy beans, ckd —*½ cup*	129	5.3	1.6
Skim milk —*1 cup*	86	5.2	0.6
Mozzarella, part-skim, low moisture —*1 oz*	79	4.6	4.6
Lima beans, large, ckd —*½ cup*	108	4.2	1.3
Cheddar cheese —*1 oz*	114	3.9	3.9
Great northern beans, ckd —*½ cup*	104	3.6	1.2
Swiss cheese —*1 oz*	107	3.6	3.6
Peanut butter —*2 Tbsp*	188	2.4	2.1
Cowpeas (black-eyed peas), ckd —*½ cup*	100	2.2	0.7
Peanuts, dry-roasted —*1 oz*	166	2.1	2.1
Pears, fresh —*1 medium*	98	1.7	0.3
Pretzels, hard, plain, salted —*1 oz*	108	1.6	1.6
Asparagus, fresh, boiled, slices — *½ cup*	22	1.5	0.5
Pecans, dried —*1 oz*	189	1.5	1.5
Spinach, fresh, boiled —*½ cup*	21	1.4	0.4
Tortillas, corn —*1 medium*	58	1.4	1.6
Almonds, dried, unblanched —*1 oz*	167	1.3	1.3
Bananas —*1 medium*	109	1.3	0.3
Carrots, fresh, raw, slices —*1 cup*	52	1.3	0.3
Garlic, raw —*3 cloves*	13	1.3	4
Parmesan cheese, grated —*1 Tbsp*	23	1.3	7.4
Walnuts —*1 oz*	182	1.3	1.3

SODIUM

SODIUM is familiar to most people as table salt—sodium chloride—which is about 40 percent sodium. When most people think about cutting back on sodium, they think about cutting back on salt, but there are many forms of sodium added to foods in processing, and sodium occurs naturally in many foods.

Many organs interact to regulate the amount of sodium in the body. The chief monitors are the kidneys, adrenal glands, heart, and brain. This regulatory system will conserve sodium if you need it and excrete it if you have an excess. Although your sodium intake may vary from day to day, the amount of sodium in your body generally does not vary by more than 2 percent.

WHAT IT DOES

All cells in the body are bathed in a fluid that maintains cell function; the minerals in this fluid are 90 to 95 percent sodium salts. The quantity of sodium in these particles determines the fluid balance of the entire body. If the body is retaining more sodium, it must also retain more water to maintain the proper the electrolyte ratio.

HOW MUCH YOU NEED

There is no RDA for sodium, but the minimum amount you need for good health is about 115 milligrams per day. To ensure an adequate intake, the National Academy of Sciences recommends consuming at least 500 milligrams a day. Considering that a single serving of many processed foods supplies twice that amount, meeting the minimum intake is hardly a problem for most people. Instead, focus on *limiting* your intake to the recommended daily maximum: 2,400 milligrams of sodium per day. People with hypertension or kidney disease may be advised to consume even less.

IF YOU GET TOO LITTLE

Because sodium is so abundant in the diet, and because the body's regulatory system is so efficient, sodium deficiencies are practically unheard of. However, severe vomiting or diarrhea, or the profuse sweating that accompanies sustained and strenuous exercise on a very hot day, may dramatically lower sodium levels. In such circumstances, the body can release a hormone called angiotensin, which promtoes sodium retention in the body. But sodium levels can rapidly fall dangerously low under conditions of extreme sweating if fluid is not adequately replaced. Should this occur, a lack of sodium can lead to cardiovascular complications, coma, and even death.

IF YOU GET TOO MUCH

Eating too much salt triggers the body's thirst mechanism and encourages you to drink more fluids, and the regulatory system in the body will then increase urine production to help excrete the excess sodium.

Researchers aren't sure how, but a high sodium intake promotes hypertension. Some people are sodium-sensitive. This means that sodium raises their blood pressure. Sodium sensitivity increases with age. Recommendations for keeping sodium intake in check apply to everyone, however, since it can be difficult to determine who is sodium-sensitive and who is not before hypertension develops. In addition, even though you may not be sodium- sensitive at 30 or 40, your sensitivity may increase with the years.

Some evidence suggests that excessive sodium intake can accelerate calcium excretion in the urine, thus contributing to osteoporosis. This loss could affect your bones even if you consume lots of calcium.

TIPS AND FACTS

• A teaspoon of salt contains 2,400 milligrams of sodium.

• About 75 percent of the sodium Americans eat comes from processed foods and fast foods, not from their salt shakers.

• Cravings for salt are not primarily based on a physiological need for more sodium. Instead, people who eat a lot of salty foods crave salt because their systems are used to it. The cycle can be broken with relative ease. If you gradually cut back on salt, in a few weeks you will no longer crave foods that are highly salted. In fact, you may begin to find salty foods unpalatable.

• Sodium comes in forms other than table salt. A few of the common sources of sodium found in foods include: baking powder, baking soda, monosodium glutamate (MSG), sodium citrate, sodium nitrate, sodium phosphate, sodium saccharin. In addition, the following flavorings are high in sodium: brine, garlic salt, kelp, onion salt, sea salt, and soy sauce.

• On packaged foods, note that unsalted does not mean sodium-free, but that no salt was added to the product. Such foods may still be naturally high in sodium. The lowest-sodium foods will be labeled "very low sodium" (35 milligrams or less per serving) or "sodium-free" (less than 5 milligrams per serving). Those labeled "low sodium" have 140 milligrams or less per serving; "reduced-sodium" on a label indicates the product has at least 25 percent less sodium than the regular version.

• Reduce the sodium content of canned vegetables, beans, and water-pack tuna by draining the liquid and rinsing the food under cold running water before using.

• Bottled water may be high in sodium, especially mineral water, sparkling water, and club soda. Seltzer is generally sodium-free. Check nutrition labels.

Where you can find it

Fresh or unprocessed fruit, vegetables, meats, and eggs are generally low in sodium. Many packaged and canned foods are high in sodium, since it is added during processing, as are condiments, cheese, and fast foods. The chart below and on the next two pages lists the sodium content of foods.

Sodium Content of Foods

	Calories	Sodium (mg)	Sodium per oz
Salt, table —*1 tsp*	0	2326	10,981
Miso —*2 oz*	188	2092	1033
Salmon, chinook, lox —*3 ½ oz*	117	2000	567
Anchovy, canned in oil, drained —*1 can*	95	1651	1039
Sardines, pacific, canned in tomato sauce, w/ bones, drained —*1 can*	659	1532	117
Ham, cured, trimmed —*3 ½ oz*	147	1516	423
Pork, arm picnic, cured, roasted, trimmed —*3 ½ oz*	170	1231	349
Corned beef, ckd —*3 ½ oz*	251	1134	321
Crab, alaska king, ckd, moist heat —*3 ½ oz*	97	1072	304
Tomato paste, w/ salt —*½ cup*	107	1035	224
Soy sauce —*1 Tbsp*	10	1029	1619
Tomato juice, canned, w/ salt —*1 cup*	41	877	102
Pickles, dill —*1 medium*	12	833	363
Breakfast strips, beef, ckd —*3 slices*	153	766	638
Tomato sauce, canned —*½ cup*	37	741	171
Canadian-style bacon, grilled —*2 slices*	86	719	438
Teriyaki sauce —*1 Tbsp*	15	690	1086
Sausage, meatless —*3 links*	192	666	252
Vegetable juice cocktail, canned —*1 cup*	46	653	77
Frankfurter, turkey —*1 frankfurter*	102	642	404
Salami, pork, dry or hard —*1 oz*	115	639	640
Beef jerky —*1 oz*	116	627	627
Clam & tomato juice, canned —*5 fl oz*	69	604	113
Navy beans, canned —*½ cup*	148	587	127
Biscuits, plain or buttermilk, from dry mix, baked —*1 biscuit*	191	544	271
Stuffing, bread, from dry mix —*½ cup*	178	543	154

Sodium Content of Foods

	Calories	Sodium (mg)	Sodium per oz
Salmon, canned, sockeye, drained, w/ bones —*3 ½ oz*	153	538	152
Baked beans, vegetarian, canned —*½ cup*	118	504	113
Tomato, purée, canned, w/ salt —*½ cup*	50	499	113
Peppers, hot chili, canned, jalapeno, chopped —*¼ cup*	8	497	415
Pretzels, hard, plain, salted —*1 oz*	108	486	486
Sausage, smoked link, pork —*2 small links*	124	480	425
Sauerkraut, canned —*½ cup*	13	469	187
Sardines, atlantic, canned in oil, w/ bones, drained —*1 can*	191	465	143
Cottage cheese, 1% fat —*½ cup*	82	459	115
Parmesan, hard —*1 oz*	111	454	454
Kidney beans, red, canned —*½ cup*	109	437	97
Oysters, eastern, ckd, moist heat —*3 ½ oz*	137	422	120
English muffins, whole-wheat —*1 muffin*	134	420	181
American cheese, processed —*1 oz*	106	406	405
Ham deli meat, extra-lean —*1 slice*	37	405	405
Lima beans, large, canned —*½ cup*	95	405	95
Pickles, sweet —*1 cup, sliced*	50	399	266
Turkey breast, w/ skin, pre-basted, roasted —*3 ½ oz*	126	397	113
Blue cheese —*1 oz*	100	396	395
Tuna, canned, white, in oil, drained —*3 ½ oz*	186	396	112
Swiss cheese, processed —*1 oz*	95	389	388
Lobster, northern, ckd, moist heat —*3 ½ oz*	98	380	108
Bagels, plain, onion, poppy, or sesame —*1 bagel*	195	379	151
Oatmeal, instant, fortified, plain, ckd —*1 cup*	138	377	46

	Calories	Sodium (mg)	Sodium per oz
Refried beans, canned —*½ cup*	118	377	85
Tuna, canned, white, in water, drained —*3 ½ oz*	128	377	107
Olives, ripe, canned —*5 jumbo*	34	373	254
Mussel, blue, ckd, moist heat —*3 ½ oz*	172	369	105
Corn, sweet, white or yellow, canned, cream style, kernels —*½ cup*	92	365	81
Chickpeas (garbanzo beans), canned —*½ cup*	143	359	85
Pinto beans, canned —*½ cup*	103	353	83
Pastrami, beef —*1 oz*	99	348	348
Pita bread, whole-wheat —*1 large*	170	341	151
Salsa —*½ cup*	29	337	73
Mushrooms, canned —*½ cup*	19	332	120
Croissants, cheese —*1 medium*	236	316	157
Bacon, pan-fried —*3 medium slices*	109	303	452
Turkey breast, deli meat —*1 slice*	23	301	405
Beets, canned, pickled, slices —*½ cup*	74	300	75
Humus, raw —*½ cup*	210	300	69
Cheese puffs —*1 oz*	157	298	298
Pastrami, turkey —*1 slice*	40	296	296
Bacon, meatless —*4 strips*	62	293	415
Tortilla chips, nacho-flavor, light —*1 oz*	126	284	284
Tomatoes, canned, wedges, in tomato juice —*½ cup*	34	283	62
Tomatoes, sun-dried, regular —*¼ cup*	35	283	594
Turkey ham, deli meat —*1 slice*	36	282	282
Pumpkin pie mix, canned —*½ cup*	140	281	59

Sodium Content of Foods

	Calories	Sodium (mg)	Sodium per oz
Crab, blue, ckd, moist heat —*3 ½ oz*	102	279	79
Rye wafers —*3 crackers*	110	262	225
Hoisin sauce —*1 Tbsp*	35	258	458
Buttermilk —*1 cup*	99	257	30
Saltines —*3 crackers*	78	234	369
French rolls —*1 roll*	105	231	173
Peanuts, dry-roasted, w/ salt —*1 oz*	166	231	230
Shrimp, ckd, moist heat —*3 ½ oz*	99	224	64
Almonds, dry-roasted, unblanched, w/ salt —*1 oz*	166	221	221
Pistachios, dry-roasted, w/ salt —*1 oz*	172	221	221
Sunflower seed kernels, dry-roasted w/ salt —*1 oz*	165	221	221
Peas, green, canned —*½ cup*	59	214	71
Salad dressing, french —*1 Tbsp*	67	214	388
Potato chips, barbecue-flavor —*1 oz*	139	213	213
Oysters, pacific, ckd, moist heat —*3 ½ oz*	163	212	60
Rye bread —*1 slice*	83	211	187
Mackerel, king, ckd, dry heat —*3 ½ oz*	134	203	58
Rolls, hamburger or hot dog, mixed grain —*1 roll*	113	197	130
Milk crackers —*3 crackers*	150	196	168
Olives, ripe, canned, —*5 large*	25	192	247
Cashews, dry-roasted, w/ salt —*1 oz*	163	181	181
Brie —*1 oz*	95	178	178
Catsup —*1 Tbsp*	16	178	336
Tomatoes, canned, whole —*½ cup*	23	178	42
Yogurt, nonfat, plain —*8 oz container*	127	174	22
Pickle relish, hamburger —*1 Tbsp*	19	164	311
Fish sticks, frozen —*1 stick*	76	163	165
Pumpkin & squash seeds, roasted, w/ salt —*1 oz*	148	163	163
Swiss chard, fresh, boiled, chopped —*½ cup*	18	157	51
Peanut butter, chunk-style, w/ salt —*2 Tbsp*	188	156	138
Cream cheese, fat-free —*1 oz*	27	155	155
Ricotta cheese, part-skim —*½ cup*	171	155	35
Tortillas, flour —*1 medium*	104	153	135
Margarine, soft —*1 Tbsp*	101	152	306
Tortilla chips, plain —*1 oz*	142	150	150
Mozzarella, part-skim, low moisture —*1 oz*	79	150	150
Whole-wheat bread —*1 slice*	69	148	149
Goat, semisoft —*1 oz*	103	146	146
Chicken egg, whole, poached —*1 large*	75	140	79
Celery, fresh, raw, stalks —*4 medium*	26	139	25
White bread —*1 slice*	67	136	152
Margarine, stick —*1 Tbsp*	101	133	267

ZINC

ZINC is plentiful in oysters, and this might be why oysters have a reputation as an aphrodisease: Zinc is essential for proper sexual maturation and the manufacture of testosterone, but megadoses of zinc (or oysters for that matter) do not actually have any effect on libido or sexual prowess. Still, zinc is a remarkable nutrient. It is present in all the body's tissues and is involved in over 100 enzymatic reactions. Yet despite its ubiquitous role, zinc wasn't considered essential to human health until the 1960s, when it was discovered that a zinc deficiency was responsible for growth retardation and delayed puberty in teenage boys in Iran and Egypt. Zinc was not included in the RDAs until 1974.

What it does

Zinc is a fundamental part of the enzymes that are used to produce DNA and RNA, the genetic material within cells, and so is used for cell duplication. This is why zinc is so necessary for proper growth. It is also involved in protein metabolism, particularly in the synthesis of collagen. It also plays a role in wound healing, helps the body use vitamin A, maintains the senses of taste and smell, aids in the use of insulin, and helps strengthen the immune system.

How Much You Need

AGE	RDA/MALE	RDA/FEMALE
19 to 24	15 mg	12 mg
25 to 50	15 mg	12 mg
51 and over	15 mg	12 mg

For recommendations for infants, children, adolescents, and pregnant or lactating women, see pages 18-19.

If you get too little

Because zinc is so widely dispered in the body's tissues, a diagnosis of mild deficiency is difficult. Some experts suggest that it is more common than most people think, especially in children, adults on special diets, and the elderly.

In infants and children, a zinc deficiency will inhibit growth and sexual maturation. Even mild deficiencies in children will dull the sense of taste, cause poor appetite, and result in suboptimal growth.

In both children and adults, a low intake can also contribute to impaired sense of taste and smell, delayed wound healing, weakened immune function (particularly in the elderly), and skin problems (especially acne). In pregnant women, a zinc deficiency can result in low-birth-weight babies.

If you get too much

As little as 18 to 25 milligrams of zinc per day, if taken for long periods, interferes with the absorption of copper. In addition, large doses can impair blood-cell formation and depress the immune system. Just 50 to 75 milligrams of zinc per day can reduce levels of HDL ("good") cholesterol. Nausea, vomiting, and diarrhea may also result from doses of 200 milligrams of zinc per day.

Tips and facts

• Small amounts of zinc taken frequently are better absorbed than a single dose of the same total amount, so try to include good sources of zinc in every meal.

• Fiber and phytates (chemicals present in some grains, such as wheat) can inhibit zinc absorption. It is possible that people on a high-fiber diet might not get enough zinc, especially if they eat little or no meat.

• There is no good evidence that excess zinc can cause Alzhemizer's disease. A 1994 study received much attention because it indicated that in a test tube, zinc produces changes in nerve cells similar to the ones that take place in the brains of people with Alzhemier's. But what happens in a laboratory experiment cannot be translated to what happens in the human body.

• Zinc may be able to ease cold symptoms. One study found that a particular brand of zinc lozenge had this effect. The theory is that zinc in the mouth and throat somehow deactivates cold viruses. (High doses of zinc will not prevent a cold, however.) But, zinc takers reported nausea, mouth irritation, and a bad taste in the mouth, and the results from the study were far from conclusive. Individuals will have to decide for themselves whether it is worth risking these side effects to possibly shorten the duration of a cold.

WHERE YOU CAN FIND IT

Red meat, shellfish (especially oysters), legumes, nuts, and organ meats are good sources of zinc. Whole grains also contain zinc, but the mineral is not as readily absorbed from them.

Leading Sources of Zinc

	Calories	Zinc (mg)	Zinc per oz
Oysters, eastern, ckd, moist heat —*3 ½ oz*	137	182	51
Oysters, pacific, ckd, moist heat —*3 ½ oz*	163	33	9.4
Crab, alaska king, ckd, moist heat —*3 ½ oz*	97	7.6	2.2
Baked beans, w/ pork & tomato sauce, canned —*½ cup*	124	7.4	1.7
Tip round, select, roasted, trimmed —*3 ½ oz*	170	7	2
Veal shoulder, whole, braised, trimmed —*3 ½ oz*	199	7	2
Wheat germ, crude —*½ cup*	207	7	3.5
Sardines, pacific, canned in tomato sauce, w/ bones, drained —*1 can*	659	5.2	0.4
Lamb, leg, whole, domestic, choice, roasted, trimmed —*3 ½ oz*	191	4.9	1.4
Chicken giblets, simmered —*3 ½ oz*	157	4.6	1.3
Turkey, dark meat, roasted —*3 ½ oz*	187	4.5	1.3
Chicken liver, simmered —*3 ½ oz*	157	4.3	1.2
Crab, blue, ckd, moist heat —*3 ½ oz*	102	4.2	1.2
Leg, whole, New Zealand, roasted, trimmed —*3 ½ oz*	181	4	1.2
Chicken, dark meat, roasted —*3 ½ oz*	205	2.8	0.8
Pork, loin, roasted, trimmed —*3 ½ oz*	209	2.5	0.7
Turkey, light meat, roasted —*3 ½ oz*	157	2	0.6
Baked beans, vegetarian, canned —*½ cup*	118	1.8	0.4
Turkey, breast meat w/o skin, roasted —*3 ½ oz*	135	1.7	0.5
Cashews, dry-roasted —*1 oz*	163	1.6	1.6
Spaghetti, spinach, ckd —*1 cup*	182	1.5	0.3
Swordfish, ckd, dry heat —*3 ½ oz*	155	1.5	.42
Tofu, raw, firm —*3 ½ oz*	144	1.5	0.5
White beans, canned —*½ cup*	153	1.5	0.3
Almonds, dry roasted, unblanched —*1 oz*	166	1.4	1.4
Avocados, florida —*1 medium*	340	1.3	0.1
Barley, pearled, ckd —*1 cup*	193	1.3	0.2
Brazil nuts, dried, unblanched —*1 oz*	186	1.3	1.3
Chickpeas (garbanzo beans), canned —*½ cup*	143	1.3	0.3
Lentils, ckd —*½ cup*	115	1.3	0.4
Chicken, light meat, roasted —*3 ½ oz*	173	1.2	0.4
Oat bran, ckd —*1 cup*	88	1.2	0.2
Oatmeal, reg/quick/instant, ckd —*1 cup*	145	1.2	0.1
Pine nuts, pignolia, dried —*1 oz*	160	1.2	1.2
Whole-wheat hot natural cereal, ckd —*1 cup*	150	1.2	0.1
Rice, brown, ckd —*1 cup*	218	1.1	0.2
Sausage, meatless —*3 links*	192	1.1	0.4
Spaghetti, whole-wheat, ckd —*1 cup*	174	1.1	0.2
English muffins, whole-wheat —*1 muffin*	134	1	0.5
Tuna, skipjack, ckd, dry heat —*3 ½ oz*	132	1	0.3

BORON

BORON was used to preserve foods such as meat, shellfish, and butter in the late nineteenth century—a function that was prized in times of poor refrigeration and food shortages. Thus, people consumed large amounts of boron with no apparent ill effects, until one study suggested that a high intake over a period of a few weeks could cause appetite loss and digestive problems. As a result, the addition of boron to foods was banned, and the mineral was pretty much forgotten. But in the late 1980s, interest in boron was revived to such an extent that exaggerated claims were being made for its health benefits. The truth is that boron is essential to human health, though nutritionists still have much to learn about its functions and its degree of importance.

WHAT IT DOES

Although the role boron plays in human health is still under investigation, research has shown that the mineral helps to maintain the structure of cell membranes. It is also involved in the metabolism of several minerals—especially calcium—and may enhance the effects of estrogen. Thus, boron helps build and preserve bone mass. It may also help regulate brain function.

IF YOU GET TOO MUCH

It is difficult to overload on boron by eating foods, but if you take supplements you might get too much. Intakes up to 10 milligrams per day appear to be safe, but daily doses above 50 milligrams may have adverse consequences. An overload of boron can cause gastrointestinal upset, skin problems, and seizures.

IF YOU GET TOO LITTLE

A poor intake of boron may increase the risk of developing osteoporosis in post-menopausal women. It may also affect motor function and cognitive performance.

TIPS AND FACTS

- Boron has been touted as a miracle mineral. Some people believe that it cures arthritis; improves memory; prevents the hot flashes that occur in menopause; and builds muscle mass. These claims have been exaggerated from the results of small, preliminary studies involving people whose intake of boron was extremely low. There's absolutely no evidence that a high intake of boron can produce any of these effects.

HOW MUCH YOU NEED

Because research into boron is in its early stages, there is no RDA and no estimated safe and adequate daily dietary intake for this mineral. However, experts believe that 1 milligram a day is enough to meet the body's need for boron. Average daily boron intake in the United States has been estimated to be between 0.5 and 3.1 milligrams per day.

WHERE YOU CAN FIND IT

Nuts, legumes, leafy green vegetables, and dried beans are good sources of boron, as are beer and wine. Animal products tend to be low in this mineral.

CHROMIUM

CHROMIUM is an essential trace mineral that the body requires in very small amounts. Several claims have been made for chromium, particularly in supplement form: that it helps burn fat and build muscle; that it is a cure for diabetes; and that it will help lower blood cholesterol levels. The real story, however, is fraught with ifs, buts, and unanswered questions.

What it does

Chromium is important in the burning of carbohydrates and fats, and in some aspects of protein metabolism. It is needed for the body to use insulin properly. Without chromium, insulin cannot make blood sugar (glucose, our basic fuel) available to cells, the exact role chromium plays in this process is not known.

If you get too little

A deficiency of chromium seems to be one factor in some cases of glucose intolerance, also called insulin resistance. In this condition, the cells do not respond to insulin, and so do not use glucose as they normally should. Although this condition is a symptom of diabetes, diabetes is not caused by a chromium deficiency, and taking supplements will not cure the disease.

There is some evidence that a lack of chromium can cause high blood cholesterol levels and low HDL ("good") cholesterol levels, but the studies have been inconsistent.

If you get too much

Chromium itself is not known to have any adverse effect in large doses. The mineral comes in many forms, however. In a laboratory study, chromium picolinate was found to cause damage to the chromosomes in the cells of hamsters, raising the question of whether the mineral can cause cancer. Other forms of chromium did not cause the same damage, so the culprit was probably the picolinate, not the chromium. Of course, no one knows if the findings would also apply to people, but since there appears to be little benefit in taking chromium supplements, it would be wise to avoid them.

Tips and facts

- Vitamin C enhances chromium absorption.
- Calorie for calorie, diets that are high in fat tend to contain less chromium than low-fat diets.
- Cooking acidic foods in stainless steel pots may boost the food's chromium content, since the mineral will leach from stainless steel.
- Chromium is not useful as a weight-loss or bodybuilding aid. In one study, chromium pills did not help football players build muscle or lose fat. There is no reason to think chromium would build muscle.

How Much You Need

It is hard to measure chromium levels in the body, so it's difficult to say exactly how much chromium you need. A range of intakes is recommended.

AGE	MALE	FEMALE
19 to 24	50 to 200 mcg	50 to 200 mcg
25 to 50	50 to 200 mcg	50 to 200 mcg
51 and over	50 to 200 mcg	50 to 200 mcg

For recommendations for infants, children, adolescents, and pregnant or lactating women, see pages 18-19.

Where you can find it

Whole grains, brewer's yeast, prunes, nuts, peanut butter, potatoes, and seafood are high in chromium.

IODINE

IODINE is closely associated with normal functioning of the thyroid gland. This small gland, located in the neck on either side of the trachea (windpipe), regulates metabolism and growth. Despite its small size—less than an ounce—the thyroid gland of a healthy adult has a remarkable ability to store iodine. The body typically contains 20 to 30 milligrams of the mineral, and 75 percent of it is stored in the thyroid gland.

WHAT IT DOES

Iodine is essential for the formation of the thyroid hormone thyroxin, which governs metabolism and growth. There is also some evidence that thyroxin is involved in the conversion of beta carotene to vitamin A, in the synthesis of protein and cholesterol, and in the absorption of carbohydrates. In addition, it is essential for reproduction.

IF YOU GET TOO LITTLE

If your diet is lacking in iodine, the thyroid gland will enlarge in an attempt to trap as much iodine from the blood as possible. Once the enlargement becomes visible, it is called a goiter. (However, not all goiters are caused by an iodine deficiency.)

A low iodine intake also causes insufficient production of thyroid hormones. Among the consequences of diminished thyroid hormone production are fatigue, skin changes, an increase in blood fats, hoarseness, delayed reflex reactions, and reduced mental functioning.

A lack of iodine in the diets of pregnant women can cause a severe form of mental retardation called cretinism in the baby. In children, an iodine deficinecy can adversely effect intellectual ability.

Fortunately, there have been no cases of iodine deficiency reported in the United States since the 1970s, although it still may be a problem in developing countries.

IF YOU GET TOO MUCH

The typical American diet contains far more iodine than the RDA with no adverse effects. Indeed iodine appears to be benign even in intakes 10 to 20 times the RDA. However, extremely high doses can also cause goiters.

TIPS AND FACTS

• Sea salt is not a good source of iodine. This type of salt, often sold in health-food stores, is made by drying sea water, but the iodine it contains is lost during the drying process.

• Although many processed foods contain added salt, iodized salt is not typically used. However, dough conditioners used in some baked goods are high in iodine, and so these foods contribute signifcant amounts of iodine to the diet.

HOW MUCH YOU NEED

AGE	RDA/MALE	RDA/FEMALE
19 to 24	150 mcg	150 mcg
25 to 50	150 mcg	150 mcg
51 and over	150 mcg	150 mcg

For recommendations for infants, children, adolescents, and pregnant or lactating women, see pages 18-19.

WHERE YOU CAN FIND IT

Iodized table salt is obviously a good source of iodine. Iodine is present in salt water, so fish and shellfish are a also good sources. Dairy products, too, contain some iodine. The amount of iodine in fruits and vegetables depends on the soil they are grown in.

MOLYBDENUM was first determined to be an essential nutrient for humans in 1953. But since it is needed in amounts far below those of other trace elements, and because deficiencies are unknown, there has been little research into the effects of molybdenum on health. Still, researchers know that molybdenum is required, and that even a poor diet seems to supply enough to meet the body's needs.

WHAT IT DOES

Molybdenum is needed to produce enzymes that aid in various chemical reactions in the body, notably those that form uric acid, a waste product that is excreted by the body through urine. It may help the body retain fluoride and aid in the release of iron from iron stores in the liver when the body requires it. It is also involved in interactions involving copper and sulfur.

IF YOU GET TOO MUCH

Megadoses of molybdenum can interfere with the absorption of copper and produce signs of copper deficiency.

IF YOU GET TOO LITTLE

There has never been a report of a molybdenum deficiency in people with normal diets. In one case where molybdenum was inadvertently omitted from a formula fed to a person receiving nutrition intravenously, the result was irritabilty, reduced uric acid and sulfur output, and ultimately, coma.

TIPS AND FACTS

• One survey found that in the United States, people generally consume between 120 and 240 micrograms of molybdenum per day. Another found the range to be between 76 and 109 micrograms. Both surveys indicate that the daily intake of this trace mineral is well above recommended guidelines.

WHERE YOU CAN FIND IT

Milk, legumes, grains, and cereals are good sources of molybdenum. The molybdenum content of plant foods depends on the soil they are grown in.

HOW MUCH YOU NEED

The estimated safe and adequate dietary intake for molybdenum is listed below.

AGE	MALE	FEMALE
19 to 24	75 to 250 mcg	75 to 250mcg
25 to 50	75 to 250 mcg	75 to 250mcg
51 and over	75 to 250 mcg	75 to 250mcg

For recommendations for infants, children, adolescents, and pregnant or lactating women, see pages 18-19.

Foods, General

Baby Foods

	Weight g	Calories	Carbohydrates g	Cholesterol mg	Dietary fiber g	Total fat g	Mono. fat g	Poly. fat g	Sat. fat g	Protein g	Calcium mg	Iron mg	Potassium mg	Sodium mg	Zinc mg	Vitamin A RE	Vitamin B_{12} mcg	Vitamin B_6 mg	Vitamin C mg	Folic acid mcg	Niacin mg	Riboflavin mg	Thiamin mg
Apples & raspberry w/ sugar																							
junior — *1 jar*	170	99	26.4	0	3.6	0.3	0	0.1	0.1	0.3	9	0	122	3	0.1	5	0	0.06	49	5.6	0.2	0.05	0.02
strained — *1 jar*	113	66	17.7	0	2.4	0.2	0	0.1	0	0.2	6	0	90	2	0	2	0	0.04	30	3.8	0.1	0.03	0.02
Apples, toddler — *1 jar*	113	58	13.7	0	1	0.1	0	0	0	0.2	11	0	57	15	0	1	0	0.06	35	1.1	0.1	0.02	0.01
Applesauce																							
junior — *1 jar*	170	63	17.5	0	2.9	0	0	0	0	0	9	0	131	3	0.1	2	0	0.05	64	2.9	0.1	0.05	0.02
strained — *1 jar*	113	46	12.3	0	1.9	0.2	0	0.1	0	0.2	5	0	80	2	0	2	0	0.04	43	2.2	0.1	0.03	0.01
Applesauce & apricots																							
junior — *1 jar*	170	80	21.1	0	3.1	0.3	0.1	0.1	0	0.3	10	0	185	5	0.1	58	0	0.05	30	2.4	0.2	0.05	0.02
strained — *1 jar*	113	51	13.1	0	2	0.2	0	0.1	0	0.2	7	0	136	3	0	44	0	0.03	21	1.5	0.2	0.03	0.02
Applesauce & cherries																							
junior — *1 jar*	170	95	24	0	1.9	0	0	0	0	0	2	1	224	2	0	7	0	0.07	73	0.7	0.2	0.05	0.02
strained — *1 jar*	113	58	15.9	0	1.2	0	0	0	0	0	1	0	149	1	0	5	0	0.04	48	0.5	0.2	0.03	0.01
Applesauce & pineapple																							
junior — *1 jar*	170	66	17.9	0	2.6	0.2	0	0.1	0	0.2	7	0	129	3	0.1	3	0	0.07	46	3.4	0.1	0.05	0.04
strained — *1 jar*	113	42	11.4	0	1.7	0.1	0	0	0	0.1	5	0	88	2	0	2	0	0.04	32	2.2	0.1	0.03	0.02
Applesauce w/ banana, junior — *1 jar*	170	112	27.5	0	2.7	0.2	0	0.1	0.1	0.6	9	0	223	5	0.1	3	0	0.17	29	5.1	0.3	0.05	0.02
Apricots w/ tapioca																							
junior — *1 jar*	170	107	29.4	0	2.6	0	0	0	0	0.5	14	0	213	10	0.1	122	0	0.05	30	2.7	0.3	0.02	0.01
strained — *1 jar*	113	68	18.4	0	1.7	0	0	0	0	0.3	10	0	137	9	0.1	81	0	0.03	24	1.7	0.2	0.01	0.01
Arrowroot cookies — *2 oz*	56.7	251	40.4	1	0.1	8.1	5.1	0.5	1.9	4.3	18	2	88	210	0.3	0	0	0.02	3	5.7	3.3	0.24	0.28
Bananas & pineapple w/ tapioca																							
junior — *1 jar*	170	116	31.3	0	2.7	0.2	0	0	0.1	0.3	12	0	133	14	0.1	7	0	0.16	36	9.4	0.3	0.03	0.03

	Weight g	Calories	Carbohydrates g	Cholesterol mg	Dietary fiber g	Total fat g	Mono. fat g	Poly. fat g	Sat. fat g	Protein g	Calcium mg	Iron mg	Potassium mg	Sodium mg	Zinc mg	Vitamin A RE	Vitamin B_{12} mcg	Vitamin B_6 mg	Vitamin C mg	Folic acid mcg	Niacin mg	Riboflavin mg	Thiamin mg
strained — *1 jar*	113	73	20.1	0	1.8	0	0	0	0	0.2	8	0	77	7	0	5	0	0.09	22	6.1	0.2	0.02	0.02
Bananas w/ tapioca																							
junior — *1 jar*	170	114	30.3	0	2.7	0.3	0	0.1	0.1	0.7	14	1	184	15	0.1	7	0	0.24	44	10.9	0.4	0.03	0.03
strained — *1 jar*	113	64	17.3	0	1.8	0.1	0	0	0	0.5	6	0	99	10	0.1	5	0	0.13	19	6.2	0.2	0.04	0.01
Beef																							
junior — *1 jar*	71	75	0	20	0	3.5	1.3	0.1	1.8	10.3	6	1	135	47	1.4	22	1	0.09	1	4.1	2.3	0.11	0.01
strained — *1 jar*	71	76	0	21	0	3.8	1.6	0.2	1.8	9.7	5	1	156	58	1.7	14	1	0.1	1	3.9	2	0.1	0.01
Beef & rice, toddler — *1 jar*	170	139	15	0	0	4.9	0	0	0	8.5	19	1	204	607	1.6	134	0.9	0.24	7	10.2	2.3	0.12	0.03
Beef lasagna, toddler — *1 jar*	170	131	17	0	0	3.6	0	0	0	7.1	31	1	207	772	1.2	265	0.9	0.12	3	10.2	2.3	0.15	0.12
Beef noodle																							
junior — *1 jar*	170	97	12.6	14	1.9	3.2	1.4	0.2	1.3	4.3	14	1	78	29	0.7	150	0.2	0.05	2	9.4	1	0.06	0.05
strained — *1 jar*	113	60	7.9	8	1.2	1.9	0.8	0.1	0.8	2.6	10	0	53	33	0.4	124	0.1	0.05	1	5.8	0.8	0.05	0.04
Beef stew, toddler — *1 jar*	170	87	9.4	21	1.9	2	0.7	0.2	1	8.7	15	1	241	587	1.5	425	0.9	0.13	5	10.2	2.2	0.11	0.02
Beef w/ vegetables & dumplings																							
junior — *1 jar*	170	82	13.6	0	0	1.4	0	0	0	3.6	24	1	80	88	0.6	151	0.2	0.08	1	12.6	0.8	0.06	0.07
strained — *1 jar*	113	54	8.7	0	0	1	0	0	0	2.3	16	0	52	55	0.5	63	0.1	0.05	1	8.1	0.6	0.05	0.06
Beets, strained — *1 jar*	113	38	8.7	0	2.1	0.1	0	0	0	1.5	16	0	206	94	0.1	3	0	0.03	3	34.8	0.1	0.05	0.01
Carrots																							
junior — *1 jar*	170	54	12.2	0	2.9	0.3	0	0.2	0.1	1.4	39	1	343	83	0.3	2008	0	0.14	9	29.4	0.8	0.07	0.04
strained — *1 jar*	113	31	6.8	0	1.9	0.1	0	0.1	0	0.9	25	0	221	42	0.2	1295	0	0.08	6	16.8	0.5	0.05	0.03
Cereal, barley, dry — *2 oz*	60	219	45.2	0	4.9	2	0.4	1.1	0.3	6.7	477	29	237	28	1.9	1	0	0.22	1	17.4	21.6	1.62	1.64
Cereal, high protein, dry — *2 oz*	60	217	28	0	4.3	3.5	0.7	1.7	0.5	21.6	434	29	812	28	2.7	1	0	0.29	1	114	20.4	1.62	1.6
Cereal, mixed, dry — *2 oz*	60	227	44	0	4.5	2.6	0.7	1	0.5	7.3	440	29	262	23	1.4	1	0	0.11	1	25.7	20.8	1.63	1.46
Cereal, oatmeal, dry — *2 oz*	60	239	41.5	0	4	4.7	1.5	1.7	0.8	8.2	440	29	282	20	2.2	1	0	0.09	2	21.2	21.6	1.56	1.73

	Weight g	Calories	Carbohydrates g	Cholesterol mg	Dietary fiber g	Total fat g	Mono. fat g	Poly. fat g	Sat. fat g	Protein g	Calcium mg	Iron mg	Potassium mg	Sodium mg	Zinc mg	Vitamin A RE	Vitamin B_{12} mcg	Vitamin B_6 mg	Vitamin C mg	Folic acid mcg	Niacin mg	Riboflavin mg	Thiamin mg
Cereal, rice, dry — *2 oz*	60	235	46.6	0	0.3	2.9	0.8	1.2	0.6	4.3	510	29	231	19	1.2	1	0	0.29	1	14.6	18.7	1.33	1.59
Cherry cobbler, junior — *2 oz*	60	47	11.5	0	0.1	0.1	0	0	0	0.2	3	0	27	26	0	2	0	0.01	6	1.2	0	0.01	0.01
Cherry vanilla pudding																							
junior — *1 jar*	170	117	31.3	17	0.5	0.3	0.1	0.1	0.1	0.3	9	0	56	26	0.1	34	0	0.02	2	0.5	0.1	0.02	0.01
strained — *1 jar*	113	77	20.1	11	0.3	0.3	0.1	0.1	0.1	0.2	6	0	38	18	0	23	0	0.01	1	0.3	0	0.01	0.01
Chicken																							
junior — *1 jar*	71	106	0	42	0	6.8	3.1	1.7	1.8	10.4	39	1	87	36	0.7	9	0.3	0.13	1	7.9	2.4	0.12	0.01
strained — *1 jar*	71	92	0.1	44	0	5.6	2.5	1.4	1.4	9.7	45	1	100	33	0.9	11	0.3	0.14	1	7.4	2.3	0.11	0.01
Chicken noodle dinner																							
junior — *1 jar*	170	87	12.8	29	1.9	2.4	1	0.5	0.7	3.2	29	1	60	29	0.5	182	0.2	0.04	2	9	0.9	0.05	0.05
strained — *1 jar*	113	59	8.5	20	1.2	1.7	0.6	0.3	0.7	2.4	25	1	44	18	0.3	127	0.1	0.04	1	6.1	0.5	0.06	0.04
Chicken soup, strained — *1 jar*	113	57	8.1	5	1.2	1.9	0.5	1	0.3	1.8	42	0	75	18	0.2	194	0.1	0.04	1	5.9	0.3	0.04	0.02
Chicken stew, toddler — *1 jar*	170	133	10.9	49	1	6.3	2.9	1.3	1.9	8.8	61	1	156	340	0.7	206	0.2	0.08	3	1.7	2	0.13	0.05
Corn, creamed																							
junior — *1 jar*	170	111	27.7	2	3.6	0.7	0.2	0.3	0.1	2.4	31	0	138	88	0.4	14	0	0.07	4	21.6	0.9	0.08	0.02
strained — *1 jar*	113	64	15.9	1	2.4	0.5	0.1	0.2	0.1	1.6	23	0	102	49	0.2	8	0	0.05	2	12.8	0.6	0.05	0.01
Custard pudding, vanilla																							
junior — *1 jar*	170	151	27.5	23	0	3.9	1.3	0.3	2	2.7	95	0	105	49	0.5	7	0	0.03	1	10.5	0.1	0.13	0.02
strained — *1 jar*	113	96	18.2	9	0	2.3	0.8	0.2	1.1	1.8	62	0	75	32	0.3	7	0	0.02	1	6.8	0	0.09	0.01
Dutch apple dessert																							
junior — *1 jar*	170	117	28.6	0	1.5	1.7	0.4	0.1	1.1	0	7	0	63	27	0	9	0	0.02	36	1.2	0.1	0.02	0.02
strained — *1 jar*	113	77	18.9	0	1	1	0.3	0	0.7	0	6	0	37	18	0	6	0	0.01	24	0.8	0.1	0.01	0.01
Green beans																							
junior — *1 jar*	170	43	9.7	0	3.2	0.2	0	0.1	0	2	111	2	218	3	0.3	73	0	0.06	14	55.6	0.5	0.17	0.04

	Weight g	Calories	Carbohydrates g	Cholesterol mg	Dietary fiber g	Total fat g	Mono. fat g	Poly. fat g	Sat. fat g	Protein g	Calcium mg	Iron mg	Potassium mg	Sodium mg	Zinc mg	Vitamin A RE	Vitamin B_{12} mcg	Vitamin B_6 mg	Vitamin C mg	Folic acid mcg	Niacin mg	Riboflavin mg	Thiamin mg
junior, creamed — *1 jar*	170	54	12.2	2	2.7	0.7	0.1	0.4	0.1	1.7	54	0	111	20	0.3	26	0.1	0.02	5	67.5	0.4	0.09	0.04
strained — *1 jar*	113	28	6.7	0	2.1	0.1	0	0.1	0	1.5	44	1	179	2	0.2	51	0	0.04	6	39.1	0.4	0.1	0.03
toddler — *1 jar*	113	33	6.4	0	1.5	0.2	0	0.1	0	1.4	31	0	131	42	0.1	40	0	0.03	2	36.2	0.3	0.05	0.02
Guava & papaya w/ tapioca, strained — *1 jar*	113	71	19.2	0	0	0.1	0	0	0	0.2	8	0	84	5	0.1	20	0	0.02	91	2.3	0.3	0.02	0.01
Guava w/ tapioca, strained — *1 jar*	113	76	20.7	0	2	0	0	0	0	0.3	8	0	82	2	0.1	34	0	0.05	85	2.3	0.4	0.08	0.02
Ham																							
junior — *1 jar*	71	89	0	21	0	4.8	2.3	0.6	1.6	10.7	4	1	149	48	1.2	7	0.1	0.14	1	1.5	2	0.14	0.1
strained — *1 jar*	71	79	0	17	0	4.1	2	0.6	1.4	9.9	4	1	145	29	1.6	8	0.1	0.18	1	1.4	1.9	0.11	0.1
Lamb																							
junior — *1 jar*	71	80	0	27	0	3.7	1.5	0.2	1.8	10.8	5	1	150	52	1.8	6	1.6	0.13	1	1.4	2.3	0.14	0.01
strained — *1 jar*	71	73	0.1	27	0	3.3	1.3	0.1	1.6	10	5	1	146	44	2	7	1.6	0.11	1	1.6	2.1	0.14	0.01
Macaroni & cheese																							
junior — *1 jar*	170	104	13.9	10	0.5	3.4	0.9	0.2	2	4.4	87	1	75	129	0.5	5	0.1	0.03	2	2.6	0.9	0.11	0.1
strained — *1 jar*	113	67	8.5	8	0.3	2.4	0.6	0.1	1.4	2.9	61	0	52	82	0.4	6	0	0.02	1	1.6	0.5	0.08	0.06
Macaroni dinner w/ tomato & beef																							
junior — *1 jar*	170	100	16	7	1.9	1.9	0.8	0.1	0.7	4.3	24	1	122	29	0.6	185	0.4	0.08	3	11.1	1.3	0.09	0.08
strained — *1 jar*	113	62	9.9	5	1.2	1.2	0.5	0.1	0.5	2.5	18	1	108	19	0.4	102	0.3	0.05	2	22.7	0.9	0.07	0.08
Mango w/ tapioca, strained — *1 jar*	113	90	24.4	0	1.1	0.2	0.1	0	0.1	0.3	5	0	67	5	0.1	76	0	0.13	141	2.3	0.3	0.03	0.03
Mixed vegetable dinner																							
junior — *1 jar*	170	56	13.4	0	0	0	0	0	0	1.7	29	1	190	15	0.4	415	0	0.13	6	11.4	0.7	0.04	0.02
strained — *1 jar*	113	46	10.7	0	0	0.1	0	0	0	1.4	25	0	137	9	0.2	308	0	0.08	3	9	0.6	0.04	0.02
Papaya & applesauce w/ tapioca, strained — *1 jar*	113	79	21.4	0	1.6	0.1	0	0	0	0.2	8	0	89	6	0	9	0	0.03	128	2.3	0.1	0.03	0.01
Peach cobbler																							
junior — *1 jar*	220	147	40.3	0	1.5	0	0	0	0	0.7	9	0	123	20	0.1	31	0	0.02	45	2.4	0.6	0.03	0.02

	Weight *g*	Calories	Carbohydrates *g*	Cholesterol *mg*	Dietary fiber *g*	Total fat *g*	Mono. fat *g*	Poly. fat *g*	Sat. fat *g*	Protein *g*	Calcium *mg*	Iron *mg*	Potassium *mg*	Sodium *mg*	Zinc *mg*	Vitamin A *RE*	Vitamin B_{12} *mcg*	Vitamin B_6 *mg*	Vitamin C *mg*	Folic acid *mcg*	Niacin *mg*	Riboflavin *mg*	Thiamin *mg*
strained — *1 jar*	113	73	20.1	0	0.8	0	0	0	0	0.3	5	0	61	8	0.3	16	0	0.01	23	1.2	0.3	0.02	0.01
Peaches																							
toddler — *1 jar*	170	87	20.1	0	1.4	0.3	0.1	0.1	0	0.9	10	0	141	9	0.2	24	0	0.07	53	8.5	0.8	0.03	0.02
Peaches w/ sugar																							
junior — *1 jar*	170	121	32.1	0	2.6	0.3	0.1	0.2	0	0.9	9	0	264	9	0.1	31	0	0.03	32	6.6	1.1	0.05	0.02
strained — *1 jar*	113	80	21.4	0	1.7	0.2	0.1	0.1	0	0.6	7	0	183	7	0.1	18	0	0.02	35	4.4	0.7	0.04	0.01
Pears																							
junior — *1 jar*	170	73	19.7	0	6.1	0.2	0	0	0	0.5	14	0	196	3	0.1	5	0	0.02	37	6.5	0.3	0.05	0.02
strained — *1 jar*	113	46	12.2	0	4.1	0.2	0	0.1	0	0.3	9	0	147	2	0.1	3	0	0.01	28	4.1	0.2	0.03	0.01
toddler — *1 jar*	170	97	23.1	0	2	0.2	0.1	0.1	0	0.5	17	0	87	10	0.2	0	0	0.07	53	1.7	0.2	0.03	0.02
Pears & pineapple																							
junior — *1 jar*	170	75	19.4	0	4.4	0.3	0.1	0.1	0	0.5	17	0	201	2	0.2	5	0	0.02	29	4.9	0.3	0.04	0.04
strained — *1 jar*	113	46	12.3	0	2.9	0.1	0	0	0	0.3	11	0	131	5	0.1	3	0	0.02	31	3.2	0.2	0.03	0.02
Peas																							
strained — *1 jar*	113	45	9.2	0	2.4	0.3	0	0.2	0.1	4	23	1	127	5	0.4	63	0	0.08	8	29.3	1.2	0.07	0.09
toddler — *1 jar*	170	109	17.5	0	6.6	1.4	0.1	0.6	0.2	6.6	36	2	138	82	0.9	51	0	0.1	10	59.5	1.4	0.1	0.17
Peas, creamed, strained — *1 jar*	113	60	10.1	5	2.1	2.1	0.5	1.1	0.5	2.5	15	1	99	16	0.4	10	0.1	0.05	2	25.7	0.9	0.06	0.1
Plums w/ tapioca																							
junior — *1 jar*	170	126	34.7	0	2	0	0	0	0	0.2	10	0	141	14	0.1	15	0	0.05	1	1.5	0.4	0.05	0.01
strained — *1 jar*	113	80	22.3	0	1.4	0	0	0	0	0.1	7	0	96	7	0.1	11	0	0.03	1	1	0.2	0.03	0.01
Pork, strained — *1 jar*	71	88	0	34	0	5	2.5	0.6	1.7	9.9	4	1	158	30	1.6	9	0.7	0.15	1	1.4	1.6	0.14	0.1
Potatoes, toddler — *1 cup*	163	83	19.2	0	1.5	0.2	0	0	0	1.6	7	0	179	93	0.3	0	0	0.11	17	9.8	0.6	0.02	0.03
Prunes w/ tapioca																							
junior — *1 jar*	170	119	31.8	0	4.6	0.2	0.1	0	0	1	26	1	275	3	0.2	70	0	0.15	1	0.3	0.9	0.14	0.04

Foods, General

	Weight g	Calories	Carbohydrates g	Cholesterol mg	Dietary fiber g	Total fat g	Mono. fat g	Poly. fat g	Sat. fat g	Protein g	Calcium mg	Iron mg	Potassium mg	Sodium mg	Zinc mg	Vitamin A RE	Vitamin B_{12} mcg	Vitamin B_6 mg	Vitamin C mg	Folic acid mcg	Niacin mg	Riboflavin mg	Thiamin mg
strained — *1 jar*	113	79	20.9	0	3.1	0.1	0.1	0	0	0.7	17	0	200	6	0.1	51	0	0.09	1	0.2	0.6	0.08	0.02
Spinach, creamed, strained — *1 jar*	113	42	6.4	6	2	1.5	0.4	0.2	0.8	2.8	101	1	216	55	0.4	471	0.1	0.08	10	68.7	0.2	0.12	0.02
Squash																							
junior — *1 jar*	170	41	9.5	0	3.6	0.3	0	0.1	0.1	1.4	41	1	315	2	0.1	342	0	0.12	13	26.2	0.6	0.11	0.02
strained — *1 jar*	113	27	6.3	0	2.4	0.2	0	0.1	0	0.9	27	0	202	2	0.2	228	0	0.07	9	17.4	0.4	0.06	0.01
Sweet potatoes																							
junior — *1 jar*	170	102	23.6	0	2.6	0.2	0	0.1	0	1.9	27	1	413	37	0.2	1129	0	0.19	16	17.5	0.7	0.06	0.04
strained — *1 jar*	113	64	14.9	0	1.7	0.1	0	0	0	1.2	18	0	297	23	0.2	728	0	0.11	11	11.1	0.4	0.04	0.03
Turkey																							
junior — *1 jar*	71	92	0	38	0	5	1.9	1.2	1.6	10.9	20	1	128	51	1.3	7	0.8	0.12	2	8.6	2.5	0.18	0.01
strained — *1 jar*	71	81	0.1	42	0	4.1	1.5	1	1.4	10.2	16	1	164	39	1.3	10	0.7	0.13	2	8	2.6	0.15	0.01
Turkey & rice																							
junior — *1 jar*	170	83	12.2	17	1.9	2.4	0.9	0.5	0.7	3.1	39	0	58	26	0.4	252	0.2	0.05	2	5.3	0.5	0.05	0.01
strained — *1 jar*	113	55	8.2	11	1.2	1.5	0.6	0.3	0.5	2.1	24	0	46	19	0.3	107	0.1	0.04	1	3.6	0.3	0.02	0.01
Turkey sticks, junior — *1 jar*	71	129	1	46	0.4	10.1	3.3	2.6	2.9	9.7	51	1	65	343	1.3	4	0.7	0.05	1	8	1.2	0.11	0.01
Turkey, rice & vegetable dinner, junior — *1 jar*	170	100	12.8	13	1.4	2.7	0.9	0.5	0.9	6.5	19	1	182	311	1	386	0.2	0.22	1	5.3	3.6	0.12	0.12
Veal																							
juinor — *1 jar*	71	78	0	19	0	3.6	1.5	0.1	1.7	10.9	4	1	168	49	1.8	11	0.9	0.08	1	4.8	2.7	0.13	0.01
strained — *1 jar*	71	72	0	18	0	3.4	1.5	0.1	1.6	9.6	5	1	153	45	1.4	10	0.9	0.11	2	4.2	2.5	0.11	0.01
Vegetables & bacon																							
junior — *1 jar*	170	121	12.9	5	1.9	6.6	3.2	0.7	2.4	3.1	19	1	146	77	0.5	371	0.2	0.11	2	15.3	0.9	0.05	0.09
strained — *1 jar*	113	78	9.7	4	1.2	3.7	1.8	0.4	1.3	1.8	16	0	101	49	0.3	337	0.1	0.09	1	10.4	0.6	0.04	0.04
Vegetables & beef																							
junior — *1 jar*	170	90	12.6	9	1.9	2.9	1.3	0.1	1.2	4.1	17	1	179	41	0.7	326	0.4	0.11	3	8.3	1.1	0.05	0.05

	Weight g	Calories	Carbohydrates g	Cholesterol mg	Dietary fiber g	Total fat g	Mono. fat g	Poly. fat g	Sat. fat g	Protein g	Calcium mg	Iron mg	Potassium mg	Sodium mg	Zinc mg	Vitamin A RE	Vitamin B_{12} mcg	Vitamin B6 mg	Vitamin C mg	Folic acid mcg	Niacin mg	Riboflavin mg	Thiamin mg
strained — *1 jar*	113	60	7.9	6	1.2	2.3	1	0.1	0.9	2.3	14	0	114	24	0.4	193	0.3	0.06	1	5.3	0.6	0.03	0.02
Vegetables & chicken dinner																							
junior — *1 jar*	170	85	14.5	17	1.9	1.9	0.7	0.4	0.5	3.2	24	1	44	15	0.5	252	0.2	0.06	2	6.5	0.6	0.03	0.02
strained — *1 jar*	113	49	7.5	15	1.2	1.2	0.5	0.3	0.3	2.1	16	0	34	12	0.3	155	0.1	0.02	1	3.6	0.2	0.02	0.01
Vegetables & ham																							
junior — *1 jar*	170	88	11.9	9	1.9	2.9	1.3	0.3	1	4.1	14	0	156	31	0.4	138	0.1	0.05	2	9	0.6	0.04	0.06
strained — *1 jar*	113	54	7.8	6	1.2	1.9	0.9	0.2	0.7	2	9	0	96	14	0.2	107	0	0.04	2	5.5	0.5	0.03	0.04
Vegetables & lamb																							
junior — *1 jar*	170	87	12.1	9	1.9	2.9	1.2	0.3	1.2	3.6	22	1	162	22	0.4	338	0.3	0.07	3	6.1	0.9	0.05	0.04
strained — *1 jar*	113	59	7.8	7	1.2	2.3	0.9	0.2	0.9	2.3	14	0	106	23	0.2	320	0.2	0.05	1	4.1	0.6	0.04	0.02
Vegetables & turkey																							
junior — *1 jar*	170	80	13.1	17	1.9	2	0.8	0.5	0.5	2.9	22	1	43	29	0.4	196	0.2	0.04	2	4.9	0.4	0.03	0.03
strained — *1 jar*	113	47	7.5	11	1.2	1.4	0.5	0.3	0.4	1.9	18	0	50	15	0.3	127	0.1	0.04	1	2.9	0.3	0.02	0.01
toddler — *1 jar*	170	136	13.6	0	0	5.8	0	0	0	8.2	78	1	282	568	0.5	457	0.7	0.1	6	5.1	1	0.15	0.03
Vegetables, noodles & chicken																							
junior — *1 jar*	170	109	15.5	0	1.9	3.7	0	0	0	2.9	44	1	100	44	0.5	221	0.2	0.04	1	5.8	1.1	0.06	0.07
strained — *1 jar*	113	71	8.9	0	1.2	2.8	0	0	0	2.3	32	0	62	23	0.3	198	0.1	0.02	1	3.6	0.5	0.06	0.04
Vegetables, noodles & turkey																							
junior — *1 jar*	170	88	12.9	0	1.9	2.6	0	0	0	3.1	54	0	124	29	0.5	226	0.2	0.03	1	4.8	0.5	0.07	0.04
strained — *1 jar*	113	50	7.7	0	1.2	1.4	0	0	0	1.4	36	0	71	24	0.3	150	0.1	0.02	1	2.7	0.3	0.05	0.02
Zwieback cookies — *1 piece*	7	30	5.2	1	0.2	0.7	0.3	0.1	0.3	0.7	1	0	21	16	0	0	0	0.01	0	1.4	0.1	0.02	0.01

Beef

	Weight g	Calories	Carbohydrates g	Cholesterol mg	Dietary fiber g	Total fat g	Mono. fat g	Poly. fat g	Sat. fat g	Protein g	Calcium mg	Iron mg	Potassium mg	Sodium mg	Zinc mg	Vitamin A RE	Vitamin B_{12} mcg	Vitamin B6 mg	Vitamin C mg	Folic acid mcg	Niacin mg	Riboflavin mg	Thiamin mg
Arm pot roast (chuck), choice, braised																							
¼" fat trim — *3 ½ oz*	100	348	0	99	0	25.8	11.1	1	10.2	27	10	3	243	59	6.7	0	2.9	0.28	0	9	3.1	0.24	0.07

	Weight g	Calories	Carbohydrates g	Cholesterol mg	Dietary fiber g	Total fat g	Mono. fat g	Poly. fat g	Sat. fat g	Protein g	Calcium mg	Iron mg	Potassium mg	Sodium mg	Zinc mg	Vitamin A RE	Vitamin B_{12} mcg	Vitamin B_6 mg	Vitamin C mg	Folic acid mcg	Niacin mg	Riboflavin mg	Thiamin mg
⅛" fat trim — *3 ½ oz*	100	323	0	100	0	22.5	9.6	0.9	8.8	28.2	10	3	252	61	7.1	0	3	0.29	0	9	3.3	0.25	0.07
0" fat trim — *3 ½ oz*	100	293	0	100	0	18.6	7.9	0.7	7.2	29.4	10	3	262	62	7.5	0	3.1	0.3	0	10	3.4	0.26	0.07
trimmed of all visible fat — *3 ½ oz*	100	219	0	101	0	8.7	3.6	0.3	3.2	33	9	4	289	66	8.7	0	3.4	0.33	0	11	3.7	0.29	0.08
Arm pot roast (chuck), select, braised																							
¼" fat trim — *3 ½ oz*	100	315	0	100	0	21.7	9.3	0.8	8.6	27.9	10	3	250	60	7	0	3	0.29	0	9	3.2	0.24	0.07
⅛" fat trim — *3 ½ oz*	100	291	0	100	0	18.6	8	0.7	7.3	29	10	3	258	61	7.4	0	3.1	0.3	0	10	3.3	0.25	0.07
0" fat trim — *3 ½ oz*	100	260	0	100	0	14.6	6.3	0.6	5.7	30.1	10	3	267	63	7.7	0	3.2	0.31	0	10	3.4	0.26	0.07
trimmed of all visible fat — *3 ½ oz*	100	198	0	101	0	6.3	2.6	0.3	2.3	33	9	4	289	66	8.7	0	3.4	0.33	0	11	3.7	0.29	0.08
Blade roast (chuck), choice, braised																							
¼" fat trim — *3 ½ oz*	100	363	0	103	0	27.8	12	1	11.1	26.2	13	3	228	64	8.1	0	2.3	0.25	0	5	2.4	0.24	0.07
⅛" fat trim — *3 ½ oz*	100	359	0	103	0	27.3	11.8	1	10.9	26.4	13	3	230	64	8.2	0	2.3	0.26	0	5	2.4	0.24	0.07
0" fat trim — *3 ½ oz*	100	348	0	104	0	25.8	11.2	0.9	10.3	27	13	3	234	65	8.5	0	2.3	0.26	0	5	2.4	0.25	0.07
trimmed of all visible fat — *3 ½ oz*	100	265	0	106	0	14.7	6.3	0.5	5.7	31.1	13	4	263	71	10.3	0	2.5	0.29	0	6	2.7	0.28	0.08
Blade roast (chuck), select, braised																							
¼" fat trim — *3 ½ oz*	100	326	0	104	0	23.4	10.1	0.8	9.3	27	13	3	234	65	8.5	0	2.3	0.26	0	5	2.4	0.25	0.07
⅛" fat trim — *3 ½ oz*	100	318	0	104	0	22.4	9.7	0.8	8.9	27.3	13	3	237	66	8.7	0	2.3	0.26	0	5	2.5	0.25	0.07
0" fat trim — *3 ½ oz*	100	313	0	104	0	21.7	9.4	0.8	8.6	27.6	13	3	239	66	8.8	0	2.3	0.26	0	5	2.5	0.25	0.07
trimmed of all visible fat — *3 ½ oz*	100	238	0	106	0	11.7	5	0.4	4.5	31.1	13	4	263	71	10.3	0	2.5	0.29	0	6	2.7	0.28	0.08
Bottom round, choice, braised																							
¼" fat trim — *3 ½ oz*	100	284	0	96	0	17.9	7.8	0.7	6.7	28.7	6	3	282	50	4.9	0	2.4	0.33	0	10	3.7	0.24	0.07
⅛" fat trim — *3 ½ oz*	100	268	0	96	0	15.9	6.9	0.6	5.9	29.4	6	3	288	50	5.1	0	2.4	0.34	0	10	3.8	0.24	0.07
0" fat trim — *3 ½ oz*	100	227	0	96	0	10.6	4.6	0.4	3.7	31	5	3	302	51	5.4	0	2.4	0.35	0	11	4	0.25	0.07
trimmed of all visible fat — *3 ½ oz*	100	213	0	96	0	8.7	3.8	0.3	2.9	31.6	5	3	308	51	5.5	0	2.5	0.36	0	11	4.1	0.26	0.07

	Weight g	Calories	Carbohydrates g	Cholesterol mg	Dietary fiber g	Total fat g	Mono. fat g	Poly. fat g	Sat. fat g	Protein g	Calcium mg	Iron mg	Potassium mg	Sodium mg	Zinc mg	Vitamin A RE	Vitamin B_{12} mcg	Vitamin B_6 mg	Vitamin C mg	Folic acid mcg	Niacin mg	Riboflavin mg	Thiamin mg
Bottom round, choice, roasted																							
¼" fat trim — *3 ½ oz*	100	260	0	80	0	16.4	7.2	0.6	6.2	26.4	6	3	355	63	4.2	0	2.6	0.34	0	11	3.8	0.22	0.08
⅛" fat trim — *3 ½ oz*	100	241	0	79	0	13.9	6.2	0.5	5.1	27.1	6	3	366	64	4.3	0	2.6	0.35	0	12	3.9	0.23	0.08
0" fat trim — *3 ½ oz*	100	203	0	78	0	9	4.1	0.4	3.1	28.4	5	3	385	65	4.6	0	2.7	0.37	0	12	4	0.24	0.08
trimmed of all visible fat — *3 ½ oz*	100	193	0	78	0	7.8	3.5	0.3	2.6	28.8	5	3	391	66	4.6	0	2.7	0.37	0	12	4.1	0.24	0.08
Bottom round, select, braised																							
¼" fat trim — *3 ½ oz*	100	259	0	96	0	15.1	6.6	0.6	5.7	28.9	6	3	283	50	5	0	2.4	0.33	0	10	3.8	0.24	0.07
⅛" fat trim — *3 ½ oz*	100	245	0	96	0	13.2	5.7	0.5	4.9	29.5	6	3	289	50	5.1	0	2.4	0.34	0	10	3.8	0.24	0.07
0" fat trim — *3 ½ oz*	100	201	0	96	0	7.6	3.3	0.3	2.7	31.2	5	3	304	51	5.4	0	2.5	0.36	0	11	4	0.26	0.07
trimmed of all visible fat — *3 ½ oz*	100	192	0	96	0	6.3	2.8	0.2	2.1	31.6	5	3	308	51	5.5	0	2.5	0.36	0	11	4.1	0.26	0.07
Bottom round, select, roasted																							
¼" fat trim — *3 ½ oz*	100	234	0	80	0	13.2	5.8	0.5	5	26.8	6	3	361	63	4.3	0	2.6	0.35	0	11	3.8	0.23	0.08
⅛" fat trim — *3 ½ oz*	100	219	0	79	0	11.3	5	0.4	4.2	27.3	5	3	369	64	4.4	0	2.6	0.36	0	12	3.9	0.23	0.08
0" fat trim — *3 ½ oz*	100	177	0	78	0	6	2.7	0.2	2.1	28.6	5	3	388	66	4.6	0	2.7	0.37	0	12	4.1	0.24	0.08
trimmed of all visible fat — *3 ½ oz*	100	171	0	78	0	5.4	2.5	0.2	1.8	28.8	5	3	391	66	4.6	0	2.7	0.37	0	12	4.1	0.24	0.08
Corned beef, cooked — *3 ½ oz*	100	251	0.5	98	0	19	9.2	0.7	6.3	18.2	8	2	145	1134	4.6	0	1.6	0.23	0	6	3	0.17	0.03
Eye of round, choice, roasted																							
¼" fat trim — *3 ½ oz*	100	241	0	72	0	14.1	6.1	0.5	5.5	26.6	6	2	359	59	4.3	0	2.1	0.35	0	6	3.5	0.16	0.08
⅛" fat trim — *3 ½ oz*	100	200	0	70	0	8.9	3.8	0.3	3.4	28.1	5	2	381	61	4.6	0	2.1	0.37	0	7	3.6	0.17	0.08
0" fat trim — *3 ½ oz*	100	180	0	69	0	6.4	2.7	0.2	2.3	28.8	5	2	392	62	4.7	0	2.2	0.38	0	7	3.7	0.17	0.09
trimmed of all visible fat — *3 ½ oz*	100	175	0	69	0	5.7	2.4	0.2	2.1	29	5	2	395	62	4.7	0	2.2	0.38	0	7	3.8	0.17	0.09
Eye of round, select, roasted																							
¼" fat trim — *3 ½ oz*	100	217	0	72	0	11.3	4.9	0.4	4.4	27	6	2	365	60	4.4	0	2.1	0.35	0	7	3.5	0.16	0.08
⅛" fat trim — *3 ½ oz*	100	186	0	70	0	7.3	3.1	0.3	2.8	28.1	5	2	381	61	4.6	0	2.1	0.37	0	7	3.6	0.17	0.08

	Weight g	Calories	Carbohydrates g	Cholesterol mg	Dietary fiber g	Total fat g	Mono. fat g	Poly. fat g	Sat. fat g	Protein g	Calcium mg	Iron mg	Potassium mg	Sodium mg	Zinc mg	Vitamin A RE	Vitamin B_{12} mcg	Vitamin B_6 mg	Vitamin C mg	Folic acid mcg	Niacin mg	Riboflavin mg	Thiamin mg
0" fat trim — *3 ½ oz*	100	161	0	69	0	4.2	1.8	0.1	1.5	28.8	5	2	392	62	4.7	0	2.2	0.38	0	7	3.7	0.17	0.09
trimmed of all visible fat — *3 ½ oz*	100	155	0	69	0	3.5	1.5	0.1	1.3	29	5	2	395	62	4.7	0	2.2	0.38	0	7	3.8	0.17	0.09
Flank, choice, braised																							
0" fat trim — *3 ½ oz*	100	263	0	72	0	16.4	6.9	0.5	6.9	27	6	3	337	70	5.8	0	3.3	0.35	0	9	4.4	0.18	0.14
trimmed of all visible fat — *3 ½ oz*	100	237	0	71	0	13	5.4	0.4	5.5	28	6	3	351	72	6.1	0	3.4	0.36	0	9	4.6	0.19	0.14
Flank, choice, broiled																							
0" fat trim — *3 ½ oz*	100	226	0	68	0	12.5	5.1	0.5	5.3	26.4	7	3	402	81	4.7	0	3.2	0.34	0	8	4.9	0.18	0.1
trimmed of all visible fat — *3 ½ oz*	100	207	0	67	0	10.1	4.1	0.4	4.4	27.1	7	3	414	83	4.8	0	3.3	0.34	0	8	5	0.19	0.11
Ground beef, extra lean, baked																							
medium — *3 ½ oz*	100	250	0	82	0	16.1	7.1	0.6	6.3	24.5	7	2	224	49	5.3	0	1.7	0.22	0	9	4.2	0.24	0.04
well done — *3 ½ oz*	100	274	0	107	0	16	7	0.6	6.3	30.3	9	3	291	64	6.9	0	1.9	0.29	0	11	5.4	0.31	0.05
Ground beef, extra lean, broiled																							
medium — *3 ½ oz*	100	256	0	84	0	16.3	7.2	0.6	6.4	25.4	7	2	313	70	5.5	0	2.2	0.27	0	9	5	0.27	0.06
well done — *3 ½ oz*	100	265	0	99	0	15.8	6.9	0.6	6.2	28.6	9	3	369	82	6.4	0	2.6	0.32	0	11	5.9	0.32	0.07
Ground beef, extra lean, pan-fried																							
medium — *3 ½ oz*	100	255	0	81	0	16.4	7.2	0.6	6.5	25	7	2	312	70	5.4	0	2	0.27	0	9	4.7	0.26	0.06
well done — *3 ½ oz*	100	263	0	93	0	16	7	0.6	6.3	28	8	3	360	81	6.3	0	2.3	0.31	0	10	5.4	0.3	0.07
Ground beef, lean, baked																							
medium — *3 ½ oz*	100	268	0	78	0	18.3	8	0.7	7.2	23.9	9	2	224	56	5.1	0	1.8	0.2	0	9	4.3	0.19	0.05
well done — *3 ½ oz*	100	292	0	99	0	18.4	8	0.7	7.2	29.6	12	3	286	71	6.5	0	2.3	0.26	0	12	5.5	0.24	0.07
Ground beef, lean, broiled																							
medium — *3 ½ oz*	100	272	0	87	0	18.5	8.1	0.7	7.3	24.7	11	2	301	77	5.4	0	2.4	0.26	0	9	5.2	0.21	0.05
well done — *3 ½ oz*	100	280	0	101	0	17.6	7.7	0.7	6.9	28.2	12	2	349	89	6.2	0	2.7	0.3	0	11	6	0.24	0.06

	Weight g	Calories	Carbohydrates g	Cholesterol mg	Dietary fiber g	Total fat g	Mono. fat g	Poly. fat g	Sat. fat g	Protein g	Calcium mg	Iron mg	Potassium mg	Sodium mg	Zinc mg	Vitamin A RE	Vitamin B_{12} mcg	Vitamin B_6 mg	Vitamin C mg	Folic acid mcg	Niacin mg	Riboflavin mg	Thiamin mg
Ground beef, lean, pan-fried																							
medium — *3 ½ oz*	100	275	0	84	0	19.1	8.3	0.7	7.5	24.2	10	2	299	77	5.2	0	2.3	0.28	0	9	4.8	0.22	0.05
well done — *3 ½ oz*	100	277	0	95	0	17.7	7.7	0.7	6.9	27.6	11	2	340	87	5.9	0	2.6	0.32	0	10	5.5	0.24	0.06
Ground beef, regular, baked																							
medium — *3 ½ oz*	100	287	0	87	0	20.9	9.2	0.8	8.2	23	10	2	221	60	4.9	0	2.3	0.23	0	9	4.8	0.16	0.03
well done — *3 ½ oz*	100	317	0	108	0	21.5	9.4	0.8	8.4	28.8	12	3	274	75	6.1	0	2.9	0.29	0	11	5.9	0.2	0.04
Ground beef, regular, broiled																							
medium — *3 ½ oz*	100	289	0	90	0	20.7	9.1	0.8	8.1	24.1	11	2	292	83	5.2	0	2.9	0.27	0	9	5.8	0.19	0.03
well done — *3 ½ oz*	100	292	0	101	0	19.5	8.5	0.7	7.7	27.2	12	3	327	93	5.8	0	3.3	0.3	0	10	6.5	0.21	0.04
Ground beef, regular, pan-fried																							
medium — *3 ½ oz*	100	306	0	89	0	22.6	9.9	0.8	8.9	23.9	11	2	300	84	5.1	0	2.7	0.24	0	9	5.8	0.2	0.03
well done — *3 ½ oz*	100	286	0	98	0	18.9	8.3	0.7	7.4	27	13	3	332	93	5.6	0	3	0.27	0	10	6.5	0.21	0.04
Porterhouse steak, choice, broiled																							
¼" fat trim — *3 ½ oz*	100	327	0	75	0	25.6	11.3	0.9	9.9	22.4	8	3	307	62	4.4	0	2.1	0.34	0	7	3.9	0.21	0.09
0" fat trim — *3 ½ oz*	100	284	0	69	0	20.3	9.4	0.7	7.5	23.6	8	3	334	65	4.8	0	2.2	0.37	0	7	4.2	0.23	0.1
⅛" fat trim — *3 ½ oz*	100	299	0	74	0	22.1	9.8	0.8	8.5	23.3	8	3	322	64	4.6	0	2.2	0.35	0	7	4.1	0.22	0.1
trimmed of all visible fat — *3 ½ oz*	100	224	0	65	0	12.8	6.3	0.4	4.3	25.5	7	3	367	69	5.3	0	2.3	0.4	0	8	4.6	0.25	0.11
Porterhouse steak, select, broiled																							
⅛" fat trim — *3 ½ oz*	100	294	0	65	0	21.2	9.1	0.9	8.3	24.1	8	3	320	64	4.6	0	2.2	0.35	0	7	4.1	0.22	0.1
0" fat trim — *3 ½ oz*	100	267	0	64	0	18	7.8	0.7	7.1	24.5	8	3	329	65	4.7	0	2.2	0.36	0	7	4.2	0.22	0.1
trimmed of all visible fat — *3 ½ oz*	100	194	0	58	0	8.8	3.8	0.4	3.3	26.9	7	3	367	69	5.3	0	2.3	0.4	0	8	4.6	0.25	0.11
Rib eye, small end, choice, broiled																							
¼" fat trim — *3 ½ oz*	100	307	0	83	0	22.3	9.5	0.8	9	24.9	13	2	344	64	6	0	3	0.35	0	7	4.2	0.19	0.09
⅛" fat trim — *3 ½ oz*	100	300	0	82	0	21.3	9.1	0.7	8.6	25.2	13	2	349	64	6.1	0	3	0.36	0	7	4.3	0.2	0.09

	Weight g	Calories	Carbohydrates g	Cholesterol mg	Dietary fiber g	Total fat g	Mono. fat g	Poly. fat g	Sat. fat g	Protein g	Calcium mg	Iron mg	Potassium mg	Sodium mg	Zinc mg	Vitamin A RE	Vitamin B_{12} mcg	Vitamin B_6 mg	Vitamin C mg	Folic acid mcg	Niacin mg	Riboflavin mg	Thiamin mg
Rib, large end, choice, broiled																							
¼" fat trim — *3 ½ oz*	100	367	0	81	0	30.8	13	1.2	12.5	21	10	2	298	63	4.9	0	2.8	0.23	0	6	2.7	0.16	0.07
⅛" fat trim — *3 ½ oz*	100	370	0	81	0	31.2	13.2	1.2	12.7	20.9	10	2	297	63	4.8	0	2.8	0.23	0	5	2.7	0.16	0.07
Rib, large end, choice, roasted																							
¼" fat trim — *3 ½ oz*	100	383	0	85	0	32	13.7	1.1	12.9	22.3	10	2	283	63	5.6	0	2.3	0.22	0	7	3.6	0.18	0.07
⅛" fat trim — *3 ½ oz*	100	378	0	85	0	31.3	13.4	1.1	12.6	22.5	10	2	286	63	5.7	0	2.3	0.22	0	7	3.6	0.18	0.07
0" fat trim — *3 ½ oz*	100	372	0	85	0	30.5	13	1.1	12.3	22.8	10	2	290	64	5.8	0	2.3	0.23	0	7	3.6	0.19	0.07
trimmed of all visible fat — *3 ½ oz*	100	253	0	81	0	15	6.3	0.4	6	27.5	8	3	357	73	7.5	0	2.6	0.26	0	9	4.5	0.22	0.09
Rib, large end, prime, broiled																							
¼" fat trim — *3 ½ oz*	100	413	0	86	0	36.2	15.8	1.3	15	20.3	10	2	291	61	4.8	0	2.8	0.26	0	6	2.6	0.17	0.07
⅛" fat trim — *3 ½ oz*	100	404	0	86	0	35	15.3	1.2	14.5	20.7	10	2	298	62	4.9	0	2.8	0.27	0	6	2.6	0.17	0.07
Rib, large end, prime, roasted																							
¼" fat trim — *3 ½ oz*	100	402	0	85	0	33.9	14.8	1.2	14.1	22.5	10	2	286	63	5.6	0	2.3	0.22	0	7	3.6	0.18	0.07
⅛" fat trim — *3 ½ oz*	100	393	0	85	0	32.7	14.3	1.1	13.6	22.9	10	2	291	64	5.8	0	2.3	0.23	0	7	3.7	0.19	0.07
Rib, large end, select, broiled																							
¼" fat trim — *3 ½ oz*	100	324	0	80	0	25.8	10.9	1	10.5	21.5	10	2	308	64	5.1	0	2.9	0.23	0	6	2.8	0.16	0.07
⅛" fat trim — *3 ½ oz*	100	324	0	80	0	25.7	10.9	1	10.4	21.6	10	2	309	64	5.1	0	2.9	0.23	0	6	2.8	0.16	0.07
Rib, large end, select, roasted																							
¼" fat trim — *3 ½ oz*	100	340	0	85	0	26.7	11.4	0.9	10.8	23.1	10	2	295	65	5.9	0	2.4	0.23	0	7	3.7	0.19	0.07
⅛" fat trim — *3 ½ oz*	100	333	0	84	0	25.8	11.1	0.9	10.4	23.4	9	2	299	65	6	0	2.4	0.23	0	8	3.7	0.19	0.07
0" fat trim — *3 ½ oz*	100	331	0	84	0	25.5	10.9	0.9	10.3	23.5	9	2	300	65	6	0	2.4	0.23	0	8	3.8	0.19	0.07
trimmed of all visible fat — *3 ½ oz*	100	220	0	81	0	11.4	4.8	0.3	4.6	27.5	8	3	357	73	7.5	0	2.6	0.26	0	9	4.5	0.22	0.09
Rib, small end, choice, broiled																							
¼" fat trim — *3 ½ oz*	100	349	0	84	0	27.6	11.9	1	11.2	23.5	13	2	322	62	5.5	0	2.9	0.33	0	7	4	0.18	0.09

	Weight g	Calories	Carbohydrates g	Cholesterol mg	Dietary fiber g	Total fat g	Mono. fat g	Poly. fat g	Sat. fat g	Protein g	Calcium mg	Iron mg	Potassium mg	Sodium mg	Zinc mg	Vitamin A RE	Vitamin B_{12} mcg	Vitamin B_6 mg	Vitamin C mg	Folic acid mcg	Niacin mg	Riboflavin mg	Thiamin mg
⅛" fat trim — *3 ½ oz*	100	343	0	84	0	26.8	11.5	0.9	10.9	23.8	13	2	326	62	5.6	0	2.9	0.34	0	7	4	0.19	0.09
0" fat trim — *3 ½ oz*	100	312	0	83	0	22.8	9.8	0.8	9.2	24.7	13	2	342	64	5.9	0	3	0.35	0	7	4.2	0.19	0.09
trimmed of all visible fat — *3 ½ oz*	100	225	0	80	0	11.7	4.9	0.3	4.7	28	13	3	394	69	7	0	3.3	0.4	0	8	4.8	0.22	0.1
Rib, small end, choice, roasted																							
¼" fat trim — *3 ½ oz*	100	367	0	84	0	30.2	13.1	1.1	12.2	22	13	2	314	62	4.8	0	2.8	0.24	0	6	3.1	0.16	0.06
⅛" fat trim — *3 ½ oz*	100	359	0	83	0	29.2	12.6	1.1	11.8	22.3	13	2	319	63	4.9	0	2.9	0.24	0	6	3.1	0.16	0.06
Rib, small end, prime, broiled																							
¼" fat trim — *3 ½ oz*	100	361	0	84	0	28.7	12.5	1	11.8	23.9	13	2	328	62	5.7	0	2.9	0.34	0	7	4	0.19	0.09
⅛" fat trim — *3 ½ oz*	100	354	0	83	0	27.9	12.1	1	11.5	24.1	13	2	332	63	5.7	0	2.9	0.34	0	7	4.1	0.19	0.09
Rib, small end, prime, roasted																							
¼" fat trim — *3 ½ oz*	100	417	0	84	0	35.9	15.6	1.3	14.8	21.9	13	2	318	65	4.8	0	2.8	0.3	0	6	3	0.16	0.06
⅛" fat trim — *3 ½ oz*	100	411	0	84	0	35.1	15.3	1.2	14.5	22.2	13	2	323	65	4.8	0	2.9	0.3	0	7	3	0.17	0.06
Rib, small end, select, broiled																							
¼" fat trim — *3 ½ oz*	100	321	0	84	0	24.3	10.4	0.9	9.8	23.9	13	2	328	62	5.7	0	2.9	0.34	0	7	4	0.19	0.09
⅛" fat trim — *3 ½ oz*	100	315	0	83	0	23.5	10.1	0.8	9.5	24.1	13	2	331	63	5.7	0	2.9	0.34	0	7	4.1	0.19	0.09
0" fat trim — *3 ½ oz*	100	285	0	83	0	19.8	8.5	0.7	8	24.9	13	2	344	64	6	0	3	0.35	0	7	4.2	0.19	0.09
trimmed of all visible fat — *3 ½ oz*	100	198	0	80	0	8.7	3.7	0.3	3.5	28	13	3	394	69	7	0	3.3	0.4	0	8	4.8	0.22	0.1
Rib, small end, select, roasted																							
¼" fat trim — *3 ½ oz*	100	331	0	83	0	26.1	11.3	1	10.5	22.5	13	2	323	63	4.9	0	2.9	0.24	0	6	3.2	0.16	0.06
⅛" fat trim — *3 ½ oz*	100	323	0	83	0	25	10.8	0.9	10.1	22.8	13	2	328	64	5	0	2.9	0.24	0	6	3.2	0.16	0.06
Rib, whole, choice, broiled																							
¼" fat trim — *3 ½ oz*	100	360	0	82	0	29.5	12.6	1.1	12	22	12	2	308	62	5.1	0	2.8	0.27	0	6	3.2	0.17	0.08
⅛" fat trim — *3 ½ oz*	100	352	0	82	0	28.5	12.1	1	11.6	22.3	11	2	313	63	5.2	0	2.9	0.27	0	6	3.3	0.17	0.08

	Weight *g*	Calories	Carbohydrates *g*	Cholesterol *mg*	Dietary fiber *g*	Total fat *g*	Mono. fat *g*	Poly. fat *g*	Sat. fat *g*	Protein *g*	Calcium *mg*	Iron *mg*	Potassium *mg*	Sodium *mg*	Zinc *mg*	Vitamin A *RE*	Vitamin B_{12} *mcg*	Vitamin B_6 *mg*	Vitamin C *mg*	Folic acid *mcg*	Niacin *mg*	Riboflavin *mg*	Thiamin *mg*
Rib, whole, choice, roasted																							
¼" fat trim — *3 ½ oz*	100	376	0	85	0	31.2	13.4	1.1	12.6	22.2	11	2	296	63	5.2	0	2.5	0.23	0	7	3.4	0.17	0.07
⅛" fat trim — *3 ½ oz*	100	365	0	84	0	29.8	12.8	1.1	12	22.6	11	2	302	64	5.4	0	2.6	0.23	0	7	3.4	0.17	0.07
Rib, whole, prime, broiled																							
¼" fat trim — *3 ½ oz*	100	392	0	85	0	33.2	14.5	1.2	13.7	21.7	11	2	306	62	5.1	0	2.8	0.29	0	6	3.2	0.17	0.08
⅛" fat trim — *3 ½ oz*	100	386	0	85	0	32.4	14.1	1.1	13.4	22	11	2	310	62	5.2	0	2.8	0.3	0	6	3.2	0.18	0.08
Rib, whole, prime, roasted																							
¼" fat trim — *3 ½ oz*	100	409	0	85	0	34.8	15.2	1.2	14.4	22.2	11	2	299	64	5.3	0	2.5	0.26	0	7	3.3	0.17	0.07
⅛" fat trim — *3 ½ oz*	100	400	0	85	0	33.7	14.7	1.2	14	22.6	11	2	304	65	5.4	0	2.6	0.26	0	7	3.4	0.18	0.07
Rib, whole, select, broiled																							
¼" fat trim — *3 ½ oz*	100	323	0	82	0	25.2	10.7	0.9	10.2	22.5	11	2	316	63	5.3	0	2.9	0.27	0	6	3.3	0.17	0.08
⅛" fat trim — *3 ½ oz*	100	315	0	81	0	24.2	10.3	0.9	9.8	22.7	11	2	321	64	5.4	0	2.9	0.28	0	6	3.3	0.17	0.08
Rib, whole, select, roasted																							
¼" fat trim — *3 ½ oz*	100	336	0	84	0	26.5	11.4	0.9	10.7	22.9	11	2	306	64	5.5	0	2.6	0.23	0	7	3.5	0.18	0.07
⅛" fat trim — *3 ½ oz*	100	330	0	84	0	25.6	11	0.9	10.3	23.1	11	2	310	65	5.6	0	2.6	0.24	0	7	3.5	0.18	0.07
Round, choice, broiled																							
¼" fat trim — *3 ½ oz*	100	240	0	80	0	13.6	5.8	0.5	5.2	27.4	6	3	392	61	4.3	0	3	0.38	0	9	4	0.21	0.09
⅛" fat trim — *3 ½ oz*	100	235	0	79	0	13	5.6	0.5	4.9	27.5	6	3	395	62	4.4	0	3	0.38	0	9	4	0.21	0.09
Round, select, broiled																							
¼" fat trim — *3 ½ oz*	100	223	0	55	0	11.7	4.6	0.4	4.1	27.4	6	3	392	62	4.3	0	3	0.38	0	9	4	0.21	0.09
⅛" fat trim — *3 ½ oz*	100	218	0	79	0	11.1	4.8	0.4	4.2	27.6	6	3	395	62	4.4	0	3	0.38	0	9	4	0.21	0.1
Shank crosscuts, choice, simmered, ¼" fat trim — *3 ½ oz*	100	263	0	80	0	14.7	6.5	0.5	5.7	30.7	30	4	404	61	9.3	0	3.5	0.34	0	9	5.3	0.2	0.12
Short ribs, choice, braised																							
trimmed of all visible fat — *3 ½ oz*	100	295	0	93	0	18.1	8	0.6	7.7	30.8	11	3	313	58	7.8	0	3.5	0.28	0	7	3.2	0.2	0.07

	Weight g	Calories	Carbohydrates g	Cholesterol mg	Dietary fiber g	Total fat g	Mono. fat g	Poly. fat g	Sat. fat g	Protein g	Calcium mg	Iron mg	Potassium mg	Sodium mg	Zinc mg	Vitamin A RE	Vitamin B_{12} mcg	Vitamin B_6 mg	Vitamin C mg	Folic acid mcg	Niacin mg	Riboflavin mg	Thiamin mg
untrimmed — *3 ½ oz*	100	471	0	94	0	42	18.9	1.5	17.8	21.6	12	2	224	50	4.9	0	2.6	0.22	0	5	2.5	0.15	0.05
T-bone steak, choice, broiled																							
¼" fat trim — *3 ½ oz*	100	309	0	67	0	23.3	10.2	0.8	9.1	23.2	8	3	321	64	4.5	0	2.1	0.33	0	7	4	0.21	0.09
⅛" fat trim — *3 ½ oz*	100	286	0	65	0	20.3	8.9	0.7	7.8	24	8	3	334	66	4.6	0	2.2	0.35	0	7	4.1	0.22	0.1
0" fat trim — *3 ½ oz*	100	255	0	57	0	16.9	7.7	0.6	6.3	24.1	7	3	347	67	4.8	0	2.2	0.36	0	7	4.3	0.23	0.1
trimmed of all visible fat — *3 ½ oz*	100	198	0	52	0	9.6	4.6	0.3	3.2	26	6	3	378	71	5.3	0	2.3	0.39	0	8	4.6	0.25	0.11
T-bone steak, select, broiled																							
¼" fat trim — *3 ½ oz*	100	280	0	58	0	19.4	8.4	0.7	7.7	24.5	8	3	334	66	4.6	0	2.2	0.35	0	7	4.1	0.22	0.1
⅛" fat trim — *3 ½ oz*	100	265	0	57	0	17.5	7.6	0.7	6.9	25	8	3	342	66	4.8	0	2.2	0.35	0	7	4.2	0.22	0.1
0" fat trim — *3 ½ oz*	100	228	0	58	0	13.7	5.9	0.6	5.3	24.5	7	3	352	68	4.9	0	2.2	0.36	0	7	4.3	0.23	0.1
trimmed of all visible fat — *3 ½ oz*	100	177	0	54	0	7.4	3.2	0.4	2.7	26	6	3	378	71	5.3	0	2.3	0.39	0	8	4.6	0.25	0.11
Tenderloin, choice, broiled																							
¼" fat trim — *3 ½ oz*	100	304	0	86	0	21.8	8.9	0.8	8.6	25.1	8	3	365	59	4.8	0	2.4	0.39	0	6	3.5	0.26	0.11
⅛" fat trim — *3 ½ oz*	100	295	0	86	0	20.7	8.4	0.8	8.1	25.4	8	3	371	59	4.9	0	2.4	0.39	0	6	3.5	0.26	0.11
0" fat trim — *3 ½ oz*	100	244	0	85	0	14.3	5.7	0.5	5.5	27	7	3	398	61	5.3	0	2.5	0.42	0	7	3.8	0.28	0.12
trimmed of all visible fat — *3 ½ oz*	100	212	0	84	0	10.1	3.8	0.4	3.8	28.3	7	4	419	63	5.6	0	2.6	0.44	0	7	3.9	0.3	0.13
Tenderloin, choice, roasted																							
¼" fat trim — *3 ½ oz*	100	339	0	86	0	26.4	10.9	1	10.4	23.6	9	3	400	65	4	0	3.3	0.47	0	8	3.8	0.27	0.15
⅛" fat trim — *3 ½ oz*	100	331	0	85	0	25.4	10.5	1	10	23.9	9	3	407	65	4	0	3.4	0.48	0	8	3.9	0.27	0.15
Tenderloin, prime, broiled																							
¼" fat trim — *3 ½ oz*	100	317	0	86	0	23.4	9.7	0.9	9.3	24.9	8	3	362	59	4.8	0	2.4	0.38	0	6	3.5	0.26	0.11
⅛" fat trim — *3 ½ oz*	100	308	0	86	0	22.2	9.2	0.9	8.9	25.3	8	3	368	59	4.9	0	2.4	0.39	0	6	3.5	0.26	0.11
Tenderloin, prime, roasted																							
¼" fat trim — *3 ½ oz*	100	353	0	88	0	27.9	11.6	1.1	11.1	23.7	9	3	330	55	4.3	0	2.5	0.33	0	7	3	0.27	0.09

	Weight g	Calories	Carbohydrates g	Cholesterol mg	Dietary fiber g	Total fat g	Mono. fat g	Poly. fat g	Sat. fat g	Protein g	Calcium mg	Iron mg	Potassium mg	Sodium mg	Zinc mg	Vitamin A RE	Vitamin B_{12} mcg	Vitamin B_6 mg	Vitamin C mg	Folic acid mcg	Niacin mg	Riboflavin mg	Thiamin mg
⅛" fat trim — *3 ½ oz*	100	343	0	88	0	26.7	11	1	10.6	24	8	3	336	55	4.4	0	2.5	0.33	0	7	3	0.27	0.09
Tenderloin, select, broiled																							
¼" fat trim — *3 ½ oz*	100	271	0	86	0	17.9	7.4	0.7	7	25.6	8	3	374	60	5	0	2.4	0.39	0	6	3.6	0.27	0.12
⅛" fat trim — *3 ½ oz*	100	266	0	86	0	17.3	7.1	0.7	6.8	25.8	8	3	377	60	5	0	2.4	0.4	0	6	3.6	0.27	0.12
0" fat trim — *3 ½ oz*	100	229	0	85	0	12.5	5	0.5	4.8	27.2	7	3	401	62	5.3	0	2.5	0.42	0	7	3.8	0.29	0.12
trimmed of all visible fat — *3 ½ oz*	100	200	0	84	0	8.8	3.3	0.3	3.3	28.3	7	4	419	63	5.6	0	2.6	0.44	0	7	3.9	0.3	0.13
Tenderloin, select, roasted																							
¼" fat trim — *3 ½ oz*	100	324	0	86	0	24.7	10.4	1	9.8	23.6	9	3	326	56	4	0	2.5	0.25	0	7	3	0.26	0.08
⅛" fat trim — *3 ½ oz*	100	316	0	85	0	23.7	9.9	1	9.4	23.9	9	3	331	57	4	0	2.5	0.25	0	8	3	0.26	0.09
Tip round, choice, roasted																							
¼" fat trim — *3 ½ oz*	100	247	0	83	0	14.9	6.2	0.6	5.7	26.5	6	3	354	62	6.4	0	2.7	0.37	0	7	3.5	0.25	0.09
⅛" fat trim — *3 ½ oz*	100	228	0	82	0	12.3	5.1	0.5	4.6	27.3	6	3	365	63	6.6	0	2.8	0.38	0	8	3.6	0.25	0.09
0" fat trim — *3 ½ oz*	100	200	0	82	0	9	3.7	0.4	3.3	28	5	3	375	64	6.8	0	2.8	0.39	0	8	3.7	0.26	0.1
trimmed of all visible fat — *3 ½ oz*	100	180	0	81	0	6.4	2.5	0.3	2.2	28.7	5	3	386	65	7.1	0	2.9	0.4	0	8	3.7	0.27	0.1
Tip round, prime, roasted, ¼" fat trim — *3 ½ oz*	100	274	0	83	0	17.9	7.6	0.7	6.9	26.4	6	3	351	62	6.3	0	2.7	0.37	0	7	3.5	0.24	0.09
Tip round, select, roasted																							
¼" fat trim — *3 ½ oz*	100	225	0	82	0	12.2	5.1	0.5	4.6	27.1	6	3	362	63	6.6	0	2.8	0.38	0	8	3.5	0.25	0.09
⅛" fat trim — *3 ½ oz*	100	210	0	82	0	10.2	4.2	0.4	3.8	27.6	6	3	370	64	6.7	0	2.8	0.38	0	8	3.6	0.26	0.09
0" fat trim — *3 ½ oz*	100	186	0	81	0	7.3	3	0.3	2.7	28.2	5	3	378	64	6.9	0	2.9	0.39	0	8	3.7	0.26	0.1
trimmed of all visible fat — *3 ½ oz*	100	170	0	81	0	5.3	2.1	0.2	1.9	28.7	5	3	386	65	7.1	0	2.9	0.4	0	8	3.7	0.27	0.1
Top loin, choice, broiled																							
¼" fat trim — *3 ½ oz*	100	298	0	79	0	21	8.8	0.8	8.3	25.4	9	2	346	63	4.5	0	1.9	0.37	0	7	4.7	0.18	0.08
⅛" fat trim — *3 ½ oz*	100	284	0	79	0	19.2	8	0.7	7.6	25.9	9	2	354	64	4.7	0	1.9	0.38	0	7	4.8	0.18	0.08
0" fat trim — *3 ½ oz*	100	228	0	77	0	12	4.9	0.4	4.7	27.9	8	2	385	67	5.1	0	2	0.41	0	8	5.2	0.19	0.09

	Weight *g*	Calories	Carbohydrates *g*	Cholesterol *mg*	Dietary fiber *g*	Total fat *g*	Mono. fat *g*	Poly. fat *g*	Sat. fat *g*	Protein *g*	Calcium *mg*	Iron *mg*	Potassium *mg*	Sodium *mg*	Zinc *mg*	Vitamin A *RE*	Vitamin B_{12} *mcg*	Vitamin B_6 *mg*	Vitamin C *mg*	Folic acid *mcg*	Niacin *mg*	Riboflavin *mg*	Thiamin *mg*
trimmed of all visible fat — *3 ½ oz*	100	209	0	76	0	9.6	3.9	0.3	3.7	28.6	8	2	396	68	5.2	0	2	0.42	0	8	5.3	0.2	0.09
Top loin, prime, broiled																							
¼" fat trim — *3 ½ oz*	100	323	0	79	0	23.8	10.1	0.9	9.6	25.4	9	2	346	63	4.5	0	1.9	0.37	0	7	4.7	0.18	0.08
⅛" fat trim — *3 ½ oz*	100	310	0	79	0	22.1	9.4	0.8	8.9	25.9	9	2	354	64	4.7	0	1.9	0.38	0	7	4.8	0.18	0.08
Top loin, select, broiled																							
¼" fat trim — *3 ½ oz*	100	266	0	79	0	17.2	7.2	0.6	6.8	25.9	9	2	354	64	4.7	0	1.9	0.38	0	7	4.8	0.18	0.08
⅛" fat trim — *3 ½ oz*	100	253	0	78	0	15.6	6.5	0.6	6.1	26.4	9	2	362	65	4.8	0	2	0.39	0	7	4.9	0.18	0.08
0" fat trim — *3 ½ oz*	100	199	0	77	0	8.8	3.6	0.3	3.4	28.1	8	2	388	67	5.1	0	2	0.41	0	8	5.2	0.19	0.09
trimmed of all visible fat — *3 ½ oz*	100	184	0	76	0	6.9	2.8	0.2	2.6	28.6	8	2	396	68	5.2	0	2	0.42	0	8	5.3	0.2	0.09
Top round, choice, braised																							
¼" fat trim — *3 ½ oz*	100	260	0	90	0	12.9	5.3	0.5	4.9	33.6	5	3	312	45	4.2	0	2.6	0.27	0	9	3.6	0.24	0.07
⅛" fat trim — *3 ½ oz*	100	250	0	90	0	11.6	4.8	0.5	4.3	34.1	5	3	317	45	4.3	0	2.6	0.27	0	9	3.6	0.24	0.07
0" fat trim — *3 ½ oz*	100	216	0	90	0	7.1	2.8	0.3	2.5	35.6	4	3	330	45	4.5	0	2.7	0.28	0	9	3.8	0.25	0.07
trimmed of all visible fat — *3 ½ oz*	100	207	0	90	0	5.8	2.3	0.3	2	36.1	4	3	334	45	4.6	0	2.7	0.28	0	9	3.8	0.25	0.07
Top round, choice, broiled																							
¼" fat trim — *3 ½ oz*	100	224	0	85	0	10.6	4.3	0.4	3.9	30.2	7	3	419	60	5.3	0	2.4	0.53	0	11	5.7	0.26	0.11
⅛" fat trim — *3 ½ oz*	100	216	0	85	0	9.4	3.8	0.4	3.5	30.5	6	3	424	60	5.3	0	2.4	0.54	0	12	5.8	0.26	0.11
Top round, choice, pan-fried																							
¼" fat trim — *3 ½ oz*	100	277	0	97	0	15.4	5.9	1.8	5.3	32.4	6	3	470	68	4.3	0	3.2	0.56	0	12	5.1	0.26	0.1
⅛" fat trim — *3 ½ oz*	100	266	0	97	0	13.8	5.2	1.7	4.6	33	6	3	480	68	4.4	0	3.3	0.57	0	12	5.2	0.26	0.11
Top round, prime, broiled																							
¼" fat trim — *3 ½ oz*	100	229	0	84	0	10.7	4.3	0.5	3.9	31.1	6	3	432	60	5.4	0	2.5	0.55	0	12	5.9	0.26	0.12
⅛" fat trim — *3 ½ oz*	100	225	0	84	0	10.1	4	0.5	3.6	31.3	6	3	436	61	5.5	0	2.5	0.55	0	12	6	0.26	0.12

	Weight g	Calories	Carbohydrates g	Cholesterol mg	Dietary fiber g	Total fat g	Mono. fat g	Poly. fat g	Sat. fat g	Protein g	Calcium mg	Iron mg	Potassium mg	Sodium mg	Zinc mg	Vitamin A RE	Vitamin B_{12} mcg	Vitamin B_6 mg	Vitamin C mg	Folic acid mcg	Niacin mg	Riboflavin mg	Thiamin mg
Top round, select, braised																							
¼" fat trim — *3 ½ oz*	100	234	0	90	0	9.9	4.1	0.4	3.7	34.1	5	3	317	45	4.3	0	2.6	0.27	0	9	3.6	0.24	0.07
⅛" fat trim — *3 ½ oz*	100	225	0	90	0	8.5	3.5	0.4	3.2	34.6	4	3	321	45	4.4	0	2.6	0.27	0	9	3.7	0.24	0.07
0" fat trim — *3 ½ oz*	100	200	0	90	0	5.3	2.1	0.2	1.9	35.6	4	3	330	45	4.5	0	2.7	0.28	0	9	3.8	0.25	0.07
trimmed of all visible fat — *3 ½ oz*	100	190	0	90	0	4	1.6	0.2	1.4	36.1	4	3	334	45	4.6	0	2.7	0.28	0	9	3.8	0.25	0.07
Top round, select, broiled																							
¼" fat trim — *3 ½ oz*	100	206	0	85	0	8.5	3.5	0.4	3.2	30.2	7	3	419	60	5.3	0	2.4	0.53	0	11	5.7	0.26	0.11
⅛" fat trim — *3 ½ oz*	100	196	0	85	0	7.3	3	0.3	2.7	30.6	6	3	425	60	5.3	0	2.4	0.54	0	12	5.8	0.26	0.11
Top sirloin, choice, broiled																							
¼" fat trim — *3 ½ oz*	100	269	0	90	0	16.7	7.2	0.6	6.7	27.6	11	3	363	62	5.8	0	2.7	0.41	0	9	3.9	0.27	0.11
⅛" fat trim — *3 ½ oz*	100	259	0	90	0	15.5	6.7	0.6	6.2	28	11	3	369	63	5.9	0	2.7	0.41	0	9	4	0.27	0.11
0" fat trim — *3 ½ oz*	100	229	0	89	0	11.6	5	0.5	4.6	29.2	11	3	386	64	6.2	0	2.8	0.43	0	10	4.1	0.28	0.12
trimmed of all visible fat — *3 ½ oz*	100	200	0	89	0	7.8	3.3	0.3	3	30.4	11	3	403	66	6.5	0	2.9	0.45	0	10	4.3	0.29	0.13
Top sirloin, choice, pan-fried																							
¼" fat trim — *3 ½ oz*	100	326	0	98	0	22.8	9.6	1.7	8.9	28.1	12	3	396	70	5.4	0	3.3	0.43	0	9	3.8	0.28	0.12
⅛" fat trim — *3 ½ oz*	100	313	0	98	0	21.1	8.9	1.7	8.2	28.8	12	3	406	71	5.6	0	3.3	0.44	0	9	3.8	0.29	0.12
Top sirloin, select, broiled																							
¼" fat trim — *3 ½ oz*	100	245	0	90	0	13.9	6	0.5	5.5	28	11	3	369	63	5.9	0	2.7	0.41	0	9	4	0.27	0.11
⅛" fat trim — *3 ½ oz*	100	240	0	90	0	13.3	5.7	0.5	5.3	28.2	11	3	372	63	6	0	2.7	0.42	0	9	4	0.27	0.12
0" fat trim — *3 ½ oz*	100	195	0	89	0	7.6	3.2	0.3	3	29.7	11	3	393	65	6.4	0	2.8	0.44	0	10	4.2	0.29	0.12
trimmed of all visible fat — *3 ½ oz*	100	180	0	89	0	5.6	2.4	0.2	2.2	30.4	11	3	403	66	6.5	0	2.9	0.45	0	10	4.3	0.29	0.13
Variety meats																							
brain, pan-fried — *3 ½ oz*	100	196	0	1995	0	15.8	4	2.3	3.7	12.6	9	2	354	158	1.4	0	15.2	0.39	3	6	3.8	0.26	0.13
liver, pan-fried — *2 oz*	57	123	4.5	273	0	4.5	0.9	1	1.5	15.2	6	4	206	60	3.1	6083	63.40	0.81	13	125	8.2	2.35	0.12

	Weight g	Calories	Carbohydrates g	Cholesterol mg	Dietary fiber g	Total fat g	Mono. fat g	Poly. fat g	Sat. fat g	Protein g	Calcium mg	Iron mg	Potassium mg	Sodium mg	Zinc mg	Vitamin A RE	Vitamin B_{12} mcg	Vitamin B_6 mg	Vitamin C mg	Folic acid mcg	Niacin mg	Riboflavin mg	Thiamin mg
lungs, braised — *3 ½ oz*	100	120	0	277	0	3.7	1	0.5	1.3	20.4	11	5	173	101	1.6	12	2.6	0.02	33	8	2.5	0.14	0.04
pancreas, braised — *3 ½ oz*	100	271	0	262	0	17.2	5.9	3.2	5.9	27.1	16	3	246	60	4.6	0	16.6	0.18	20	3	4	0.49	0.18
spleen, braised — *3 ½ oz*	100	145	0	347	0	4.2	1.1	0.3	1.4	25.1	12	39	284	57	2.8	0	5	0.04	50	4	5.6	0.3	0.05
thymus, braised — *3 ½ oz*	100	319	0	294	0	25	8.6	4.7	8.6	21.9	10	1	433	116	2.2	0	1.5	0.08	30	1	1.8	0.23	0.08
tongue, simmered — *3 ½ oz*	100	283	0.3	107	0	20.7	9.5	0.8	8.9	22.1	7	3	180	60	4.8	0	5.9	0.16	1	5	2.2	0.35	0.03

Beverages: Alcoholic

	Weight g	Calories	Carbohydrates g	Cholesterol mg	Dietary fiber g	Total fat g	Mono. fat g	Poly. fat g	Sat. fat g	Protein g	Calcium mg	Iron mg	Potassium mg	Sodium mg	Zinc mg	Vitamin A RE	Vitamin B_{12} mcg	Vitamin B_6 mg	Vitamin C mg	Folic acid mcg	Niacin mg	Riboflavin mg	Thiamin mg
Beer																							
light — *12 fl oz*	354	99	4.6	0	0	0	0	0	0	0.7	18	0	64	11	0.1	0	0	0.12	0	14.5	1.4	0.11	0.03
regular — *12 fl oz*	356	146	13.2	0	0.7	0	0	0	0	1.1	18	0	89	18	0.1	0	0.1	0.18	0	21.4	1.6	0.09	0.02
Bloody Mary — *5 fl oz*	148	115	4.9	0	0.4	0.1	0	0	0	0.7	10	1	216	332	0.1	50	0	0.11	20	19.7	0.6	0.03	0.05
Bourbon & soda — *4 fl oz*	116	104	0	0	0	0	0	0	0	0	3	0	2	16	0.1	0	0	0	0	0	0	0	0
Coffee liqueur																							
53 proof — *1 ½ fl oz jigger*	52	175	24.3	0	0	0.2	0	0.1	0.1	0.1	1	0	16	4	0	0	0	0	0	0	0.1	0.01	0
63 proof — *1 ½ fl oz jigger*	52	160	16.7	0	0	0.2	0	0.1	0.1	0.1	1	0	16	4	0	0	0	0	0	0	0.1	0.01	0
w/ cream, 34 proof — *1 ½ fl oz jigger*	47	154	9.8	7	0	7.4	2.1	0.3	4.5	1.3	8	0	15	43	0.1	20	0.1	0.01	0	0	0	0.03	0
Creme de menthe, 72 proof — *1 ½ fl oz jigger*	50	186	20.8	0	0	0.2	0	0.1	0	0	0	0	0	3	0	0	0	0	0	0	0	0	0
Daiquiri																							
canned — *6.8 fl oz*	207	259	32.5	0	0	0	0	0	0	0	0	0	23	83	0.1	0	0	0.01	3	1.7	0	0	0
from recipe — *2 fl oz*	60	112	4.1	0	0	0.1	0	0	0	0.1	2	0	13	3	0	0	0	0	1	1.2	0	0	0.01
Distilled spirits																							
gin, rum, vodka, whiskey, 100 proof — *1 ½ fl oz jigger*	42	124	0	0	0	0	0	0	0	0	0	0	1	0	0	0	0	0	0	0	0	0	0
gin, rum, vodka, whiskey, 86 proof — *1 ½ fl oz jigger*	42	105	0	0	0	0	0	0	0	0	0	0	1	0	0	0	0	0	0	0	0	0	0
gin, rum, vodka, whiskey, 90 proof — *1 ½ fl oz jigger*	42	110	0	0	0	0	0	0	0	0	0	0	1	0	0	0	0	0	0	0	0	0	0
Gin & tonic — *7 ½ fl oz*	225	171	15.8	0	0	0	0	0	0	0	5	0	11	9	0.2	0	0	0	1	1.1	0	0	0

	Weight g	Calories	Carbohydrates g	Cholesterol mg	Dietary fiber g	Total fat g	Mono. fat g	Poly. fat g	Sat. fat g	Protein g	Calcium mg	Iron mg	Potassium mg	Sodium mg	Zinc mg	Vitamin A RE	Vitamin B_{12} mcg	Vitamin B_6 mg	Vitamin C mg	Folic acid mcg	Niacin mg	Riboflavin mg	Thiamin mg
Manhattan — *2 fl oz*	57	128	1.8	0	0	0	0	0	0	0.1	1	0	15	2	0	0	0	0	0	0.1	0.1	0	0.01
Martini — *2 ½ fl oz*	70	156	0.2	0	0	0	0	0	0	0	1	0	13	2	0	0	0	0	0	0.1	0	0	0
Piña colada																							
canned — *6.8 fl oz*	222	526	61.3	0	0.2	16.9	1	0.3	14.6	1.3	2	0	184	158	0.4	4	0	0.04	3	13.3	0.2	0.01	0.04
from recipe — *4 ½ fl oz*	141	262	39.9	0	0.8	2.7	0.2	0.5	1.2	0.6	11	0	100	8	0.2	0	0	0.06	7	14.4	0.2	0.02	0.04
Screwdriver — *7 fl oz*	213	175	18.3	0	0.4	0	0	0	0	1.1	15	0	326	2	0.1	13	0	0.07	66	74.8	0.3	0.03	0.14
Tequila sunrise, canned — *6.8 fl oz*	211	232	23.8	0	0	0.2	0	0	0	0.6	0	0	21	120	1.3	21	0	0.11	41	22.4	0.4	0.03	0.08
Tom Collins — *7 ½ oz*	222	122	2.9	0	0	0	0	0	0	0	9	0	18	38	0.2	0	0	0.01	4	1.6	0	0	0.01
Whiskey sour																							
canned — *6.8 fl oz*	209	249	28	0	0.2	0	0	0	0	0	0	0	23	92	0.1	2	0	0	3	0	0	0.01	0.02
from powdered mix — *1 packet*	618	1014	98.3	0	0	0	0	0	0	0.6	278	0	25	284	0.3	0	0	0	2	0	0.1	0	0.02
from recipe — *3 fl oz*	90	122	5	0	0.2	0.1	0	0	0	0.2	5	0	48	10	0	1	0	0.02	11	4.7	0.1	0	0.19
Wine																							
dessert, dry — *3 ½ fl oz*	103	130	4.2	0	0	0	0	0	0	0.2	8	0	95	9	0.1	0	0	0	0	0.4	0.2	0.02	0.02
dessert, sweet — *3 ½ fl oz*	103	158	12.2	0	0	0	0	0	0	0.2	8	0	95	9	0.1	0	0	0	0	0.4	0.2	0.02	0.02
table, red — *3 ½ fl oz*	103	74	1.8	0	0	0	0	0	0	0.2	8	0	115	5	0.1	0	0	0.04	0	2.1	0.1	0.03	0.01
table, rose — *3 ½ fl oz*	103	73	1.4	0	0	0	0	0	0	0.2	8	0	102	5	0.1	0	0	0.02	0	1.1	0.1	0.02	0
table, white — *3 ½ fl oz*	103	70	0.8	0	0	0	0	0	0	0.1	9	0	82	5	0.1	0	0	0.01	0	0.2	0.1	0.01	0

Beverages: Non-Alcoholic

	Weight g	Calories	Carbohydrates g	Cholesterol mg	Dietary fiber g	Total fat g	Mono. fat g	Poly. fat g	Sat. fat g	Protein g	Calcium mg	Iron mg	Potassium mg	Sodium mg	Zinc mg	Vitamin A RE	Vitamin B_{12} mcg	Vitamin B_6 mg	Vitamin C mg	Folic acid mcg	Niacin mg	Riboflavin mg	Thiamin mg
Acerola juice — *1 cup*	242	51	11.6	0	0.7	0.7	0.2	0.2	0.2	1	24	1	235	7	0.2	123	0	0.01	3872	33.9	1	0.15	0.05
Apple juice																							
canned or bottled, unsweetened — *1 cup*	248	117	29	0	0.2	0.3	0	0.1	0	0.1	17	1	295	7	0.1	0	0	0.07	2	0.3	0.2	0.04	0.05
canned or bottled, unsweetened w/ vitamin C — *1 cup*	248	117	29	0	0.2	0.3	0	0.1	0	0.1	17	1	295	7	0.1	0	0	0.07	103	0.3	0	0.04	0.05
concentrate only, unsweetened — *1 fl oz*	28	47	11.7	0	0.1	0.1	0	0	0	0.1	6	0	128	7	0	0	0	0.03	1	0.3	0	0.02	0

	Weight *g*	Calories	Carbohydrates *g*	Cholesterol *mg*	Dietary fiber *g*	Total fat *g*	Mono. fat *g*	Poly. fat *g*	Sat. fat *g*	Protein *g*	Calcium *mg*	Iron *mg*	Potassium *mg*	Sodium *mg*	Zinc *mg*	Vitamin A *RE*	Vitamin B_{12} *mcg*	Vitamin B_6 *mg*	Vitamin C *mg*	Folic acid *mcg*	Niacin *mg*	Riboflavin *mg*	Thiamin *mg*
from frozen concentrate, unsweetened — *1 cup*	239	112	27.6	0	0.2	0.2	0	0.1	0	0.3	14	1	301	17	0.1	0	0	0.08	1	0.7	0.1	0.04	0.01
from frozen concentrate w/ vitamin C — *1 cup*	239	112	27.6	0	0.2	0.2	0	0.1	0	0.3	14	1	301	17	0.1	0	0	0.08	60	0.7	0.1	0.04	0.01
Apricot nectar																							
canned — *1 cup*	251	141	36.1	0	1.5	0.2	0.1	0	0	0.9	18	1	286	8	0.2	331	0	0.06	2	3.3	0.7	0.04	0.02
canned, w/ vitamin C — *1 cup*	251	141	36.1	0	1.5	0.2	0.1	0	0	0.9	18	1	286	8	0.2	331	0	0.06	137	3.3	0.7	0.04	0.02
Beef broth & tomato juice, canned — *8 fl oz*	244	90	20.7	0	0.2	0.2	0.1	0.1	0.1	1.5	27	1	234	320	0	32	0.1	0.06	2	10.5	0.4	0.07	0
Carrot juice, canned — *1 cup*	236	94	21.9	0	1.9	0.4	0	0.2	0.1	2.2	57	1	689	68	0.4	6077	0	0.51	20	9	0.9	0.13	0.22
Citrus fruit juice drink, from frozen concentrate — *1 cup*	248	114	28.5	0	0	0	0	0	0	0.7	22	3	278	7	0.1	10	0	0.06	67	5	0.4	0.03	0.03
Clam & tomato juice, canned — *5 fl oz*	151	69	16.5	0	0.3	0.2	0	0	0	0.9	18	1	136	604	1.6	33	46.2	0.13	6	24	0.3	0.05	0.06
Club soda — *12 fl oz*	355	0	0	0	0	0	0	0	0	0	18	0	7	75	0.4	0	0	0	0	0	0	0	0
Coffee																							
brewed — *6 fl oz*	178	4	0.7	0	0	0	0	0	0	0.2	4	0	96	4	0	0	0	0	0	0.2	0.4	0	0
espresso — *3 fl oz*	90	8	1.4	0	0	0.2	0	0.1	0.1	0	2	0	104	13	0	0	0	0	0	0.9	4.7	0.16	0
instant — *6 fl oz*	179	4	0.7	0	0	0	0	0	0	0.2	5	0	64	5	0.1	0	0	0	0	0	0.5	0	0
instant, cappuccino-flavored — *6 fl oz*	192	61	10.8	0	0	2.1	0.1	0	1.8	0.4	8	0	119	104	0.1	0	0	0	0	0	0.3	0.01	0.02
instant, decaffeinated — *6 fl oz*	179	4	0.7	0	0	0	0	0	0	0.2	5	0	63	5	0.1	0	0	0	0	0	0.5	0.03	0
instant w/ chicory — *6 fl oz*	179	7	1.3	0	0	0	0	0	0	0.2	5	0	61	11	0.1	0	0	0	0	0	0.4	0.01	0
Coffee substitute (grain beverage) — *6 fl oz*	180	9	1.8	0	0	0	0	0	0	0.2	5	0	43	7	0.1	0	0	0.02	0	0.5	0.4	0	0.01
Cola																							
diet w/ sodium saccharin — *12 fl oz*	355	0	0.4	0	0	0	0	0	0	0	14	0	7	57	0.2	0	0	0	0	0	0	0	0
low-calorie w/ aspartame — *12 fl oz*	355	4	0.4	0	0	0	0	0	0	0.4	14	0	0	21	0.3	0	0	0	0	0	0	0.08	0.02
regular — *12 fl oz*	370	152	38.5	0	0	0	0	0	0	0	11	0	4	15	0	0	0	0	0	0	0	0	0
Cranberry juice cocktail																							
from frozen concentrate — *1 cup*	250	138	35	0	0.3	0	0	0	0	0	13	0	35	8	0.1	3	0	0.04	25	0	0	0.02	0.02

	Weight g	Calories	Carbohydrates g	Cholesterol mg	Dietary fiber g	Total fat g	Mono. fat g	Poly. fat g	Sat. fat g	Protein g	Calcium mg	Iron mg	Potassium mg	Sodium mg	Zinc mg	Vitamin A RE	Vitamin B_{12} mcg	Vitamin B_6 mg	Vitamin C mg	Folic acid mcg	Niacin mg	Riboflavin mg	Thiamin mg
low-calorie — *1 cup*	237	45	11.1	0	0	0	0	0	0	0	21	0	52	7	0	0	0	0.05	76	0.5	0.1	0.02	0.02
regular — *1 cup*	253	144	36.4	0	0.3	0.3	0	0.1	0	0	8	0	46	5	0.2	0	0	0.05	90	0.5	0.1	0.02	0.02
Cranberry-apple juice drink — *1 cup*	245	164	41.9	0	0.2	0	0	0	0	0.2	17	0	66	5	0.1	0	0	0.05	78	0.5	0.1	0.05	0.01
Cranberry-apricot juice drink — *1 cup*	245	157	39.7	0	0.2	0	0	0	0	0.5	22	0	149	5	0.1	113	0	0.05	0	1.5	0.3	0.02	0.01
Cranberry-grape juice drink — *1 cup*	245	137	34.3	0	0.2	0.2	0	0.1	0.1	0.5	20	0	59	7	0.1	0	0	0.07	78	1.7	0.3	0.04	0.02
Cream soda — *12 fl oz*	371	189	49.3	0	0	0	0	0	0	0	19	0	4	45	0.3	0	0	0	0	0	0	0	0
Eggnog																							
from powder, prepared w/ milk — *8 fl oz*	272	261	38.9	33	0.8	8.4	2.5	0.3	5.1	8.2	291	0	370	163	0.9	76	0.9	0.1	2	12.2	0.2	0.39	0.09
from recipe — *1 cup*	254	342	34.4	149	0	19	5.7	0.9	11.3	9.7	330	1	420	138	1.2	203	1.1	0.13	4	2.3	0.3	0.48	0.09
Fruit punch drink																							
from frozen concentrate — *1 cup*	247	114	28.9	0	0.2	0	0	0	0	0	10	0	32	10	0.1	2	0	0.01	108	2.2	0.1	0.03	0.02
canned — *1 cup*	248	117	29.5	0	0.2	0	0	0	0	0	20	1	62	55	0.3	2	0	0	73	3.2	0.1	0.06	0.05
Fruit punch juice drink, from frozen concentrate — *1 cup*	248	124	30.3	0	0.2	0.5	0.1	0.1	0.1	0.2	17	1	191	12	0.5	2	0	0.03	14	0	0.1	0.16	0
Fruit punch-flavor drink, from powder — *1 cup*	262	97	24.9	0	0	0	0	0	0	0	42	0	3	37	0.1	0	0	0	31	0.3	0	0.01	0
Ginger ale — *12 fl oz*	366	124	31.8	0	0	0	0	0	0	0	11	1	4	26	0.2	0	0	0	0	0	0	0	0
Grape drink, canned — *1 cup*	250	113	28.8	0	0	0	0	0	0	0	8	0	13	15	0.3	0	0	0.02	85	0.8	0.1	0.01	0.01
Grape juice																							
canned or bottled, unsweetened — *1 cup*	253	154	37.8	0	0.3	0.2	0	0.1	0.1	1.4	23	1	334	8	0.1	3	0	0.16	0	6.6	0.7	0.09	0.07
from frozen concentrate, sweetened — *1 cup*	250	128	31.9	0	0.3	0.2	0	0.1	0.1	0.5	10	0	53	5	0.1	3	0	0.11	60	3.3	0.3	0.07	0.04
Grape juice drink, canned — *1 cup*	250	125	32.3	0	0.3	0	0	0	0	0.3	8	0	88	3	0.1	0	0	0.05	40	2	0.3	0.03	0.03
Grape soda — *12 fl oz*	372	160	41.7	0	0	0	0	0	0	0	11	0	4	56	0.3	0	0	0	0	0	0	0	0
Grapefruit juice																							
canned, sweetened — *1 cup*	250	115	27.8	0	0.3	0.2	0	0.1	0	1.5	20	1	405	5	0.2	0	0	0.05	67	26	0.8	0.06	0.1
canned, unsweetened — *1 cup*	247	94	22.1	0	0.2	0.2	0	0.1	0	1.3	17	0	378	2	0.2	2	0	0.05	72	25.7	0.6	0.05	0.1

	Weight g	Calories	Carbohydrates g	Cholesterol mg	Dietary fiber g	Total fat g	Mono. fat g	Poly. fat g	Sat. fat g	Protein g	Calcium mg	Iron mg	Potassium mg	Sodium mg	Zinc mg	Vitamin A RE	Vitamin B_{12} mcg	Vitamin B_6 mg	Vitamin C mg	Folic acid mcg	Niacin mg	Riboflavin mg	Thiamin mg
fresh, pink — *1 cup*	247	96	22.7	0	0	0.2	0	0.1	0	1.2	22	0	400	2	0.1	109	0	0.11	94	25.2	0.5	0.05	0.1
fresh, white — *1 cup*	247	96	22.7	0	0.2	0.2	0	0.1	0	1.2	22	0	400	2	0.1	2	0	0.11	94	25.2	0.5	0.05	0.1
from frozen concentrate, unsweetened — *1 cup*	247	101	24	0	0.2	0.3	0	0.1	0	1.4	20	0	336	2	0.1	2	0	0.11	83	8.9	0.5	0.05	0.1
Lemon-lime soda — *12 fl oz*	368	147	38.3	0	0	0	0	0	0	0	7	0	4	40	0.2	0	0	0	0	0	0.1	0	0
Lemonade																							
from frozen concentrate — *1 cup*	248	99	26	0	0.2	0	0	0	0	0.2	7	0	37	7	0.1	5	0	0.01	10	5.5	0	0.05	0.01
from powdered mix — *1 cup*	264	103	26.9	0	0	0	0	0	0	0	71	0	34	13	0.1	0	0	0.01	8	3.4	0	0	0.01
from powdered mix, low-calorie — *1 cup*	237	5	1.2	0	0	0	0	0	0	0	50	0	0	7	0.1	0	0	0	6	0.2	0	0	0
Lemonade-flavor drink, from powdered mix — *1 cup*	266	112	28.7	0	0	0	0	0	0	0	29	0	3	19	0.1	0	0	0	34	0	0	0	0
Limeade, from frozen concentrate — *1 cup*	247	101	27.2	0	0.2	0	0	0	0	0	7	0	32	5	0	0	0	0	7	2.5	0.1	0	0
Malt beverage — *1 cup*	237	142	31.9	0	0	0.3	0	0.1	0.1	0.7	12	0	19	31	0	0	0	0.06	1	33.2	2.6	0.11	0.04
Malted milk-flavor mix, made w/ whole milk — *1 cup*	265	231	28.4	34	0	8.7	2.5	0.4	5.4	9.8	371	4	572	204	1.1	742	1	0.87	29	21.7	10.4	1.14	0.71
Orange & apricot juice drink, canned — *1 cup*	250	128	31.8	0	0.3	0.3	0.1	0.1	0	0.8	13	0	200	5	0.1	145	0	0.07	50	14.5	0.5	0.03	0.05
Orange drink, canned — *1 cup*	248	126	32	0	0.2	0	0	0	0	0	15	1	45	40	0.2	5	0	0.02	85	5.5	0.1	0.01	0.01
Orange juice																							
canned, unsweetened — *1 cup*	249	105	24.5	0	0.5	0.3	0.1	0.1	0	1.5	20	1	436	5	0.2	45	0	0.22	86	45.1	0.8	0.07	0.15
fresh — *1 cup*	248	112	25.8	0	0.5	0.5	0.1	0.1	0.1	1.7	27	0	496	2	0.1	50	0	0.1	124	75.1	1	0.07	0.22
from frozen concentrate, unsweetened — *1 cup*	249	112	26.8	0	0.5	0.1	0	0	0	1.7	22	0	473	2	0.1	20	0	0.11	97	109.1	0.5	0.04	0.2
Orange soda — *12 fl oz*	372	179	45.8	0	0	0	0	0	0	0	19	0	7	45	0.4	0	0	0	0	0	0	0	0
Orange-flavor drink, breakfast type, from powder — *1 cup*	248	114	29.3	0	0	0	0	0	0	0	62	0	50	12	0.1	551	0	0	121	142.9	0	0.04	0
Orange-grapefruit juice, canned, unsweetened — *1 cup*	247	106	25.4	0	0.2	0.2	0	0	0	1.5	20	1	390	7	0.2	30	0	0.06	72	35.3	0.8	0.07	0.14
Papaya nectar — *1 cup*	250	143	36.3	0	1.5	0.4	0.1	0.1	0.1	0.4	25	1	78	13	0.4	28	0	0.02	8	5.3	0.4	0.01	0.02
Passion-fruit juice																							
purple — *1 cup*	247	126	33.6	0	0.5	0.1	0	0.1	0	1	10	1	687	15	0.1	178	0	0.12	74	17.3	3.6	0.32	0

	Weight *g*	Calories	Carbohydrates *g*	Cholesterol *mg*	Dietary fiber *g*	Total fat *g*	Mono. fat *g*	Poly. fat *g*	Sat. fat *g*	Protein *g*	Calcium *mg*	Iron *mg*	Potassium *mg*	Sodium *mg*	Zinc *mg*	Vitamin A *RE*	Vitamin B_{12} *mcg*	Vitamin B_6 *mg*	Vitamin C *mg*	Folic acid *mcg*	Niacin *mg*	Riboflavin *mg*	Thiamin *mg*
yellow — *1 cup*	247	148	35.7	0	0.5	0.4	0.1	0.3	0	1.7	10	1	687	15	0.1	595	0	0.15	45	19.8	5.5	0.25	0
Peach nectar																							
canned — *1 cup*	249	134	34.7	0	1.5	0	0	0	0	0.7	12	0	100	17	0.2	65	0	0.02	13	3.5	0.7	0.03	0.01
canned w/ vitamin C — *1 cup*	249	134	34.7	0	1.5	0	0	0	0	0.7	12	0	100	17	0.2	65	0	0.02	67	3.5	0.7	0.03	0.01
Pear nectar																							
canned — *1 cup*	250	150	39.4	0	1.5	0	0	0	0	0.3	13	1	33	10	0.2	0	0	0.04	3	3	0.3	0.03	0.01
canned w/ vitamin C — *1 cup*	250	150	39.4	0	1.5	0	0	0	0	0.3	13	1	33	10	0.2	0	0	0.04	68	3	0.3	0.03	0.01
Pepper-type soda — *12 fl oz*	368	151	38.3	0	0	0.4	0	0	0.3	0	11	0	4	37	0.1	0	0	0	0	0	0	0	0
Pineapple & grapefruit juice drink, canned — *1 cup*	250	118	29	0	0.3	0.3	0	0.1	0	0.5	18	1	153	35	0.2	10	0	0.11	115	26.3	0.7	0.04	0.08
Pineapple & orange juice drink, canned — *1 cup*	250	125	29.5	0	0.3	0	0	0	0	3.3	13	1	115	8	0.2	133	0	0.12	56	27.3	0.5	0.05	0.08
Pineapple juice																							
canned, unsweetened — *1 cup*	250	140	34.5	0	0.5	0.2	0	0.1	0	0.8	43	1	335	3	0.3	0	0	0.24	27	57.8	0.6	0.06	0.14
canned, unsweetened w/ vitamin C — *1 cup*	250	140	34.5	0	0.5	0.2	0	0.1	0	0.8	43	1	335	3	0.3	0	0	0.24	60	57.8	0.6	0.06	0.14
from frozen concentrate, unsweetened — *1 cup*	250	130	31.9	0	0.5	0.1	0	0	0	1	28	1	340	3	0.3	3	0	0.19	30	26.5	0.5	0.05	0.18
Prune juice, canned — *1 cup*	256	182	44.7	0	2.6	0.1	0.1	0	0	1.6	31	3	707	10	0.5	0	0	0.56	10	1	2	0.18	0.04
Root beer — *12 fl oz*	370	152	39.2	0	0	0	0	0	0	0	19	0	4	48	0.3	0	0	0	0	0	0	0	0
Tangerine juice																							
canned, sweetened — *1 cup*	249	125	29.9	0	0.5	0.5	0	0.1	0	1.2	45	0	443	2	0.1	105	0	0.08	55	11.5	0.2	0.05	0.15
fresh — *1 cup*	247	106	24.9	0	0.5	0.5	0.1	0.1	0.1	1.2	44	0	440	2	0.1	104	0	0.1	77	11.4	0.2	0.05	0.15
from frozen concentrate, sweetened — *1 cup*	241	111	26.7	0	0	0.3	0	0	0	1	19	0	272	2	0.1	137	0	0.1	58	11.1	0.2	0.05	0.13
Tea																							
brewed — *6 fl oz*	178	2	0.5	0	0	0	0	0	0	0	0	0	66	5	0	0	0	0	0	9.3	0	0.02	0
herb, chamomile, brewed — *6 fl oz*	178	2	0.4	0	0	0	0	0	0	0	4	0	16	2	0.1	4	0	0	0	1.1	0	0.01	0.02
herb, other than chamomile, brewed — *6 fl oz*	237	2	0.5	0	0	0	0	0	0	0	5	0	21	2	0.1	0	0	0	0	1.4	0	0.01	0.02

	Weight *g*	Calories	Carbohydrates *g*	Cholesterol *mg*	Dietary fiber *g*	Total fat *g*	Mono. fat *g*	Poly. fat *g*	Sat. fat *g*	Protein *g*	Calcium *mg*	Iron *mg*	Potassium *mg*	Sodium *mg*	Zinc *mg*	Vitamin A *RE*	Vitamin B12 *mcg*	Vitamin B6 *mg*	Vitamin C *mg*	Folic acid *mcg*	Niacin *mg*	Riboflavin *mg*	Thiamin *mg*
Tea, instant																							
low-calorie, lemon-flavored — *1 cup*	237	5	1.2	0	0	0	0	0	0	0	5	0	40	24	0.1	0	0	0	0	4.5	0.1	0.01	0
sweetened, lemon-flavored — *1 cup*	259	88	22	0	0	0	0	0	0	0.3	5	0	49	8	0.1	0	0	0.01	0	9.6	0.1	0.05	0
sweetened, lemon-flavored w/ vitamin C — *1 cup*	259	88	22	0	0	0	0	0	0	0.3	5	0	49	8	0.1	0	0	0.01	23	9.6	0.1	0.05	0
unsweetened, lemon-flavored — *1 cup*	238	5	1	0	0	0	0	0	0	0	5	0	50	14	0.1	0	0	0	0	0.7	0.1	0.02	0
unsweetened, regular, prepared — *1 cup*	237	2	0.5	0	0	0	0	0	0	0	5	0	47	7	0.1	0	0	0	0	0.7	0.1	0	0
Tomato juice																							
canned w/ salt — *1 cup*	243	41	10.3	0	1	0.1	0	0.1	0	1.8	22	1	535	877	0.3	136	0	0.27	44	48.4	1.6	0.08	0.11
canned w/o salt — *1 cup*	243	41	10.3	0	1.9	0.1	0	0.1	0	1.8	22	1	535	24	0.3	136	0	0.27	44	48.4	1.6	0.08	0.11
Vegetable juice cocktail, canned — *1 cup*	242	46	11	0	1.9	0.2	0	0.1	0	1.5	27	1	467	653	0.5	283	0	0.34	67	51.1	1.8	0.07	0.1

Breads & Breadstuffs

	Weight *g*	Calories	Carbohydrates *g*	Cholesterol *mg*	Dietary fiber *g*	Total fat *g*	Mono. fat *g*	Poly. fat *g*	Sat. fat *g*	Protein *g*	Calcium *mg*	Iron *mg*	Potassium *mg*	Sodium *mg*	Zinc *mg*	Vitamin A *RE*	Vitamin B12 *mcg*	Vitamin B6 *mg*	Vitamin C *mg*	Folic acid *mcg*	Niacin *mg*	Riboflavin *mg*	Thiamin *mg*
Bagels																							
cinnamon-raisin — *1 bagel*	71	195	39.2	0	1.6	1.2	0.1	0.5	0.2	7	13	3	108	229	0.5	6	0	0.04	0	14.9	2.2	0.2	0.27
egg — *1 bagel*	71	197	37.6	17	1.6	1.5	0.3	0.5	0.3	7.5	9	3	48	359	0.5	23	0.1	0.06	0	15.6	2.4	0.17	0.38
oat bran — *1 bagel*	71	181	37.8	0	2.6	0.9	0.2	0.3	0.1	7.6	9	2	145	360	1.5	0	0	0.14	0	32.7	2.1	0.24	0.24
plain, onion, poppy, or sesame — *1 bagel*	71	195	37.9	0	1.6	1.1	0.1	0.5	0.2	7.5	53	3	72	379	0.6	0	0	0.04	0	15.6	3.2	0.22	0.38
Biscuits, plain or buttermilk																							
from dry mix, baked — *1 biscuit*	57	191	27.6	2	1	6.9	2.4	2.5	1.6	4.2	105	1	107	544	0.3	15	0.1	0.04	0	3.4	1.7	0.2	0.2
refrigerated dough, lower fat, baked — *1 biscuit*	21	63	11.6	0	0.4	1.1	0.6	0.2	0.3	1.6	4	1	39	305	0.1	0	0	0.01	0	1.1	0.7	0.05	0.09
refrigerated dough, regular, baked — *1 biscuit*	27	93	12.8	0	0.4	4	2.2	0.5	1	1.8	5	1	42	325	0.1	0	0	0.01	0	1.1	0.8	0.06	0.09
Boston brown bread, canned — *1 slice*	45	88	19.5	0	2.1	0.7	0.1	0.3	0.1	2.3	32	1	143	284	0.2	5	0	0.04	0	3.2	0.5	0.05	0.01
Bread crumbs																							
dry, plain — *¼ cup*	27	107	19.6	0	0.6	1.5	0.6	0.4	0.3	3.4	61	2	60	233	0.3	0	0	0.03	0	6.8	1.8	0.12	0.21
dry, seasoned — *¼ cup*	30	110	21.1	1	1.3	0.8	0.3	0.2	0.2	4.3	30	1	81	795	0.3	1	0	0.04	0	6	0.8	0.05	0.05

	Weight g	Calories	Carbohydrates g	Cholesterol mg	Dietary fiber g	Total fat g	Mono. fat g	Poly. fat g	Sat. fat g	Protein g	Calcium mg	Iron mg	Potassium mg	Sodium mg	Zinc mg	Vitamin A RE	Vitamin B_{12} mcg	Vitamin B_6 mg	Vitamin C mg	Folic acid mcg	Niacin mg	Riboflavin mg	Thiamin mg
fresh — *¼ cup*	11	30	5.6	0	0.3	0.4	0.2	0.1	0.1	0.9	12	0	13	61	0.1	0	0	0.01	0	3.8	0.4	0.04	0.05
Bread sticks, plain — *2 medium*	20	82	13.7	0	0.6	1.9	0.7	0.7	0.3	2.4	4	1	25	131	0.2	0	0	0.01	0	6	1.1	0.11	0.12
Cornbread, from dry mix, baked — *1 piece*	60	188	28.9	37	1.4	6	3.1	0.7	1.6	4.3	44	1	77	467	0.4	26	0.1	0.06	0	6.6	1.2	0.16	0.15
Cracked-wheat bread — *1 slice*	25	65	12.4	0	1.4	1	0.5	0.2	0.2	2.2	11	1	44	135	0.3	0	0	0.08	0	9.8	0.9	0.06	0.09
Croissants																							
apple — *1 medium*	57	145	21.1	29	1.4	5	1.4	0.4	2.5	4.2	17	1	51	156	0.6	42	0.1	0.02	0	7.4	0.9	0.09	0.13
butter — *1 medium*	57	231	26.1	43	1.5	12	3.3	0.7	6.7	4.7	21	1	67	424	0.4	78	0.2	0.03	0	16	1.2	0.14	0.22
cheese — *1 medium*	57	236	26.8	36	1.5	11.9	3.7	1.5	5.5	5.2	30	1	75	316	0.5	89	0.2	0.04	0	18.8	1.2	0.19	0.3
Croutons																							
plain — *¼ cup*	8	31	5.5	0	0.4	0.5	0.3	0.1	0.1	0.9	6	0	9	52	0.1	0	0	0	0	1.7	0.4	0.02	0.05
seasoned — *¼ cup*	10	47	6.4	0	0.5	1.8	1	0.2	0.5	1.1	10	0	18	124	0.1	1	0	0.01	0	4	0.5	0.04	0.05
Egg bread — *1 slice*	40	115	19.1	20	0.9	2.4	1.1	0.4	0.6	3.8	37	1	46	197	0.3	9	0	0.03	0	28	1.9	0.17	0.18
Egg roll wrappers — *1 wrapper*	32	93	18.5	3	0.6	0.5	0.1	0.2	0.1	3.1	15	1	26	183	0.2	1	0	0.01	0	5.4	1.7	0.12	0.17
English muffins																							
mixed-grain — *1 muffin*	66	155	30.6	0	1.8	1.2	0.5	0.4	0.2	6	129	2	103	275	0.6	1	0	0.06	0	23.1	2.4	0.21	0.28
plain — *1 muffin*	57	134	26.2	0	1.5	1	0.2	0.5	0.1	4.4	99	1	75	264	0.4	0	0	0.02	0	21.1	2.2	0.16	0.25
raisin-cinnamon — *1 muffin*	57	139	27.8	0	1.7	1.5	0.3	0.8	0.2	4.3	84	1	119	255	0.6	0	0	0.04	0	18.2	2	0.17	0.22
wheat — *1 muffin*	57	127	25.5	0	2.6	1.1	0.2	0.5	0.2	5	101	2	106	218	0.6	0	0	0.05	0	22.2	1.9	0.17	0.25
whole-wheat — *1 muffin*	66	134	26.7	0	4.4	1.4	0.3	0.6	0.2	5.8	175	2	139	420	1.1	0	0	0.11	0	32.3	2.3	0.09	0.2
French bread (including sourdough) — *1 slice*	25	69	13	0	0.8	0.8	0.3	0.2	0.2	2.2	19	1	28	152	0.2	0	0	0.01	0	7.8	1.2	0.08	0.13
Irish soda bread — *1 slice*	60	174	33.6	11	1.6	3	1.2	0.9	0.7	4	49	2	160	239	0.3	30	0	0.05	0	6	1.4	0.16	0.18
Italian bread — *1 slice*	20	54	10	0	0.5	0.7	0.2	0.3	0.2	1.8	16	1	22	117	0.2	0	0	0.01	0	6	0.9	0.06	0.09
Mixed-grain bread — *1 slice*	26	65	12.1	0	1.7	1	0.4	0.2	0.2	2.6	24	1	53	127	0.3	0	0	0.09	0	12.5	1.1	0.09	0.11

	Weight g	Calories	Carbohydrates g	Cholesterol mg	Dietary fiber g	Total fat g	Mono. fat g	Poly. fat g	Sat. fat g	Protein g	Calcium mg	Iron mg	Potassium mg	Sodium mg	Zinc mg	Vitamin A RE	Vitamin B_{12} mcg	Vitamin B_6 mg	Vitamin C mg	Folic acid mcg	Niacin mg	Riboflavin mg	Thiamin mg
Oat bran bread																							
reduced-calorie — *1 slice*	23	46	9.5	0	2.8	0.7	0.2	0.4	0.1	1.8	13	1	23	81	0.2	0	0	0.02	0	7.8	0.9	0.05	0.08
regular — *1 slice*	30	71	11.9	0	1.4	1.3	0.5	0.5	0.2	3.1	20	1	34	122	0.3	0	0	0.01	0	7.5	1.4	0.1	0.15
Oatmeal bread																							
reduced-calorie — *1 slice*	23	48	10	0	0	0.8	0.2	0.3	0.1	1.7	26	1	35	89	0.2	0	0	0.01	0	7.8	0.7	0.06	0.08
regular — *1 slice*	27	73	13.1	0	1.1	1.2	0.4	0.5	0.2	2.3	18	1	38	162	0.3	1	0	0.02	0	7.3	0.8	0.06	0.11
Pita bread																							
white — *1 large*	60	165	33.4	0	1.3	0.7	0.1	0.3	0.1	5.5	52	2	72	322	0.5	0	0	0.02	0	14.4	2.8	0.2	0.36
whole-wheat — *1 large*	64	170	35.2	0	4.7	1.7	0.2	0.7	0.3	6.3	10	2	109	340	1	0	0	0.15	0	22.4	1.8	0.05	0.22
Pumpernickel bread — *1 slice*	26	65	12.4	0	1.7	0.8	0.2	0.3	0.1	2.3	18	1	54	174	0.4	0	0	0.03	0	8.8	0.8	0.08	0.09
Raisin bread — *1 slice*	26	71	13.6	0	1.1	1.1	0.6	0.2	0.3	2.1	17	1	59	101	0.2	0	0	0.02	0	8.8	0.9	0.1	0.09
Rice bran bread — *1 slice*	27	66	11.7	0	1.3	1.2	0.4	0.5	0.2	2.4	19	1	53	119	0.3	0	0	0.06	0	8.1	1.8	0.08	0.18
Rolls, dinner																							
egg — *1 roll*	35	107	18.2	18	1.3	2.2	1.1	0.4	0.6	3.3	21	1	37	191	0.3	8	0.1	0.03	0	18.6	1.2	0.18	0.18
oat bran — *1 roll*	33	78	13.3	0	1.4	1.5	0.5	0.5	0.2	3.1	28	1	36	136	0.3	0	0	0.01	0	10.2	1.6	0.1	0.15
plain — *1 roll*	28	85	14.3	0	0.9	2.1	1.1	0.3	0.5	2.4	34	1	38	148	0.2	0	0	0.02	0	8.5	1.1	0.09	0.14
rye — *1 roll*	28	81	15.1	0	1.4	1	0.4	0.2	0.2	2.9	9	1	51	253	0.3	0	0	0.02	0	6.2	1.1	0.08	0.11
wheat — *1 roll*	28	77	13	0	1.1	1.8	0.9	0.3	0.4	2.4	50	1	38	96	0.3	0	0	0.02	0	4.3	1.2	0.08	0.12
whole-wheat — *1 roll*	28	75	14.5	0	2.1	1.3	0.3	0.6	0.2	2.5	30	1	77	136	0.6	0	0	0.06	0	8.5	1	0.04	0.07
Rolls, french — *1 roll*	38	105	19.1	0	1.2	1.6	0.7	0.3	0.4	3.3	35	1	43	231	0.3	0	0	0.02	0	12.5	1.7	0.11	0.2
Rolls, hamburger or hot dog																							
mixed-grain — *1 roll*	43	113	19.2	0	1.6	2.6	1.3	0.5	0.6	4.1	41	2	65	197	0.5	0	0	0.04	0	12	1.9	0.13	0.2
plain — *1 roll*	43	123	21.6	0	1.2	2.2	1.1	0.4	0.5	3.7	60	1	61	241	0.3	0	0	0.02	0	11.6	1.7	0.13	0.21
reduced-calorie — *1 roll*	43	84	18.1	0	2.7	0.9	0.2	0.3	0.1	3.6	25	1	34	190	0.4	0	0.1	0.02	0	12.9	2.1	0.08	0.17

	Weight g	Calories	Carbohydrates g	Cholesterol mg	Dietary fiber g	Total fat g	Mono. fat g	Poly. fat g	Sat. fat g	Protein g	Calcium mg	Iron mg	Potassium mg	Sodium mg	Zinc mg	Vitamin A RE	Vitamin B_{12} mcg	Vitamin B_6 mg	Vitamin C mg	Folic acid mcg	Niacin mg	Riboflavin mg	Thiamin mg
Rolls, hard (including kaiser) — *1 roll*	57	167	30	0	1.3	2.5	0.6	1	0.3	5.6	54	2	62	310	0.5	0	0	0.03	0	8.6	2.4	0.19	0.27
Rye bread																							
reduced-calorie — *1 slice*	23	47	9.3	0	2.8	0.7	0.2	0.2	0.1	2.1	17	1	23	93	0.2	0	0	0.01	0	5.3	0.6	0.06	0.08
regular — *1 slice*	32	83	15.5	0	1.9	1.1	0.4	0.3	0.2	2.7	23	1	53	211	0.4	0	0	0.02	0	16.3	1.2	0.11	0.14
Stuffing																							
cornbread, from dry mix — *½ cup*	100	179	21.9	0	2.9	8.8	3.9	2.7	1.8	2.9	26	1	62	455	0.2	85	0	0.04	1	8	1.2	0.09	0.12
regular, from dry mix — *½ cup*	100	178	21.7	0	2.9	8.6	3.8	2.6	1.7	3.2	32	1	74	543	0.3	81	0	0.04	0	17	1.5	0.11	0.14
Taco shells, baked — *1 medium*	13.3	62	8.3	0	1	3	1.3	1.1	0.4	1	21	0	24	49	0.2	5	0	0.05	0	0.8	0.2	0.01	0.03
Tortillas																							
corn — *1 medium*	26	58	12.1	0	1.4	0.7	0.2	0.3	0.1	1.5	46	0	40	42	0.2	6	0	0.06	0	3.9	0.4	0.02	0.03
flour — *1 medium*	32	104	17.8	0	1.1	2.3	0.9	0.9	0.4	2.8	40	1	42	153	0.2	0	0	0.02	0	3.8	1.1	0.09	0.17
Wheat bran bread — *1 slice*	36	89	17.2	0	1.4	1.2	0.6	0.2	0.3	3.2	27	1	82	175	0.5	0	0	0.06	0	9	1.6	0.1	0.14
Wheat bread																							
reduced-calorie — *1 slice*	23	46	10	0	2.8	0.5	0.1	0.2	0.1	2.1	18	1	29	118	0.2	0	0	0.03	0	6.4	0.9	0.07	0.1
regular — *1 slice*	25	65	11.8	0	1.1	1	0.4	0.2	0.2	2.3	26	1	50	133	0.3	0	0	0.02	0	10.3	1	0.07	0.1
Wheat germ bread — *1 slice*	28	73	13.5	0	0.6	0.8	0.4	0.2	0.2	2.7	25	1	71	155	0.4	0	0	0.03	0	15.4	1.3	0.11	0.1
White bread																							
no salt — *1 slice*	25	67	12.4	0	0.6	0.9	0.4	0.2	0.2	2.1	27	1	30	7	0.2	0	0	0.02	0	8.5	1	0.09	0.12
reduced-calorie — *1 slice*	23	48	10.2	0	2.2	0.6	0.2	0.1	0.1	2	22	1	17	104	0.3	0	0.1	0.01	0	7.8	0.8	0.07	0.09
regular — *1 slice*	25	67	12.4	0	0.6	0.9	0.4	0.2	0.2	2.1	27	1	30	135	0.2	0	0	0.02	0	8.5	1	0.09	0.12
Whole-wheat bread — *1 slice*	28	69	12.9	0	1.9	1.2	0.5	0.3	0.3	2.7	20	1	71	148	0.5	0	0	0.05	0	14	1.1	0.06	0.1
Wonton wrappers — *1 wrapper*	8	23	4.6	1	0.1	0.1	0	0	0	0.8	4	0	7	46	0.1	0	0	0	0	1.4	0.4	0.03	0.04

Cheese

	Weight g	Calories	Carbohydrates g	Cholesterol mg	Dietary fiber g	Total fat g	Mono. fat g	Poly. fat g	Sat. fat g	Protein g	Calcium mg	Iron mg	Potassium mg	Sodium mg	Zinc mg	Vitamin A RE	Vitamin B_{12} mcg	Vitamin B_6 mg	Vitamin C mg	Folic acid mcg	Niacin mg	Riboflavin mg	Thiamin mg
American, processed — *1 oz*	28	106	0.5	27	0	8.9	2.5	0.3	5.6	6.3	174	0	46	406	0.8	82	0.2	0.02	0	2.2	0	0.1	0.01
Blue — *1 oz*	28	100	0.7	21	0	8.1	2.2	0.2	5.3	6.1	150	0	73	396	0.8	65	0.3	0.05	0	10.3	0.3	0.11	0.01
Brick — *1 oz*	28	105	0.8	27	0	8.4	2.4	0.2	5.3	6.6	191	0	38	159	0.7	86	0.4	0.02	0	5.8	0	0.1	0
Brie — *1 oz*	28	95	0.1	28	0	7.8	2.3	0.2	4.9	5.9	52	0	43	178	0.7	52	0.5	0.07	0	18.4	0.1	0.15	0.02
Camembert — *1 oz*	28	85	0.1	20	0	6.9	2	0.2	4.3	5.6	110	0	53	239	0.7	71	0.4	0.06	0	17.6	0.2	0.14	0.01
Caraway — *1 oz*	28	107	0.9	26	0	8.3	2.3	0.2	5.3	7.1	191	0	26	196	0.8	82	0.1	0.02	0	5.2	0.1	0.13	0.01
Cheddar																							
low-fat — *1 oz*	28	49	0.5	6	0	2	0.6	0.1	1.2	6.9	118	0	19	174	0.5	18	0.1	0.01	0	3.1	0	0.06	0
low-sodium — *1 oz*	28	113	0.5	28	0	9.2	2.6	0.3	5.9	6.9	199	0	32	6	0.9	82	0.2	0.02	0	5.1	0	0.11	0.01
regular — *1 oz*	28	114	0.4	30	0	9.4	2.7	0.3	6	7.1	204	0	28	176	0.9	86	0.2	0.02	0	5.2	0	0.11	0.01
Cheese food																							
american — *1 oz*	28	93	2.1	18	0	7	2	0.2	4.4	5.6	163	0	79	452	0.8	62	0.3	0.04	0	2.1	0	0.13	0.01
american, cold-pack — *1 oz*	28	94	2.4	18	0	6.9	2	0.2	4.4	5.6	141	0	103	274	0.9	57	0.4	0.04	0	1.5	0	0.13	0.01
swiss — *1 oz*	28	92	1.3	23	0	6.8	1.9	0.2	4.4	6.2	205	0	81	440	1	69	0.7	0.01	0	1.6	0	0.11	0
Cheese spread, american — *1 oz*	28	82	2.5	16	0	6	1.8	0.2	3.8	4.7	159	0	69	381	0.7	54	0.1	0.03	0	2	0	0.12	0.01
Cheshire — *1 oz*	28	110	1.4	29	0	8.7	2.5	0.2	5.5	6.6	182	0	27	198	0.8	69	0.2	0.02	0	5.2	0	0.08	0.01
Colby																							
low-fat — *1 oz*	28	49	0.5	6	0	2	0.6	0.1	1.2	6.9	118	0	19	174	0.5	18	0.1	0.01	0	3.1	0	0.06	0
low-sodium — *1 oz*	28	113	0.5	28	0	9.2	2.6	0.3	5.9	6.9	199	0	32	6	0.9	82	0.2	0.02	0	5.1	0	0.11	0.01
regular — *1 oz*	28	112	0.7	27	0	9.1	2.6	0.3	5.7	6.7	194	0	36	171	0.9	78	0.2	0.02	0	5.2	0	0.11	0
Cottage cheese																							
1% fat — *½ cup*	113	82	3.1	5	0	1.2	0.3	0	0.7	14	69	0	97	459	0.4	12	0.7	0.08	0	14	0.1	0.19	0.02
2% fat — *½ cup*	113	101	4.1	9	0	2.2	0.6	0.1	1.4	15.5	77	0	109	459	0.5	23	0.8	0.09	0	14.8	0.2	0.21	0.03

	Weight g	Calories	Carbohydrates g	Cholesterol mg	Dietary fiber g	Total fat g	Mono. fat g	Poly. fat g	Sat. fat g	Protein g	Calcium mg	Iron mg	Potassium mg	Sodium mg	Zinc mg	Vitamin A RE	Vitamin B_{12} mcg	Vitamin B_6 mg	Vitamin C mg	Folic acid mcg	Niacin mg	Riboflavin mg	Thiamin mg
creamed, large curd — *½ cup*	105	109	2.8	16	0	4.7	1.3	0.1	3	13.1	63	0	89	425	0.4	50	0.7	0.07	0	12.8	0.1	0.17	0.02
creamed, small curd — *½ cup*	113	116	3	17	0	5.1	1.4	0.2	3.2	14.1	68	0	95	455	0.4	54	0.7	0.08	0	13.7	0.1	0.18	0.02
creamed w/ fruit — *½ cup*	113	140	15	13	0	3.8	1.1	0.1	2.4	11.2	54	0	76	457	0.3	41	0.6	0.06	0	11	0.1	0.15	0.02
dry — *½ cup*	73	61	1.3	5	0	0.3	0.1	0	0.2	12.5	23	0	23	9	0.3	6	0.6	0.06	0	10.7	0.1	0.1	0.02
Cream cheese																							
fat-free — *1 oz*	28	27	1.6	2	0	0.4	0.1	0	0.3	4.1	52	0	46	155	0.2	79	0.2	0.01	0	10.5	0	0.05	0.01
regular — *1 oz*	28	99	0.8	31	0	9.9	2.8	0.4	6.2	2.1	23	0	34	84	0.2	124	0.1	0.01	0	3.7	0	0.06	0
Edam — *1 oz*	28	101	0.4	25	0	7.9	2.3	0.2	5	7.1	207	0	53	274	1.1	72	0.4	0.02	0	4.6	0	0.11	0.01
Feta — *1 oz*	28	75	1.2	25	0	6	1.3	0.2	4.2	4	140	0	18	316	0.8	36	0.5	0.12	0	9.1	0.3	0.24	0.04
Fontina — *1 oz*	28	110	0.4	33	0	8.8	2.5	0.5	5.4	7.3	156	0	18	227	1	82	0.5	0.02	0	1.7	0	0.06	0.01
Goat																							
hard — *1 oz*	28	128	0.6	30	0	10.1	2.3	0.2	7	8.7	254	1	14	98	0.5	135	0	0.02	0	1.1	0.7	0.34	0.04
semisoft — *1 oz*	28	103	0.7	22	0	8.5	1.9	0.2	5.9	6.1	84	0	45	146	0.2	113	0.1	0.02	0	0.6	0.3	0.19	0.02
soft — *1 oz*	28	76	0.3	13	0	6	1.4	0.1	4.1	5.3	40	1	7	104	0.3	80	0.1	0.07	0	3.4	0.1	0.11	0.02
Gouda — *1 oz*	28	101	0.6	32	0	7.8	2.2	0.2	5	7.1	198	0	34	232	1.1	49	0.4	0.02	0	5.9	0	0.09	0.01
Gruyere — *1 oz*	28	117	0.1	31	0	9.2	2.8	0.5	5.4	8.5	287	0	23	95	1.1	85	0.5	0.02	0	3	0	0.08	0.02
Limburger — *1 oz*	28	93	0.1	26	0	7.7	2.4	0.1	4.7	5.7	141	0	36	227	0.6	90	0.3	0.02	0	16.3	0	0.14	0.02
Monterey — *1 oz*	28	106	0.2	25	0	8.6	2.5	0.3	5.4	6.9	212	0	23	152	0.9	72	0.2	0.02	0	5.2	0	0.11	0
Mozzarella																							
part skim — *1 oz*	28	72	0.8	16	0	4.5	1.3	0.1	2.9	6.9	183	0	24	132	0.8	50	0.2	0.02	0	2.5	0	0.09	0.01
part skim, low moisture — *1 oz*	28	79	0.9	15	0	4.9	1.4	0.1	3.1	7.8	207	0	27	150	0.9	54	0.3	0.02	0	2.8	0	0.1	0.01
part skim, low moisture, shredded — *¼ cup*	28	79	0.9	15	0	4.8	1.4	0.1	3.1	7.8	207	0	27	149	0.9	54	0.3	0.02	0	2.8	0	0.1	0.01
whole milk — *1 oz*	28	80	0.6	22	0	6.1	1.9	0.2	3.7	5.5	147	0	19	106	0.6	68	0.2	0.02	0	2	0	0.07	0
whole milk, low moisture — *1 oz*	28	90	0.7	25	0	7	2	0.2	4.4	6.1	163	0	21	118	0.7	78	0.2	0.02	0	2.2	0	0.08	0

	Weight g	Calories	Carbohydrates g	Cholesterol mg	Dietary fiber g	Total fat g	Mono. fat g	Poly. fat g	Sat. fat g	Protein g	Calcium mg	Iron mg	Potassium mg	Sodium mg	Zinc mg	Vitamin A RE	Vitamin B_{12} mcg	Vitamin B_6 mg	Vitamin C mg	Folic acid mcg	Niacin mg	Riboflavin mg	Thiamin mg
whole milk, shredded — *¼ cup*	28	79	0.6	22	0	6	1.8	0.2	3.7	5.4	145	0	19	104	0.6	67	0.2	0.02	0	2	0	0.07	0
Muenster — *1 oz*	28	104	0.3	27	0	8.5	2.5	0.2	5.4	6.6	203	0	38	178	0.8	90	0.4	0.02	0	3.4	0	0.09	0
Neufchatel — *1 oz*	28	74	0.8	22	0	6.6	1.9	0.2	4.2	2.8	21	0	32	113	0.1	75	0.1	0.01	0	3.2	0	0.06	0
Parmesan																							
grated — *1 Tbsp*	5	23	0.2	4	0	1.5	0.4	0	1	2.1	69	0	5	93	0.2	9	0.1	0.01	0	0.4	0	0.02	0
hard — *1 oz*	28	111	0.9	19	0	7.3	2.1	0.2	4.7	10.1	336	0	26	454	0.8	42	0.3	0.03	0	2	0.1	0.09	0.01
shredded — *1 Tbsp*	5	21	0.2	4	0	1.4	0.4	0	0.9	1.9	63	0	5	85	0.2	9	0.1	0.01	0	0.4	0	0.02	0
Pimento, processed — *1 oz*	28	106	0.5	27	0	8.8	2.5	0.3	5.6	6.3	174	0	46	405	0.8	91	0.2	0.02	1	2.2	0	0.1	0.01
Port de salut — *1 oz*	28	100	0.2	35	0	8	2.6	0.2	4.7	6.7	184	0	38	151	0.7	105	0.4	0.02	0	5.2	0	0.07	0
Provolone — *1 oz*	28	100	0.6	20	0	7.5	2.1	0.2	4.8	7.3	214	0	39	248	0.9	75	0.4	0.02	0	3	0	0.09	0.01
Queso anejo — *1 oz*	28	106	1.3	30	0	8.5	2.4	0.3	5.4	6.1	193	0	25	321	0.8	18	0.4	0.01	0	0.3	0	0.06	0.01
Queso asadero — *1 oz*	28	101	0.8	30	0	8	2.3	0.2	5.1	6.4	187	0	24	186	0.9	18	0.3	0.02	0	2.3	0.1	0.06	0.01
Queso chihuahua — *1 oz*	28	106	1.6	30	0	8.4	2.4	0.3	5.3	6.1	185	0	15	175	1	18	0.3	0.02	0	0.6	0	0.06	0.01
Ricotta																							
part skim — *½ cup*	124	171	6.4	38	0	9.8	2.9	0.3	6.1	14.1	337	1	155	155	1.7	140	0.4	0.02	0	16.2	0.1	0.23	0.03
whole milk — *½ cup*	124	216	3.8	63	0	16.1	4.5	0.5	10.3	14	257	0	130	104	1.4	166	0.4	0.05	0	15.1	0.1	0.24	0.02
Romano — *1 oz*	28	110	1	29	0	7.6	2.2	0.2	4.9	9	302	0	24	340	0.7	40	0.3	0.02	0	1.9	0	0.1	0.01
Roquefort — *1 oz*	28	105	0.6	26	0	8.7	2.4	0.4	5.5	6.1	188	0	26	513	0.6	85	0.2	0.04	0	13.9	0.2	0.17	0.01
Swiss																							
processed — *1 oz*	28	95	0.6	24	0	7.1	2	0.2	4.5	7	219	0	61	388	1	65	0.3	0.01	0	1.7	0	0.08	0
regular — *1 oz*	28	107	1	26	0	7.8	2.1	0.3	5	8.1	272	0	31	74	1.1	72	0.5	0.02	0	1.8	0	0.1	0.01
Tilsit — *1 oz*	28	96	0.5	29	0	7.4	2	0.2	4.8	6.9	198	0	18	213	1	82	0.6	0.02	0	5.7	0.1	0.1	0.02

Chicken

	Weight g	Calories	Carbohydrates g	Cholesterol mg	Dietary fiber g	Total fat g	Mono. fat g	Poly. fat g	Sat. fat g	Protein g	Calcium mg	Iron mg	Potassium mg	Sodium mg	Zinc mg	Vitamin A RE	Vitamin B_{12} mcg	Vitamin B_6 mg	Vitamin C mg	Folic acid mcg	Niacin mg	Riboflavin mg	Thiamin mg
Back meat																							
fried — *3 ½ oz*	100	288	5.7	93	0	15.3	5.7	3.6	4.1	30	26	2	251	99	2.8	29	0.3	0.35	0	9	7.7	0.25	0.11
roasted — *3 ½ oz*	100	239	0	90	0	13.2	4.8	3.1	3.6	28.2	24	1	237	96	2.7	28	0.3	0.34	0	7	7.1	0.22	0.07
stewed — *3 ½ oz*	100	209	0	85	0	11.2	4	2.6	3	25.3	21	1	158	67	2.4	27	0.2	0.2	0	7	4.6	0.17	0.05
Back meat w/ skin																							
fried, batter-dipped — *3 ½ oz*	100	331	10.3	88	0	21.9	8.9	5.2	5.8	22	26	1	180	317	2	36	0.3	0.23	0	9	5.8	0.21	0.12
fried, flour-coated — *3 ½ oz*	100	331	6.5	89	0	20.7	8.2	4.8	5.6	27.8	24	2	226	90	2.5	37	0.3	0.3	0	8	7.3	0.24	0.11
roasted — *3 ½ oz*	100	300	0	88	0	21	8.3	4.6	5.8	26	21	1	210	87	2.3	99	0.3	0.27	0	6	6.7	0.2	0.06
stewed — *3 ½ oz*	100	258	0	78	0	18.1	7.1	4	5	22.2	18	1	145	64	1.9	88	0.2	0.15	0	5	4.3	0.15	0.04
Breast meat																							
fried — *3 ½ oz*	100	187	0.5	91	0	4.7	1.7	1.1	1.3	33.4	16	1	276	79	1.1	7	0.4	0.64	0	4	14.8	0.13	0.08
roasted — *3 ½ oz*	100	165	0	85	0	3.6	1.2	0.8	1	31	15	1	256	74	1	6	0.3	0.6	0	4	13.7	0.11	0.07
stewed — *3 ½ oz*	100	151	0	77	0	3	1	0.7	0.9	29	13	1	187	63	1	6	0.2	0.33	0	3	8.5	0.12	0.04
Breast meat w/ skin																							
fried, batter-dipped — *3 ½ oz*	100	260	9	85	0.3	13.2	5.5	3.1	3.5	24.8	20	1	201	275	1	20	0.3	0.43	0	6	10.5	0.15	0.12
fried, flour-coated — *3 ½ oz*	100	222	1.6	89	0.1	8.9	3.5	2	2.5	31.8	16	1	259	76	1.1	15	0.3	0.58	0	4	13.7	0.13	0.08
roasted — *3 ½ oz*	100	197	0	84	0	7.8	3	1.7	2.2	29.8	14	1	245	71	1	27	0.3	0.56	0	4	12.7	0.12	0.07
stewed — *3 ½ oz*	100	184	0	75	0	7.4	2.9	1.6	2.1	27.4	13	1	178	62	1	24	0.2	0.29	0	3	7.8	0.12	0.04
Capon, meat & skin, roasted — *3 ½ oz*	100	229	0	86	0	11.7	4.8	2.5	3.3	29	14	1	255	49	1.7	20	0.3	0.43	0	6	8.9	0.17	0.07
Chicken giblets																							
fried — *3 ½ oz*	100	277	4.4	446	0	13.5	4.4	3.4	3.8	32.5	18	10	330	113	6.3	3579	13.3	0.61	9	379	11	1.52	0.1
simmered — *3 ½ oz*	100	157	1	393	0	4.8	1.2	1.1	1.5	25.9	12	6	158	58	4.6	2229	10.1	0.34	8	376	4.1	0.95	0.09
Chicken liver, simmered — *3 ½ oz*	100	157	0.9	631	0	5.5	1.3	0.9	1.8	24.4	14	8	140	51	4.3	4913	19.4	0.58	16	770	4.5	1.75	0.15

	Weight *g*	Calories	Carbohydrates *g*	Cholesterol *mg*	Dietary fiber *g*	Total fat *g*	Mono. fat *g*	Poly. fat *g*	Sat. fat *g*	Protein *g*	Calcium *mg*	Iron *mg*	Potassium *mg*	Sodium *mg*	Zinc *mg*	Vitamin A *RE*	Vitamin B_{12} *mcg*	Vitamin B_6 *mg*	Vitamin C *mg*	Folic acid *mcg*	Niacin *mg*	Riboflavin *mg*	Thiamin *mg*
Chicken skin — *1 oz*	28	129	0	24	0	11.5	4.8	2.4	3.2	5.8	4	0	39	18	0.3	22	0.1	0.03	0	0.6	1.6	0.04	0.01
Chicken, canned, meat only w/ broth — *3 ½ oz*	100	165	0	62	0	8	3.2	1.8	2.2	21.8	14	2	138	503	1.4	34	0.3	0.35	2	4	6.3	0.13	0.02
Cornish game hen																							
meat only, roasted — *3 ½ oz*	100	134	0	106	0	3.9	1.2	0.9	1	23.3	13	1	250	63	1.5	20	0.3	0.36	1	2	6.3	0.23	0.08
meat w/ skin, roasted — *3 ½ oz*	100	260	0	131	0	18.2	8	3.6	5.1	22.3	13	1	245	64	1.5	32	0.3	0.31	1	2	5.9	0.2	0.07
Dark meat																							
fried — *3 ½ oz*	100	239	2.6	96	0	11.6	4.3	2.8	3.1	29	18	1	253	97	2.9	24	0.3	0.37	0	9	7.1	0.25	0.09
from roaster chicken, roasted — *3 ½ oz*	100	178	0	75	0	8.8	3.3	2	2.4	23.3	11	1	224	95	2.1	16	0.3	0.31	0	7	5.7	0.19	0.06
roasted — *3 ½ oz*	100	205	0	93	0	9.7	3.6	2.3	2.7	27.4	15	1	240	93	2.8	22	0.3	0.36	0	8	6.5	0.23	0.07
stewed — *3 ½ oz*	100	192	0	88	0	9	3.3	2.1	2.5	26	14	1	181	74	2.7	21	0.2	0.21	0	7	4.7	0.2	0.06
Dark meat w/ skin																							
fried, batter-dipped — *3 ½ oz*	100	298	9.4	89	0	18.6	7.6	4.4	5	21.9	21	1	185	295	2.1	31	0.3	0.25	0	9	5.6	0.22	0.12
fried, flour-coated — *3 ½ oz*	100	285	4.1	92	0	16.9	6.7	3.9	4.6	27.2	17	2	230	89	2.6	31	0.3	0.32	0	8	6.8	0.24	0.1
roasted — *3 ½ oz*	100	253	0	91	0	15.8	6.2	3.5	4.4	26	15	1	220	87	2.5	58	0.3	0.31	0	7	6.4	0.21	0.07
stewed — *3 ½ oz*	100	233	0	82	0	14.7	5.8	3.2	4.1	23.5	14	1	166	70	2.3	54	0.2	0.17	0	6	4.5	0.18	0.05
Drumstick																							
fried — *3 ½ oz*	100	195	0	94	0	8.1	2.9	2	2.1	28.6	12	1	249	96	3.2	18	0.4	0.39	0	9	6.1	0.24	0.08
roasted — *3 ½ oz*	100	172	0	93	0	5.7	1.9	1.4	1.5	28.3	12	1	246	95	3.2	18	0.3	0.39	0	9	6.1	0.23	0.08
stewed — *3 ½ oz*	100	169	0	88	0	5.7	1.9	1.4	1.5	27.5	11	1	199	80	3	17	0.2	0.23	0	8	4.3	0.21	0.05
Drumstick w/ skin																							
fried, batter-dipped — *3 ½ oz*	100	268	8.3	86	0.3	15.8	6.4	3.8	4.1	22	17	1	186	269	2.3	26	0.3	0.27	0	9	5.1	0.22	0.11
fried, flour-coated — *3 ½ oz*	100	245	1.6	90	0.1	13.7	5.4	3.2	3.7	27	12	1	229	89	2.9	25	0.3	0.35	0	8	6	0.23	0.08
roasted — *3 ½ oz*	100	216	0	91	0	11.2	4.3	2.5	3.1	27	12	1	229	90	2.9	30	0.3	0.34	0	8	6	0.22	0.07
stewed — *3 ½ oz*	100	204	0	83	0	10.6	4.1	2.4	2.9	25.3	11	1	184	76	2.7	27	0.2	0.19	0	7	4.2	0.19	0.05

	Weight g	Calories	Carbohydrates g	Cholesterol mg	Dietary fiber g	Total fat g	Mono. fat g	Poly. fat g	Sat. fat g	Protein g	Calcium mg	Iron mg	Potassium mg	Sodium mg	Zinc mg	Vitamin A RE	Vitamin B_{12} mcg	Vitamin B_6 mg	Vitamin C mg	Folic acid mcg	Niacin mg	Riboflavin mg	Thiamin mg
Leg meat																							
fried — *3 ½ oz*	100	208	0.7	99	0	9.3	3.4	2.2	2.5	28.4	13	1	254	96	3	20	0.3	0.39	0	9	6.7	0.25	0.08
roasted — *3 ½ oz*	100	191	0	94	0	8.4	3.1	2	2.3	27	12	1	242	91	2.9	19	0.3	0.37	0	8	6.3	0.23	0.08
stewed — *3 ½ oz*	100	185	0	89	0	8.1	2.9	1.9	2.2	26.3	11	1	190	78	2.8	18	0.2	0.21	0	8	4.8	0.22	0.06
Leg meat w/ skin																							
fried, batter-dipped — *3 ½ oz*	100	273	8.7	90	0.3	16.2	6.6	3.9	4.3	21.8	18	1	189	279	2.2	27	0.3	0.27	0	9	5.4	0.22	0.12
fried, flour-coated — *3 ½ oz*	100	254	2.5	94	0.1	14.4	5.7	3.3	3.9	26.8	13	1	233	88	2.7	28	0.3	0.34	0	8	6.5	0.24	0.09
stewed — *3 ½ oz*	100	220	0	84	0	12.9	5	2.9	3.6	24.2	11	1	176	73	2.4	36	0.2	0.18	0	6	4.6	0.19	0.05
Light & dark meat																							
fried — *3 ½ oz*	100	219	1.7	94	0.1	9.1	3.4	2.2	2.5	30.6	17	1	257	91	2.2	18	0.3	0.48	0	7	9.7	0.2	0.09
from roaster chicken, roasted — *3 ½ oz*	100	167	0	75	0	6.6	2.5	1.5	1.8	25	12	1	229	75	1.5	12	0.3	0.41	0	5	7.9	0.15	0.06
Light & dark meat w/ skin																							
fried, batter-dipped — *3 ½ oz*	100	289	9.4	87	0.3	17.4	7.1	4.1	4.6	22.5	21	1	185	292	1.7	28	0.3	0.31	0	8	7	0.19	0.12
fried, flour-coated — *3 ½ oz*	100	269	3.2	90	0.1	14.9	5.9	3.4	4.1	28.6	17	1	234	84	2	27	0.3	0.41	0	6	9	0.19	0.09
from roaster chicken, roasted — *3 ½ oz*	100	223	0	76	0	13.4	5.4	2.9	3.7	24	12	1	211	73	1.5	25	0.3	0.35	0	5	7.4	0.14	0.06
roasted — *3 ½ oz*	100	239	0	88	0	13.6	5.3	3	3.8	27.3	15	1	223	82	1.9	47	0.3	0.4	0	5	8.5	0.17	0.06
stewed — *3 ½ oz*	100	219	0	78	0	12.6	4.9	2.7	3.5	24.7	13	1	166	67	1.8	42	0.2	0.22	0	5	5.6	0.15	0.05
Light meat																							
fried — *3 ½ oz*	100	192	0.4	90	0	5.5	2	1.3	1.5	32.8	16	1	263	81	1.3	9	0.4	0.63	0	4	13.4	0.13	0.07
from roaster chicken, roasted — *3 ½ oz*	100	153	0	75	0	4.1	1.5	0.9	1.1	27.1	13	1	236	51	0.8	8	0.3	0.54	0	3	10.5	0.09	0.06
roasted — *3 ½ oz*	100	173	0	85	0	4.5	1.5	1	1.3	30.9	15	1	247	77	1.2	9	0.3	0.6	0	4	12.4	0.12	0.07
stewed — *3 ½ oz*	100	159	0	77	0	4	1.4	0.9	1.1	28.9	13	1	180	65	1.2	8	0.2	0.33	0	3	7.8	0.12	0.04
Light meat w/ skin																							
fried, batter-dipped — *3 ½ oz*	100	277	9.5	84	0	15.4	6.4	3.6	4.1	23.6	20	1	185	287	1.1	24	0.3	0.39	0	6	9.2	0.15	0.11

	Weight g	Calories	Carbohydrates g	Cholesterol mg	Dietary fiber g	Total fat g	Mono. fat g	Poly. fat g	Sat. fat g	Protein g	Calcium mg	Iron mg	Potassium mg	Sodium mg	Zinc mg	Vitamin A RE	Vitamin B_{12} mcg	Vitamin B_6 mg	Vitamin C mg	Folic acid mcg	Niacin mg	Riboflavin mg	Thiamin mg
fried, flour-coated — *3 ½ oz*	100	246	1.8	87	0.1	12.1	4.8	2.7	3.3	30.5	16	1	239	77	1.3	20	0.3	0.54	0	4	12	0.13	0.08
roasted — *3 ½ oz*	100	222	0	84	0	10.9	4.3	2.3	3.1	29	15	1	227	75	1.2	32	0.3	0.52	0	3	11.1	0.12	0.06
stewed — *3 ½ oz*	100	201	0	74	0	10	3.9	2.1	2.8	26.1	13	1	167	63	1.1	28	0.2	0.27	0	3	6.9	0.11	0.04
Neck meat																							
fried — *3 ½ oz*	100	229	1.8	105	0	11.9	4.6	3	3	26.9	41	3	213	99	4.2	49	0.3	0.35	0	8	5	0.32	0.07
simmered — *3 ½ oz*	100	179	0	79	0	8.2	2.5	2	2.1	24.6	44	3	140	64	3.8	36	0.2	0.16	0	6	4	0.28	0.05
Neck meat w/ skin																							
fried, batter-dipped — *3 ½ oz*	100	330	8.7	91	0	23.5	9.8	5.6	6.2	19.8	31	2	151	276	2.5	51	0.2	0.21	0	7	4.5	0.24	0.1
fried, flour-coated — *3 ½ oz*	100	332	4.2	94	0	23.6	9.7	5.5	6.3	24	31	2	180	82	3.1	57	0.3	0.25	0	6	5.3	0.26	0.08
simmered — *3 ½ oz*	100	247	0	70	0	18.1	7.2	3.9	5	19.6	27	2	108	52	2.7	48	0.1	0.1	0	3	3.3	0.25	0.04
Thigh meat																							
fried — *3 ½ oz*	100	218	1.2	102	0	10.3	3.8	2.4	2.8	28.2	13	1	259	95	2.8	21	0.3	0.38	0	9	7.1	0.26	0.09
roasted — *3 ½ oz*	100	209	0	95	0	10.9	4.2	2.5	3	25.9	12	1	238	88	2.6	20	0.3	0.35	0	8	6.5	0.23	0.07
stewed — *3 ½ oz*	100	195	0	90	0	9.8	3.7	2.2	2.7	25	11	1	183	75	2.6	19	0.2	0.21	0	7	5.2	0.22	0.06
Thigh meat w/ skin																							
fried, batter-dipped — *3 ½ oz*	100	277	9.1	93	0.3	16.5	6.7	3.9	4.4	21.6	18	1	192	288	2	29	0.3	0.26	0	9	5.7	0.23	0.12
fried, flour-coated — *3 ½ oz*	100	262	3.2	97	0.1	15	5.9	3.4	4.1	26.8	14	1	237	88	2.5	29	0.3	0.33	0	8	6.9	0.24	0.09
roasted — *3 ½ oz*	100	247	0	93	0	15.5	6.2	3.4	4.3	25.1	12	1	222	84	2.4	48	0.3	0.31	0	7	6.4	0.21	0.07
stewed — *3 ½ oz*	100	232	0	84	0	14.7	5.8	3.3	4.1	23.3	11	1	170	71	2.3	44	0.2	0.17	0	6	4.9	0.19	0.06
Wing meat																							
fried — *3 ½ oz*	100	211	0	84	0	9.2	3.1	2.1	2.5	30.2	15	1	208	91	2.1	18	0.3	0.59	0	4	7.2	0.13	0.05
roasted — *3 ½ oz*	100	203	0	85	0	8.1	2.6	1.8	2.3	30.5	16	1	210	92	2.1	18	0.3	0.59	0	4	7.3	0.13	0.05
stewed — *3 ½ oz*	100	181	0	74	0	7.2	2.3	1.6	2	27.2	13	1	153	73	2	16	0.2	0.32	0	3	5.2	0.11	0.04

	Weight *g*	Calories	Carbohydrates *g*	Cholesterol *mg*	Dietary fiber *g*	Total fat *g*	Mono. fat *g*	Poly. fat *g*	Sat. fat *g*	Protein *g*	Calcium *mg*	Iron *mg*	Potassium *mg*	Sodium *mg*	Zinc *mg*	Vitamin A *RE*	Vitamin B_{12} *mcg*	Vitamin B_6 *mg*	Vitamin C *mg*	Folic acid *mcg*	Niacin *mg*	Riboflavin *mg*	Thiamin *mg*
Wing meat w/ skin																							
fried, batter-dipped — *3 ½ oz*	100	324	10.9	79	0.3	21.8	9	5.1	5.8	19.9	20	1	138	320	1.4	34	0.3	0.3	0	6	5.3	0.15	0.11
fried, flour-coated — *3 ½ oz*	100	321	2.4	81	0.1	22.2	8.9	5	6.1	26.1	15	1	177	77	1.8	38	0.3	0.41	0	3	6.7	0.14	0.06
roasted — *3 ½ oz*	100	290	0	84	0	19.5	7.6	4.1	5.5	26.9	15	1	184	82	1.8	47	0.3	0.42	0	3	6.6	0.13	0.04
stewed — *3 ½ oz*	100	249	0	70	0	16.8	6.6	3.6	4.7	22.8	12	1	139	67	1.6	40	0.2	0.22	0	3	4.6	0.1	0.04

Condiments

	Weight *g*	Calories	Carbohydrates *g*	Cholesterol *mg*	Dietary fiber *g*	Total fat *g*	Mono. fat *g*	Poly. fat *g*	Sat. fat *g*	Protein *g*	Calcium *mg*	Iron *mg*	Potassium *mg*	Sodium *mg*	Zinc *mg*	Vitamin A *RE*	Vitamin B_{12} *mcg*	Vitamin B_6 *mg*	Vitamin C *mg*	Folic acid *mcg*	Niacin *mg*	Riboflavin *mg*	Thiamin *mg*
Catsup																							
low-sodium — *1 Tbsp*	15	16	4.1	0	0.2	0.1	0	0	0	0.2	3	0	72	3	0	15	0	0.03	2	2.3	0.2	0.01	0.01
regular — *1 Tbsp*	15	16	4.1	0	0.2	0.1	0	0	0	0.2	3	0	72	178	0	15	0	0.03	2	2.3	0.2	0.01	0.01
Cranberry sauce, canned, sweetened — *¼ cup*	69	105	26.9	0	0.7	0.1	0	0	0	0.1	3	0	18	20	0	1	0	0.01	1	0.7	0.1	0.01	0.01
Cranberry-orange relish, canned — *¼ cup*	69	122	31.8	0	0	0.1	0	0	0	0.2	8	0	26	22	0	5	0	0	12	0	0.1	0.01	0.02
Hoisin sauce — *1 Tbsp*	16	35	7.1	0	0.4	0.5	0.2	0.3	0.1	0.5	5	0	19	258	0.1	0	0	0.01	0	3.7	0.2	0.03	0
Mayonnaise																							
imitation, soybean — *1 Tbsp*	15	35	2.4	4	0	2.9	0.7	1.6	0.5	0	0	0	2	75	0	0	0	0	0	0	0	0	0
imitation, soybean w/o cholesterol — *1 Tbsp*	14	68	2.2	0	0	6.7	1.5	3.9	1.1	0	0	0	1	50	0	0	0	0	0	0	0	0	0
soybean & safflower oil — *1 Tbsp*	14	99	0.4	8	0	11	1.8	7.6	1.2	0.2	2	0	5	78	0	12	0	0.08	0	1.1	0	0	0
soybean oil — *1 Tbsp*	14	99	0.4	8	0	11	3.1	5.7	1.6	0.2	2	0	5	78	0	12	0	0.08	0	1.1	0	0	0
Olives, ripe, canned																							
extra large — *5 olives*	22	25	1.4	0	0.7	2.3	1.7	0.2	0.3	0.2	19	1	2	192	0	9	0	0	0	0	0	0	0
jumbo — *5 olives*	42	34	2.3	0	1	2.9	2.1	0.2	0.4	0.4	39	1	4	373	0.1	15	0	0	1	0	0	0	0
Oyster sauce — *1 tsp*	4	2	0.4	0	0	0	0	0	0	0.1	1	0	2	109	0	0	0	0	0	0.6	0.1	0	0
Pepper or hot sauce — *1 tsp*	5	1	0.1	0	0.1	0	0	0	0	0	0	0	7	124	0	1	0	0.01	4	0.3	0	0	0
Pickle relish																							
hamburger — *1 Tbsp*	15	19	5.2	0	0.5	0.1	0	0	0	0.1	1	0	11	164	0	4	0	0	0	0.2	0.1	0.01	0

	Weight g	Calories	Carbohydrates g	Cholesterol mg	Dietary fiber g	Total fat g	Mono. fat g	Poly. fat g	Sat. fat g	Protein g	Calcium mg	Iron mg	Potassium mg	Sodium mg	Zinc mg	Vitamin A RE	Vitamin B12 mcg	Vitamin B6 mg	Vitamin C mg	Folic acid mcg	Niacin mg	Riboflavin mg	Thiamin mg
hot dog — *1 Tbsp*	15	14	3.5	0	0.2	0.1	0	0	0	0.2	1	0	12	164	0	3	0	0	0	0.2	0.1	0.01	0.01
sweet — *1 Tbsp*	15	20	5.3	0	0.2	0.1	0	0	0	0.1	0	0	4	122	0	2	0	0	0	0.2	0	0	0
Pickles																							
dill — *1 medium*	65	12	2.7	0	0.8	0.1	0	0.1	0	0.4	6	0	75	833	0.1	21	0	0.01	1	0.7	0	0.02	0.01
dill, low-sodium — *1 medium*	65	12	2.7	0	0.8	0.1	0	0.1	0	0.4	6	0	75	12	0.1	21	0	0.01	1	0.7	0	0.02	0.01
sour, low-sodium, slices — *¼ cup*	39	4	0.9	0	0.5	0.1	0	0	0	0.1	0	0	9	7	0	6	0	0	0	0.3	0	0	0
sweet, low-sodium, sliced — *¼ cup*	43	50	13.5	0	0.5	0.1	0	0	0	0.2	2	0	14	8	0	6	0	0.01	1	0.4	0.1	0.01	0
sweet, slices — *1 cup*	43	50	13.5	0	0.5	0.1	0	0	0	0.2	2	0	14	399	0	6	0	0.01	1	0.4	0.1	0.01	0
Pimento, canned — *½ cup*	96	22	4.9	0	1.8	0.3	0	0.2	0	1.1	6	2	152	13	0.2	255	0	0.21	82	5.8	0.6	0.06	0.02
Plum sauce — *1 Tbsp*	19	35	8.1	0	0.1	0.2	0	0.1	0	0.2	2	0	49	102	0	1	0	0.01	0	1.1	0.2	0.02	0
Salsa — *½ cup*	130	29	6.4	0	2.5	0.3	0	0.2	0	1.4	60	1	241	337	0.4	86	0	0.14	26	18.2	0.9	0.04	0.05
Sandwich spread w/ chopped pickle — *1 Tbsp*	15	60	3.4	12	0.1	5.2	1.1	3.1	0.8	0.1	2	0	5	153	0.1	13	0	0	0	0.9	0	0	0
Soy sauce — *1 Tbsp*	18	10	1.5	0	0	0	0	0	0	0.9	3	0	32	1029	0.1	0	0	0.03	0	2.8	0.6	0.02	0.01
Teriyaki sauce — *1 Tbsp*	18	15	2.9	0	0	0	0	0	0	1.1	5	0	41	690	0	0	0	0.02	0	3.6	0.2	0.01	0.01

Crackers

	Weight g	Calories	Carbohydrates g	Cholesterol mg	Dietary fiber g	Total fat g	Mono. fat g	Poly. fat g	Sat. fat g	Protein g	Calcium mg	Iron mg	Potassium mg	Sodium mg	Zinc mg	Vitamin A RE	Vitamin B12 mcg	Vitamin B6 mg	Vitamin C mg	Folic acid mcg	Niacin mg	Riboflavin mg	Thiamin mg
Cheese crackers																							
low-sodium — *10 crackers*	10	50	5.8	1	0.2	2.5	0.9	0.5	0.9	1	15	0	11	46	0.1	3	0	0.06	0	2.5	0.5	0.04	0.06
Crispbread, rye — *1 crispbread*	10	37	8.2	0	1.7	0.1	0	0.1	0	0.8	3	0	32	26	0.2	0	0	0.02	0	2.2	0.1	0.01	0.02
Matzo																							
egg — *1 matzo*	28	111	22.3	25	0.8	0.6	0.2	0.1	0.2	3.5	11	1	43	6	0.2	4	0.1	0.02	0	8.2	1.4	0.18	0.18
plain — *1 matzo*	28	112	23.7	0	0.9	0.4	0	0.2	0.1	2.8	4	1	32	1	0.2	0	0	0.03	0	4	1.1	0.08	0.11
whole-wheat — *1 matzo*	28	100	22.4	0	3.3	0.4	0.1	0.2	0.1	3.7	7	1	90	1	0.7	0	0	0.05	0	9.9	1.5	0.08	0.1
Melba toast																							
plain — *2 toasts*	10	39	7.7	0	0.6	0.3	0.1	0.1	0	1.2	9	0	20	83	0.2	0	0	0.01	0	2.6	0.4	0.03	0.04

	Weight g	Calories	Carbohydrates g	Cholesterol mg	Dietary fiber g	Total fat g	Mono. fat g	Poly. fat g	Sat. fat g	Protein g	Calcium mg	Iron mg	Potassium mg	Sodium mg	Zinc mg	Vitamin A RE	Vitamin B_{12} mcg	Vitamin B_6 mg	Vitamin C mg	Folic acid mcg	Niacin mg	Riboflavin mg	Thiamin mg
plain, no salt — *2 toasts*	10	39	7.7	0	0.6	0.3	0.1	0.1	0	1.2	9	0	20	2	0.2	0	0	0.01	0	2.6	0.4	0.03	0.04
rye/pumpernickel — *2 toasts*	10	39	7.7	0	0.8	0.3	0.1	0.1	0	1.2	8	0	19	90	0.1	0	0	0.01	0	2.2	0.5	0.03	0.05
wheat — *2 toasts*	10	37	7.6	0	0.7	0.2	0.1	0.1	0	1.3	4	0	15	84	0.2	0	0	0.01	0	2.4	0.5	0.03	0.04
Milk crackers — *3 crackers*	33	150	23	5	0.6	5.2	2.9	0.7	1	2.5	57	1	38	195	0.2	3	0	0.01	0	5.3	1.5	0.14	0.18
Oyster crackers — *¼ cup*	11	49	8	0	0.3	1.3	0.7	0.2	0.2	1	13	1	14	146	0.1	0	0	0	0	3.5	0.6	0.05	0.06
Rusk toast — *2 toasts*	20	81	14.5	6	0	1.4	0.7	0.2	0.3	2.7	5	1	49	51	0.2	3	0	0.01	0	12.8	0.9	0.08	0.08
Rye wafers — *3 crackers*	33	110	26.5	0	7.6	0.3	0.1	0.1	0	3.2	13	2	163	262	0.9	1	0	0.09	0	14.9	0.5	0.1	0.14
Saltines																							
fat-free, low-sodium — *3 crackers*	15	59	12.3	0	0.4	0.2	0	0.1	0	1.6	3	1	17	95	0.1	0	0	0.01	0	2	0.9	0.09	0.08
low-sodium — *3 crackers*	9	39	6.4	0	0.3	1.1	0.6	0.2	0.2	0.8	11	0	65	57	0.1	0	0	0	0	2.8	0.5	0.04	0.05
regular — *3 crackers*	9	39	6.4	0	0.3	1.1	0.6	0.2	0.2	0.8	11	0	12	117	0.1	0	0	0	0	2.8	0.5	0.04	0.05
unsalted tops — *3 crackers*	9	39	6.4	0	0.2	1.1	0.6	0.2	0.2	0.8	11	0	12	69	0.1	0	0	0	0	2.8	0.5	0.04	0.05
Wheat crackers																							
low-sodium — *5 crackers*	15	71	9.7	0	0.7	3.1	1.8	0.5	0.6	1.3	7	1	30	42	0.2	0	0	0.02	0	2.7	0.7	0.05	0.08
regular — *5 crackers*	15	71	9.7	0	0.7	3.1	1.8	0.5	0.6	1.3	7	1	27	119	0.2	0	0	0.02	0	2.7	0.7	0.05	0.08
Whole-wheat crackers																							
low-sodium — *5 crackers*	20	89	13.7	0	2.1	3.4	1.9	0.5	0.6	1.8	10	1	59	49	0.4	0	0	0.04	0	5.6	0.9	0.02	0.04
regular — *5 crackers*	20	89	13.7	0	2.1	3.4	1.9	0.5	0.6	1.8	10	1	59	132	0.4	0	0	0.04	0	5.6	0.9	0.02	0.04

Cream

	Weight g	Calories	Carbohydrates g	Cholesterol mg	Dietary fiber g	Total fat g	Mono. fat g	Poly. fat g	Sat. fat g	Protein g	Calcium mg	Iron mg	Potassium mg	Sodium mg	Zinc mg	Vitamin A RE	Vitamin B_{12} mcg	Vitamin B_6 mg	Vitamin C mg	Folic acid mcg	Niacin mg	Riboflavin mg	Thiamin mg
Cream substitute, powdered — *1 tsp*	2	11	1.1	0	0	0.7	0	0	0.7	0.1	0	0	16	4	0	0	0	0	0	0	0	0	0
Dessert topping																							
frozen — *¼ cup*	19	60	4.3	0	0	4.7	0.3	0.1	4.1	0.2	1	0	3	5	0	16	0	0	0	0	0	0	0
powdered, made w/ milk — *¼ cup*	20	38	3.3	2	0	2.5	0.2	0	2.1	0.7	18	0	30	13	0.1	10	0.1	0.01	0	0.7	0	0.02	0.01
pressurized — *¼ cup*	18	46	2.8	0	0	3.9	0.3	0	3.3	0.2	1	0	3	11	0	8	0	0	0	0	0	0	0

	Weight g	Calories	Carbohydrates g	Cholesterol mg	Dietary fiber g	Total fat g	Mono. fat g	Poly. fat g	Sat. fat g	Protein g	Calcium mg	Iron mg	Potassium mg	Sodium mg	Zinc mg	Vitamin A RE	Vitamin B_{12} mcg	Vitamin B_6 mg	Vitamin C mg	Folic acid mcg	Niacin mg	Riboflavin mg	Thiamin mg
Half & half — *1 Tbsp*	15	20	0.6	6	0	1.7	0.5	0.1	1.1	0.4	16	0	19	6	0.1	16	0	0.01	0	0.4	0	0.02	0.01
Light cream (coffee/table) — *1 Tbsp*	15	29	0.5	10	0	2.9	0.8	0.1	1.8	0.4	14	0	18	6	0	27	0	0	0	0.4	0	0.02	0
Medium cream, 25% fat — *1 Tbsp*	15	37	0.5	13	0	3.8	1.1	0.1	2.3	0.4	14	0	17	6	0	35	0	0	0	0.4	0	0.02	0
Sour cream																							
cultured — *¼ cup*	58	123	2.5	26	0	12.1	3.5	0.4	7.5	1.8	67	0	83	31	0.2	112	0.2	0.01	0	6.2	0	0.09	0.02
half & half, cultured — *½ cup*	121	163	5.2	47	0	14.5	4.2	0.5	9	3.6	126	0	156	49	0.6	136	0.4	0.02	1	13.1	0.1	0.18	0.04
imitation — *¼ cup*	58	120	3.8	0	0	11.2	0.3	0	10.2	1.4	1	0	92	59	0.7	0	0	0	0	0	0	0	0
Whipping cream																							
heavy fluid — *1 Tbsp*	15	52	0.4	21	0	5.6	1.6	0.2	3.5	0.3	10	0	11	6	0	63	0	0	0	0.6	0	0.02	0
heavy, whipped — *¼ cup*	30	103	0.8	41	0	11.1	3.2	0.4	6.9	0.6	19	0	23	11	0.1	126	0.1	0.01	0	1.1	0	0.03	0.01
light, fluid — *1 Tbsp*	15	44	0.4	17	0	4.6	1.4	0.1	2.9	0.3	10	0	15	5	0	44	0	0	0	0.6	0	0.02	0
light, whipped — *¼ cup*	30	88	0.9	33	0	9.3	2.7	0.3	5.8	0.7	21	0	29	10	0.1	89	0.1	0.01	0	1.1	0	0.04	0.01
pressurized — *¼ cup*	15	39	1.9	11	0	3.3	1	0.1	2.1	0.5	15	0	22	20	0.1	31	0	0.01	0	0.4	0	0.01	0.01

Duck

	Weight g	Calories	Carbohydrates g	Cholesterol mg	Dietary fiber g	Total fat g	Mono. fat g	Poly. fat g	Sat. fat g	Protein g	Calcium mg	Iron mg	Potassium mg	Sodium mg	Zinc mg	Vitamin A RE	Vitamin B_{12} mcg	Vitamin B_6 mg	Vitamin C mg	Folic acid mcg	Niacin mg	Riboflavin mg	Thiamin mg
Domestic, meat & skin, roasted — *3 ½ oz*	100	337	0	84	0	28.4	12.9	3.7	9.7	19	11	3	204	59	1.9	63	0.3	0.18	0	6	4.8	0.27	0.17
Domestic, meat only, roasted — *3 ½ oz*	100	201	0	89	0	11.2	3.7	1.4	4.2	23.5	12	3	252	65	2.6	23	0.4	0.25	0	10	5.1	0.47	0.26
Duck liver, raw — *3 ½ oz*	100	136	3.5	515	0	4.6	0.7	0.6	1.4	18.7	11	31	230	140	3.1	11946	54	0.76	5	738	6.5	0.89	0.56
Wild duck																							
breast, raw — *3 ½ oz*	100	123	0	77	0	4.3	1.2	0.6	1.3	19.9	3	5	268	57	0.7	16	0.8	0.63	6	25	3.4	0.31	0.42
meat & skin, raw — *3 ½ oz*	100	211	0	80	0	15.2	6.8	2	5	17.4	5	4	249	56	0.8	26	0.7	0.53	5	21	3.3	0.27	0.35

Eggs

	Weight g	Calories	Carbohydrates g	Cholesterol mg	Dietary fiber g	Total fat g	Mono. fat g	Poly. fat g	Sat. fat g	Protein g	Calcium mg	Iron mg	Potassium mg	Sodium mg	Zinc mg	Vitamin A RE	Vitamin B_{12} mcg	Vitamin B_6 mg	Vitamin C mg	Folic acid mcg	Niacin mg	Riboflavin mg	Thiamin mg
Chicken egg																							
white, raw — *1 large*	33	17	0.3	0	0	0	0	0	0	3.5	2	0	48	55	0	0	0.1	0	0	1	0	0.15	0
whole, fried — *1 large*	46	92	0.6	211	0	6.9	2.7	1.3	1.9	6.2	25	1	61	162	0.5	114	0.4	0.07	0	17.5	0	0.24	0.03

	Weight g	Calories	Carbohydrates g	Cholesterol mg	Dietary fiber g	Total fat g	Mono. fat g	Poly. fat g	Sat. fat g	Protein g	Calcium mg	Iron mg	Potassium mg	Sodium mg	Zinc mg	Vitamin A RE	Vitamin B_{12} mcg	Vitamin B_6 mg	Vitamin C mg	Folic acid mcg	Niacin mg	Riboflavin mg	Thiamin mg
whole, hard-boiled — *1 large*	50	78	0.6	212	0	5.3	2	0.7	1.6	6.3	25	1	63	62	0.5	84	0.6	0.06	0	22	0	0.26	0.03
whole, poached — *1 large*	50	75	0.6	212	0	5	1.9	0.7	1.5	6.2	25	1	60	140	0.6	95	0.4	0.06	0	17.5	0	0.22	0.02
whole, raw — *1 extra large*	58	86	0.7	247	0	5.8	2.2	0.8	1.8	7.2	28	1	70	73	0.6	111	0.6	0.08	0	27.3	0	0.29	0.04
whole, raw — *1 jumbo*	65	97	0.8	276	0	6.5	2.5	0.9	2	8.1	32	1	79	82	0.7	124	0.7	0.09	0	30.6	0	0.33	0.04
whole, raw — *1 large*	50	75	0.6	213	0	5	1.9	0.7	1.6	6.2	25	1	61	63	0.6	96	0.5	0.07	0	23.5	0	0.25	0.03
whole, scrambled — *1 large*	61	101	1.3	215	0	7.4	2.9	1.3	2.2	6.8	43	1	84	171	0.6	119	0.5	0.07	0	18.3	0	0.27	0.03
yolk, raw — *1 large*	17	59	0.3	213	0	5.1	1.9	0.7	1.6	2.8	23	1	16	7	0.5	97	0.5	0.07	0	24.2	0	0.11	0.03
Duck egg, whole, raw — *1 egg*	70	130	1	619	0	9.6	4.6	0.9	2.6	9	45	3	156	102	1	279	3.8	0.18	0	56	0.1	0.28	0.11
Egg substitute																							
frozen — *¼ cup*	60	96	1.9	1	0	6.7	1.5	3.7	1.2	6.8	44	1	128	120	0.6	81	0.2	0.08	0	9.8	0.1	0.23	0.07
liquid — *¼ cup*	63	53	0.4	1	0	2.1	0.6	1	0.4	7.5	33	1	207	111	0.8	136	0.2	0	0	9.4	0.1	0.19	0.07
powdered — *1 oz*	28	126	6.2	162	0	3.7	1.5	0.5	1.1	15.7	92	1	211	227	0.5	104	1	0.04	0	35.4	0.2	0.5	0.06
Goose egg, whole, raw — *1 egg*	144	267	1.9	1227	0	19.1	8.3	2.4	5.2	20	87	5	302	199	1.9	553	7.3	0.34	0	108.9	0.3	0.55	0.21
Quail egg, whole, raw — *1 egg*	9	14	0	76	0	1	0.4	0.1	0.3	1.2	6	0	12	13	0.1	8	0.1	0.01	0	6	0	0.07	0.01
Turkey egg, whole, raw — *1 egg*	79	135	0.9	737	0	9.4	3.6	1.3	2.9	10.8	78	3	112	120	1.2	131	1.3	0.1	0	56.2	0	0.37	0.09

Fats & Oils

	Weight g	Calories	Carbohydrates g	Cholesterol mg	Dietary fiber g	Total fat g	Mono. fat g	Poly. fat g	Sat. fat g	Protein g	Calcium mg	Iron mg	Potassium mg	Sodium mg	Zinc mg	Vitamin A RE	Vitamin B_{12} mcg	Vitamin B_6 mg	Vitamin C mg	Folic acid mcg	Niacin mg	Riboflavin mg	Thiamin mg
Almond oil — *1 Tbsp*	14	120	0	0	0	13.6	9.5	2.4	1.1	0	0	0	0	0	0	0	0	0	0	0	0	0	0
Apricot kernel oil — *1 Tbsp*	14	120	0	0	0	13.6	8.2	4	0.9	0	0	0	0	0	0	0	0	0	0	0	0	0	0
Avocado oil — *1 Tbsp*	14	124	0	0	0	14	9.9	1.9	1.6	0	0	0	0	0	0	0	0	0	0	0	0	0	0
Beef tallow — *1 Tbsp*	13	115	0	14	0	12.8	5.4	0.5	6.4	0	0	0	0	0	0	0	0	0	0	0	0	0	0
Butter																							
salted — *1 Tbsp*	14	102	0	31	0	11.5	3.3	0.4	7.2	0.1	3	0	4	117	0	107	0	0	0	0.4	0	0	0
unsalted — *1 Tbsp*	14	102	0	31	0	11.5	3.3	0.4	7.2	0.1	3	0	4	2	0	107	0	0	0	0.4	0	0	0
whipped — *1 Tbsp*	9	67	0	21	0	7.6	2.2	0.3	4.7	0.1	2	0	2	78	0	71	0	0	0	0.3	0	0	0

	Weight g	Calories	Carbohydrates g	Cholesterol mg	Dietary fiber g	Total fat g	Mono. fat g	Poly. fat g	Sat. fat g	Protein g	Calcium mg	Iron mg	Potassium mg	Sodium mg	Zinc mg	Vitamin A RE	Vitamin B_{12} mcg	Vitamin B_6 mg	Vitamin C mg	Folic acid mcg	Niacin mg	Riboflavin mg	Thiamin mg
Butter/vegetable oil blend, 60% corn oil & 40% butter — *1 Tbsp*	14	102	0.1	12	0	11.5	4.7	2.3	4	0.1	4	0	5	127	0	113	0	0	0	0.3	0	0	0
Canola oil — *1 Tbsp*	14	124	0	0	0	14	8.2	4.1	1	0	0	0	0	0	0	0	0	0	0	0	0	0	0
Chicken fat — *1 Tbsp*	13	115	0	11	0	12.8	5.7	2.7	3.8	0	0	0	0	0	0	0	0	0	0	0	0	0	0
Coconut oil — *1 Tbsp*	14	117	0	0	0	13.6	0.8	0.2	11.8	0	0	0	0	0	0	0	0	0	0	0	0	0	0
Cod liver oil — *1 Tbsp*	14	123	0	78	0	13.6	6.4	3.1	3.1	0	0	0	0	0	0	4080	0	0	0	0	0	0	0
Corn oil — *1 Tbsp*	14	120	0	0	0	13.6	3.3	8	1.7	0	0	0	0	0	0	0	0	0	0	0	0	0	0
Cottonseed oil — *1 Tbsp*	14	120	0	0	0	13.6	2.4	7.1	3.5	0	0	0	0	0	0	0	0	0	0	0	0	0	0
Duck fat — *1 Tbsp*	13	115	0	13	0	12.8	6.3	1.7	4.2	0	0	0	0	0	0	0	0	0	0	0	0	0	0
Goose fat — *1 Tbsp*	13	115	0	13	0	12.8	7.3	1.4	3.5	0	0	0	0	0	0	0	0	0	0	0	0	0	0
Grape seed oil — *1 Tbsp*	14	120	0	0	0	13.6	2.2	9.5	1.3	0	0	0	0	0	0	0	0	0	0	0	0	0	0
Hazelnut oil — *1 Tbsp*	14	120	0	0	0	13.6	10.6	1.4	1	0	0	0	0	0	0	0	0	0	0	0	0	0	0
Herring oil — *1 Tbsp*	14	123	0	104	0	13.6	7.7	2.1	2.9	0	0	0	0	0	0	0	0	0	0	0	0	0	0
Lard — *1 Tbsp*	13	115	0	12	0	12.8	5.8	1.4	5	0	0	0	0	0	0	0	0	0	0	0	0	0	0
Margarine, imitation																							
corn (hydg & regular) — *1 Tbsp*	14	50	0.1	0	0	5.6	2.1	2.3	0.9	0.1	3	0	4	138	0	115	0	0	0	0.1	0	0	0
soybean (hydg) — *1 Tbsp*	14	50	0.1	0	0	5.6	2.4	2	0.9	0.1	3	0	4	138	0	115	0	0	0	0.1	0	0	0
soybean (hydg) & cottonseed — *1 Tbsp*	5	17	0	0	0	1.9	0.7	0.7	0.4	0	1	0	1	46	0	38	0	0	0	0	0	0	0
soybean (hydg) & cottonseed (hydg) — *1 Tbsp*	5	17	0	0	0	1.9	0.9	0.5	0.3	0	1	0	1	46	0	38	0	0	0	0	0	0	0
soybean (hydg) & palm (hydg & regular) — *1 Tbsp*	14	50	0.1	0	0	5.6	2	1.8	1.5	0.1	3	0	4	138	0	115	0	0	0	0.1	0	0	0
Margarine, liquid, soybean (hydg & regular) & cottonseed — *1 Tbsp*	14	102	0	0	0	11.4	4	5.1	1.9	0.3	9	0	13	111	0	113	0	0	0	0.4	0	0.01	0
Margarine, hard, soybean (hydg & regular) & cottonseed (hydg) — *1 Tbsp*	14	101	0.1	0	0	11.4	5.8	2.8	2.2	0.1	4	0	6	133	0	113	0	0	0	0.2	0	0.01	0
Margarine, soft																							
corn (hydg & regular) — *1 Tbsp*	14	101	0.1	0	0	11.3	4.5	4.4	2	0.1	4	0	5	152	0	113	0	0	0	0.2	0	0	0
safflower & cottonseed (hydg) & peanut (hydg) — *1 Tbsp*	14	101	0.1	0	0	11.3	2	7	1.9	0.1	4	0	5	152	0	113	0	0	0	0.2	0	0	0

	Weight g	Calories	Carbohydrates g	Cholesterol mg	Dietary fiber g	Total fat g	Mono. fat g	Poly. fat g	Sat. fat g	Protein g	Calcium mg	Iron mg	Potassium mg	Sodium mg	Zinc mg	Vitamin A RE	Vitamin B_{12} mcg	Vitamin B_6 mg	Vitamin C mg	Folic acid mcg	Niacin mg	Riboflavin mg	Thiamin mg
safflower (hydg & regular) — *1 Tbsp*	14	101	0.1	0	0	11.3	3.3	6.3	1.3	0.1	4	0	5	152	0	113	0	0	0	0.15	0	0	0
soybean (hydg & regular) & cottonseed (hydg) — *1 Tbsp*	14	101	0.1	0	0	11.3	5	3.6	2.2	0.1	4	0	5	152	0	113	0	0	0	0.2	0	0	0
soybean (hydg & regular) & cottonseed (hydg) — *1 Tbsp*	14	101	0.1	0	0	11.3	4.3	4.2	2.3	0.1	4	0	5	152	0	113	0	0	0	0.2	0	0	0
soybean (hydg & regular) w/ salt — *1 Tbsp*	14	101	0.1	0	0	11.3	5.1	3.8	1.9	0.1	4	0	5	152	0	113	0	0	0	0.2	0	0	0
soybean (hydg & regular) w/o salt — *1 Tbsp*	14	101	0.1	0	0	11.3	5.1	3.8	1.9	0.1	4	0	5	4	0	113	0	0	0	0.2	0	0	0
soybean (hydg) & cottonseed — *1 Tbsp*	14	101	0.1	0	0	11.3	4.4	4.1	2.3	0.1	4	0	5	152	0	113	0	0	0	0.2	0	0	0
soybean (hydg) & cottonseed (hydg) w/ salt — *1 Tbsp*	14	101	0.1	0	0	11.3	5.4	3.5	2	0.1	4	0	5	152	0	113	0	0	0	0.2	0	0	0
soybean (hydg) & cottonseed (hydg), w/o salt — *1 Tbsp*	14	101	0.1	0	0	11.3	5.4	3.5	2	0.1	4	0	5	4	0	113	0	0	0	0.2	0	0	0
soybean (hydg) & palm (hydg & regular) — *1 Tbsp*	14	101	0.1	0	0	11.3	3.6	4.9	2.4	0.1	4	0	5	152	0	113	0	0	0	0.2	0	0	0
soybean (hydg) & safflower — *1 Tbsp*	14	101	0.1	0	0	11.3	4.4	5	1.5	0.1	4	0	5	152	0	113	0	0	0	0.2	0	0	0
sunflower & cottonseed (hydg) & peanut (hydg) — *1 Tbsp*	14	101	0.1	0	0	11.3	2.3	6.8	1.8	0.1	4	0	5	152	0	113	0	0	0	0.2	0	0	0
unspecified oils — *1 Tbsp*	14	101	0.1	0	0	11.3	4	4.9	1.9	0.1	4	0	5	152	0	113	0	0	0	0.2	0	0	0
Margarine, stick																							
coconut (hydg & regular) & safflower & palm (hydg) — *1 Tbsp*	14	101	0.1	0	0	11.4	1.2	1.6	8	0.1	4	0	6	133	0	113	0	0	0	0.2	0	0.01	0
corn & soybean (hydg) & cottonseed (hydg) w/ salt — *1 Tbsp*	14	101	0.1	0	0	11.4	5.2	3.5	2.1	0.1	4	0	6	133	0	113	0	0	0	0.2	0	0.01	0
corn & soybean (hydg) & cottonseed (hydg) w/o salt — *1 Tbsp*	14	101	0.1	0	0	11.3	5.2	3.5	2.1	0.1	2	0	3	0	0	113	0	0	0	0.1	0	0	0
corn (hydg) — *1 Tbsp*	14	101	0.1	0	0	11.4	6.5	2.5	1.9	0.1	4	0	6	133	0	113	0	0	0	0.2	0	0.01	0
corn (hydg & regular) — *1 Tbsp*	14	101	0.1	0	0	11.4	5.5	3.4	2	0.1	4	0	6	133	0	113	0	0	0	0.2	0	0.01	0
lard (hydg) — *1 Tbsp*	14	103	0.1	7	0	11.4	5.3	1.1	4.5	0.1	0	0	6	133	0	0	0	0	0	0	0	0	0
safflower & soybean (hydg & regular) & cottonseed (hydg) — *1 Tbsp*	14	101	0.1	0	0	11.4	4.3	4.6	2	0.1	4	0	6	133	0	113	0	0	0	0.2	0	0.01	0
safflower & soybean (hydg) — *1 Tbsp*	14	101	0.1	0	0	11.4	4.5	4.4	1.9	0.1	4	0	6	133	0	113	0	0	0	0.2	0	0.01	0
safflower & soybean (hydg) & cottonseed (hydg) — *1 Tbsp*	14	101	0.1	0	0	11.4	3.2	5.7	1.9	0.1	4	0	6	133	0	113	0	0	0	0.2	0	0.01	0
soybean (hydg & regular) — *1 Tbsp*	14	101	0.1	0	0	11.4	5.3	3.7	1.8	0.1	4	0	6	133	0	113	0	0	0	0.2	0	0.01	0
soybean (hydg & regular) & cottonseed (hydg) — *1 Tbsp*	14	101	0.1	0	0	11.4	5.1	3.6	2.2	0.1	4	0	6	133	0	113	0	0	0	0.2	0	0.01	0

	Weight g	Calories	Carbohydrates g	Cholesterol mg	Dietary fiber g	Total fat g	Mono. fat g	Poly. fat g	Sat. fat g	Protein g	Calcium mg	Iron mg	Potassium mg	Sodium mg	Zinc mg	Vitamin A RE	Vitamin B_{12} mcg	Vitamin B_6 mg	Vitamin C mg	Folic acid mcg	Niacin mg	Riboflavin mg	Thiamin mg
soybean (hydg) — *1 Tbsp*	14	101	0.1	0	0	11.4	5.5	2.9	2.4	0.1	4	0	6	133	0	113	0	0	0	0.2	0	0.01	0
soybean (hydg) & corn & cottonseed (hydg) — *1 Tbsp*	14	101	0.1	0	0	11.4	4.5	3.5	2.8	0.1	4	0	6	133	0	113	0	0	0	0.2	0	0.01	0
soybean (hydg) & cottonseed — *1 Tbsp*	14	101	0.1	0	0	11.4	5.7	2.8	2.3	0.1	4	0	6	133	0	113	0	0	0	0.2	0	0.01	0
soybean (hydg) & cottonseed (hydg) — *1 Tbsp*	14	101	0.1	0	0	11.4	6.7	2.1	2.1	0.1	4	0	6	133	0	113	0	0	0	0.2	0	0.01	0
soybean (hydg) & palm (hydg & regular) — *1 Tbsp*	14	101	0.1	0	0	11.4	4.4	4	2.5	0.1	4	0	6	133	0	113	0	0	0	0.2	0	0.01	0
soybean (hydg) & palm (hydg) — *1 Tbsp*	14	101	0.1	0	0	11.4	4.5	4.2	2.1	0.1	4	0	6	133	0	113	0	0	0	0.2	0	0.01	0
sunflower & soybean (hydg) & cottonseed (hydg) — *1 Tbsp*	14	101	0.1	0	0	11.4	4	5.2	1.7	0.1	4	0	6	133	0	113	0	0	0	0.2	0	0.01	0
unspecified oils — *1 Tbsp*	14	101	0.1	0	0	11.4	5	3.6	2.2	0.1	4	0	6	133	0	113	0	0	0	0.2	0	0.01	0
Mutton tallow — *1 Tbsp*	13	115	0	13	0	12.8	5.2	1	6.1	0	0	0	0	0	0	0	0	0	0	0	0	0	0
Olive oil — *1 Tbsp*	13	119	0	0	0	13.5	9.9	1.1	1.8	0	0	0	0	0	0	0	0	0	0	0	0	0	0
Palm kernel oil — *1 Tbsp*	14	117	0	0	0	13.6	1.6	0.2	11.1	0	0	0	0	0	0	0	0	0	0	0	0	0	0
Palm oil — *1 Tbsp*	14	120	0	0	0	13.6	5	1.3	6.7	0	0	0	0	0	0	0	0	0	0	0	0	0	0
Peanut oil — *1 Tbsp*	14	119	0	0	0	13.5	6.2	4.3	2.3	0	0	0	0	0	0	0	0	0	0	0	0	0	0
Poppyseed oil — *1 Tbsp*	14	120	0	0	0	13.6	2.7	8.5	1.8	0	0	0	0	0	0	0	0	0	0	0	0	0	0
Rice bran oil — *1 Tbsp*	14	120	0	0	0	13.6	5.3	4.8	2.7	0	0	0	0	0	0	0	0	0	0	0	0	0	0
Safflower oil, linoleic (over 70%) — *1 Tbsp*	14	120	0	0	0	13.6	1.6	10.1	1.2	0	0	0	0	0	0	0	0	0	0	0	0	0	0
Safflower oil, oleic (over 70%) — *1 Tbsp*	14	120	0	0	0	13.6	10.2	1.9	0.8	0	0	0	0	0	0	0	0	0	0	0	0	0	0
Salad dressing																							
bleu cheese w/ salt — *1 Tbsp*	15	77	1.1	3	0	8	1.9	4.3	1.5	0.7	12	0	6	167	0	10	0	0.01	0	1.2	0	0.02	0
french — *1 Tbsp*	16	67	2.7	0	0	6.4	1.2	3.4	1.5	0.1	2	0	12	214	0	20	0	0	0	0.7	0	0	0
french, diet — *1 Tbsp*	16	22	3.5	0	0	0.9	0.2	0.6	0.1	0	2	0	13	128	0	21	0	0	0	0	0	0	0
italian — *1 Tbsp*	15	69	1.5	0	0	7.1	1.6	4.1	1	0.1	1	0	2	116	0	4	0	0	0	0.7	0	0	0
italian, diet — *1 Tbsp*	15	16	0.7	1	0	1.5	0.3	0.9	0.2	0	0	0	2	118	0	0	0	0	0	0	0	0	0
mayonnaise type — *1 Tbsp*	15	57	3.5	4	0	4.9	1.3	2.6	0.7	0.1	2	0	1	104	0	12	0	0	0	0.9	0	0	0

	Weight *g*	Calories	Carbohydrates *g*	Cholesterol *mg*	Dietary fiber *g*	Total fat *g*	Mono. fat *g*	Poly. fat *g*	Sat. fat *g*	Protein *g*	Calcium *mg*	Iron *mg*	Potassium *mg*	Sodium *mg*	Zinc *mg*	Vitamin A *RE*	Vitamin B_{12} *mcg*	Vitamin B_6 *mg*	Vitamin C *mg*	Folic acid *mcg*	Niacin *mg*	Riboflavin *mg*	Thiamin *mg*
russian — *1 Tbsp*	15	76	1.6	3	0	7.8	1.8	4.5	1.1	0.2	3	0	24	133	0.1	32	0	0	1	1.6	0.1	0.01	0.01
russian, low-calorie — *1 Tbsp*	16	23	4.5	1	0	0.7	0.1	0.4	0.1	0.1	3	0	26	141	0	3	0	0	1	0.6	0	0	0
sesame seed — *1 Tbsp*	15	68	1.3	0	0.2	6.9	1.8	3.8	0.9	0.5	3	0	24	153	0	32	0	0	0	0	0	0	0
thousand island — *1 Tbsp*	16	59	2.4	4	0	5.6	1.3	3.1	0.9	0.1	2	0	18	109	0	15	0	0	0	1	0	0	0
thousand island, diet — *1 Tbsp*	15	24	2.5	2	0.2	1.6	0.4	0.9	0.2	0.1	2	0	17	153	0	15	0	0	0	0.9	0	0	0
Salmon oil — *1 Tbsp*	14	123	0	66	0	13.6	3.9	5.5	2.7	0	0	0	0	0	0	0	0	0	0	0	0	0	0
Sardine oil — *1 Tbsp*	14	123	0	97	0	13.6	4.6	4.3	4.1	0	0	0	0	0	0	0	0	0	0	0	0	0	0
Sesame oil — *1 Tbsp*	14	120	0	0	0	13.6	5.4	5.7	1.9	0	0	0	0	0	0	0	0	0	0	0	0	0	0
Shortening																							
coconut (hydg) &/or palm kernel (hydg) — *1 Tbsp*	13	113	0	0	0	12.8	0.3	0.1	11.7	0	0	0	0	0	0	0	0	0	0	0	0	0	0
frying (heavy duty), soybean (hydg), linoleic (less than 1%) — *1 Tbsp*	13	113	0	0	0	12.8	9.4	0.1	2.7	0	0	0	0	0	0	0	0	0	0	0	0	0	0
frying, beef tallow & cottonseed — *1 Tbsp*	13	115	0	13	0	12.8	4.9	1.1	5.7	0	0	0	0	0	0	0	0	0	0	0	0	0	0
frying, soybean (hydg) & cottonseed (hydg) — *1 Tbsp*	13	113	0	0	0	12.8	7.4	2.8	2	0	0	0	0	0	0	0	0	0	0	0	0	0	0
lard & vegetable oil — *1 Tbsp*	13	115	0	7	0	12.8	5.7	1.4	5.2	0	0	0	0	0	0	0	0	0	0	0	0	0	0
multipurpose, soybean (hydg) & palm (hydg) — *1 Tbsp*	13	113	0	0	0	12.8	6.5	1.8	3.9	0	0	0	0	0	0	0	0	0	0	0	0	0	0
soybean-cottonseed — *1 Tbsp*	13	113	0	0	0	12.8	5.7	3.3	3.2	0	0	0	0	0	0	0	0	0	0	0	0	0	0
Soybean (hydg) & cottonseed oil — *1 Tbsp*	14	120	0	0	0	13.6	4	6.5	2.4	0	0	0	0	0	0	0	0	0	0	0	0	0	0
Soybean lecithin oil — *1 Tbsp*	14	104	0	0	0	13.6	1.5	6.2	2	0	0	0	0	0	0	0	0	0	0	0	0	0	0
Soybean oil — *1 Tbsp*	14	120	0	0	0	13.6	3.2	7.9	2	0	0	0	0	0	0	0	0	0	0	0	0	0	0
Sunflower oil																							
linoleic (60% & over) — *1 Tbsp*	14	120	0	0	0	13.6	2.7	8.9	1.4	0	0	0	0	0	0	0	0	0	0	0	0	0	0
linoleic (hydg) — *1 Tbsp*	14	120	0	0	0	13.6	6.3	5	1.8	0	0	0	0	0	0	0	0	0	0	0	0	0	0
oleic (70% & over) — *1 Tbsp*	14	124	0	0	0	14	11.7	0.5	1.4	0	0	0	0	0	0	0	0	0	0	0	0	0	0
regular — *1 Tbsp*	14	120	0	0	0	13.6	6.2	5.5	1.4	0	0	0	0	0	0	0	0	0	0	0	0	0	0

	Weight g	Calories	Carbohydrates g	Cholesterol mg	Dietary fiber g	Total fat g	Mono. fat g	Poly. fat g	Sat. fat g	Protein g	Calcium mg	Iron mg	Potassium mg	Sodium mg	Zinc mg	Vitamin A RE	Vitamin B_{12} mcg	Vitamin B_6 mg	Vitamin C mg	Folic acid mcg	Niacin mg	Riboflavin mg	Thiamin mg
Tea seed oil — *1 Tbsp*	14	120	0	0	0	13.6	7	3.1	2.9	0	0	0	0	0	0	0	0	0	0	0	0	0	0
Tomato seed oil — *1 Tbsp*	14	120	0	0	0	13.6	3.1	7.2	2.7	0	0	0	0	0	0	0	0	0	0	0	0	0	0
Turkey fat — *1 Tbsp*	13	115	0	13	0	12.8	5.5	3	3.8	0	0	0	0	0	0	0	0	0	0	0	0	0	0
Vegetable oil spread																							
stick, soybean (hydg) & palm (hydg) — *1 Tbsp*	14	78	0	0	0	8.8	3.7	2.6	2	0.1	3	0	4	143	0	115	0	0	0	0.1	0	0	0
tub, hydg soybean & hydg cottonseed — *1 Tbsp*	14	78	0	0	0	8.8	5.6	1	1.7	0.1	3	0	4	143	0	115	0	0	0	0.1	0	0	0
tub, soybean (hydg) & palm (hydg & regular) — *1 Tbsp*	14	78	0	0	0	8.8	3.5	2.9	1.9	0.1	3	0	4	143	0	115	0	0	0	0.1	0	0	0
tub, unspecified oils — *1 Tbsp*	14	78	0	0	0	8.8	4.5	2	1.8	0.1	3	0	4	143	0	115	0	0	0	0.1	0	0	0
Walnut oil — *1 Tbsp*	14	120	0	0	0	13.6	3.1	8.6	1.2	0	0	0	0	0	0	0	0	0	0	0	0	0	0
Wheat germ oil — *1 Tbsp*	14	120	0	0	0	13.6	2.1	8.4	2.6	0	0	0	0	0	0	0	0	0	0	0	0	0	0

Fish

	Weight g	Calories	Carbohydrates g	Cholesterol mg	Dietary fiber g	Total fat g	Mono. fat g	Poly. fat g	Sat. fat g	Protein g	Calcium mg	Iron mg	Potassium mg	Sodium mg	Zinc mg	Vitamin A RE	Vitamin B_{12} mcg	Vitamin B_6 mg	Vitamin C mg	Folic acid mcg	Niacin mg	Riboflavin mg	Thiamin mg
Anchovy, canned in oil, drained — *1 can*	45	95	0	38	0	4.4	1.7	1.2	1	13	104	2	245	1651	1.1	9	0.4	0.09	0	5.6	9	0.16	0.04
Bass																							
freshwater, ckd, dry heat — *3 ½ oz*	100	146	0	87	0	4.7	1.8	1.4	1	24.2	103	2	456	90	0.8	35	2.3	0.14	2	17	1.5	0.09	0.09
striped, ckd, dry heat — *3 ½ oz*	100	124	0	103	0	3	0.8	1	0.7	22.7	19	1	328	88	0.5	31	4.4	0.35	0	10	2.6	0.04	0.12
Bluefish, ckd, dry heat — *3 ½ oz*	100	159	0	76	0	5.4	2.3	1.4	1.2	25.7	9	1	477	77	1	138	6.2	0.46	0	2	7.2	0.1	0.07
Burbot, ckd, dry heat — *3 ½ oz*	100	115	0	77	0	1	0.2	0.4	0.2	24.8	64	1	518	124	1	5	0.9	0.35	0	1	2	0.17	0.43
Butterfish, ckd, dry heat — *3 ½ oz*	100	187	0	83	0	10.3	0	0	0	22.2	28	1	481	114	1	33	1.8	0.35	0	17	5.8	0.19	0.15
Carp, ckd, dry heat — *3 ½ oz*	100	162	0	84	0	7.2	3	1.8	1.4	22.9	52	2	427	63	1.9	9	1.5	0.22	2	17.3	2.1	0.07	0.14
Catfish, channel																							
ckd, dry heat — *3 ½ oz*	100	152	0	64	0	8	4.2	1.4	1.8	18.7	9	1	321	80	1.1	15	2.8	0.16	1	7	2.5	0.07	0.42
fried, breaded — *3 ½ oz*	100	229	8	81	0.7	13.3	5.6	3.3	3.3	18.1	44	1	340	280	0.9	8	1.9	0.19	0	16.5	2.3	0.13	0.07
Caviar, black & red, granular — *1 Tbsp*	16	40	0.6	94	0	2.9	0.7	1.2	0.6	3.9	44	2	29	240	0.2	90	3.2	0.05	0	8	0	0.1	0.03
Cisco, smoked — *3 ½ oz*	100	177	0	32	0	11.9	5.5	2.3	1.7	16.4	26	0	293	481	0.3	283	4.3	0.27	0	2.1	2.3	0.16	0.05

	Weight g	Calories	Carbohydrates g	Cholesterol mg	Dietary fiber g	Total fat g	Mono. fat g	Poly. fat g	Sat. fat g	Protein g	Calcium mg	Iron mg	Potassium mg	Sodium mg	Zinc mg	Vitamin A RE	Vitamin B_{12} mcg	Vitamin B_6 mg	Vitamin C mg	Folic acid mcg	Niacin mg	Riboflavin mg	Thiamin mg
Cod, atlantic																							
canned, undrained — *3 ½ oz*	100	105	0	55	0	0.9	0.1	0.3	0.2	22.8	21	0	528	218	0.6	14	1	0.28	1	8.1	2.5	0.08	0.09
ckd, dry heat — *3 ½ oz*	100	105	0	55	0	0.9	0.1	0.3	0.2	22.8	14	0	244	78	0.6	14	1	0.28	1	8.1	2.5	0.08	0.09
dried & salted — *3 ½ oz*	100	290	0	152	0	2.4	0.3	0.8	0.5	62.8	160	3	1458	7027	1.6	42	10	0.86	4	24.7	7.5	0.24	0.27
Cod, pacific, ckd, dry heat — *3 ½ oz*	100	105	0	47	0	0.8	0.1	0.3	0.1	23	9	0	517	91	0.5	10	1	0.46	3	8	2.5	0.05	0.03
Croaker, atlantic, fried, breaded — *3 ½ oz*	100	221	7.5	84	0.4	12.7	5.3	2.9	3.5	18.2	32	1	340	348	0.5	22	2.1	0.26	0	18.1	4.3	0.13	0.09
Cusk, ckd, dry heat — *3 ½ oz*	100	112	0	53	0	0.9	0	0	0	24.4	13	1	503	40	0.5	21	1.2	0.45	0	2	3.3	0.16	0.05
Dolphinfish, ckd, dry heat — *3 ½ oz*	100	109	0	94	0	0.9	0.2	0.2	0.2	23.7	19	1	533	113	0.6	62	0.7	0.46	0	6	7.4	0.09	0.02
Drum, freshwater, ckd, dry heat — *3 ½ oz*	100	153	0	82	0	6.3	2.8	1.5	1.4	22.5	77	1	353	96	0.9	59	2.3	0.35	1	17	2.9	0.21	0.08
Eel, raw — *3 ½ oz*	100	184	0	126	0	11.7	7.2	0.9	2.4	18.4	20	1	272	51	1.6	1043	3	0.07	2	15	3.5	0.04	0.15
Fish sticks, frozen — *1 stick*	28	76	6.7	31	0	3.4	1.4	0.9	0.9	4.4	6	0	73	163	0.2	9	0.5	0.02	0	5.1	0.6	0.05	0.04
Flatfish (flounder & sole), ckd, dry heat — *3 ½ oz*	100	117	0	68	0	1.5	0.2	0.6	0.4	24.2	18	0	344	105	0.6	11	2.5	0.24	0	9.2	2.2	0.11	0.08
Gefiltefish, jarred, sweet recipe — *3 ½ oz*	100	84	7.4	30	0	1.7	0.8	0.3	0.4	9.1	23	2	91	524	0.8	27	0.8	0.08	1	2.8	1	0.06	0.07
Grouper, ckd, dry heat — *3 ½ oz*	100	118	0	47	0	1.3	0.3	0.4	0.3	24.8	21	1	475	53	0.5	50	0.7	0.35	0	10.2	0.4	0.01	0.08
Haddock																							
ckd, dry heat — *3 ½ oz*	100	112	0	74	0	0.9	0.2	0.3	0.2	24.2	42	1	399	87	0.5	19	1.4	0.35	0	13.3	4.6	0.05	0.04
smoked — *3 ½ oz*	100	116	0	77	0	1	0.2	0.3	0.2	25.2	49	1	415	763	0.5	22	1.6	0.4	0	15.3	5.1	0.05	0.05
Halibut																							
atlantic & pacific, ckd, dry heat — *3 ½ oz*	100	140	0	41	0	2.9	1	0.9	0.4	26.7	60	1	576	69	0.5	54	1.4	0.4	0	13.8	7.1	0.09	0.07
greenland, ckd, dry heat — *3 ½ oz*	100	239	0	59	0	17.7	10.7	1.8	3.1	18.4	4	1	344	103	0.5	18	1	0.49	0	1	1.9	0.1	0.07
Herring																							
atlantic, ckd, dry heat — *3 ½ oz*	100	203	0	77	0	11.6	4.8	2.7	2.6	23	74	1	419	115	1.3	31	13.1	0.35	1	11.5	4.1	0.3	0.11
atlantic, kippered — *3 ½ oz*	100	217	0	82	0	12.4	5.1	2.9	2.8	24.6	84	2	447	918	1.4	39	18.7	0.41	1	13.7	4.4	0.32	0.13
atlantic, pickled — *3 ½ oz*	100	262	9.6	13	0	18	11.9	1.7	2.4	14.2	77	1	69	870	0.5	258	4.3	0.17	0	2.4	3.3	0.14	0.04

	Weight g	Calories	Carbohydrates g	Cholesterol mg	Dietary fiber g	Total fat g	Mono. fat g	Poly. fat g	Sat. fat g	Protein g	Calcium mg	Iron mg	Potassium mg	Sodium mg	Zinc mg	Vitamin A RE	Vitamin B_{12} mcg	Vitamin B_6 mg	Vitamin C mg	Folic acid mcg	Niacin mg	Riboflavin mg	Thiamin mg
pacific, ckd, dry heat — *3 ½ oz*	100	250	0	99	0	17.8	8.8	3.1	4.2	21	106	1	542	95	0.7	35	9.6	0.52	0	6	2.8	0.26	0.07
Ling, ckd, dry heat — *3 ½ oz*	100	111	0	51	0	0.8	0	0	0	24.4	44	1	486	173	1	35	0.7	0.35	0	8	2.8	0.23	0.13
Lingcod, ckd, dry heat — *3 ½ oz*	100	109	0	67	0	1.4	0.4	0.4	0.3	22.6	18	0	560	76	0.6	17	4.2	0.35	0	10	2.3	0.14	0.04
Lox — *3 ½ oz*	100	117	0	23	0	4.3	2	1	0.9	18.3	11	1	175	2000	0.3	26	3.3	0.28	0	1.9	4.7	0.1	0.02
Mackerel																							
atlantic, ckd, dry heat — *3 ½ oz*	100	262	0	75	0	17.8	7	4.3	4.2	23.9	15	2	401	83	0.9	54	19	0.46	0	1.5	6.9	0.41	0.16
jack, canned, drained — *3 ½ oz*	100	156	0	79	0	6.3	2.2	1.7	1.9	23.2	241	2	194	379	1	130	6.9	0.21	1	5	6.2	0.21	0.04
pacific & jack, ckd, dry heat — *3 ½ oz*	100	201	0	60	0	10.1	3.4	2.5	2.9	25.7	29	1	521	110	0.9	14	4.2	0.38	2	2	10.7	0.54	0.14
spanish, ckd, dry heat — *3 ½ oz*	100	158	0	73	0	6.3	2.1	1.8	1.8	23.6	13	1	554	66	0.6	33	7	0.46	2	1.2	5	0.21	0.13
king, ckd, dry heat — *3 ½ oz*	100	134	0	68	0	2.6	1	0.6	0.5	26	40	2	558	203	0.7	252	18	0.51	2	9	10.5	0.58	0.12
Milkfish, ckd, dry heat — *3 ½ oz*	100	190	0	67	0	8.6	0	0	0	26.3	65	0	374	92	1.1	33	3.3	0.49	0	18	8.3	0.07	0.02
Monkfish, ckd, dry heat — *3 ½ oz*	100	97	0	32	0	2	0	0	0	18.6	10	0	513	23	0.5	14	1	0.28	1	8	2.6	0.07	0.03
Mullet, striped, ckd, dry heat — *3 ½ oz*	100	150	0	63	0	4.9	1.4	0.9	1.4	24.8	31	1	458	71	0.9	42	0.3	0.49	1	9.8	6.3	0.1	0.1
Ocean perch, atlantic, ckd, dry heat — *3 ½ oz*	100	121	0	54	0	2.1	0.8	0.5	0.3	23.9	137	1	350	96	0.6	14	1.2	0.27	1	10.4	2.4	0.13	0.13
Orange roughy, ckd, dry heat — *3 ½ oz*	100	89	0	26	0	0.9	0.6	0	0	18.9	38	0	385	81	1	24	2.3	0.35	0	8	3.7	0.18	0.12
Perch, ckd, dry heat — *3 ½ oz*	100	117	0	115	0	1.2	0.2	0.5	0.2	24.9	102	1	344	79	1.4	10	2.2	0.14	2	5.8	1.9	0.12	0.08
Pike																							
northern, ckd, dry heat — *3 ½ oz*	100	113	0	50	0	0.9	0.2	0.3	0.2	24.7	73	1	331	49	0.9	24	2.3	0.14	4	17.3	2.8	0.08	0.07
walleye, ckd, dry heat — *3 ½ oz*	100	119	0	110	0	1.6	0.4	0.6	0.3	24.5	141	2	499	65	0.8	24	2.3	0.14	0	17	2.8	0.2	0.31
Pollock																							
atlantic, ckd, dry heat — *3 ½ oz*	100	118	0	91	0	1.3	0.1	0.6	0.2	24.9	77	1	456	110	0.6	12	3.7	0.33	0	3	4	0.23	0.05
walleye, ckd, dry heat — *3 ½ oz*	100	113	0	96	0	1.1	0.2	0.5	0.2	23.5	6	0	387	116	0.6	23	4.2	0.07	0	3.6	1.7	0.08	0.07
Pompano, florida, ckd, dry heat — *3 ½ oz*	100	211	0	64	0	12.1	3.3	1.5	4.5	23.7	43	1	636	76	0.7	36	1.2	0.23	0	17.3	3.8	0.15	0.68
Pout, ocean, ckd, dry heat — *3 ½ oz*	100	102	0	67	0	1.2	0.4	0	0.4	21.3	13	0	513	78	1.3	14	1	0.28	0	8	2.6	0.07	0.09

Foods, General

	Weight g	Calories	Carbohydrates g	Cholesterol mg	Dietary fiber g	Total fat g	Mono. fat g	Poly. fat g	Sat. fat g	Protein g	Calcium mg	Iron mg	Potassium mg	Sodium mg	Zinc mg	Vitamin A RE	Vitamin B_{12} mcg	Vitamin B_6 mg	Vitamin C mg	Folic acid mcg	Niacin mg	Riboflavin mg	Thiamin mg
Rockfish, pacific, ckd, dry heat — *3 ½ oz*	100	121	0	44	0	2	0.4	0.6	0.5	24	12	1	520	77	0.5	66	1.2	0.27	0	10.4	3.9	0.08	0.04
Roe, ckd, dry heat — *3 ½ oz*	100	204	1.9	479	0	8.2	2.1	3.4	1.9	28.6	28	1	283	117	1.3	91	11.5	0.19	16	92	2.2	0.95	0.28
Sablefish																							
ckd, dry heat — *3 ½ oz*	100	250	0	63	0	19.6	10.3	2.6	4.1	17.2	45	2	459	72	0.4	101	1.4	0.35	0	17	5.1	0.12	0.12
smoked — *3 ½ oz*	100	257	0	64	0	20.1	10.6	2.7	4.2	17.7	50	2	471	737	0.4	122	2	0.39	0	19.7	5.3	0.12	0.13
Salmon nuggets, breaded, frozen, heated — *3 ½ oz*	100	212	14	26	0	11.7	4.6	3	1.6	12.7	8	1	165	173	0.5	6	2.1	0.22	0	6	4.5	0.16	0.21
Salmon, atlantic, ckd, dry heat — *3 ½ oz*	100	206	0	63	0	12.4	4.4	4.4	2.5	22.1	15	0	384	61	0.4	15	2.8	0.65	4	34	8	0.14	0.34
Salmon, canned w/ bones																							
chum w/o salt, drained — *3 ½ oz*	100	141	0	39	0	5.5	1.9	1.5	1.5	21.4	249	1	300	75	1	18	4.4	0.38	0	20	7	0.16	0.02
pink, undrained — *3 ½ oz*	100	139	0	55	0	6.1	1.8	2	1.5	19.8	213	1	326	554	0.9	17	4.4	0.3	0	15.4	6.5	0.19	0.02
pink w/o salt, undrained — *3 ½ oz*	100	139	0	55	0	6.1	1.8	2	1.5	19.8	213	1	326	75	0.9	17	4.4	0.3	0	15.4	6.5	0.19	0.02
sockeye, drained — *3 ½ oz*	100	153	0	44	0	7.3	3.2	1.9	1.6	20.5	239	1	377	538	1	53	0.3	0.3	0	9.8	5.5	0.19	0.02
sockeye w/o salt, drained — *3 ½ oz*	100	153	0	44	0	7.3	2.8	2.3	1.6	20.5	239	1	377	75	1	53	0.3	0.3	0	9.8	5.5	0.19	0.02
Salmon, chinook																							
ckd, dry heat — *3 ½ oz*	100	231	0	85	0	13.4	5.7	2.7	3.2	25.7	28	1	505	60	0.6	149	2.9	0.46	4	35	10	0.15	0.04
smoked — *3 ½ oz*	100	117	0	23	0	4.3	2	1	0.9	18.3	11	1	175	784	0.3	26	3.3	0.28	0	1.9	4.7	0.1	0.02
Salmon, chum																							
ckd, dry heat — *3 ½ oz*	100	154	0	95	0	4.8	2	1.2	1.1	25.8	14	1	550	64	0.6	34	3.5	0.46	0	5	8.5	0.22	0.09
drained — *3 ½ oz*	100	141	0	39	0	5.5	1.9	1.5	1.5	21.4	249	1	300	487	1	18	4.4	0.38	0	20	7	0.16	0.02
Salmon, coho																							
ckd, moist heat — *3 ½ oz*	100	184	0	57	0	7.5	2.7	2.5	1.6	27.4	46	1	455	53	0.5	32	4.5	0.56	1	9	7.8	0.16	0.12
Salmon, coho, ckd, dry heat — *3 ½ oz*	100	178	0	63	0	8.2	3.6	2	1.9	24.3	12	0	460	52	0.5	59	3.2	0.57	2	14	7.4	0.11	0.1
Salmon, pink, ckd, dry heat — *3 ½ oz*	100	149	0	67	0	4.4	1.2	1.7	0.7	25.6	17	1	414	86	0.7	41	3.5	0.23	0	5	8.5	0.07	0.2
Salmon, sockeye, ckd, dry heat — *3 ½ oz*	100	216	0	87	0	11	5.3	2.4	1.9	27.3	7	1	375	66	0.5	63	5.8	0.22	0	5	6.7	0.17	0.22

	Weight g	Calories	Carbohydrates g	Cholesterol mg	Dietary fiber g	Total fat g	Mono. fat g	Poly. fat g	Sat. fat g	Protein g	Calcium mg	Iron mg	Potassium mg	Sodium mg	Zinc mg	Vitamin A RE	Vitamin B_{12} mcg	Vitamin B_6 mg	Vitamin C mg	Folic acid mcg	Niacin mg	Riboflavin mg	Thiamin mg
Sardines																							
atlantic, canned in oil w/ bones, drained — *1 can*	92	191	0	131	0	10.5	3.6	4.7	1.4	22.7	351	3	365	465	1.2	62	8.2	0.15	0	10.9	4.8	0.21	0.07
pacific, canned in tomato sauce w/ bones, drained — *1 can*	370	659	0	226	0	44.3	20.5	9	11.4	60.5	888	9	1262	1532	5.2	259	33.3	0.46	4	89.9	15.5	0.86	0.16
Scup, ckd, dry heat — *3 ½ oz*	100	135	0	67	0	3.5	0	0	0	24.2	51	1	368	54	0.6	31	1.6	0.35	0	17	5	0.12	0.13
Sea bass, ckd, dry heat — *3 ½ oz*	100	124	0	53	0	2.6	0.5	1	0.7	23.6	13	0	328	87	0.5	64	0.3	0.46	0	5.8	1.9	0.15	0.13
Seatrout, ckd, dry heat — *3 ½ oz*	100	133	0	106	0	4.6	1.1	0.9	1.3	21.5	22	0	437	74	0.6	35	3.5	0.46	0	6	2.9	0.21	0.07
Shad, american, ckd, dry heat — *3 ½ oz*	100	252	0	96	0	17.7	0	0	0	21.7	60	1	492	65	0.5	36	0.1	0.46	0	17	10.8	0.31	0.18
Shark																							
fried, batter-dipped — *3 ½ oz*	100	228	6.4	59	0	13.8	5.9	3.7	3.2	18.6	50	1	155	122	0.5	54	1.2	0.3	0	5.2	2.8	0.1	0.07
raw — *3 ½ oz*	100	130	0	51	0	4.5	1.8	1.2	0.9	21	34	1	160	79	0.4	70	1.5	0.4	0	3.2	2.9	0.06	0.04
Sheepshead, ckd, dry heat — *3 ½ oz*	100	126	0	64	0	1.6	0.4	0.4	0.4	26	37	1	512	73	0.6	35	2.3	0.35	0	17.3	1.8	0.05	0.01
Smelt, rainbow, ckd, dry heat — *3 ½ oz*	100	124	0	90	0	3.1	0.8	1.1	0.6	22.6	77	1	372	77	2.1	17	4	0.17	0	4.6	1.8	0.15	0.01
Snapper, ckd, dry heat — *3 ½ oz*	100	128	0	47	0	1.7	0.3	0.6	0.4	26.3	40	0	522	57	0.4	35	3.5	0.46	2	5.8	0.3	0	0.05
Spot, ckd, dry heat — *3 ½ oz*	100	158	0	77	0	6.3	1.7	1.4	1.9	23.7	18	0	636	37	0.7	35	3.5	0.46	0	6	8.5	0.27	0.19
Sturgeon																							
ckd, dry heat — *3 ½ oz*	100	135	0	77	0	5.2	2.5	0.9	1.2	20.7	17	1	364	69	0.5	242	2.5	0.23	0	17.3	10.1	0.09	0.08
smoked — *3 ½ oz*	100	173	0	80	0	4.4	2.4	0.4	1	31.2	17	1	379	739	0.6	280	2.9	0.27	0	20	11.1	0.09	0.09
Sucker, white, ckd, dry heat — *3 ½ oz*	100	119	0	53	0	3	0.9	1	0.6	21.5	90	2	487	51	1	59	2.3	0.23	0	17	1.5	0.09	0.01
Sunfish, pumpkin seed, ckd, dry heat — *3 ½ oz*	100	114	0	86	0	0.9	0.2	0.3	0.2	24.9	103	2	449	103	2	17	2.3	0.14	1	17	1.5	0.09	0.09
Surimi — *3 ½ oz*	100	99	6.9	30	0	0.9	0.1	0.5	0.2	15.2	9	0	112	143	0.3	20	1.6	0.03	0	1.6	0.2	0.02	0.02
Swordfish, ckd, dry heat — *3 ½ oz*	100	155	0	50	0	5.1	2	1.2	1.4	25.4	6	1	369	115	1.5	41	2	0.38	1	2.3	11.8	0.12	0.04
Tilefish, ckd, dry heat — *3 ½ oz*	100	147	0	64	0	4.7	1.3	1.2	0.9	24.5	26	0	512	59	0.5	21	2.5	0.3	0	17.3	3.5	0.19	0.14
Trout																							
mixed species, ckd, dry heat — *3 ½ oz*	100	190	0	74	0	8.5	4.2	1.9	1.5	26.6	55	2	463	67	0.9	19	7.5	0.23	1	15	5.8	0.42	0.43

	Weight g	Calories	Carbohydrates g	Cholesterol mg	Dietary fiber g	Total fat g	Mono. fat g	Poly. fat g	Sat. fat g	Protein g	Calcium mg	Iron mg	Potassium mg	Sodium mg	Zinc mg	Vitamin A RE	Vitamin B_{12} mcg	Vitamin B_6 mg	Vitamin C mg	Folic acid mcg	Niacin mg	Riboflavin mg	Thiamin mg
rainbow, ckd, dry heat — *3 ½ oz*	100	150	0	69	0	5.8	1.7	1.8	1.6	22.9	86	0	448	56	0.5	15	6.3	0.35	2	19	5.8	0.1	0.15
Tuna salad — *3 ½ oz*	100	187	9.4	13	0	9.3	2.9	4.1	1.5	16	17	1	178	402	0.6	27	1.2	0.08	2	7.3	6.7	0.07	0.03
Tuna, canned, light																							
in oil, drained — *3 ½ oz*	100	198	0	18	0	8.2	2.9	2.9	1.5	29.1	13	1	207	354	0.9	23	2.2	0.11	0	5.3	12.4	0.12	0.04
in oil w/o salt, drained — *3 ½ oz*	100	198	0	18	0	8.2	2.9	2.9	1.5	29.1	13	1	207	50	0.9	23	2.2	0.11	0	5.3	12.4	0.12	0.04
in water, drained — *3 ½ oz*	100	116	0	30	0	0.8	0.2	0.3	0.2	25.5	11	2	237	338	0.8	17	3	0.35	0	4	13.3	0.07	0.03
in water w/o salt, drained — *3 ½ oz*	100	131	0	18	0	0.5	0.1	0.1	0.2	29.6	12	3	314	50	0.4	23	2.2	0.38	0	4.7	12.4	0.12	0.04
Tuna, canned, white																							
in oil, drained — *3 ½ oz*	100	186	0	31	0	8.1	2.5	3.4	1.7	26.5	4	1	333	396	0.5	24	2.2	0.43	0	4.6	11.7	0.08	0.02
in oil w/o salt, drained — *3 ½ oz*	100	186	0	31	0	8.1	2.5	3.4	1.7	26.5	4	1	333	50	0.5	24	2.2	0.43	0	4.6	11.7	0.08	0.02
in water, drained — *3 ½ oz*	100	128	0	42	0	3	0.8	1.1	0.8	23.6	14	1	237	377	0.5	6	1.2	0.22	0	2	5.8	0.04	0.01
in water w/o salt, drained — *3 ½ oz*	100	128	0	42	0	3	0.8	1.1	0.8	23.6	14	1	237	50	0.5	6	1.2	0.22	0	2	5.8	0.04	0.01
Tuna, fresh																							
bluefin, ckd, dry heat — *3 ½ oz*	100	184	0	49	0	6.3	2.1	1.8	1.6	29.9	10	1	323	50	0.8	756	10.9	0.53	0	2.2	10.5	0.31	0.28
skipjack, ckd, dry heat — *3 ½ oz*	100	132	0	60	0	1.3	0.2	0.4	0.4	28.2	37	2	522	47	1.1	18	2.2	0.98	1	10	18.8	0.12	0.04
yellowfin, ckd, dry heat — *3 ½ oz*	100	139	0	58	0	1.2	0.2	0.4	0.3	30	21	1	569	47	0.7	20	0.6	1.04	1	2	11.9	0.06	0.5
Turbot, ckd, dry heat — *3 ½ oz*	100	122	0	62	0	3.8	0	0	0	20.6	23	0	305	192	0.3	12	2.5	0.24	2	9	2.7	0.1	0.08
Whitefish																							
ckd, dry heat — *3 ½ oz*	100	172	0	77	0	7.5	2.6	2.8	1.2	24.5	33	0	406	65	1.3	39	1	0.35	0	17	3.8	0.15	0.17
smoked — *3 ½ oz*	100	108	0	33	0	0.9	0.3	0.3	0.2	23.4	18	1	423	1019	0.5	57	3.3	0.39	0	7.3	2.4	0.1	0.03
Whitting, ckd, dry heat — *3 ½ oz*	100	116	0	84	0	1.7	0.4	0.6	0.4	23.5	62	0	434	132	0.5	34	2.6	0.18	0	15	1.7	0.06	0.07
Wolffish, atlantic, ckd, dry heat — *3 ½ oz*	100	123	0	59	0	3.1	1.1	1.1	0.5	22.4	8	0	385	109	1	130	2.4	0.46	0	6	2.6	0.1	0.21
Yellowtail, ckd, dry heat — *3 ½ oz*	100	187	0	71	0	6.7	0	0	0	29.7	29	1	538	50	0.7	31	1.3	0.19	3	4	8.7	0.05	0.18

Flours

	Weight g	Calories	Carbohydrates g	Cholesterol mg	Dietary fiber g	Total fat g	Mono. fat g	Poly. fat g	Sat. fat g	Protein g	Calcium mg	Iron mg	Potassium mg	Sodium mg	Zinc mg	Vitamin A RE	Vitamin B_{12} mcg	Vitamin B_6 mg	Vitamin C mg	Folic acid mcg	Niacin mg	Riboflavin mg	Thiamin mg
Acorn flour, full-fat — *1 oz*	28	142	15.5	0	0	8.6	5.4	1.6	1.1	2.1	12	0	202	0	0.2	1	0	0.2	0	32.2	0.7	0.04	0.04
Arrowroot flour — *¼ cup*	32	114	28.2	0	1.1	0	0	0	0	0.1	13	0	4	1	0	0	0	0	0	2.2	0	0	0
Buckwheat flour — *1 cup*	120	402	84.7	0	12	3.7	1.1	1.1	0.8	15.1	49	5	692	13	3.7	0	0	0.7	0	64.8	7.4	0.23	0.5
Carob flour — *1 cup*	103	185	91.5	0	41	0.7	0.2	0.2	0.1	4.8	358	3	852	36	0.9	1	0	0.38	0	29.9	2	0.47	0.05
Corn flour																							
masa, enriched — *1 cup*	114	416	86.9	0	10.9	4.3	1.1	2	0.6	10.6	161	8	340	6	2	0	0	0.42	0	27.4	11.2	0.86	1.63
masa, enriched, yellow — *1 cup*	114	416	86.9	0	0	4.3	1.1	2	0.6	10.6	161	8	340	6	2	54	0	0.42	0	27.4	11.2	0.86	1.63
whole-grain, yellow — *1 cup*	117	422	89.9	0	15.7	4.5	1.2	2.1	0.6	8.1	8	3	369	6	2	55	0	0.43	0	29.3	2.2	0.09	0.29
Cornstarch — *¼ cup*	32	122	29.2	0	0.3	0	0	0	0	0.1	1	0	1	3	0	0	0	0	0	0	0	0	0
Peanut flour																							
defatted — *½ cup*	30	98	10.4	0	4.7	0.2	0.1	0	0	15.7	42	1	387	54	1.5	0	0	0.15	0	74.5	8.1	0.14	0.21
low-fat — *½ cup*	30	128	9.4	0	4.7	6.6	3.3	2.1	0.9	10.1	39	1	407	0	1.8	0	0	0.09	0	40	3.4	0.05	0.14
Pecan flour — *1 oz*	28	93	14.4	0	0	0.4	0.2	0.1	0	9	9	1	95	0	1.5	3	0	0.05	1	10.4	0.2	0.03	0.23
Potato flour — *1 cup*	179	628	143	0	10.9	1.4	0	0.6	0.4	14.3	59	31	2843	61	2.9	0	0	0.01	34	90.6	6.1	0.25	0.75
Rice flour																							
brown — *1 cup*	158	574	120.8	0	7.3	4.4	1.6	1.6	0.9	11.4	17	3	457	13	3.9	0	0	1.16	0	25.3	10	0.13	0.7
white — *1 cup*	158	578	126.6	0	3.8	2.2	0.7	0.6	0.6	9.4	16	1	120	0	1.3	0	0	0.69	0	6.3	4.1	0.03	0.22
Rye flour																							
dark — *1 cup*	128	415	88	0	28.9	3.4	0.4	1.5	0.4	18	72	8	934	1	7.2	0	0	0.57	0	76.8	5.5	0.32	0.4
light — *1 cup*	102	374	81.8	0	14.9	1.4	0.2	0.6	0.1	8.6	21	2	238	2	1.8	0	0	0.24	0	22.4	0.8	0.09	0.34
medium — *1 cup*	102	361	79	0	14.9	1.8	0.2	0.8	0.2	9.6	24	2	347	3	2	0	0	0.27	0	19.4	1.8	0.12	0.29
Semolina, enriched — *1 cup*	167	601	121.6	0	6.5	1.8	0.2	0.7	0.3	21.2	28	7	311	2	1.8	0	0	0.17	0	120.2	10	0.95	1.35

	Weight g	Calories	Carbohydrates g	Cholesterol mg	Dietary fiber g	Total fat g	Mono. fat g	Poly. fat g	Sat. fat g	Protein g	Calcium mg	Iron mg	Potassium mg	Sodium mg	Zinc mg	Vitamin A RE	Vitamin B_{12} mcg	Vitamin B_6 mg	Vitamin C mg	Folic acid mcg	Niacin mg	Riboflavin mg	Thiamin mg
Sesame flour																							
high-fat — *1 oz*	28	149	7.5	0	0	10.5	4	4.6	1.5	8.7	45	4	120	12	3	2	0	0.04	0	8.7	3.8	0.08	0.76
low-fat — *1 oz*	28	94	10.1	0	0	0.5	0.2	0.2	0.1	14.2	42	4	113	11	2.8	2	0	0.04	0	8.2	3.6	0.08	0.71
partially defatted — *1 oz*	28	108	10	0	0	3.4	1.2	1.4	0.5	11.4	43	4	120	12	3	2	0	0.04	0	8.2	3.6	0.08	0.72
Soy flour																							
defatted — *1 cup*	100	329	38.4	0	17.5	1.2	0.2	0.5	0.1	47	241	9	2384	20	2.5	4	0	0.57	0	305.4	2.6	0.25	0.7
full-fat, raw — *1 cup*	84	366	29.6	0	8.1	17.3	3.8	9.8	2.5	29	173	5	2113	11	3.3	10	0	0.39	0	289.8	3.6	0.97	0.49
full-fat, roasted — *1 cup*	85	375	28.6	0	8.2	18.6	4.1	10.5	2.7	29.6	160	5	1735	10	3	9	0	0.3	0	193.3	2.8	0.8	0.35
low-fat — *1 cup*	88	287	33.4	0	9	5.9	1.3	3.3	0.9	40.9	165	5	2262	16	1	4	0	0.46	0	360.8	1.9	0.25	0.33
Sunflower seed flour, partially defatted — *½ cup*	32	104	11.5	0	1.7	0.5	0.1	0.3	0	15.4	36	2	21	1	1.6	2	0	0.24	0	71.1	2.3	0.09	1.02
Triticale flour, whole-grain — *1 cup*	130	439	95.1	0	19	2.4	0.2	1	0.4	17.1	46	3	606	3	3.5	0	0	0.52	0	96.2	3.7	0.17	0.49
Wheat flour, white																							
all-purpose, enriched, bleached — *1 cup*	125	455	95.4	0	3.4	1.2	0.1	0.5	0.2	12.9	19	6	134	3	0.9	0	0	0.06	0	32.5	7.4	0.62	0.98
all-purpose, enriched, calcium-fortified — *1 cup*	125	455	95.4	0	3.4	1.2	0.1	0.5	0.2	12.9	315	6	134	3	0.9	0	0	0.06	0	32.5	7.4	0.62	0.98
all-purpose, enriched, unbleached — *1 cup*	125	455	95.4	0	3.4	1.2	0.1	0.5	0.2	12.9	19	6	134	3	0.9	0	0	0.06	0	32.5	7.4	0.62	0.98
all-purpose, self-rising, enriched — *1 cup*	125	443	92.8	0	3.4	1.2	0.1	0.5	0.2	12.4	423	6	155	1588	0.8	0	0	0.06	0	52.5	7.3	0.52	0.84
bread, enriched — *1 cup*	137	495	99.4	0	3.3	2.3	0.2	1	0.3	16.4	21	6	137	3	1.2	0	0	0.05	0	39.7	10.3	0.7	1.11
cake, enriched, unsifted — *1 cup*	137	496	106.9	0	2.3	1.2	0.1	0.5	0.2	11.2	19	10	144	3	0.8	0	0	0.05	0	26	9.3	0.59	1.22
Wheat flour, whole-wheat — *1 cup*	120	407	87.1	0	14.6	2.2	0.3	0.9	0.4	16.4	41	5	486	6	3.5	0	0	0.41	0	52.8	7.6	0.26	0.54
Fruits																							
Acerola (west indian cherry), fresh — *1 cup*	98	31	7.5	0	1.1	0.3	0.1	0.1	0.1	0.4	12	0	143	7	0.1	75	0	0.01	1644	13.7	0.4	0.06	0.02
Apple butter — *1 Tbsp*	18	33	8.6	0	0.2	0.1	0	0	0	0	1	0	16	0	0	0	0	0.01	0	0	0	0	0
Apples																							
canned, sweetened — *½ cup*	102	68	17	0	1.7	0.5	0	0.1	0.1	0.2	4	0	69	3	0	5	0	0.04	0	0.3	0.1	0.01	0.01

	Weight g	Calories	Carbohydrates g	Cholesterol mg	Dietary fiber g	Total fat g	Mono. fat g	Poly. fat g	Sat. fat g	Protein g	Calcium mg	Iron mg	Potassium mg	Sodium mg	Zinc mg	Vitamin A RE	Vitamin B_{12} mcg	Vitamin B_6 mg	Vitamin C mg	Folic acid mcg	Niacin mg	Riboflavin mg	Thiamin mg
dehydrated, sulfured — *1 cup*	60	208	56.1	0	7.4	0.3	0	0.1	0.1	0.8	11	1	384	74	0.2	5	0	0.17	1	0.6	0.4	0.08	0.03
dehydrated, sulfured, stewed — *1 cup*	193	143	38.4	0	5	0.2	0	0.1	0	0.5	8	1	262	50	0.1	4	0	0.1	1	0.2	0.3	0.06	0.02
dried, sulfured — *1 cup*	86	209	56.7	0	7.5	0.3	0	0.1	0	0.8	12	1	387	75	0.2	0	0	0.11	3	0	0.8	0.14	0
fresh — *1 medium*	138	81	21	0	3.7	0.5	0	0.1	0.1	0.3	10	0	159	0	0.1	7	0	0.07	8	3.9	0.1	0.02	0.02
fresh, peeled, slices — *1 cup*	110	63	16.3	0	2.1	0.3	0	0.1	0.1	0.2	4	0	124	0	0	4	0	0.05	4	0.4	0.1	0.01	0.02
fresh, peeled, slices, cooked — *1 cup*	171	91	23.3	0	4.1	0.6	0	0.2	0.1	0.4	9	0	150	2	0.1	7	0	0.08	0	1	0.2	0.02	0.03
fresh, slices — *1 cup*	110	65	16.8	0	3	0.4	0	0.1	0.1	0.2	8	0	127	0	0	6	0	0.05	6	3.1	0.1	0.02	0.02
frozen, cooked — *1 cup*	206	97	24.7	0	3.9	0.7	0	0.2	0.1	0.6	10	0	157	6	0.1	4	0	0.07	1	1.2	0.1	0.02	0.03
frozen, slices — *1 cup*	173	83	21.3	0	3.3	0.6	0	0.2	0.1	0.5	7	0	133	5	0.1	5	0	0.06	0	1.2	0.1	0.02	0.02
Applesauce																							
canned, sweetened — *½ cup*	128	97	25.4	0	1.5	0.2	0	0.1	0	0.2	5	0	78	4	0.1	1	0	0.03	2	0.8	0.2	0.04	0.02
canned, unsweetened — *1 cup*	244	105	27.5	0	2.9	0.1	0	0	0	0.4	7	0	183	5	0.1	7	0	0.06	3	1.5	0.5	0.06	0.03
canned, unsweetened w/ vitamin C — *½ cup*	122	52	13.8	0	1.5	0.1	0	0	0	0.2	4	0	92	2	0	4	0	0.03	26	0.7	0.2	0.03	0.02
Apricots																							
canned, extra heavy syrup — *½ cup*	123	118	30.6	0	2	0	0	0	0	0.7	10	1	155	16	0.1	181	0	0.07	3	2	0.4	0.03	0.02
canned, extra light syrup — *½ cup*	124	61	15.4	0	2	0.1	0.1	0	0	0.7	12	0	173	2	0.1	157	0	0.07	5	2.1	0.7	0.02	0.02
canned, heavy syrup — *½ cup*	129	107	27.7	0	2.1	0.1	0	0	0	0.7	12	0	181	5	0.1	159	0	0.07	4	2.2	0.5	0.03	0.03
canned, juice-pack — *½ cup*	122	59	15.1	0	2	0	0	0	0	0.8	15	0	201	5	0.1	206	0	0.07	6	2.1	0.4	0.02	0.02
canned, light syrup — *½ cup*	127	80	20.9	0	2	0.1	0	0	0	0.7	14	0	175	5	0.1	167	0	0.07	3	2.2	0.4	0.03	0.02
canned, water-pack — *½ cup*	122	33	7.8	0	1.9	0.2	0.1	0	0	0.9	10	0	233	4	0.1	157	0	0.07	4	2.1	0.5	0.03	0.03
dehydrated, sulfured — *½ cup*	60	190	49.3	0	0	0.4	0.2	0.1	0	2.9	36	4	1101	8	0.6	754	0	0.31	6	2.6	2.1	0.09	0.03
dehydrated, sulfured, stewed — *½ cup*	125	157	40.6	0	0	0.3	0.1	0.1	0	2.4	30	3	906	6	0.5	549	0	0.2	9	1.9	2	0.08	0.02
dried, sulfured — *1 cup*	130	309	80.3	0	11.7	0.6	0.3	0.1	0	4.7	59	6	1791	13	1	941	0	0.2	3	13.4	3.9	0.2	0.01
fresh — *3 apricots*	105	50	11.7	0	2.5	0.4	0.2	0.1	0	1.5	15	1	311	1	0.3	274	0	0.06	11	9	0.6	0.04	0.03

	Weight g	Calories	Carbohydrates g	Cholesterol mg	Dietary fiber g	Total fat g	Mono. fat g	Poly. fat g	Sat. fat g	Protein g	Calcium mg	Iron mg	Potassium mg	Sodium mg	Zinc mg	Vitamin A RE	Vitamin B_{12} mcg	Vitamin B_6 mg	Vitamin C mg	Folic acid mcg	Niacin mg	Riboflavin mg	Thiamin mg
fresh, halved — *½ cup*	77.5	37	8.6	0	1.9	0.3	0.1	0.1	0	1.1	11	0	229	1	0.2	202	0	0.04	8	6.7	0.5	0.03	0.02
frozen, sweetened — *1 cup*	242	237	60.7	0	5.3	0.2	0.1	0	0	1.7	24	2	554	10	0.2	407	0	0.15	22	4.1	1.9	0.1	0.05
Avocados, fresh																							
california — *1 medium*	173	306	12	0	8.5	30	19.4	3.5	4.5	3.7	19	2	1097	21	0.7	106	0	0.48	14	113.3	3.3	0.21	0.19
california, pureed — *¼ cup*	58	102	4	0	2.8	10	6.4	1.2	1.5	1.2	6	1	365	7	0.2	35	0	0.16	5	37.7	1.1	0.07	0.06
florida — *1 medium*	304	340	27.1	0	16.1	27	14.8	4.5	5.3	4.8	33	2	1484	15	1.3	185	0	0.85	24	162	5.8	0.37	0.33
florida, puréed — *¼ cup*	58	64	5.1	0	3	5.1	2.8	0.9	1	0.9	6	0	281	3	0.2	35	0	0.16	5	30.7	1.1	0.07	0.06
Bananas, fresh																							
slices — *1 cup*	150	138	35.1	0	3.6	0.7	0.1	0.1	0.3	1.5	9	0	594	2	0.2	12	0	0.87	14	28.7	0.8	0.15	0.07
whole — *1 medium*	118	109	27.6	0	2.8	0.6	0	0.1	0.2	1.2	7	0	467	1	0.2	9	0	0.68	11	22.5	0.6	0.12	0.05
Blackberries																							
canned, heavy syrup — *1 cup*	256	236	59.1	0	8.7	0.4	0	0.2	0	3.4	54	2	253	8	0.5	56	0	0.09	7	67.8	0.7	0.1	0.07
fresh — *1 cup*	144	75	18.4	0	7.6	0.6	0.1	0.3	0	1	46	1	282	0	0.4	23	0	0.08	30	49	0.6	0.06	0.04
frozen, unsweetened — *1 cup*	151	97	23.7	0	7.6	0.6	0.1	0.4	0	1.8	44	1	211	2	0.4	17	0	0.09	5	51.3	1.8	0.07	0.04
Blueberries																							
canned, heavy syrup — *½ cup*	128	113	28.2	0	1.9	0.4	0.1	0.2	0	0.8	6	0	51	4	0.1	8	0	0.05	1	2.1	0.1	0.07	0.04
fresh — *1 cup*	145	81	20.5	0	3.9	0.6	0.1	0.2	0	1	9	0	129	9	0.2	15	0	0.05	19	9.3	0.5	0.07	0.07
frozen, sweetened — *1 cup*	230	186	50.5	0	4.8	0.3	0	0.1	0	0.9	14	1	138	2	0.1	9	0	0.14	2	15.4	0.6	0.12	0.05
frozen, unsweetened — *1 cup*	155	79	18.9	0	4.2	1	0.1	0.4	0.1	0.7	12	0	84	2	0.1	12	0	0.09	4	10.4	0.8	0.06	0.05
Boysenberries																							
canned, heavy syrup — *½ cup*	128	113	28.6	0	3.3	0.2	0	0.1	0	1.3	23	1	115	4	0.2	5	0	0.05	8	44	0.3	0.04	0.03
frozen, unsweetened — *1 cup*	132	66	16.1	0	5.1	0.3	0	0.2	0	1.5	36	1	183	1	0.3	9	0	0.07	4	83.6	1	0.05	0.07
Breadfruit, fresh — *¼ small fruit*	96	99	26	0	4.7	0.2	0	0.1	0	1	16	1	470	2	0.1	4	0	0.1	28	13.4	0.9	0.03	0.11

	Weight g	Calories	Carbohydrates g	Cholesterol mg	Dietary fiber g	Total fat g	Mono. fat g	Poly. fat g	Sat. fat g	Protein g	Calcium mg	Iron mg	Potassium mg	Sodium mg	Zinc mg	Vitamin A RE	Vitamin B_{12} mcg	Vitamin B_6 mg	Vitamin C mg	Folic acid mcg	Niacin mg	Riboflavin mg	Thiamin mg
Cantaloupe, fresh																							
diced — *1 cup*	156	55	13	0	1.2	0.4	0	0.2	0.1	1.4	17	0	482	14	0.2	502	0	0.18	66	26.5	0.9	0.03	0.06
wedges — *1 wedge*	55	19	4.6	0	0.4	0.2	0	0.1	0	0.5	6	0	170	5	0.1	177	0	0.06	23	9.4	0.3	0.01	0.02
Cape gooseberries, fresh — *1 cup*	140	74	15.7	0	0	1	0	0	0	2.7	13	1	0	0	0	101	0	0	15	0	3.9	0.06	0.15
Carambola (starfruit), fresh — *1 medium*	91	30	7.1	0	2.5	0.3	0	0.2	0	0.5	4	0	148	2	0.1	45	0	0.09	19	12.7	0.4	0.02	0.03
Carissa (natal-plum), fresh, slices — *1 cup*	150	93	20.4	0	0	2	0	0	0	0.8	17	2	390	5	0	6	0	0	57	0	0.3	0.09	0.06
Casaba melon, fresh, cubes — *1 cup*	170	44	10.5	0	1.4	0.2	0	0.1	0	1.5	9	1	357	20	0.3	5	0	0.2	27	28.9	0.7	0.03	0.1
Cherimoya, fresh — *1 medium*	547	514	131.3	0	13.1	2.2	0	0	0	7.1	126	3	0	0	0	5	0	0	49	0	7.1	0.6	0.55
Cherries, sour, red																							
canned, extra heavy syrup — *½ cup*	131	149	38.1	0	1	0.1	0	0	0	0.9	13	2	119	9	0.1	91	0	0.06	2	9.7	0.2	0.05	0.02
canned, heavy syrup — *½ cup*	128	116	29.8	0	1.4	0.1	0	0	0	0.9	13	2	119	9	0.1	91	0	0.06	3	9.7	0.2	0.05	0.02
canned, light syrup — *½ cup*	126	95	24.3	0	1	0.1	0	0	0	0.9	13	2	120	9	0.1	92	0	0.06	3	9.7	0.2	0.05	0.02
canned, water-pack — *½ cup*	122	44	10.9	0	1.3	0.1	0	0	0	0.9	13	2	120	9	0.1	92	0	0.05	3	9.8	0.2	0.05	0.02
fresh — *1 cup*	155	78	18.9	0	2.5	0.5	0.1	0.1	0.1	1.6	25	0	268	5	0.2	198	0	0.07	16	11.6	0.6	0.06	0.05
frozen — *1 cup*	155	71	17.1	0	2.5	0.7	0.2	0.2	0.2	1.4	20	1	192	2	0.2	135	0	0.1	3	7	0.2	0.05	0.07
Cherries, sweet																							
canned, extra heavy syrup — *½ cup*	131	133	34.2	0	2	0.2	0.1	0.1	0	0.8	12	0	185	4	0.1	20	0	0.04	5	5.5	0.5	0.05	0.03
canned, heavy syrup — *½ cup*	127	105	26.9	0	1.9	0.2	0.1	0.1	0	0.8	11	0	183	4	0.1	19	0	0.04	5	5.3	0.5	0.05	0.03
canned, juice-pack — *½ cup*	125	68	17.3	0	1.9	0	0	0	0	1.1	18	1	164	4	0.1	16	0	0.04	3	5.3	0.5	0.03	0.02
canned, light syrup — *½ cup*	126	84	21.8	0	1.9	0.2	0.1	0.1	0	0.8	11	0	186	4	0.1	20	0	0.04	5	5.3	0.5	0.05	0.03
canned, water-pack — *½ cup*	124	57	14.6	0	1.9	0.2	0	0	0	1	14	0	162	1	0.1	20	0	0.04	3	5.2	0.5	0.05	0.03
fresh — *1 cup*	145	104	24	0	3.3	1.4	0.4	0.4	0.3	1.7	22	1	325	0	0.1	30	0	0.05	10	6.1	0.6	0.09	0.07
frozen, sweetened — *1 cup*	259	231	57.9	0	5.4	0.3	0.1	0.1	0.1	3	31	1	515	3	0.1	49	0	0.09	3	10.9	0.5	0.12	0.07
Crabapples, fresh, slices — *1 cup*	110	84	21.9	0	0	0.3	0	0.1	0.1	0.4	20	0	213	1	0	4	0	0	9	0	0.1	0.02	0.03

	Weight g	Calories	Carbohydrates g	Cholesterol mg	Dietary fiber g	Total fat g	Mono. fat g	Poly. fat g	Sat. fat g	Protein g	Calcium mg	Iron mg	Potassium mg	Sodium mg	Zinc mg	Vitamin A RE	Vitamin B_{12} mcg	Vitamin B_6 mg	Vitamin C mg	Folic acid mcg	Niacin mg	Riboflavin mg	Thiamin mg
Cranberries, fresh — *1 cup*	95	47	12	0	4	0.2	0	0.1	0	0.4	7	0	67	1	0.1	5	0	0.06	13	1.6	0.1	0.02	0.03
Currants, fresh																							
european black — *1 cup*	112	71	17.2	0	0	0.5	0.1	0.2	0	1.6	62	2	361	2	0.3	26	0	0.07	203	0	0.3	0.06	0.06
red & white — *1 cup*	112	63	15.5	0	4.8	0.2	0	0.1	0	1.6	37	1	308	1	0.3	13	0	0.08	46	9	0.1	0.06	0.04
zante — *¼ cup*	36	102	26.7	0	2.4	0.1	0	0.1	0	1.5	31	1	321	3	0.2	3	0	0.11	2	3.7	0.6	0.05	0.06
Custard-apple (bullock's-heart), fresh — *1 fruit*	0	0	0	0	0	0	0	0	0	0	0	0	0	0	0	0	0	0	0	0	0	0	0
Dates, domestic, fresh or dried — *5 dates*	42	114	30.5	0	3.1	0.2	0.1	0	0.1	0.8	13	0	271	1	0.1	2	0	0.08	0	5.2	0.9	0.04	0.04
Elderberries, fresh — *1 cup*	145	106	26.7	0	10.2	0.7	0.1	0.4	0	1	55	2	406	9	0.2	87	0	0.33	52	8.7	0.7	0.09	0.1
Feijoa, fresh, puréed — *1 cup*	243	119	25.8	0	0	1.9	0	0	0	3	41	0	377	7	0.1	0	0	0.12	49	92.3	0.7	0.08	0.02
Figs																							
canned, extra heavy syrup — *½ cup*	131	140	36.4	0	0	0.1	0	0.1	0	0.5	34	0	127	1	0.1	5	0	0	1	0	0.5	0.05	0.03
canned, heavy syrup — *½ cup*	130	114	29.7	0	2.8	0.1	0	0.1	0	0.5	35	0	128	1	0.1	5	0	0.09	1	2.6	0.6	0.05	0.03
canned, light syrup — *½ cup*	126	87	22.6	0	2.3	0.1	0	0.1	0	0.5	34	0	129	1	0.1	5	0	0.09	1	2.5	0.6	0.05	0.03
canned, water-pack — *½ cup*	124	66	17.3	0	2.7	0.1	0	0.1	0	0.5	35	0	128	1	0.1	5	0	0.09	1	2.5	0.6	0.05	0.03
dried — *¼ cup*	50	127	32.5	0	4.6	0.6	0.1	0.3	0.1	1.5	72	1	354	5	0.3	6	0	0.11	0	3.7	0.3	0.04	0.04
dried, stewed — *½ cup*	130	140	35.7	0	6.2	0.6	0.1	0.3	0.1	1.7	79	1	390	6	0.3	21	0	0.17	6	1.3	0.8	0.14	0.01
fresh — *2 medium*	100	74	19.2	0	3.3	0.3	0.1	0.1	0.1	0.8	35	0	232	1	0.2	14	0	0.11	2	6	0.4	0.05	0.06
Fruit cocktail																							
canned, extra heavy syrup — *½ cup*	130	114	29.8	0	1.4	0.1	0	0	0	0.5	8	0	112	8	0.1	26	0	0.06	2	3.4	0.5	0.02	0.02
canned, extra light syrup — *½ cup*	62	28	7.2	0	0.7	0	0	0	0	0.2	5	0	64	2	0	14	0	0.03	2	1.7	0.3	0.01	0.02
canned, heavy syrup — *½ cup*	124	91	23.4	0	1.2	0.1	0	0	0	0.5	7	0	109	7	0.1	25	0	0.06	2	3.2	0.5	0.02	0.02
canned, juice-pack — *½ cup*	119	55	14.1	0	1.2	0	0	0	0	0.5	9	0	113	5	0.1	37	0	0.06	3	3	0.5	0.02	0.01
canned, light syrup — *½ cup*	121	69	18.1	0	1.2	0.1	0	0	0	0.5	7	0	108	7	0.1	25	0	0.06	2	3.3	0.5	0.02	0.02
canned, water-pack — *½ cup*	119	38	10.1	0	1.2	0.1	0	0	0	0.5	6	0	111	5	0.1	30	0	0.06	2	3.2	0.4	0.01	0.02

	Weight g	Calories	Carbohydrates g	Cholesterol mg	Dietary fiber g	Total fat g	Mono. fat g	Poly. fat g	Sat. fat g	Protein g	Calcium mg	Iron mg	Potassium mg	Sodium mg	Zinc mg	Vitamin A RE	Vitamin B_{12} mcg	Vitamin B_6 mg	Vitamin C mg	Folic acid mcg	Niacin mg	Riboflavin mg	Thiamin mg
Gooseberries																							
canned, light syrup — *½ cup*	126	92	23.6	0	3	0.3	0	0.1	0	0.8	20	0	97	3	0.1	18	0	0.02	13	4	0.2	0.07	0.03
fresh — *1 cup*	150	66	15.3	0	6.5	0.9	0.1	0.5	0.1	1.3	38	0	297	2	0.2	44	0	0.12	42	9	0.5	0.05	0.06
Grapefruit																							
canned, juice-pack — *½ cup*	125	46	11.5	0	0.5	0.1	0	0	0	0.9	19	0	210	9	0.1	0	0	0.02	42	11	0.3	0.02	0.04
canned, light syrup — *½ cup*	127	76	19.6	0	0.5	0.1	0	0	0	0.7	18	1	164	3	0.1	0	0	0.03	27	10.8	0.3	0.03	0.05
canned, water-pack — *½ cup*	122	44	11.2	0	0.5	0.1	0	0	0	0.7	18	1	161	2	0.1	0	0	0.02	27	10.7	0.3	0.03	0.05
fresh, pink & red — *½ grapefruit*	123	37	9.4	0	0	0.1	0	0	0	0.7	14	0	159	0	0.1	32	0	0.05	47	15	0.2	0.02	0.04
fresh, white — *½ grapefruit*	59	19	5	0	0.6	0.1	0	0	0	0.4	7	0	87	0	0	1	0	0.03	20	5.9	0.2	0.01	0.02
Grapes																							
canned, thompson seedless, heavy syrup — *½ cup*	128	93	25.2	0	0.5	0.1	0	0	0	0.6	13	1	132	6	0.1	8	0	0.08	1	3.3	0.2	0.03	0.04
canned, thompson seedless, water-pack — *½ cup*	123	49	12.6	0	1.2	0.1	0	0	0	0.6	12	1	131	7	0.1	9	0	0.08	1	3.2	0.2	0.03	0.04
fresh, american type (slip skin) — *1 cup*	92	58	15.8	0	0.9	0.3	0	0.1	0.1	0.6	13	0	176	2	0	9	0	0.1	4	3.6	0.3	0.05	0.08
fresh, european type (adherent skin), seedless — *1 cup*	160	114	28.4	0	1.6	0.9	0	0.3	0.3	1.1	18	0	296	3	0.1	11	0	0.18	17	6.2	0.5	0.09	0.15
Guavas, fresh																							
common — *1 medium*	90	46	10.7	0	4.9	0.5	0	0.2	0.2	0.7	18	0	256	3	0.2	71	0	0.13	165	12.6	1.1	0.05	0.05
strawberry — *1 medium*	6	4	1	0	0	0	0	0	0	0	1	0	18	2	0	1	0	0	2	0	0	0	0
Honeydew melon, fresh, diced — *1 cup*	170	60	15.6	0	1	0.2	0	0.1	0	0.8	10	0	461	17	0.1	7	0	0.1	42	10.2	1	0.03	0.13
Jackfruit, fresh, slices — *1 cup*	165	155	39.6	0	2.6	0.5	0.1	0.1	0.1	2.4	56	1	500	5	0.7	50	0	0.18	11	23.1	0.7	0.18	0.05
Java-plum (jambolan), fresh — *3 plums*	9	5	1.4	0	0	0	0	0	0	0.1	2	0	7	1	0	0	0	0	1	0	0	0	0
Jujube, fresh — *3 ½ oz*	100	79	20.2	0	0	0.2	0	0	0	1.2	21	0	250	3	0.1	4	0	0.08	69	0	0.9	0.04	0.02
Kiwi fruit, fresh, skinned — *1 medium*	76	46	11.3	0	2.6	0.3	0	0.2	0	0.8	20	0	252	4	0.1	14	0	0.07	74	28.9	0.4	0.04	0.02
Kumquats, fresh — *5 kumquats*	95	60	15.6	0	6.3	0.1	0	0	0	0.9	42	0	185	6	0.1	29	0	0.06	36	15.2	0.5	0.1	0.08
Lemons, fresh — *1 medium*	58	17	5.4	0	1.6	0.2	0	0.1	0	0.6	15	0	80	1	0	2	0	0.05	31	6.2	0.1	0.01	0.02

	Weight g	Calories	Carbohydrates g	Cholesterol mg	Dietary fiber g	Total fat g	Mono. fat g	Poly. fat g	Sat. fat g	Protein g	Calcium mg	Iron mg	Potassium mg	Sodium mg	Zinc mg	Vitamin A RE	Vitamin B_{12} mcg	Vitamin B_6 mg	Vitamin C mg	Folic acid mcg	Niacin mg	Riboflavin mg	Thiamin mg
Limes, fresh — *1 medium*	67	20	7.1	0	1.9	0.1	0	0	0	0.5	22	0	68	1	0.1	1	0	0.03	19	5.5	0.1	0.01	0.02
Litchis																							
dried — *5 medium*	13	35	8.8	0	0.6	0.2	0	0	0	0.5	4	0	139	0	0	0	0	0.01	23	1.5	0.4	0.07	0
fresh — *1 cup*	190	125	31.4	0	2.5	0.8	0.2	0.3	0.2	1.6	10	1	325	2	0.1	0	0	0.19	136	26.6	1.1	0.12	0.02
Loganberries, frozen — *1 cup*	147	81	19.1	0	7.2	0.5	0	0.3	0	2.2	38	1	213	1	0.5	6	0	0.1	22	37.8	1.2	0.05	0.07
Longans																							
dried — *3 ½ oz*	100	286	74	0	0	0.4	0	0	0	4.9	45	5	658	48	0.2	0	0	0	28	0	1	0.5	0.04
fresh — *1 medium*	3	2	0.5	0	0	0	0	0	0	0	0	0	9	0	0	0	0	0	3	0	0	0	0
Loquats, fresh — *1 medium*	16	8	1.9	0	0.3	0	0	0	0	0.1	3	0	43	0	0	24	0	0.02	0	2.2	0	0	0
Mammy-apple (mamey), fresh — *1 fruit*	846	431	105.8	0	25.4	4.2	1.7	0.7	1.2	4.2	93	6	398	127	0.8	195	0	0.85	118	118.4	3.4	0.34	0.17
Mangos, fresh, slices — *1 cup*	165	107	28.1	0	3	0.4	0.2	0.1	0.1	0.8	17	0	257	3	0.1	642	0	0.22	46	23.1	1	0.09	0.1
Mulberries, fresh — *1 cup*	140	60	13.7	0	2.4	0.5	0.1	0.3	0	2	55	3	272	14	0.2	4	0	0.07	51	8.4	0.9	0.14	0.04
Nectarines, fresh — *1 nectarine*	136	67	16	0	2.2	0.6	0.2	0.3	0.1	1.3	7	0	288	0	0.1	101	0	0.03	7	5	1.3	0.06	0.02
Oheloberries, fresh — *1 cup*	140	39	9.6	0	0	0.3	0	0	0	0.5	10	0	53	1	0	116	0	0	8	0	0.4	0.05	0.02
Oranges, fresh																							
navel — *1 orange*	140	64	16.3	0	3.4	0.1	0	0	0	1.4	56	0	249	1	0.1	25	0	0.1	80	47.2	0.4	0.06	0.12
valencia — *1 orange*	121	59	14.4	0	3	0.4	0.1	0.1	0	1.3	48	0	217	0	0.1	28	0	0.08	59	46.7	0.3	0.05	0.11
Papayas, fresh, cubes — *1 cup*	140	55	13.7	0	2.5	0.2	0.1	0	0.1	0.9	34	0	360	4	0.1	39	0	0.03	87	53.2	0.5	0.04	0.04
Passion-fruit, purple, fresh — *1 fruit*	18	17	4.2	0	1.9	0.1	0	0.1	0	0.4	2	0	63	5	0	13	0	0.02	5	2.5	0.3	0.02	0
Peaches																							
canned, extra heavy syrup — *½ cup*	131	126	34.1	0	1.3	0	0	0	0	0.6	4	0	109	10	0.1	17	0	0.02	2	4.1	0.7	0.03	0.01
canned, extra light syrup — *½ cup*	0	0	0	0	0	0	0	0	0	0	0	0	0	0	0	0	0	0	0	0	0	0	0
canned, heavy syrup — *½ cup*	131	97	26.1	0	1.7	0.1	0	0.1	0	0.6	4	0	121	8	0.1	43	0	0.02	4	4.2	0.8	0.03	0.01
canned, juice-pack — *½ cup*	125	55	14.5	0	1.6	0	0	0	0	0.8	8	0	160	5	0.1	48	0	0.02	5	4.3	0.7	0.02	0.01

	Weight g	Calories	Carbohydrates g	Cholesterol mg	Dietary fiber g	Total fat g	Mono. fat g	Poly. fat g	Sat. fat g	Protein g	Calcium mg	Iron mg	Potassium mg	Sodium mg	Zinc mg	Vitamin A RE	Vitamin B_{12} mcg	Vitamin B_6 mg	Vitamin C mg	Folic acid mcg	Niacin mg	Riboflavin mg	Thiamin mg
canned, light syrup — *½ cup*	126	68	18.3	0	1.6	0	0	0	0	0.6	4	0	122	6	0.1	44	0	0.02	3	4.1	0.7	0.03	0.01
canned, spiced, heavy syrup — *1 cup*	242	182	48.6	0	3.1	0.2	0.1	0.1	0	1	15	1	206	10	0.2	77	0	0.05	13	7.7	1.3	0.08	0.03
canned, water-pack — *1 cup*	244	59	14.9	0	3.2	0.1	0.1	0.1	0	1.1	5	1	242	7	0.2	129	0	0.05	7	8.3	1.3	0.05	0.02
dehydrated, sulfured — *1 cup*	116	377	96.5	0	0	1.2	0.4	0.6	0.1	5.7	44	6	1567	12	0.9	165	0	0.18	12	7.7	5.6	0.13	0.05
dehydrated, sulfured, stewed — *1 cup*	242	322	82.6	0	0	1	0.4	0.5	0.1	4.9	39	5	1341	10	0.8	97	0	0.13	16	6.8	4.9	0.15	0.02
dried, sulfured — *¼ cup*	40	96	24.5	0	3.3	0.3	0.1	0.1	0	1.4	11	2	398	3	0.2	86	0	0.03	2	0.1	1.8	0.08	0
fresh — *1 medium*	98	42	10.9	0	2	0.1	0	0	0	0.7	5	0	193	0	0.1	53	0	0.02	6	3.3	1	0.04	0.02
frozen, sweetened — *1 cup*	250	235	60	0	4.5	0.3	0.1	0.2	0	1.6	8	1	325	15	0.1	70	0	0.05	236	8	1.6	0.09	0.03
Pears																							
canned, extra heavy syrup — *½ cup*	133	129	33.6	0	2.1	0.2	0	0	0	0.3	7	0	85	7	0.1	0	0	0.02	1	1.6	0.3	0.03	0.01
canned, extra light syrup — *½ cup*	124	58	15.1	0	2	0.1	0	0	0	0.4	9	0	56	2	0.1	0	0	0.02	2	1.5	0.5	0.02	0.01
canned, heavy syrup — *½ cup*	133	98	25.5	0	2.1	0.2	0	0	0	0.3	7	0	86	7	0.1	0	0	0.02	1	1.6	0.3	0.03	0.01
canned, juice-pack — *½ cup*	124	62	16	0	2	0.1	0	0	0	0.4	11	0	119	5	0.1	1	0	0.02	2	1.5	0.2	0.01	0.01
canned, light syrup — *½ cup*	126	72	19	0	2	0	0	0	0	0.2	6	0	83	6	0.1	0	0	0.02	1	1.5	0.2	0.02	0.01
canned, water-pack — *½cup*	122	35	9.5	0	2	0	0	0	0	0.2	5	0	65	2	0.1	0	0	0.02	1	1.5	0.1	0.01	0.01
dried, sulfured — *¼ cup*	45	118	31.4	0	3.4	0.3	0.1	0.1	0	0.8	15	1	240	3	0.2	0	0	0.03	3	0	0.6	0.07	0
fresh — *1 medium*	166	98	25.1	0	4	0.7	0.1	0.2	0	0.6	18	0	208	0	0.2	3	0	0.03	7	12.1	0.2	0.07	0.03
Pears, asian, fresh — *1 medium*	275	116	29.3	0	9.9	0.6	0.1	0.2	0	1.4	11	0	333	0	0.1	0	0	0.06	10	22	0.6	0.03	0.02
Persimmons, japanese																							
dried — *1 persimmon*	34	93	25	0	4.9	0.2	0	0	0	0.5	9	0	273	1	0.1	19	0	0	0	0	0.1	0.01	0
fresh — *1 persimmon*	168	118	31.2	0	6	0.3	0.1	0.1	0	1	13	0	270	2	0.2	365	0	0.17	13	12.6	0.2	0.03	0.05
Pineapple																							
canned, extra heavy syrup — *½ cup*	130	108	28	0	1	0.1	0	0	0	0.4	18	0	133	1	0.1	1	0	0.1	9	6	0.4	0.03	0.12
canned, heavy syrup — *½ cup*	127	99	25.7	0	1	0.1	0	0.1	0	0.4	18	0	132	1	0.2	1	0	0.09	9	5.8	0.4	0.03	0.11

	Weight g	Calories	Carbohydrates g	Cholesterol mg	Dietary fiber g	Total fat g	Mono. fat g	Poly. fat g	Sat. fat g	Protein g	Calcium mg	Iron mg	Potassium mg	Sodium mg	Zinc mg	Vitamin A RE	Vitamin B_{12} mcg	Vitamin B_6 mg	Vitamin C mg	Folic acid mcg	Niacin mg	Riboflavin mg	Thiamin mg
canned, juice-pack — *1 cup*	249	149	39.1	0	2	0.2	0	0.1	0	1	35	1	304	2	0.2	10	0	0.18	24	12	0.7	0.05	0.24
canned, light syrup — *½ cup*	126	66	16.9	0	1	0.2	0	0.1	0	0.5	18	0	132	1	0.2	1	0	0.09	9	5.9	0.4	0.03	0.11
canned, water-pack — *1 cup*	246	79	20.4	0	2	0.2	0	0.1	0	1.1	37	1	312	2	0.3	5	0	0.18	19	11.8	0.7	0.06	0.23
fresh, diced — *1 cup*	155	76	19.2	0	1.9	0.7	0.1	0.2	0	0.6	11	1	175	2	0.1	3	0	0.13	24	16.4	0.7	0.06	0.14
frozen, sweetened — *1 cup*	245	208	54.4	0	2.7	0.2	0	0.1	0	1	22	1	245	5	0.3	7	0	0.18	20	26	0.7	0.07	0.25
Pitanga (surinam-cherry), fresh — *1 cup*	173	57	13	0	0	0.7	0	0	0	1.4	16	0	178	5	0	260	0	0	45	0	0.5	0.07	0.05
Plantains																							
cooked, slices — *1 cup*	154	179	48	0	3.5	0.3	0	0.1	0.1	1.2	3	1	716	8	0.2	140	0	0.37	17	40	1.2	0.08	0.07
fresh, slices — *1 cup*	148	181	47.2	0	3.4	0.5	0	0.1	0.2	1.9	4	1	739	6	0.2	167	0	0.44	27	32.6	1	0.08	0.08
Plums																							
canned, extra heavy syrup — *1 cup*	261	264	68.7	0	2.6	0.3	0.2	0.1	0	0.9	23	2	232	50	0.2	65	0	0.07	1	6.5	0.7	0.1	0.04
canned, heavy syrup — *½ cup*	129	115	30	0	1.3	0.1	0.1	0	0	0.5	12	1	117	25	0.1	34	0	0.03	1	3.2	0.4	0.05	0.02
canned, juice-pack — *½ cup*	126	73	19.1	0	1.3	0	0	0	0	0.6	13	0	194	1	0.1	127	0	0.03	4	3.3	0.6	0.07	0.03
canned, light syrup — *½ cup*	126	79	20.5	0	1.3	0.1	0.1	0	0	0.5	11	1	117	25	0.1	33	0	0.03	1	3.3	0.4	0.05	0.02
canned, water-pack — *½ cup*	125	51	13.7	0	1.2	0	0	0	0	0.5	9	0	157	1	0.1	113	0	0.03	3	3.2	0.5	0.05	0.03
fresh — *1 fruit*	66	36	8.6	0	1	0.4	0.3	0.1	0	0.5	3	0	114	0	0.1	21	0	0.05	6	1.5	0.3	0.06	0.03
Pomegranates, fresh — *1 pomegranate*	154	105	26.4	0	0.9	0.5	0.1	0.1	0.1	1.5	5	0	399	5	0.2	0	0	0.16	9	9.2	0.5	0.05	0.05
Prickly pears, fresh — *1 cup*	149	61	14.3	0	5.4	0.8	0.1	0.3	0.1	1.1	83	0	328	7	0.2	7	0	0.09	21	8.9	0.7	0.09	0.02
Prunes																							
canned, heavy syrup — *1 cup*	117	123	32.5	0	4.4	0.2	0.2	0.1	0	1	20	0	264	4	0.2	94	0	0.24	3	0.1	1	0.14	0.04
dehydrated — *1 cup*	132	447	117.6	0	0	1	0.6	0.2	0.1	4.9	95	5	1397	7	1	232	0	0.98	0	2.5	4	0.22	0.16
dehydrated, stewed — *1 cup*	280	316	83.2	0	0	0.7	0.5	0.1	0.1	3.4	67	3	988	6	0.7	146	0	0.53	0	0.6	2.8	0.08	0.13
dried — *¼ cup*	43	102	26.7	0	3	0.2	0.1	0	0	1.1	22	1	317	2	0.2	85	0	0.11	1	1.6	0.8	0.07	0.03
dried, stewed — *1 cup*	248	265	69.6	0	16.4	0.6	0.4	0.1	0	2.9	57	3	828	5	0.6	77	0	0.54	7	0.3	1.8	0.25	0.06

	Weight g	Calories	Carbohydrates g	Cholesterol mg	Dietary fiber g	Total fat g	Mono. fat g	Poly. fat g	Sat. fat g	Protein g	Calcium mg	Iron mg	Potassium mg	Sodium mg	Zinc mg	Vitamin A RE	Vitamin B_{12} mcg	Vitamin B_6 mg	Vitamin C mg	Folic acid mcg	Niacin mg	Riboflavin mg	Thiamin mg
dried, stewed w/ sugar — *1 cup*	248	308	81.5	0	9.4	0.5	0.4	0.1	0	2.7	52	3	774	5	0.5	72	0	0.5	7	0.3	1.7	0.23	0.05
Pummelo, fresh, sectioned — *1 cup*	190	72	18.3	0	1.9	0.1	0	0	0	1.4	8	0	410	2	0.2	0	0	0.07	116	0	0.4	0.05	0.06
Quinces, fresh — *1 quince*	92	52	14.1	0	1.7	0.1	0	0	0	0.4	10	1	181	4	0	4	0	0.04	14	2.8	0.2	0.03	0.02
Raisins																							
golden seedless — *¼ cup*	41	125	32.8	0	1.7	0.2	0	0.1	0.1	1.4	22	1	308	5	0.1	2	0	0.13	1	1.4	0.5	0.08	0
seedless — *¼ cup*	41	124	32.6	0	1.7	0.2	0	0.1	0.1	1.3	20	1	310	5	0.1	0	0	0.1	1	1.4	0.3	0.04	0.06
Raspberries																							
canned, red, heavy syrup — *½ cup*	128	116	29.9	0	4.2	0.2	0	0.1	0	1.1	14	1	120	4	0.2	4	0	0.05	11	13.4	0.6	0.04	0.03
fresh — *1 cup*	123	60	14.2	0	8.4	0.7	0.1	0.4	0	1.1	27	1	187	0	0.6	16	0	0.07	31	32	1.1	0.11	0.04
frozen, sweetened — *1 cup*	250	258	65.4	0	11	0.4	0	0.2	0	1.8	38	2	285	3	0.5	15	0	0.09	41	65	0.6	0.11	0.05
Rhubarb																							
fresh, diced — *1 cup*	122	26	5.5	0	2.2	0.2	0	0.1	0.1	1.1	105	0	351	5	0.1	12	0	0.03	10	8.7	0.4	0.04	0.02
frozen, cooked w/ sugar — *1 cup*	240	278	74.9	0	4.8	0.1	0	0.1	0	0.9	348	1	230	2	0.2	17	0	0.05	8	12.7	0.5	0.06	0.04
frozen, diced, uncooked — *1 cup*	137	29	7	0	2.5	0.2	0	0.1	0	0.8	266	0	148	3	0.1	15	0	0.03	7	11.2	0.3	0.04	0.04
Roselle, fresh — *1 cup*	57	28	6.4	0	0	0.4	0	0	0	0.5	123	1	119	3	0	17	0	0	7	0	0.2	0.02	0.01
Sapodilla, fresh — *1 sapodilla*	170	141	33.9	0	9	1.9	0.9	0	0.3	0.7	36	1	328	20	0.2	10	0	0.06	25	23.8	0.3	0.03	0
Sapotes, fresh — *1 sapote*	225	302	76	0	5.9	1.4	0	0	0	4.8	88	2	774	23	0	92	0	0	45	0	4.1	0.05	0.02
Soursop, fresh — *1 soursop*	625	413	105.3	0	20.6	1.9	0.6	0.4	0.3	6.3	88	4	1738	88	0.6	0	0	0.37	129	87.5	5.6	0.31	0.44
Strawberries																							
canned, heavy syrup — *½ cup*	127	117	29.9	0	2.2	0.3	0	0.2	0	0.7	17	1	109	5	0.1	4	0	0.06	40	35.6	0.1	0.04	0.03
fresh, halves — *1 cup*	152	46	10.7	0	3.5	0.6	0.1	0.3	0	0.9	21	1	252	2	0.2	5	0	0.09	86	26.9	0.3	0.1	0.03
frozen — *1 cup*	221	77	20.2	0	4.6	0.2	0	0.1	0	1	35	2	327	4	0.3	9	0	0.06	91	37.1	1	0.08	0.05
frozen, sweetened, slices — *1 cup*	255	245	66.1	0	4.8	0.3	0	0.2	0	1.4	28	2	250	8	0.2	5	0	0.08	106	38	1	0.13	0.04
frozen, sweetened, whole — *1 cup*	255	199	53.6	0	4.8	0.4	0	0.2	0	1.3	28	1	250	3	0.1	8	0	0.07	101	9.7	0.7	0.2	0.04

	Weight g	Calories	Carbohydrates g	Cholesterol mg	Dietary fiber g	Total fat g	Mono. fat g	Poly. fat g	Sat. fat g	Protein g	Calcium mg	Iron mg	Potassium mg	Sodium mg	Zinc mg	Vitamin A RE	Vitamin B_{12} mcg	Vitamin B6 mg	Vitamin C mg	Folic acid mcg	Niacin mg	Riboflavin mg	Thiamin mg
Sugar-apples, fresh — *1 fruit*	155	146	36.6	0	6.8	0.4	0.2	0.1	0.1	3.2	37	1	383	14	0.2	2	0	0.31	56	21.7	1.4	0.18	0.17
Tamarind, fresh — *1 tamarind*	2	5	1.3	0	0.1	0	0	0	0	0.1	1	0	13	1	0	0	0	0	0	0.3	0	0	0.01
Tangerines																							
canned, juice-pack — *½ cup*	125	46	11.9	0	0.9	0	0	0	0	0.8	14	0	166	6	0.6	106	0	0.05	43	5.7	0.6	0.04	0.1
canned, light syrup — *½ cup*	126	77	20.4	0	0.9	0.1	0	0	0	0.6	9	0	98	8	0.3	106	0	0.05	25	5.8	0.6	0.06	0.07
fresh — *1 medium*	195	86	21.8	0	4.5	0.4	0.1	0.1	0	1.2	27	0	306	2	0.5	179	0	0.13	60	39.8	0.3	0.04	0.2
Watermelon, fresh, diced — *1 cup*	152	49	10.9	0	0.8	0.7	0.2	0.2	0.1	0.9	12	0	176	3	0.1	56	0	0.22	15	3.3	0.3	0.03	0.12

Game

	Weight g	Calories	Carbohydrates g	Cholesterol mg	Dietary fiber g	Total fat g	Mono. fat g	Poly. fat g	Sat. fat g	Protein g	Calcium mg	Iron mg	Potassium mg	Sodium mg	Zinc mg	Vitamin A RE	Vitamin B_{12} mcg	Vitamin B6 mg	Vitamin C mg	Folic acid mcg	Niacin mg	Riboflavin mg	Thiamin mg
Antelope, roasted — *3 ½ oz*	100	150	0	126	0	2.7	0.6	0.6	1	29.5	4	4	372	54	1.7	0	0	0	0	0	0	0.73	0.26
Bear, simmered — *3 ½ oz*	100	259	0	98	0	13.4	5.7	2.4	3.5	32.4	5	11	263	71	10.3	0	2.5	0.29	0	6	3.4	0.82	0.1
Beaver, roasted — *3 ½ oz*	100	212	0	117	0	7	1.9	1.4	2.1	34.9	22	10	403	59	2.3	0	8.3	0.47	3	11	2.2	0.31	0.05
Beefalo, roasted — *3 ½ oz*	100	188	0	58	0	6.3	2.7	0.2	2.7	30.7	24	3	459	82	6.4	0	2.6	0	9	18	4.9	0.11	0.03
Bison, roasted — *3 ½ oz*	100	143	0	82	0	2.4	1	0.2	0.9	28.4	8	3	361	57	3.7	0	2.9	0.4	0	8	3.7	0.27	0.1
Caribou, roasted — *3 ½ oz*	100	167	0	109	0	4.4	1.3	0.6	1.7	29.8	22	6	310	60	5.3	0	6.6	0.32	3	5	5.8	0.9	0.25
Deer, roasted — *3 ½ oz*	100	158	0	112	0	3.2	0.9	0.6	1.3	30.2	7	4	335	54	2.8	0	0	0	0	0	6.7	0.6	0.18
Elk, roasted — *3 ½ oz*	100	146	0	73	0	1.9	0.5	0.4	0.7	30.2	5	4	328	61	3.2	0	0	0	0	0	0	0	0
Goat, roasted — *3 ½ oz*	100	143	0	75	0	3	1.4	0.2	0.9	27.1	17	4	405	86	5.3	0	1.2	0	0	5	4	0.61	0.09
Moose, roasted — *3 ½ oz*	100	134	0	78	0	1	0.2	0.3	0.3	29.3	6	4	334	69	3.7	0	6.3	0.37	5	4	5.3	0.34	0.05
Muskrat, roasted — *3 ½ oz*	100	234	0	121	0	11.7	0	0	0	30.1	36	7	320	95	2.3	0	8.3	0.47	7	11	7.2	0.71	0.08
Opossum, roasted — *3 ½ oz*	100	221	0	129	0	10.2	3.8	3	1.2	30.2	17	5	438	58	2.3	0	8.3	0.47	0	10	8.4	0.37	0.1
Pheasant																							
breast, raw — *3 ½ oz*	100	133	0	58	0	3.3	1	0.6	1.1	24.4	3	1	242	33	0.6	44	0.8	0.74	6	4	8.6	0.12	0.08
leg, raw — *3 ½ oz*	100	134	0	80	0	4.3	1.4	0.7	1.5	22.2	29	2	296	45	1.5	58	0.8	0.74	6	10	3.7	0.21	0.07
meat & skin, raw — *3 ½ oz*	100	181	0	71	0	9.3	4.3	1.2	2.7	22.7	12	1	243	40	1	53	0.8	0.66	5	6	6.4	0.14	0.07

	Weight g	Calories	Carbohydrates g	Cholesterol mg	Dietary fiber g	Total fat g	Mono. fat g	Poly. fat g	Sat. fat g	Protein g	Calcium mg	Iron mg	Potassium mg	Sodium mg	Zinc mg	Vitamin A RE	Vitamin B_{12} mcg	Vitamin B_6 mg	Vitamin C mg	Folic acid mcg	Niacin mg	Riboflavin mg	Thiamin mg
meat only, raw — *3 ½ oz*	100	133	0	66	0	3.6	1.2	0.6	1.2	23.6	13	1	262	37	1	49	0.8	0.74	6	6	6.8	0.15	0.08
Quail																							
breast, raw — *3 ½ oz*	100	123	0	58	0	3	0.8	0.8	0.9	22.6	10	2	260	55	2.7	11	0.5	0.53	5	4	8.2	0.24	0.24
meat & skin, raw — *3 ½ oz*	100	192	0	76	0	12.1	4.2	3	3.4	19.6	13	4	216	53	2.4	73	0.4	0.6	6	8	7.5	0.26	0.24
meat only, raw — *3 ½ oz*	100	134	0	70	0	4.5	1.3	1.2	1.3	21.8	13	5	237	51	2.7	17	0.5	0.53	7	7	8.2	0.29	0.28
Rabbit, domesticated																							
roasted — *3 ½ oz*	100	197	0	82	0	8.1	2.2	1.6	2.4	29.1	19	2	383	47	2.3	0	8.3	0.47	0	11	8.4	0.21	0.09
stewed — *3 ½ oz*	100	206	0	86	0	8.4	2.3	1.6	2.5	30.4	20	2	300	37	2.4	0	6.5	0.34	0	9	7.2	0.17	0.06
Rabbit, wild, stewed — *3 ½ oz*	100	173	0	123	0	3.5	1	0.7	1.1	33	18	5	343	45	2.4	0	6.5	0.34	0	8	6.4	0.07	0.02
Raccoon, roasted — *3 ½ oz*	100	255	0	97	0	14.5	5.2	2.1	4.1	29.2	14	7	398	79	2.3	0	8.3	0.47	0	11	4.7	0.52	0.59
Squab (pigeon)																							
light meat, raw — *3 ½ oz*	100	134	0	90	0	4.5	1.6	1	1.2	21.8	10	2	260	55	2.7	17	0.5	0.53	5	4	7.3	0.24	0.24
meat & skin, raw — *3 ½ oz*	100	294	0	95	0	23.8	9.7	3.1	8.4	18.5	12	4	199	54	2.2	73	0.4	0.41	5	6	6	0.22	0.21
meat only, raw — *3 ½ oz*	100	142	0	90	0	7.5	2.7	1.6	2	17.5	13	5	237	51	2.7	28	0.5	0.53	7	7	6.9	0.29	0.28
Squirrel, roasted — *3 ½ oz*	100	173	0	121	0	4.7	1.3	1.5	0.9	30.8	3	7	352	119	1.8	0	6.5	0.37	0	9	4.6	0.29	0.06
Water buffalo, roasted — *3 ½ oz*	100	131	0	61	0	1.8	0.6	0.4	0.6	26.8	15	2	313	56	2.5	0	1.8	0.46	0	9	6.3	0.25	0.03
Wild boar, roasted — *3 ½ oz*	100	160	0	77	0	4.4	1.7	0.6	1.3	28.3	16	1	396	60	3	0	0.7	0.42	0	6	4.2	0.14	0.31

Goose

	Weight g	Calories	Carbohydrates g	Cholesterol mg	Dietary fiber g	Total fat g	Mono. fat g	Poly. fat g	Sat. fat g	Protein g	Calcium mg	Iron mg	Potassium mg	Sodium mg	Zinc mg	Vitamin A RE	Vitamin B_{12} mcg	Vitamin B_6 mg	Vitamin C mg	Folic acid mcg	Niacin mg	Riboflavin mg	Thiamin mg
Goose liver																							
Paté de foie gras, canned, smoked — *3 ½ oz*	100	462	4.7	150	0	43.8	25.6	0.8	14.5	11.4	70	6	138	697	0.9	1000	9.4	0.06	2	60	2.5	0.3	0.09
raw — *3 ½ oz*	100	133	6.3	515	0	4.3	0.8	0.3	1.6	16.4	43	31	230	140	3.1	9285	54	0.76	5	738	6.5	0.89	0.56
Meat & skin, roasted — *3 ½ oz*	100	305	0	91	0	21.9	10.3	2.5	6.9	25.2	13	3	329	70	2.6	21	0.4	0.37	0	2	4.2	0.32	0.08
Meat only, roasted — *3 ½ oz*	100	238	0	96	0	12.7	4.3	1.5	4.6	29	14	3	388	76	3.2	12	0.5	0.47	0	12	4.1	0.39	0.09

Foods, General

	Weight g	Calories	Carbohydrates g	Cholesterol mg	Dietary fiber g	Total fat g	Mono. fat g	Poly. fat g	Sat. fat g	Protein g	Calcium mg	Iron mg	Potassium mg	Sodium mg	Zinc mg	Vitamin A RE	Vitamin B_{12} mcg	Vitamin B_6 mg	Vitamin C mg	Folic acid mcg	Niacin mg	Riboflavin mg	Thiamin mg
Grains																							
Amaranth, dry — *½ cup*	98	365	64.5	0	14.8	6.3	1.4	2.8	1.6	14.1	149	7	357	20	3.1	0	0	0.22	4	47.8	1.3	0.2	0.08
Barley																							
dry, whole — *½ cup*	92	326	67.6	0	15.9	2.1	0.3	1	0.4	11.5	30	3	416	11	2.5	2	0	0.29	0	17.5	4.2	0.26	0.59
pearled, cooked — *1 cup*	157	193	44.3	0	6	0.7	0.1	0.3	0.1	3.5	17	2	146	5	1.3	2	0	0.18	0	25.1	3.2	0.1	0.13
pearled, dry — *½ cup*	100	352	77.7	0	15.6	1.2	0.1	0.6	0.2	9.9	29	3	280	9	2.1	2	0	0.26	0	23	4.6	0.11	0.19
Buckwheat																							
dry — *½ cup*	85	292	60.8	0	8.5	2.9	0.9	0.9	0.6	11.3	15	2	391	1	2	0	0	0.18	0	25.5	6	0.36	0.09
groats, roasted, cooked — *1 cup*	168	155	33.5	0	4.5	1	0.3	0.3	0.2	5.7	12	1	148	7	1	0	0	0.13	0	23.5	1.6	0.07	0.07
groats, roasted, dry — *½ cup*	82	284	61.5	0	8.4	2.2	0.7	0.7	0.5	9.6	14	2	262	9	2	0	0	0.29	0	34.4	4.2	0.22	0.18
Bulgur																							
cooked — *1 cup*	182	151	33.8	0	8.2	0.4	0.1	0.2	0.1	5.6	18	2	124	9	1	0	0	0.15	0	32.8	1.8	0.05	0.1
dry — *½ cup*	70	239	53.1	0	12.8	0.9	0.1	0.4	0.2	8.6	25	2	287	12	1.4	0	0	0.24	0	18.9	3.6	0.08	0.16
Corn																							
dry, white — *½ cup*	83	303	61.6	0	0	3.9	1	1.8	0.6	7.8	6	2	238	29	1.8	0	0	0.52	0	0	3	0.17	0.32
dry, yellow — *½ cup*	83	303	61.6	0	0	3.9	1	1.8	0.6	7.8	6	2	238	29	1.8	39	0	0.52	0	15.8	3	0.17	0.32
Corn bran, crude — *1 cup*	76	170	65.1	0	65	0.7	0.2	0.3	0.1	6.4	32	2	33	5	1.2	5	0	0.12	0	3	2.1	0.08	0.01
Corn grits, regular/quick																							
white, cooked — *1 cup*	242	145	31.5	0	0.5	0.5	0.1	0.2	0.1	3.4	0	2	53	0	0.2	0	0	0.06	0	2.4	2	0.15	0.24
white, dry — *½ cup*	78	289	62.1	0	1.2	0.9	0.2	0.4	0.1	6.9	2	3	107	1	0.3	0	0	0.11	0	3.9	3.9	0.3	0.5
yellow, enriched, cooked — *1 cup*	242	145	31.5	0	0.5	0.5	0.1	0.2	0.1	3.4	0	2	53	0	0.2	15	0	0.06	0	2.4	2	0.15	0.24
yellow, enriched, dry — *½ cup*	78	289	62.1	0	1.2	0.9	0.2	0.4	0.1	6.9	2	3	107	1	0.3	34	0	0.11	0	3.9	3.9	0.3	0.5
Cornmeal																							
degermed, enriched, white — *1 cup*	138	505	107	0	10.2	2.3	0.6	1	0.3	11.7	7	6	224	4	1	0	0	0.35	0	66.2	6.9	0.56	0.99

	Weight *g*	Calories	Carbohydrates *g*	Cholesterol *mg*	Dietary fiber *g*	Total fat *g*	Mono. fat *g*	Poly. fat *g*	Sat. fat *g*	Protein *g*	Calcium *mg*	Iron *mg*	Potassium *mg*	Sodium *mg*	Zinc *mg*	Vitamin A *RE*	Vitamin B_{12} *mcg*	Vitamin B_6 *mg*	Vitamin C *mg*	Folic acid *mcg*	Niacin *mg*	Riboflavin *mg*	Thiamin *mg*
degermed, enriched, yellow — *1 cup*	138	505	107	0	10.2	2.3	0.6	1	0.3	11.7	7	6	224	4	1	57	0	0.35	0	66.2	6.9	0.56	0.99
self-rising, degermed, enriched, white — *1 cup*	138	490	103	0	9.8	2.4	0.6	1	0.3	11.6	483	7	235	1860	1.4	0	0	0.54	0	42.8	6.3	0.53	0.94
self-rising, degermed, enriched, yellow — *1 cup*	138	490	103	0	9.8	2.4	0.6	1	0.3	11.6	483	7	235	1860	1.4	57	0	0.54	0	42.8	6.3	0.53	0.94
self-rising, enriched, yellow w/ wheat flour — *1 cup*	170	592	125	0	10.7	4.8	1.3	2.2	0.7	14.3	508	8	352	2242	2.4	49	0	0.65	0	112.2	8.8	0.74	1.21
self-rising, plain, enriched, white — *1 cup*	122	407	85.7	0	8.2	4.1	1.1	1.9	0.6	10.1	440	7	311	1521	2.4	0	0	0.66	0	69.5	6.5	0.49	0.81
self-rising, plain, enriched, yellow — *1 cup*	122	407	85.7	0	8.2	4.1	1.1	1.9	0.6	10.1	440	7	311	1521	2.4	57	0	0.66	0	69.5	6.5	0.49	0.81
whole-grain, white — *1 cup*	122	442	93.8	0	8.9	4.4	1.2	2	0.6	9.9	7	4	350	43	2.2	0	0	0.37	0	31	4.4	0.25	0.47
whole-grain, yellow — *1 cup*	122	442	93.8	0	8.9	4.4	1.2	2	0.6	9.9	7	4	350	43	2.2	57	0	0.37	0	31	4.4	0.25	0.47
Cream of rice																							
cooked — *1 cup*	244	127	27.8	0	0.2	0.2	0.1	0.1	0.1	2.2	7	0	49	2	0.4	0	0	0.07	0	7.3	1	0	0
dry — *½ cup*	87	320	71.3	0	0.6	0.4	0.1	0.1	0.1	5.4	21	1	124	5	1	0	0	0.17	0	25.1	2.6	0.09	0.17
Cream of wheat																							
cooked — *1 cup*	251	133	27.6	0	1.8	0.5	0.1	0.3	0.1	3.8	50	10	43	3	0.3	0	0	0.04	0	10	1.5	0	0.25
dry — *½ cup*	87	320	66.2	0	3.3	1.3	0.2	0.7	0.2	9.1	122	25	104	6	0.8	0	0	0.09	0	29.4	3.6	0.17	0.43
Farina																							
cooked — *1 cup*	233	117	24.7	0	3.3	0.2	0	0.1	0	3.3	5	1	30	0	0.2	0	0	0.02	0	4.7	1.3	0.12	0.19
dry — *½ cup*	88	325	68.6	0	1.7	0.4	0.1	0.2	0.1	9.3	12	3	83	3	0.5	0	0	0.05	0	21.1	3.6	0.32	0.5
Hominy, canned																							
white — *½ cup*	83	59	11.8	0	2.1	0.7	0.2	0.3	0.1	1.2	8	1	7	173	0.9	0	0	0	0	0.8	0	0	0
yellow — *½ cup*	80	58	11.4	0	2	0.7	0.2	0.3	0.1	1.2	8	0	7	168	0.8	9	0	0	0	0.8	0	0	0
Millet																							
cooked — *1 cup*	240	286	56.8	0	3.1	2.4	0.4	1.2	0.4	8.4	7	2	149	5	2.2	0	0	0.26	0	45.6	3.2	0.2	0.25
dry — *½ cup*	100	378	72.9	0	8.5	4.2	0.8	2.1	0.7	11	8	3	195	5	1.7	0	0	0.38	0	85	4.7	0.29	0.42

	Weight g	Calories	Carbohydrates g	Cholesterol mg	Dietary fiber g	Total fat g	Mono. fat g	Poly. fat g	Sat. fat g	Protein g	Calcium mg	Iron mg	Potassium mg	Sodium mg	Zinc mg	Vitamin A RE	Vitamin B_{12} mcg	Vitamin B_6 mg	Vitamin C mg	Folic acid mcg	Niacin mg	Riboflavin mg	Thiamin mg
Oat bran																							
cooked — *1 cup*	219	88	25.1	0	5.7	1.9	0.6	0.7	0.4	7	22	2	201	2	1.2	0	0	0.05	0	13.1	0.3	0.07	0.35
dry — *½ cup*	47	116	31.1	0	7.2	3.3	1.1	1.3	0.6	8.1	27	3	266	2	1.5	0	0	0.08	0	24.4	0.4	0.1	0.55
Oatmeal, instant, fortified																							
plain, cooked — *1 cup*	234	138	23.9	0	4	2.3	0.7	0.9	0.4	5.9	215	8	131	377	1.1	599	0	0.98	0	198.9	7.2	0.37	0.7
plain, dry — *1 packet*	28	103	17.9	0	3.1	1.7	0.5	0.6	0.3	4.3	161	6	99	283	0.9	449	0	0.73	0	148.7	5.4	0.29	0.52
Oatmeal, regular/quick/instant																							
cooked — *1 cup*	234	145	25.3	0	4	2.3	0.7	0.9	0.4	6.1	19	2	131	2	1.1	5	0	0.05	0	9.4	0.3	0.05	0.26
dry — *½ cup*	41	156	27.1	0	4.3	2.6	0.8	0.9	0.4	6.5	21	2	142	2	1.2	4	0	0.05	0	13	0.3	0.06	0.3
Oats, dry — *½ cup*	78	303	51.7	0	8.3	5.4	1.7	2	0.9	13.2	42	4	335	2	3.1	0	0	0.09	0	43.7	0.7	0.11	0.6
Quinoa, dry — *½ cup*	85	318	58.6	0	5	4.9	1.3	2	0.5	11.1	51	8	629	18	2.8	0	0	0.19	0	41.7	2.5	0.34	0.17
Rice bran, crude — *½ cup*	59	186	29.3	0	12.4	12.3	4.5	4.4	2.5	7.9	34	11	876	3	3.6	0	0	2.4	0	37.2	20.1	0.17	1.62
Rice, brown, long-grain																							
cooked — *1 cup*	195	216	44.8	0	3.5	1.8	0.6	0.6	0.4	5	20	1	84	10	1.2	0	0	0.28	0	7.8	3	0.05	0.19
dry — *½ cup*	93	342	71.4	0	3.2	2.7	1	1	0.5	7.3	21	1	206	6	1.9	0	0	0.47	0	18.5	4.7	0.09	0.37
Rice, brown, medium-grain																							
cooked — *1 cup*	195	218	45.8	0	3.5	1.6	0.6	0.6	0.3	4.5	20	1	154	2	1.2	0	0	0.29	0	7.8	2.6	0.02	0.2
dry — *½ cup*	95	344	72.4	0	3.2	2.5	0.9	0.9	0.5	7.1	31	2	255	4	1.9	0	0	0.48	0	19	4.1	0.04	0.39
Rice, white, glutinous																							
cooked — *1 cup*	174	169	36.7	0	1.7	0.3	0.1	0.1	0.1	3.5	3	0	17	9	0.7	0	0	0.05	0	1.7	0.5	0.02	0.03
dry — *½ cup*	93	342	75.6	0	2.6	0.5	0.2	0.2	0.1	6.3	10	1	71	6	1.1	0	0	0.1	0	6.5	2	0.05	0.17
Rice, white, long-grain																							
enriched, cooked — *1 cup*	158	205	44.5	0	0.6	0.4	0.1	0.1	0.1	4.3	16	2	55	2	0.8	0	0	0.15	0	4.7	2.3	0.02	0.26
enriched, raw — *½ cup*	93	338	74	0	1.2	0.6	0.2	0.2	0.2	6.6	26	4	106	5	1	0	0	0.15	0	7.4	3.9	0.05	0.53

	Weight g	Calories	Carbohydrates g	Cholesterol mg	Dietary fiber g	Total fat g	Mono. fat g	Poly. fat g	Sat. fat g	Protein g	Calcium mg	Iron mg	Potassium mg	Sodium mg	Zinc mg	Vitamin A RE	Vitamin B_{12} mcg	Vitamin B_6 mg	Vitamin C mg	Folic acid mcg	Niacin mg	Riboflavin mg	Thiamin mg
Rice, white, long-grain, instant, enriched, dry — *½ cup*	93	351	77.3	0	1.5	0.3	0.1	0.1	0.1	7.1	17	4	17	6	0.9	0	0	0.04	0	5.6	5.1	0.06	0.57
Rice, white, long-grain, parboiled																							
enriched, cooked — *1 cup*	175	200	43.3	0	0.7	0.5	0.1	0.1	0.1	4	33	2	65	5	0.5	0	0	0.03	0	7	2.5	0.03	0.44
enriched, dry — *½ cup*	93	343	75.6	0	1.6	0.5	0.2	0.1	0.1	6.3	56	3	111	5	0.9	0	0	0.32	0	15.7	3.4	0.06	0.55
enriched, cooked — *1 cup*	165	162	35.1	0	1	0.3	0.1	0.1	0.1	3.4	13	1	7	5	0.4	0	0	0.02	0	6.6	1.5	0.08	0.12
Rice, white, medium-grain																							
enriched, cooked — *1 cup*	186	242	53.2	0	0.6	0.4	0.1	0.1	0.1	4.4	6	3	54	0	0.8	0	0	0.09	0	3.7	3.4	0.03	0.31
enriched, dry — *½ cup*	98	351	77.4	0	1.4	0.6	0.2	0.2	0.2	6.4	9	4	84	1	1.1	0	0	0.14	0	8.8	5	0.05	0.56
Rice, white, short-grain																							
cooked — *1 cup*	186	242	53.4	0	0	0.4	0.1	0.1	0.1	4.4	2	3	48	0	0.7	0	0	0.11	0	3.7	2.8	0.03	0.31
dry — *½ cup*	100	358	79.2	0	2.8	0.5	0.2	0.1	0.1	6.5	3	4	76	1	1.1	0	0	0.17	0	6	4.1	0.05	0.57
Rye, dry — *½ cup*	85	283	58.9	0	12.3	2.1	0.3	0.9	0.2	12.5	28	2	223	5	3.2	0	0	0.25	0	50.7	3.6	0.21	0.27
Sorghum, dry — *½ cup*	96	325	71.6	0	0	3.2	1	1.3	0.4	10.8	27	4	336	6	0	0	0	0	0	0	2.8	0.14	0.23
Tapioca, pearl, dry — *½ cup*	76	272	67.4	0	0.7	0	0	0	0	0.1	15	1	8	1	0.1	0	0	0.01	0	3	0	0	0
Triticale, dry — *½ cup*	96	323	69.2	0	0	2	0.2	0.9	0.4	12.5	36	2	319	5	3.3	0	0	0.13	0	70.1	1.4	0.13	0.4
Wheat bran, crude — *½ cup*	29	63	18.7	0	12.4	1.2	0.2	0.6	0.2	4.5	21	3	343	1	2.1	0	0	0.38	0	22.9	3.9	0.17	0.15
Wheat germ, crude — *½ cup*	58	207	29.8	0	7.6	5.6	0.8	3.5	1	13.3	22	4	513	7	7.1	0	0	0.75	0	161.6	3.9	0.29	1.08
Wheat, sprouted — *½ cup*	54	107	23	0	0.6	0.7	0.1	0.3	0.1	4	15	1	91	9	0.9	0	0	0.14	1	20.5	1.7	0.08	0.12
Whole-wheat hot natural cereal																							
cooked — *1 cup*	242	150	33.2	0	3.9	1	0.1	0.5	0.1	4.8	17	2	172	0	1.2	0	0	0.18	0	26.6	2.2	0.12	0.17
dry — *½ cup*	47	161	35.3	0	4.5	0.9	0.1	0.5	0.1	5.3	19	2	183	1	1.3	0	0	0.18	0	36.7	2.3	0.14	0.19
Wild rice																							
cooked — *1 cup*	164	166	35	0	3	0.6	0.1	0.3	0.1	6.5	5	1	166	5	2.2	0	0	0.22	0	42.6	2.1	0.14	0.09
dry — *½ cup*	80	286	59.9	0	5	0.9	0.1	0.5	0.1	11.8	17	2	342	6	4.8	2	0	0.31	0	76	5.4	0.21	0.09

Herbs, Spices & Flavorings

	Weight g	Calories	Carbohydrates g	Cholesterol mg	Dietary fiber g	Total fat g	Mono. fat g	Poly. fat g	Sat. fat g	Protein g	Calcium mg	Iron mg	Potassium mg	Sodium mg	Zinc mg	Vitamin A RE	Vitamin B_{12} mcg	Vitamin B_6 mg	Vitamin C mg	Folic acid mcg	Niacin mg	Riboflavin mg	Thiamin mg
Allspice, ground — *1 tsp*	2	5	1.4	0	0.4	0.2	0	0	0	0.1	13	0	20	1	0	1	0	0.01	1	0.7	0.1	0	0
Anise seed — *1 tsp*	2	7	1.1	0	0.3	0.3	0.2	0.1	0	0.4	14	1	30	0	0.1	1	0	0.01	0	0.2	0.1	0.01	0.01
Basil																							
dried, ground — *1 tsp*	1	4	0.9	0	0.6	0.1	0	0	0	0.2	30	1	48	0	0.1	13	0	0.02	1	3.8	0.1	0	0
fresh — *1 Tbsp*	3	1	0.1	0	0.1	0	0	0	0	0.1	4	0	12	0	0	10	0	0	0	1.7	0	0	0
Bay leaf, crumbled — *1 tsp*	0.6	2	0.4	0	0.2	0.1	0	0	0	0	5	0	3	0	0	4	0	0.01	0	1.1	0	0	0
Caraway seed — *1 tsp*	2	7	1	0	0.8	0.3	0.1	0.1	0	0.4	14	0	28	0	0.1	1	0	0.01	0	0.2	0.1	0.01	0.01
Cardamom, ground — *1 tsp*	2	6	1.4	0	0.6	0.1	0	0	0	0.2	8	0	22	0	0.1	0	0	0	0	0	0	0	0
Celery seed — *1 tsp*	2	8	0.8	0	0.2	0.5	0.3	0.1	0	0.4	35	1	28	3	0.1	0	0	0.01	0	0.2	0.1	0.01	0.01
Chervil, dried — *1 tsp*	0.6	1	0.3	0	0.1	0	0	0	0	0.1	8	0	28	0	0.1	4	0	0.01	0	1.6	0	0	0
Chili powder — *1 tsp*	3	8	1.4	0	0.9	0.4	0.1	0.2	0.1	0.3	7	0	50	26	0.1	91	0	0.05	2	2.6	0.2	0.02	0.01
Chives																							
freeze-dried — *1 Tbsp*	0.2	1	0.1	0	0.1	0	0	0	0	0	2	0	6	0	0	14	0	0	1	0.2	0	0	0
fresh, chopped — *1 Tbsp*	3	1	0.1	0	0.1	0	0	0	0	0.1	3	0	9	0	0	13	0	0	2	3.2	0	0	0
Cinnamon, ground — *1 tsp*	2	6	1.8	0	1.2	0.1	0	0	0	0.1	28	1	11	1	0	1	0	0.01	1	0.7	0	0	0
Cloves, ground — *1 tsp*	2	7	1.3	0	0.7	0.4	0	0.1	0.1	0.1	14	0	23	5	0	1	0	0.03	2	2	0	0.01	0
Coriander																							
fresh (cilantro) — *¼ cup*	4	1	0.1	0	0.1	0	0	0	0	0.1	4	0	22	1	0	11	0	0	0	0.4	0	0	0
leaf, dried — *1 tsp*	0.6	2	0.3	0	0.1	0	0	0	0	0.1	7	0	27	1	0	4	0	0.01	3	1.6	0.1	0.01	0.01
seed — *1 tsp*	2	5	1	0	0.8	0.3	0.2	0	0	0.2	13	0	23	1	0.1	0	0	0	0	0	0	0.01	0
Cumin seed — *1 tsp*	2	8	0.9	0	0.2	0.5	0.3	0.1	0	0.4	20	1	38	4	0.1	3	0	0.01	0	0.2	0.1	0.01	0.01
Curry powder — *1 tsp*	2	7	1.2	0	0.7	0.3	0.1	0.1	0	0.3	10	1	31	1	0.1	2	0	0.01	0	3.1	0.1	0.01	0.01
Dill seed — *1 tsp*	2	6	1.2	0	0.4	0.3	0.2	0	0	0.3	32	0	25	0	0.1	0	0	0.01	0	0.2	0.1	0.01	0.01

	Weight *g*	Calories	Carbohydrates *g*	Cholesterol *mg*	Dietary fiber *g*	Total fat *g*	Mono. fat *g*	Poly. fat *g*	Sat. fat *g*	Protein *g*	Calcium *mg*	Iron *mg*	Potassium *mg*	Sodium *mg*	Zinc *mg*	Vitamin A *RE*	Vitamin B_{12} *mcg*	Vitamin B_6 *mg*	Vitamin C *mg*	Folic acid *mcg*	Niacin *mg*	Riboflavin *mg*	Thiamin *mg*
Dill weed																							
dried — *1 tsp*	1	3	0.6	0	0.1	0	0	0	0	0.2	18	0	33	2	0	6	0	0.01	1	0	0	0	0
fresh — *5 sprigs*	1	0	0.1	0	0	0	0	0	0	0	2	0	7	1	0	8	0	0	1	1.5	0	0	0
Fennel seed — *1 tsp*	2	7	1	0	0.8	0.3	0.2	0	0	0.3	24	0	34	2	0.1	0	0	0	0	0	0.1	0.01	0.01
Fenugreek seed — *1 tsp*	4	12	2.2	0	0.9	0.2	0	0	0.1	0.9	6	1	28	2	0.1	0	0	0	0	2.1	0.1	0.01	0.01
Garlic powder — *1 tsp*	3	9	2	0	0.3	0	0	0	0	0.5	2	0	31	1	0.1	0	0	0.08	1	0.1	0	0	0.01
Garlic, raw — *3 cloves*	9	13	3	0	0.2	0	0	0	0	0.6	16	0	36	2	0.1	0	0	0.11	3	0.3	0.1	0.01	0.02
Ginger root, raw — *1 tsp*	2	1	0.3	0	0	0	0	0	0	0	0	0	8	0	0	0	0	0	0	0.2	0	0	0
Ginger, ground — *1 tsp*	2	6	1.3	0	0.2	0.1	0	0	0	0.2	2	0	24	1	0.1	0	0	0.02	0	0.7	0.1	0	0
Lemon juice																							
canned or bottled — *½ cup*	122	26	7.9	0	0.5	0.4	0	0.1	0	0.5	13	0	124	26	0.1	2	0	0.05	30	12.3	0.2	0.01	0.05
fresh — *½ cup*	122	31	10.5	0	0.5	0	0	0	0	0.5	9	0	151	1	0.1	2	0	0.06	56	15.7	0.1	0.01	0.04
frozen, single strength — *½ cup*	122	27	7.9	0	0.5	0.4	0	0.1	0.1	0.6	10	0	109	1	0.1	1	0	0.07	38	11.6	0.2	0.02	0.07
Lemon peel, fresh — *1 Tbsp*	6	3	1	0	0.6	0	0	0	0	0.1	8	0	10	0	0	0	0	0.01	8	0.8	0	0	0
Lime juice																							
canned or bottled — *½ cup*	123	26	8.2	0	0.5	0.3	0	0.1	0	0.3	15	0	92	20	0.1	2	0	0.03	8	9.7	0.2	0	0.04
fresh — *½ cup*	123	33	11.1	0	0.5	0.1	0	0	0	0.5	11	0	134	1	0.1	1	0	0.05	36	10.1	0.1	0.01	0.02
Mace, ground — *1 tsp*	2	8	0.9	0	0.3	0.6	0.2	0.1	0.2	0.1	4	0	8	1	0	1	0	0.01	0	1.3	0	0.01	0.01
Marjoram, dried — *1 tsp*	0.6	2	0.4	0	0.2	0	0	0	0	0.1	12	0	9	0	0	5	0	0.01	0	1.6	0	0	0
Mustard seed, yellow — *1 tsp*	3	15	1.2	0	0.5	0.9	0.7	0.2	0	0.8	17	0	23	0	0.2	0	0	0.01	0	2.5	0.3	0.01	0.02
Nutmeg, ground — *1 tsp*	2	12	1.1	0	0.5	0.8	0.1	0	0.6	0.1	4	0	8	0	0	0	0	0.01	0	1.7	0	0	0.01
Onion powder — *1 tsp*	2	7	1.7	0	0.1	0	0	0	0	0.2	8	0	20	1	0	0	0	0.03	0	3.5	0	0	0.01
Onion, dehydrated flakes — *1 Tbsp*	5	16	4.2	0	0.5	0	0	0	0	0.4	13	0	81	1	0.1	0	0	0.08	4	8.3	0	0.01	0.03
Orange peel, fresh — *1 Tbsp*	6	6	1.5	0	0.6	0	0	0	0	0.1	10	0	13	0	0	3	0	0.01	8	1.8	0.1	0.01	0.01

	Weight *g*	**Calories**	**Carbohydrates** *g*	**Cholesterol** *mg*	**Dietary fiber** *g*	**Total fat** *g*	**Mono. fat** *g*	**Poly. fat** *g*	**Sat. fat** *g*	**Protein** *g*	**Calcium** *mg*	**Iron** *mg*	**Potassium** *mg*	**Sodium** *mg*	**Zinc** *mg*	**Vitamin A** *RE*	**Vitamin B12** *mcg*	**Vitamin B6** *mg*	**Vitamin C** *mg*	**Folic acid** *mcg*	**Niacin** *mg*	**Riboflavin** *mg*	**Thiamin** *mg*
Oregano, ground — *1 tsp*	2	5	1	0	0.6	0.2	0	0.1	0	0.2	24	1	25	0	0.1	10	0	0.02	1	4.1	0.1	0	0.01
Paprika — *1 tsp*	2	6	1.2	0	0.4	0.3	0	0.2	0	0.3	4	0	49	1	0.1	127	0	0.04	1	2.2	0.3	0.04	0.01
Parsley																							
dried — *1 tsp*	0.3	1	0.2	0	0.1	0	0	0	0	0.1	4	0	11	1	0	7	0	0	0	0.5	0	0	0
freeze-dried — *1 Tbsp*	0.4	1	0.2	0	0.1	0	0	0	0	0.1	1	0	25	2	0	25	0	0.01	1	6.1	0	0.01	0
fresh — *¼ cup*	15	5	0.9	0	0.5	0.1	0	0	0	0.4	21	1	83	8	0.2	78	0	0.01	20	22.8	0.2	0.01	0.01
Pepper																							
black — *1 tsp*	2	5	1.4	0	0.6	0.1	0	0	0	0.2	9	1	26	1	0	0	0	0.01	0	0.2	0	0.01	0
red or cayenne — *1 tsp*	2	6	1	0	0.5	0.3	0	0.2	0.1	0.2	3	0	36	1	0	75	0	0.04	1	1.9	0.2	0.02	0.01
white — *1 tsp*	2	7	1.6	0	0.6	0.1	0	0	0	0.2	6	0	2	0	0	0	0	0.01	1	0.2	0	0	0
Peppermint, fresh — *1 Tbsp*	2	1	0.2	0	0.1	0	0	0	0	0.1	4	0	9	0	0	7	0	0	1	1.8	0	0	0
Poppy seed — *1 tsp*	3	15	0.7	0	0.3	1.3	0.2	0.9	0.1	0.5	41	0	20	1	0.3	0	0	0.01	0	1.6	0	0	0.02
Poultry seasoning — *1 tsp*	2	5	1	0	0.2	0.1	0	0	0	0.1	15	1	10	0	0	4	0	0.01	0	2.1	0	0	0
Pumpkin pie spice — *1 tsp*	2	6	1.2	0	0.3	0.2	0	0	0.1	0.1	12	0	11	1	0	0	0	0.01	0	0.9	0	0	0
Rosemary																							
dried — *1 tsp*	1	4	0.8	0	0.5	0.2	0	0	0.1	0.1	15	0	11	1	0	4	0	0	1	0	0	0	0.01
fresh — *1 Tbsp*	2	2	0.4	0	0.2	0.1	0	0	0	0.1	5	0	11	0	0	5	0	0.01	0	1.9	0	0	0
Saffron — *1 tsp*	0.7	2	0.5	0	0	0	0	0	0	0.1	1	0	12	1	0	0	0	0.01	1	0.7	0	0	0
Sage, ground — *1 tsp*	0.7	2	0.4	0	0.3	0.1	0	0	0	0.1	12	0	7	0	0	4	0	0.01	0	1.9	0	0	0.01
Salt, table — *1 tsp*	6	0	0	0	0	0	0	0	0	0	1	0	0	2325	0	0	0	0	0	0	0	0	0
Savory, ground — *1 tsp*	1	4	1	0	0.6	0.1	0	0	0	0.1	30	1	15	0	0.1	7	0	0	1	0	0.1	0	0.01
Spearmint																							
dried — *1 tsp*	0.5	1	0.3	0	0.1	0	0	0	0	0.1	7	0	10	2	0	5	0	0.01	0	2.7	0	0.01	0
fresh — *1 Tbsp*	6	3	0.5	0	0.4	0	0	0	0	0.2	11	1	26	2	0.1	23	0	0.01	1	6	0.1	0.01	0

	Weight g	Calories	Carbohydrates g	Cholesterol mg	Dietary fiber g	Total fat g	Mono. fat g	Poly. fat g	Sat. fat g	Protein g	Calcium mg	Iron mg	Potassium mg	Sodium mg	Zinc mg	Vitamin A RE	Vitamin B_{12} mcg	Vitamin B_6 mg	Vitamin C mg	Folic acid mcg	Niacin mg	Riboflavin mg	Thiamin mg
Tarragon, ground — *1 tsp*	2	5	0.8	0	0.1	0.1	0	0.1	0	0.4	18	1	48	1	0.1	7	0	0.02	1	4.4	0.1	0.02	0
Thyme																							
dried, ground — *1 tsp*	1	4	0.9	0	0.5	0.1	0	0	0	0.1	26	2	11	1	0.1	5	0	0.02	1	3.8	0.1	0.01	0.01
fresh — *1 Tbsp*	2	2	0.6	0	0.3	0	0	0	0	0.1	10	0	15	0	0	11	0	0.01	4	1.1	0	0.01	0
Turmeric, ground — *1 tsp*	2	8	1.4	0	0.5	0.2	0	0	0.1	0.2	4	1	56	1	0.1	0	0	0.04	1	0.9	0.1	0.01	0
Vanilla extract																							
imitation w/ alcohol — *1 tsp*	4	10	0.1	0	0	0	0	0	0	0	0	0	4	0	0	0	0	0	0	0	0	0	0
imitation w/o alcohol — *1 tsp*	4	2	0.6	0	0	0	0	0	0	0	0	0	0	0	0	0	0	0	0	0	0	0	0
pure extract — *1 tsp*	4	12	0.5	0	0	0	0	0	0	0	0	0	6	0	0	0	0	0	0	0	0	0	0
Vinegar, cider — *1 Tbsp*	15	2	0.9	0	0	0	0	0	0	0	1	0	15	0	0	0	0	0	0	0	0	0	0

Ice Cream & Frozen Desserts

	Weight g	Calories	Carbohydrates g	Cholesterol mg	Dietary fiber g	Total fat g	Mono. fat g	Poly. fat g	Sat. fat g	Protein g	Calcium mg	Iron mg	Potassium mg	Sodium mg	Zinc mg	Vitamin A RE	Vitamin B_{12} mcg	Vitamin B_6 mg	Vitamin C mg	Folic acid mcg	Niacin mg	Riboflavin mg	Thiamin mg
Frozen yogurt																							
chocolate, soft serve — *½ cup*	72	115	17.9	4	1.6	4.3	1.3	0.2	2.6	2.9	106	1	188	71	0.4	31	0.2	0.05	0	7.9	0.2	0.15	0.03
vanilla, soft serve — *½ cup*	72	114	17.4	1	0	4	1.1	0.2	2.5	2.9	103	0	152	63	0.3	41	0.2	0.06	1	4.3	0.2	0.16	0.03
Fruit & juice bars — *1 bar*	77	63	15.6	0	0	0.1	0	0	0	0.9	4	0	41	3	0	2	0	0.02	7	4.6	0.1	0.01	0.01
Fruit ice																							
frozen, lime — *½ cup*	99	77	32.3	0	0	0	0	0	0	0.4	2	0	3	22	0	0	0	0	1	0	0	0	0
w/ aspartame — *1 bar*	51	12	3.2	0	0	0.1	0	0	0	0.3	1	0	13	3	0	0	0	0	0	0	0.1	0	0
Ice cream																							
chocolate — *½ cup*	66	143	18.6	22	0.8	7.3	2.1	0.3	4.5	2.5	72	1	164	50	0.4	79	0.2	0.04	0	10.6	0.1	0.13	0.03
french vanilla, soft-serve — *½ cup*	86	185	19.1	78	0	11.2	3	0.4	6.4	3.5	113	0	152	52	0.4	132	0.4	0.04	1	7.7	0.1	0.16	0.04
strawberry — *½ cup*	66	127	18.2	19	0.2	5.5	0	0	3.4	2.1	79	0	124	40	0.2	51	0.2	0.03	5	7.9	0.1	0.17	0.03
vanilla — *½ cup*	66	133	15.6	29	0	7.3	2.1	0.3	4.5	2.3	84	0	131	53	0.5	77	0.3	0.03	0	3.3	0.1	0.16	0.03
vanilla, rich — *½ cup*	74	178	16.6	45	0	12	3.4	0.4	7.4	2.6	87	0	118	41	0.3	136	0.3	0.03	1	3.7	0.1	0.12	0.03

	Weight g	Calories	Carbohydrates g	Cholesterol mg	Dietary fiber g	Total fat g	Mono. fat g	Poly. fat g	Sat. fat g	Protein g	Calcium mg	Iron mg	Potassium mg	Sodium mg	Zinc mg	Vitamin A RE	Vitamin B_{12} mcg	Vitamin B_6 mg	Vitamin C mg	Folic acid mcg	Niacin mg	Riboflavin mg	Thiamin mg
Ice milk																							
vanilla — *½ cup*	66	92	15	9	0	2.8	0.8	0.1	1.7	2.5	92	0	139	56	0.3	31	0.4	0.04	1	4	0.1	0.17	0.04
vanilla, soft serve — *½ cup*	88	111	19.2	11	0	2.3	0.7	0.1	1.4	4.3	138	0	194	62	0.5	26	0.4	0.04	1	5.3	0.1	0.17	0.05
Ice pops — *1 bar*	59	42	11.2	0	0	0	0	0	0	0	0	0	2	7	0	0	0	0	0	0	0	0	0
Milkshake, thick																							
chocolate — *8 fl oz*	227	269	48	24	0.7	6.1	1.8	0.2	3.8	6.9	299	1	508	252	1.1	48	0.7	0.06	0	11.1	0.3	0.5	0.11
vanilla — *8 fl oz*	227	254	40.3	27	0	6.9	2	0.3	4.3	8.8	331	0	414	216	0.9	64	1.2	0.1	0	15	0.3	0.44	0.07
Sherbet, orange — *½ cup*	99	137	30.1	5	0.5	2	0.5	0.1	1.1	1.1	53	0	95	46	0.5	14	0.1	0.03	4	4	0.1	0.07	0.02

Lamb

	Weight g	Calories	Carbohydrates g	Cholesterol mg	Dietary fiber g	Total fat g	Mono. fat g	Poly. fat g	Sat. fat g	Protein g	Calcium mg	Iron mg	Potassium mg	Sodium mg	Zinc mg	Vitamin A RE	Vitamin B_{12} mcg	Vitamin B_6 mg	Vitamin C mg	Folic acid mcg	Niacin mg	Riboflavin mg	Thiamin mg
Foreshank, domestic, choice, braised																							
¼" fat trim — *3 ½ oz*	100	243	0	106	0	13.5	5.7	1	5.6	28.4	20	2	257	72	7.7	0	2.3	0.1	0	17	5.5	0.19	0.05
⅛" fat trim — *3 ½ oz*	100	243	0	106	0	13.5	5.7	1	5.6	28.4	20	2	257	72	7.7	0	2.3	0.1	0	17	5.5	0.19	0.05
trimmed of all visible fat — *3 ½ oz*	100	187	0	104	0	6	2.6	0.4	2.2	31	20	2	267	74	8.7	0	2.3	0.11	0	19	5.1	0.19	0.04
Foreshank, new zealand, braised																							
⅛" fat trim — *3 ½ oz*	100	258	0	102	0	15.8	6.1	0.7	7.8	27	14	2	118	47	4.8	0	2.4	0.08	0	1	6.1	0.33	0.07
trimmed of all visible fat — *3 ½ oz*	100	186	0	101	0	6	2.4	0.3	2.6	30.8	10	2	125	49	5.6	0	2.5	0.09	0	1	5.6	0.36	0.07
Ground lamb, broiled — *3 ½ oz*	100	283	0	97	0	19.7	8.3	1.4	8.1	24.8	22	2	339	81	4.7	0	2.6	0.14	0	19	6.7	0.25	0.1
Leg, shank half, domestic, choice, roasted																							
¼" fat trim — *3 ½ oz*	100	225	0	90	0	12.5	5.3	0.9	5.1	26.4	10	2	326	65	4.7	0	2.7	0.16	0	22	6.6	0.27	0.1
⅛" fat trim — *3 ½ oz*	100	217	0	90	0	11.4	4.9	0.8	4.6	26.7	9	2	329	65	4.7	0	2.7	0.16	0	23	6.5	0.27	0.1
trimmed of all visible fat — *3 ½ oz*	100	180	0	87	0	6.7	2.9	0.4	2.4	28.2	8	2	342	66	5	0	2.7	0.17	0	24	6.4	0.28	0.11
Leg, sirloin half, domestic, choice, roasted																							
¼" fat trim — *3 ½ oz*	100	292	0	97	0	20.7	8.7	1.5	8.7	24.6	11	2	301	68	4.1	0	2.5	0.14	0	17	6.6	0.28	0.11
⅛" fat trim — *3 ½ oz*	100	284	0	96	0	19.7	8.3	1.4	8.3	25	11	2	304	68	4.2	0	2.5	0.14	0	17	6.6	0.28	0.11

	Weight g	Calories	Carbohydrates g	Cholesterol mg	Dietary fiber g	Total fat g	Mono. fat g	Poly. fat g	Sat. fat g	Protein g	Calcium mg	Iron mg	Potassium mg	Sodium mg	Zinc mg	Vitamin A RE	Vitamin B_{12} mcg	Vitamin B_6 mg	Vitamin C mg	Folic acid mcg	Niacin mg	Riboflavin mg	Thiamin mg
trimmed of all visible fat — *3 ½ oz*	100	204	0	92	0	9.2	4	0.6	3.3	28.4	8	2	333	71	4.9	0	2.6	0.17	0	21	6.3	0.31	0.12
Leg, whole, domestic, choice, roasted																							
¼" fat trim — *3 ½ oz*	100	258	0	93	0	16.5	7	1.2	6.9	25.6	11	2	313	66	4.4	0	2.6	0.15	0	20	6.6	0.27	0.1
⅛" fat trim — *3 ½ oz*	100	242	0	92	0	14.4	6.1	1	5.9	26.2	10	2	319	67	4.5	0	2.6	0.15	0	20	6.5	0.28	0.11
trimmed of all visible fat — *3 ½ oz*	100	191	0	89	0	7.7	3.4	0.5	2.8	28.3	8	2	338	68	4.9	0	2.6	0.17	0	23	6.3	0.29	0.11
Leg, whole, new zealand, roasted																							
⅛" fat trim — *3 ½ oz*	100	234	0	101	0	14	5.4	0.7	6.8	25.3	9	2	170	44	3.7	0	2.6	0.13	0	1	7.6	0.46	0.12
trimmed of all visible fat — *3 ½ oz*	100	181	0	100	0	7	2.8	0.4	3.1	27.7	7	2	183	45	4	0	2.6	0.14	0	0	7.5	0.5	0.12
Loin, domestic, choice, broiled																							
¼" fat trim — *3 ½ oz*	100	316	0	100	0	23.1	9.7	1.7	9.8	25.2	20	2	327	77	3.5	0	2.5	0.13	0	18	7.1	0.25	0.1
⅛" fat trim — *3 ½ oz*	100	297	0	99	0	20.6	8.7	1.5	8.7	26.1	20	2	336	78	3.6	0	2.5	0.13	0	19	7.1	0.26	0.11
trimmed of all visible fat — *3 ½ oz*	100	216	0	95	0	9.7	4.3	0.6	3.5	30	19	2	376	84	4.1	0	2.5	0.16	0	24	6.9	0.28	0.11
Loin, domestic, choice, roasted																							
¼" fat trim — *3 ½ oz*	100	309	0	95	0	23.6	9.7	1.9	10.2	22.6	18	2	246	64	3.4	0	2.2	0.11	0	19	7.1	0.24	0.1
⅛" fat trim — *3 ½ oz*	100	290	0	93	0	21.1	8.7	1.7	9.1	23.3	18	2	250	64	3.5	0	2.2	0.13	0	20	7.1	0.24	0.1
trimmed of all visible fat — *3 ½ oz*	100	202	0	87	0	9.8	4	0.9	3.7	26.6	17	2	267	66	4.1	0	2.2	0.16	0	25	6.8	0.27	0.1
Loin, new zealand, broiled																							
⅛" fat trim — *3 ½ oz*	100	296	0	113	0	21.3	8.2	1	10.6	24.4	23	2	164	50	2.8	0	2.5	0.11	0	1	7.9	0.37	0.12
trimmed of all visible fat — *3 ½ oz*	100	199	0	114	0	8.2	3.2	0.5	3.6	29.3	21	2	189	55	3.3	0	2.6	0.14	0	0	7.9	0.43	0.13
Rib, domestic, choice, broiled																							
¼" fat trim — *3 ½ oz*	100	361	0	99	0	29.6	12.1	2.4	12.7	22.1	19	2	270	76	4	0	2.5	0.11	0	14	7	0.22	0.09
⅛" fat trim — *3 ½ oz*	100	340	0	98	0	26.8	11	2.2	11.4	23.1	18	2	277	77	4.2	0	2.6	0.11	0	15	6.9	0.23	0.09
trimmed of all visible fat — *3 ½ oz*	100	235	0	91	0	13	5.2	1.2	4.7	27.7	16	2	313	85	5.3	0	2.6	0.15	0	21	6.6	0.25	0.1

	Weight g	Calories	Carbohydrates g	Cholesterol mg	Dietary fiber g	Total fat g	Mono. fat g	Poly. fat g	Sat. fat g	Protein g	Calcium mg	Iron mg	Potassium mg	Sodium mg	Zinc mg	Vitamin A RE	Vitamin B_{12} mcg	Vitamin B_6 mg	Vitamin C mg	Folic acid mcg	Niacin mg	Riboflavin mg	Thiamin mg
Rib, domestic, choice, roasted																							
¼" fat trim — *3 ½ oz*	100	359	0	97	0	29.8	12.5	2.2	12.8	21.1	22	2	271	73	3.5	0	2.2	0.11	0	15	6.8	0.21	0.09
⅛" fat trim — *3 ½ oz*	100	341	0	96	0	27.5	11.6	2	11.7	21.8	22	2	277	74	3.6	0	2.2	0.12	0	16	6.7	0.21	0.09
trimmed of all visible fat — *3 ½ oz*	100	232	0	88	0	13.3	5.8	0.9	4.8	26.2	21	2	315	81	4.5	0	2.2	0.15	0	22	6.2	0.23	0.09
Rib, new zealand, roasted																							
⅛" fat trim — *3 ½ oz*	100	317	0	99	0	25.7	9.9	1.2	12.8	19.9	18	2	128	44	2.7	0	2.3	0.08	0	1	6.7	0.28	0.1
trimmed of all visible fat — *3 ½ oz*	100	196	0	94	0	10.2	4	0.6	4.4	24.4	14	2	146	48	3.4	0	2.3	0.11	0	0	6.1	0.33	0.11
Shoulder, arm, domestic, choice, braised																							
¼" fat trim — *3 ½ oz*	100	346	0	120	0	24	10.2	1.7	9.9	30.4	25	2	306	72	6.1	0	2.6	0.11	0	18	6.7	0.25	0.07
⅛" fat trim — *3 ½ oz*	100	337	0	120	0	22.7	9.6	1.6	9.2	31.1	25	2	311	72	6.2	0	2.6	0.11	0	19	6.6	0.25	0.07
trimmed of all visible fat — *3 ½ oz*	100	279	0	121	0	14.1	6.2	0.9	5	35.5	26	3	338	76	7.3	0	2.7	0.13	0	22	6.3	0.27	0.07
Shoulder, arm, domestic, choice, broiled																							
¼" fat trim — *3 ½ oz*	100	281	0	96	0	19.6	8	1.6	8.4	24.4	18	2	309	77	4.9	0	2.9	0.12	0	18	7	0.27	0.1
⅛" fat trim — *3 ½ oz*	100	269	0	96	0	18.1	7.4	1.5	7.7	24.9	18	2	314	78	5	0	2.9	0.12	0	19	7	0.27	0.1
trimmed of all visible fat — *3 ½ oz*	100	200	0	92	0	9	3.7	0.8	3.4	27.7	17	2	340	82	5.7	0	3	0.14	0	23	6.8	0.29	0.1
Shoulder, arm, domestic, choice, roasted																							
¼" fat trim — *3 ½ oz*	100	279	0	92	0	20.2	8.3	1.6	8.7	22.5	18	2	259	65	4.5	0	2.6	0.12	0	20	6.7	0.25	0.09
⅛" fat trim — *3 ½ oz*	100	267	0	91	0	18.8	7.7	1.5	8	22.9	17	2	262	65	4.6	0	2.6	0.13	0	21	6.6	0.25	0.09
trimmed of all visible fat — *3 ½ oz*	100	192	0	86	0	9.3	3.8	0.8	3.6	25.5	16	2	277	67	5.3	0	2.6	0.14	0	25	6.3	0.27	0.1
Shoulder, blade, domestic, choice, braised																							
¼" fat trim — *3 ½ oz*	100	345	0	116	0	24.7	10.1	2	10.3	28.5	27	2	243	75	6.9	0	2.8	0.11	0	18	6	0.21	0.06
⅛" fat trim — *3 ½ oz*	100	339	0	116	0	23.9	9.7	2	9.9	28.9	27	2	244	75	7	0	2.8	0.11	0	18	6	0.21	0.06
trimmed of all visible fat — *3 ½ oz*	100	288	0	117	0	16.6	6.7	1.5	6.4	32.4	28	3	254	79	8.1	0	2.9	0.12	0	21	5.6	0.22	0.06

	Weight g	Calories	Carbohydrates g	Cholesterol mg	Dietary fiber g	Total fat g	Mono. fat g	Poly. fat g	Sat. fat g	Protein g	Calcium mg	Iron mg	Potassium mg	Sodium mg	Zinc mg	Vitamin A RE	Vitamin B_{12} mcg	Vitamin B_6 mg	Vitamin C mg	Folic acid mcg	Niacin mg	Riboflavin mg	Thiamin mg
Shoulder, blade, domestic, choice, broiled																							
¼" fat trim — *3 ½ oz*	100	278	0	95	0	19.9	8.5	1.4	8.2	23.1	24	2	336	82	5.6	0	2.7	0.15	0	18	6.4	0.25	0.09
⅛" fat trim — *3 ½ oz*	100	267	0	95	0	18.5	7.9	1.3	7.5	23.5	24	2	341	83	5.8	0	2.7	0.15	0	18	6.3	0.25	0.09
trimmed of all visible fat — *3 ½ oz*	100	211	0	91	0	11.3	5	0.7	4	25.5	24	2	368	88	6.5	0	2.8	0.17	0	21	6.1	0.26	0.1
Shoulder, blade, domestic, choice, roasted																							
¼" fat trim — *3 ½ oz*	100	281	0	92	0	20.6	8.4	1.7	8.6	22.3	21	2	246	66	5.6	0	2.7	0.11	0	21	5.9	0.23	0.09
⅛" fat trim — *3 ½ oz*	100	270	0	92	0	19.2	7.8	1.6	8	22.6	21	2	248	67	5.7	0	2.7	0.13	0	21	5.8	0.24	0.09
trimmed of all visible fat — *3 ½ oz*	100	209	0	87	0	11.6	4.7	1	4.3	24.6	21	2	258	68	6.5	0	2.7	0.15	0	25	5.5	0.25	0.09
Shoulder, domestic, choice, braised																							
¼" fat trim — *3 ½ oz*	100	344	0	116	0	24.6	10	2	10.3	28.7	25	2	248	75	6.4	0	2.8	0.1	0	17	6.3	0.22	0.07
⅛" fat trim — *3 ½ oz*	100	338	0	117	0	23.6	9.7	1.9	9.7	29.5	27	2	261	74	6.8	0	2.8	0.11	0	18	6.2	0.22	0.07
trimmed of all visible fat — *3 ½ oz*	100	283	0	117	0	15.9	6.5	1.4	6.2	32.8	26	3	261	79	7.5	0	2.9	0.12	0	21	6	0.23	0.06
Shoulder, domestic, choice, broiled																							
¼" fat trim — *3 ½ oz*	100	278	0	97	0	19.3	7.9	1.6	8	24.4	21	2	301	78	5.7	0	3	0.12	0	19	6.5	0.26	0.09
⅛" fat trim — *3 ½ oz*	100	268	0	95	0	18.4	7.8	1.3	7.5	23.8	23	2	335	82	5.6	0	2.8	0.14	0	18	6.5	0.26	0.1
trimmed of all visible fat — *3 ½ oz*	100	210	0	93	0	10.5	4.2	0.9	3.9	27.1	21	2	324	83	6.6	0	3.1	0.14	0	23	6.2	0.28	0.1
Shoulder, domestic, choice, roasted																							
¼" fat trim — *3 ½ oz*	100	276	0	92	0	20	8.2	1.6	8.4	22.5	20	2	251	66	5.2	0	2.6	0.13	0	21	6.2	0.24	0.09
⅛" fat trim — *3 ½ oz*	100	269	0	91	0	19.1	7.8	1.6	8	22.7	20	2	251	66	5.4	0	2.7	0.13	0	21	6	0.24	0.09
trimmed of all visible fat — *3 ½ oz*	100	204	0	87	0	10.8	4.4	1	4.1	24.9	19	2	265	68	6	0	2.7	0.15	0	25	5.8	0.26	0.09
Shoulder, whole, new zealand, braised																							
⅛" fat trim — *3 ½ oz*	100	342	0	123	0	24	9.4	1.3	11.5	29.4	27	2	151	52	4.8	0	3.5	0.07	0	1	6.3	0.33	0.08
trimmed of all visible fat — *3 ½ oz*	100	285	0	127	0	15.5	6.1	1	6.8	34.1	27	2	166	56	5.6	0	3.7	0.08	0	0	5.9	0.36	0.08
untrimmed — *3 ½ oz*	100	357	0	123	0	26.3	10.2	1.3	12.7	28.2	27	2	147	51	4.5	0	3.4	0.07	0	1	6.4	0.32	0.08

	Weight g	Calories	Carbohydrates g	Cholesterol mg	Dietary fiber g	Total fat g	Mono. fat g	Poly. fat g	Sat. fat g	Protein g	Calcium mg	Iron mg	Potassium mg	Sodium mg	Zinc mg	Vitamin A RE	Vitamin B_{12} mcg	Vitamin B_6 mg	Vitamin C mg	Folic acid mcg	Niacin mg	Riboflavin mg	Thiamin mg
Variety meats																							
brain, braised — *3 ½ oz*	100	145	0	2043	0	10.2	1.8	1	2.6	12.6	12	2	205	134	1.4	0	9.3	0.11	12	5	2.5	0.24	0.11
brain, pan-fried — *3 ½ oz*	100	273	0	2504	0	22.2	4	2.3	5.7	17	21	2	358	157	2	0	24.1	0.23	23	7	4.6	0.37	0.17
heart, braised — *3 ½ oz*	100	185	1.9	249	0	7.9	2.2	0.8	3.1	25	14	6	188	63	3.7	0	11.2	0.3	7	2	4.4	1.19	0.17
kidneys, braised — *3 ½ oz*	100	137	1	565	0	3.6	0.8	0.7	1.2	23.7	18	12	178	151	3.8	137	78.9	0.12	12	81	6	2.07	0.35
liver, pan-fried — *3 ½ oz*	100	238	3.8	493	0	12.7	2.6	1.9	4.9	25.5	9	10	352	124	5.6	7806	85.7	0.95	13	400	16.7	4.59	0.35
lungs, braised — *3 ½ oz*	100	113	0	284	0	3.1	0.8	0.4	1.1	19.9	12	5	127	84	1.9	32	2.5	0.06	28	8	2.4	0.14	0.03
pancreas, braised — *3 ½ oz*	100	234	0	400	0	15.1	5.5	0.7	6.8	22.8	12	2	291	52	2.7	0	5.5	0.05	20	13	2.6	0.21	0.02
spleen, braised — *3 ½ oz*	100	156	0	385	0	4.8	1.3	0.4	1.6	26.5	13	39	248	58	3.9	0	5.3	0.08	26	4	5.9	0.32	0.05

Legumes

	Weight g	Calories	Carbohydrates g	Cholesterol mg	Dietary fiber g	Total fat g	Mono. fat g	Poly. fat g	Sat. fat g	Protein g	Calcium mg	Iron mg	Potassium mg	Sodium mg	Zinc mg	Vitamin A RE	Vitamin B_{12} mcg	Vitamin B_6 mg	Vitamin C mg	Folic acid mcg	Niacin mg	Riboflavin mg	Thiamin mg
Adzuki beans																							
canned, sweetened — *½ cup*	148	351	81.4	0	0	0	0	0	0	5.6	33	2	176	323	2.3	1	0	0.12	0	157.8	0.9	0.08	0.15
cooked — *½ cup*	115	147	28.5	0	0	0.1	0	0	0	8.6	32	2	612	9	2	1	0	0.11	0	139.3	0.8	0.07	0.13
Baked beans, canned																							
vegetarian — *½ cup*	127	118	26	0	6.4	0.6	0	0.2	0.1	6.1	64	0	376	504	1.8	22	0	0.17	4	30.4	0.5	0.08	0.19
w/ beef — *½ cup*	133	161	22.5	29	0	4.6	1.8	0.3	2.2	8.5	60	2	426	632	1.6	28	0	0.12	2	57.7	1.3	0.06	0.07
w/ franks — *½ cup*	130	184	19.9	8	8.9	8.5	3.7	1.1	3	8.7	62	2	304	557	2.4	19	0	0.06	3	38.9	1.2	0.07	0.08
w/ pork — *½ cup*	127	134	25.3	9	7	2	0.9	0.3	0.8	6.6	67	2	391	524	1.8	23	0	0.08	3	45.9	0.6	0.05	0.07
w/ pork & sweet sauce — *½ cup*	127	140	26.6	9	6.6	1.8	0.8	0.2	0.7	6.7	77	2	336	425	1.9	14	0	0.11	4	47.3	0.4	0.08	0.06
w/ pork & tomato sauce — *½ cup*	127	124	24.5	9	6.1	1.3	0.6	0.2	0.5	6.5	71	4	380	557	7.4	15	0	0.09	4	28.5	0.6	0.06	0.07
Black beans, cooked — *½ cup*	86	114	20.4	0	7.5	0.5	0	0.2	0.1	7.6	23	2	305	1	1	1	0	0.06	0	128	0.4	0.05	0.21
Black turtle soup beans																							
canned — *½ cup*	120	109	19.9	0	8.3	0.3	0	0.2	0.1	7.2	42	2	370	461	0.6	0	0	0.07	3	73	0.7	0.14	0.17
cooked — *½ cup*	93	120	22.5	0	4.9	0.3	0	0.1	0.1	7.6	51	3	401	3	0.7	1	0	0.07	0	79.1	0.5	0.05	0.21

	Weight g	Calories	Carbohydrates g	Cholesterol mg	Dietary fiber g	Total fat g	Mono. fat g	Poly. fat g	Sat. fat g	Protein g	Calcium mg	Iron mg	Potassium mg	Sodium mg	Zinc mg	Vitamin A RE	Vitamin B_{12} mcg	Vitamin B_6 mg	Vitamin C mg	Folic acid mcg	Niacin mg	Riboflavin mg	Thiamin mg
Chickpeas (garbanzo beans)																							
canned — *½ cup*	120	143	27.1	0	5.3	1.4	0.3	0.6	0.1	5.9	38	2	206	359	1.3	2	0	0.57	5	80.2	0.2	0.04	0.03
cooked — *½ cup*	82	134	22.5	0	6.2	2.1	0.5	0.9	0.2	7.3	40	2	239	6	1.3	2	0	0.11	1	141	0.4	0.05	0.1
Cowpeas (black-eyed peas)																							
canned — *½ cup*	120	92	16.4	0	4	0.7	0.1	0.3	0.2	5.7	24	1	206	359	0.8	1	0	0.05	3	61.4	0.4	0.09	0.09
canned, w/ pork — *½ cup*	120	100	19.8	8	4	1.9	0.8	0.3	0.7	3.3	20	2	214	420	1.2	0	0	0.05	0	61.2	0.5	0.06	0.08
cooked — *½ cup*	86	100	17.9	0	5.6	0.5	0	0.2	0.1	6.6	21	2	239	3	1.1	2	0	0.09	0	178.8	0.4	0.05	0.17
Cowpeas, catjang, cooked — *½ cup*	86	100	17.4	0	3.1	0.6	0.1	0.3	0.2	7	22	3	321	16	1.6	1	0	0.08	0	121	0.6	0.04	0.14
Cranberry beans																							
canned — *½ cup*	130	108	19.7	0	8.2	0.4	0	0.2	0.1	7.2	44	2	338	432	1.1	0	0	0.07	1	100.6	0.7	0.05	0.05
cooked — *½ cup*	89	120	21.6	0	8.9	0.4	0	0.2	0.1	8.3	44	2	342	1	1	0	0	0.07	0	183	0.5	0.06	0.19
Falafel — *3 patties*	51	170	16.2	0	0	9.1	5.2	2.1	1.2	6.8	28	2	298	150	0.8	1	0	0.06	1	39.6	0.5	0.08	0.07
Fava beans (broad beans)																							
canned — *½ cup*	128	91	15.9	0	4.7	0.3	0.1	0.1	0	7	33	1	310	580	0.8	1	0	0.06	2	41.9	1.2	0.06	0.03
cooked — *½ cup*	85	94	16.7	0	4.6	0.3	0.1	0.1	0.1	6.5	31	1	228	4	0.9	2	0	0.06	0	88.5	0.6	0.08	0.08
French beans, cooked — *½ cup*	89	114	21.3	0	8.3	0.7	0	0.4	0.1	6.2	56	1	327	5	0.6	0	0	0.09	1	66.1	0.5	0.05	0.12
Great northern beans																							
canned — *½ cup*	131	149	27.5	0	6.4	0.5	0	0.2	0.2	9.7	69	2	460	5	0.9	0	0	0.14	2	106.5	0.6	0.08	0.19
cooked — *½ cup*	89	104	18.7	0	6.2	0.4	0	0.2	0.1	7.4	60	2	346	2	0.8	0	0	0.1	1	90.5	0.6	0.05	0.14
Humus, raw — *½ cup*	123	210	24.8	0	6.3	10.4	4.4	3.9	1.6	6	62	2	214	300	1.4	2	0	0.49	10	73.1	0.5	0.07	0.11
Hyacinth beans, cooked — *½ cup*	97	113	20.1	0	0	0.6	0	0	0.1	7.9	39	4	327	7	2.8	0	0	0.04	0	3.7	0.4	0.04	0.26
Kidney beans																							
red, canned — *½ cup*	128	109	20	0	8.2	0.4	0	0.2	0.1	6.7	31	2	329	436	0.7	0	0	0.03	1	64.8	0.6	0.11	0.13
red, cooked — *½ cup*	89	112	20.2	0	6.5	0.4	0	0.2	0.1	7.7	25	3	357	2	0.9	0	0	0.11	1	114.7	0.5	0.05	0.14

	Weight g	Calories	Carbohydrates g	Cholesterol mg	Dietary fiber g	Total fat g	Mono. fat g	Poly. fat g	Sat. fat g	Protein g	Calcium mg	Iron mg	Potassium mg	Sodium mg	Zinc mg	Vitamin A RE	Vitamin B_{12} mcg	Vitamin B_6 mg	Vitamin C mg	Folic acid mcg	Niacin mg	Riboflavin mg	Thiamin mg
royal red, cooked — *½ cup*	89	109	19.3	0	8.2	0.2	0	0.1	0	8.4	39	2	335	4	0.8	0	0	0.09	1	65.2	0.5	0.06	0.08
Lentils, cooked — *½ cup*	99	115	19.9	0	7.8	0.4	0.1	0.2	0.1	8.9	19	3	365	2	1.3	1	0	0.18	1	179	1	0.07	0.17
Lima beans, baby, cooked — *½ cup*	91	115	21.2	0	7	0.3	0	0.2	0.1	7.3	26	2	365	3	0.9	0	0	0.07	0	136.4	0.6	0.05	0.15
Lima beans, large																							
canned — *½ cup*	121	95	18	0	5.8	0.2	0	0.1	0	5.9	25	2	265	405	0.8	0	0	0.11	0	60.7	0.3	0.04	0.07
cooked — *½ cup*	94	108	19.6	0	6.6	0.4	0	0.2	0.1	7.3	16	2	478	2	0.9	0	0	0.15	0	78.1	0.4	0.05	0.15
Lupins, cooked — *½ cup*	83	99	8.2	0	2.3	2.4	1	0.6	0.3	12.9	42	1	203	3	1.1	1	0	0.01	1	49.2	0.4	0.04	0.11
Mothbeans, cooked — *½ cup*	89	104	18.5	0	0	0.5	0	0.2	0.1	6.9	3	3	269	9	0.5	1	0	0.08	1	126.8	0.6	0.02	0.11
Mung beans, cooked — *½ cup*	101	106	19.3	0	7.7	0.4	0.1	0.1	0.1	7.1	27	1	269	2	0.8	2	0	0.07	1	160.4	0.6	0.06	0.17
Mungo beans, cooked — *½ cup*	90	95	16.5	0	5.8	0.5	0	0.3	0	6.8	48	2	208	6	0.7	3	0	0.05	1	85	1.4	0.07	0.14
Navy beans																							
canned — *½ cup*	131	148	26.8	0	6.7	0.6	0	0.2	0.1	9.9	62	2	377	587	1	0	0	0.13	1	81.6	0.6	0.07	0.18
cooked — *½ cup*	91	129	23.9	0	5.8	0.5	0	0.2	0.1	7.9	64	2	335	1	1	0	0	0.15	1	127.3	0.5	0.06	0.18
Pigeon peas, cooked — *½ cup*	84	102	19.5	0	5.6	0.3	0	0.2	0.1	5.7	36	1	323	4	0.8	0	0	0.04	0	93.1	0.7	0.05	0.12
Pink beans, cooked — *½ cup*	85	126	23.6	0	4.5	0.4	0	0.2	0.1	7.7	44	2	429	2	0.8	0	0	0.15	0	142.2	0.5	0.05	0.22
Pinto beans																							
canned — *½ cup*	120	103	18.3	0	5.5	1	0.2	0.3	0.2	5.8	52	2	292	353	0.8	2	0	0.09	1	72.2	0.4	0.08	0.12
cooked — *½ cup*	86	117	21.9	0	7.4	0.4	0.1	0.2	0.1	7	41	2	400	2	0.9	0	0	0.13	2	147.1	0.3	0.08	0.16
Refried beans, canned — *½ cup*	126	118	19.6	10	6.7	1.6	0.7	0.2	0.6	6.9	44	2	336	377	1.5	0	0	0.18	8	13.9	0.4	0.02	0.03
Small white beans, cooked — *½ cup*	90	127	23.1	0	9.3	0.6	0.1	0.2	0.1	8	65	3	414	2	1	0	0	0.11	0	122.5	0.2	0.05	0.21
Soy meal, defatted, raw — *½ cup*	61	207	24.5	0	0	1.5	0.2	0.6	0.2	27.4	149	8	1519	2	3.1	2	0	0.35	0	184.6	1.6	0.15	0.42
Soybeans																							
cooked — *½ cup*	86	149	8.5	0	5.2	7.7	1.7	4.4	1.1	14.3	88	4	443	1	1	1	0	0.2	1	46.3	0.3	0.25	0.13
dry-roasted — *½ cup*	86	387	28.1	0	7	18.6	4.1	10.5	2.7	34	232	3	1173	2	4.1	2	0	0.19	4	176	0.9	0.65	0.37

	Weight g	Calories	Carbohydrates g	Cholesterol mg	Dietary fiber g	Total fat g	Mono. fat g	Poly. fat g	Sat. fat g	Protein g	Calcium mg	Iron mg	Potassium mg	Sodium mg	Zinc mg	Vitamin A RE	Vitamin B12 mcg	Vitamin B6 mg	Vitamin C mg	Folic acid mcg	Niacin mg	Riboflavin mg	Thiamin mg
roasted, salted — *½ cup*	86	405	28.9	0	15.2	21.8	4.8	12.3	3.2	30.3	119	3	1264	140	2.7	17	0	0.18	2	181.5	1.2	0.12	0.09
Split peas, cooked — *½ cup*	98	116	20.7	0	8.1	0.4	0.1	0.2	0.1	8.2	14	1	355	2	1	1	0	0.05	0	63.6	0.9	0.05	0.19
White beans																							
canned — *½ cup*	131	153	28.7	0	6.3	0.4	0	0.2	0.1	9.5	96	4	595	7	1.5	0	0	0.1	0	85.7	0.1	0.05	0.13
cooked — *½ cup*	90	124	22.5	0	5.6	0.3	0	0.1	0.1	8.7	81	3	502	5	1.2	0	0	0.08	0	72.2	0.1	0.04	0.11
Winged beans, cooked — *½ cup*	86	126	12.8	0	0	5	1.9	1.3	0.7	9.1	122	4	241	11	1.2	0	0	0.04	0	8.9	0.7	0.11	0.25
Yardlong beans, cooked — *½ cup*	86	101	18	0	3.2	0.4	0	0.2	0.1	7.1	36	2	269	4	0.9	2	0	0.08	0	124.6	0.5	0.05	0.18
Yellow beans, cooked — *½ cup*	89	127	22.4	0	9.2	1	0.1	0.4	0.2	8.1	55	2	288	4	0.9	0	0	0.11	2	71.6	0.6	0.09	0.17

Luncheon Meats & Sausages

	Weight g	Calories	Carbohydrates g	Cholesterol mg	Dietary fiber g	Total fat g	Mono. fat g	Poly. fat g	Sat. fat g	Protein g	Calcium mg	Iron mg	Potassium mg	Sodium mg	Zinc mg	Vitamin A RE	Vitamin B12 mcg	Vitamin B6 mg	Vitamin C mg	Folic acid mcg	Niacin mg	Riboflavin mg	Thiamin mg
Barbecue loaf, pork & beef — *1 oz*	28	49	1.8	10	0	2.5	1.2	0.2	0.9	4.5	16	0	93	378	0.7	2	0.5	0.07	0	2.6	0.6	0.07	0.1
Beef																							
loaved lunch meat — *1 slice*	28	87	0.8	18	0	7.4	3.5	0.2	3.2	4.1	3	1	59	377	0.7	0	1.1	0.05	0	1.4	1	0.06	0.03
thin sliced lunch meat — *1 oz*	28	50	1.6	12	0	1.1	0.5	0.1	0.5	8	3	1	122	408	1.1	0	0.7	0.1	0	3.1	1.5	0.05	0.02
Beef, cured																							
chopped beef, smoked — *1 oz*	28	35	0.5	13	0	1.3	0.5	0.1	0.5	5.7	2	1	107	357	1.1	0	0.5	0.1	0	2.3	1.3	0.05	0.02
dried beef — *1 oz*	28	47	0.4	12	0	1.1	0.5	0.1	0.5	8.2	2	1	126	984	1.5	0	0.8	0.1	0	3.1	1.5	0.06	0.02
luncheon meat, jellied — *1 oz*	28	31	0	10	0	0.9	0.4	0	0.4	5.4	3	1	114	375	1	0	1.5	0.07	0	2	1.4	0.08	0.04
sausage, cooked, smoked — *1 oz*	28	88	0.7	19	0	7.6	3.7	0.3	3.2	4	2	0	50	321	0.8	0	0.5	0.03	0	1.1	0.9	0.04	0.01
thin-sliced — *1 oz*	28	50	1.6	12	0	1.1	0.5	0.1	0.5	8	3	1	122	408	1.1	0	0.7	0.1	0	3.1	1.5	0.05	0.02
Berliner, pork & beef — *1 oz*	28	65	0.7	13	0	4.9	2.3	0.4	1.7	4.3	3	0	80	368	0.7	0	0.8	0.06	0	1.4	0.9	0.06	0.11
Blood sausage — *1 oz*	28	107	0.4	34	0	9.8	4.5	1	3.8	4.1	2	2	11	193	0.4	0	0.3	0.01	0	1.4	0.3	0.04	0.02
Bockwurst (pork, veal, milk), raw — *1 link*	65	200	0.3	38	0	17.9	8.5	1.9	6.6	8.7	10	0	176	718	1	4	0.5	0.15	0	3.9	2.7	0.11	0.27
Bologna																							
beef — *1 slice*	23	72	0.2	13	0	6.6	3.2	0.3	2.8	2.8	3	0	36	226	0.5	0	0.3	0.03	0	1.2	0.6	0.03	0.01

	Weight *g*	Calories	Carbohydrates *g*	Cholesterol *mg*	Dietary fiber *g*	Total fat *g*	Mono. fat *g*	Poly. fat *g*	Sat. fat *g*	Protein *g*	Calcium *mg*	Iron *mg*	Potassium *mg*	Sodium *mg*	Zinc *mg*	Vitamin A *RE*	Vitamin B_{12} *mcg*	Vitamin B_6 *mg*	Vitamin C *mg*	Folic acid *mcg*	Niacin *mg*	Riboflavin *mg*	Thiamin *mg*
beef & pork — *1 slice*	23	73	0.6	13	0	6.5	3.1	0.6	2.5	2.7	3	0	41	234	0.4	0	0.3	0.04	0	1.2	0.6	0.03	0.04
pork — *1 slice*	23	57	0.2	14	0	4.6	2.2	0.5	1.6	3.5	3	0	65	272	0.5	0	0.2	0.06	0	1.2	0.9	0.04	0.12
turkey — *1 slice*	28	56	0.3	28	0	4.3	1.4	1.2	1.4	3.9	24	0	56	249	0.5	0	0.1	0.06	0	2	1	0.05	0.02
Bratwurst, pork, cooked — *1 link*	85	256	1.8	51	0	22	10.4	2.3	7.9	12	37	1	180	473	2	0	0.8	0.18	1	1.7	2.7	0.16	0.43
Braunschweiger, pork — *1 oz*	28	102	0.9	44	0	9.1	4.2	1.1	3.1	3.8	3	3	56	324	0.8	1196	5.7	0.09	0	12.5	2.4	0.43	0.07
Breakfast strips, cooked																							
beef — *3 slices*	34	153	0.5	40	0	11.7	5.7	0.5	4.9	10.6	3	1	140	766	2.2	0	1.2	0.11	0	2.7	2.2	0.09	0.03
pork — *3 slices*	34	156	0.4	36	0	12.5	5.6	1.9	4.3	9.8	5	1	158	714	1.3	0	0.6	0.12	0	1.4	2.6	0.13	0.25
Brotwurst (pork, beef, & nonfat dry milk) — *1 link*	70	226	2.1	44	0	19.5	9.3	2	7	10	34	1	197	778	1.5	0	1.4	0.09	0	3.5	2.3	0.16	0.18
Chicken roll, light meat — *1 slice*	28	45	0.7	14	0	2.1	0.8	0.5	0.6	5.5	12	0	65	166	0.2	7	0	0.06	0	0.6	1.5	0.04	0.02
Chicken spread, canned — *1 oz*	28	54	1.5	15	0	3.3	1.4	0.7	1	4.4	35	1	30	109	0.3	7	0	0.04	0	0.9	0.8	0.03	0
Chorizo, pork & beef — *1 link*	60	273	1.1	53	0	23	11	2.1	8.6	14.5	5	1	239	741	2	0	1.2	0.32	0	1.2	3.1	0.18	0.38
Corned beef loaf, jellied — *1 slice*	28	43	0	13	0	1.7	0.8	0.1	0.7	6.5	3	1	29	270	1.2	0	0.4	0.03	0	2.3	0.5	0.03	0
Corned beef, canned — *1 oz*	28	71	0	24	0	4.2	1.7	0.2	1.8	7.7	3	1	39	285	1	0	0.5	0.04	0	2.6	0.7	0.04	0.01
Dutch brand loaf, pork & beef — *1 slice*	28	68	1.6	13	0	5.1	2.4	0.5	1.8	3.8	24	0	107	354	0.5	0	0.4	0.07	0	0.6	0.7	0.08	0.09
Frankfurter																							
beef — *1 frankfurter*	45	142	0.8	27	0	12.8	6.1	0.6	5.4	5.4	9	1	75	462	1	0	0.7	0.05	0	1.8	1.1	0.05	0.02
beef & pork — *1 frankfurter*	45	144	1.1	23	0	13.1	6.2	1.2	4.8	5.1	5	1	75	504	0.8	0	0.6	0.06	0	1.8	1.2	0.05	0.09
chicken — *1 frankfurter*	45	116	3.1	45	0	8.8	3.8	1.8	2.5	5.8	43	1	38	617	0.5	17	0.1	0.14	0	1.8	1.4	0.05	0.03
turkey — *1 frankfurter*	45	102	0.7	48	0	8	2.5	2.3	2.7	6.4	48	1	81	642	1.4	0	0.1	0.1	0	3.6	1.9	0.08	0.02
Ham																							
chopped, canned — *1 oz*	28	68	0.1	14	0	5.3	2.6	0.6	1.8	4.6	2	0	81	387	0.5	0	0.2	0.09	1	0.3	0.9	0.05	0.15
extra lean — *1 slice*	28	37	0.3	13	0	1.4	0.7	0.1	0.5	5.5	2	0	99	405	0.5	0	0.2	0.13	0	1.1	1.4	0.06	0.26
minced — *1 slice*	21	55	0.4	15	0	4.3	2	0.5	1.5	3.4	2	0	65	261	0.4	0	0.2	0.05	0	0.2	0.9	0.04	0.15

	Weight g	Calories	Carbohydrates g	Cholesterol mg	Dietary fiber g	Total fat g	Mono. fat g	Poly. fat g	Sat. fat g	Protein g	Calcium mg	Iron mg	Potassium mg	Sodium mg	Zinc mg	Vitamin A RE	Vitamin B_{12} mcg	Vitamin B_6 mg	Vitamin C mg	Folic acid mcg	Niacin mg	Riboflavin mg	Thiamin mg
regular — *1 slice*	28	52	0.9	16	0	3	1.4	0.3	1	5	2	0	94	373	0.6	0	0.2	0.1	0	0.9	1.5	0.07	0.24
turkey — *1 slice*	28	36	0.1	16	0	1.4	0.3	0.4	0.5	5.4	3	1	92	282	0.8	0	0.1	0.07	0	1.7	1	0.07	0.01
Ham & cheese loaf — *1 slice*	28	73	0.4	16	0	5.7	2.6	0.6	2.1	4.7	16	0	83	381	0.6	7	0.2	0.07	0	0.9	1	0.05	0.17
Headcheese, pork — *1 slice*	28	60	0.1	23	0	4.5	2.3	0.5	1.4	4.5	5	0	9	356	0.4	0	0.3	0.05	0	0.6	0.3	0.05	0.01
Honey loaf, pork & beef — *1 slice*	28	36	1.5	10	0	1.3	0.6	0.1	0.4	4.5	5	0	97	374	0.7	0	0.3	0.09	0	2.3	0.9	0.07	0.14
Honey roll sausage, beef — *1 oz*	28	52	0.6	14	0	3	1.4	0.1	1.2	5.3	3	1	82	375	0.9	0	0.7	0.08	0	1.1	1.2	0.05	0.02
Italian sausage, pork, cooked — *1 link*	67	216	1	52	0	17.2	8	2.2	6.1	13.4	16	1	204	618	1.6	0	0.9	0.22	1	3.4	2.8	0.16	0.42
Kielbasa/kolbassy (pork, beef, & nonfat dry milk) — *1 oz*	28	88	0.6	19	0	7.7	3.7	0.9	2.8	3.8	12	0	77	305	0.6	0	0.5	0.05	0	1.4	0.8	0.06	0.06
Knackwurst/knockwurst, pork & beef — *1 oz*	28	87	0.5	16	0	7.9	3.6	0.8	2.9	3.4	3	0	56	286	0.5	0	0.3	0.05	0	0.6	0.8	0.04	0.1
Lebanon bologna, beef — *1 slice*	23	49	0.6	16	0	3	1.4	0.1	1.3	4.4	3	1	69	308	0.9	0	0.6	0.06	0	0.7	1	0.04	0.01
Liver cheese, pork — *1 oz*	28	86	0.6	49	0	7.3	3.5	1	2.5	4.3	2	3	64	347	1	1489	7	0.13	1	29.5	3.3	0.63	0.06
Liver sausage/liverwurst, pork — *1 oz*	28	92	0.6	45	0	8.1	3.8	0.7	3	4	7	2	48	244	0.7	2353	3.8	0.05	0	8.5	1.2	0.29	0.08
Luncheon sausage, pork & beef — *1 oz*	28	74	0.4	18	0	5.9	2.8	0.6	2.2	4.4	4	0	69	335	0.7	0	0.6	0.06	0	0.9	1	0.06	0.06
Luxury loaf, pork — *1 slice*	28	40	1.4	10	0	1.4	0.7	0.1	0.4	5.2	10	0	107	347	0.9	0	0.4	0.09	0	0.6	1	0.08	0.2
Mortadella, beef & pork — *1 slice*	15	47	0.5	8	0	3.8	1.7	0.5	1.4	2.5	3	0	24	187	0.3	0	0.2	0.02	0	0.5	0.4	0.02	0.02
Mother's loaf, pork — *1 slice*	21	59	1.6	9	0	4.7	2.2	0.5	1.7	2.5	9	0	47	237	0.3	0	0.2	0.04	0	1.7	0.7	0.04	0.12
New england brand sausage, pork & beef — *1 oz*	28	46	1.4	14	0	2.1	1	0.2	0.7	4.9	2	0	91	346	0.8	0	0.4	0.1	0	2	1	0.07	0.18
Olive loaf, pork — *1 slice*	28	67	2.6	11	0	4.7	2.2	0.5	1.7	3.3	31	0	84	421	0.4	6	0.4	0.07	0	0.6	0.5	0.07	0.08
Pastrami																							
beef — *1 oz*	28	99	0.9	26	0	8.3	4.1	0.3	3	4.9	3	1	65	348	1.2	0	0.5	0.05	0	2	1.4	0.05	0.03
turkey — *1 slice*	28	40	0.5	15	0	1.8	0.6	0.5	0.5	5.2	3	0	74	296	0.6	0	0.1	0.08	0	1.4	1	0.07	0.02
Paté																							
chicken liver, canned — *1 oz*	28	57	1.9	111	0	3.7	1.5	0.7	1.1	3.8	3	3	27	109	0.6	62	2.3	0.07	3	91	2.1	0.4	0.01
goose liver, smoked, canned — *1 oz*	28	131	1.3	43	0	12.4	7.3	0.2	4.1	3.2	20	2	39	198	0.3	284	2.7	0.02	0	17	0.7	0.08	0.02

Food	Weight *g*	Calories	Carbohydrates *g*	Cholesterol *mg*	Dietary fiber *g*	Total fat *g*	Mono. fat *g*	Poly. fat *g*	Sat. fat *g*	Protein *g*	Calcium *mg*	Iron *mg*	Potassium *mg*	Sodium *mg*	Zinc *mg*	Vitamin A *RE*	Vitamin B_{12} *mcg*	Vitamin B_6 *mg*	Vitamin C *mg*	Folic acid *mcg*	Niacin *mg*	Riboflavin *mg*	Thiamin *mg*
Peppered loaf, pork & beef — *1 slice*	28	42	1.3	13	0	1.8	0.9	0.1	0.6	4.9	15	0	112	432	0.9	0	0.6	0.08	0	0.6	0.9	0.09	0.11
Pepperoni, pork & beef — *1 slice*	6	27	0.2	4	0	2.4	1.2	0.2	0.9	1.2	1	0	19	112	0.1	0	0.1	0.01	0	0.2	0.3	0.01	0.02
Pickle & pimento loaf, pork — *1 slice*	28	74	1.7	10	0	6	2.7	0.7	2.2	3.3	27	0	96	394	0.4	2	0.3	0.05	0	1.4	0.6	0.07	0.08
Picnic loaf, pork & beef — *1 slice*	28	66	1.3	11	0	4.7	2.2	0.5	1.7	4.2	13	0	76	330	0.6	0	0.4	0.09	0	0.6	0.7	0.07	0.11
Polish sausage, pork — *1 oz*	28	92	0.5	20	0	8.1	3.8	0.9	2.9	4	3	0	67	248	0.5	0	0.3	0.05	0	0.6	1	0.04	0.14
Pork & beef lunch meat — *1 slice*	28	100	0.7	16	0	9.1	4.3	1.1	3.3	3.6	3	0	57	367	0.5	0	0.4	0.06	0	1.7	0.8	0.04	0.09
Pork lunch meat, canned — *1 oz*	28	95	0.6	18	0	8.6	4.1	1	3.1	3.5	2	0	61	365	0.4	0	0.3	0.06	0	1.7	0.9	0.05	0.1
Salami																							
beef — *1 oz*	28	74	0.8	18	0	5.9	2.7	0.3	2.6	4.3	3	1	64	333	0.6	0	0.9	0.05	0	0.6	0.9	0.05	0.03
beef & pork — *1 oz*	28	71	0.6	18	0	5.7	2.6	0.6	2.3	3.9	4	1	56	302	0.6	0	1	0.06	0	0.6	1	0.11	0.07
beerwurst, beef — *1 slice*	23	76	0.4	14	0	6.9	3.2	0.3	3	2.9	2	0	40	236	0.6	0	0.5	0.04	0	0.7	0.8	0.03	0.02
beerwurst, pork — *1 slice*	23	55	0.5	14	0	4.3	2.1	0.5	1.4	3.3	2	0	58	285	0.4	0	0.2	0.08	0	0.7	0.7	0.04	0.13
turkey — *1 oz*	28	56	0.2	23	0	3.9	1.3	1	1.1	4.6	6	0	69	285	0.5	0	0.1	0.07	0	1.1	1	0.05	0.02
Salami, dry or hard																							
pork — *1 oz*	28	115	0.5	22	0	9.5	4.5	1.1	3.4	6.4	4	0	107	638	1.2	0	0.8	0.16	0	0.6	1.6	0.09	0.26
pork & beef — *1 oz*	28	118	0.7	22	0	9.7	4.8	0.9	3.4	6.5	2	0	107	525	0.9	0	0.5	0.14	0	0.6	1.4	0.08	0.17
Sandwich spread																							
ham & cheese — *1 oz*	28	69	0.6	17	0	5.3	2	0.4	2.4	4.6	62	0	46	339	0.6	26	0.2	0.04	0	0.9	0.6	0.06	0.09
ham salad — *1 oz*	28	61	3	10	0	4.4	2	0.8	1.4	2.5	2	0	43	259	0.3	0	0.2	0.04	0	0.3	0.6	0.03	0.12
pork & beef — *1 oz*	28	67	3.4	11	0.1	4.9	2.2	0.7	1.7	2.2	3	0	31	287	0.3	3	0.3	0.03	0	0.6	0.5	0.04	0.05
poultry salad — *1 oz*	28	57	2.1	9	0	3.8	0.9	1.8	1	3.3	3	0	52	107	0.3	12	0.1	0.03	0	1.4	0.5	0.02	0.01
Sausage, fresh																							
pork & beef, cooked — *1 patty*	27	107	0.7	19	0	9.8	4.6	1.1	3.5	3.7	3	0	51	217	0.5	0	0.1	0.01	0	0.5	0.9	0.04	0.1
pork, cooked — *1 patty*	27	100	0.3	22	0	8.4	3.8	1	2.9	5.3	9	0	97	349	0.7	0	0.5	0.09	1	0.5	1.2	0.07	0.2

	Weight g	Calories	Carbohydrates g	Cholesterol mg	Dietary fiber g	Total fat g	Mono. fat g	Poly. fat g	Sat. fat g	Protein g	Calcium mg	Iron mg	Potassium mg	Sodium mg	Zinc mg	Vitamin A RE	Vitamin B_{12} mcg	Vitamin B_6 mg	Vitamin C mg	Folic acid mcg	Niacin mg	Riboflavin mg	Thiamin mg
Sausage, smoked link																							
pork — *2 small links*	32	124	0.7	22	0	10.1	4.7	1.2	3.6	7.1	10	0	108	480	0.9	0	0.5	0.11	1	1.6	1.5	0.08	0.22
pork & beef — *2 small links*	32	108	0.5	23	0	9.7	4.5	1	3.4	4.3	3	0	60	302	0.7	0	0.5	0.05	0	0.6	1	0.05	0.08
pork & beef w/ flour & nonfat dry milk — *2 small links*	32	86	1.3	28	0	6.9	3.2	0.7	2.5	4.5	6	0	50	348	0.6	0	0.4	0.04	1	0.6	0.9	0.06	0.08
pork & beef w/ nonfat dry milk — *2 small links*	32	100	0.6	21	0	8.8	4	1	3.1	4.2	13	0	92	375	0.6	0	0.5	0.06	0	0.6	0.9	0.07	0.06
Thuringer (cervelat/summer sausage), beef & pork — *1 oz*	28	95	0.1	21	0	8.4	3.7	0.3	3.4	4.5	4	1	77	352	0.7	0	1.6	0.07	0	0.6	1.2	0.09	0.04
Turkey breast — *1 slice*	21	23	0	9	0	0.3	0.1	0.1	0.1	4.7	1	0	58	301	0.2	0	0.4	0.08	0	0.8	1.7	0.02	0.01
Turkey roll																							
light & dark meat — *1 oz*	28	42	0.6	16	0	2	0.7	0.5	0.6	5.1	9	0	77	166	0.6	0	0.1	0.08	0	1.4	1.4	0.08	0.03
light meat — *1 oz*	28	42	0.2	12	0	2	0.7	0.5	0.6	5.3	11	0	71	139	0.4	0	0.1	0.09	0	1.1	2	0.06	0.03
Vienna sausage, beef & pork, canned — *3 sausages*	48	134	1	25	0	12.1	6	0.8	4.5	4.9	5	0	48	457	0.8	0	0.5	0.06	0	1.9	0.8	0.05	0.04

Meat Substitutes

	Weight g	Calories	Carbohydrates g	Cholesterol mg	Dietary fiber g	Total fat g	Mono. fat g	Poly. fat g	Sat. fat g	Protein g	Calcium mg	Iron mg	Potassium mg	Sodium mg	Zinc mg	Vitamin A RE	Vitamin B_{12} mcg	Vitamin B_6 mg	Vitamin C mg	Folic acid mcg	Niacin mg	Riboflavin mg	Thiamin mg
Bacon, meatless — *4 strips*	20	62	1.3	0	0.5	5.9	1.4	3.1	0.9	2.1	5	0	34	293	0.1	2	0	0.1	0	8.3	1.5	0.1	0.88
Meat extender — *1 oz*	28	89	10.9	0	5	0.8	0.2	0.5	0.1	10.8	58	3	539	3	0.6	1	1.7	0.38	0	56.1	6.2	0.25	0.2
Miso — *3 ½ oz*	100	207	28.1	0	5.4	6.1	1.3	3.4	0.9	11.9	66	3	165	3661	3.3	9	0	0.22	0	33.1	0.9	0.25	0.1
Natto — *3 ½ oz*	100	211	14.3	0	5.4	11	2.4	6.2	1.6	17.7	216	9	727	7	3	0	0	0.13	13	8	0	0.19	0.16
Sausage, meatless — *3 links*	75	192	7.4	0	2.1	13.6	3.4	7	2.2	13.9	47	3	173	666	1.1	48	0	0.62	0	19.5	8.4	0.3	1.76
Tempeh — *3 ½ oz*	100	198	17	0	0	7.6	1.7	4.3	1.1	18.9	93	2	366	6	1.8	69	1	0.3	0	51.8	4.6	0.11	0.13
Tofu																							
fried — *3 ½ oz*	99	269	10.4	0	3.9	20	4.4	11.3	2.9	17.1	369	5	145	16	2	0	0	0.1	0	26.6	0.1	0.05	0.17
okara — *3 ½ oz*	100	77	12.5	0	0	1.7	0.3	0.8	0.2	3.2	80	1	213	9	0.6	0	0	0.12	0	26.4	0.1	0.02	0.02
raw, firm — *3 ½ oz*	100	144	4.3	0	2.3	8.7	1.9	4.9	1.3	15.7	204	10	236	14	1.6	17	0	0.09	0	29.2	0.4	0.1	0.16
raw, regular — *3 ½ oz*	100	76	1.9	0	1.2	4.8	1.1	2.7	0.7	8.1	105	5	121	7	0.8	9	0	0.05	0	15	0.2	0.05	0.08
salted & fermented (fuyu) — *3 ½ oz*	99	115	5.1	0	0	7.9	1.7	4.5	1.1	8.1	46	2	74	2844	1.5	17	0	0.09	0	28.8	0.4	0.1	0.16

Milk

	Weight g	Calories	Carbohydrates g	Cholesterol mg	Dietary fiber g	Total fat g	Mono. fat g	Poly. fat g	Sat. fat g	Protein g	Calcium mg	Iron mg	Potassium mg	Sodium mg	Zinc mg	Vitamin A RE	Vitamin B_{12} mcg	Vitamin B_6 mg	Vitamin C mg	Folic acid mcg	Niacin mg	Riboflavin mg	Thiamin mg
1% fat milk																							
protein fortified — *1 cup*	246	119	13.6	10	0	2.9	0.8	0.1	1.8	9.7	349	0	444	143	1.1	145	1	0.12	3	14.5	0.2	0.47	0.11
regular — *1 cup*	244	102	11.7	10	0	2.6	0.7	0.1	1.6	8	300	0	381	123	1	144	0.9	0.1	2	12.4	0.2	0.41	0.1
w/ added nonfat milk solids — *1 cup*	245	104	12.2	10	0	2.4	0.7	0.1	1.5	8.5	313	0	397	128	1	145	0.9	0.11	2	13	0.2	0.42	0.1
2% fat milk																							
protein fortified — *1 cup*	246	137	13.5	19	0	4.9	1.4	0.2	3	9.7	352	0	447	145	1.1	140	1.1	0.13	3	14.8	0.2	0.48	0.11
regular — *1 cup*	244	121	11.7	18	0	4.7	1.4	0.2	2.9	8.1	297	0	377	122	1	139	0.9	0.1	2	12.4	0.2	0.4	0.1
w/ added nonfat milk solids — *1 cup*	245	125	12.2	18	0	4.7	1.4	0.2	2.9	8.5	313	0	397	128	1	140	0.9	0.11	2	13	0.2	0.42	0.1
Buttermilk																							
cultured — *1 cup*	245	99	11.7	9	0	2.2	0.6	0.1	1.3	8.1	285	0	371	257	1	20	0.5	0.08	2	12.3	0.1	0.38	0.08
Chocolate milk, whole																							
carob-flavored powder — *1 cup*	256	195	22.5	33	1	8.2	2.4	0.3	5.1	8.2	292	1	369	133	0.9	77	0.9	0.12	2	12.3	0.3	0.39	0.09
chocolate-flavored powder — *1 cup*	266	226	30.9	32	1.3	8.8	2.6	0.3	5.5	8.8	301	1	497	165	1.3	77	0.9	0.1	2	12.2	0.3	0.43	0.1
chocolate syrup — *1 cup*	282	231	33.6	34	0.6	8.5	2.5	0.3	5.3	8.7	296	1	454	155	1.2	76	0.9	0.1	2	13.8	0.3	0.41	0.1
Condensed, sweetened, canned — *½ cup*	153	491	83.2	52	0	13.3	3.7	0.5	8.4	12.1	434	0	568	194	1.4	124	0.7	0.08	4	17.1	0.3	0.64	0.14
Dry milk																							
buttermilk — *¼ cup*	30	116	14.7	21	0	1.7	0.5	0.1	1.1	10.3	355	0	478	155	1.2	16	1.1	0.1	2	14.2	0.3	0.47	0.12
skim, calcium-reduced — *¼ cup*	19	66	9.7	0	0	0	0	0	0	6.6	52	0	127	427	0.8	0	0.7	0.06	1	9.3	0.1	0.31	0.03
skim, instant, nonfat solids — *¼ cup*	17	61	8.9	3	0	0.1	0	0	0.1	6	209	0	290	93	0.7	1	0.7	0.06	1	8.5	0.2	0.3	0.07
skim, instant w/ nonfat solids — *¼ cup*	17	61	8.9	3	0	0.1	0	0	0.1	6	209	0	290	93	0.7	121	0.7	0.06	1	8.5	0.2	0.3	0.07
skim, regular w/ nonfat solids — *¼ cup*	30	109	15.6	6	0	0.2	0.1	0	0.1	10.8	377	0	538	161	1.2	198	1.2	0.11	2	15	0.3	0.47	0.12
whole — *¼ cup*	32	159	12.3	31	0	8.5	2.5	0.2	5.4	8.4	292	0	426	119	1.1	90	1	0.1	3	11.8	0.2	0.39	0.09

	Weight g	Calories	Carbohydrates g	Cholesterol mg	Dietary fiber g	Total fat g	Mono. fat g	Poly. fat g	Sat. fat g	Protein g	Calcium mg	Iron mg	Potassium mg	Sodium mg	Zinc mg	Vitamin A RE	Vitamin B_{12} mcg	Vitamin B_6 mg	Vitamin C mg	Folic acid mcg	Niacin mg	Riboflavin mg	Thiamin mg
Evaporated milk																							
skim — *½ cup*	128	100	14.5	5	0	0.3	0.1	0	0.2	9.7	371	0	424	147	1.2	150	0.3	0.07	2	11	0.2	0.4	0.06
whole — *½ cup*	126	169	12.7	37	0	9.5	2.9	0.3	5.8	8.6	329	0	382	133	1	68	0.2	0.06	2	10	0.2	0.4	0.06
Goat milk — *1 cup*	244	168	10.9	28	0	10.1	2.7	0.4	6.5	8.7	326	0	499	122	0.7	137	0.2	0.11	3	1.5	0.7	0.34	0.12
Indian buffalo milk — *1 cup*	244	236	12.6	46	0	16.8	4.4	0.4	11.2	9.2	412	0	434	127	0.5	129	0.9	0.06	5	13.7	0.2	0.33	0.13
Sheep milk — *1 cup*	245	264	13.1	66	0	17.2	4.2	0.8	11.3	14.7	474	0	334	108	1.3	103	1.7	0.15	10	17.2	1	0.87	0.16
Skim milk																							
protein-fortified — *1 cup*	246	100	13.7	5	0	0.6	0.2	0	0.4	9.7	352	0	446	144	1.1	150	1.1	0.12	3	14.8	0.2	0.48	0.11
regular — *1 cup*	245	86	11.9	4	0	0.4	0.1	0	0.3	8.4	302	0	406	126	1	149	0.9	0.1	2	12.7	0.2	0.34	0.09
w/ added nonfat milk solids — *1 cup*	245	90	12.3	5	0	0.6	0.2	0	0.4	8.7	316	0	418	130	1	149	0.9	0.11	2	13.2	0.2	0.43	0.1
Soy milk, fluid — *1 cup*	245	81	4.4	0	3.2	4.7	0.8	2	0.5	6.7	10	1	345	29	0.6	7	0	0.1	0	3.7	0.4	0.17	0.39
Whole milk																							
3.3% fat — *1 cup*	244	150	11.4	33	0	8.1	2.4	0.3	5.1	8	291	0	370	120	0.9	76	0.9	0.1	2	12.2	0.2	0.4	0.09
low-sodium — *1 cup*	244	149	10.9	33	0	8.4	2.4	0.3	5.3	7.6	246	0	617	6	0.9	78	0.9	0.08	2	12.2	0.1	0.26	0.05

Nuts & Seeds

	Weight g	Calories	Carbohydrates g	Cholesterol mg	Dietary fiber g	Total fat g	Mono. fat g	Poly. fat g	Sat. fat g	Protein g	Calcium mg	Iron mg	Potassium mg	Sodium mg	Zinc mg	Vitamin A RE	Vitamin B_{12} mcg	Vitamin B_6 mg	Vitamin C mg	Folic acid mcg	Niacin mg	Riboflavin mg	Thiamin mg
Acorns																							
dried — *1 oz*	28	144	15.2	0	0	8.9	5.6	1.7	1.2	2.3	15	0	201	0	0.2	0	0	0.2	0	32.5	0.7	0.04	0.04
raw — *1 oz*	28	110	11.6	0	0	6.8	4.3	1.3	0.9	1.7	12	0	153	0	0.1	1	0	0.15	0	24.7	0.5	0.03	0.03
Almond butter																							
honey/cinnamon — *1 Tbsp*	16	96	4.3	0	0	8.4	5.4	1.8	0.8	2.5	43	1	120	2	0.5	0	0	0.01	0	10.3	0.5	0.1	0.02
honey/cinnamon w/ salt — *1 Tbsp*	16	96	4.3	0	0.6	8.4	5.4	1.8	0.8	2.5	43	1	120	27	0.5	0	0	0.01	0	10.3	0.5	0.1	0.02
unsalted — *1 Tbsp*	16	101	3.4	0	0.6	9.5	6.1	2	0.9	2.4	43	1	121	2	0.5	0	0	0.01	0	10.4	0.5	0.1	0.02
w/ salt — *1 Tbsp*	16	101	3.4	0	0.6	9.5	6.1	2	0.9	2.4	43	1	121	72	0.5	0	0	0.01	0	10.4	0.5	0.1	0.02
Almond meal, partially defatted — *1 oz*	28	116	8.2	0	0	5.2	3.4	1.1	0.5	11.2	120	2	397	2	0.8	0	0	0.03	0	16.2	1.8	0.48	0.09

	Weight g	Calories	Carbohydrates g	Cholesterol mg	Dietary fiber g	Total fat g	Mono. fat g	Poly. fat g	Sat. fat g	Protein g	Calcium mg	Iron mg	Potassium mg	Sodium mg	Zinc mg	Vitamin A RE	Vitamin B_{12} mcg	Vitamin B_6 mg	Vitamin C mg	Folic acid mcg	Niacin mg	Riboflavin mg	Thiamin mg
Almond paste — *1 oz*	28	130	13.6	0	1.4	7.9	5.1	1.6	0.7	2.6	49	0	89	3	0.4	0	0	0.01	0	20.7	0.4	0.12	0.02
Almond powder																							
full-fat — *1 oz*	28	168	6.3	0	0	14.6	9.5	3.1	1.4	5.6	62	1	201	2	0.1	0	0	0.03	0	16.8	0.7	0.33	0.06
partially defatted — *1 oz*	28	111	9	0	0	4.5	2.9	1	0.4	10.6	67	1	204	3	0.9	0	0	0.03	0	10.4	0.9	0.18	0.04
Almonds																							
dried, blanched — *1 oz*	28	166	5.3	0	1.9	14.9	9.7	3.1	1.4	5.8	70	1	213	3	0.9	0	0	0.03	0	10.9	0.9	0.19	0.05
dried, unblanched — *1 oz*	28	167	5.8	0	3.1	14.8	9.6	3.1	1.4	5.7	75	1	208	3	0.8	0	0	0.03	0	16.6	1	0.22	0.06
dried, unblanched, slices — *½ cup*	48	280	9.7	0	5.2	24.8	16.1	5.2	2.4	9.5	126	2	348	5	1.4	0	0	0.05	0	27.9	1.6	0.37	0.1
dried, unblanched, slivers — *½ cup*	54	318	11	0	5.9	28.2	18.3	5.9	2.7	10.8	144	2	395	6	1.6	0	0	0.06	0	31.7	1.8	0.42	0.11
dry-roasted, unblanched — *1 oz*	28	166	6.9	0	3.9	14.6	9.5	3.1	1.4	4.6	80	1	218	3	1.4	0	0	0.02	0	18.1	0.8	0.17	0.04
dry-roasted, unblanched w/ salt — *1 oz*	28	166	6.9	0	3.9	14.6	9.5	3.1	1.4	4.6	80	1	218	221	1.4	0	0	0.02	0	18.1	0.8	0.17	0.04
honey-roasted, unblanched — *1 oz*	28	168	7.9	0	3.9	14.1	9.2	3	1.3	5.2	75	1	159	37	0.7	0	0	0.02	0	9.1	0.8	0.27	0.03
oil-roasted, blanched — *1 oz*	28	174	5.1	0	3.2	16	10.4	3.4	1.5	5.4	55	2	196	3	0.4	0	0	0.03	0	18	1.1	0.08	0.02
oil-roasted, unblanched — *1 oz*	28	175	4.5	0	3.2	16.3	10.6	3.4	1.5	5.8	66	1	194	3	1.4	0	0	0.02	0	18.1	1	0.28	0.04
oil-roasted, unblanched w/ salt — *1 oz*	28	175	4.5	0	3.2	16.3	10.6	3.4	1.5	5.8	66	1	194	221	1.4	0	0	0.02	0	18.1	1	0.28	0.04
toasted, unblanched — *1 oz*	28	167	6.5	0	3.2	14.4	9.3	3	1.4	5.8	80	1	219	3	1.4	0	0	0.02	0	18.2	0.8	0.17	0.04
Beechnuts, dried — *1 oz*	28	163	9.5	0	0	14.2	6.2	5.7	1.6	1.8	0	1	288	11	0.1	0	0	0.19	4	32	0.2	0.11	0.09
Brazilnuts, dried, unblanched — *1 oz*	28	186	3.6	0	1.5	18.8	6.5	6.8	4.6	4.1	50	1	170	1	1.3	0	0	0.07	0	1.1	0.5	0.03	0.28
Breadfruit seeds																							
boiled — *1 oz*	28	48	9.1	0	0	0.7	0.1	0.3	0.2	1.5	17	0	248	7	0.2	7	0	0.08	2	13.9	1.5	0.05	0.08
raw — *1 oz*	28	54	8.3	0	0	1.6	0.2	0.8	0.4	2.1	10	1	267	7	0.3	7	0	0.09	2	15	0.1	0.09	0.14
roasted — *1 oz*	28	59	11.4	0	0	0.8	0.1	0.4	0.2	1.8	24	0	307	8	0.3	8	0	0.12	2	16.8	2.1	0.07	0.12
Breadnuttree seeds																							
dried — *1 oz*	28	104	22.5	0	4.2	0.5	0.1	0.3	0.1	2.4	27	1	570	15	0.5	6	0	0.19	13	32	0.6	0.04	0.01

	Weight *g*	Calories	Carbohydrates *g*	Cholesterol *mg*	Dietary fiber *g*	Total fat *g*	Mono. fat *g*	Poly. fat *g*	Sat. fat *g*	Protein *g*	Calcium *mg*	Iron *mg*	Potassium *mg*	Sodium *mg*	Zinc *mg*	Vitamin A *RE*	Vitamin B_{12} *mcg*	Vitamin B_6 *mg*	Vitamin C *mg*	Folic acid *mcg*	Niacin *mg*	Riboflavin *mg*	Thiamin *mg*
raw — *1 oz*	28	62	13.1	0	0	0.3	0	0.1	0.1	1.7	28	1	335	9	0.3	7	0	0.11	8	18.8	0.2	0.02	0.02
Butternuts, dried — *1 oz*	28	174	3.4	0	1.3	16.2	3	12.1	0.4	7.1	15	1	119	0	0.9	3	0	0.16	1	18.8	0.3	0.04	0.11
Cashew butter																							
unsalted — *1 Tbsp*	16	94	4.4	0	0.3	7.9	4.7	1.3	1.6	2.8	7	1	87	2	0.8	0	0	0.04	0	10.9	0.3	0.03	0.05
w/ salt — *1 Tbsp*	16	94	4.4	0	0.3	7.9	4.7	1.3	1.6	2.8	7	1	87	98	0.8	0	0	0.04	0	10.9	0.3	0.03	0.05
Cashews																							
dry-roasted — *1 oz*	28	163	9.3	0	0.9	13.1	7.7	2.2	2.6	4.3	13	2	160	5	1.6	0	0	0.07	0	19.6	0.4	0.06	0.06
dry-roasted w/ salt — *1 oz*	28	163	9.3	0	0.9	13.1	7.7	2.2	2.6	4.3	13	2	160	181	1.6	0	0	0.07	0	19.6	0.4	0.06	0.06
oil-roasted — *1 oz*	28	163	8.1	0	1.1	13.7	8.1	2.3	2.7	4.6	12	1	150	5	1.3	0	0	0.07	0	19.2	0.5	0.05	0.12
oil-roasted w/ salt — *1 oz*	28	163	8.1	0	1.1	13.7	8.1	2.3	2.7	4.6	12	1	150	177	1.3	0	0	0.07	0	19.2	0.5	0.05	0.12
Chestnuts, chinese																							
boiled & steamed — *1 oz*	28	43	9.5	0	0	0.2	0.1	0.1	0	0.8	3	0	87	1	0.2	4	0	0.08	7	13.2	0.2	0.03	0.03
dried — *1 oz*	28	103	22.6	0	0	0.5	0.3	0.1	0.1	1.9	8	1	206	1	0.4	9	0	0.19	17	31.2	0.4	0.08	0.07
raw — *1 oz*	28	64	13.9	0	0	0.3	0.2	0.1	0	1.2	5	0	127	1	0.2	6	0	0.12	10	19.2	0.2	0.05	0.05
roasted — *1 oz*	28	68	14.8	0	0	0.3	0.2	0.1	0	1.3	5	0	135	1	0.3	0	0	0.12	11	20.5	0.4	0.03	0.04
Chestnuts, european																							
boiled & steamed — *1 oz*	28	37	7.9	0	0	0.4	0.1	0.2	0.1	0.6	13	0	203	8	0.1	1	0	0.07	8	10.9	0.2	0.03	0.04
dried — *1 oz*	28	105	22.2	0	0	1.1	0.4	0.4	0.2	1.4	18	1	281	10	0.1	0	0	0.19	4	31.2	0.2	0.02	0.1
raw — *1 oz*	28	56	12.5	0	0	0.4	0.1	0.1	0.1	0.5	5	0	137	1	0.1	1	0	0.1	11	16.4	0.3	0	0.04
roasted — *1 oz*	28	69	15	0	1.4	0.6	0.2	0.2	0.1	0.9	8	0	168	1	0.2	1	0	0.14	7	19.9	0.4	0.05	0.07
Chestnuts, japanese																							
boiled & steamed — *1 oz*	28	16	3.6	0	0	0.1	0	0	0	0.2	3	0	34	1	0.1	0	0	0.03	3	4.8	0.2	0.02	0.04
dried — *1 oz*	28	102	23.1	0	0	0.4	0.2	0.1	0.1	1.5	20	1	218	10	0.7	3	0	0.19	17	30.8	1	0.11	0.23
raw — *1 oz*	28	44	9.9	0	0	0.2	0.1	0	0	0.6	9	0	93	4	0.3	1	0	0.08	7	13.2	0.4	0.05	0.1

	Weight g	Calories	Carbohydrates g	Cholesterol mg	Dietary fiber g	Total fat g	Mono. fat g	Poly. fat g	Sat. fat g	Protein g	Calcium mg	Iron mg	Potassium mg	Sodium mg	Zinc mg	Vitamin A RE	Vitamin B_{12} mcg	Vitamin B_6 mg	Vitamin C mg	Folic acid mcg	Niacin mg	Riboflavin mg	Thiamin mg
roasted — *1 oz*	28	57	12.8	0	0	0.2	0.1	0.1	0	0.8	10	1	121	5	0.4	2	0	0.12	8	16.7	0.2	0	0.13
Chia seeds, dried — *1 oz*	28	134	13.6	0	0	7.4	2.1	2.1	3	4.7	150	3	292	11	1.5	1	0	0.2	4	32.4	1.6	0.05	0.25
Coconut																							
dried, creamed — *1 oz*	28	194	6.1	0	0	19.6	0.8	0.2	17.4	1.5	7	1	156	10	0.6	0	0	0.09	0	2.6	0.2	0.03	0.02
dried, sweetened, flaked, canned — *½ cup*	39	171	15.8	0	1.7	12.2	0.5	0.1	10.8	1.3	5	1	125	8	0.6	0	0	0.09	0	2.7	0.1	0.01	0.01
dried, sweetened, flaked, packaged — *½ cup*	37	175	17.6	0	1.6	11.9	0.5	0.1	10.5	1.2	5	1	117	95	0.6	0	0	0.1	0	2.9	0.1	0.01	0.01
dried, sweetened, shredded — *½ cup*	47	233	22.2	0	2.1	16.5	0.7	0.2	14.6	1.3	7	1	157	122	0.8	0	0	0.13	0	3.8	0.2	0.01	0.01
dried, toasted — *1 oz*	28	168	12.6	0	0	13.3	0.6	0.1	11.8	1.5	8	1	157	10	0.6	0	0	0.09	0	2.6	0.2	0.03	0.02
dried, unsweetened — *1 oz*	28	187	6.9	0	4.6	18.3	0.8	0.2	16.2	2	7	1	154	10	0.6	0	0	0.09	0	2.6	0.2	0.03	0.02
raw — *1 piece*	45	159	6.9	0	4.1	15.1	0.6	0.2	13.4	1.5	6	1	160	9	0.5	0	0	0.02	1	11.9	0.2	0.01	0.03
raw, shredded — *½ cup*	40	142	6.1	0	3.6	13.4	0.6	0.1	11.9	1.3	6	1	142	8	0.4	0	0	0.02	1	10.6	0.2	0.01	0.03
Coconut cream																							
canned — *½ cup*	148	284	12.4	0	3.3	26.2	1.1	0.3	23.3	4	1	1	149	74	0.9	0	0	0.04	3	21.2	0.1	0.06	0.03
raw — *½ cup*	120	396	8	0	2.6	41.6	1.8	0.5	36.9	4.4	13	3	390	5	1.2	0	0	0.06	3	27.6	1.1	0	0.04
Coconut milk																							
canned — *½ cup*	113	223	3.2	0	0	24.1	1	0.3	21.4	2.3	20	4	249	15	0.6	0	0	0.03	1	15.3	0.7	0	0.02
raw — *½ cup*	120	276	6.6	0	2.6	28.6	1.2	0.3	25.4	2.7	19	2	316	18	0.8	0	0	0.04	3	19.3	0.9	0	0.03
Coconut water — *½ cup*	120	23	4.5	0	1.3	0.2	0	0	0.2	0.9	29	0	300	126	0.1	0	0	0.04	3	3	0.1	0.07	0.04
Filberts (hazelnuts)																							
dried, blanched — *1 oz*	28	191	4.5	0	1.8	19.1	15	1.8	1.4	3.6	55	1	131	1	0.7	2	0	0.18	0	21.1	0.3	0.03	0.15
dried, unblanched — *1 oz*	28	179	4.3	0	1.7	17.8	13.9	1.7	1.3	3.7	53	1	126	1	0.7	2	0	0.17	0	20.4	0.3	0.03	0.14
dried, unblanched, chopped — *½ cup*	58	363	8.8	0	3.5	36	28.2	3.5	2.6	7.5	108	2	256	2	1.4	4	0	0.35	1	41.3	0.7	0.06	0.29
dry-roasted, unblanched — *1 oz*	28	188	5.1	0	2	18.8	14.7	1.8	1.4	2.8	55	1	131	1	0.7	2	0	0.18	0	21.1	0.8	0.06	0.06
oil-roasted, unblanched — *1 oz*	28	187	5.4	0	1.8	18	14.1	1.7	1.3	4	56	1	132	1	0.7	2	0	0.18	0	21.3	0.8	0.06	0.06

	Weight *g*	Calories	Carbohydrates *g*	Cholesterol *mg*	Dietary fiber *g*	Total fat *g*	Mono. fat *g*	Poly. fat *g*	Sat. fat *g*	Protein *g*	Calcium *mg*	Iron *mg*	Potassium *mg*	Sodium *mg*	Zinc *mg*	Vitamin A *RE*	Vitamin B_{12} *mcg*	Vitamin B_6 *mg*	Vitamin C *mg*	Folic acid *mcg*	Niacin *mg*	Riboflavin *mg*	Thiamin *mg*
Ginkgo nuts																							
canned — *1 oz*	28	31	6.3	0	2.6	0.5	0.2	0.2	0.1	0.6	1	0	51	87	0.1	10	0	0.06	3	9.3	1	0.02	0.04
dried — *1 oz*	28	99	20.5	0	0	0.6	0.2	0.2	0.1	2.9	6	0	283	4	0.2	31	0	0.18	8	30	3.3	0.05	0.12
raw — *1 oz*	28	52	10.7	0	0	0.5	0.2	0.2	0.1	1.2	1	0	145	2	0.1	16	0	0.09	4	15.3	1.7	0.03	0.06
Hickorynuts, dried — *1 oz*	28	186	5.2	0	1.8	18.2	9.2	6.2	2	3.6	17	1	124	0	1.2	4	0	0.05	1	11.3	0.3	0.04	0.25
Lotus seeds																							
dried — *1 oz*	28	94	18.3	0	0	0.6	0.1	0.3	0.1	4.4	46	1	388	1	0.3	1	0	0.18	0	29.4	0.5	0.04	0.18
raw — *1 oz*	28	25	4.9	0	0	0.2	0	0.1	0	1.2	12	0	104	0	0.1	0	0	0.05	0	7.9	0.1	0.01	0.05
Macadamia nuts																							
dried — *1 oz*	28	199	3.9	0	2.6	20.9	16.5	0.4	3.1	2.4	20	1	104	1	0.5	0	0	0.06	0	4.5	0.6	0.03	0.1
oil-roasted — *½ cup*	67	481	8.6	0	6.2	51.3	40.5	0.9	7.7	4.9	30	1	220	5	0.7	1	0	0.13	0	10.7	1.4	0.07	0.14
oil-roasted w/ salt — *1 oz*	28	204	3.7	0	2.6	21.7	17.1	0.4	3.2	2.1	13	1	93	74	0.3	0	0	0.06	0	4.5	0.6	0.03	0.06
Mixed nuts																							
dry-roasted w/ peanuts — *1 oz*	28	168	7.2	0	2.6	14.6	8.9	3.1	2	4.9	20	1	169	3	1.1	0	0	0.08	0	14.3	1.3	0.06	0.06
dry-roasted w/ peanuts, w/ salt — *1 oz*	28	168	7.2	0	2.6	14.6	8.9	3.1	2	4.9	20	1	169	190	1.1	0	0	0.08	0	14.3	1.3	0.06	0.06
oil-roasted w/ peanuts — *1 oz*	28	175	6.1	0	2.8	16	9	3.8	2.5	4.8	31	1	165	3	1.4	1	0	0.07	0	23.5	1.4	0.06	0.14
oil-roasted w/ peanuts, w/ salt — *1 oz*	28	175	6.1	0	2.6	16	9	3.8	2.5	4.8	31	1	165	185	1.4	1	0	0.07	0	23.5	1.4	0.06	0.14
oil-roasted w/o peanuts — *1 oz*	28	174	6.3	0	1.6	15.9	9.4	3.2	2.6	4.4	30	1	154	3	1.3	1	0	0.05	0	16	0.6	0.14	0.14
Nuts, wheat-based formulated																							
macadamia-flavored — *1 oz*	28	175	7.9	0	1.5	16	6.7	6.2	2.4	3.2	6	1	74	13	0.8	0	0	0.07	0	26.6	0.3	0.06	0.06
unflavored w/salt — *1 oz*	28	176	6.7	0	1.5	16.4	6.7	6.4	2.5	3.9	7	1	90	143	0.8	0	0	0.11	0	40.3	0.4	0.09	0.09
Peanut butter																							
chunk-style w/ salt — *2 Tbsp*	32	188	6.9	0	2.1	16	7.5	4.5	3.1	7.7	13	1	239	156	0.9	0	0	0.14	0	29.4	4.4	0.04	0.04
chunk-style w/o salt — *1 Tbsp*	16	94	3.5	0	1.1	8	3.8	2.3	1.5	3.8	7	0	120	3	0.4	0	0	0.07	0	14.7	2.2	0.02	0.02

	Weight *g*	Calories	Carbohydrates *g*	Cholesterol *mg*	Dietary fiber *g*	Total fat *g*	Mono. fat *g*	Poly. fat *g*	Sat. fat *g*	Protein *g*	Calcium *mg*	Iron *mg*	Potassium *mg*	Sodium *mg*	Zinc *mg*	Vitamin A *RE*	Vitamin B_{12} *mcg*	Vitamin B_6 *mg*	Vitamin C *mg*	Folic acid *mcg*	Niacin *mg*	Riboflavin *mg*	Thiamin *mg*
smooth-style w/o salt — *1 Tbsp*	16	95	3.1	0	0.9	8.2	3.9	2.2	1.7	4	6	0	107	3	0.5	0	0	0.07	0	11.8	2.1	0.02	0.01
smooth-style w/ salt — *2 Tbsp*	32	190	6.2	0	1.9	16.3	7.8	4.4	3.3	8.1	12	1	214	149	0.9	0	0	0.15	0	23.7	4.3	0.03	0.03
Peanuts																							
boiled w/ salt — *1 oz, shelled*	28	90	6	0	2.5	6.2	3.1	2	0.9	3.8	16	0	51	213	0.5	0	0	0.04	0	21.2	1.5	0.02	0.07
dry-roasted w/ salt — *1 oz*	28	166	6.1	0	2.3	14.1	7	4.4	2	6.7	15	1	187	230	0.9	0	0	0.07	0	41.2	3.8	0.03	0.12
dry-roasted w/o salt — *1 oz*	28	166	6.1	0	2.3	14.1	7	4.4	2	6.7	15	1	187	2	0.9	0	0	0.07	0	41.2	3.8	0.03	0.12
oil-roasted w/ salt — *1 oz*	29	167	5.5	0	2.6	14.2	7	4.5	2	7.6	25	1	196	125	1.9	0	0	0.07	0	36.2	4.1	0.03	0.07
oil-roasted w/o salt — *1 oz*	28	165	5.4	0	2	14	6.9	4.4	1.9	7.5	25	1	193	2	1.9	0	0	0.07	0	35.6	4	0.03	0.07
raw — *1 oz*	28	161	4.6	0	2.4	14	6.9	4.4	1.9	7.3	26	1	200	5	0.9	0	0	0.1	0	68	3.4	0.04	0.18
Peanuts, spanish																							
oil-roasted w/ salt — *1 oz*	28	164	4.9	0	2.5	13.9	6.3	4.8	2.1	7.9	28	1	220	123	0.6	0	0	0.07	0	35.7	4.2	0.02	0.09
oil-roasted w/o salt — *1 oz*	28	164	4.9	0	2.5	13.9	6.3	4.8	2.1	7.9	28	1	220	2	0.6	0	0	0.07	0	35.7	4.2	0.02	0.09
raw — *1 oz*	28	162	4.5	0	2.7	14.1	6.3	4.9	2.2	7.4	30	1	211	6	0.6	0	0	0.1	0	68	4.5	0.04	0.19
Peanuts, valencia																							
oil-roasted w/ salt — *1 oz*	28	167	4.6	0	2.5	14.5	6.5	5	2.2	7.7	15	0	174	219	0.9	0	0	0.07	0	35.6	4.1	0.04	0.03
oil-roasted w/o salt — *1 oz*	28	167	4.6	0	2.5	14.5	6.5	5	2.2	7.7	15	0	174	2	0.9	0	0	0.07	0	35.6	4.1	0.04	0.03
raw — *1 oz*	28	162	5.9	0	2.5	13.5	6.1	4.7	2.1	7.1	18	1	94	0	0.9	0	0	0.1	0	69.6	3.7	0.09	0.18
Peanuts, virginia																							
oil-roasted w/ salt — *1 oz*	28	164	5.6	0	2.5	13.8	7.2	4.2	1.8	7.3	24	0	185	123	1.9	0	0	0.07	0	35.6	4.2	0.03	0.08
oil-roasted w/o salt — *1 oz*	28	164	5.6	0	2.5	13.8	7.2	4.2	1.8	7.3	24	0	185	2	1.9	0	0	0.07	0	35.6	4.2	0.03	0.08
raw — *1 oz*	28	160	4.7	0	2.4	13.8	7.2	4.2	1.8	7.1	25	1	196	3	1.3	0	0	0.1	0	67.7	3.5	0.04	0.19
Pecans																							
dried — *1 oz*	28	189	5.2	0	2.2	19.2	12	4.7	1.5	2.2	10	1	111	0	1.6	4	0	0.05	1	11.1	0.3	0.04	0.24
dried, chopped — *½ cup*	60	397	10.9	0	4.5	40.2	25.1	10	3.2	4.6	21	1	233	1	3.3	8	0	0.11	1	23.3	0.5	0.08	0.5

	Weight g	Calories	Carbohydrates g	Cholesterol mg	Dietary fiber g	Total fat g	Mono. fat g	Poly. fat g	Sat. fat g	Protein g	Calcium mg	Iron mg	Potassium mg	Sodium mg	Zinc mg	Vitamin A RE	Vitamin B_{12} mcg	Vitamin B_6 mg	Vitamin C mg	Folic acid mcg	Niacin mg	Riboflavin mg	Thiamin mg
dry-roasted — *1 oz*	28	187	6.3	0	2.6	18.3	11.4	4.5	1.5	2.3	10	1	105	0	1.6	4	0	0.06	1	11.5	0.3	0.03	0.09
oil-roasted — *1 oz*	28	194	4.6	0	1.9	20.2	12.6	5	1.6	2	10	1	102	0	1.6	4	0	0.05	1	11.2	0.3	0.03	0.09
Pilinuts, dried — *1 oz*	28	204	1.1	0	0	22.6	10.6	2.2	8.8	3.1	41	1	144	1	0.8	1	0	0.03	0	16.9	0.1	0.03	0.26
Pine nuts																							
pignolia, dried — *1 oz*	28	160	4	0	1.3	14.4	5.4	6.1	2.2	6.8	7	3	170	1	1.2	1	0	0.03	1	16.2	1	0.05	0.23
pinyon, dried — *1 oz*	28	178	5.5	0	3	17.3	6.5	7.3	2.7	3.3	2	1	178	20	1.2	1	0	0.03	1	16.4	1.2	0.06	0.35
Pistachios																							
dried — *1 oz*	28	164	7	0	3.1	13.7	9.3	2.1	1.7	5.8	38	2	310	2	0.4	7	0	0.07	2	16.4	0.3	0.05	0.23
dry-roasted — *1 oz*	28	172	7.8	0	3.1	15	10.1	2.3	1.9	4.2	20	1	275	2	0.4	7	0	0.07	2	16.8	0.4	0.07	0.12
dry-roasted w/ salt — *1 oz*	28	172	7.8	0	3.1	15	10.1	2.3	1.9	4.2	20	1	275	221	0.4	7	0	0.07	2	16.8	0.4	0.07	0.12
Pumpkin or squash seeds																							
dried, hulled — *1 oz*	28	153	5	0	1.1	13	4	5.9	2.5	7	12	4	229	5	2.1	11	0	0.06	1	16.3	0.5	0.09	0.06
roasted, hulled — *1 oz*	28	148	3.8	0	1.1	11.9	3.7	5.4	2.3	9.3	12	4	229	5	2.1	11	0	0.03	1	16.3	0.5	0.09	0.06
roasted w/ salt — *1 oz*	28	148	3.8	0	1.1	11.9	3.7	5.4	2.3	9.3	12	4	229	163	2.1	11	0	0.03	1	16.3	0.5	0.09	0.06
whole, roasted — *1 oz*	28	126	15.2	0	1.1	5.5	1.7	2.5	1	5.3	16	1	261	5	2.9	2	0	0.01	0	2.6	0.1	0.01	0.01
whole, roasted w/ salt — *1 oz*	28	126	15.2	0	1.5	5.5	1.7	2.5	1	5.3	16	1	261	163	2.9	2	0	0.01	0	2.6	0.1	0.01	0.01
Safflower seed kernels, dried — *1 oz*	28	147	9.7	0	0	10.9	1.4	8	1	4.6	22	1	195	1	1.4	1	0	0.33	0	45.5	0.6	0.12	0.33
Safflower seed meal, partially defatted — *1 oz*	28	97	13.8	0	0	0.7	0.1	0.4	0.1	10.1	22	1	19	1	1.4	1	0	0.33	0	45.1	0.6	0.12	0.33
Sesame meal, partially defatted — *1 oz*	28	161	7.4	0	0	13.6	5.1	6	1.9	4.8	43	4	115	11	2.9	2	0	0.04	0	8.4	3.6	0.08	0.73
Sesame seed paste — *1 Tbsp*	16	95	4.1	0	0.9	8.1	3.1	3.6	1.1	2.9	154	3	93	2	1.2	1	0	0.13	0	16	1.1	0.03	0.04
Sesame seeds																							
kernels, toasted — *1 oz*	28	161	7.4	0	4.8	13.6	5.1	6	1.9	4.8	37	2	115	11	2.9	2	0	0.04	0	27.2	1.5	0.13	0.34
toasted — *1 oz*	28	160	7.3	0	4	13.6	5.1	6	1.9	4.8	280	4	135	3	2	0	0	0.23	0	27.8	1.3	0.07	0.23
whole, dried — *1 Tbsp*	9	52	2.1	0	1.1	4.5	1.7	2	0.6	1.6	88	1	42	1	0.7	0	0	0.07	0	8.7	0.4	0.02	0.07

	Weight g	Calories	Carbohydrates g	Cholesterol mg	Dietary fiber g	Total fat g	Mono. fat g	Poly. fat g	Sat. fat g	Protein g	Calcium mg	Iron mg	Potassium mg	Sodium mg	Zinc mg	Vitamin A RE	Vitamin B_{12} mcg	Vitamin B_6 mg	Vitamin C mg	Folic acid mcg	Niacin mg	Riboflavin mg	Thiamin mg
Sunflower seed butter																							
unsalted — *1 Tbsp*	16	93	4.4	0	0	7.6	1.5	5	0.8	3.1	20	1	12	0	0.8	1	0	0.13	0	38	0.9	0.05	0.05
w/ salt — *1 Tbsp*	16	93	4.4	0	0	7.6	1.5	5	0.8	3.1	20	1	12	83	0.8	1	0	0.13	0	38	0.9	0.05	0.05
Sunflower seed kernels																							
dried — *½ cup*	72	410	13.5	0	7.6	35.7	6.8	23.6	3.7	16.4	84	5	496	2	3.6	4	0	0.55	1	163.7	3.2	0.18	1.65
dry-roasted — *1 oz*	28	165	6.8	0	3.1	14.1	2.7	9.3	1.5	5.5	20	1	241	1	1.5	0	0	0.23	0	67.3	2	0.07	0.03
dry-roasted w/ salt — *1 oz*	28	165	6.8	0	2.6	14.1	2.7	9.3	1.5	5.5	20	1	241	221	1.5	0	0	0.23	0	67.3	2	0.07	0.03
oil-roasted — *1 oz*	28	174	4.2	0	1.9	16.3	3.1	10.8	1.7	6.1	16	2	137	1	1.5	1	0	0.22	0	66.3	1.2	0.08	0.09
toasted — *1 oz*	28	175	5.8	0	3.3	16.1	3.1	10.6	1.7	4.9	16	2	139	1	1.5	0	0	0.23	0	67.4	1.2	0.08	0.09
toasted w/ salt — *1 oz*	28	175	5.8	0	3.3	16.1	3.1	10.6	1.7	4.9	16	2	139	174	1.5	0	0	0.23	0	67.4	1.2	0.08	0.09
Tahini (sesame butter)																							
from raw & stone ground seeds — *1 Tbsp*	15	86	3.9	0	1.4	7.2	2.7	3.2	1	2.7	63	0	62	11	0.7	1	0	0.02	0	14.7	0.9	0.08	0.19
from roasted seeds — *1 Tbsp*	15	89	3.2	0	1.4	8.1	3	3.5	1.1	2.6	64	1	62	17	0.7	1	0	0.02	0	14.7	0.8	0.07	0.18
from unroasted seeds — *1 Tbsp*	14	85	2.5	0	1.3	7.9	3	3.5	1.1	2.5	20	1	64	0	1.5	1	0	0.02	0	13.7	0.8	0.02	0.22
Walnuts																							
black, dried — *1 oz*	28	172	3.4	0	1.4	16	3.6	10.6	1	6.9	16	1	149	0	1	9	0	0.16	1	18.6	0.2	0.03	0.06
english/persian, dried — *1 oz*	28	182	5.2	0	1.4	17.5	4	11.1	1.6	4.1	27	1	142	3	0.8	3	0	0.16	1	18.7	0.3	0.04	0.11
english/persian, dried, chopped — *½ cup*	60	385	11	0	2.9	37.1	8.5	23.5	3.4	8.6	56	1	301	6	1.6	7	0	0.33	2	39.6	0.6	0.09	0.23
Watermelon seeds, dried — *1 oz*	28	158	4.3	0	0	13.4	2.1	8	2.8	8	15	2	184	28	2.9	0	0	0.03	0	16.4	1	0.04	0.05

Pasta

	Weight g	Calories	Carbohydrates g	Cholesterol mg	Dietary fiber g	Total fat g	Mono. fat g	Poly. fat g	Sat. fat g	Protein g	Calcium mg	Iron mg	Potassium mg	Sodium mg	Zinc mg	Vitamin A RE	Vitamin B_{12} mcg	Vitamin B_6 mg	Vitamin C mg	Folic acid mcg	Niacin mg	Riboflavin mg	Thiamin mg
Corn																							
cooked — *1 cup*	140	176	39.1	0	6.7	1	0.3	0.5	0.1	3.7	1	0	43	0	0.9	8	0	0.08	0	8.4	0.8	0.03	0.07
dry — *2 oz*	57	203	45.2	0	6.3	1.2	0.3	0.5	0.2	4.3	2	1	168	2	1	10	0	0.12	0	14.3	1.4	0.05	0.13

	Weight *g*	Calories	Carbohydrates *g*	Cholesterol *mg*	Dietary fiber *g*	Total fat *g*	Mono. fat *g*	Poly. fat *g*	Sat. fat *g*	Protein *g*	Calcium *mg*	Iron *mg*	Potassium *mg*	Sodium *mg*	Zinc *mg*	Vitamin A *RE*	Vitamin B_{12} *mcg*	Vitamin B_6 *mg*	Vitamin C *mg*	Folic acid *mcg*	Niacin *mg*	Riboflavin *mg*	Thiamin *mg*
Couscous																							
cooked — *1 cup*	157	176	36.5	0	2.2	0.3	0	0.1	0	6	13	1	91	8	0.4	0	0	0.08	0	23.6	1.5	0.04	0.1
dry — *½ cup*	87	325	67	0	4.3	0.6	0.1	0.2	0.1	11	21	1	144	9	0.7	0	0	0.1	0	17.3	3	0.07	0.14
Egg noodles																							
cooked — *1 cup*	160	213	39.7	53	1.8	2.4	0.7	0.7	0.5	7.6	19	3	45	11	1	10	0.1	0.06	0	11.2	2.4	0.13	0.3
dry — *2 oz*	57	217	40.5	54	1.5	2.4	0.7	0.7	0.5	8	18	3	133	12	0.9	10	0.2	0.07	0	16.5	4.6	0.27	0.6
Egg noodles, spinach																							
cooked — *1 cup*	160	211	38.8	53	3.7	2.5	0.8	0.6	0.6	8.1	30	2	59	19	1	22	0.2	0.18	0	33.6	2.4	0.2	0.39
dry — *2 oz*	57	218	40.1	54	3.9	2.6	0.8	0.6	0.6	8.3	32	2	202	41	1	25	0.2	0.23	0	50.2	3.7	0.27	0.62
Macaroni, elbows																							
cooked — *1 cup*	140	197	39.7	0	1.8	0.9	0.1	0.4	0.1	6.7	10	2	43	1	0.7	0	0	0.05	0	9.8	2.3	0.14	0.29
dry — *2 oz*	57	211	42.6	0	1.4	0.9	0.1	0.4	0.1	7.3	10	2	92	4	0.7	0	0	0.06	0	10.3	4.3	0.25	0.59
Macaroni, elbows, whole-wheat																							
cooked — *1 cup*	140	174	37.2	0	3.9	0.8	0.1	0.3	0.1	7.5	21	1	62	4	1.1	0	0	0.11	0	7	1	0.06	0.15
dry — *2 oz*	57	198	42.8	0	4.7	0.8	0.1	0.3	0.1	8.3	23	2	123	5	1.4	0	0	0.13	0	32.5	2.9	0.08	0.28
Macaroni, protein-fortified, small shells																							
cooked — *1 cup*	115	189	36.4	0	0	0.2	0	0.1	0	9.3	12	1	48	6	0.6	0	0	0.07	0	12.7	2.1	0.19	0.34
dry — *2 oz*	57	214	38.5	0	1.4	1.3	0.2	0.6	0.2	11.3	22	2	115	5	1	0	0	0.1	0	11.4	4.4	0.27	0.68
Macaroni, vegetable																							
cooked — *1 cup*	134	172	35.7	0	5.8	0.1	0	0.1	0	6.1	15	1	42	8	0.6	7	0	0.03	0	8	1.4	0.08	0.15
dry — *2 oz*	57	209	42.7	0	2.5	0.6	0.1	0.2	0.1	7.5	19	2	162	25	0.4	9	0	0.07	0	9.7	4.2	0.3	0.59
Mung bean (cellophane) noodles, dry — *½ cup*	70	246	60.3	0	0.4	0	0	0	0	0.1	18	2	7	7	0.3	0	0	0.04	0	1.4	0.1	0	0.11
Pasta, fresh, plain																							
cooked — *2 oz*	57	75	14.2	19	0	0.6	0.1	0.2	0.1	2.9	3	1	14	3	0.3	3	0.1	0.02	0	4	0.6	0.09	0.12

	Weight *g*	Calories	Carbohydrates *g*	Cholesterol *mg*	Dietary fiber *g*	Total fat *g*	Mono. fat *g*	Poly. fat *g*	Sat. fat *g*	Protein *g*	Calcium *mg*	Iron *mg*	Potassium *mg*	Sodium *mg*	Zinc *mg*	Vitamin A *RE*	Vitamin B_{12} *mcg*	Vitamin B_6 *mg*	Vitamin C *mg*	Folic acid *mcg*	Niacin *mg*	Riboflavin *mg*	Thiamin *mg*
uncooked — *2 oz*	57	164	31	42	0	1.3	0.2	0.5	0.2	6.4	9	2	102	15	0.7	1	0.2	0.05	0	12.5	1.9	0.25	0.4
Pasta, fresh, spinach																							
cooked — *2 oz*	57	74	14.3	19	0	0.5	0.2	0.1	0.1	2.9	10	1	21	3	0.4	8	0.1	0.06	0	10.3	0.6	0.08	0.1
uncooked — *2 oz*	57	165	31.8	42	0	1.2	0.4	0.3	0.3	6.4	25	2	155	15	0.8	19	0.2	0.18	0	31.9	2	0.23	0.35
Soba noodles																							
cooked — *1 cup*	114	113	24.4	0	0	0.1	0	0	0	5.8	5	1	40	68	0.1	0	0	0.05	0	8	0.6	0.03	0.11
dry — *2 oz*	57	192	42.5	0	0	0.4	0.1	0.1	0.1	8.2	20	2	144	451	1	0	0	0.14	0	34.2	1.8	0.07	0.27
Somen noodles																							
cooked — *1 cup*	176	231	48.5	0	0	0.3	0	0.1	0	7	14	1	51	283	0.4	0	0	0.02	0	3.5	0.2	0.06	0.04
dry — *1 oz*	29	101	21.1	0	1.2	0.2	0	0.1	0	3.2	7	0	47	524	0.1	0	0	0.01	0	4	0.2	0.01	0.03
Spaghetti																							
cooked — *1 cup*	140	197	39.7	0	2.4	0.9	0.1	0.4	0.1	6.7	10	2	43	1	0.7	0	0	0.05	0	9.8	2.3	0.14	0.29
dry — *2 oz*	57	211	42.6	0	1.4	0.9	0.1	0.4	0.1	7.3	10	2	92	4	0.7	0	0	0.06	0	10.3	4.3	0.25	0.59
Spaghetti, protein-fortified																							
cooked — *1 cup*	140	230	44.3	0	2.4	0.3	0	0.1	0	11.3	14	1	59	7	0.7	0	0	0.09	0	15.4	2.6	0.23	0.42
dry — *2 oz*	57	214	38.5	0	0	1.3	0.2	0.6	0.2	11.3	22	2	115	5	1	0	0	0.1	0	11.4	4.4	0.27	0.68
Spaghetti, spinach																							
cooked — *1 cup*	140	182	36.6	0	0	0.9	0.1	0.4	0.1	6.4	42	1	81	20	1.5	21	0	0.13	0	16.8	2.1	0.14	0.14
dry — *2 oz*	57	212	42.6	0	6	0.9	0.1	0.4	0.1	7.6	33	1	214	21	1.6	26	0	0.18	0	27.4	2.6	0.11	0.21
Spaghetti, whole-wheat																							
cooked — *1 cup*	140	174	37.2	0	6.3	0.8	0.1	0.3	0.1	7.5	21	1	62	4	1.1	0	0	0.11	0	7	1	0.06	0.15
dry — *2 oz*	57	198	42.8	0	0	0.8	0.1	0.3	0.1	8.3	23	2	123	5	1.4	0	0	0.13	0	32.5	2.9	0.08	0.28

Pork

	Weight g	Calories	Carbohydrates g	Cholesterol mg	Dietary fiber g	Total fat g	Mono. fat g	Poly. fat g	Sat. fat g	Protein g	Calcium mg	Iron mg	Potassium mg	Sodium mg	Zinc mg	Vitamin A RE	Vitamin B_{12} mcg	Vitamin B_6 mg	Vitamin C mg	Folic acid mcg	Niacin mg	Riboflavin mg	Thiamin mg
Arm picnic, braised																							
trimmed of all visible fat — *3 ½ oz*	100	248	0	114	0	12.2	5.8	1.2	4.2	32.3	8	2	405	102	5	2	0.7	0.41	0	5	5.9	0.36	0.6
untrimmed — *3 ½ oz*	100	329	0	109	0	23.2	10.4	2.3	8.5	28	18	2	369	88	4.2	3	0.7	0.35	0	4	5.2	0.31	0.54
Arm picnic, cured, roasted																							
trimmed of all visible fat — *3 ½ oz*	100	170	0	48	0	7	3.2	0.8	2.4	24.9	11	1	292	1231	2.9	0	1.1	0.37	0	4	4.8	0.23	0.73
untrimmed — *3 ½ oz*	100	280	0	58	0	21.4	10.1	2.3	7.7	20.4	10	1	258	1072	2.5	0	0.9	0.28	0	3	4.1	0.19	0.61
Arm picnic, roasted																							
trimmed of all visible fat — *3 ½ oz*	100	228	0	95	0	12.6	6	1.2	4.3	26.7	9	1	351	80	4.1	2	0.8	0.41	0	5	4.3	0.36	0.58
untrimmed — *3 ½ oz*	100	317	0	94	0	24	10.7	2.4	8.8	23.5	19	1	325	70	3.5	2	0.7	0.35	0	4	3.9	0.3	0.52
Backribs, roasted, untrimmed — *3 ½ oz*	100	370	0	118	0	29.6	13.5	2.3	11	24.3	45	1	315	101	3.4	3	0.6	0.31	0	3	3.6	0.2	0.43
Bacon, pan-fried — *3 medium slices*	19	109	0.1	16	0	9.4	4.5	1.1	3.3	5.8	2	0	92	303	0.6	0	0.3	0.05	0	1	1.4	0.05	0.13
Blade roll, cured, roasted, untrimmed — *3 ½ oz*	100	287	0.4	67	0	23.5	11	2.5	8.4	17.3	7	1	194	973	2.5	0	1.1	0.21	3	3	2.4	0.29	0.46
Boston blade, braised																							
trimmed of all visible fat — *3 ½ oz*	100	273	0	116	0	15.6	7	1.3	5.5	31.1	29	2	412	75	5.6	3	1	0.29	0	2	4.3	0.4	0.72
untrimmed — *3 ½ oz*	100	319	0	113	0	21.7	9.6	2	7.9	28.7	32	2	389	70	5	3	0.9	0.27	0	2	4.1	0.36	0.67
Boston blade, broiled																							
trimmed of all visible fat — *3 ½ oz*	100	227	0	94	0	12.5	5.6	1.1	4.5	26.7	33	2	343	74	5	2	1.1	0.31	0	5	4.3	0.44	0.75
untrimmed — *3 ½ oz*	100	259	0	95	0	16.6	7.4	1.5	6	25.6	36	1	326	69	4.5	3	1.1	0.28	0	4	4.1	0.4	0.7
Boston blade, roasted																							
trimmed of all visible fat — *3 ½ oz*	100	232	0	85	0	14.3	6.3	1.3	5.2	24.2	27	2	427	88	4.2	3	1.2	0.44	1	8	5	0.4	1.12
untrimmed — *3 ½ oz*	100	269	0	86	0	18.9	8.3	1.8	7	23.1	28	1	332	67	4	2	0.9	0.23	1	5	4.1	0.36	0.64
Canadian-style bacon, grilled — *2 slices*	47	86	0.6	27	0	3.9	1.9	0.4	1.3	11.3	5	0	181	719	0.8	0	0.4	0.21	0	1.9	3.2	0.09	0.38

	Weight g	Calories	Carbohydrates g	Cholesterol mg	Dietary fiber g	Total fat g	Mono. fat g	Poly. fat g	Sat. fat g	Protein g	Calcium mg	Iron mg	Potassium mg	Sodium mg	Zinc mg	Vitamin A RE	Vitamin B_{12} mcg	Vitamin B_6 mg	Vitamin C mg	Folic acid mcg	Niacin mg	Riboflavin mg	Thiamin mg
Center rib (chops or roasts), braised																							
trimmed of all visible fat — *3 ½ oz*	100	211	0	71	0	10.1	4.9	0.7	4	28	5	1	405	41	2.2	2	0.4	0.33	0	4	4.5	0.26	0.55
untrimmed — *3 ½ oz*	100	255	0	73	0	15.8	7.2	1.3	6.1	26.3	5	1	387	40	2.1	2	0.4	0.31	0	4	4.3	0.24	0.53
Center rib (chops or roasts), broiled																							
trimmed of all visible fat — *3 ½ oz*	100	216	0	81	0	10.1	4.6	0.6	3.6	29.5	31	1	420	65	2.4	2	0.7	0.4	0	9	5.2	0.32	0.89
untrimmed — *3 ½ oz*	100	260	0	82	0	15.8	7	1.2	5.8	27.6	28	1	401	62	2.3	2	0.7	0.37	0	8	4.9	0.3	0.83
Center rib (chops or roasts), pan-fried																							
trimmed of all visible fat — *3 ½ oz*	100	224	0	70	0	11.8	5.3	1.5	4.3	27.7	5	1	454	52	2.1	2	0.6	0.39	0	8	5.1	0.34	0.76
untrimmed — *3 ½ oz*	100	224	0	70	0	11.8	5.3	1.5	4.3	27.7	5	1	454	52	2.1	2	0.6	0.39	0	8	5.1	0.34	0.76
Center rib (chops or roasts), roasted																							
trimmed of all visible fat — *3 ½ oz*	100	214	0	83	0	10.1	4.5	0.9	3.5	28.8	6	1	363	50	2.8	2	0.6	0.4	0	9	5.4	0.31	0.64
untrimmed — *3 ½ oz*	100	252	0	81	0	15.2	6.7	1.3	5.4	27	6	1	346	48	2.6	3	0.6	0.36	0	8	5	0.29	0.6
Country-style ribs, braised																							
trimmed of all visible fat — *3 ½ oz*	100	234	0	86	0	13.6	5.9	1.1	4.9	26	25	1	345	63	4	2	0.7	0.36	1	3	4.1	0.28	0.55
untrimmed — *3 ½ oz*	100	296	0	87	0	21.5	9.3	1.9	8	23.9	29	1	328	59	3.6	2	0.7	0.33	1	3	3.8	0.26	0.51
Country-style ribs, roasted																							
trimmed of all visible fat — *3 ½ oz*	100	247	0	93	0	14.8	6.5	1.1	5.3	26.6	29	1	349	29	3.8	2	0.8	0.44	0	5	4.7	0.34	0.57
untrimmed — *3 ½ oz*	100	328	0	92	0	25.3	11	2	9.2	23.4	25	1	344	52	2.4	3	0.8	0.44	0	5	4.3	0.34	0.89
Ground pork, cooked — *3 ½ oz*	100	297	0	94	0	20.8	9.3	1.9	7.7	25.7	22	1	362	73	3.2	2	0.5	0.39	1	6	4.2	0.22	0.71
Ham, cured, center slice, unheated — *3 ½ oz*	100	203	0.1	54	0	12.9	6.1	1.4	4.6	20.2	7	1	337	1386	1.9	0	0.8	0.47	0	4	4.8	0.21	0.85
Ham, cured, extra lean																							
canned, roasted — *3 ½ oz*	100	136	0.5	30	0	4.9	2.5	0.4	1.6	21.2	6	1	348	1135	2.2	0	0.7	0.45	0	5	4.9	0.25	1.04
canned, unheated — *3 ½ oz*	99	119	0	38	0	4.5	2.2	0.4	1.5	18.3	6	1	361	1245	1.9	0	0.8	0.45	0	6	5.3	0.23	0.83
roasted — *3 ½ oz*	100	145	1.5	53	0	5.5	2.6	0.5	1.8	20.9	8	1	287	1203	2.9	0	0.7	0.4	0	3	4	0.2	0.75

	Weight g	Calories	Carbohydrates g	Cholesterol mg	Dietary fiber g	Total fat g	Mono. fat g	Poly. fat g	Sat. fat g	Protein g	Calcium mg	Iron mg	Potassium mg	Sodium mg	Zinc mg	Vitamin A RE	Vitamin B_{12} mcg	Vitamin B_6 mg	Vitamin C mg	Folic acid mcg	Niacin mg	Riboflavin mg	Thiamin mg
Ham, cured, ham steak — *3 ½ oz*	100	122	0	45	0	4.3	2	0.5	1.4	19.6	4	1	325	1269	2	0	0.8	0.37	32	4	5.1	0.2	0.8
Ham, cured, patties																							
grilled — *1 patty*	60	203	1	43	0	18.4	8.7	2	6.6	7.9	5	1	145	632	1.1	0	0.4	0.1	0	1.8	1.9	0.11	0.21
unheated — *1 patty*	65	205	1.1	46	0	18.4	8.6	2	6.6	8.3	5	1	156	709	1	0	0.7	0.1	0	2	2	0.1	0.3
Ham, cured, regular																							
canned, roasted — *3 ½ oz*	100	226	0.4	62	0	15.2	7.1	1.8	5	20.5	8	1	357	941	2.5	0	1.1	0.3	14	5	5.3	0.26	0.82
canned, unheated — *3 ½ oz*	100	190	0	39	0	13	6.2	1.5	4.3	17	6	1	316	1240	1.7	0	0.8	0.48	0	5	3.2	0.23	0.96
roasted — *3 ½ oz*	100	178	0	59	0	9	4.4	1.4	3.1	22.6	8	1	409	1500	2.5	0	0.7	0.31	0	3	6.2	0.33	0.73
Ham, cured, whole																							
trimmed of all visible fat, roasted — *3 ½ oz*	100	157	0	55	0	5.5	2.5	0.6	1.8	25.1	7	1	316	1327	2.6	0	0.7	0.47	0	4	5	0.25	0.68
trimmed of all visible fat, unheated — *3 ½ oz*	100	147	0.1	52	0	5.7	2.6	0.7	1.9	22.3	7	1	371	1516	2	0	0.9	0.53	0	4	5.3	0.23	0.93
untrimmed, roasted — *3 ½ oz*	100	243	0	62	0	16.8	7.9	1.8	6	21.6	7	1	286	1187	2.3	0	0.6	0.38	0	3	4.5	0.22	0.6
untrimmed, unheated — *3 ½ oz*	100	246	0.1	56	0	18.5	8.7	1.6	6.6	18.5	7	1	310	1284	1.8	0	0.7	0.41	0	4	4.5	0.19	0.78
Leg, roasted																							
trimmed of all visible fat — *3 ½ oz*	100	211	0	94	0	9.4	4.5	0.9	3.3	29.4	7	1	373	64	3.3	3	0.7	0.45	0	12	4.9	0.35	0.69
untrimmed — *3 ½ oz*	100	273	0	94	0	17.6	7.9	1.7	6.5	26.8	14	1	352	60	3	3	0.7	0.4	0	10	4.6	0.31	0.64
Loin, braised																							
trimmed of all visible fat — *3 ½ oz*	100	204	0	79	0	9.1	4.2	0.7	3.4	28.6	18	1	387	50	2.5	2	0.6	0.39	1	4	4.6	0.27	0.66
untrimmed — *3 ½ oz*	100	239	0	80	0	13.6	6.1	1.2	5.1	27.2	21	1	374	48	2.4	2	0.5	0.37	1	3	4.4	0.25	0.63
Loin, broiled																							
trimmed of all visible fat — *3 ½ oz*	100	210	0	79	0	9.8	4.5	0.8	3.6	28.6	17	1	438	64	2.5	2	0.7	0.49	1	6	5.2	0.34	0.92
untrimmed — *3 ½ oz*	100	242	0	80	0	13.9	6.2	1.2	5.2	27.3	19	1	423	62	2.4	2	0.7	0.46	1	5	5	0.32	0.88
Loin, roasted																							
trimmed of all visible fat — *3 ½ oz*	100	209	0	81	0	9.6	4.3	0.8	3.5	28.6	18	1	425	58	2.5	2	0.7	0.55	1	7	5.9	0.33	1.02

	Weight g	Calories	Carbohydrates g	Cholesterol mg	Dietary fiber g	Total fat g	Mono. fat g	Poly. fat g	Sat. fat g	Protein g	Calcium mg	Iron mg	Potassium mg	Sodium mg	Zinc mg	Vitamin A RE	Vitamin B_{12} mcg	Vitamin B_6 mg	Vitamin C mg	Folic acid mcg	Niacin mg	Riboflavin mg	Thiamin mg
untrimmed — *3 ½ oz*	100	248	0	82	0	14.7	6.5	1.2	5.4	27.1	19	1	408	59	2.3	3	0.7	0.52	1	6	5.6	0.31	0.99
Rump, roasted																							
trimmed of all visible fat — *3 ½ oz*	100	206	0	96	0	8.1	3.8	0.8	2.9	30.9	7	1	391	65	3	3	0.8	0.34	0	3	4.9	0.36	0.8
untrimmed — *3 ½ oz*	100	252	0	96	0	14.3	6.4	1.4	5.3	28.9	12	1	374	62	2.8	3	0.7	0.32	0	3	4.7	0.33	0.75
Shank, roasted																							
trimmed of all visible fat — *3 ½ oz*	100	215	0	92	0	10.5	5	0.9	3.6	28.2	7	1	360	64	3.5	2	0.7	0.46	0	6	4.9	0.34	0.63
untrimmed — *3 ½ oz*	100	289	0	92	0	20.1	9	1.9	7.4	25.3	15	1	338	59	3.1	3	0.7	0.4	0	5	4.5	0.3	0.58
Shoulder, roasted																							
trimmed of all visible fat — *3 ½ oz*	100	230	0	90	0	13.5	6.2	1.3	4.8	25.3	18	2	346	75	4.2	2	0.9	0.32	1	5	4.3	0.37	0.63
untrimmed — *3 ½ oz*	100	292	0	90	0	21.4	9.5	2.1	7.9	23.3	24	1	329	68	3.7	2	0.8	0.29	1	5	4	0.33	0.58
Sirloin (chops or roasts), braised																							
trimmed of all visible fat — *3 ½ oz*	100	175	0	81	0	6.6	2.9	0.6	2.3	27	13	1	356	46	2.4	2	0.6	0.44	1	3	4	0.28	0.7
untrimmed — *3 ½ oz*	100	189	0	81	0	8.4	3.7	0.8	3	26.5	13	1	352	46	2.3	2	0.6	0.43	1	3	3.9	0.28	0.69
Sirloin (chops or roasts), broiled																							
trimmed of all visible fat — *3 ½ oz*	100	193	0	92	0	6.7	2.9	0.5	2.2	31.1	18	1	377	56	2.7	2	0.8	0.54	0	6	4.8	0.4	1.03
untrimmed — *3 ½ oz*	100	208	0	91	0	8.6	3.8	0.7	2.9	30.5	18	1	372	56	2.6	2	0.8	0.53	0	6	4.7	0.39	1.01
Sirloin (chops or roasts), roasted, trimmed of all visible fat — *3 ½ oz*	100	198	0	86	0	8.3	3.6	0.7	3	28.9	17	1	405	56	2.5	2	0.8	0.48	1	5	5.1	0.38	0.89
Spareribs, briased, untrimmed — *3 ½ oz*	100	397	0	121	0	30.3	13.5	2.7	11.1	29.1	47	2	320	93	4.6	3	1.1	0.35	0	4	5.5	0.38	0.41
Tenderloin, broiled																							
trimmed of all visible fat — *3 ½ oz*	100	187	0	94	0	6.3	2.6	0.6	2.2	30.4	5	1	451	65	3	2	1	0.53	1	6	5.1	0.39	0.99
untrimmed — *3 ½ oz*	100	201	0	94	0	8.1	3.3	0.7	2.9	29.9	5	1	444	64	2.9	2	1	0.52	1	6	5.1	0.38	0.97
Tenderloin, roasted																							
trimmed of all visible fat — *3 ½ oz*	100	164	0	79	0	4.8	1.9	0.4	1.7	28.1	6	1	437	56	2.6	2	0.6	0.42	0	6	4.7	0.39	0.94
untrimmed — *3 ½ oz*	100	173	0	79	0	6.1	2.5	0.5	2.1	27.8	6	1	433	55	2.6	2	0.6	0.41	0	6	4.7	0.38	0.93

	Weight g	Calories	Carbohydrates g	Cholesterol mg	Dietary fiber g	Total fat g	Mono. fat g	Poly. fat g	Sat. fat g	Protein g	Calcium mg	Iron mg	Potassium mg	Sodium mg	Zinc mg	Vitamin A RE	Vitamin B_{12} mcg	Vitamin B_6 mg	Vitamin C mg	Folic acid mcg	Niacin mg	Riboflavin mg	Thiamin mg
Top loin (chops or roasts), braised																							
trimmed of all visible fat — *3 ½ oz*	100	202	0	73	0	8.6	4	0.6	3.1	29.1	23	1	421	42	2.2	2	0.5	0.35	0	5	4.7	0.27	0.57
untrimmed — *3 ½ oz*	100	233	0	75	0	12.7	5.7	1	4.7	27.8	21	1	407	42	2.1	2	0.5	0.33	0	4	4.5	0.26	0.55
Top loin (chops or roasts), broiled																							
trimmed of all visible fat — *3 ½ oz*	100	203	0	80	0	7.8	3.6	0.5	2.7	31.1	31	1	420	65	2.4	2	0.7	0.4	0	9	5.2	0.32	0.89
untrimmed — *3 ½ oz*	100	229	0	81	0	11.2	5.2	0.7	4	30	29	1	405	63	2.3	2	0.7	0.38	0	8	5	0.31	0.85
Top loin (chops or roasts), pan-fried																							
trimmed of all visible fat — *3 ½ oz*	100	225	0	77	0	10.5	4.6	1.3	3.6	30.5	22	1	500	57	2.3	2	0.7	0.43	0	8	5.6	0.38	0.84
untrimmed — *3 ½ oz*	100	257	0	78	0	14.8	6.5	1.7	5.3	29	21	1	479	55	2.2	2	0.7	0.4	0	8	5.4	0.35	0.8
Variety meats																							
brain, cooked — *3 ½ oz*	100	138	0	2552	0	9.5	1.7	1.5	2.2	12.1	9	2	195	91	1.5	0	1.4	0.14	14	4	3.3	0.22	0.08
chitterlings, simmered — *3 ½ oz*	100	303	0	143	0	28.8	9.7	7.2	10.1	10.3	27	4	8	39	5.1	0	1	0.01	0	3	0.1	0.08	0
ears, simmered — *1 ear*	111	184	0.2	100	0	12	5.5	1.3	4.3	17.7	20	2	44	185	0.2	0	0	0.01	0	0	0.6	0.08	0.02
feet, pickled — *3 ½ oz*	99	201	0	91	0	16	7.5	1.7	5.5	13.4	32	1	233	916	1.2	0	0.6	0.38	0	4	0.4	0.04	0.01
feet, simmered — *3 ½ oz*	100	194	0	100	0	12.4	5.8	1.4	4.3	19.2	45	0	146	30	1.1	0	0.2	0.09	0	1	0.5	0.06	0.01
heart, braised — *1 heart*	129	191	0.5	285	0	6.5	1.5	1.7	1.7	30.4	9	8	266	45	4	9	4.9	0.5	3	5.2	7.8	2.2	0.72
kidney, braised — *3 ½ oz*	100	151	0	480	0	4.7	1.6	0.4	1.5	25.4	13	5	143	80	4.2	78	7.8	0.46	11	41	5.8	1.59	0.4
liver, braised — *3 ½ oz*	100	165	3.8	355	0	4.4	0.6	1.1	1.4	26	10	18	150	49	6.7	5399	18.7	0.57	24	163	8.4	2.2	0.26
lungs, braised — *3 ½ oz*	100	99	0	387	0	3.1	0.7	0.4	1.1	16.6	8	16	151	81	2.5	0	2	0.08	8	2	1.4	0.32	0.08
pancreas, braised — *3 ½ oz*	100	219	0	315	0	10.8	3.8	2	3.7	28.5	16	3	168	42	4.3	0	17.1	0.44	6	5	3.2	0.66	0.09
spleen, braised — *3 ½ oz*	100	149	0	504	0	3.2	0.9	0.2	1.1	28.2	13	22	227	107	3.5	0	2.8	0.06	12	4	5.9	0.26	0.14
tail, simmered — *3 ½ oz*	100	396	0	129	0	35.8	16.9	3.9	12.5	17	14	1	157	25	1.6	0	0.6	0.27	0	4	1.1	0.07	0.07
tongue, braised — *3 ½ oz*	100	271	0	146	0	18.6	8.8	1.9	6.4	24.1	19	5	237	109	4.5	0	2.4	0.23	2	4	5.3	0.51	0.32

Shellfish

	Weight g	Calories	Carbohydrates g	Cholesterol mg	Dietary fiber g	Total fat g	Mono. fat g	Poly. fat g	Sat. fat g	Protein g	Calcium mg	Iron mg	Potassium mg	Sodium mg	Zinc mg	Vitamin A RE	Vitamin B_{12} mcg	Vitamin B_6 mg	Vitamin C mg	Folic acid mcg	Niacin mg	Riboflavin mg	Thiamin mg
Abalone, fried — *3 ½ oz*	100	189	11.1	94	0	6.8	2.7	1.7	1.6	19.6	37	4	284	591	1	2	0.7	0.15	2	5.4	1.9	0.13	0.22
Clams																							
canned, drained — *3 ½ oz*	100	148	5.1	67	0	2	0.2	0.6	0.2	25.6	92	28	628	112	2.7	171	98.9	0.11	22	28.8	3.4	0.43	0.15
ckd, moist heat — *3 ½ oz*	100	148	5.1	67	0	2	0.2	0.6	0.2	25.6	92	28	628	112	2.7	171	98.9	0.11	22	28.8	3.4	0.43	0.15
fried, breaded — *3 ½ oz*	100	202	10.3	61	0	11.2	4.5	2.9	2.7	14.2	63	14	326	364	1.5	90	40.3	0.06	10	18.2	2.1	0.24	0.1
raw — *3 ½ oz*	100	74	2.6	34	0	1	0.1	0.3	0.7	1	46	14	314	56	1.4	90	49.4	0.06	13	16	1.8	0.21	0.08
Crab, alaska king																							
ckd, moist heat — *3 ½ oz*	100	97	0	53	0	1.5	0.2	0.5	0.1	19.4	59	1	262	1072	7.6	9	11.5	0.18	8	51	1.3	0.06	0.05
imitation, made from surimi — *3 ½ oz*	100	102	10.2	20	0	1.3	0.2	0.7	0.3	12	13	0	90	841	0.3	20	1.6	0.03	0	1.6	0.2	0.03	0.03
Crab, blue																							
canned — *3 ½ oz*	100	99	0	89	0	1.2	0.2	0.4	0.3	20.5	101	1	374	333	4	2	0.5	0.15	3	42.5	1.4	0.08	0.08
ckd, moist heat — *3 ½ oz*	100	102	0	100	0	1.8	0.3	0.7	0.2	20.2	104	1	324	279	4.2	2	7.3	0.18	3	50.8	3.3	0.05	0.1
crab cakes — *3 ½ oz*	100	155	0.5	150	0	7.5	2.8	2.3	1.5	20.2	105	1	324	330	4.1	81	5.9	0.17	3	41.5	2.9	0.08	0.09
Crab, dungeness, ckd, moist heat — *3 ½ oz*	100	110	1	76	0	1.2	0.2	0.4	0.2	22.3	59	0	408	378	5.5	31	10.4	0.17	4	42	3.6	0.2	0.06
Crab, queen, ckd, moist heat — *3 ½ oz*	100	115	0	71	0	1.5	0.3	0.5	0.2	23.7	33	3	200	691	3.6	52	10.4	0.17	7	42	2.9	0.24	0.1
Crayfish, ckd, moist heat — *3 ½ oz*	100	87	0	137	0	1.3	0.3	0.4	0.2	17.5	51	1	238	97	1.5	15	3.1	0.13	1	11	1.7	0.08	0.05
Cuttlefish, ckd, moist heat — *3 ½ oz*	100	158	1.6	224	0	1.4	0.2	0.3	0.2	32.5	180	11	637	744	3.5	203	5.4	0.27	9	24	2.2	1.73	0.02
Lobster, northern, ckd, moist heat — *3 ½ oz*	100	98	1.3	72	0	0.6	0.2	0.1	0.1	20.5	61	0	352	380	2.9	26	3.1	0.08	0	11.1	1.1	0.07	0.01
Mussels, blue, ckd, moist heat — *3 ½ oz*	100	172	7.4	56	0	4.5	1	1.2	0.9	23.8	33	7	268	369	2.7	91	24	0.1	14	75.6	3	0.42	0.3
Octopus, ckd, moist heat — *3 ½ oz*	100	164	4.4	96	0	2.1	0.3	0.5	0.5	29.8	106	10	630	460	3.4	81	36	0.65	8	24	3.8	0.08	0.06
Oysters																							
eastern, canned — *3 ½ oz*	100	69	3.9	55	0	2.5	0.3	0.7	0.6	7.1	45	7	229	112	91	90	19.1	0.1	5	8.9	1.2	0.17	0.15
eastern, ckd, dry heat — *3 ½ oz*	100	79	7.3	38	0	2.1	0.2	0.7	0.7	7	56	8	152	163	45.2	19	24.3	0.08	6	24	1.8	0.06	0.13

	Weight g	Calories	Carbohydrates g	Cholesterol mg	Dietary fiber g	Total fat g	Mono. fat g	Poly. fat g	Sat. fat g	Protein g	Calcium mg	Iron mg	Potassium mg	Sodium mg	Zinc mg	Vitamin A RE	Vitamin B_{12} mcg	Vitamin B_6 mg	Vitamin C mg	Folic acid mcg	Niacin mg	Riboflavin mg	Thiamin mg
eastern, ckd, moist heat — *3 ½ oz*	100	137	7.8	105	0	4.9	0.6	1.9	1.5	14.1	90	12	281	422	181.6	54	35	0.12	6	14	2.5	0.18	0.19
eastern, fried, breaded — *3 ½ oz*	100	197	11.6	81	0	12.6	4.7	3.3	3.2	8.8	62	7	244	417	87.1	90	15.6	0.06	4	13.6	1.7	0.2	0.15
eastern, raw — *3 ½ oz*	100	68	3.9	53	0	2.5	0.3	1	0.8	7.1	45	7	156	211	90.8	30	19.5	0.06	4	10	1.4	0.1	0.1
pacific, ckd, moist heat — *3 ½ oz*	100	163	9.9	100	0	4.6	0.7	1.8	1	18.9	16	9	302	212	33.2	146	28.8	0.09	13	15	3.6	0.44	0.13
pacific, raw — *3 ½ oz*	100	81	5	50	0	2.3	0.4	0.9	0.5	9.5	8	5	168	106	16.6	81	16	0.05	8	10	2	0.23	0.07
Scallops																							
fried, breaded — *3 ½ oz*	100	215	10.1	61	0	10.9	4.5	2.9	2.7	18.1	42	1	333	464	1.1	22	1.3	0.14	2	18.2	1.5	0.11	0.04
imitation, made from surimi — *3 ½ oz*	100	99	10.6	22	0	0.4	0.1	0.2	0.1	12.8	8	0	103	795	0.3	20	1.6	0.03	0	1.6	0.3	0.02	0.01
raw — *3 ½ oz*	100	88	2.4	33	0	0.8	0	0.3	0.1	16.8	24	0	322	161	1	15	1.5	0.15	3	16	1.2	0.07	0.01
Shrimp																							
canned — *3 ½ oz*	100	120	1	173	0	2	0.3	0.8	0.4	23.1	59	3	210	169	1.3	18	1.1	0.11	2	1.8	2.8	0.04	0.03
ckd, moist heat — *3 ½ oz*	100	99	0	195	0	1.1	0.2	0.4	0.3	20.9	39	3	182	224	1.6	66	1.5	0.13	2	3.5	2.6	0.03	0.03
fried, breaded — *3 ½ oz*	100	242	11.5	177	0.4	12.3	3.8	5.1	2.1	21.4	67	1	225	344	1.4	56	1.9	0.1	2	8.1	3.1	0.14	0.13
imitation, made from surimi — *3 ½ oz*	100	101	9.1	36	0	1.5	0.2	0.8	0.3	12.4	19	1	89	705	0.3	20	1.6	0.03	0	1.6	0.2	0.03	0.02
Spiny lobster, ckd, moist heat — *3 ½ oz*	100	143	3.1	90	0	1.9	0.4	0.8	0.3	26.4	63	1	208	227	7.3	6	4	0.17	2	1	4.9	0.06	0.01
Squid																							
fried — *3 ½ oz*	100	175	7.8	260	0	7.5	2.7	2.1	1.9	17.9	39	1	279	306	1.7	11	1.2	0.06	4	5.3	2.6	0.46	0.06
raw — *3 ½ oz*	100	92	3.1	233	0	1.4	0.1	0.5	0.4	15.6	32	1	246	44	1.5	10	1.3	0.06	5	4.9	2.2	0.41	0.02
Whelk, ckd, moist heat — *3 ½ oz*	100	275	15.5	130	0	0.8	0.1	0	0.1	47.7	113	10	694	412	3.3	49	18.1	0.65	7	11.4	2	0.21	0.05

Snacks

	Weight g	Calories	Carbohydrates g	Cholesterol mg	Dietary fiber g	Total fat g	Mono. fat g	Poly. fat g	Sat. fat g	Protein g	Calcium mg	Iron mg	Potassium mg	Sodium mg	Zinc mg	Vitamin A RE	Vitamin B_{12} mcg	Vitamin B_6 mg	Vitamin C mg	Folic acid mcg	Niacin mg	Riboflavin mg	Thiamin mg
Beef jerky — *1 oz*	28	116	3.1	14	0.5	7.3	3.2	0.3	3.1	9.4	6	2	169	627	2.3	0	0.3	0.05	0	38	0.5	0.04	0.04
Cheese puffs — *1 oz*	28	157	15.3	1	0.3	9.8	5.7	1.3	1.9	2.2	16	0	47	298	0.1	10	0	0.04	0	34	0.3	0.06	0.07
Chow mein noodles — *½ cup*	23	119	12.9	0	0.9	6.9	1.7	3.9	1	1.9	5	1	27	99	0.3	2	0	0.02	0	5	1.3	0.09	0.13
Corn cakes — *1 cake*	9	35	7.5	0	0.2	0.2	0.1	0.1	0	0.7	2	0	14	44	0.2	2	0	0.01	0	1.7	0.5	0	0.02

	Weight g	Calories	Carbohydrates g	Cholesterol mg	Dietary fiber g	Total fat g	Mono. fat g	Poly. fat g	Sat. fat g	Protein g	Calcium mg	Iron mg	Potassium mg	Sodium mg	Zinc mg	Vitamin A RE	Vitamin B12 mcg	Vitamin B6 mg	Vitamin C mg	Folic acid mcg	Niacin mg	Riboflavin mg	Thiamin mg
Cornnuts, plain — *1 oz*	28	124	20.8	0	2	4	2.1	0.9	0.7	2.4	3	0	79	156	0.5	0	0	0.06	0	0	0.5	0.04	0.01
Oriental mix, rice-based — *1 oz*	28	156	14.6	0	3.7	7.3	2.8	3	1.1	4.9	15	1	93	117	0.8	0	0	0.02	0	10.8	0.9	0.04	0.09
Popcorn																							
air-popped — *1 cup*	8	31	6.2	0	1.2	0.3	0.1	0.2	0	1	1	0	24	0	0.3	2	0	0.02	0	1.8	0.2	0.02	0.02
caramel-coated — *1 oz*	28	122	22.4	1	1.5	3.6	0.8	1.3	1	1.1	12	0	31	58	0.2	3	0	0.01	0	0.6	0.6	0.02	0.02
caramel-coated w/ peanuts — *1 oz*	28	113	22.9	0	1.1	2.2	0.8	0.9	0.3	1.8	19	1	101	84	0.4	2	0	0.05	0	4.5	0.6	0.04	0.01
cheese-flavored — *1 cup*	11	58	5.7	1	1.1	3.7	1.1	1.7	0.7	1	12	0	29	98	0.2	5	0.1	0.03	0	1.2	0.2	0.03	0.01
oil-popped — *1 cup*	11	55	6.3	0	1.1	3.1	0.9	1.5	0.5	1	1	0	25	97	0.3	2	0	0.02	0	1.9	0.2	0.01	0.01
Popcorn cakes — *1 cake*	10	38	8	0	0.3	0.3	0.1	0.1	0	1	1	0	33	29	0.4	1	0	0.02	0	1.8	0.6	0.02	0.01
Pork skins, plain — *1 oz*	28	155	0	27	0	8.9	4.2	1	3.2	17.4	9	0	36	521	0.2	11	0.2	0.01	0	0	0.4	0.08	0.03
Potato chips																							
barbecue-flavor — *1 oz*	28	139	15	0	1.2	9.2	1.9	4.6	2.3	2.2	14	1	357	213	0.3	6	0	0.18	10	23.5	1.3	0.06	0.06
cheese-flavor — *1 oz*	28	141	16.4	1	1.5	7.7	2.2	2.7	2.4	2.4	20	1	433	225	0.3	2	0	0.1	15	0	1.4	0.04	0.04
light — *1 oz*	28	134	19	0	1.7	5.9	1.4	3.1	1.2	2	6	0	494	139	0	0	0	0.19	7	7.7	2	0.08	0.06
plain, salted — *1 oz*	28	152	15	0	1.3	9.8	2.8	3.5	3.1	2	7	0	361	168	0.3	0	0	0.19	9	12.8	1.1	0.06	0.05
plain, unsalted — *1 oz*	28	152	15	0	1.4	9.8	2.8	3.5	3.1	2	7	0	361	2	0.3	0	0	0.19	9	12.8	1.1	0.06	0.05
sour cream & onion-flavor — *1 oz*	28	151	14.6	2	1.5	9.6	1.7	4.9	2.5	2.3	20	0	377	177	0.3	6	0.3	0.19	11	17.6	1.1	0.06	0.05
Potato chips, made from dried potatoes																							
cheese-flavor — *1 oz*	28	156	14.3	1	0.9	10.5	2	5.3	2.7	2	31	0	108	214	0.2	0	0	0.15	2	5.1	0.7	0.03	0.05
light — *1 oz*	28	142	18.4	0	1	7.3	1.7	3.8	1.5	1.6	10	0	285	121	0.2	0	0	0.22	3	6.5	1.2	0.02	0.05
plain — *1 oz*	28	158	14.5	0	1	10.9	2.1	5.7	2.7	1.7	7	0	286	186	0.2	0	0	0.04	2	2	0.9	0.03	0.06
sour cream & onion-flavor — *1 oz*	28	155	14.5	1	0.3	10.5	2	5.3	2.7	1.9	18	0	141	204	0.2	28	0	0.13	3	6.5	0.7	0.03	0.05
Potato sticks — *1 oz*	28	148	15.1	0	1	9.8	1.7	5.1	2.5	1.9	5	1	351	71	0.3	0	0	0.09	13	11.3	1.4	0.03	0.03

	Weight g	Calories	Carbohydrates g	Cholesterol mg	Dietary fiber g	Total fat g	Mono. fat g	Poly. fat g	Sat. fat g	Protein g	Calcium mg	Iron mg	Potassium mg	Sodium mg	Zinc mg	Vitamin A RE	Vitamin B_{12} mcg	Vitamin B_6 mg	Vitamin C mg	Folic acid mcg	Niacin mg	Riboflavin mg	Thiamin mg
Pretzels																							
chocolate-flavor coated — *1 oz*	28	130	20.1	0	0	4.7	1.5	0.6	2.2	2.1	21	1	64	161	0.3	1	0	0.05	0	2.6	0.2	0.06	0.03
plain, salted — *1 oz*	28	108	22.5	0	0.9	1	0.4	0.3	0.2	2.6	10	1	41	486	0.2	0	0	0.03	0	23.5	1.5	0.18	0.13
unsalted — *1 oz*	28	108	22.5	0	0.8	1	0.4	0.3	0.2	2.6	10	1	41	82	0.2	0	0	0.03	0	23.5	1.5	0.18	0.13
whole-wheat — *1 oz*	28	103	23	0	2.2	0.7	0.3	0.2	0.2	3.1	8	1	122	58	0.2	0	0	0.08	0	15.3	1.9	0.08	0.12
Rice cakes																							
buckwheat — *1 cake*	9	34	7.2	0	0.3	0.3	0.1	0.1	0.1	0.8	1	0	27	10	0.2	0	0	0.01	0	1.9	0.7	0.01	0.01
corn — *1 cake*	9	35	7.3	0	0.3	0.3	0.1	0.1	0.1	0.8	1	0	25	26	0.2	0	0	0.01	0	1.7	0.6	0.01	0.01
multigrain — *1 cake*	9	35	7.2	0	0.3	0.3	0.1	0.1	0.1	0.8	2	0	26	23	0.2	0	0	0.01	0	1.8	0.6	0.02	0.01
plain — *1 cake*	9	35	7.3	0	0.4	0.3	0.1	0.1	0.1	0.7	1	0	26	29	0.3	0	0	0.01	0	1.9	0.7	0.01	0.01
plain, unsalted — *1 cake*	9	35	7.3	0	0.4	0.3	0.1	0.1	0.1	0.7	1	0	26	2	0.3	0	0	0.01	0	1.9	0.7	0.01	0.01
sesame seed — *1 cake*	9	35	7.3	0	0.5	0.3	0.1	0.1	0	0.7	1	0	26	20	0.3	0	0	0.01	0	1.6	0.6	0.01	0
Taro chips — *1 oz*	28	141	19.3	0	2	7.1	1.3	3.7	1.8	0.7	17	0	214	97	0.1	0	0	0.12	1	5.7	0.1	0.01	0.05
Tortilla chips																							
nacho-flavor — *1 oz*	28	141	17.7	1	1.5	7.3	4.3	1	1.4	2.2	42	0	61	201	0.3	12	0	0.08	1	4	0.4	0.05	0.04
nacho-flavor, light — *1 oz*	28	126	20.3	1	1.4	4.3	2.5	0.6	0.8	2.5	45	0	77	284	0	12	0	0.07	0	7.4	0.1	0.08	0.06
plain — *1 oz*	28	142	17.8	0	1.8	7.4	4.4	1	1.4	2	44	0	56	150	0.4	6	0	0.08	0	2.8	0.4	0.05	0.02
ranch-flavor — *1 oz*	28	139	18.3	0	1.1	6.7	4	0.9	1.3	2.2	40	0	69	174	0.4	8	0	0.06	0	4.8	0.4	0.07	0.03
Trail mix																							
regular — *1 oz*	28	131	12.7	0	0	8.3	3.6	2.7	1.6	3.9	22	1	194	65	0.9	1	0	0.08	0	20.1	1.3	0.06	0.13
tropical — *1 oz*	28	115	18.6	0	0	4.8	0.7	1.5	2.4	1.8	16	1	201	3	0.3	1	0	0.09	2	11.9	0.4	0.03	0.13
unsalted — *1 oz*	28	131	12.7	0	0	8.3	3.6	2.7	1.6	3.9	22	1	194	3	0.9	1	0	0.08	0	20.1	1.3	0.06	0.13
w/ chocolate chips, nuts & seeds, unsalted — *1 oz*	28	137	12.7	1	0	9	3.8	3.2	1.7	4	31	1	184	8	0.9	1	0	0.07	0	18.4	1.2	0.06	0.12
w/ chocolate chips, salted nuts & seeds — *1 oz*	28	137	12.7	1	0	9	3.8	3.2	1.7	4	31	1	184	34	0.9	1	0	0.07	0	18.4	1.2	0.06	0.12

Sweets

Food	Weight g	Calories	Carbohydrates g	Cholesterol mg	Dietary fiber g	Total fat g	Mono. fat g	Poly. fat g	Sat. fat g	Protein g	Calcium mg	Iron mg	Potassium mg	Sodium mg	Zinc mg	Vitamin A RE	Vitamin B_{12} mcg	Vitamin B_6 mg	Vitamin C mg	Folic acid mcg	Niacin mg	Riboflavin mg	Thiamin mg
Butterscotch candy — *1 oz*	28	112	27	3	0	1	0.1	0	0.3	0	1	0	1	12	0	10	0	0	0	0	0	0.01	0
Candy, hard — *1 oz*	28	106	27.8	0	0	0	0	0	0	0	1	0	1	11	0	0	0	0	0	0	0	0	0
Caramels — *3 pieces*	30	116	23.3	2	0.4	2.5	0.3	0.1	2	1.4	42	0	65	74	0.1	2	0	0.01	0	1.5	0.1	0.05	0
Caramels, chocolate-flavor roll — *3 pieces*	21	76	18.3	0	0.2	0.5	0.2	0.2	0.1	0.4	5	0	21	5	0.1	0	0	0	0	0.2	0	0.01	0
Chocolate																							
baking, mexican — *1 square*	20	85	15.5	0	0.8	3.1	1	0.2	1.7	0.7	7	0	79	1	0.3	0	0	0.01	0	356.8	0.4	0.02	0.01
baking, unsweetened — *1 square*	28	148	8	0	4.4	15.7	5.2	0.5	9.2	2.9	21	2	236	4	1.1	3	0	0.03	0	2	0.3	0.05	0.02
milk chocolate — *1 oz*	28	144	16.7	6	1	8.6	2.8	0.3	5.2	1.9	54	0	108	23	0.4	15	0.1	0.01	0	2.3	0.1	0.08	0.02
milk chocolate w/ almonds — *1 oz*	29	150	15.2	5	1.8	9.8	3.9	0.7	4.9	2.6	64	0	127	21	0.4	4	0.2	0.01	0	3.2	0.2	0.12	0.02
milk chocolate w/ rice cereal — *1 oz*	28	141	18	5	0.7	7.5	2.5	0.2	4.5	1.8	49	0	97	41	0.3	3	0.1	0.02	0	2.6	0.1	0.08	0.02
semisweet chips — *½ cup*	84	402	53	0	5	25.2	8.4	0.8	14.9	3.5	27	3	307	9	1.4	2	0	0.03	0	2.5	0.4	0.08	0.05
Chocolate-coated peanuts — *10 pieces*	40	208	19.8	4	1.7	13.4	5.2	1.7	5.8	5.2	42	1	201	16	0.8	0	0.2	0.08	0	3.2	1.7	0.07	0.05
Chocolate-coated raisins — *10 pieces*	10	39	6.8	0	0.4	1.5	0.5	0.1	0.9	0.4	9	0	51	4	0.1	1	0	0.01	0	0.5	0	0.02	0.01
Cocoa																							
dry powder, unsweetened — *1 Tbsp*	5	12	2.9	0	1.8	0.7	0.2	0	0.4	1.1	7	1	82	1	0.4	0	0	0.01	0	1.7	0.1	0.01	0
hot, homemade — *1 cup*	250	193	29.5	20	2	5.8	1.7	0.2	3.6	9.8	315	1	500	128	1.5	138	0.9	0.12	3	15	0.4	0.44	0.1
low-calorie, prepared w/ water — *1 packet*	192	48	8.4	2	0.4	0.4	0.1	0	0.3	3.8	90	1	405	173	0.6	0	0.3	0.05	0	2.3	0.2	0.21	0.04
prepared w/ water — *1 packet*	206	103	22.5	2	2.5	1.2	0.4	0	0.7	3.1	97	0	202	148	0.5	0	0.4	0.03	0	0	0.2	0.16	0.03
Fudge																							
chocolate — *1 piece*	17	65	13.5	2	0.1	1.4	0.4	0.1	0.9	0.3	7	0	18	11	0.1	8	0	0	0	0.3	0	0.01	0
chocolate w/ nuts — *1 piece*	19	81	13.8	3	0.2	3.1	0.8	1	1.1	0.6	10	0	30	11	0.1	9	0	0.02	0	1.9	0	0.02	0.01
peanut butter — *1 piece*	16	59	12.5	1	0.1	1	0.5	0.3	0.2	0.6	7	0	21	12	0.1	2	0	0.01	0	1.8	0.2	0.01	0
vanilla — *1 piece*	16	59	13.2	3	0	0.9	0.2	0	0.5	0.2	6	0	8	11	0	8	0	0	0	0.2	0	0.01	0

Food	Weight g	Calories	Carbohydrates g	Cholesterol mg	Dietary fiber g	Total fat g	Mono. fat g	Poly. fat g	Sat. fat g	Protein g	Calcium mg	Iron mg	Potassium mg	Sodium mg	Zinc mg	Vitamin A RE	Vitamin B_{12} mcg	Vitamin B_6 mg	Vitamin C mg	Folic acid mcg	Niacin mg	Riboflavin mg	Thiamin mg
Gumdrops — *10 gumdrops*	36	139	35.6	0	0	0	0	0	0	0	1	0	2	16	0	0	0	0	0	0	0	0	0
Gummy bears — *10 gummy bears*	22	85	21.8	0	0	0	0	0	0	0	1	0	1	10	0	0	0	0	0	0	0	0	0
Halavah, plain — *1 oz*	28	133	17.1	0	1.3	6.1	2.3	2.4	1.2	3.5	9	1	53	55	1.2	0	0	0.1	0	18.4	0.8	0.02	0.12
Jams & preserves — *1 Tbsp*	20	48	12.9	0	0.2	0	0	0	0	0.1	4	0	15	8	0	0	0	0	2	6.6	0	0	0
Jellies — *1 Tbsp*	19	51	13.5	0	0.2	0	0	0	0	0.1	2	0	12	7	0	0	0	0	0	0.2	0	0	0
Jellybeans — *10 large*	28	104	26.4	0	0	0.1	0.1	0	0	0	1	0	10	7	0	0	0	0	0	0	0	0	0
Marmalade, orange — *1 Tbsp*	20	49	13.3	0	0	0	0	0	0	0.1	8	0	7	11	0	1	0	0	1	7.2	0	0	0
Marshmallows — *3 regular*	22	69	17.6	0	0	0	0	0	0	0.4	1	0	1	10	0	0	0	0	0	0.2	0	0	0
Peanut brittle — *1 oz*	28	128	19.6	4	0.6	5.4	2.4	1.3	1.4	2.1	9	0	59	128	0.3	13	0	0.03	0	19.9	1	0.01	0.05
Pralines — *1 piece*	39	177	24.2	0	1.1	9.5	5.9	2.4	0.7	1.1	12	0	82	24	0.8	2	0	0.03	0	5.5	0.1	0.02	0.12
Sesame sticks — *1 oz*	28	153	13.2	0	0.8	10.4	3.1	4.9	1.8	3.1	48	0	50	422	0.3	3	0	0.02	0	6.2	0.4	0.02	0.03
Taffy — *1 piece*	15	56	13.7	1	0	0.5	0.1	0	0.3	0	0	0	1	13	0	5	0	0	0	0	0	0	0
Toffee — *1 piece*	12	65	7.7	13	0	3.9	1.1	0.1	2.5	0.1	4	0	6	22	0	38	0	0	0	0.2	0	0.01	0

Turkey

Food	Weight g	Calories	Carbohydrates g	Cholesterol mg	Dietary fiber g	Total fat g	Mono. fat g	Poly. fat g	Sat. fat g	Protein g	Calcium mg	Iron mg	Potassium mg	Sodium mg	Zinc mg	Vitamin A RE	Vitamin B_{12} mcg	Vitamin B_6 mg	Vitamin C mg	Folic acid mcg	Niacin mg	Riboflavin mg	Thiamin mg
Back meat w/ skin, roasted — *3 ½ oz*	100	243	0	91	0	14.4	5	3.7	4.2	26.6	33	2	260	73	3.9	0	0.3	0.3	0	8	3.4	0.22	0.05
Breast meat w/ skin																							
pre-basted, roasted — *3 ½ oz*	100	126	0	42	0	3.5	1.1	0.8	1	22.2	9	1	248	397	1.5	0	0.3	0.32	0	5	9.1	0.13	0.05
roasted — *3 ½ oz*	100	189	0	74	0	7.4	2.5	1.8	2.1	28.7	21	1	288	63	2	0	0.4	0.48	0	6	6.4	0.13	0.06
Breast meat w/o skin, roasted — *3 ½ oz*	100	135	0	83	0	0.7	0.1	0.2	0.2	30.1	12	2	292	52	1.7	0	0.4	0.56	0	6	7.5	0.13	0.04
Dark meat w/ skin, roasted — *3 ½ oz*	100	221	0	89	0	11.5	3.7	3.1	3.5	27.5	33	2	274	76	4.2	0	0.4	0.32	0	9	3.5	0.24	0.06
Dark meat, roasted — *3 ½ oz*	100	187	0	85	0	7.2	1.6	2.2	2.4	28.6	32	2	290	79	4.5	0	0.4	0.36	0	9	3.6	0.25	0.06
Ground turkey, cooked — *3 ½ oz*	100	235	0	102	0	13.2	4.9	3.2	3.4	27.4	25	2	270	107	2.9	0	0.3	0.39	0	7	4.8	0.17	0.05
Leg meat w/skin, roasted — *3 ½ oz*	100	208	0	85	0	9.8	2.9	2.7	3.1	27.9	32	2	280	77	4.3	0	0.4	0.33	0	9	3.6	0.24	0.06
Leg meat, roasted — *3 ½ oz*	100	159	0	119	0	3.8	0.9	1.1	1.3	29.2	22	3	258	81	4.3	0	0.4	0.37	0	10	3.3	0.27	0.05

	Weight g	Calories	Carbohydrates g	Cholesterol mg	Dietary fiber g	Total fat g	Mono. fat g	Poly. fat g	Sat. fat g	Protein g	Calcium mg	Iron mg	Potassium mg	Sodium mg	Zinc mg	Vitamin A RE	Vitamin B_{12} mcg	Vitamin B_6 mg	Vitamin C mg	Folic acid mcg	Niacin mg	Riboflavin mg	Thiamin mg
Light & dark meat																							
frozen, seasoned, roasted — *3 ½ oz*	100	155	3.1	53	0	5.8	1.2	1.7	1.9	21.3	5	2	298	680	2.5	0	1.5	0.27	0	5	6.3	0.16	0.05
roasted — *3 ½ oz*	100	170	0	76	0	5	1	1.4	1.6	29.3	25	2	298	70	3.1	0	0.4	0.46	0	7	5.4	0.18	0.06
w/ skin, roasted — *3 ½ oz*	100	208	0	82	0	9.7	3.2	2.5	2.8	28.1	26	2	280	68	3	0	0.4	0.41	0	7	5.1	0.18	0.06
Light meat w/ skin, roasted — *3 ½ oz*	100	197	0	76	0	8.3	2.8	2	2.3	28.6	21	1	285	63	2	0	0.4	0.47	0	6	6.3	0.13	0.06
Light meat, roasted — *3 ½ oz*	100	157	0	69	0	3.2	0.6	0.9	1	29.9	19	1	305	64	2	0	0.4	0.54	0	6	6.8	0.13	0.06
Neck, simmered — *3 ½ oz*	100	180	0	122	0	7.3	1.7	2.2	2.4	26.8	37	2	149	56	7.1	0	0.2	0.21	0	8	1.7	0.19	0.04
Thigh w/ skin, prebasted, roasted — *3 ½ oz*	100	157	0	62	0	8.5	2.5	2.4	2.7	18.8	8	2	241	437	4.1	0	0.2	0.23	0	6	2.4	0.26	0.08
Turkey giblets, simmered — *3 ½ oz*	100	167	2.1	418	0	5.1	1.2	1.2	1.5	26.6	13	7	200	59	3.7	1795	24	0.33	2	345	4.5	0.9	0.05
Turkey skin — *1 oz*	28	125	0	32	0	11.2	4.8	2.6	2.9	5.6	10	1	45	15	0.6	0	0.1	0.02	0	1.1	0.8	0.04	0.01
Turkey, canned w/ broth — *3 ½ oz*	100	163	0	66	0	6.9	2.3	1.8	2	23.7	12	2	224	467	2.4	0	0.3	0.33	2	6	6.6	0.17	0.01
Wing w/ skin, roasted — *3 ½ oz*	100	229	0	81	0	12.4	4.7	2.9	3.4	27.4	24	1	266	61	2.1	0	0.3	0.42	0	6	5.7	0.13	0.05

Veal

	Weight g	Calories	Carbohydrates g	Cholesterol mg	Dietary fiber g	Total fat g	Mono. fat g	Poly. fat g	Sat. fat g	Protein g	Calcium mg	Iron mg	Potassium mg	Sodium mg	Zinc mg	Vitamin A RE	Vitamin B_{12} mcg	Vitamin B_6 mg	Vitamin C mg	Folic acid mcg	Niacin mg	Riboflavin mg	Thiamin mg
Ground veal, broiled — *3 ½ oz*	100	172	0	103	0	7.6	2.8	0.6	3	24.4	17	1	337	83	3.9	0	1.3	0.39	0	11	8	0.27	0.07
Leg (top round), braised																							
trimmed of all visible fat — *3 ½ oz*	100	203	0	135	0	5.1	1.8	0.4	1.9	36.7	9	1	387	67	4	0	1.2	0.37	0	18	10.7	0.36	0.06
untrimmed — *3 ½ oz*	100	211	0	134	0	6.3	2.4	0.5	2.5	36.2	8	1	383	67	4	0	1.2	0.36	0	18	10.6	0.35	0.06
Leg (top round), pan-fried																							
trimmed of all visible fat — *3 ½ oz*	100	183	0	107	0	4.6	1.7	0.4	1.3	33.2	7	1	442	77	3.4	0	1.5	0.51	0	16	12.6	0.37	0.07
untrimmed — *3 ½ oz*	100	211	0	105	0	8.4	3.2	0.6	3.2	31.8	6	1	425	76	3.2	0	1.5	0.49	0	15	12.1	0.35	0.07
Leg (top round), pan-fried, breaded																							
trimmed of all visible fat — *3 ½ oz*	100	206	9.8	113	0.2	6.3	2.2	1.4	1.6	28.4	39	2	383	455	2.9	10	1.3	0.42	0	20	10.8	0.36	0.16
untrimmed — *3 ½ oz*	100	228	9.9	112	0.3	9.2	3.4	1.5	3.1	27.3	39	2	371	454	2.8	10	1.2	0.4	0	19	10.3	0.35	0.16

	Weight g	Calories	Carbohydrates g	Cholesterol mg	Dietary fiber g	Total fat g	Mono. fat g	Poly. fat g	Sat. fat g	Protein g	Calcium mg	Iron mg	Potassium mg	Sodium mg	Zinc mg	Vitamin A RE	Vitamin B_{12} mcg	Vitamin B_6 mg	Vitamin C mg	Folic acid mcg	Niacin mg	Riboflavin mg	Thiamin mg
Leg (top round), roasted																							
trimmed of all visible fat — *3 ½ oz*	100	150	0	103	0	3.4	1.2	0.3	1.2	28.1	6	1	393	68	3.1	0	1.2	0.31	0	16	10.1	0.33	0.06
untrimmed — *3 ½ oz*	100	160	0	103	0	4.7	1.7	0.4	1.8	27.7	6	1	389	68	3	0	1.2	0.31	0	16	9.9	0.32	0.06
Loin, braised																							
trimmed of all visible fat — *3 ½ oz*	100	226	0	125	0	9.2	3.3	0.8	2.6	33.6	32	1	297	84	4.1	0	1.3	0.28	0	15	10.1	0.34	0.05
untrimmed — *3 ½ oz*	100	284	0	118	0	17.2	6.7	1.2	6.7	30.2	28	1	280	80	3.6	0	1.2	0.26	0	14	9	0.3	0.04
Loin, roasted																							
trimmed of all visible fat — *3 ½ oz*	100	175	0	106	0	6.9	2.5	0.6	2.6	26.3	21	1	340	96	3.2	0	1.3	0.37	0	16	9.5	0.3	0.06
untrimmed — *3 ½ oz*	100	217	0	103	0	12.3	4.8	0.8	5.3	24.8	19	1	325	93	3	0	1.2	0.34	0	15	8.9	0.28	0.05
Rib, braised																							
trimmed of all visible fat — *3 ½ oz*	100	218	0	144	0	7.8	2.6	0.7	2.6	34.4	24	1	318	99	6	0	1.5	0.34	0	16	7.9	0.31	0.06
untrimmed — *3 ½ oz*	100	251	0	139	0	12.5	4.7	0.9	5	32.4	22	1	306	95	5.6	0	1.5	0.32	0	16	7.5	0.29	0.05
Rib, roasted																							
trimmed of all visible fat — *3 ½ oz*	100	177	0	115	0	7.4	2.7	0.7	2.1	25.8	12	1	311	97	4.5	0	1.6	0.27	0	14	7.5	0.29	0.06
untrimmed — *3 ½ oz*	100	228	0	110	0	14	5.4	1	5.4	24	11	1	295	92	4.1	0	1.5	0.25	0	13	7	0.27	0.05
Shoulder, arm, braised																							
trimmed of all visible fat — *3 ½ oz*	100	201	0	155	0	5.3	1.9	0.5	1.5	35.7	30	1	347	90	6.2	0	1.8	0.3	0	19	10.7	0.33	0.06
untrimmed — *3 ½ oz*	100	236	0	148	0	10.2	4	0.7	4	33.6	28	1	333	87	5.8	0	1.7	0.29	0	18	10.1	0.31	0.06
Shoulder, arm, roasted																							
trimmed of all visible fat — *3 ½ oz*	100	164	0	109	0	5.8	2.2	0.4	2.3	26.1	27	1	356	91	4.3	0	1.6	0.3	0	17	8.2	0.33	0.07
untrimmed — *3 ½ oz*	100	183	0	108	0	8.3	3.2	0.5	3.5	25.5	26	1	348	90	4.2	0	1.5	0.29	0	17	8	0.32	0.06
Shoulder, blade, braised																							
trimmed of all visible fat — *3 ½ oz*	100	198	0	158	0	6.5	2.3	0.6	1.8	32.7	40	1	305	101	7.4	0	2	0.25	0	15	5.7	0.36	0.06
untrimmed — *3 ½ oz*	100	225	0	153	0	10.1	3.9	0.7	3.6	31.3	38	1	297	98	7	0	1.9	0.24	0	15	5.5	0.35	0.06

	Weight g	Calories	Carbohydrates g	Cholesterol mg	Dietary fiber g	Total fat g	Mono. fat g	Poly. fat g	Sat. fat g	Protein g	Calcium mg	Iron mg	Potassium mg	Sodium mg	Zinc mg	Vitamin A RE	Vitamin B_{12} mcg	Vitamin B_6 mg	Vitamin C mg	Folic acid mcg	Niacin mg	Riboflavin mg	Thiamin mg
Shoulder, blade, roasted																							
trimmed of all visible fat — *3 ½ oz*	100	171	0	119	0	6.9	2.5	0.6	2.6	25.6	28	1	310	102	5.7	0	2.1	0.24	0	11	5.8	0.36	0.07
untrimmed — *3 ½ oz*	100	186	0	117	0	8.7	3.2	0.6	3.5	25.2	28	1	306	100	5.6	0	2	0.24	0	11	5.7	0.35	0.07
Shoulder, whole, braised																							
trimmed of all visible fat — *3 ½ oz*	100	199	0	130	0	6.1	2.2	0.6	1.7	33.7	37	1	319	97	7	0	1.9	0.26	0	16	6.7	0.35	0.06
untrimmed — *3 ½ oz*	100	228	0	126	0	10.1	3.9	0.7	3.8	32.1	35	1	309	95	6.6	0	1.8	0.25	0	15	6.4	0.34	0.06
Shoulder, whole, roasted																							
trimmed of all visible fat — *3 ½ oz*	100	170	0	114	0	6.6	2.4	0.5	2.5	25.8	27	1	327	97	5.3	0	1.9	0.26	0	13	6.4	0.34	0.07
untrimmed — *3 ½ oz*	100	184	0	113	0	8.4	3.2	0.6	3.4	25.3	27	1	322	96	5.1	0	1.8	0.26	0	12	6.3	0.34	0.07
Sirloin, braised																							
trimmed of all visible fat — *3 ½ oz*	100	204	0	113	0	6.5	2.3	0.6	1.8	34	19	1	339	81	4.8	0	1.6	0.38	0	16	7.1	0.38	0.06
untrimmed — *3 ½ oz*	100	252	0	108	0	13.1	5.2	0.9	5.2	31.3	17	1	321	79	4.3	0	1.5	0.35	0	15	6.6	0.35	0.05
Sirloin, roasted																							
trimmed of all visible fat — *3 ½ oz*	100	168	0	104	0	6.2	2.3	0.5	2.4	26.3	14	1	365	85	3.5	0	1.5	0.34	0	16	9.3	0.37	0.06
untrimmed — *3 ½ oz*	100	202	0	102	0	10.5	4.1	0.7	4.5	25.1	13	1	351	83	3.4	0	1.4	0.32	0	15	8.9	0.35	0.06
Variety meats																							
brain, pan-fried — *3 ½ oz*	100	213	0	2120	0	16.8	4.2	2.4	4	14.5	10	1	472	176	1.8	0	21.3	0.33	15	6	5.6	0.36	0.15
heart, braised — *3 ½ oz*	100	186	0.1	176	0	6.8	1.4	1.8	1.8	29.1	8	4	199	58	2.2	0	14.5	0.21	10	2	4.9	0.93	0.35
kidneys, braised — *3 ½ oz*	100	163	0	791	0	5.7	1.2	1.1	1.7	26.3	29	3	159	110	4.3	201	36.9	0.18	8	21	4.6	1.99	0.19
liver, pan-fried — *3 ½ oz*	100	245	3.9	330	0	11.4	2.5	1.8	4.2	29.8	12	5	438	132	7.9	5628	64	0.86	22	320	16.9	3.36	0.25
lungs, braised — *3 ½ oz*	100	104	0	263	0	2.6	0.7	0.4	0.9	18.7	7	4	142	56	1.2	0	2.4	0.06	34	8	2.3	0.13	0.03
pancreas, braised — *3 ½ oz*	100	256	0	0	0	14.6	5	2.7	5	29.1	18	2	278	68	5.2	0	17.3	0.19	6	3	4.1	0.51	0.19
spleen, braised — *3 ½ oz*	100	129	0	447	0	2.9	0.8	0.2	1	24.1	7	7	215	58	1.9	0	4.8	0.07	40	4	5.3	0.29	0.05
thymus, braised — *3 ½ oz*	100	174	0	469	0	4.3	1.5	0.8	1.5	31.6	3	2	342	66	3.1	0	2.2	0.09	74	1	2	0.16	0.06

Vegetables

	Weight g	Calories	Carbohydrates g	Cholesterol mg	Dietary fiber g	Total fat g	Mono. fat g	Poly. fat g	Sat. fat g	Protein g	Calcium mg	Iron mg	Potassium mg	Sodium mg	Zinc mg	Vitamin A RE	Vitamin B_{12} mcg	Vitamin B_6 mg	Vitamin C mg	Folic acid mcg	Niacin mg	Riboflavin mg	Thiamin mg
Amaranth leaves																							
fresh, boiled — *½ cup*	66	14	2.7	0	0	0.1	0	0.1	0	1.4	138	1	423	14	0.6	183	0	0.12	27	37.5	0.4	0.09	0.01
fresh, raw — *1 cup*	28	7	1.1	0	0	0.1	0	0	0	0.7	60	1	171	6	0.3	82	0	0.05	12	23.9	0.2	0.04	0.01
Arrowhead																							
fresh, boiled — *1 medium*	12	9	1.9	0	0	0	0	0	0	0.5	1	0	106	2	0	0	0	0.02	0	1.1	0.1	0.01	0.02
fresh, raw — *1 medium*	12	12	2.4	0	0	0	0	0	0	0.6	1	0	111	3	0	0	0	0.03	0	1.7	0.2	0.01	0.02
Artichoke																							
fresh, boiled — *1 medium*	120	60	13.4	0	6.5	0.2	0	0.1	0	4.2	54	2	425	114	0.6	22	0	0.13	12	61.2	1.2	0.08	0.08
fresh, raw — *1 medium*	128	60	13.5	0	6.9	0.2	0	0.1	0	4.2	56	2	474	120	0.6	23	0	0.15	15	87	1.3	0.08	0.09
frozen — *4 ½ oz*	128	48	9.9	0	5	0.5	0	0.2	0.1	3.4	24	1	316	60	0.4	19	0	0.1	7	160.1	1.1	0.18	0.07
frozen, boiled — *½ cup*	84	38	7.7	0	3.9	0.4	0	0.2	0.1	2.6	18	0	222	45	0.3	13	0	0.07	4	99.8	0.8	0.13	0.05
Artichoke hearts, boiled — *½ cup*	84	42	9.4	0	4.5	0.1	0	0.1	0	2.9	38	1	297	80	0.4	15	0	0.09	8	42.8	0.8	0.06	0.05
Arugula, fresh, raw — *1 cup*	20	5	0.7	0	0.3	0.1	0	0.1	0	0.5	32	0	74	5	0.1	47	0	0.01	3	19.4	0.1	0.02	0.01
Asparagus																							
canned — *½ cup*	121	23	3	0	1.9	0.8	0	0.3	0.2	2.6	19	2	208	347	0.5	64	0	0.13	22	115.7	1.2	0.12	0.07
fresh, boiled, slices — *½ cup*	90	22	3.8	0	1.4	0.3	0	0.1	0.1	2.3	18	1	144	10	0.4	49	0	0.11	10	131.4	1	0.11	0.11
fresh, boiled, spears — *4 medium*	60	14	2.5	0	1	0.2	0	0.1	0	1.6	12	0	96	7	0.3	32	0	0.07	6	87.6	0.6	0.08	0.07
fresh, raw, slices — *1 cup*	134	31	6.1	0	2.8	0.3	0	0.1	0.1	3.1	28	1	366	3	0.6	78	0	0.18	18	171.5	1.6	0.17	0.19
fresh, raw, spears — *4 medium*	64	15	2.9	0	1.3	0.1	0	0.1	0	1.5	13	1	175	1	0.3	37	0	0.08	8	81.9	0.7	0.08	0.09
frozen, boiled, slices — *½ cup*	90	25	4.4	0	1.4	0.4	0	0.2	0.1	2.7	21	1	196	4	0.5	74	0	0.02	22	121.2	0.9	0.09	0.06
frozen, boiled, spears — *4 medium*	60	17	2.9	0	1	0.3	0	0.1	0.1	1.8	14	0	131	2	0.3	49	0	0.01	15	80.8	0.6	0.06	0.04
frozen, spears — *4 medium*	58	14	2.4	0	1.1	0.1	0	0.1	0	1.9	15	0	147	5	0.3	55	0	0.06	18	110.6	0.7	0.08	0.07

	Weight g	Calories	Carbohydrates g	Cholesterol mg	Dietary fiber g	Total fat g	Mono. fat g	Poly. fat g	Sat. fat g	Protein g	Calcium mg	Iron mg	Potassium mg	Sodium mg	Zinc mg	Vitamin A RE	Vitamin B_{12} mcg	Vitamin B_6 mg	Vitamin C mg	Folic acid mcg	Niacin mg	Riboflavin mg	Thiamin mg
Balsam-pear, leafy tips																							
fresh, boiled — *½ cup*	29	10	2	0	0.6	0.1	0	0	0	1	12	0	175	4	0.1	50	0	0.22	16	25.4	0.3	0.08	0.04
fresh, raw — *1 cup*	48	14	1.6	0	0	0.3	0	0	0	2.5	40	1	292	5	0.1	83	0	0.39	42	61.5	0.5	0.17	0.09
Balsam-pear, pods																							
fresh, boiled — *½ cup*	62	12	2.7	0	1.2	0.1	0	0	0	0.5	6	0	198	4	0.5	7	0	0.03	20	31.7	0.2	0.03	0.03
fresh, raw — *1 cup*	93	16	3.4	0	2.6	0.2	0	0	0	0.9	18	0	275	5	0.7	35	0	0.04	78	67	0.4	0.04	0.04
Bamboo shoots																							
canned — *½ cup*	66	12	2.1	0	0.9	0.3	0	0.1	0.1	1.1	5	0	52	5	0.4	1	0	0.09	1	2.1	0.1	0.02	0.02
fresh, boiled — *½ cup*	60	7	1.2	0	0.6	0.1	0	0.1	0	0.9	7	0	320	2	0.3	0	0	0.06	0	1.4	0.2	0.03	0.01
fresh, raw — *1 cup*	151	41	7.9	0	3.3	0.5	0	0.2	0.1	3.9	20	1	805	6	1.7	3	0	0.36	6	10.7	0.9	0.11	0.23
Beans, snap, green																							
canned — *½ cup*	68	14	3	0	1.3	0.1	0	0	0	0.8	18	1	74	177	0.2	24	0	0.02	3	21.5	0.1	0.04	0.01
fresh, boiled — *½ cup*	63	22	4.9	0	2	0.2	0	0.1	0	1.2	29	1	187	2	0.2	42	0	0.04	6	20.8	0.4	0.06	0.05
fresh, raw — *1 cup*	110	34	7.9	0	3.7	0.1	0	0.1	0	2	41	1	230	7	0.3	74	0	0.08	18	40.2	0.8	0.12	0.09
frozen — *1 cup*	124	41	9.4	0	3.5	0.3	0	0.1	0.1	2.2	52	1	231	4	0.3	60	0	0.05	16	18.2	0.6	0.11	0.12
frozen, boiled — *½ cup*	68	19	4.4	0	2	0.1	0	0.1	0	1	33	1	85	6	0.3	27	0	0.04	3	15.5	0.3	0.06	0.02
Beans, snap, yellow																							
canned — *½ cup*	68	14	3	0	0.9	0.1	0	0	0	0.8	18	1	74	169	0.2	7	0	0.02	3	21.5	0.1	0.04	0.01
canned w/o salt — *½ cup*	68	14	3.1	0	0.9	0.1	0	0	0	0.8	18	1	74	1	0.2	7	0	0.03	3	21.6	0.1	0.04	0.01
fresh, boiled — *½ cup*	63	22	4.9	0	2.1	0.2	0	0.1	0	1.2	29	1	187	2	0.2	5	0	0.04	6	20.8	0.4	0.06	0.05
fresh, raw — *1 cup*	110	34	7.9	0	3.7	0.1	0	0.1	0	2	41	1	230	7	0.3	12	0	0.08	18	40.2	0.8	0.12	0.09
frozen — *1 cup*	124	41	9.4	0	3.5	0.3	0	0.1	0.1	2.2	52	1	231	4	0.3	16	0	0.05	16	18.2	0.6	0.11	0.12
frozen, boiled — *½ cup*	68	19	4.4	0	2	0.1	0	0.1	0	1	33	1	85	6	0.3	7	0	0.04	3	15.5	0.3	0.06	0.02

	Weight g	Calories	Carbohydrates g	Cholesterol mg	Dietary fiber g	Total fat g	Mono. fat g	Poly. fat g	Sat. fat g	Protein g	Calcium mg	Iron mg	Potassium mg	Sodium mg	Zinc mg	Vitamin A RE	Vitamin B_{12} mcg	Vitamin B6 mg	Vitamin C mg	Folic acid mcg	Niacin mg	Riboflavin mg	Thiamin mg
Beet greens																							
fresh, boiled, chopped — *½ cup*	72	19	3.9	0	2.1	0.1	0	0.1	0	1.9	82	1	654	174	0.4	367	0	0.1	18	10.3	0.4	0.21	0.08
fresh, raw, chopped — *1 cup*	38	7	1.5	0	1.4	0	0	0	0	0.7	45	1	208	76	0.1	232	0	0.04	11	5.6	0.2	0.08	0.04
Beets																							
canned, harvard, slices — *½ cup*	123	90	22.4	0	3.1	0.1	0	0	0	1	14	0	202	199	0.3	1	0	0.07	3	35.7	0.1	0.06	0.01
canned, pickled, slices — *½ cup*	114	74	18.5	0	0	0.1	0	0	0	0.9	12	0	168	300	0.3	1	0	0.06	3	30.1	0.3	0.05	0.01
canned, slices — *½ cup*	85	26	6.1	0	1.4	0.1	0	0	0	0.8	13	2	126	165	0.2	1	0	0.05	3	25.7	0.1	0.03	0.01
fresh, boiled, slices — *½ cup*	85	37	8.5	0	1.7	0.2	0	0.1	0	1.4	14	1	259	65	0.3	3	0	0.06	3	68	0.3	0.03	0.02
fresh, raw — *1 cup*	136	58	13	0	3.8	0.2	0	0.1	0	2.2	22	1	442	106	0.5	5	0	0.09	7	148.2	0.5	0.05	0.04
Borage																							
fresh, boiled — *3 ½ oz*	100	25	3.6	0	0	0.8	0.2	0.1	0.2	2.1	102	4	491	88	0.2	438	0	0.09	33	10	0.9	0.17	0.06
fresh, raw, chopped — *1 cup*	89	19	2.7	0	0	0.6	0.2	0.1	0.2	1.6	83	3	418	71	0.2	374	0	0.07	31	11.8	0.8	0.13	0.05
Broadbeans																							
fresh, boiled — *3 ½ oz*	100	56	10.1	0	3.6	0.5	0	0.3	0.1	4.8	18	2	193	41	0.5	27	0	0.03	20	57.8	1.2	0.09	0.13
fresh, raw — *1 cup*	109	78	12.8	0	4.6	0.7	0	0.3	0.2	6.1	24	2	273	55	0.6	38	0	0.04	36	105	1.6	0.12	0.19
Broccoli																							
fresh, boiled, chopped — *½ cup*	78	22	3.9	0	2.3	0.3	0	0.1	0	2.3	36	1	228	20	0.3	108	0	0.11	58	39	0.4	0.09	0.04
fresh, boiled, spears — *1 medium*	37	10	1.9	0	1.1	0.1	0	0.1	0	1.1	17	0	108	10	0.1	51	0	0.05	28	18.5	0.2	0.04	0.02
fresh, raw, chopped — *1 cup*	88	25	4.6	0	2.6	0.3	0	0.1	0	2.6	42	1	286	24	0.4	136	0	0.14	82	62.5	0.6	0.1	0.06
fresh, raw, spears — *1 medium*	31	9	1.6	0	0.9	0.1	0	0.1	0	0.9	15	0	101	8	0.1	48	0	0.05	29	22	0.2	0.04	0.02
frozen, boiled, chopped — *½ cup*	92	26	4.9	0	2.8	0.1	0	0.1	0	2.9	47	1	166	22	0.3	174	0	0.12	37	51.9	0.4	0.07	0.05
frozen, chopped — *1 cup*	156	41	7.5	0	4.7	0.5	0	0.2	0.1	4.4	87	1	331	37	0.7	323	0	0.2	88	104.5	0.7	0.15	0.08
Broccoli leaves, fresh, raw — *3 ½ oz*	100	28	5.2	0	0	0.4	0	0.2	0.1	3	48	1	325	27	0.4	1600	0	0.16	93	71	0.6	0.12	0.07

	Weight g	Calories	Carbohydrates g	Cholesterol mg	Dietary fiber g	Total fat g	Mono. fat g	Poly. fat g	Sat. fat g	Protein g	Calcium mg	Iron mg	Potassium mg	Sodium mg	Zinc mg	Vitamin A RE	Vitamin B_{12} mcg	Vitamin B_6 mg	Vitamin C mg	Folic acid mcg	Niacin mg	Riboflavin mg	Thiamin mg
Brussels sprouts																							
fresh, boiled — *½ cup*	78	30	6.8	0	2	0.4	0	0.2	0.1	2	28	1	247	16	0.3	56	0	0.14	48	46.8	0.5	0.06	0.08
fresh, raw — *1 cup*	88	38	7.9	0	3.3	0.3	0	0.1	0.1	3	37	1	342	22	0.4	77	0	0.19	75	53.8	0.7	0.08	0.12
frozen — *5 oz*	142	58	11.2	0	5.4	0.6	0	0.3	0.1	5.4	37	1	525	14	0.4	115	0	0.29	105	175.2	0.9	0.17	0.15
frozen, boiled — *½ cup*	78	33	6.4	0	3.2	0.3	0	0.2	0.1	2.8	19	1	252	18	0.3	46	0	0.22	35	78.4	0.4	0.09	0.08
Burdock root																							
fresh, boiled — *½ cup*	63	55	13.2	0	1.1	0.1	0	0	0	1.3	31	0	225	3	0.2	0	0	0.17	2	12.2	0.2	0.04	0.02
fresh, raw — *1 cup*	118	85	20.5	0	3.9	0.2	0	0.1	0	1.8	48	1	363	6	0.4	0	0	0.28	4	26.9	0.4	0.04	0.01
Butterbur (fuki)																							
canned, chopped — *½ cup*	62	2	0.2	0	0	0.1	0	0	0	0.1	21	0	7	2	0	0	0	0.02	7	1.6	0.1	0	0
fresh, boiled — *3 ½ oz*	100	8	2.2	0	0	0	0	0	0	0.2	59	0	354	4	0.1	3	0	0.05	19	4.1	0.1	0.01	0.01
fresh, raw — *1 cup*	94	13	3.4	0	0	0	0	0	0	0.4	97	0	616	7	0.2	5	0	0.09	30	9.8	0.2	0.02	0.02
Cabbage																							
fresh, boiled, shredded — *½ cup*	75	17	3.3	0	1.7	0.3	0	0.1	0	0.8	23	0	73	6	0.1	10	0	0.08	15	15	0.2	0.04	0.04
fresh, raw, chopped — *1 cup*	89	22	4.8	0	2	0.2	0	0.1	0	1.3	42	1	219	16	0.2	12	0	0.09	29	38.3	0.3	0.04	0.04
fresh, raw, shredded — *1 cup*	70	18	3.8	0	1.6	0.2	0	0.1	0	1	33	0	172	13	0.1	9	0	0.07	23	30.1	0.2	0.03	0.04
Cabbage, chinese (pak-choi)																							
fresh, boiled, shredded — *½ cup*	85	10	1.5	0	1.4	0.1	0	0.1	0	1.3	79	1	315	29	0.1	218	0	0.14	22	34.5	0.4	0.05	0.03
fresh, raw, shredded — *1 cup*	70	9	1.5	0	0.7	0.1	0	0.1	0	1.1	74	1	176	46	0.1	210	0	0.14	32	46	0.4	0.05	0.03
Cabbage, chinese (pe-tsai)																							
fresh, boiled, shredded — *½ cup*	60	8	1.4	0	1.6	0.1	0	0	0	0.9	19	0	134	5	0.1	58	0	0.11	9	31.8	0.3	0.03	0.03
fresh, raw, shredded — *1 cup*	76	12	2.5	0	2.4	0.2	0	0.1	0	0.9	59	0	181	7	0.2	91	0	0.18	21	59.8	0.3	0.04	0.03
Cabbage, red																							
fresh, boiled, shredded — *½ cup*	75	16	3.5	0	1.5	0.2	0	0.1	0	0.8	28	0	105	6	0.1	2	0	0.11	26	9.5	0.2	0.02	0.03

	Weight g	Calories	Carbohydrates g	Cholesterol mg	Dietary fiber g	Total fat g	Mono. fat g	Poly. fat g	Sat. fat g	Protein g	Calcium mg	Iron mg	Potassium mg	Sodium mg	Zinc mg	Vitamin A RE	Vitamin B_{12} mcg	Vitamin B_6 mg	Vitamin C mg	Folic acid mcg	Niacin mg	Riboflavin mg	Thiamin mg
fresh, raw, chopped — *1 cup*	89	24	5.4	0	1.8	0.2	0	0.1	0	1.2	45	0	183	10	0.2	4	0	0.19	51	18.4	0.3	0.03	0.04
fresh, raw, shredded — *1 cup*	70	19	4.3	0	1.4	0.2	0	0.1	0	1	36	0	144	8	0.1	3	0	0.15	40	14.5	0.2	0.02	0.04
Cabbage, savoy																							
fresh, boiled, shredded — *½ cup*	73	17	3.9	0	2	0.1	0	0	0	1.3	22	0	133	17	0.2	65	0	0.11	12	33.6	0	0.01	0.04
fresh, raw, shredded — *1 cup*	70	19	4.3	0	2.2	0.1	0	0	0	1.4	25	0	161	20	0.2	70	0	0.13	22	56.1	0.2	0.02	0.05
Cardoon																							
fresh, boiled — *3 ½ oz*	100	22	5.3	0	1.7	0.1	0	0	0	0.8	72	1	392	176	0.2	12	0	0.04	2	21.6	0.3	0.03	0.02
fresh, raw, shredded — *1 cup*	178	36	8.7	0	2.8	0.2	0	0.1	0	1.2	125	1	712	303	0.3	21	0	0.08	4	50.4	0.5	0.05	0.04
Carrots																							
canned, slices — *½ cup*	73	17	4	0	1.1	0.1	0	0.1	0	0.5	18	0	131	177	0.2	1005	0	0.08	2	6.7	0.4	0.02	0.01
fresh, boiled, slices — *½ cup*	78	35	8.2	0	2.6	0.1	0	0.1	0	0.9	24	0	177	51	0.2	1915	0	0.19	2	10.8	0.4	0.04	0.03
fresh, raw — *1 medium*	61	26	6.2	0	1.8	0.1	0	0	0	0.6	16	0	197	21	0.1	1716	0	0.09	6	8.5	0.6	0.04	0.06
fresh, raw, baby — *5 large*	75	29	6.1	0	1.4	0.4	0	0.2	0.1	0.6	17	1	209	26	0.1	148	0	0.06	6	24.8	0.7	0.04	0.02
fresh, raw, grated — *1 cup*	110	47	11.2	0	3.3	0.2	0	0.1	0	1.1	30	1	355	39	0.2	3094	0	0.16	10	15.4	1	0.06	0.11
fresh, raw, slices — *1 cup*	122	52	12.4	0	3.7	0.2	0	0.1	0	1.3	33	1	394	43	0.2	3432	0	0.18	11	17.1	1.1	0.07	0.12
frozen, boiled, slices — *½ cup*	73	26	6	0	2.6	0.1	0	0	0	0.9	20	0	115	43	0.2	1292	0	0.09	2	7.9	0.3	0.03	0.02
frozen, slices — *1 cup*	128	50	11.5	0	4.1	0.3	0	0.1	0	1.4	41	1	232	76	0.3	2724	0	0.23	6	12.3	0.8	0.06	0.05
Cassava, fresh, raw — *1 cup*	206	247	55.5	0	3.3	0.8	0.2	0.1	0.2	6.4	187	7	1574	16	0.5	2	0	0.63	99	45.5	2.9	0.21	0.46
Cauliflower																							
fresh, boiled — *½ cup*	62	14	2.5	0	1.7	0.3	0	0.1	0	1.1	10	0	88	9	0.1	1	0	0.11	27	27.3	0.3	0.03	0.03
fresh, raw — *1 cup*	100	25	5.2	0	2.5	0.2	0	0.1	0	2	22	0	303	30	0.3	2	0	0.22	46	57	0.5	0.06	0.06
frozen — *1 cup*	132	32	6.2	0	3	0.4	0	0.2	0.1	2.7	29	1	255	32	0.2	4	0	0.16	64	84.4	0.6	0.09	0.07
frozen, boiled — *½ cup*	90	17	3.4	0	2.4	0.2	0	0.1	0	1.4	15	0	125	16	0.1	2	0	0.08	28	36.9	0.3	0.05	0.03

Food	Weight g	Calories	Carbohydrates g	Cholesterol mg	Dietary fiber g	Total fat g	Mono. fat g	Poly. fat g	Sat. fat g	Protein g	Calcium mg	Iron mg	Potassium mg	Sodium mg	Zinc mg	Vitamin A RE	Vitamin B_{12} mcg	Vitamin B_6 mg	Vitamin C mg	Folic acid mcg	Niacin mg	Riboflavin mg	Thiamin mg
Cauliflower, green																							
fresh, boiled — *3 ½ oz*	100	32	6.3	0	3.3	0.3	0	0.1	0	3	32	1	278	23	0.6	14	0	0.21	73	41	0.7	0.1	0.07
fresh, raw — *1 cup*	64	20	3.9	0	2	0.2	0	0.1	0	1.9	21	0	192	15	0.4	10	0	0.14	56	36.5	0.5	0.07	0.05
Celeriac																							
fresh, boiled — *3 ½ oz*	100	25	5.9	0	1.2	0.2	0	0	0	1	26	0	173	61	0.2	0	0	0.1	4	3.4	0.4	0.04	0.03
fresh, raw — *1 cup*	156	61	14.4	0	2.8	0.5	0.1	0.2	0.1	2.3	67	1	468	156	0.5	0	0	0.26	12	11.9	1.1	0.09	0.08
Celery																							
fresh, boiled, diced — *½ cup*	75	14	3	0	1.2	0.1	0	0.1	0	0.6	32	0	213	68	0.1	10	0	0.06	5	16.5	0.2	0.04	0.03
fresh, raw, diced — *1 cup*	120	19	4.4	0	2	0.2	0	0.1	0	0.9	48	0	344	104	0.2	16	0	0.1	8	33.6	0.4	0.05	0.06
fresh, raw, stalks — *4 medium*	160	26	5.8	0	2.7	0.2	0	0.1	0.1	1.2	64	1	459	139	0.2	21	0	0.14	11	44.8	0.5	0.07	0.07
Celtuce, fresh, raw — *5 leaves*	40	9	1.5	0	0.7	0.1	0	0	0	0.3	16	0	132	4	0.1	140	0	0.02	8	18.2	0.2	0.03	0.02
Chayote																							
fresh, boiled — *½ cup*	80	19	4.1	0	2.2	0.4	0	0	0	0.5	10	0	138	1	0.2	4	0	0.09	6	14.5	0.3	0.03	0.02
fresh, raw — *1 cup*	132	32	7.1	0	4	0.4	0	0.2	0.1	1.2	25	1	198	5	0.5	8	0	0.17	15	36.4	0.7	0.05	0.04
Chicory greens, fresh, raw, chopped — *1 cup*	180	41	8.5	0	7.2	0.5	0	0.2	0.1	3.1	180	2	756	81	0.8	720	0	0.19	43	197.1	0.9	0.18	0.11
Chicory roots, fresh, raw — *1 cup*	90	66	15.8	0	0	0.2	0	0.1	0	1.3	37	1	261	45	0.3	1	0	0.22	5	20.6	0.4	0.03	0.04
Chicory, witloof, fresh, raw — *1 cup*	90	15	3.6	0	2.8	0.1	0	0	0	0.8	17	0	190	2	0.1	3	0	0.04	3	33.3	0.1	0.02	0.06
Coleslaw — *½ cup*	60	41	7.4	5	0.9	1.6	0.4	0.8	0.2	0.8	27	0	109	14	0.1	49	0	0.08	20	15.9	0.2	0.04	0.04
Collards																							
fresh, boiled, chopped — *½ cup*	95	26	5.8	0	2.7	0.2	0	0.1	0	1.3	22	0	124	15	0.1	259	0	0.05	11	5.7	0.3	0.05	0.02
fresh, raw, chopped — *1 cup*	36	11	2.6	0	1.3	0.1	0	0	0	0.6	10	0	61	7	0	120	0	0.02	8	4.3	0.1	0.02	0.01
frozen, boiled, chopped — *½ cup*	85	31	6	0	2.4	0.3	0	0.2	0.1	2.5	179	1	213	43	0.2	508	0	0.1	22	64.7	0.5	0.1	0.04
frozen, chopped — *3 ½ oz*	100	33	6.5	0	3.6	0.4	0	0	0	2.7	201	1	253	48	0.3	571	0	0.12	40	73.1	0.6	0.11	0.05

	Weight g	Calories	Carbohydrates g	Cholesterol mg	Dietary fiber g	Total fat g	Mono. fat g	Poly. fat g	Sat. fat g	Protein g	Calcium mg	Iron mg	Potassium mg	Sodium mg	Zinc mg	Vitamin A RE	Vitamin B_{12} mcg	Vitamin B_6 mg	Vitamin C mg	Folic acid mcg	Niacin mg	Riboflavin mg	Thiamin mg
Corn, sweet, white																							
canned — *½ cup*	82	66	15.2	0	1.6	0.8	0.2	0.4	0.1	2.1	4	1	160	265	0.3	0	0	0.04	7	39.9	1	0.06	0.03
canned, cream-style — *½ cup*	128	92	23.2	0	1.5	0.5	0.2	0.3	0.1	2.2	4	0	172	365	0.7	0	0	0.08	6	57.3	1.2	0.07	0.03
canned, cream-style w/o salt — *½ cup*	128	92	23.2	0	1.5	0.5	0.2	0.3	0.1	2.2	4	0	172	4	0.7	0	0	0.08	6	57.3	1.2	0.07	0.03
canned, vacuum pack — *½ cup*	105	83	20.4	0	2.1	0.5	0.2	0.2	0.1	2.5	5	0	195	286	0.5	0	0	0.06	9	51.8	1.2	0.08	0.04
canned, vacuum pack w/o salt — *½ cup*	105	83	20.4	0	2.1	0.5	0.2	0.2	0.1	2.5	5	0	195	3	0.5	0	0	0.06	9	51.8	1.2	0.08	0.04
fresh, boiled — *½ cup*	82	89	20.6	0	2.2	1	0.3	0.5	0.2	2.7	2	1	204	14	0.4	0	0	0.05	5	38.1	1.3	0.06	0.18
fresh, boiled, on the cob — *1 large ear*	77	83	19.3	0	2.1	1	0.3	0.5	0.2	2.6	2	0	192	13	0.4	0	0	0.05	5	35.7	1.2	0.06	0.17
fresh, raw — *1 cup*	154	132	29.3	0	4.2	1.8	0.5	0.9	0.3	5	3	1	416	23	0.7	0	0	0.08	10	70.5	2.6	0.09	0.31
fresh, raw, on the cob — *1 large ear*	73	63	13.9	0	2	0.9	0.3	0.4	0.1	2.4	1	0	197	11	0.3	0	0	0.4	5	33.4	1.2	0.04	0.15
frozen — *1 cup*	164	144	34.1	0	3.9	1.3	0.4	0.6	0.2	5	7	1	344	5	0.6	0	0	0.29	10	58.6	2.8	0.11	0.14
frozen, boiled — *½ cup*	82	66	16	0	2	0.4	0.1	0.2	0.1	2.3	3	0	121	4	0.3	0	0	0.11	3	25.4	1.1	0.06	0.07
frozen, boiled, on the cob — *1 ear*	63	59	14.1	0	1.3	0.5	0.1	0.2	0.1	2	2	0	158	3	0.4	0	0	0.14	3	19.2	1	0.04	0.11
frozen, on the cob — *1 ear*	125	123	29.4	0	3.5	1	0.3	0.5	0.2	4.1	5	1	368	6	0.9	0	0	0.22	9	50.1	2.1	0.11	0.13
Corn, sweet, yellow																							
canned — *½ cup*	82	66	15.2	0	1.6	0.8	0.2	0.4	0.1	2.1	4	1	160	175	0.3	13	0	0.04	7	39.9	1	0.06	0.03
canned, cream-style — *½ cup*	128	92	23.2	0	1.5	0.5	0.2	0.3	0.1	2.2	4	0	172	365	0.7	13	0	0.08	6	57.3	1.2	0.07	0.03
canned, vacuum pack — *½ cup*	105	83	20.4	0	2.1	0.5	0.2	0.2	0.1	2.5	5	0	195	286	0.5	25	0	0.06	9	51.8	1.2	0.08	0.04
canned, vacuum pack w/o salt — *½ cup*	105	83	20.4	0	2.1	0.5	0.2	0.2	0.1	2.5	5	0	195	3	0.5	25	0	0.06	9	51.8	1.2	0.08	0.04
fresh, boiled — *½ cup*	82	89	20.6	0	2.3	1	0.3	0.5	0.2	2.7	2	1	204	14	0.4	18	0	0.05	5	38.1	1.3	0.06	0.18
fresh, raw — *1 cup*	154	132	29.3	0	4.2	1.8	0.5	0.9	0.3	5	3	1	416	23	0.7	43	0	0.08	10	70.5	2.6	0.09	0.31
fresh, raw, on the cob — *1 large ear*	143	123	27.2	0	3.9	1.7	0.5	0.8	0.3	4.6	3	1	386	21	0.6	40	0	0.08	10	65.5	2.4	0.09	0.29
frozen — *1 cup*	164	144	34.1	0	3.9	1.3	0.4	0.6	0.2	5	7	1	344	5	0.6	21	0	0.29	10	58.6	2.8	0.11	0.14
frozen, boiled — *½ cup*	82	66	16	0	2	0.4	0.1	0.2	0.1	2.3	3	0	121	4	0.3	18	0	0.11	3	25.4	1.1	0.06	0.07

	Weight *g*	Calories	Carbohydrates *g*	Cholesterol *mg*	Dietary fiber *g*	Total fat *g*	Mono. fat *g*	Poly. fat *g*	Sat. fat *g*	Protein *g*	Calcium *mg*	Iron *mg*	Potassium *mg*	Sodium *mg*	Zinc *mg*	Vitamin A *RE*	Vitamin B_{12} *mcg*	Vitamin B_6 *mg*	Vitamin C *mg*	Folic acid *mcg*	Niacin *mg*	Riboflavin *mg*	Thiamin *mg*
frozen, boiled, on the cob — *1 ear*	63	59	14.1	0	1.8	0.5	0.1	0.2	0.1	2	2	0	158	3	0.4	13	0	0.14	3	19.2	1	0.04	0.11
frozen, on the cob — *1 ear*	125	123	29.4	0	3.5	1	0.3	0.5	0.2	4.1	5	1	368	6	0.9	31	0	0.22	9	50.1	2.1	0.11	0.13
Cornsalad, raw — *1 cup*	56	12	2	0	0	0.2	0	0	0	1.1	21	1	257	2	0.3	397	0	0.15	21	7.6	0.2	0.05	0.04
Cowpeas																							
fresh, boiled — *½ cup*	83	80	16.8	0	4.1	0.3	0	0.1	0.1	2.6	106	1	345	3	0.8	65	0	0.05	2	104.8	1.2	0.12	0.08
fresh, raw — *1 cup*	145	131	27.4	0	7.3	0.5	0	0.2	0.1	4.3	183	2	625	6	1.5	119	0	0.1	4	243.6	2.1	0.21	0.16
frozen — *1 cup*	160	222	40.2	0	8	1.1	0.1	0.5	0.3	14.4	42	4	706	10	2.5	13	0	0.17	6	298.9	1.3	0.11	0.39
frozen, boiled — *½ cup*	85	112	20.2	0	5.4	0.6	0.1	0.2	0.1	7.2	20	2	319	4	1.2	7	0	0.08	2	120.1	0.6	0.05	0.22
Cowpeas, pods																							
fresh, boiled — *½ cup*	48	16	3.3	0	0	0.1	0	0.1	0	1.2	26	0	93	1	0.1	67	0	0.06	8	12.2	0.4	0.04	0.04
fresh, raw — *1 cup*	94	41	8.9	0	0	0.3	0	0.1	0.1	3.1	61	1	202	4	0.3	150	0	0.16	31	49.4	1.1	0.13	0.14
Cucumber, fresh, raw, slices — *1 cup*	104	14	2.9	0	0.8	0.1	0	0.1	0	0.7	15	0	150	2	0.2	22	0	0.04	6	13.5	0.2	0.02	0.02
Dandelion greens																							
fresh, boiled, chopped — *½ cup*	53	17	3.4	0	1.5	0.3	0	0.1	0.1	1.1	74	1	122	23	0.1	614	0	0.08	9	6.6	0.3	0.09	0.07
fresh, raw, chopped — *1 cup*	55	25	5.1	0	1.9	0.4	0	0.2	0.1	1.5	103	2	218	42	0.2	770	0	0.14	19	15	0.4	0.14	0.1
Dock																							
fresh, boiled — *3 ½ oz*	100	20	2.9	0	2.6	0.6	0	0	0	1.8	38	2	321	3	0.2	347	0	0.1	26	7.8	0.4	0.09	0.03
fresh, raw, chopped — *1 cup*	133	29	4.3	0	3.9	0.9	0	0	0	2.7	59	3	519	5	0.3	532	0	0.16	64	17.6	0.7	0.13	0.05
Eggplant																							
fresh, boiled, cubes — *½ cup*	99	28	6.6	0	2.5	0.2	0	0.1	0	0.8	6	0	246	3	0.1	6	0	0.09	1	14.3	0.6	0.02	0.08
fresh, raw, cubes — *1 cup*	82	21	5	0	2.1	0.1	0	0.1	0	0.8	6	0	178	2	0.1	7	0	0.07	1	15.6	0.5	0.03	0.04
Endive, fresh, raw, chopped — *1 cup*	50	9	1.7	0	1.6	0.1	0	0	0	0.6	26	0	157	11	0.4	103	0	0.01	3	71	0.2	0.04	0.04
Eppaw, fresh, raw — *1 cup*	100	150	31.7	0	0	1.8	0	0	0	4.6	110	1	340	12	1.2	0	0	0.18	13	24.3	0.3	0.12	0.11
Fennel, bulb, fresh, raw, slices — *1 cup*	87	27	6.3	0	2.7	0.2	0	0	0	1.1	43	1	360	45	0.2	11	0	0.04	10	23.5	0.6	0.03	0.01

	Weight g	Calories	Carbohydrates g	Cholesterol mg	Dietary fiber g	Total fat g	Mono. fat g	Poly. fat g	Sat. fat g	Protein g	Calcium mg	Iron mg	Potassium mg	Sodium mg	Zinc mg	Vitamin A RE	Vitamin B_{12} mcg	Vitamin B_6 mg	Vitamin C mg	Folic acid mcg	Niacin mg	Riboflavin mg	Thiamin mg
Garden cress																							
fresh, boiled — *½ cup*	68	16	2.6	0	0.5	0.4	0.1	0.1	0	1.3	41	1	240	5	0.1	524	0	0.11	16	25.2	0.5	0.11	0.04
fresh, raw — *1 cup*	50	16	2.8	0	0.6	0.4	0.1	0.1	0	1.3	41	1	303	7	0.1	465	0	0.12	35	40.2	0.5	0.13	0.04
Gourd, dishcloth (towelgourd)																							
fresh, boiled, slices — *½ cup*	89	50	12.8	0	0	0.3	0.1	0.1	0	0.6	8	0	403	19	0.2	23	0	0.09	5	10.7	0.2	0.04	0.04
fresh, raw, slices — *1 cup*	95	19	4.1	0	0	0.2	0	0.1	0	1.1	19	0	132	3	0.1	39	0	0.04	11	6.4	0.4	0.06	0.05
Gourd, white-flowered (calabash)																							
fresh, boiled, cubes — *½ cup*	73	11	2.7	0	0	0	0	0	0	0.4	18	0	124	1	0.5	0	0	0.03	6	3.1	0.3	0.02	0.02
fresh, raw, slices — *1 cup*	116	16	3.9	0	0	0	0	0	0	0.7	30	0	174	2	0.8	2	0	0.05	12	6.8	0.4	0.03	0.03
Hearts of palm, canned — *½ cup*	73	20	3.4	0	1.8	0.5	0.1	0.1	0.1	1.8	42	2	129	311	0.8	0	0	0.02	6	28.5	0.3	0.04	0.01
Horseradish-tree																							
leafy tips, fresh, boiled, chopped — *½ cup*	21	13	2.3	0	0.4	0.2	0.1	0	0	1.1	32	0	72	2	0.1	147	0	0.2	7	4.7	0.4	0.11	0.05
leafy tips, fresh, raw, chopped — *1 cup*	21	13	1.7	0	0.4	0.3	0	0	0	2	39	1	71	2	0.1	159	0	0.25	11	8.4	0.5	0.14	0.05
Horseradish-tree pods																							
fresh, boiled, slices — *½ cup*	59	21	4.8	0	2.5	0.1	0.1	0	0	1.2	12	0	270	25	0.2	4	0	0.07	57	17.9	0.3	0.04	0.03
fresh, raw, slices — *1 cup*	100	37	8.5	0	3.2	0.2	0.1	0	0	2.1	30	0	461	42	0.5	7	0	0.12	141	44.3	0.6	0.07	0.05
Hyacinth-bean																							
fresh, boiled — *½ cup*	44	22	4	0	0	0.1	0.1	0	0.1	1.3	18	0	114	1	0.2	6	0	0.01	2	20.2	0.2	0.04	0.02
fresh, raw — *1 cup*	80	37	7.4	0	0	0.2	0.1	0	0.1	1.7	40	1	202	2	0.3	9	0	0.02	10	49.2	0.4	0.07	0.06
Jerusalem-artichokes, fresh, raw, slices — *1 cup*	150	114	26.2	0	2.4	0	0	0	0	3	21	5	644	6	0.2	3	0	0.12	6	20.1	2	0.09	0.3
Jew's ear (pepeao)																							
dried — *1 cup*	24	72	19.4	0	0	0.1	0	0	0	1.2	27	1	170	17	1.8	0	0	0.23	0	38.5	0.7	0.08	0.2
fresh, raw, slices — *1 cup*	99	25	6.7	0	0	0	0	0	0	0.5	16	1	43	9	0.7	0	0	0.09	1	18.9	0.1	0.2	0.08

	Weight g	Calories	Carbohydrates g	Cholesterol mg	Dietary fiber g	Total fat g	Mono. fat g	Poly. fat g	Sat. fat g	Protein g	Calcium mg	Iron mg	Potassium mg	Sodium mg	Zinc mg	Vitamin A RE	Vitamin B_{12} mcg	Vitamin B_6 mg	Vitamin C mg	Folic acid mcg	Niacin mg	Riboflavin mg	Thiamin mg
Jute, potherb																							
fresh, boiled — *½ cup*	44	16	3.2	0	0.9	0.1	0	0	0	1.6	92	1	239	5	0.3	226	0	0.25	14	45.2	0.4	0.08	0.04
fresh, raw — *1 cup*	28	10	1.6	0	0	0.1	0	0	0	1.3	58	1	157	2	0.2	156	0	0.17	10	34.4	0.4	0.15	0.04
Kale																							
fresh, boiled, chopped — *½ cup*	65	21	3.7	0	1.3	0.3	0	0.1	0	1.2	47	1	148	15	0.2	481	0	0.09	27	8.7	0.3	0.05	0.03
fresh, raw, chopped — *1 cup*	67	34	6.7	0	1.3	0.5	0	0.2	0.1	2.2	90	1	299	29	0.3	596	0	0.18	80	19.6	0.7	0.09	0.07
frozen — *3 ½ oz*	100	28	4.9	0	2	0.5	0	0.2	0.1	2.7	136	1	333	15	0.2	625	0	0.09	39	16.7	0.7	0.11	0.06
frozen, boiled, chopped — *½ cup*	65	20	3.4	0	1.3	0.3	0	0.2	0	1.8	90	1	209	10	0.1	413	0	0.06	16	9.3	0.4	0.07	0.03
Kale, scotch																							
fresh, boiled, chopped — *½ cup*	65	18	3.7	0	0.8	0.3	0	0.1	0	1.2	86	1	178	29	0.2	129	0	0.09	34	8.7	0.5	0.03	0.03
fresh, raw, chopped — *1 cup*	67	28	5.6	0	1.1	0.4	0	0.2	0.1	1.9	137	2	302	47	0.2	208	0	0.15	87	18.8	0.9	0.04	0.05
Kanpyo (dried gourd strips) — *½ cup*	27	70	17.6	0	0	0.2	0	0.1	0	2.3	76	1	427	4	1.6	0	0	0.14	0	16.5	0.8	0.01	0
Kohlrabi																							
fresh, boiled, slices — *½ cup*	83	24	5.5	0	0.9	0.1	0	0	0	1.5	21	0	281	17	0.3	3	0	0.13	45	10	0.3	0.02	0.03
fresh, raw — *1 cup*	135	36	8.4	0	4.9	0.1	0	0.1	0	2.3	32	1	473	27	0	5	0	0.2	84	21.7	0.5	0.03	0.07
Lambsquarters																							
fresh, boiled, chopped — *½ cup*	90	29	4.5	0	1.9	0.6	0.1	0.3	0	2.9	232	1	259	26	0.3	873	0	0.16	33	12.2	0.8	0.23	0.09
fresh, raw — *3 ½ oz*	100	43	7.3	0	4	0.8	0.2	0.4	0.1	4.2	309	1	452	43	0.4	1160	0	0.27	80	29.6	1.2	0.44	0.16
Leeks (bulb & lower leaf-portion)																							
fresh, boiled — *1 medium*	124	38	9.4	0	1.2	0.2	0	0.1	0	1	37	1	108	12	0.1	6	0	0.14	5	30.1	0.2	0.02	0.03
fresh, raw — *1 medium*	89	54	12.6	0	1.6	0.3	0	0.1	0	1.3	53	2	160	18	0.1	9	0	0.21	11	57.1	0.4	0.03	0.05
Lettuce, fresh, raw																							
butterhead/boston/bibb, shredded — *1 cup*	55	7	1.3	0	0.6	0.1	0	0.1	0	0.7	18	0	141	3	0.1	53	0	0.03	4	40.3	0.2	0.03	0.03
cos or romaine, shredded — *1 cup*	56	9	1.3	0	1	0.1	0	0.1	0	0.9	20	1	162	4	0.1	146	0	0.03	13	76	0.3	0.06	0.06

	Weight g	Calories	Carbohydrates g	Cholesterol mg	Dietary fiber g	Total fat g	Mono. fat g	Poly. fat g	Sat. fat g	Protein g	Calcium mg	Iron mg	Potassium mg	Sodium mg	Zinc mg	Vitamin A RE	Vitamin B_{12} mcg	Vitamin B_6 mg	Vitamin C mg	Folic acid mcg	Niacin mg	Riboflavin mg	Thiamin mg
iceberg, shredded — *1 cup*	55	7	1.1	0	0.8	0.1	0	0.1	0	0.6	10	0	87	5	0.1	18	0	0.02	2	30.8	0.1	0.02	0.03
looseleaf, shredded — *1 cup*	56	10	2	0	1.1	0.2	0	0.1	0	0.7	38	1	148	5	0.2	106	0	0.03	10	27.9	0.2	0.04	0.03
Lima beans																							
canned w/o salt — *½ cup*	124	88	16.5	0	4.5	0.4	0	0.2	0.1	5	35	2	353	5	0.8	19	0	0.08	11	19.8	0.7	0.05	0.04
fresh, boiled — *½ cup*	85	105	20.1	0	4.5	0.3	0	0.1	0.1	5.8	27	2	485	14	0.7	31	0	0.16	9	22.4	0.9	0.08	0.12
fresh, raw — *1 cup*	156	176	31.4	0	7.6	1.3	0.1	0.7	0.3	10.7	53	5	729	12	1.2	47	0	0.32	37	53	2.3	0.16	0.34
Lima beans, baby																							
frozen — *1 cup*	164	216	41.2	0	9.8	0.7	0	0.4	0.2	12.4	57	4	741	85	1	31	0	0.26	14	45.3	1.7	0.12	0.19
frozen, boiled — *½ cup*	90	95	17.5	0	5.4	0.3	0	0.1	0.1	6	25	2	370	26	0.5	15	0	0.1	5	14	0.7	0.05	0.06
Lima beans, fordhook																							
frozen — *1 cup*	160	170	31.7	0	8.8	0.6	0	0.3	0.1	10.2	38	2	765	93	0.8	35	0	0.22	31	51	1.9	0.11	0.15
frozen, boiled — *½ cup*	85	85	16	0	4.9	0.3	0	0.1	0.1	5.2	19	1	347	45	0.4	16	0	0.1	11	18	0.9	0.05	0.06
Lotus root																							
fresh, boiled — *10 slices*	89	59	14.3	0	2.8	0.1	0	0	0	1.4	23	1	323	40	0.3	0	0	0.19	24	7	0.3	0.01	0.11
fresh, raw — *10 slices*	81	45	14	0	4	0.1	0	0	0	2.1	36	1	450	32	0.3	0	0	0.21	36	10.3	0.3	0.18	0.13
Mountain yam, hawaii																							
fresh, raw, cubes — *1 cup*	136	91	22.2	0	0	0.1	0	0.1	0	1.8	35	1	568	18	0.4	0	0	0.24	4	19	0.7	0.03	0.14
fresh, steamed, cubes — *½ cup*	73	59	14.5	0	0	0.1	0	0	0	1.3	6	0	359	9	0.2	0	0	0.15	0	8.8	0.1	0.01	0.06
Mushrooms																							
canned — *½ cup*	78	19	3.9	0	1.9	0.2	0	0.1	0	1.5	9	1	101	332	0.6	0	0	0.05	0	9.6	1.2	0.02	0.07
fresh, boiled, slices — *½ cup*	78	21	4	0	1.7	0.4	0	0.1	0	1.7	5	1	278	2	0.7	0	0	0.07	3	14.2	3.5	0.23	0.06
fresh, raw, slices — *1 cup*	70	18	3.3	0	0.8	0.3	0	0.1	0	1.5	4	1	259	3	0.5	0	0	0.07	2	14.8	2.9	0.31	0.07
Mushrooms, enoki, fresh, raw — *10 medium*	30	10	2.1	0	0.8	0.1	0	0	0	0.7	0	0	114	1	0.2	0	0	0.01	4	9	1.1	0.03	0.03

	Weight g	Calories	Carbohydrates g	Cholesterol mg	Dietary fiber g	Total fat g	Mono. fat g	Poly. fat g	Sat. fat g	Protein g	Calcium mg	Iron mg	Potassium mg	Sodium mg	Zinc mg	Vitamin A RE	Vitamin B_{12} mcg	Vitamin B_6 mg	Vitamin C mg	Folic acid mcg	Niacin mg	Riboflavin mg	Thiamin mg
Mushrooms, shiitake																							
cooked — *4 mushrooms*	72	40	10.3	0	1.5	0.2	0	0	0	1.1	2	0	84	3	1	0	0	0.11	0	15.1	1.1	0.12	0.03
dried — *4 mushrooms*	15	44	11.3	0	1.7	0.1	0	0	0	1.4	2	0	230	2	1.1	0	0	0.14	1	24.5	2.1	0.19	0.05
Mustard greens																							
fresh, boiled, chopped — *½ cup*	70	11	1.5	0	1.4	0.2	0.1	0	0	1.6	52	0	141	11	0.1	212	0	0.07	18	51.4	0.3	0.04	0.03
fresh, raw, chopped — *1 cup*	56	15	2.7	0	1.8	0.1	0.1	0	0	1.5	58	1	198	14	0.1	297	0	0.1	39	104.9	0.4	0.06	0.04
frozen, boiled, chopped — *½ cup*	75	14	2.3	0	2.1	0.2	0.1	0	0	1.7	76	1	104	19	0.2	335	0	0.08	10	52.1	0.2	0.04	0.03
frozen, chopped — *1 cup*	146	29	5	0	4.8	0.4	0.2	0.1	0	3.6	169	2	248	42	0.3	752	0	0.19	37	201.9	0.5	0.09	0.07
Mustard spinach (tendergreen)																							
fresh, boiled, chopped — *½ cup*	90	14	2.5	0	1.8	0.2	0	0	0	1.5	142	1	257	13	0.1	738	0	0.09	59	65.5	0.4	0.06	0.04
fresh, raw, chopped — *1 cup*	150	33	5.9	0	4.2	0.5	0	0	0	3.3	315	2	674	32	0.3	1485	0	0.23	195	238.4	1	0.14	0.1
New zealand spinach																							
fresh, boiled, chopped — *½ cup*	90	11	2	0	0	0.2	0	0.1	0	1.2	43	1	92	96	0.3	326	0	0.21	14	7.5	0.4	0.1	0.03
fresh, raw, chopped — *1 cup*	56	8	1.4	0	0	0.1	0	0	0	0.8	32	0	73	73	0.2	246	0	0.17	17	8.3	0.3	0.07	0.02
Nopales																							
fresh, cooked — *1 cup*	149	22	4.9	0	3	0.1	0	0	0	2	244	1	291	30	0.3	69	0	0.1	8	4.5	0.4	0.06	0.02
fresh, raw, slices — *1 cup*	86	14	2.9	0	2	0.1	0	0	0	1.1	140	1	274	19	0.2	35	0	0.06	12	2.6	0.5	0.04	0.01
Okra																							
fresh, boiled, slices — *½ cup*	80	26	5.8	0	2	0.1	0	0	0	1.5	50	0	258	4	0.4	46	0	0.15	13	36.6	0.7	0.04	0.11
fresh, raw — *1 cup*	100	38	7.6	0	3.2	0.1	0	0	0	2	81	1	303	8	0.6	66	0	0.22	21	87.8	1	0.06	0.2
frozen — *3 ½ oz*	100	30	6.6	0	2.2	0.3	0	0.1	0.1	1.7	81	1	211	3	0.5	46	0	0.04	12	147.6	0.7	0.11	0.09
frozen, boiled, slices — *½ cup*	92	34	5.3	0	2.6	0.3	0	0.1	0.1	1.9	88	1	215	3	0.6	47	0	0.04	11	134	0.7	0.11	0.09
Onions																							
fresh, raw, chopped — *1 cup*	160	61	13.8	0	2.9	0.3	0	0.1	0	1.9	32	0	251	5	0.3	0	0	0.19	10	30.4	0.2	0.03	0.07

	Weight g	Calories	Carbohydrates g	Cholesterol mg	Dietary fiber g	Total fat g	Mono. fat g	Poly. fat g	Sat. fat g	Protein g	Calcium mg	Iron mg	Potassium mg	Sodium mg	Zinc mg	Vitamin A RE	Vitamin B_{12} mcg	Vitamin B_6 mg	Vitamin C mg	Folic acid mcg	Niacin mg	Riboflavin mg	Thiamin mg
fresh, raw, whole — *1 medium*	110	42	9.5	0	2	0.2	0	0.1	0	1.3	22	0	173	3	0.2	0	0	0.13	7	20.9	0.2	0.02	0.05
frozen, boiled, whole — *½ cup*	105	29	7	0	1.5	0.1	0	0	0	0.7	28	0	106	8	0.1	2	0	0.07	5	14.1	0.1	0.02	0.02
frozen, whole — *3 ½ oz*	100	35	8.4	0	1.7	0.1	0	0	0	0.9	36	0	142	10	0.1	3	0	0.09	8	21.2	0.2	0.02	0.03
Onions, spring, tops & bulbs, fresh, raw, chopped — *1 cup*	100	32	7.3	0	2.6	0.2	0	0.1	0	1.8	72	1	276	16	0.4	39	0	0.06	19	64	0.5	0.08	0.06
Parsnips																							
fresh, boiled, slices — *½ cup*	78	63	15.2	0	3.1	0.2	0.1	0	0	1	29	0	286	8	0.2	0	0	0.07	10	45.4	0.6	0.04	0.06
fresh, raw, slices — *1 cup*	133	100	23.9	0	6.5	0.4	0.1	0.1	0.1	1.6	48	1	499	13	0.8	0	0	0.12	23	88.8	0.9	0.07	0.12
Peas & carrots																							
frozen — *1 cup*	140	74	15.6	0	4.8	0.7	0.1	0.3	0.1	4.8	38	2	272	111	0.7	1330	0	0.14	16	50	2	0.11	0.27
frozen, boiled — *½ cup*	80	38	8.1	0	2.5	0.3	0	0.2	0.1	2.5	18	1	126	54	0.4	621	0	0.07	6	20.8	0.9	0.05	0.18
Peas & onions																							
frozen — *1 cup*	138	97	18.6	0	4.8	0.4	0	0.2	0.1	5.5	32	2	280	84	0.7	75	0	0.2	19	61.4	2.4	0.16	0.41
frozen, boiled — *½ cup*	90	41	7.8	0	2	0.2	0	0.1	0	2.3	13	1	105	33	0.3	32	0	0.08	6	17.9	0.9	0.06	0.14
Peas, edible-pod																							
fresh, boiled — *½ cup*	80	34	5.6	0	2.2	0.2	0	0.1	0	2.6	34	2	192	3	0.3	10	0	0.12	38	23.3	0.4	0.06	0.1
fresh, raw — *1 cup*	63	26	4.8	0	1.6	0.1	0	0.1	0	1.8	27	1	126	3	0.2	9	0	0.1	38	26.3	0.4	0.05	0.09
frozen — *1 cup*	144	60	10.4	0	4.5	0.4	0	0.2	0.1	4	72	3	276	6	0.6	20	0	0.22	32	57.9	0.7	0.14	0.09
frozen, boiled — *½ cup*	80	42	7.2	0	2.5	0.3	0	0.1	0.1	2.8	47	2	174	4	0.4	14	0	0.14	18	28.2	0.5	0.1	0.05
Peas, green																							
canned — *½ cup*	85	59	10.7	0	3.5	0.3	0	0.1	0.1	3.8	17	1	147	214	0.6	65	0	0.05	8	37.7	0.6	0.07	0.1
fresh, boiled — *½ cup*	80	67	12.5	0	4.4	0.2	0	0.1	0	4.3	22	1	217	2	1	48	0	0.17	11	50.6	1.6	0.12	0.21
fresh, raw — *1 cup*	145	117	21	0	7.4	0.6	0.1	0.3	0.1	7.9	36	2	354	7	1.8	93	0	0.25	58	94.3	3	0.19	0.39
frozen — *1 cup*	144	111	19.7	0	6.8	0.5	0	0.3	0.1	7.5	32	2	215	161	1.2	105	0	0.18	26	76.5	2.5	0.14	0.37
frozen, boiled — *½ cup*	80	62	11.4	0	4.4	0.2	0	0.1	0	4.1	19	1	134	70	0.8	54	0	0.09	8	46.9	1.2	0.08	0.23

	Weight g	Calories	Carbohydrates g	Cholesterol mg	Dietary fiber g	Total fat g	Mono. fat g	Poly. fat g	Sat. fat g	Protein g	Calcium mg	Iron mg	Potassium mg	Sodium mg	Zinc mg	Vitamin A RE	Vitamin B_{12} mcg	Vitamin B_6 mg	Vitamin C mg	Folic acid mcg	Niacin mg	Riboflavin mg	Thiamin mg
Peppers, hot chili																							
canned, jalapeño, chopped — *¼ cup*	34	8	1.7	0	0.6	0.2	0	0.1	0	0.3	9	1	46	497	0.1	58	0	0.07	4	4.6	0.2	0.02	0.01
fresh, raw, green, chopped — *¼ cup*	38	15	3.5	0	0.6	0.1	0	0	0	0.8	7	0	128	3	0.1	29	0	0.1	91	8.8	0.4	0.03	0.03
fresh, raw, red, chopped — *¼ cup*	38	15	3.5	0	0.6	0.1	0	0	0	0.8	7	0	128	3	0.1	403	0	0.1	91	8.8	0.4	0.03	0.03
sun-dried, whole — *2 peppers*	1	3	0.8	0	0.3	0.1	0	0	0	0.1	0	0	20	1	0	29	0	0.01	0	0.6	0.1	0.01	0
Peppers, sweet, green																							
fresh, boiled, chopped — *½ cup*	68	19	4.6	0	0.8	0.1	0	0.1	0	0.6	6	0	113	1	0.1	40	0	0.16	51	10.9	0.3	0.02	0.04
fresh, raw, chopped — *1 cup*	149	40	9.6	0	2.7	0.3	0	0.2	0	1.3	13	1	264	3	0.2	94	0	0.37	133	32.8	0.8	0.04	0.1
frozen, boiled, chopped — *3 ½ oz*	100	18	3.9	0	0.9	0.2	0	0.1	0	1	8	1	72	4	0.1	29	0	0.11	41	9.9	1.1	0.03	0.05
frozen, chopped — *3 ½ oz*	100	20	4.5	0	1.6	0.2	0	0.1	0	1.1	9	1	91	5	0.1	37	0	0.14	59	14.1	1.4	0.04	0.07
Peppers, sweet, red																							
fresh, boiled, chopped — *½ cup*	68	19	4.6	0	0.8	0.1	0	0.1	0	0.6	6	0	113	1	0.1	256	0	0.16	116	10.9	0.3	0.02	0.04
fresh, raw, chopped — *1 cup*	149	40	9.6	0	3	0.3	0	0.2	0	1.3	13	1	264	3	0.2	849	0	0.37	283	32.8	0.8	0.04	0.1
frozen, boiled, chopped — *3 ½ oz*	100	18	3.9	0	0	0.2	0	0.1	0	1	8	1	72	4	0.1	334	0	0.11	41	9.9	1.1	0.03	0.05
frozen, chopped — *3 ½ oz*	100	20	4.5	0	1.6	0.2	0	0.1	0	1.1	9	1	91	5	0.1	476	0	0.14	59	14.1	1.4	0.04	0.07
Peppers, sweet, yellow, fresh, raw — *½ large pepper*	93	25	5.9	0	0.8	0.2	0	0	0	0.9	10	0	197	2	0.2	22	0	0.16	171	24.2	0.8	0.02	0.03
Pickles, sour, slices — *¼ cup*	39	4	0.9	0	0.5	0.1	0	0	0	0.1	0	0	9	468	0	6	0	0	0	0.3	0	0	0
Pigeonpeas																							
fresh, boiled — *½ cup*	77	85	14.9	0	4.7	1	0	0.7	0.3	4.6	31	1	349	4	0.6	10	0	0.04	21	76.5	1.6	0.13	0.27
fresh, raw — *1 cup*	154	209	36.8	0	7.9	2.5	0	1.3	0.5	11.1	65	2	850	8	1.6	22	0	0.1	60	266.3	3.4	0.26	0.62
Pinto beans																							
frozen — *3 ½ oz*	100	170	32.5	0	5.7	0.5	0	0.3	0.1	9.8	58	3	756	92	0.8	0	0	0.22	1	50.4	0.7	0.12	0.34
frozen, boiled — *3 ½ oz*	100	162	30.9	0	8.6	0.5	0	0.3	0.1	9.3	52	3	646	83	0.7	0	0	0.19	1	33.5	0.6	0.11	0.27
Poi — *1 cup*	240	269	65.4	0	1	0.3	0	0.1	0.1	0.9	38	2	439	29	0.5	5	0	0.66	10	51.4	2.6	0.1	0.31

	Weight g	Calories	Carbohydrates g	Cholesterol mg	Dietary fiber g	Total fat g	Mono. fat g	Poly. fat g	Sat. fat g	Protein g	Calcium mg	Iron mg	Potassium mg	Sodium mg	Zinc mg	Vitamin A RE	Vitamin B_{12} mcg	Vitamin B_6 mg	Vitamin C mg	Folic acid mcg	Niacin mg	Riboflavin mg	Thiamin mg
Pokeberry shoots (poke)																							
fresh, boiled — *½ cup*	83	17	2.6	0	1.2	0.3	0	0.1	0.1	1.9	44	1	152	15	0.2	718	0	0.09	68	7.2	0.9	0.21	0.06
fresh, raw — *1 cup*	160	37	5.9	0	2.7	0.6	0	0	0	4.2	85	3	387	37	0.4	1392	0	0.23	218	25.3	1.9	0.53	0.13
Potatoes																							
canned — *½ cup*	90	54	12.2	0	2.1	0.2	0	0.1	0	1.3	5	1	206	197	0.3	0	0	0.17	5	5.6	0.8	0.01	0.06
fresh, baked w/o skin — *½ cup*	61	57	13.2	0	0.9	0.1	0	0	0	1.2	3	0	239	3	0.2	0	0	0.18	8	5.6	0.9	0.01	0.06
fresh, baked w/ skin — *1 potato*	202	220	51	0	4.8	0.2	0	0.1	0.1	4.6	20	3	844	16	0.6	0	0	0.7	26	22.2	3.3	0.07	0.22
fresh, boiled w/o skin — *½ cup*	78	67	15.6	0	1.4	0.1	0	0	0	1.3	6	0	256	4	0.2	0	0	0.21	6	6.9	1	0.01	0.08
fresh, microwaved w/ skin — *1 potato*	202	212	48.7	0	4.6	0.2	0	0.1	0.1	4.9	22	3	903	16	0.7	0	0	0.69	31	24.2	3.5	0.06	0.24
fresh, microwaved w/o skin — *½ cup*	78	78	18.2	0	1.2	0.1	0	0	0	1.6	4	0	321	5	0.3	0	0	0.25	12	9.7	1.3	0.02	0.1
fresh, raw w/ skin — *1 large*	184	145	33.1	0	2.9	0.2	0	0.1	0	3.8	13	1	999	11	0.7	0	0	0.48	36	23.6	2.7	0.06	0.16
frozen, boiled — *3 ½ oz*	100	65	14.5	0	1.4	0.1	0	0.1	0	2	7	1	287	20	0.3	0	0	0.2	9	8.4	1.3	0.03	0.1
frozen, whole — *1 cup*	182	142	31.8	0	2.2	0.3	0	0.1	0.1	4.3	15	2	630	46	0.5	0	0	0.47	26	22.9	3.1	0.06	0.28
Potatoes, french fried, frozen, cooked — *10 strips*	50	100	15.6	0	1.6	3.8	2.4	0.4	0.6	1.6	4	1	209	15	0.2	0	0	0.15	5	6	1	0.01	0.06
Potatoes, mashed																							
dehydrated, flakes w/ whole milk & butter — *½ cup*	105	119	15.8	15	2.4	5.9	1.7	0.3	3.6	2	51	0	245	349	0.2	22	0.1	0.01	10	7.8	0.7	0.05	0.12
dehydrated, granules w/ whole milk & butter — *½ cup*	105	113	15.1	15	2.3	5.2	1.5	0.2	3.2	2.2	37	0	151	270	0.3	20	0	0.01	6	8.4	0.8	0.08	0.08
fresh w/ whole milk — *½ cup*	105	81	18.4	2	2.1	0.6	0.2	0.1	0.3	2	27	0	314	318	0.3	6	0	0.24	7	8.6	1.2	0.04	0.09
fresh w/ whole milk & butter — *½ cup*	105	111	17.5	13	2.1	4.4	1.2	0.2	2.9	2	27	0	303	310	0.3	21	0	0.24	6	8.3	1.1	0.04	0.09
fresh w/ whole milk & margarine — *½ cup*	105	111	17.5	2	2.1	4.4	1.9	1.3	1.1	2	27	0	303	310	0.3	21	0	0.24	6	8.3	1.1	0.04	0.09
Pumpkin																							
canned — *½ cup*	123	42	9.9	0	3.6	0.3	0	0	0.2	1.3	32	2	252	6	0.2	2702	0	0.07	5	15.1	0.4	0.07	0.03
fresh, boiled, mashed — *½ cup*	123	25	6	0	1.3	0.1	0	0	0	0.9	18	1	282	1	0.3	132	0	0.05	6	10.4	0.5	0.1	0.04
fresh, raw, cubes — *1 cup*	116	30	7.5	0	0.6	0.1	0	0	0.1	1.2	24	1	394	1	0.4	186	0	0.07	10	18.8	0.7	0.13	0.06

	Weight g	Calories	Carbohydrates g	Cholesterol mg	Dietary fiber g	Total fat g	Mono. fat g	Poly. fat g	Sat. fat g	Protein g	Calcium mg	Iron mg	Potassium mg	Sodium mg	Zinc mg	Vitamin A RE	Vitamin B_{12} mcg	Vitamin B_6 mg	Vitamin C mg	Folic acid mcg	Niacin mg	Riboflavin mg	Thiamin mg
Pumpkin flowers																							
fresh, boiled — *½ cup*	67	10	2.2	0	0.6	0.1	0	0	0	0.7	25	1	71	4	0.1	116	0	0.03	3	27.3	0.2	0.02	0.01
fresh, raw — *1 cup*	33	5	1.1	0	0	0	0	0	0	0.3	13	0	57	2	0	64	0	0	9	19.4	0.2	0.02	0.01
Pumpkin leaves																							
fresh, boiled — *½ cup*	36	7	1.2	0	1	0.1	0	0	0	1	15	1	155	3	0.1	88	0	0.07	0	8.8	0.3	0.05	0.02
fresh, raw — *1 cup*	39	7	0.9	0	0	0.2	0	0	0.1	1.2	15	1	170	4	0.1	76	0	0.08	4	14.1	0.4	0.05	0.04
Pumpkin pie mix, canned — *½ cup*	135	140	35.6	0	11.2	0.2	0	0	0.1	1.5	50	1	186	281	0.4	1121	0	0.21	5	47.3	0.5	0.16	0.02
Purslane																							
fresh, boiled — *½ cup*	58	10	2	0	0	0.1	0	0	0	0.9	45	0	281	25	0.1	106	0	0.04	6	4.9	0.3	0.05	0.02
fresh, raw — *1 cup*	43	7	1.5	0	0	0	0	0	0	0.6	28	1	212	19	0.1	57	0	0.03	9	5	0.2	0.05	0.02
Radicchio, fresh, raw, shredded — *1 cup*	40	9	1.8	0	0.4	0.1	0	0	0	0.6	8	0	121	9	0.2	1	0	0.02	3	24	0.1	0.01	0.01
Radishes, fresh, raw, slices — *1 cup*	116	20	4.2	0	1.9	0.6	0	0.1	0	0.7	24	0	269	28	0.3	1	0	0.08	26	31.3	0.3	0.05	0.01
Radishes, oriental																							
fresh, boiled, slices — *½ cup*	74	12	2.5	0	1.2	0.2	0	0.1	0.1	0.5	12	0	209	10	0.1	0	0	0.03	11	12.8	0.1	0.02	0
fresh, raw — *1 radish*	338	61	13.9	0	5.4	0.3	0.1	0.2	0.1	2	91	1	767	71	0.5	0	0	0.16	74	95.3	0.7	0.07	0.07
Radishes, white icicle, fresh, raw, slices — *1 cup*	100	14	2.6	0	1.4	0.1	0	0	0	1.1	27	1	280	16	0.1	0	0	0.08	29	14	0.3	0.02	0.03
Rutabegas																							
fresh, boiled, mashed — *½ cup*	120	47	10.5	0	2.2	0.3	0	0.1	0	1.5	58	1	391	24	0.4	67	0	0.12	23	18	0.9	0.05	0.1
fresh, raw, cubes — *1 cup*	140	50	11.4	0	3.5	0.3	0	0.1	0	1.7	66	1	472	28	0.5	81	0	0.14	35	29.4	1	0.06	0.13
Salsify																							
fresh, boiled, slices — *½ cup*	68	46	10.4	0	2.1	0.1	0	0	0	1.8	32	0	191	11	0.2	0	0	0.15	3	10.3	0.3	0.12	0.04
fresh, raw, slices — *1 cup*	133	109	24.7	0	4.4	0.3	0	0	0	4.4	80	1	505	27	0.5	0	0	0.37	11	35	0.7	0.29	0.11
Sauerkraut, canned — *½ cup*	71	13	3	0	1.8	0.1	0	0	0	0.6	21	1	121	469	0.1	1	0	0.09	10	16.8	0.1	0.02	0.01

	Weight *g*	Calories	Carbohydrates *g*	Cholesterol *mg*	Dietary fiber *g*	Total fat *g*	Mono. fat *g*	Poly. fat *g*	Sat. fat *g*	Protein *g*	Calcium *mg*	Iron *mg*	Potassium *mg*	Sodium *mg*	Zinc *mg*	Vitamin A *RE*	Vitamin B_{12} *mcg*	Vitamin B_6 *mg*	Vitamin C *mg*	Folic acid *mcg*	Niacin *mg*	Riboflavin *mg*	Thiamin *mg*
Seaweed																							
agar, dried — *2 oz*	57	174	45.9	0	4.4	0.2	0	0.1	0	3.5	354	12	638	58	3.3	0	0	0.17	0	329	0.1	0.13	0.01
agar, raw — *¼ cup*	20	5	1.4	0	0.1	0	0	0	0	0.1	11	0	45	2	0.1	0	0	0.01	0	17	0	0	0
irishmoss, raw — *¼ cup*	20	10	2.5	0	0.3	0	0	0	0	0.3	14	2	13	13	0.4	2	0	0.01	1	36.5	0.1	0.09	0
kelp, raw — *¼ cup*	20	9	1.9	0	0.3	0.1	0	0	0	0.3	34	1	18	47	0.2	2	0	0	1	36	0.1	0.03	0.01
laver, raw — *¼ cup*	20	7	1	0	0.1	0.1	0	0	0	1.2	14	0	71	10	0.2	104	0	0.03	8	29.3	0.3	0.09	0.02
spirulina, dried — *½ cup*	4	11	0.9	0	0.1	0.3	0	0.1	0.1	2.2	5	1	51	39	0.1	2	0	0.01	0	3.5	0.5	0.14	0.09
spirulina, raw — *3 ½ oz*	100	26	2.4	0	0	0.4	0	0.1	0.1	5.9	12	3	127	98	0.2	6	0	0.03	1	9.2	1.2	0.34	0.22
wakame, raw — *¼ cup*	20	9	1.8	0	0.1	0.1	0	0	0	0.6	30	0	10	174	0.1	7	0	0	1	39.1	0.3	0.05	0.01
Sesbania flower																							
fresh, raw — *1 cup*	20	5	1.3	0	0	0	0	0	0	0.3	4	0	37	3	0	0	0	0	15	20.4	0.1	0.02	0.02
fresh, steamed — *½ cup*	52	11	2.7	0	0	0	0	0	0	0.6	11	0	56	6	0	0	0	0	19	29.6	0.1	0.02	0.02
Shallots, fresh, raw, chopped — *¼ cup*	40	29	6.7	0	0	0	0	0	0	1	15	0	134	5	0.2	499	0	0.14	3	13.7	0.1	0.01	0.02
Soybeans																							
fresh, boiled — *½ cup*	90	127	9.9	0	3.8	5.8	1.1	2.7	0.7	11.1	131	2	485	13	0.8	14	0	0.05	15	99.9	1.1	0.14	0.23
fresh, raw — *1 cup*	256	376	28.3	0	10.8	17.4	3.3	8.2	2	33.2	504	9	1587	38	2.5	46	0	0.17	74	422.4	4.2	0.45	1.11
Spinach																							
canned — *½ cup*	107	25	3.6	0	2.6	0.5	0	0.2	0.1	3	136	2	370	29	0.5	939	0	0.11	15	104.7	0.4	0.15	0.02
fresh, boiled — *½ cup*	90	21	3.4	0	2.2	0.2	0	0.1	0	2.7	122	3	419	63	0.7	737	0	0.22	9	131.2	0.4	0.21	0.09
fresh, raw — *1 cup*	30	7	1.1	0	0.8	0.1	0	0	0	0.9	30	1	167	24	0.2	202	0	0.06	8	58.3	0.2	0.06	0.02
frozen, boiled, chopped — *½ cup*	95	27	5.1	0	2.9	0.2	0	0.1	0	3	139	1	283	82	0.7	739	0	0.14	12	102.1	0.4	0.16	0.06
frozen, chopped — *1 cup*	156	37	6.2	0	4.7	0.5	0	0.2	0.1	4.6	173	3	504	115	0.7	1211	0	0.22	38	186.6	0.7	0.24	0.13
Sprouts																							
alfalfa, fresh — *¼ cup*	8	2	0.3	0	0.2	0.1	0	0	0	0.3	3	0	7	0	0.1	1	0	0	1	3	0	0.01	0.01

	Weight *g*	Calories	Carbohydrates *g*	Cholesterol *mg*	Dietary fiber *g*	Total fat *g*	Mono. fat *g*	Poly. fat *g*	Sat. fat *g*	Protein *g*	Calcium *mg*	Iron *mg*	Potassium *mg*	Sodium *mg*	Zinc *mg*	Vitamin A *RE*	Vitamin B_{12} *mcg*	Vitamin B_6 *mg*	Vitamin C *mg*	Folic acid *mcg*	Niacin *mg*	Riboflavin *mg*	Thiamin *mg*
kidney bean, boiled — *1 oz*	28	9	1.3	0	0	0.2	0	0.1	0	1.4	5	0	55	2	0.1	0	0	0.03	10	13.4	0.9	0.08	0.1
kidney bean, fresh — *¼ cup*	46	13	1.9	0	0	0.2	0	0.1	0	1.9	8	0	86	3	0.2	0	0	0.04	18	27.1	1.3	0.12	0.17
lentil, fresh — *¼ cup*	19	20	4.3	0	0	0.1	0	0	0	1.7	5	1	62	2	0.3	1	0	0.04	3	19.2	0.2	0.02	0.04
lentil, stir-fried — *1 oz*	28	29	6	0	0	0.1	0	0.1	0	2.5	4	1	81	3	0.5	1	0	0.05	4	19	0.3	0.03	0.06
mung bean, boiled — *¼ cup*	31	7	1.3	0	0.2	0	0	0	0	0.6	4	0	31	3	0.1	0	0	0.02	4	9.1	0.3	0.03	0.02
mung bean, canned — *¼ cup*	31	4	0.7	0	0.3	0	0	0	0	0.4	4	0	8	44	0.1	1	0	0.01	0	3	0.1	0.02	0.01
mung bean, fresh — *¼ cup*	26	8	1.5	0	0.5	0	0	0	0	0.8	3	0	39	2	0.1	1	0	0.02	3	15.8	0.2	0.03	0.02
mung bean, stir-fried — *¼ cup*	31	16	3.3	0	0.6	0.1	0	0	0	1.3	4	1	68	3	0.3	1	0	0.04	5	21.6	0.4	0.06	0.04
navy bean, boiled — *1 oz*	28	22	4.3	0	0	0.2	0	0.1	0	2	5	1	90	4	0.3	0	0	0.06	5	30.1	0.4	0.07	0.11
navy bean, fresh — *¼ cup*	26	17	3.4	0	0	0.2	0	0.1	0	1.6	4	1	80	3	0.2	0	0	0.05	5	34.3	0.3	0.06	0.1
pea, boiled — *1 oz*	28	33	6.2	0	0	0.1	0	0.1	0	2	7	0	76	1	0.2	3	0	0.04	2	10.3	0.3	0.08	0.06
pea, fresh — *¼ cup*	30	38	8.5	0	0	0.2	0	0.1	0	2.6	11	1	114	6	0.3	5	0	0.08	3	43.2	0.9	0.05	0.07
pinto bean, boiled — *1 oz*	28	6	1.2	0	0	0.1	0	0.1	0	0.5	4	0	28	14	0	0	0	0.02	2	8.3	0.2	0.02	0.02
pinto bean, fresh — *1 oz*	28	18	3.3	0	0	0.3	0	0.1	0	1.5	12	1	87	43	0.1	0	0	0.05	6	33.6	0.6	0.05	0.07
radish seed, fresh — *¼ cup*	10	4	0.3	0	0	0.2	0	0.1	0.1	0.4	5	0	8	1	0.1	4	0	0.03	3	9	0.3	0.01	0.01
soybean, fresh — *¼ cup*	18	21	1.7	0	0.2	1.2	0.3	0.7	0.2	2.3	12	0	85	2	0.2	0	0	0.03	3	30.1	0.2	0.02	0.06
soybean, steamed — *¼ cup*	24	19	1.5	0	0.2	1	0.2	0.6	0.1	2	14	0	83	2	0.2	0	0	0.02	2	18.8	0.3	0.01	0.05
soybean, stir-fried — *1 oz*	28	35	2.7	0	0.2	2	0.5	1.1	0.3	3.7	23	0	161	4	0.6	1	0	0.05	3	36	0.3	0.05	0.12
Squash, summer, crookneck & straightneck																							
canned — *½ cup*	108	14	3.2	0	1.5	0.1	0	0	0	0.7	13	1	104	5	0.3	13	0	0.05	3	11.2	0.5	0.03	0.02
fresh, boiled, slices — *½ cup*	90	18	3.9	0	1.3	0.3	0	0.1	0.1	0.8	24	0	173	1	0.4	26	0	0.08	5	18.1	0.5	0.04	0.04
fresh, raw, slices — *1 cup*	130	25	5.3	0	2.5	0.3	0	0.1	0.1	1.2	27	1	276	3	0.4	44	0	0.14	11	29.8	0.6	0.06	0.07
frozen, boiled, slices — *½ cup*	96	24	5.3	0	1.3	0.2	0	0.1	0	1.2	19	0	243	6	0.3	19	0	0.1	7	12.2	0.4	0.05	0.03
frozen, slices — *1 cup*	130	26	6.2	0	1.6	0.2	0	0.1	0	1.1	23	1	272	7	0.5	36	0	0.11	8	15.3	0.5	0.06	0.05

	Weight *g*	Calories	Carbohydrates *g*	Cholesterol *mg*	Dietary fiber *g*	Total fat *g*	Mono. fat *g*	Poly. fat *g*	Sat. fat *g*	Protein *g*	Calcium *mg*	Iron *mg*	Potassium *mg*	Sodium *mg*	Zinc *mg*	Vitamin A *RE*	Vitamin B_{12} *mcg*	Vitamin B_6 *mg*	Vitamin C *mg*	Folic acid *mcg*	Niacin *mg*	Riboflavin *mg*	Thiamin *mg*
Squash, summer, scallop																							
fresh, boiled, slices — *½ cup*	90	14	3	0	1.7	0.2	0	0.1	0	0.9	14	0	126	1	0.2	8	0	0.08	10	18.6	0.4	0.02	0.05
fresh, raw, slices — *1 cup*	130	23	5	0	0	0.3	0	0.1	0.1	1.6	25	1	237	1	0.4	14	0	0.14	23	39.1	0.8	0.04	0.09
Squash, summer, zucchini																							
canned, italian style — *½ cup*	114	33	7.8	0	0	0.1	0	0.1	0	1.2	19	1	311	424	0.3	61	0	0.17	3	34.3	0.6	0.05	0.05
fresh, boiled, slices — *½ cup*	90	14	3.5	0	1.3	0	0	0	0	0.6	12	0	228	3	0.2	22	0	0.07	4	15.1	0.4	0.04	0.04
fresh, raw, baby — *4 medium*	44	9	1.4	0	0.5	0.2	0	0.1	0	1.2	9	0	202	1	0.4	22	0	0.06	15	8.8	0.3	0.02	0.02
fresh, raw, slices — *1 cup*	113	16	3.3	0	1.4	0.2	0	0.1	0	1.3	17	0	280	3	0.2	38	0	0.1	10	25	0.5	0.03	0.08
frozen — *3 ½ oz*	100	17	3.6	0	1.3	0.1	0	0.1	0	1.2	18	1	218	2	0.2	48	0	0.05	5	9.9	0.4	0.04	0.05
frozen, boiled — *½ cup*	112	19	4	0	1.4	0.1	0	0.1	0	1.3	19	1	216	2	0.2	48	0	0.05	4	8.7	0.4	0.04	0.05
Squash, winter, acorn																							
fresh, baked, cubes — *½ cup*	103	57	14.9	0	4.5	0.1	0	0.1	0	1.1	45	1	448	4	0.2	44	0	0.2	11	19.2	0.9	0.01	0.17
fresh, boiled, mashed — *½ cup*	123	42	10.8	0	3.2	0.1	0	0	0	0.8	32	1	322	4	0.1	32	0	0.14	8	13.8	0.7	0.01	0.12
fresh, raw., cubes — *1 cup*	140	56	14.6	0	2.1	0.1	0	0.1	0	1.1	46	1	486	4	0.2	48	0	0.22	15	23.4	1	0.01	0.2
Squash, winter, butternut																							
fresh, baked, cubes — *½ cup*	103	41	10.8	0	0	0.1	0	0	0	0.9	42	1	291	4	0.1	718	0	0.13	15	19.7	1	0.02	0.07
fresh, boiled, mashed — *½ cup*	120	47	12.1	0	0	0.1	0	0	0	1.5	23	1	160	2	0.1	401	0	0.08	4	19.7	0.6	0.05	0.06
fresh, raw, cubes — *1 cup*	140	63	16.4	0	0	0.1	0	0.1	0	1.4	67	1	493	6	0.2	1092	0	0.22	29	37.4	1.7	0.03	0.14
frozen — *3 ½ oz*	100	57	14.4	0	1.3	0.1	0	0	0	1.8	29	1	212	2	0.2	479	0	0.11	6	23.6	0.7	0.06	0.09
Squash, winter, hubbard																							
fresh, baked, cubes — *½ cup*	103	51	11.1	0	0	0.6	0	0.3	0.1	2.5	17	0	367	8	0.2	619	0	0.18	10	16.6	0.6	0.05	0.08
fresh, boiled, mashed — *½ cup*	118	35	7.6	0	3.4	0.4	0	0.2	0.1	1.7	12	0	253	6	0.1	473	0	0.12	8	11.5	0.4	0.03	0.05
fresh, raw, cubes — *1 cup*	116	46	10.1	0	0	0.6	0	0.2	0.1	2.3	16	0	371	8	0.2	626	0	0.18	13	19	0.6	0.05	0.08

	Weight g	Calories	Carbohydrates g	Cholesterol mg	Dietary fiber g	Total fat g	Mono. fat g	Poly. fat g	Sat. fat g	Protein g	Calcium mg	Iron mg	Potassium mg	Sodium mg	Zinc mg	Vitamin A RE	Vitamin B_{12} mcg	Vitamin B_6 mg	Vitamin C mg	Folic acid mcg	Niacin mg	Riboflavin mg	Thiamin mg
Squash, winter, spaghetti																							
fresh raw — *1 cup*	101	33	7	0	0	0.6	0	0.2	0.1	0.6	23	0	109	17	0.2	5	0	0.1	2	12.1	1	0.02	0.04
fresh, boiled — *½ cup*	78	22	5	0	1.1	0.2	0	0.1	0	0.5	16	0	91	14	0.2	9	0	0.08	3	6.2	0.6	0.02	0.03
Succotash (corn & limas)																							
canned w/ cream-style corn — *½ cup*	133	102	23.4	0	4	0.7	0.1	0.3	0.1	3.5	15	1	243	326	0.6	19	0	0.17	9	58.9	0.8	0.09	0.04
fresh, boiled — *½ cup*	96	110	23.4	0	4.3	0.8	0.1	0.4	0.1	4.9	16	1	394	16	0.6	28	0	0.11	8	31.5	1.3	0.09	0.16
fresh, raw — *3 ½ oz*	100	99	19.6	0	3.8	1	0.2	0.5	0.2	5	18	2	369	4	0.6	29	0	0.13	15	39.9	1.6	0.08	0.21
frozen — *1 cup*	156	145	31.1	0	6.2	1.4	0.3	0.7	0.3	6.7	25	1	460	70	0.7	41	0	0.16	13	64.9	2.1	0.11	0.14
frozen, boiled — *½ cup*	85	79	17	0	3.5	0.8	0.1	0.4	0.1	3.7	13	1	225	38	0.4	20	0	0.08	5	28.2	1.1	0.06	0.06
Swamp cabbage																							
fresh, raw, chopped — *1 cup*	56	11	1.8	0	1.2	0.1	0	0	0	1.5	43	1	175	63	0.1	353	0	0.05	31	32	0.5	0.06	0.02
fresh, raw, chopped — *½ cup*	49	10	1.8	0	0.9	0.1	0	0	0	1	26	1	139	60	0.1	255	0	0.04	8	17.1	0.2	0.04	0.02
Sweet potato																							
candied — *1 piece*	105	144	29.3	8	2.5	3.4	0.7	0.2	1.4	0.9	27	1	198	74	0.2	440	0	0.04	7	12	0.4	0.04	0.02
canned, mashed — *½ cup*	128	129	29.6	0	2.2	0.3	0	0.1	0.1	2.5	38	2	268	96	0.3	1929	0	0.3	7	13.6	1.2	0.11	0.03
canned, syrup pack — *½ cup*	98	106	24.9	0	2.9	0.3	0	0.1	0.1	1.3	17	1	189	38	0.2	702	0	0.06	11	7.7	0.3	0.04	0.02
canned, vacuum pack, mashed — *½ cup*	128	116	26.9	0	2.3	0.3	0	0.1	0.1	2.1	28	1	398	68	0.2	1017	0	0.24	34	21.2	0.9	0.07	0.05
fresh, baked — *1 medium*	114	117	27.7	0	3.4	0.1	0	0.1	0	2	32	1	397	11	0.3	2487	0	0.27	28	25.8	0.7	0.14	0.08
fresh, boiled, mashed — *½ cup*	164	172	39.8	0	3	0.5	0	0.2	0.1	2.7	34	1	302	21	0.4	2796	0	0.4	28	18.2	1	0.23	0.09
fresh, raw — *1 medium*	130	137	31.6	0	3.9	0.4	0	0.2	0.1	2.1	29	1	265	17	0.4	2608	0	0.33	30	17.9	0.9	0.19	0.09
frozen, baked, cubes — *½ cup*	88	88	20.6	0	1.6	0.1	0	0	0	1.5	31	0	332	7	0.3	1444	0	0.16	8	19.6	0.5	0.05	0.06
frozen, cubes — *1 cup*	176	169	39.1	0	3	0.3	0	0.1	0.1	3	65	1	642	11	0.5	3281	0	0.31	23	37.5	1.1	0.09	0.12
Sweet potato leaves																							
fresh, raw, chopped — *1 cup*	35	12	2.2	0	0.7	0.1	0	0	0	1.4	13	0	181	3	0.1	36	0	0.07	4	28	0.4	0.12	0.05

	Weight g	Calories	Carbohydrates g	Cholesterol mg	Dietary fiber g	Total fat g	Mono. fat g	Poly. fat g	Sat. fat g	Protein g	Calcium mg	Iron mg	Potassium mg	Sodium mg	Zinc mg	Vitamin A RE	Vitamin B_{12} mcg	Vitamin B_6 mg	Vitamin C mg	Folic acid mcg	Niacin mg	Riboflavin mg	Thiamin mg
fresh, steamed — *½ cup*	32	11	2.3	0	0.6	0.1	0	0	0	0.7	8	0	153	4	0.1	29	0	0.05	0	15.6	0.3	0.09	0.04
Swiss chard																							
fresh, boiled, chopped — *½ cup*	88	18	3.6	0	1.8	0.1	0	0	0	1.6	51	2	480	157	0.3	275	0	0.07	16	7.5	0.3	0.08	0.03
fresh, raw — *1 cup*	36	7	1.3	0	0.6	0.1	0	0	0	0.6	18	1	136	77	0.1	119	0	0.04	11	5	0.1	0.03	0.01
Taro																							
fresh, cooked, slices — *½ cup*	66	94	22.8	0	3.4	0.1	0	0	0	0.3	12	0	319	10	0.2	0	0	0.22	3	12.7	0.3	0.02	0.07
fresh, raw, slices — *1 cup*	104	111	27.5	0	4.3	0.2	0	0.1	0	1.6	45	1	615	11	0.2	0	0	0.29	5	23.1	0.6	0.03	0.1
Taro leaves																							
fresh, raw — *1 cup*	28	12	1.9	0	1	0.2	0	0.1	0	1.4	30	1	181	1	0.1	135	0	0.04	15	35.2	0.4	0.13	0.06
fresh, steamed — *½ cup*	73	17	2.9	0	1.5	0.3	0	0.1	0.1	2	62	1	334	1	0.2	307	0	0.05	26	35	0.9	0.28	0.1
Taro shoots																							
fresh, cooked, slices — *½ cup*	70	10	2.2	0	0	0.1	0	0	0	0.5	10	0	241	1	0.4	4	0	0.08	13	1.8	0.6	0.04	0.03
fresh, raw, slices — *1 cup*	86	9	2	0	0	0.1	0	0	0	0.8	10	1	286	1	0.4	4	0	0.1	18	2.8	0.7	0.04	0.03
Taro, tahitian																							
fresh, cooked, slices — *½ cup*	69	30	4.7	0	0	0.5	0	0.2	0.1	2.8	102	1	427	37	0.1	121	0	0.08	26	4.9	0.3	0.14	0.03
fresh, raw, slices — *1 cup*	125	50	8.6	0	0	1.2	0.1	0.5	0.2	3.5	161	2	758	63	0.1	256	0	0.15	120	11.4	1.2	0.31	0.08
Tomatillos, fresh, raw, chopped — *1 cup*	132	42	7.7	0	2.5	1.3	0.2	0.6	0.2	1.3	9	1	354	1	0.3	15	0	0.07	15	9.2	2.4	0.05	0.06
Tomato products, canned																							
paste w/ salt — *½ cup*	131	107	25.3	0	5.4	0.7	0.1	0.3	0.1	4.8	46	3	1227	1035	1	320	0	0.5	56	29.3	4.2	0.25	0.2
paste w/o salt — *½ cup*	131	107	25.3	0	5.4	0.7	0.1	0.3	0.1	4.8	46	3	1227	115	1	320	0	0.5	56	29.3	4.2	0.25	0.2
purée w/ salt — *½ cup*	125	50	12	0	2.5	0.2	0	0.1	0	2.1	21	2	533	499	0.3	160	0	0.19	13	13.8	2.1	0.07	0.09
puree w/o salt — *½ cup*	125	50	12	0	2.5	0.2	0	0.1	0	2.1	21	2	533	43	0.3	160	0	0.19	13	13.8	2.1	0.07	0.09
sauce — *½ cup*	123	37	8.8	0	1.7	0.2	0	0.1	0	1.6	17	1	454	741	0.3	120	0	0.19	16	11.5	1.4	0.07	0.08
sauce, spanish style — *½ cup*	122	40	8.8	0	1.7	0.3	0	0.1	0	1.8	21	4	450	576	0.4	121	0	0.22	10	16.5	1.6	0.08	0.09

	Weight g	Calories	Carbohydrates g	Cholesterol mg	Dietary fiber g	Total fat g	Mono. fat g	Poly. fat g	Sat. fat g	Protein g	Calcium mg	Iron mg	Potassium mg	Sodium mg	Zinc mg	Vitamin A RE	Vitamin B_{12} mcg	Vitamin B_6 mg	Vitamin C mg	Folic acid mcg	Niacin mg	Riboflavin mg	Thiamin mg
sauce w/ herbs & cheese — *½ cup*	122	72	12.5	4	2.7	2.4	0.5	1	0.8	2.6	45	1	434	662	0.4	121	0	0.02	12	9.9	1.5	0.15	0.09
sauce w/ mushrooms — *½ cup*	123	43	10.3	0	1.8	0.2	0	0.1	0	1.8	16	1	466	554	0.3	116	0	0.16	15	11.5	1.5	0.13	0.09
sauce w/ onions — *½ cup*	123	51	12.2	0	2.2	0.2	0	0.1	0	1.9	21	1	506	675	0.3	104	0	0.33	16	27.4	1.5	0.16	0.09
sauce w/ onions, green peppers, & celery — *½ cup*	125	51	11	0	1.8	0.9	0.1	0.4	0.2	1.2	16	1	498	683	0.4	101	0	0.24	17	17.6	1.4	0.15	0.08
sauce w/ tomato tidbits — *½ cup*	122	39	8.6	0	1.7	0.5	0.1	0.2	0.1	1.6	12	1	455	18	0.2	98	0	0.19	26	11.5	1.4	0.12	0.09
Tomatoes, canned																							
crushed — *3 ½ oz*	100	32	7.3	0	1.9	0.3	0	0.1	0	1.6	34	1	293	132	0.3	70	0	0.15	9	13	1.2	0.05	0.08
stewed — *½ cup*	128	36	8.6	0	1.3	0.2	0	0.1	0	1.2	42	1	303	282	0.2	69	0	0.02	15	6.9	0.9	0.04	0.06
w/ green chilies — *½ cup*	121	18	4.4	0	0	0.1	0	0	0	0.8	24	0	129	483	0.2	47	0	0.12	7	11	0.8	0.02	0.04
wedges, in tomato juice — *½ cup*	131	34	8.2	0	0	0.2	0	0.1	0	1	34	1	328	283	0.2	76	0	0.15	19	13.2	0.9	0.04	0.07
whole — *½ cup*	120	23	5.2	0	1.2	0.2	0	0.1	0	1.1	36	1	265	178	0.2	72	0	0.11	17	9.4	0.9	0.04	0.05
whole w/o salt — *½ cup*	120	23	5.2	0	1.2	0.2	0	0.1	0	1.1	36	1	272	12	0.2	72	0	0.11	17	9.4	0.9	0.04	0.05
Tomatoes, fresh																							
boiled — *½ cup*	120	32	7	0	1.2	0.5	0.1	0.2	0.1	1.3	7	1	335	13	0.1	89	0	0.11	27	15.6	0.9	0.07	0.08
raw — *1 large*	182	38	8.4	0	2	0.6	0.1	0.2	0.1	1.5	9	1	404	16	0.2	113	0	0.15	35	27.3	1.1	0.09	0.11
raw, cherry, whole — *1 cup*	149	31	6.9	0	1.6	0.5	0.1	0.2	0.1	1.3	7	1	331	13	0.1	92	0	0.12	28	22.4	0.9	0.07	0.09
raw, green — *1 large*	182	44	9.3	0	2	0.4	0.1	0.1	0.1	2.2	24	1	371	24	0.1	116	0	0.15	43	16	0.9	0.07	0.11
raw, plum — *1 medium*	62	13	2.9	0	0.7	0.2	0	0.1	0	0.5	3	0	138	6	0.1	38	0	0.05	12	9.3	0.4	0.03	0.04
stewed — *½ cup*	51	40	6.6	0	0.9	1.4	0.5	0.4	0.3	1	13	1	125	230	0.1	34	0	0.04	9	5.6	0.6	0.04	0.05
Tomatoes, sun-dried																							
not oil-packed — *¼ cup*	14	35	7.5	0	1.7	0.4	0.1	0.2	0.1	1.9	15	1	463	283	0.3	12	0	0.04	5	9.2	1.2	0.07	0.07
oil-packed, drained — *¼ cup*	28	59	6.4	0	1.6	3.9	2.4	0.6	0.5	1.4	13	1	430	73	0.2	35	0	0.09	28	6.3	1	0.11	0.05
Tree fern, fresh, cooked, chopped — *½ cup*	71	28	7.8	0	2.6	0	0	0	0	0.2	6	0	4	4	0.2	14	0	0.13	21	10.7	2.5	0.21	0

	Weight g	Calories	Carbohydrates g	Cholesterol mg	Dietary fiber g	Total fat g	Mono. fat g	Poly. fat g	Sat. fat g	Protein g	Calcium mg	Iron mg	Potassium mg	Sodium mg	Zinc mg	Vitamin A RE	Vitamin B_{12} mcg	Vitamin B_6 mg	Vitamin C mg	Folic acid mcg	Niacin mg	Riboflavin mg	Thiamin mg
Turnip greens																							
fresh, boiled, chopped — *½ cup*	72	14	3.1	0	2.5	0.2	0	0.1	0	0.8	99	1	146	21	0.1	396	0	0.13	20	85.3	0.3	0.05	0.03
fresh, raw, chopped — *1 cup*	55	15	3.2	0	1.8	0.2	0	0.1	0	0.8	105	1	163	22	0.1	418	0	0.14	33	106.9	0.3	0.06	0.04
frozen, boiled — *½ cup*	82	25	4.1	0	2.8	0.3	0	0.1	0.1	2.7	125	2	184	12	0.3	654	0	0.05	18	32.3	0.4	0.06	0.04
frozen, chopped — *1 cup*	164	36	6	0	4.1	0.5	0	0.2	0.1	4.1	194	2	302	20	0.3	1014	0	0.16	44	120.7	0.6	0.15	0.07
Turnips																							
fresh, boiled, cubes — *½ cup*	78	14	3.8	0	1.6	0.1	0	0	0	0.6	17	0	105	39	0.2	0	0	0.05	9	7.2	0.2	0.02	0.02
fresh, boiled, mashed — *½ cup*	115	21	5.6	0	2.3	0.1	0	0	0	0.8	25	0	155	58	0.2	0	0	0.08	13	10.6	0.3	0.03	0.03
fresh, raw, cubes — *1 cup*	130	35	8.1	0	2.3	0.1	0	0.1	0	1.2	39	0	248	87	0.4	0	0	0.12	27	18.9	0.5	0.04	0.05
frozen, boiled — *½ cup*	78	18	3.4	0	1.6	0.2	0	0.1	0	1.2	25	1	142	28	0.2	2	0	0.05	3	6.2	0.4	0.02	0.03
frozen, mashed — *3 ½ oz*	100	16	2.9	0	1.8	0.2	0	0.1	0	1	23	1	137	25	0.1	3	0	0.05	4	7.7	0.4	0.02	0.03
Vinespinach (basella), fresh, raw — *3 ½ oz*	100	19	3.4	0	0	0.3	0	0	0	1.8	109	1	510	24	0.4	800	0	0.24	102	140.1	0.5	0.16	0.05
Waterchestnuts, chinese																							
canned, slices — *½ cup*	70	35	8.7	0	1.8	0	0	0	0	0.6	3	1	83	6	0.3	0	0	0.11	1	4.1	0.3	0.02	0.01
fresh, raw, slices — *1 cup*	124	131	29.7	0	3.7	0.1	0	0.1	0	1.7	14	0	724	17	0.6	0	0	0.41	5	20	1.2	0.25	0.17
Watercress, fresh, raw, chopped — *1 cup*	34	4	0.4	0	0.5	0	0	0	0	0.8	41	0	112	14	0	160	0	0.04	15	3.1	0.1	0.04	0.03
Waxgourd																							
fresh, boiled, cubes — *½ cup*	88	11	2.7	0	0.9	0.2	0	0.1	0	0.4	16	0	4	94	0.5	0	0	0.03	9	3.2	0.3	0	0.03
fresh, raw, cubes — *1 cup*	132	17	4	0	3.8	0.3	0	0.1	0	0.5	25	1	8	147	0.8	0	0	0.05	17	6.9	0.5	0.15	0.05
Winged bean leaves, fresh, raw — *3 ½ oz*	100	74	14.1	0	0	1.1	0.3	0.2	0.3	5.9	224	4	176	9	1.3	809	0	0.23	45	15.5	3.5	0.6	0.83
Winged beans																							
fresh, boiled — *½ cup*	31	12	1	0	0	0.2	0.1	0	0.1	1.6	19	0	85	1	0.1	3	0	0.03	3	10.9	0.2	0.02	0.03
fresh, raw — *1 cup*	44	22	1.9	0	0	0.4	0.1	0.1	0.1	3.1	37	1	98	2	0.2	6	0	0.05	8	28.9	0.4	0.04	0.06

	Weight g	Calories	Carbohydrates g	Cholesterol mg	Dietary fiber g	Total fat g	Mono. fat g	Poly. fat g	Sat. fat g	Protein g	Calcium mg	Iron mg	Potassium mg	Sodium mg	Zinc mg	Vitamin A RE	Vitamin B_{12} mcg	Vitamin B_6 mg	Vitamin C mg	Folic acid mcg	Niacin mg	Riboflavin mg	Thiamin mg
Yam																							
fresh, boiled, cubes — *½ cup*	68	79	18.8	0	2.7	0.1	0	0	0	1	10	0	456	5	0.1	0	0	0.16	8	10.9	0.4	0.02	0.06
fresh, raw, cubes — *1 cup*	150	177	41.8	0	6.2	0.3	0	0.1	0.1	2.3	26	1	1224	14	0.4	0	0	0.44	26	34.5	0.8	0.05	0.17
Yambean																							
fresh, boiled — *3 ½ oz*	100	38	8.8	0	0	0.1	0	0	0	0.7	11	1	135	4	0.2	2	0	0.04	14	8	0.2	0.03	0.02
fresh, raw — *1 cup*	120	46	10.6	0	5.9	0.1	0	0.1	0	0.9	14	1	180	5	0.2	2	0	0.05	24	14.4	0.2	0.03	0.02
Yardlong bean																							
fresh, boiled, slices — *½ cup*	52	24	4.8	0	0	0.1	0	0	0	1.3	23	1	151	2	0.2	23	0	0.01	8	23.1	0.3	0.05	0.04
fresh, raw, slices — *1 cup*	91	43	7.6	0	0	0.4	0	0.2	0.1	2.5	46	0	218	4	0.3	78	0	0.02	17	56.1	0.4	0.1	0.1

Yogurt

	Weight g	Calories	Carbohydrates g	Cholesterol mg	Dietary fiber g	Total fat g	Mono. fat g	Poly. fat g	Sat. fat g	Protein g	Calcium mg	Iron mg	Potassium mg	Sodium mg	Zinc mg	Vitamin A RE	Vitamin B_{12} mcg	Vitamin B_6 mg	Vitamin C mg	Folic acid mcg	Niacin mg	Riboflavin mg	Thiamin mg
Low-fat																							
fruit — *8 oz*	227	225	42.3	10	0	2.6	0.7	0.1	1.7	9	314	0	402	121	1.5	27	1	0.08	1	19.3	0.2	0.37	0.08
plain — *8 oz*	227	144	16	14	0	3.5	1	0.1	2.3	11.9	415	0	531	159	2	36	1.3	0.11	2	25.4	0.3	0.49	0.1
vanilla — *8 oz*	227	194	31.3	11	0	2.8	0.8	0.1	1.8	11.2	389	0	498	149	1.9	30	1.2	0.1	2	23.8	0.2	0.46	0.1
Nonfat																							
plain — *8 oz*	227	127	17.4	4	0	0.4	0.1	0	0.3	13	452	0	579	174	2.2	5	1.4	0.12	2	27.7	0.3	0.53	0.11
Whole milk																							
plain — *8 oz*	227	139	10.6	29	0	7.4	2	0.2	4.8	7.9	274	0	351	105	1.3	68	0.8	0.07	1	16.8	0.2	0.32	0.07

Foods, Brand Name

Bacon & Sausage

	Weight g	Calories	Calories from fat	Total fat g	Sat. fat g	Cholesterol mg	Sodium mg	Carbohydrates g	Dietary fiber g	Sugars g	Protein g	Vitamin A % DV	Vitamin C % DV	Calcium % DV	Iron % DV
Goya Vienna Sausages — *3 links*	n/a	130	110	12	4	50	320	1	0	0	5	2	0	4	4
Green Giant Breakfast Patties — *2 patties*	57	100	40	4.5	0.5	0	360	5	3	<1	9	0	0	4	8
Healthy Choice Breakfast, w/ Pork or Turkey Sausage — *2 links*	45	50	10	1.5	0.5	15	300	3	0	1	7	0	0	0	0
Healthy Choice Low-Fat Smoked Sausage															
beef — *2 oz*	56	70	15	1.5	0.5	20	480	7	0	2	8	0	4	0	2
kielbasa, regular or polska — *2 oz*	56	70	15	1.5	0.5	25	480	5	0	2	9	0	4	0	2
Healthy Choice Polska Kielbasa Low-Fat — *1 link*	75	100	25	3	1	35	480	7	0	2	11	0	8	2	2
Hebrew National Beef Knockwurst — *1 link*	85	260	210	25	9	55	670	1	0	0	10	0	0	0	6
Louis Rich Turkey Bacon — *1 slice*	14	30	20	2.5	0.5	10	190	0	0	0	2	0	0	0	0
Louis Rich Turkey Sausage															
kielbasa, polska — *2 oz*	56	90	45	5	1.5	35	500	1	0	1	8	0	0	0	4
smoked — *2 oz*	56	90	50	5	1.5	35	510	2	0	2	8	0	0	0	4
turkey (hot & original) — *2 ½ oz*	70	120	70	8	2.5	55	430	1	0	0	0	0	0	4	6
Mr Turkey Sausage															
polish — *3 ½ oz*	100	161	81	9	4	55	1080	5	<1	4	15	3	34	3	62
smoked, hot — *3 ½ oz*	100	157	81	9	4	51	864	5	<1	4	15	4	27	3	60
smoked, italian — *3 ½ oz*	100	158	81	9	4	53	928	5	<1	3	15	3	51	2	53
turkey — *3 ½ oz*	100	190	126	14	4	92	664	<1	0	<1	17	1	2	6	12
Mr Turkey Turkey Bacon — *3 ½ oz*	100	196	117	13	5	88	1188	2	0	2	19	<1	2	0	7

Bean Products, Canned

	Weight g	Calories	Calories from fat	Total fat g	Sat. fat g	Cholesterol mg	Sodium mg	Carbohydrates g	Dietary fiber g	Sugars g	Protein g	Vitamin A % DV	Vitamin C % DV	Calcium % DV	Iron % DV
B & M Baked Beans															
bacon & onion w/ brown sugar — *½ cup*	131	190	20	2	0.5	<5	450	36	8	14	8	0	0	6	15
barbecue — *½ cup*	130	170	10	1	0	0	460	33	6	12	7	0	0	8	15

	Weight g	Calories	Calories from fat	Total fat g	Sat. fat g	Cholesterol mg	Sodium mg	Carbohydrates g	Dietary fiber g	Sugars g	Protein g	Vitamin A % DV	Vitamin C % DV	Calcium % DV	Iron % DV
natural honey flavor — ½ cup	134	170	15	1.5	0	0	450	30	8	7	8	0	0	6	15
pork — ½ cup	131	180	20	2	0.5	<5	430	33	7	11	8	0	0	6	15
red kidney — ½ cup	132	170	20	2	0.5	<5	440	32	6	10	7	0	0	6	15
vegetarian — ½ cup	130	170	10	1	0	0	220	31	7	8	8	0	0	6	20
yellow eye — ½ cup	130	180	25	3	0.5	<5	450	30	8	10	8	0	0	6	15
Campbell's Baked Beans															
barbecue — ½ cup	n/a	170	25	2.5	0.5	5	460	29	6	10	7	4	0	8	10
brown sugar & bacon-flavored — ½ cup	n/a	170	30	3	1	5	490	29	7	13	5	0	0	8	10
new england-style — ½ cup	n/a	180	30	3	1	5	460	32	6	14	5	0	2	8	10
Chi-Chi's Refried Beans															
fat-free — ½ cup	120	90	0	0	0	0	570	17	0	1	5	4	0	4	8
regular — ½ cup	120	100	10	1	0	0	580	18	4	1	5	4	0	2	8
vegetarian — ½ cup	120	100	10	1	0	0	580	18	0	1	5	4	0	4	8
Friends Baked Beans															
original — ½ cup	131	170	10	1	0	<5	390	32	7	10	8	0	0	6	25
red kidney — ½ cup	132	170	10	1	0	<5	510	32	6	10	7	0	0	6	20
Old El Paso Refried Beans															
black — ½ cup	120	110	20	2	0	0	340	18	6	2	6	0	0	6	10
fat-free — ½ cup	124	100	0	0	0	0	480	18	6	1	6	0	0	4	10
regular — ½ cup	120	110	20	2	1	<5	500	17	6	1	6	0	0	4	10
vegetarian — ½ cup	118	100	10	1	0	0	490	17	6	2	6	0	0	4	10
w/ cheese — ½ cup	120	130	30	3.5	1.5	5	500	18	6	1	7	0	0	8	10
w/ green chiles — ½ cup	122	100	5	0.5	0	<5	720	17	6	1	6	0	0	4	10
w/ sausage — ½ cup	118	200	120	13	5	10	360	14	4	1	7	0	0	4	10

Beverages: Beers

	Weight g	Calories	Calories from fat	Total fat g	Sat. fat g	Cholesterol mg	Sodium mg	Carbohydrates g	Dietary fiber g	Sugars g	Protein g	Vitamin A % DV	Vitamin C % DV	Calcium % DV	Iron % DV
Black & Tan — *12 fl oz*	n/a	192	0	0	0	0	9	22.6	n/a	n/a	2.5	n/a	n/a	n/a	n/a
Budweiser															
Bud Dry — *12 fl oz*	n/a	130	0	0	0	0	9	8.2	n/a	n/a	1.2	n/a	n/a	n/a	n/a
Bud Ice Light — *12 fl oz*	n/a	96	0	0	0	0	9	3.5	n/a	n/a	0.8	n/a	n/a	n/a	n/a
Bud Ice — *12 fl oz*	n/a	148	0	0	0	0	9	9.2	n/a	n/a	1.3	n/a	n/a	n/a	n/a
Bud Light — *12 fl oz*	n/a	110	0	0	0	0	9	6.6	n/a	n/a	0.9	n/a	n/a	n/a	n/a
regular — *12 fl oz*	n/a	147	0	0	0	0	9	11.4	n/a	n/a	1.2	n/a	n/a	n/a	n/a
Busch															
Busch Ice — *12 fl oz*	n/a	169	0	0	0	0	9	12.8	n/a	n/a	1.3	n/a	n/a	n/a	n/a
Busch NA (non-alcoholic) — *12 fl oz*	n/a	60	0	0	0	0	9	13.0	n/a	n/a	0.6	n/a	n/a	n/a	n/a
Light — *12 fl oz*	n/a	110	0	0	0	0	9	6.7	n/a	n/a	0.8	n/a	n/a	n/a	n/a
Natural Light — *12 fl oz*	n/a	110	0	0	0	0	9	6.7	n/a	n/a	0.9	n/a	n/a	n/a	n/a
regular — *12 fl oz*	n/a	143	0	0	0	0	9	10.9	n/a	n/a	1.1	n/a	n/a	n/a	n/a
Coors															
Cutter (non-alcoholic) — *12 fl oz*	n/a	78	0	0	0	0	9	15.7	n/a	n/a	0.7	n/a	n/a	<2	n/a
Dry — *12 fl oz*	n/a	122	0	0	0	0	11	5.9	n/a	n/a	0.8	n/a	n/a	1	n/a
Extra Gold — *12 fl oz*	n/a	150	0	0	0	0	11	11.7	n/a	n/a	1.2	n/a	n/a	1	n/a
Light — *12 fl oz*	n/a	101	0	0	0	0	11	4.3	n/a	n/a	0.7	n/a	n/a	1	n/a
regular — *12 fl oz*	n/a	148	0	0	0	0	11	11.8	n/a	n/a	0.9	n/a	n/a	<1	n/a
Elk Mountain															
Amber Ale — *12 fl oz*	n/a	190	0	0	0	0	9	17.4	n/a	n/a	2.7	n/a	n/a	n/a	n/a
Red — *12 fl oz*	n/a	160	0	0	0	0	9	14.2	n/a	n/a	2.2	n/a	n/a	n/a	n/a
Faust — *12 fl oz*	n/a	168	0	0	0	0	9	15.4	n/a	n/a	2.4	n/a	n/a	n/a	n/a

	Weight *g*	Calories	Calories from fat	Total fat *g*	Sat. fat *g*	Cholesterol *mg*	Sodium *mg*	Carbohydrates *g*	Dietary fiber *g*	Sugars *g*	Protein *g*	Vitamin A *% DV*	Vitamin C *% DV*	Calcium *% DV*	Iron *% DV*
Herman Joseph — *12 fl oz*	n/a	152	0	0	0	0	11	12.2	n/a	n/a	1.3	n/a	n/a	<1	n/a
Hurricane — *12 fl oz*	n/a	158	0	0	0	0	9	9.2	n/a	n/a	1.6	n/a	n/a	n/a	n/a
Keystone															
Amber Light — *12 fl oz*	n/a	111	0	0	0	0	11	7.9	n/a	n/a	1	n/a	n/a	1	n/a
Dry — *12 fl oz*	n/a	122	0	0	0	0	11	5.9	n/a	n/a	0.8	n/a	n/a	1	n/a
Ice — *12 fl oz*	n/a	146	0	0	0	0	12	9	n/a	n/a	1.1	n/a	n/a	<1	n/a
Light — *12 fl oz*	n/a	100	0	0	0	0	11	4.6	n/a	n/a	0.8	n/a	n/a	1	n/a
regular — *12 fl oz*	n/a	123	0	0	0	0	11	6.1	n/a	n/a	1.5	n/a	n/a	1	n/a
Killian															
Brown — *12 fl oz*	n/a	174	0	0	0	0	11	15.3	n/a	n/a	1.9	n/a	n/a	2	n/a
regular — *12 fl oz*	n/a	159	0	0	0	0	11	13.5	n/a	n/a	1.5	n/a	n/a	<1	n/a
Wild Honey — *12 fl oz*	n/a	171	0	0	0	0	5	14.4	n/a	n/a	1.9	n/a	n/a	1	n/a
King Cobra — *12 fl oz*	n/a	177	0	0	0	0	9	14.1	n/a	n/a	1.7	n/a	n/a	n/a	n/a
Lowenbrau, Dark or Special — *12 fl oz*	n/a	158	0	0	0	0	7	14.3	n/a	n/a	1.4	n/a	n/a	n/a	n/a
Michelob															
Amber Bock — *12 fl oz*	n/a	159	0	0	0	0	9	14.3	n/a	n/a	1.4	n/a	n/a	n/a	n/a
Classic Dark — *12 fl oz*	n/a	163	0	0	0	0	9	14.8	n/a	n/a	1.5	n/a	n/a	n/a	n/a
Dry — *12 fl oz*	n/a	130	0	0	0	0	9	7.9	n/a	n/a	1.2	n/a	n/a	n/a	n/a
Golden Draft — *12 fl oz*	n/a	151	0	0	0	0	9	13.1	n/a	n/a	1.6	n/a	n/a	n/a	n/a
Golden Draft Light — *12 fl oz*	n/a	110	0	0	0	0	9	6.7	n/a	n/a	1	n/a	n/a	n/a	n/a
Light — *12 fl oz*	n/a	134	0	0	0	0	9	11.5	n/a	n/a	1	n/a	n/a	n/a	n/a
Malt — *12 fl oz*	n/a	160	0	0	0	0	9	9.8	n/a	n/a	1.4	n/a	n/a	n/a	n/a
regular — *12 fl oz*	n/a	157	0	0	0	0	9	13.5	n/a	n/a	1.3	n/a	n/a	n/a	n/a

	Weight *g*	Calories	Calories from fat	Total fat *g*	Sat. fat *g*	Cholesterol *mg*	Sodium *mg*	Carbohydrates *g*	Dietary fiber *g*	Sugars *g*	Protein *g*	Vitamin A *% DV*	Vitamin C *% DV*	Calcium *% DV*	Iron *% DV*
Miller															
Genuine Draft — *12 fl oz*	n/a	143	0	0	0	0	7	13.1	n/a	n/a	1	n/a	n/a	n/a	n/a
Genuine Draft Light — *12 fl oz*	n/a	110	0	0	0	0	6	7	n/a	n/a	0.8	n/a	n/a	n/a	n/a
High Life — *12 fl oz*	n/a	143	0	0	0	0	7	13.1	n/a	n/a	1	n/a	n/a	n/a	n/a
High Life Ice — *12 fl oz*	n/a	156	0	0	0	0	9	11	n/a	n/a	1.1	n/a	n/a	n/a	n/a
High Life Lite — *12 fl oz*	n/a	110	0	0	0	0	6	7	n/a	n/a	1	n/a	n/a	n/a	n/a
Lite — *12 fl oz*	n/a	96	0	0	0	0	6	3.2	n/a	n/a	0.9	n/a	n/a	n/a	n/a
regular — *12 fl oz*	n/a	150	0	0	0	0	4	13.2	n/a	n/a	1.1	n/a	n/a	n/a	n/a
Muenchener — *12 fl oz*	n/a	178	0	0	0	0	9	11.9	n/a	n/a	2.5	n/a	n/a	n/a	n/a
Natural Ice — *12 fl oz*	n/a	158	0	0	0	0	9	9.4	n/a	n/a	1.3	n/a	n/a	n/a	n/a
Natural Pilsner — *12 fl oz*	n/a	145	0	0	0	0	9	11.1	n/a	n/a	1.1	n/a	n/a	n/a	n/a
O'Doul's (non-alcoholic) — *12 fl oz*	n/a	70	0	0	0	0	9	14.0	n/a	n/a	0.7	n/a	n/a	n/a	n/a
Red Dog — *12 fl oz*	n/a	147	0	0	0	0	4	14.1	n/a	n/a	0.7	n/a	n/a	n/a	n/a
Red Wolf — *12 fl oz*	n/a	160	0	0	0	0	9	11.6	n/a	n/a	1.5	n/a	n/a	n/a	n/a
Sharp's (non-alcoholic) — *12 fl oz*	n/a	58	0	0	0	0	3	12.1	n/a	n/a	0.4	n/a	n/a	n/a	n/a
Ziegenbock — *12 fl oz*	n/a	154	0	0	0	0	9	11.1	n/a	n/a	1.3	n/a	n/a	n/a	n/a

Beverages: Carbonated

	Weight *g*	Calories	Calories from fat	Total fat *g*	Sat. fat *g*	Cholesterol *mg*	Sodium *mg*	Carbohydrates *g*	Dietary fiber *g*	Sugars *g*	Protein *g*	Vitamin A *% DV*	Vitamin C *% DV*	Calcium *% DV*	Iron *% DV*
A & W															
cream soda — *8 fl oz*	n/a	110	0	0	0	0	30	28	0	28	0	0	0	0	0
cream soda, diet — *8 fl oz*	n/a	0	0	0	0	0	45	0	0	0	0	0	0	0	0
root beer — *8 fl oz*	n/a	120	0	0	0	0	30	31	0	31	0	0	0	0	0
root beer, diet — *8 fl oz*	n/a	0	0	0	0	0	45	0	0	0	0	0	0	0	0
AriZona															
Cowboy-Style Chocolate-Flavored Drink — *7 ½ fl oz*	n/a	130	3	0	0	1	120	30	0.3	25	3	8	1	12	2

	Weight g	Calories	Calories from fat	Total fat g	Sat. fat g	Cholesterol mg	Sodium mg	Carbohydrates g	Dietary fiber g	Sugars g	Protein g	Vitamin A % DV	Vitamin C % DV	Calcium % DV	Iron % DV
Lite Chocolate Fudge Float — *8 fl oz*	n/a	60	0	0	0	0	15	9	0	8	0	0	0	0	0
Piña Colada Virgin Cocktail — *8 fl oz*	n/a	140	0	1	0	0	30	34	0	33	0	0	0	0	0
Root Beer Float Sparkling Soda — *8 fl oz*	n/a	120	0	0	0	0	30	30	0	29	0	0	0	0	0
Strawberry Banana Colada Virgin Cocktail — *8 fl oz*	n/a	140	0	0.5	0	0	25	34	0	33	0	0	0	0	0
Vanilla Cola Sparkling Soda — *8 fl oz*	n/a	110	0	0	0	0	25	29	0	29	0	0	0	0	0
Canada Dry															
Cactus Cooler — *8 fl oz*	n/a	100	0	0	0	0	25	27	0	27	0	0	0	0	0
club soda — *8 fl oz*	n/a	0	0	0	0	0	60	0	0	0	0	0	0	0	0
club soda, sodium-free — *8 fl oz*	n/a	0	0	0	0	0	0	0	0	0	0	0	0	0	0
collins mixer — *8 fl oz*	n/a	90	0	0	0	0	15	21	0	21	0	0	0	0	0
seltzer, lemon lime or mandarin orange — *8 fl oz*	n/a	0	0	0	0	0	10	0	0	0	0	0	0	0	0
seltzer, plain — *8 fl oz*	n/a	0	0	0	0	0	0	0	0	0	0	0	0	0	0
tonic water — *8 fl oz*	n/a	90	0	0	0	0	15	24	0	24	0	0	0	0	0
tonic water, diet — *8 fl oz*	n/a	0	0	0	0	0	35	0	0	0	0	0	0	0	0
Canada Dry Ginger Ale															
diet — *8 fl oz*	n/a	0	0	0	0	0	60	0	0	0	0	0	0	0	0
golden — *8 fl oz*	n/a	90	0	0	0	0	10	24	0	24	0	0	0	0	0
lemon — *8 fl oz*	n/a	90	0	0	0	0	15	25	0	25	0	0	0	0	0
lemon, diet — *8 fl oz*	n/a	0	0	0	0	0	60	0	0	0	0	0	0	0	0
regular — *8 fl oz*	n/a	80	0	0	0	0	25	22	0	22	0	0	0	0	0
Coca-Cola															
Cherry Coke — *8 fl oz*	n/a	104	0	0	0	0	4	28	0	28	0	0	0	0	0
Cherry Coke, diet — *8 fl oz*	n/a	1	0	0	0	0	4	<1	0	0.1	0	0	0	0	0
Classic Coke — *8 fl oz*	n/a	97	0	0	0	0	9	27	0	27	0	0	0	0	0

	Weight g	Calories	Calories from fat	Total fat g	Sat. fat g	Cholesterol mg	Sodium mg	Carbohydrates g	Dietary fiber g	Sugars g	Protein g	Vitamin A % DV	Vitamin C % DV	Calcium % DV	Iron % DV
Coke II — *8 fl oz*	n/a	105	0	0	0	0	4	29	0	29	0	0	0	0	0
Diet Coke — *8 fl oz*	n/a	1	0	0	0	0	4	<1	0	<1	0	0	0	0	0
Crush															
orange — *8 fl oz*	n/a	120	0	0	0	0	30	34	0	34	0	0	0	0	0
orange, diet — *8 fl oz*	n/a	10	0	0	0	0	30	4	0	4	0	0	0	0	0
Dr. Pepper															
diet — *8 fl oz*	n/a	0	0	0	0	0	35	0	0	0	0	0	0	0	0
diet, sodium-free — *8 fl oz*	n/a	0	0	0	0	0	0	0	0	0	0	0	0	0	0
regular — *8 fl oz*	n/a	100	0	0	0	0	35	27	0	27	0	0	0	0	0
regular, sodium-free — *8 fl oz*	n/a	100	0	0	0	0	0	27	0	27	0	0	0	0	0
Fanta															
ginger ale — *8 fl oz*	n/a	86	0	0	0	0	4	23	0	23	0	0	0	0	0
grape — *8 fl oz*	n/a	117	0	0	0	0	9	31	0	31	0	0	0	0	0
orange — *8 fl oz*	n/a	118	0	0	0	0	9	32	0	32	0	0	0	0	0
root beer — *8 fl oz*	n/a	111	0	0	0	0	4	29	0	29	0	0	0	0	0
Fresca — *8 fl oz*	n/a	2.8	0	0	0	0	<1	0.2	0	<1	0	0	0	0	0
Hires															
cream soda — *8 fl oz*	n/a	120	0	0	0	0	30	32	0	32	0	0	0	0	0
cream soda, diet — *8 fl oz*	n/a	0	0	0	0	0	35	0	0	0	0	0	0	0	0
root beer — *8 fl oz*	n/a	120	0	0	0	0	45	31	0	31	0	0	0	0	0
root beer, diet — *8 fl oz*	n/a	0	0	0	0	0	70	0	0	0	0	0	0	0	0
Mello Yello															
diet — *8 fl oz*	n/a	3.3	0	0	0	0	<1	<1	0	<1	0	0	0	0	0
regular — *8 fl oz*	n/a	119	0	0	0	0	9	32	0	32	0	0	0	0	0

	Weight *g*	Calories	Calories from fat	Total fat *g*	Sat. fat *g*	Cholesterol *mg*	Sodium *mg*	Carbohydrates *g*	Dietary fiber *g*	Sugars *g*	Protein *g*	Vitamin A *% DV*	Vitamin C *% DV*	Calcium *% DV*	Iron *% DV*
Mountain Dew															
diet — *12 fl oz*	n/a	0	0	0	0	0	35	0	0	0	0	0	0	0	0
regular — *12 fl oz*	n/a	170	0	0	0	0	70	46	0	46	0	0	0	0	0
Mr. Pibb															
diet — *8 fl oz*	n/a	1.3	0	0	0	0	2	<1	0	<1	0	0	0	0	0
regular — *8 fl oz*	n/a	97	0	0	0	0	7	26	0	26	0	0	0	0	0
Mug															
cream soda — *12 fl oz*	n/a	170	0	0	0	0	65	48	0	48	0	0	0	0	0
cream soda, diet — *12 fl oz*	n/a	5	0	0	0	0	80	0	0	0	0	0	0	0	0
root beer — *12 fl oz*	n/a	160	0	0	0	0	65	43	0	43	0	0	0	0	0
root beer, diet — *12 fl oz*	n/a	0	0	0	0	0	65	0	0	0	0	0	0	0	0
Orangina Sparkling Citrus Beverage — *8 fl oz*	n/a	90	0	0	0	0	90	23	0	21	0	0	15	4	2
Pepsi															
diet — *12 fl oz*	n/a	0	0	0	0	0	35	0	0	0	0	0	0	0	0
regular — *12 fl oz*	n/a	150	0	0	0	0	35	41	0	41	0	0	0	0	0
Wild Cherry — *12 fl oz*	n/a	160	0	0	0	0	35	43	0	43	0	0	0	0	0
Schweppes															
bitter lemon — *8 fl oz*	n/a	110	0	0	0	0	20	28	0	28	0	0	0	0	0
club soda — *8 fl oz*	n/a	0	0	0	0	0	45	0	0	0	0	0	0	0	0
ginger ale — *8 fl oz*	n/a	80	0	0	0	0	25	22	0	22	0	0	0	0	0
ginger ale, diet — *8 fl oz*	n/a	0	0	0	0	0	60	0	0	0	0	0	0	0	0
7-Up															
cherry — *8 fl oz*	n/a	100	0	0	0	0	25	26	0	26	0	0	0	0	0
cherry, diet, low-sodium — *8 fl oz*	n/a	0	0	0	0	0	50	0	0	0	0	0	0	0	0

	Weight g	Calories	Calories from fat	Total fat g	Sat. fat g	Cholesterol mg	Sodium mg	Carbohydrates g	Dietary fiber g	Sugars g	Protein g	Vitamin A % DV	Vitamin C % DV	Calcium % DV	Iron % DV
cherry, low-sodium — *8 fl oz*	n/a	100	0	0	0	0	50	26	0	26	0	0	0	0	0
diet, low-sodium — *8 fl oz*	n/a	0	0	0	0	0	50	0	0	0	0	0	0	0	0
diet, no sodium — *8 fl oz*	n/a	0	0	0	0	0	0	0	0	0	0	0	0	0	0
diet, regular or cherry — *8 fl oz*	n/a	0	0	0	0	0	25	0	0	0	0	0	0	0	0
regular — *8 fl oz*	n/a	100	0	0	0	0	50	26	0	26	0	0	0	0	0
regular, low-sodium — *8 fl oz*	n/a	100	0	0	0	0	25	26	0	26	0	0	0	0	0
Slice															
lemon-lime — *12 fl oz*	n/a	150	0	0	0	0	55	40	0	39	0	0	0	0	0
lemon-lime, diet — *12 fl oz*	n/a	0	0	0	0	0	35	1	0	0	0	0	0	0	0
mandarin orange — *12 fl oz*	n/a	190	0	0	0	0	55	51	0	50	0	0	0	0	0
mandarin orange, diet — *12 fl oz*	n/a	0	0	0	0	0	50	1	0	0	0	0	0	0	0
Sprite															
diet — *8 fl oz*	n/a	2.7	0	0	0	0	0	0	0	0	0	0	0	0	0
regular — *8 fl oz*	n/a	96	0	0	0	0	23	26	0	26	0	0	0	0	0
Squirt															
diet — *8 fl oz*	n/a	0	0	0	0	0	15	0	0	0	0	0	0	0	0
regular — *8 fl oz*	n/a	100	0	0	0	0	15	27	0	27	0	0	0	0	0
Ruby Red — *8 fl oz*	n/a	120	0	0	0	0	15	31	0	31	0	0	0	0	0
Ruby Red, diet — *8 fl oz*	n/a	5	0	0	0	0	20	1	0	1	0	0	0	0	0
Sunkist															
citrus — *8 fl oz*	n/a	90	0	0	0	0	25	25	0	25	0	0	0	0	0
citrus, diet — *8 fl oz*	n/a	0	0	0	0	0	85	0	0	0	0	0	0	0	0
lemonade — *8 fl oz*	n/a	120	0	0	0	0	35	30	0	30	0	0	0	0	0
lemonade, diet — *8 fl oz*	n/a	0	0	0	0	0	85	0	0	0	0	0	0	0	0

	Weight *g*	Calories	Calories from fat	Total fat *g*	Sat. fat *g*	Cholesterol *mg*	Sodium *mg*	Carbohydrates *g*	Dietary fiber *g*	Sugars *g*	Protein *g*	Vitamin A *% DV*	Vitamin C *% DV*	Calcium *% DV*	Iron *% DV*
orange — *8 fl oz*	n/a	130	0	0	0	0	30	35	0	35	0	0	0	0	0
orange, diet — *8 fl oz*	n/a	0	0	0	0	0	65	0	0	0	0	0	0	0	0
Tab — *8 fl oz*	n/a	0.8	0	0	0	0	4	<1	0	<1	0	0	0	0	0

Beverages: Fruit & Vegetable Drinks & Juices

	Weight *g*	Calories	Calories from fat	Total fat *g*	Sat. fat *g*	Cholesterol *mg*	Sodium *mg*	Carbohydrates *g*	Dietary fiber *g*	Sugars *g*	Protein *g*	Vitamin A *% DV*	Vitamin C *% DV*	Calcium *% DV*	Iron *% DV*
All Sport (all varieties) — *12 fl oz*	n/a	70	0	0	0	0	55	20	0	19	0	n/a	n/a	n/a	n/a
AriZona															
grape/kiwi — *8 fl oz*	n/a	120	0	0	0	0	20	29	0	28	0	n/a	n/a	n/a	n/a
kiwi/strawberry — *8 fl oz*	n/a	120	0	0	0	0	20	29	0	28	0	n/a	n/a	n/a	n/a
lemonade — *8 fl oz*	n/a	110	0	0	0	0	25	27	0	26	0	n/a	n/a	n/a	n/a
lemonade, pink — *8 fl oz*	n/a	110	0	0	0	0	25	28	0	27	0	n/a	n/a	n/a	n/a
Mucho Mango — *8 fl oz*	n/a	100	0	0	0	0	20	27	0	25	0	n/a	n/a	n/a	n/a
Campbell's Tomato Juice															
low-sodium — *8 fl oz*	n/a	50	0	0	0	0	140	10	1	8	2	15	100	4	2
regular — *8 fl oz*	n/a	50	0	0	0	0	860	9	1	7	2	20	40	2	8
Capri Sun															
fruit punch — *6 ¾ fl oz*	n/a	100	0	0	0	0	20	26	0	26	0	0	0	0	0
grape — *6 ¾ fl oz*	n/a	110	0	0	0	0	20	28	0	28	0	0	0	0	0
orange — *6 ¾ fl oz*	n/a	100	0	0	0	0	25	26	0	26	0	0	0	0	0
red berry — *6 ¾ fl oz*	n/a	100	0	0	0	0	20	28	0	28	0	0	0	0	0
wild cherry — *6 ¾ fl oz*	n/a	110	0	0	0	0	20	30	0	30	0	0	0	0	0
Country Time															
lemonade — *8 fl oz*	n/a	90	0	0	0	0	90	23	0	23	0	n/a	n/a	n/a	n/a
lemonade, pink — *8 fl oz*	n/a	90	0	0	0	0	75	23	0	23	0	n/a	n/a	n/a	n/a

	Weight *g*	Calories	Calories from fat	Total fat *g*	Sat. fat *g*	Cholesterol *mg*	Sodium *mg*	Carbohydrates *g*	Dietary fiber *g*	Sugars *g*	Protein *g*	Vitamin A *% DV*	Vitamin C *% DV*	Calcium *% DV*	Iron *% DV*
Crystal Light															
citrus blend — *8 fl oz*	n/a	5	0	0	0	0	0	0	0	0	0	0	10	0	0
lemon-lime — *8 fl oz*	n/a	5	0	0	0	0	0	0	0	0	0	0	10	0	0
pink grapefruit — *8 fl oz*	n/a	5	0	0	0	0	0	0	0	0	0	0	10	0	0
Dole															
Apple Berry Burst — *8 fl oz*	n/a	120	0	0	0	0	20	31	0	29	0	0	100	0	0
country raspberry — *8 fl oz*	n/a	140	0	0	0	0	30	34	n/a	28	<1	n/a	25	2	4
cranberry apple — *8 fl oz*	n/a	120	0	0	0	0	35	30	n/a	26	0	n/a	100	n/a	n/a
Fruit Fiesta — *8 fl oz*	n/a	140	0	0	0	0	20	34	n/a	33	0	n/a	100	n/a	n/a
Lanai Breeze — *8 fl oz*	n/a	120	0	0	0	0	20	30	0	27	0	4	100	0	0
orange/peach/mango — *8 fl oz*	n/a	120	0	0	0	0	35	28	n/a	22	<1	n/a	100	n/a	n/a
orange/strawberry/banana — *8 fl oz*	n/a	120	0	0	0	0	30	28	n/a	24	<1	n/a	100	n/a	n/a
Pacific Pink Grapefruit — *8 fl oz*	n/a	140	0	0	0	0	20	34	0	31	0	0	100	0	0
pineapple/orange/banana — *10 fl oz*	n/a	150	0	0	0	0	25	36	n/a	26	<2	2	100	4	2
Raspberry Lemon Splash — *8 fl oz*	n/a	120	0	0	0	0	20	31	0	28	0	0	100	0	0
spicy vegetable blend — *12 fl oz*	n/a	80	0	0	0	0	950	16	2	11	<3	50	200	4	6
Tropical Breeze — *8 fl oz*	n/a	120	0	0	0	0	20	30	0	27	0	4	100	0	0
Dole 100% Fruit Juices															
pine/passion/banana — *8 fl oz*	n/a	120	0	0	0	0	20	29	0	26	2	4	100	0	0
pineapple/orange — *8 fl oz*	n/a	120	0	0	0	0	20	27	0	21	2	2	100	4	2
pineapple/orange/banana — *8 fl oz*	n/a	120	0	0	0	0	20	29	0	21	2	2	100	4	2
pineapple/orange/berry — *8 fl oz*	n/a	130	0	0	0	0	20	32	0	28	1	0	100	4	4
pineapple/orange/guava — *8 fl oz*	n/a	120	0	0	0	0	20	29	0	27	1	4	100	4	9
pineapple/orange/strawberry — *8 fl oz*	n/a	130	0	0	0	0	20	29	0	28	1	0	100	4	0

	Weight g	Calories	Calories from fat	Total fat g	Sat. fat g	Cholesterol mg	Sodium mg	Carbohydrates g	Dietary fiber g	Sugars g	Protein g	Vitamin A % DV	Vitamin C % DV	Calcium % DV	Iron % DV
Fruitopia															
Fruit Integration — *8 fl oz*	n/a	125	0	0	0	0	26	31	0	30	0	n/a	n/a	0	n/a
Fruit Integration, plus calcium — *8 fl oz*	n/a	111	0	0	0	0	22	29	0	29	0	n/a	n/a	12	n/a
Pink Lemonade Euphoria — *8 fl oz*	n/a	117	0	0	0	0	26	29	0	28	0	n/a	n/a	0	n/a
Raspberry Psychic Lemonade — *8 fl oz*	n/a	121	0	0	0	0	26	29	0	29	0	n/a	n/a	0	n/a
Strawberry Passion Awareness — *8 fl oz*	n/a	124	0	0	0	0	30	31	0	30	0	n/a	n/a	0	n/a
Tangerine Wavelength — *8 fl oz*	n/a	119	0	0	0	0	24	30	0	29	0	n/a	n/a	0	n/a
Tangerine Wavelength, plus calcium — *8 fl oz*	n/a	110	0	0	0	0	21	29	0	28	0	n/a	n/a	11	n/a
The Grape Beyond — *8 fl oz*	n/a	127	0	0	0	0	26	32	0	31	0	n/a	n/a	0	n/a
The Grape Beyond, plus calcium — *8 fl oz*	n/a	113	0	0	0	0	21	30	0	30	0	n/a	n/a	12	n/a
Gatorade, All Flavors — *8 fl oz*	n/a	50	0	0	0	0	110	14	0	14	0	n/a	n/a	n/a	n/a
Goya Nectar															
apricot — *1 can*	n/a	130	0	0	0	0	15	31	0	27	1	15	4	2	4
pear — *1 can*	n/a	240	0	0	0	0	20	59	2	49	1	2	100	4	6
Juicy Juice (Libby's)															
apple/grape — *8.45 fl oz*	n/a	140	0	0	0	0	15	34	0	30	0	0	130	0	2
orange punch — *8.45 fl oz*	n/a	130	0	0	0	0	15	33	0	28	0	0	130	0	0
punch — *8.45 fl oz*	n/a	150	0	0	0	0	15	38	0	33	0	0	130	0	0
tropical — *8.45 fl oz*	n/a	140	0	0	0	0	15	34	0	24	0	0	130	0	0
Kool-Aid Bursts															
cherry — *6 ¾ fl oz*	n/a	100	0	0	0	0	35	25	0	25	0	0	0	0	0
grape — *6 ¾ fl oz*	n/a	100	0	0	0	0	30	25	0	25	0	0	0	0	0
orange or tropical punch — *6 ¾ fl oz*	n/a	100	0	0	0	0	30	24	0	24	0	0	0	0	0

	Weight g	Calories	Calories from fat	Total fat g	Sat. fat g	Cholesterol mg	Sodium mg	Carbohydrates g	Dietary fiber g	Sugars g	Protein g	Vitamin A % DV	Vitamin C % DV	Calcium % DV	Iron % DV
Kool-Aid (sugar-free, low-calorie)															
cherry — *8 fl oz*	n/a	5	0	0	0	0	5	0	0	0	0	0	10	0	0
grape — *8 fl oz*	n/a	5	0	0	0	0	0	0	0	0	0	0	10	0	0
tropical punch — *8 fl oz*	n/a	5	0	0	0	0	10	0	0	0	0	0	10	0	0
Kool-Aid (sugar-sweetened)															
lemonade — *8 fl oz*	n/a	70	0	0	0	0	0	17	0	17	0	0	10	0	0
orange — *8 fl oz*	n/a	60	0	0	0	0	5	16	0	16	0	0	10	0	0
raspberry — *8 fl oz*	n/a	60	0	0	0	0	0	17	0	17	0	0	10	0	0
strawberry — *8 fl oz*	n/a	60	0	0	0	0	0	16	0	16	0	0	10	0	0
Kool-Aid (unsweetened)															
grape — *8 fl oz*	n/a	100	0	0	0	0	15	25	0	25	0	0	10	0	0
lemon-lime — *8 fl oz*	n/a	100	0	0	0	0	10	25	0	25	0	0	10	0	0
orange — *8 fl oz*	n/a	100	0	0	0	0	15	25	0	25	0	0	10	0	0
raspberry or strawberry — *8 fl oz*	n/a	100	0	0	0	0	35	25	0	25	0	0	10	0	0
tropical punch — *8 fl oz*	n/a	100	0	0	0	0	20	25	0	25	0	0	10	0	0
Libby's Nectar															
apricot — *11 ½ fl oz*	n/a	220	0	0	0	0	10	52	0	44	1	70	100	4	2
guava — *11 ½ fl oz*	n/a	220	0	0	0	0	10	54	0	47	0	0	100	2	0
papaya — *11 ½ fl oz*	n/a	210	0	0	0	0	10	51	0	47	<1	0	100	4	0
peach — *11 ½ fl oz*	n/a	210	0	0	0	0	5	52	0	46	1	6	100	2	4
strawberry — *11 ½ fl oz*	n/a	210	0	0	0	0	10	52	0	46	0	0	100	4	4
Minute Maid															
Concord Punch — *8 fl oz*	n/a	127	0	0	n/a	n/a	26	32	n/a	31	0	n/a	0	n/a	n/a
cranberry/apple/raspberry blend — *8 fl oz*	n/a	123	0	0	n/a	n/a	24	33	n/a	31	0	n/a	0	n/a	n/a

	Weight *g*	Calories	Calories from fat	Total fat *g*	Sat. fat *g*	Cholesterol *mg*	Sodium *mg*	Carbohydrates *g*	Dietary fiber *g*	Sugars *g*	Protein *g*	Vitamin A *% DV*	Vitamin C *% DV*	Calcium *% DV*	Iron *% DV*
fruit punch — *8 fl oz*	n/a	112	0	0	0	0	22	30	n/a	29	0	n/a	0	n/a	n/a
orange juice blend — *8 fl oz*	n/a	124	0	0	0	0	33	32	n/a	31	0	n/a	100	n/a	n/a
pink grapefruit blend — *8 fl oz*	n/a	124	0	0	0	0	32	30	n/a	28	0	n/a	0	n/a	n/a
Nestlé Sweet Success															
mixed berry, or orange/pineapple — *1 can*	n/a	200	5	0.5	0	25	140	39	4	33	9	50	100	25	25
strawberry/banana — *1 can*	n/a	200	5	0.5	0	25	130	39	4	33	9	50	100	25	25
Newman's Own Lemonade — *10 fl oz*	n/a	140	0	0	0	0	45	34	0	34	0	0	4	0	0
Ocean Spray															
Cran-Blueberry — *8 fl oz*	n/a	160	0	0	0	0	35	41	0	41	0	0	100	n/a	n/a
Cran-Cherry — *8 fl oz*	n/a	160	0	0	0	0	35	39	0	39	0	0	100	n/a	n/a
Cran-Currant — *8 fl oz*	n/a	140	0	0	0	0	35	33	2	33	0	0	100	n/a	n/a
Cran-Grape — *8 fl oz*	n/a	170	0	0	0	0	35	41	0	41	0	0	100	n/a	n/a
Cran-Raspberry — *8 fl oz*	n/a	140	0	0	0	0	35	36	0	36	0	0	100	n/a	n/a
Cran-Strawberry — *8 fl oz*	n/a	140	0	0	0	0	35	36	1	35	0	0	100	n/a	n/a
Cranapple — *8 fl oz*	n/a	160	0	0	0	0	35	41	1	40	0	0	100	n/a	n/a
cranberry juice cocktail — *8 fl oz*	n/a	140	0	0	0	0	35	34	0	34	0	0	100	n/a	n/a
Cranberry Pineapple Caribbean Colada — *8 fl oz*	n/a	130	0	0	0	0	35	32	0	32	0	0	100	n/a	n/a
Cranicot — *8 fl oz*	n/a	160	0	0	0	0	35	40	0	40	0	30	0	n/a	n/a
Crantastic Fruit Punch — *8 fl oz*	n/a	150	0	0	0	0	35	37	0	37	0	0	100	n/a	n/a
fruit punch — *8 fl oz*	n/a	130	0	0	0	0	35	32	0	32	0	0	100	n/a	n/a
grapefruit juice cocktail, pink — *8 fl oz*	n/a	120	0	0	0	0	35	30	0	30	0	0	100	n/a	n/a
kiwi/strawberry juice drink — *8 fl oz*	n/a	120	0	0	0	0	35	31	0	31	0	2	100	n/a	n/a
Mandarin Magic — *8 fl oz*	n/a	120	0	0	0	0	35	31	0	31	0	25	100	n/a	n/a
Ruby Red & Tangerine Grapefruit Juice Drink — *8 fl oz*	n/a	130	0	0	0	0	35	32	0	32	0	0	100	n/a	n/a

	Weight g	Calories	Calories from fat	Total fat g	Sat. fat g	Cholesterol mg	Sodium mg	Carbohydrates g	Dietary fiber g	Sugars g	Protein g	Vitamin A % DV	Vitamin C % DV	Calcium % DV	Iron % DV
Ruby Red Grapefruit Juice Drink — *8 fl oz*	n/a	130	0	0	0	0	35	33	0	33	0	0	100	n/a	n/a
Summer Cooler — *8 fl oz*	n/a	120	0	0	0	0	35	31	0	31	0	12	100	n/a	n/a
Ocean Spray, From Concentrate															
Cran-Raspberry, reduced-calorie — *8 fl oz*	n/a	50	0	0	0	0	35	13	0	13	0	0	100	n/a	n/a
Cranapple, reduced-calorie — *8 fl oz*	n/a	50	0	0	0	0	35	13	0	13	0	0	100	n/a	n/a
cranberry juice cocktail, reduced-calorie — *8 fl oz*	n/a	50	0	0	0	0	35	13	0	13	0	0	100	n/a	n/a
Ocean Spray, Lightstyle (low calorie)															
Cran-Grape — *8 fl oz*	n/a	40	0	0	0	0	35	9	0	9	0	0	100	n/a	n/a
Cran-Raspberry — *8 fl oz*	n/a	40	0	9	0	0	35	10	0	10	0	0	100	n/a	n/a
cranberry juice cocktail — *8 fl oz*	n/a	40	0	0	0	0	35	10	0	10	0	0	100	n/a	n/a
pink grapefruit juice cocktail — *8 fl oz*	n/a	40	0	0	0	0	35	9	0	9	0	0	100	n/a	n/a
Ocean Spray, Mauna La'i Hawaiian															
hawaiian guava & passion fruit juice drink — *8 fl oz*	n/a	130	0	0	0	0	35	32	0	32	0	10	100	n/a	n/a
hawaiian guava fruit juice drink — *8 fl oz*	n/a	130	0	0	0	0	35	32	0	32	0	0	100	n/a	n/a
Powerade (all flavors) — *8 fl oz*	n/a	72	0	0	0	0	28	19	0	15	0	n/a	n/a	n/a	n/a
Snap-E-Tom Tomato & Chile Vegetable Cocktail — *6 fl oz*	n/a	40	0	0	0	0	500	8	1	4	2	50	20	0	6
Tang															
mango-flavored — *8 fl oz*	n/a	100	0	0	0	0	0	25	0	25	0	10	100	4	0
orange-flavored — *8 fl oz*	n/a	100	0	0	0	0	0	24	0	24	0	10	100	8	0
orange-flavored, sugar-free, low-calorie — *8 fl oz*	n/a	5	0	0	0	0	0	1	0	n/a	0	10	100	0	0
Tropicana Punch															
berry — *8 fl oz*	n/a	130	0	0	0	0	15	32	0	30	0	n/a	n/a	n/a	n/a
citrus — *8 fl oz*	n/a	140	0	0	0	0	15	36	0	32	0	n/a	n/a	n/a	n/a

	Weight g	Calories	Calories from fat	Total fat g	Sat. fat g	Cholesterol mg	Sodium mg	Carbohydrates g	Dietary fiber g	Sugars g	Protein g	Vitamin A % DV	Vitamin C % DV	Calcium % DV	Iron % DV
Tropicana Pure Tropics															
orange/kiwi/passion — *8 fl oz*	n/a	100	0	0	0	0	15	26	0	23	<1	n/a	10	2	n/a
orange/peach/mango — *8 fl oz*	n/a	110	0	0	0	0	15	28	0	24	<1	n/a	10	2	n/a
orange/pineapple — *8 fl oz*	n/a	110	0	0	0	0	15	27	0	24	<1	n/a	10	2	n/a
orange/strawberry/banana — *8 fl oz*	n/a	110	0	0	0	0	5	27	0	23	<1	n/a	10	2	n/a
Tropicana Season's Best															
Citrus Medley — *8 fl oz*	n/a	120	0	0	0	0	25	31	0	27	<1	n/a	35	2	n/a
Fruit Medley — *8 fl oz*	n/a	130	0	0	0	0	25	32	0	27	<1	n/a	6	2	n/a
Ruby Red Grapefruit Cocktail — *8 fl oz*	n/a	120	0	0	0	0	20	29	0	28	<1	n/a	100	n/a	n/a
Tropicana Twister															
apple/berry/pear — *8 fl oz*	n/a	140	0	0	0	0	20	34	0	32	0	n/a	n/a	n/a	n/a
apple/cranberry — *11 ½ fl oz*	n/a	190	0	0	0	0	25	48	0	45	0	n/a	n/a	n/a	n/a
apple/raspberry/blackberry — *8 fl oz*	n/a	130	0	0	0	0	20	32	0	31	0	n/a	n/a	n/a	n/a
cranberry punch — *10 fl oz*	n/a	170	0	0	0	0	20	43	0	41	0	n/a	n/a	n/a	n/a
cranberry/raspberry/strawberry — *8 fl oz*	n/a	120	0	0	0	0	5	31	0	30	0	n/a	n/a	n/a	n/a
fruit punch — *8 fl oz*	n/a	130	0	0	0	0	25	32	0	30	0	n/a	n/a	n/a	n/a
orange/cranberry — *10 fl oz*	n/a	160	0	0	0	0	20	40	0	39	0	n/a	6	n/a	n/a
orange/peach/strawberry — *8 fl oz*	n/a	130	0	0	0	0	20	32	0	31	0	n/a	n/a	n/a	n/a
orange/strawberry/banana — *8 fl oz*	n/a	120	0	0	0	0	20	29	0	28	0	n/a	10	n/a	n/a
Tropicana Twister, Light															
cranberry/raspberry/strawberry, light — *8 fl oz*	n/a	45	0	0	0	0	10	11	0	9	0	n/a	100	n/a	n/a
orange/cranberry, light — *8 fl oz*	n/a	30	0	0	0	0	20	7	0	5	0	n/a	100	n/a	n/a
orange/strawberry/banana, light — *8 fl oz*	n/a	35	0	0	0	0	20	9	0	6	<1	n/a	100	n/a	n/a

Foods, Brand Name

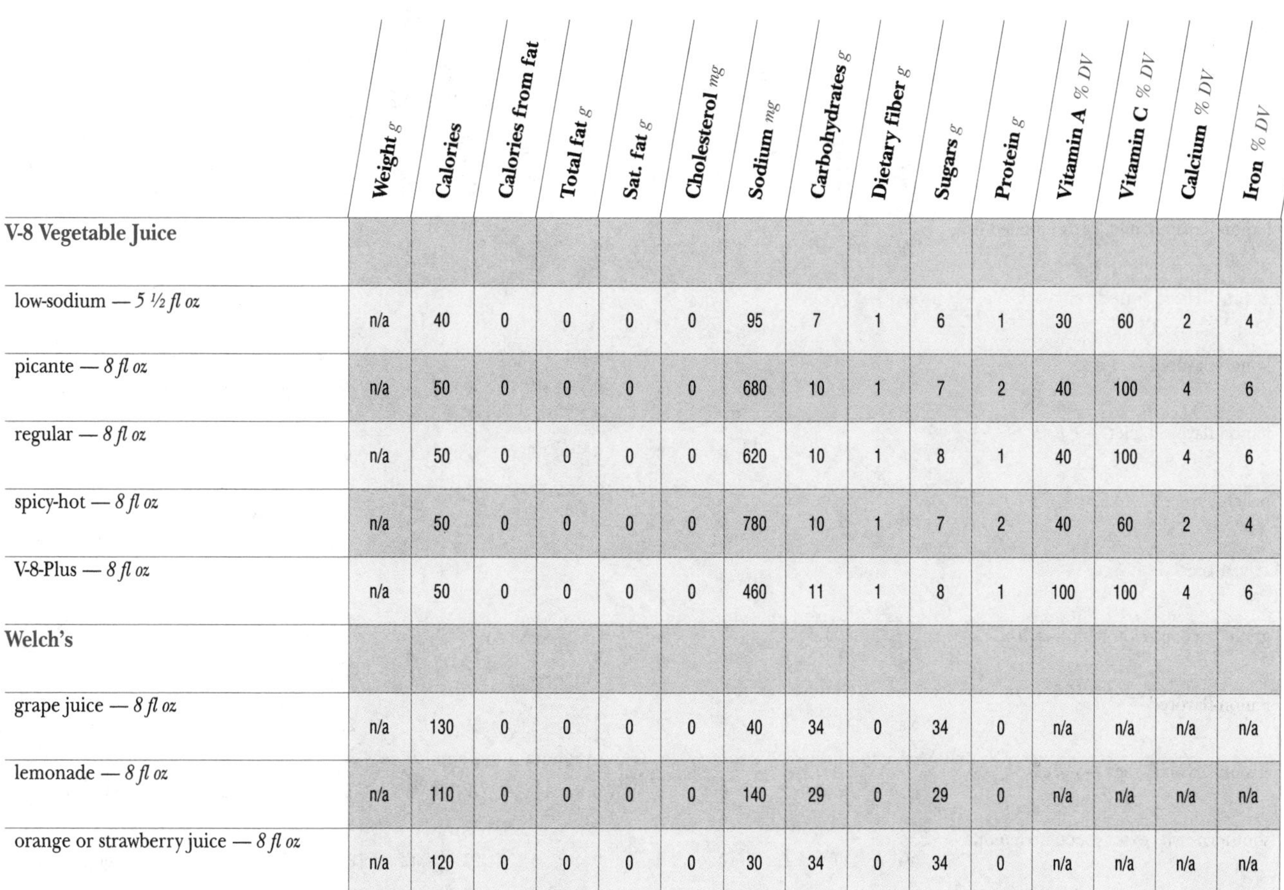

	Weight g	Calories	Calories from fat	Total fat g	Sat. fat g	Cholesterol mg	Sodium mg	Carbohydrates g	Dietary fiber g	Sugars g	Protein g	Vitamin A % DV	Vitamin C % DV	Calcium % DV	Iron % DV
V-8 Vegetable Juice															
low-sodium — *5 ½ fl oz*	n/a	40	0	0	0	0	95	7	1	6	1	30	60	2	4
picante — *8 fl oz*	n/a	50	0	0	0	0	680	10	1	7	2	40	100	4	6
regular — *8 fl oz*	n/a	50	0	0	0	0	620	10	1	8	1	40	100	4	6
spicy-hot — *8 fl oz*	n/a	50	0	0	0	0	780	10	1	7	2	40	60	2	4
V-8-Plus — *8 fl oz*	n/a	50	0	0	0	0	460	11	1	8	1	100	100	4	6
Welch's															
grape juice — *8 fl oz*	n/a	130	0	0	0	0	40	34	0	34	0	n/a	n/a	n/a	n/a
lemonade — *8 fl oz*	n/a	110	0	0	0	0	140	29	0	29	0	n/a	n/a	n/a	n/a
orange or strawberry juice — *8 fl oz*	n/a	120	0	0	0	0	30	34	0	34	0	n/a	n/a	n/a	n/a

Beverages: Iced Teas

	Weight g	Calories	Calories from fat	Total fat g	Sat. fat g	Cholesterol mg	Sodium mg	Carbohydrates g	Dietary fiber g	Sugars g	Protein g	Vitamin A % DV	Vitamin C % DV	Calcium % DV	Iron % DV
AriZona															
decaffeinated, light — *8 fl oz*	n/a	65	0	0	0	0	20	16	0	15	0	n/a	n/a	n/a	n/a
diet — *8 fl oz*	n/a	4	0	0	0	0	15	0	0	0	0	n/a	n/a	n/a	n/a
ginseng — *8 fl oz*	n/a	60	0	0	0	0	20	15	0	14	0	n/a	n/a	n/a	n/a
green tea w/ ginseng & honey — *8 fl oz*	n/a	70	0	0	0	0	20	18	0	17	0	n/a	n/a	n/a	n/a
lemon, raspberry, or peach — *8 fl oz*	n/a	95	0	0	0	0	20	25	0	24	0	n/a	n/a	n/a	n/a
sun-brewed-style w/ tropical flavors — *8 fl oz*	n/a	95	0	0	0	0	20	25	0	24	0	n/a	n/a	n/a	n/a
Country Time, Sugar-Sweetened — *8 fl oz*	n/a	70	0	0	0	0	0	17	0	17	0	0	10	0	0
Crystal Light															
decaffeinated — *8 fl oz*	n/a	5	0	0	0	0	0	0	0	0	0	0	10	0	0
regular — *8 fl oz*	n/a	5	0	0	0	0	0	0	0	0	0	0	10	0	0
Lipton Brisk															
Carribean Cooler — *1 can*	n/a	130	0	0	0	0	75	34	0	34	0	n/a	0	n/a	n/a

	Weight g	Calories	Calories from fat	Total fat g	Sat. fat g	Cholesterol mg	Sodium mg	Carbohydrates g	Dietary fiber g	Sugars g	Protein g	Vitamin A % DV	Vitamin C % DV	Calcium % DV	Iron % DV
lemon-flavored, diet, decaffeinated — *1 can*	n/a	5	0	0	0	0	75	1	0	0	0	0	0	0	0
Lipton Brisk Chilled															
lemon-flavored — *8 fl oz*	n/a	80	0	0	0	0	15	20	0	20	0	n/a	25	n/a	n/a
lemon-flavored, diet — *8 fl oz*	n/a	0	0	0	0	0	10	0	0	0	0	n/a	0	n/a	n/a
peach-flavored — *8 fl oz*	n/a	80	0	0	0	0	15	20	0	20	0	n/a	0	n/a	n/a
Lipton Iced Tea Mix															
green tea & passion fruit — *8 fl oz*	n/a	80	0	0	0	0	5	19	0	19	0	n/a	0	n/a	n/a
lemon-flavored — *8 fl oz*	n/a	90	0	0	0	0	5	21	0	21	0	n/a	0	n/a	n/a
lemon-flavored, diet — *8 fl oz*	n/a	5	0	0	0	0	5	0	0	0	0	n/a	0	n/a	n/a
southern-style, extra-sweet, no lemon — *8 fl oz*	n/a	120	0	0	0	0	5	29	n/a	29	0	n/a	0	n/a	n/a
southern-style, sweetened, no lemon — *8 fl oz*	n/a	100	0	0	0	0	5	24	n/a	24	0	n/a	0	n/a	n/a
tea & lemonade — *8 fl oz*	n/a	110	0	0	0	0	5	26	n/a	26	0	n/a	0	n/a	n/a
Nestea															
Cool — *8 fl oz*	n/a	82	0	0	0	0	33	22	n/a	22	0	n/a	n/a	n/a	n/a
Cool, diet — *8 fl oz*	n/a	2	0	0	0	0	27	0.1	n/a	0.1	0	n/a	n/a	n/a	n/a
earl grey — *8 fl oz*	n/a	68	0	0	0	0	2	18	n/a	18	0	n/a	n/a	n/a	n/a
lemon, diet — *8 fl oz*	n/a	3	0	0	0	0	<1	1.2	n/a	1.2	0	n/a	n/a	n/a	n/a
lemon-sweetened — *8 fl oz*	n/a	68	0	0	0	0	<1	22	n/a	22	0	n/a	n/a	n/a	n/a
sweetened — *8 fl oz*	n/a	65	0	0	0	0	<1	18	n/a	18	0	n/a	n/a	n/a	n/a
Nestea Iced Tea Mixes (unprepared)															
lemon — *2 Tbsp*	1.4	5	0	0	0	0	0	1	0	0	0	0	0	0	0
lemon & sugar — *2 Tbsp*	1.9	80	0	0	0	0	0	19	0	19	0	0	0	0	0
lemonade tea — *2 Tbsp*	1.9	80	0	0	0	0	0	19	0	17	0	0	0	0	0
sugar-free — *2 Tbsp*	1.9	5	0	0	0	0	0	1	0	0	0	0	0	0	0

	Weight *g*	Calories	Calories from fat	Total fat *g*	Sat. fat *g*	Cholesterol *mg*	Sodium *mg*	Carbohydrates *g*	Dietary fiber *g*	Sugars *g*	Protein *g*	Vitamin A *% DV*	Vitamin C *% DV*	Calcium *% DV*	Iron *% DV*
Nestea, Pitcher-Style															
extra-sweet, w/ lemon — *8 fl oz*	n/a	100	0	0	0	0	<1	27	0	27	0	n/a	n/a	n/a	n/a
lightly sweetened, w/ lemon — *8 fl oz*	n/a	54	0	0	0	0	<1	14	0	14	0	n/a	n/a	n/a	n/a
unsweetened — *8 fl oz*	n/a	0.6	0	0	0	0	<1	0.2	0	0.2	0	n/a	n/a	n/a	n/a
Snapple, Diet															
lemon — *8 fl oz*	n/a	100	0	0	0	0	10	25	0	23	0	n/a	n/a	n/a	n/a
peach — *8 fl oz*	n/a	0	0	0	0	0	10	1	0	0	0	n/a	n/a	n/a	n/a
raspberry — *8 fl oz*	n/a	0	0	0	0	0	10	1	0	0	0	n/a	n/a	n/a	n/a

Beverages: Other

	Weight *g*	Calories	Calories from fat	Total fat *g*	Sat. fat *g*	Cholesterol *mg*	Sodium *mg*	Carbohydrates *g*	Dietary fiber *g*	Sugars *g*	Protein *g*	Vitamin A *% DV*	Vitamin C *% DV*	Calcium *% DV*	Iron *% DV*
Carnation Hot Cocoa Mix (prepared w/ water)															
fat-free w/ marshmallows — *1 serving*	12	45	0	0	0	0	100	10	<1	7	2	0	0	4	2
Marshmallow Blizzard — *1 serving*	44	180	15	1.5	0	<5	140	39	<1	33	2	0	0	6	2
raspberry, fat-free — *1 serving*	8	30	0	0	0	0	150	4	1	3	2	0	0	6	2
rich chocolate, fat-free — *1 serving*	8	25	0	0	0	0	135	4	1	3	2	0	0	6	2
70 Calorie — *1 serving*	20	70	0	0	0	0	140	15	<1	15	3	0	0	8	2
Carnation Instant Breakfast Drink															
cafe mocha — *1 can*	n/a	220	25	2.5	0.5	5	210	35	0	33	12	45	50	50	25
creamy milk chocolate — *1 can*	n/a	220	25	2.5	1	10	230	37	2	34	12	45	50	50	25
french vanilla — *1 can*	n/a	200	25	3	0.5	10	180	31	0	29	12	45	50	50	25
strawberry creme — *1 can*	n/a	220	25	3	0.5	10	210	35	0	33	12	45	50	50	25
Carnation Instant Breakfast Powder (unprepared)															
cafe mocha — *1 packet*	n/a	130	5	0.5	0	<5	100	28	<1	23	4	35	45	35	25
classic chocolate malt — *1 packet*	n/a	130	10	1.5	0.5	<5	130	26	1	17	4	35	45	25	25
creamy milk chocolate — *1 packet*	n/a	130	10	1	0.5	<5	100	28	1	20	4	35	45	30	25

	Weight *g*	Calories	Calories from fat	Total fat *g*	Sat. fat *g*	Cholesterol *mg*	Sodium *mg*	Carbohydrates *g*	Dietary fiber *g*	Sugars *g*	Protein *g*	Vitamin A *% DV*	Vitamin C *% DV*	Calcium *% DV*	Iron *% DV*
french vanilla — *1 packet*	n/a	130	0	0	0	<5	95	27	0	17	4	35	45	35	25
french vanilla, no-sugar-added — *1 packet*	n/a	70	0	0	0	<5	95	12	0	7	4	35	45	35	25
strawberry creme — *1 packet*	n/a	130	0	0	0	<5	160	28	0	18	4	35	45	35	25
strawberry creme, no-sugar-added — *1 packet*	n/a	70	0	0	0	<5	95	12	0	7	4	35	45	35	25
Heinz Shake Mix (prepared w/ water)															
chocolate — *8 fl oz*	n/a	70	0	0	0	2	140	12	2	7	6	2	2	30	6
double fudge — *8 fl oz*	n/a	70	0	0.5	0	5	150	11	2	3	6	4	0	35	8
strawberry — *8 fl oz*	n/a	70	0	0	0	5	170	11	1	9	6	2	0	30	0
vanilla — *8 fl oz*	n/a	70	0	0	0	5	170	11	1	10	6	0	0	30	0
Nestlé Hot Cocoa Mix (prepared w/ water)															
rich chocolate — *1 envelope*	28	110	10	1	0.5	0	60	24	<1	19	1	0	0	4	0
rich chocolate w/ marshmallows — *1 envelope*	28	110	10	1	0.5	0	60	24	<1	19	1	0	0	4	0
Nestlé Quik Chocolate Mix — *2 Tbsp*	22	90	5	0.5	0.5	0	30	19	1	18	1	0	0	0	0
Nestlé Quik Flavored Milk															
banana, low-fat — *1 cup*	n/a	200	50	5	3	20	95	30	0	30	7	10	0	25	0
chocolate, low-fat — *1 cup*	n/a	190	40	5	3	20	150	29	0	29	8	10	0	25	0
strawberry — *1 cup*	n/a	230	80	9	5	30	100	31	0	30	7	6	0	25	0
strawberry, low-fat — *1 cup*	n/a	200	40	5	3	20	120	32	0	32	8	10	0	25	0
Nestlé Quik Syrup															
chocolate — *2 Tbsp*	38	100	5	0.5	0	0	30	23	<1	17	1	0	0	0	2
strawberry — *2 Tbsp*	40	110	0	0	0	0	0	27	0	26	0	0	0	0	0
Nestlé Sweet Success															
Creamy Milk Chocolate — *1 can*	n/a	200	25	2.5	0.5	<5	230	36	3	30	10	25	25	35	25
Creamy Vanilla Delight — *1 can*	n/a	200	25	3	0.5	5	220	37	3	30	10	25	25	35	25

	Weight g	Calories	Calories from fat	Total fat g	Sat. fat g	Cholesterol mg	Sodium mg	Carbohydrates g	Dietary fiber g	Sugars g	Protein g	Vitamin A % DV	Vitamin C % DV	Calcium % DV	Iron % DV
Strawberries 'n' Cream — *1 can*	n/a	200	25	3	0.5	5	230	37	3	30	10	25	25	35	25
Swiss Miss Hot Cocoa Mix (prepared w/ water)															
lite — *1 envelope*	n/a	70	5	0.5	0	0	200	17	2	16	1	<2	<2	4	2
milk chocolate w/ marshmallows — *1 envelope*	n/a	120	25	2.5	1	0	125	22	1	17	1	<2	<2	4	2
Tollhouse Syrup															
mint-chocolate — *2 Tbsp*	42	130	30	3	2	0	30	25	1	22	1	0	0	0	2
semi-sweet chocolate — *2 Tbsp*	42	130	30	3.5	2	0	30	24	1	22	1	0	0	0	2
Weight Watchers Hot Cocoa Mix — *1 envelope*	19	70	0	0	0	0	160	10	1	7	6	6	0	25	0
Weight Watchers Shake Mix, Chocolate Fudge (unprepared) — *1 packet*	21	80	10	1	0	0	140	12	2	6	6	6	0	25	2
Biscuits & Breadsticks															
Arnold Old Fashioned Biscuits — *2 biscuits*	38	130	50	5	1	0	250	18	<1	4	3	0	0	4	0
Australian Toaster Biscuits, Orowheat															
corn — *1 biscuit*	69	200	25	2.5	0.5	0	210	39	2	9	5	4	0	0	8
Honey Mates — *1 biscuit*	66	210	50	5	1.5	0	410	36	1	9	4	0	0	2	8
raisin — *1 biscuit*	66	190	35	4	1	0	380	35	1	9	4	0	0	4	5
Gold Medal Biscuit Mix — *2 biscuits prepared*	n/a	180	50	6	2.5	0	480	27	<1	3	4	0	0	8	6
Hungry Jack Biscuits (refrigerated)															
Butter Tastin' Flaky — *1 biscuit*	34	100	40	4.5	1	0	350	14	0	2	2	0	0	0	4
flaky — *1 biscuit*	34	100	40	4.5	1	0	360	40	0	2	2	0	0	0	4
flaky buttermilk — *1 biscuit*	34	100	40	4.5	1	0	360	14	0	2	2	0	0	0	4
southern-style, flaky — *1 biscuit*	34	100	40	4.5	1	0	360	14	0	2	2	0	0	0	4
Pepperidge Farm Brown & Serve Breadsticks — *1 breadstick*	57	150	10	1.5	0.5	0	290	28	1	2	7	0	0	6	15
Pepperidge Farm Heat & Serve Butter Crescent Rolls — *1 roll*	31	110	45	5	3	15	160	13	1	<1	3	0	0	2	4

	Weight g	Calories	Calories from fat	Total fat g	Sat. fat g	Cholesterol mg	Sodium mg	Carbohydrates g	Dietary fiber g	Sugars g	Protein g	Vitamin A % DV	Vitamin C % DV	Calcium % DV	Iron % DV
Pepperidge Farm Thin Breadsticks															
cheddar cheese — *7 breadsticks*	17	70	25	2.5	1	5	120	10	<1	0	2	0	0	2	6
onion — *7 breadsticks*	255	70	20	2	0	0	115	11	<1	1	2	0	0	0	6
sesame — *7 breadsticks*	17	60	15	1.5	0	0	125	11	<1	<1	2	0	0	2	6
Pillsbury Breadsticks (refrigerated) — *1 breadstick*	39	110	25	2.5	0.5	0	290	18	<1	1	3	0	0	0	6
Pillsbury Biscuits (refrigerated)															
butter — *3 biscuits*	64	150	20	2	0	0	550	29	<1	3	4	0	0	0	10
buttermilk — *3 biscuits*	64	150	20	2	0	0	540	29	<1	3	4	0	0	0	10
country — *3 biscuits*	64	150	20	2	0	0	540	29	<1	3	4	0	0	0	10
Tender Layer Buttermilk — *3 biscuits*	64	160	40	4.5	1	0	520	27	<1	3	4	0	0	0	8
Stella D'oro Breadsticks, Sodium-Free — *1 breadstick*	10	45	10	1	0	0	0	7	0	<1	1	0	0	0	2
Stella D'oro Snack Stix															
cracked pepper — *4 breadsticks*	16	70	15	2	0	0	290	11	<1	<1	2	0	0	0	4
salsa-flavored — *4 breadsticks*	16	70	15	1.5	0	0	250	11	<1	1	2	0	0	0	4

Butter, Margarine & Spreads

	Weight g	Calories	Calories from fat	Total fat g	Sat. fat g	Cholesterol mg	Sodium mg	Carbohydrates g	Dietary fiber g	Sugars g	Protein g	Vitamin A % DV	Vitamin C % DV	Calcium % DV	Iron % DV
Fleischmann's Original Margarine — *1 Tbsp*	14	100	99	11	2	0	95	0	0	0	0	10	<2	<2	<2
I Can't Believe It's Not Butter (fat-free) — *1 Tbsp*	14	5	0	0	0	0	90	0	0	0	0	10	0	0	0
Kraft Touch of Butter															
squeeze — *1 Tbsp*	14	80	80	9	1.5	0	115	0	0	0	0	10	0	0	0
stick — *1 Tbsp*	14	90	90	10	2	0	110	0	0	0	0	10	0	0	0
tub — *1 Tbsp*	14	60	60	7	1.5	0	110	0	0	0	0	10	0	0	0
Land O'Lakes Butter															
honey butter — *1 Tbsp*	14	90	70	8	4	15	35	0	0	0	0	6	n/a	n/a	n/a
roasted garlic butter — *1 Tbsp*	14	100	100	11	5	20	95	0	0	0	0	8	n/a	n/a	n/a

	Weight g	Calories	Calories from fat	Total fat g	Sat. fat g	Cholesterol mg	Sodium mg	Carbohydrates g	Dietary fiber g	Sugars g	Protein g	Vitamin A % DV	Vitamin C % DV	Calcium % DV	Iron % DV
stick, light, salted — *1 Tbsp*	14	50	50	6	4	20	70	0	0	0	0	10	n/a	n/a	n/a
stick, light, unsalted — *1 Tbsp*	14	50	50	6	4	20	0	0	0	0	0	10	n/a	n/a	n/a
whipped, light, salted — *1 Tbsp*	9	35	30	3.5	2.5	10	45	0	0	0	0	6	n/a	n/a	n/a
Land O'Lakes Country Morning Blend															
stick, light, salted — *1 Tbsp*	14	50	50	6	3	10	110	0	0	0	0	10	n/a	n/a	n/a
stick, salted — *1 Tbsp*	14	100	100	10	2.5	0	90	0	0	0	0	10	n/a	n/a	n/a
stick, unsalted — *1 Tbsp*	14	100	100	11	2.5	0	0	0	0	0	0	10	n/a	n/a	n/a
tub — *1 Tbsp*	14	100	100	11	2	0	80	0	0	0	0	10	n/a	n/a	n/a
tub, light — *1 Tbsp*	14	50	50	6	2.5	5	110	0	0	0	0	10	n/a	n/a	n/a
Land O'Lakes Spread w/ Sweet Cream															
stick, salted — *1 Tbsp*	14	90	90	10	2.5	0	90	0	0	0	0	8	n/a	n/a	n/a
stick, unsalted — *1 Tbsp*	14	90	90	10	2.5	0	0	0	0	0	0	8	n/a	n/a	n/a
tub — *1 Tbsp*	14	80	80	8	2	0	70	0	0	0	0	8	n/a	n/a	n/a
Parkay Margarine															
squeeze — *1 Tbsp*	14	80	80	9	1.5	0	120	<1	0	0	0	10	0	0	0
stick — *1 Tbsp*	14	90	90	10	2	0	110	0	0	0	0	10	0	0	0
stick, ⅓ less fat — *1 Tbsp*	14	70	70	7	1.5	0	120	0	0	0	0	10	0	0	0
Parkay Soft Margarine															
tub — *1 Tbsp*	14	100	100	11	2	0	105	0	0	0	0	10	0	0	0
tub, diet — *1 Tbsp*	14	50	50	6	1	0	110	0	0	0	0	10	0	0	0
Promise Spread															
Ultra, Easy Squeeze, fat-free — *1 Tbsp*	14	5	0	0	0	0	115	0	0	0	0	15	0	0	0
Ultra, fat-free — *1 Tbsp*	14	5	0	0	0	0	90	0	0	0	0	15	0	0	0

	Weight g	Calories	Calories from fat	Total fat g	Sat. fat g	Cholesterol mg	Sodium mg	Carbohydrates g	Dietary fiber g	Sugars g	Protein g	Vitamin A % DV	Vitamin C % DV	Calcium % DV	Iron % DV
Weight Watchers Margarine															
light — *1 Tbsp*	n/a	45	35	4	1	0	70	2	0	0	0	10	0	0	0
light, sodium-free — *1 Tbsp*	n/a	45	35	4	1	0	0	2	0	0	0	10	0	0	0
Cake: Frozen															
Pepperidge Farm All-Butter Pound Cake — *1/5 cake*	79	290	110	13	7	110	280	39	<1	21	5	0	0	4	4
Pepperidge Farm Layer Cake (large)															
chocolate fudge — *1/6 cake*	82	300	140	16	5	35	230	38	2	18	2	0	0	2	6
devil's food — *1/6 cake*	82	290	120	14	5	35	220	40	2	18	2	0	0	2	6
german chocolate — *1/6 cake*	82	300	140	16	4	35	280	37	2	18	2	0	0	4	4
golden — *1/6 cake*	82	290	120	14	3	50	230	40	n/a	36	3	0	0	4	6
vanilla — *1/6 cake*	82	290	120	13	2.5	45	190	41	<1	23	2	0	0	2	2
Pepperidge Farm Special Recipe															
boston cream — *1/8 cake*	82	260	80	9	2.5	45	120	42	<1	18	3	0	0	4	4
chocolate mousse — *1/8 cake*	74	250	100	10	3	25	120	35	2	20	2	0	0	0	6
deluxe carrot — *1/8 cake*	82	310	150	16	4	40	320	39	1	23	2	60	0	4	2
strawberry cream w/ coconut — *1/9 cake*	76	230	80	9	3	30	115	38	1	23	2	0	0	0	6
Sara Lee															
banana cake — *1/5 cake*	78	270	90	10	3.5	25	260	44	<1	33	2	2	0	<2	4
carrot cake — *1/6 cake*	90	320	150	17	3.5	30	340	39	2	35	4	40	0	2	6
chocolate swirl cake — *1/4 cake*	83	330	140	16	8	75	350	42	<1	31	5	4	0	6	10
strawberry shortcake — *1/8 cake*	71	180	70	7	5	15	140	27	<1	15	2	<2	15	2	2
Sara Lee Butter Streusel Coffee Cake — *1/6 cake*	54	220	110	12	6	35	240	25	<1	11	4	6	0	2	4
Sara Lee Cheesecake															
cherry cream — *1/4 cake*	135	350	100	12	5	35	310	55	2	35	6	2	25	4	6

	Weight g	Calories	Calories from fat	Total fat g	Sat. fat g	Cholesterol mg	Sodium mg	Carbohydrates g	Dietary fiber g	Sugars g	Protein g	Vitamin A % DV	Vitamin C % DV	Calcium % DV	Iron % DV
chocolate chip — *¼ cake*	120	410	180	21	14	65	300	47	2	43	8	6	2	6	10
crumb — *⅛ cake*	57	220	80	9	1.5	15	210	32	<1	17	3	<2	0	2	4
french — *⅓ cake*	133	410	230	25	16	25	330	41	1	27	6	2	2	6	6
original cream — *¼ cake*	121	350	160	18	9	50	320	39	1	30	7	2	0	8	4
pecan — *⅙ cake*	54	230	110	12	4.5	25	170	24	<1	9	4	2	0	2	6
raspberry — *⅙ cake*	54	200	70	8	2.5	15	220	27	<1	13	3	<2	0	<2	4
reduced-fat cheese — *⅙ cake*	54	180	50	6	1.5	20	230	28	0	11	3	0	0	4	4
reduced-fat cream — *¼ cake*	120	310	120	13	8	70	310	40	2	28	9	6	0	10	8
strawberry cream — *¼ cake*	135	330	110	12	5	40	310	49	2	36	6	<2	30	4	6
strawberry french — *⅙ cake*	123	320	130	14	9	20	230	43	1	26	4	<2	20	4	4
Sara Lee Chocolate Mousse Cake — *⅓ cake*	122	400	230	25	20	30	190	37	2	27	5	4	0	6	10
Sara Lee Layer Cake															
chocolate — *⅛ cake*	83	280	130	15	11	30	160	34	2	30	4	2	<2	4	6
double chocolate — *⅛ cake*	80	260	120	13	11	25	180	33	2	29	3	2	0	4	8
flaky coconut — *⅛ cake*	81	280	130	14	12	30	170	34	2	25	3	<2	0	4	8
fudge golden — *⅛ cake*	80	270	120	13	11	25	130	34	1	27	3	2	0	4	4
vanilla — *⅛ cake*	80	250	120	13	10	35	140	31	0	25	2	<2	0	2	4
Sara Lee Pound Cake															
family — *⅙ cake*	76	320	150	16	9	85	280	38	<1	21	4	8	<2	2	6
Free & Light — *¼ cake*	71	200	35	4	1	0	290	39	1	21	3	10	0	2	20
golden — *¼ cake*	76	300	120	13	3.5	75	250	41	<1	29	4	2	0	2	6
reduced-fat — *¼ cake*	76	280	100	11	3	65	350	42	<1	26	4	6	0	2	8
regular — *¼ cake*	76	320	150	16	9	85	280	38	<1	21	4	8	<2	2	6
strawberry swirl — *¼ cake*	83	290	100	11	3	60	140	44	<1	25	4	2	0	4	5

	Weight g	Calories	Calories from fat	Total fat g	Sat. fat g	Cholesterol mg	Sodium mg	Carbohydrates g	Dietary fiber g	Sugars g	Protein g	Vitamin A % DV	Vitamin C % DV	Calcium % DV	Iron % DV
Weight Watchers Cheesecake															
french-style — *1 cake*	110	180	45	5	2	15	230	28	2	9	7	4	4	8	2
new york-style — *1 cake*	71	150	45	5	2	10	140	21	0	17	6	0	0	8	0
triple chocolate — *1 cake*	89	200	45	5	2.5	10	200	32	1	20	7	0	0	8	6

Cake: Mixes

	Weight g	Calories	Calories from fat	Total fat g	Sat. fat g	Cholesterol mg	Sodium mg	Carbohydrates g	Dietary fiber g	Sugars g	Protein g	Vitamin A % DV	Vitamin C % DV	Calcium % DV	Iron % DV
Aunt Jemima Easy Mix Coffee Cake — *1/3 cup unprepared*	39	168	45	5	<1	<1	243	30	<1	17	2	0	0	6	7
Betty Crocker Classic Dessert Mix															
boston cream pie — *1/10 cake*	n/a	200	40	4.5	1.5	25	300	38	0	28	3	0	0	10	4
chocolate pudding cake — *1/8 cake*	n/a	170	30	3.5	1	25	180	33	<1	21	2	0	0	2	4
gingerbread cake — *1/8 cake*	n/a	230	60	7	2	25	370	38	0	20	3	0	0	6	8
golden pound cake — *1/8 cake*	n/a	290	110	13	3.5	55	240	41	0	23	4	0	0	4	6
lemon chiffon cake — *1/16 cake*	n/a	140	30	3	0.5	25	140	26	0	16	3	0	0	2	2
lemon pudding cake — *1/8 cake*	n/a	180	35	4	1	35	210	33	0	24	2	0	0	2	2
pineapple upside down cake — *1/6 cake*	n/a	400	130	15	4	35	350	63	<1	43	3	4	0	6	4
Betty Crocker Super Moist															
butter chocolate — *1/12 cake*	n/a	270	120	13	7	75	380	34	1	21	4	6	0	4	8
butter pecan — *1/12 cake*	n/a	250	100	11	2.5	55	300	34	0	20	3	0	0	8	4
butter yellow — *1/12 cake*	n/a	260	100	11	6	75	330	37	0	23	3	6	0	6	4
carrot cake — *1/10 cake*	n/a	300	120	13	3	65	360	41	0	25	4	0	0	6	6
cherry chip — *1/10 cake*	n/a	280	110	12	3	0	350	40	0	23	3	0	0	8	4
chocolate chip — *1/12 cake*	n/a	280	130	14	3	55	290	35	0	20	3	0	0	8	4
chocolate fudge — *1/12 cake*	n/a	250	100	11	3	55	430	34	1	20	3	0	0	6	6
devil's food — *1/12 cake*	n/a	250	110	12	3	55	380	33	1	20	3	0	0	4	6
double chocolate swirl — *1/12 cake*	n/a	250	100	12	3	55	390	33	1	20	4	0	0	6	8

	Weight g	Calories	Calories from fat	Total fat g	Sat. fat g	Cholesterol mg	Sodium mg	Carbohydrates g	Dietary fiber g	Sugars g	Protein g	Vitamin A % DV	Vitamin C % DV	Calcium % DV	Iron % DV
french vanilla — *1/12 cake*	n/a	250	90	10	2.5	55	280	35	0	20	3	0	0	8	4
fudge marble — *1/12 cake*	n/a	250	100	11	2.5	55	270	35	0	21	3	0	0	8	4
german chocolate — *1/12 cake*	n/a	250	100	11	3	55	410	34	<1	20	3	0	0	2	6
golden vanilla — *1/12 cake*	n/a	280	130	14	3	55	260	35	0	20	3	0	0	6	6
lemon — *1/12 cake*	n/a	250	100	11	2.5	55	260	36	0	21	3	0	0	8	6
milk chocolate — *1/12 cake*	n/a	250	110	12	3	55	320	33	1	21	3	0	0	6	6
Party Swirl — *1/12 cake*	n/a	250	100	11	2.5	55	280	35	0	21	3	0	0	8	4
peanut butter chocolate swirl — *1/12 cake*	n/a	240	90	10	2.5	55	320	34	0	19	4	0	0	8	6
rainbow chip — *1/12 cake*	n/a	250	100	11	3	55	310	34	0	20	3	0	0	8	4
sour cream white — *1/10 cake*	n/a	280	110	12	3	0	380	39	0	22	4	0	0	8	4
spice — *1/12 cake*	n/a	250	100	11	2.5	55	310	35	0	20	3	0	0	10	6
strawberry swirl — *1/12 cake*	n/a	290	110	12	3	65	330	41	0	25	5	0	0	8	6
white — *1/12 cake*	n/a	240	90	10	2.5	0	310	34	0	19	3	0	0	6	4
white chocolate swirl — *1/12 cake*	n/a	250	100	11	2.5	55	290	36	0	20	4	0	0	8	6
yellow — *1/12 cake*	n/a	250	90	10	2.5	55	300	36	0	22	3	0	0	8	4
yellow, light — *1/10 cake*	n/a	230	40	4.5	2	65	350	43	0	25	4	0	0	8	6
Betty Crocker Super Moist Angel Food															
chocolate swirl — *1/12 cake*	n/a	150	0	0	0	0	280	34	0	24	3	0	0	6	0
Confetti — *1/12 cake*	n/a	150	0	0	0	0	300	34	0	23	3	0	0	6	0
lemon custard — *1/12 cake*	n/a	140	0	0	0	0	290	33	0	22	3	0	0	6	0
One-Step white — *1/12 cake*	n/a	140	0	0	0	0	280	32	0	23	3	0	0	15	0
traditional — *1/12 cake*	n/a	130	0	0	0	0	160	30	0	23	3	0	0	4	0
Betty Crocker Super Moist Light															
devil's food — *1/10 cake*	n/a	230	40	4.5	2	65	400	43	2	25	4	0	0	8	10

	Weight *g*	Calories	Calories from fat	Total fat *g*	Sat. fat *g*	Cholesterol *mg*	Sodium *mg*	Carbohydrates *g*	Dietary fiber *g*	Sugars *g*	Protein *g*	Vitamin A *% DV*	Vitamin C *% DV*	Calcium *% DV*	Iron *% DV*
white — *1/10 cake*	n/a	210	30	3.5	1.5	0	390	43	0	24	3	0	0	10	6
Duncan Hines															
angel food 1-step — *1/12 cake*	n/a	130	0	0	0	0	320	30	0	22	3	<2	<2	2	2
angel food 2-step — *1/12 cake*	n/a	140	0	0	0	0	115	30	1	24	4	<2	<2	2	2
chocolate-based — *1/12 cake*	n/a	290	130	15	3	50	360	34	1	20	4	<2	<2	6	6
white (made w/ egg whites) — *1/12 cake*	n/a	240	90	10	2	0	220	36	n/a	21	2	<2	<2	6	6
yellow-based — *1/12 cake*	n/a	250	100	11	2	50	290	36	n/a	22	3	<2	<2	8	6
Pillsbury Bundt Cake Mix															
chocolate caramel nut — *1/16 cake*	n/a	290	170	18	4	40	210	28	<1	18	3	0	0	4	8
hot fudge — *1/12 cake*	n/a	350	180	20	6	55	280	39	1	24	4	0	0	6	10
strawberry cream cheese — *1/16 cake*	n/a	300	150	17	4.5	60	200	34	0	21	3	2	0	4	6
Pillsbury Gingerbread Mix — *1/8 cake*	n/a	220	45	5	1.5	0	340	40	<1	20	3	0	0	4	15
Pillsbury Moist Supreme															
angel food — *1/12 cake*	n/a	140	0	0	0	0	330	31	0	23	3	0	0	4	2
banana — *1/12 cake*	n/a	260	100	11	2.5	55	280	36	0	21	3	0	0	4	6
butter-recipe chocolate — *1/12 cake*	n/a	270	120	13	7	75	420	33	1	18	3	8	0	4	10
carrot — *1/12 cake*	n/a	260	110	12	2.5	55	290	35	<1	19	3	10	0	4	8
chocolate — *1/12 cake*	n/a	250	100	11	2.5	35	280	35	<1	20	3	0	0	2	6
devil's food — *1/12 cake*	n/a	270	130	14	3	55	340	33	1	18	4	0	0	2	10
french vanilla — *1/10 cake*	n/a	300	120	13	3	45	350	42	1	23	0	0	0	0	8
fudge swirl — *1/12 cake*	n/a	250	90	10	2.5	55	290	37	1	22	3	0	0	0	0
Funfetti — *1/12 cake*	n/a	240	80	9	2	0	290	36	<1	20	3	0	0	0	6
german chocolate — *1/12 cake*	n/a	250	100	11	2.5	35	280	34	<1	18	3	0	0	4	8
lemon — *1/10 cake*	n/a	300	120	13	3	65	350	42	1	23	4	0	0	4	8

	Weight *g*	Calories	Calories from fat	Total fat *g*	Sat. fat *g*	Cholesterol *mg*	Sodium *mg*	Carbohydrates *g*	Dietary fiber *g*	Sugars *g*	Protein *g*	Vitamin A *% DV*	Vitamin C *% DV*	Calcium *% DV*	Iron *% DV*
white — *1/10 cake*	n/a	280	100	11	2.5	0	350	41	<1	23	3	0	0	0	6
yellow — *1/12 cake*	n/a	240	90	10	2.5	55	290	35	<1	19	3	0	0	0	6
Pillsbury Streusel Swirl, Cinnamon — *1/16 cake*	n/a	260	100	11	2.5	40	220	37	0	22	3	0	0	4	6
SnackWell's															
devil's food — *1/6 cake*	n/a	200	35	4	1.5	35	380	38	2	23	3	0	0	15	10
white — *1/6 cake*	n/a	210	40	4.5	1.5	35	320	39	1	23	3	0	0	8	6
yellow — *1/6 cake*	n/a	210	40	4.5	1.5	35	320	39	1	24	3	0	0	8	6
Sweet Rewards Fat-Free															
apple cinnamon — *1/8 cake*	n/a	170	0	0	0	0	250	39	0	26	2	0	0	8	4
banana — *1/8 cake*	n/a	170	0	0	0	0	280	39	0	27	3	0	0	6	4
chocolate — *1/8 cake*	n/a	170	0	0	0	0	390	38	<1	24	3	0	0	6	8
lemon — *1/8 cake*	n/a	170	0	0	0	0	270	39	0	27	2	0	0	4	4
Sweet Rewards Reduced-Fat															
devil's food — *1/12 cake*	n/a	220	70	7	2	55	370	35	1	20	4	0	0	4	6
white — *1/12 cake*	n/a	210	50	6	1.5	0	300	35	0	20	3	0	0	6	4
yellow — *1/12 cake*	n/a	220	60	6	1.5	55	300	36	0	20	3	0	0	8	4

Cake: Ready-to-eat

	Weight *g*	Calories	Calories from fat	Total fat *g*	Sat. fat *g*	Cholesterol *mg*	Sodium *mg*	Carbohydrates *g*	Dietary fiber *g*	Sugars *g*	Protein *g*	Vitamin A *% DV*	Vitamin C *% DV*	Calcium *% DV*	Iron *% DV*
Entenmann's															
all-butter loaf — *1/6 loaf*	57	220	90	10	6	80	290	30	1	18	3	8	0	2	0
apple topped cake, fat-free — *1/6 cake*	80	180	0	0	0	0	210	43	1	30	2	0	0	0	0
carrot cake, fat-free — *1/8 cake*	71	170	0	0	0	0	230	40	1	27	3	45	0	4	4
chocolate chip crumb, filled — *1/8 cake*	78	360	180	20	4.5	35	180	45	1	33	3	0	0	2	2
chocolate fudge — *1/6 cake*	85	310	130	14	4.5	20	290	46	2	36	3	0	0	4	15
chocolate, creme-filled — *1/8 cake*	74	300	150	16	4.5	30	230	40	1	31	3	2	0	4	10

	Weight *g*	Calories	Calories from fat	Total fat *g*	Sat. fat *g*	Cholesterol *mg*	Sodium *mg*	Carbohydrates *g*	Dietary fiber *g*	Sugars *g*	Protein *g*	Vitamin A *% DV*	Vitamin C *% DV*	Calcium *% DV*	Iron *% DV*
coffee cake, cinnamon apple, fat-free — *1/9 cake*	54	130	0	0	0	0	110	29	2	16	2	0	0	2	2
coffee cake, crumb — *1/10 cake*	57	250	110	12	3	15	210	33	1	13	4	4	0	2	2
crumb coffee cake, cheese-filled — *1/8 cake*	57	200	90	10	3	35	190	25	1	12	4	2	0	2	0
crumb loaf, chocolate chip — *1/8 loaf*	57	250	110	12	3	45	220	33	1	18	3	0	0	2	2
danish ring, walnut — *1/8 danish*	53	230	130	14	3	30	160	23	1	11	4	4	0	4	4
danish twist, raspberry — *1/8 danish*	53	220	100	11	3	20	190	28	1	14	3	4	0	4	2
devil's food, marshmallow- iced — *1/6 cake*	85	340	160	18	4.5	20	320	44	1	35	3	0	0	4	4
devil's food, marshmallow-iced, fat-free — *1/6 cake*	83	200	0	0	0	0	320	48	2	35	3	0	0	0	6
golden loaf, fat-free — *1/8 loaf*	48	130	0	0	0	0	160	28	1	17	2	2	0	0	0
Louisiana Crunch Cake — *1/9 cake*	76	310	120	13	3.5	50	290	45	1	32	3	0	0	4	2
Louisiana Crunch Cake, fat-free — *1/6 cake*	76	220	0	0	0	0	220	51	1	35	3	6	0	2	0
sponge ring, lemon-glazed — *1/5 cake*	74	270	80	9	2	60	310	46	0	35	3	2	0	6	0

Cake: Snack Cakes & Cupcakes

	Weight *g*	Calories	Calories from fat	Total fat *g*	Sat. fat *g*	Cholesterol *mg*	Sodium *mg*	Carbohydrates *g*	Dietary fiber *g*	Sugars *g*	Protein *g*	Vitamin A *% DV*	Vitamin C *% DV*	Calcium *% DV*	Iron *% DV*
Ding Dong (Hostess) — *2 cakes*	78	360	170	19	12	15	230	44	1	32	3	0	0	2	10
Entenmann's Creme-Filled Chocolate Cupcakes, Fat-Free — *1 cake*	57	160	0	0	0	0	150	40	1	33	1	0	0	15	4
HoHo (Hostess) — *2 cakes*	57	250	110	12	8	20	140	33	1	23	2	0	0	2	6
Hostess Chocolate Cupcake															
light — *1 cake*	48	140	15	1.5	0.5	0	180	29	0	19	1	0	0	0	4
regular — *1 cake*	50	180	50	6	2.5	5	280	30	1	17	2	0	0	10	6
Pop-Tarts (Kellogg's)															
blueberry — *1 pastry*	52	210	60	7	1	0	210	36	1	16	2	10	0	0	10
blueberry, frosted — *1 pastry*	52	200	50	5	1	0	210	37	1	16	2	10	0	0	10
blueberry, low-fat — *1 pastry*	52	190	25	3	0.5	0	220	40	1	19	2	10	0	0	10
chocolate fudge, frosted — *1 pastry*	52	200	40	5	1	0	200	37	1	20	3	10	0	0	10

	Weight g	Calories	Calories from fat	Total fat g	Sat. fat g	Cholesterol mg	Sodium mg	Carbohydrates g	Dietary fiber g	Sugars g	Protein g	Vitamin A % DV	Vitamin C % DV	Calcium % DV	Iron % DV
frosted chocolate fudge, low-fat — *1 pastry*	52	190	25	3	0.5	0	250	39	1	19	3	10	0	0	10
milk chocolate graham — *1 pastry*	52	210	50	6	1.5	0	230	36	1	18	3	10	0	0	10
strawberry — *1 pastry*	52	200	50	5	1.5	0	180	37	1	17	2	10	0	0	10
strawberry, frosted — *1 pastry*	52	200	50	5	1.5	0	170	38	1	19	2	10	0	0	10
strawberry, frosted, low-fat — *1 pastry*	52	190	25	3	0.5	0	200	40	1	21	2	10	0	0	10
strawberry, low-fat — *1 pastry*	52	190	25	3	0.5	0	220	40	1	19	2	10	0	0	10
Toast-R-Cakes (Thomas')															
banana nut — *1 cake*	33	110	40	5	0.5	<5	170	16	<1	8	2	0	0	0	4
blueberry — *1 cake*	33	100	25	3	0.5	<5	160	17	<1	9	1	0	0	0	2
chocolate chip — *1 cake*	33	100	35	4	n/a	n/a	150	15	2	n/a	2	n/a	n/a	n/a	2
corn — *1 cake*	33	110	35	4	0.5	<5	180	19	<1	8	2	0	0	0	2
raisin bran — *1 cake*	33	90	25	3	0	<5	170	17	1	9	2	0	0	0	4
Toaster Strudel Breakfast Pastries (Pillsbury)															
apple — *1 pastry*	54	180	60	7	1.5	5	190	27	<1	10	3	0	0	0	4
blueberry — *1 pastry*	54	180	60	7	1.5	5	200	26	<1	10	3	0	0	0	4
cherry — *1 pastry*	54	180	60	7	1.5	5	200	26	<1	11	3	0	0	0	4
cinnamon — *1 pastry*	54	190	70	8	1.5	5	200	26	<1	10	3	0	0	0	4
cream cheese & blueberry — *1 pastry*	54	190	80	9	3	10	220	24	<1	9	3	0	0	0	6
cream cheese & strawberry — *1 pastry*	54	190	80	9	3	10	220	24	<1	9	3	0	0	0	6
strawberry — *1 pastry*	54	180	60	7	1.5	5	200	26	<1	10	3	0	0	0	4
Twinkie (Hostess)															
light — *1 cake*	43	130	15	1.5	0.5	10	190	27	0	16	1	0	0	0	2
regular — *1 cake*	43	150	45	5	2	20	190	25	0	14	1	0	0	0	2

Candy: Baking

	Weight g	Calories	Calories from fat	Total fat g	Sat. fat g	Cholesterol mg	Sodium mg	Carbohydrates g	Dietary fiber g	Sugars g	Protein g	Vitamin A % DV	Vitamin C % DV	Calcium % DV	Iron % DV
Hershey's Bits for Baking															
Almond Joy coconut & almond — *2 Tbsp*	n/a	60	30	3.5	2	n/a	0	7	n/a	6	<1	0	0	0	0
holiday — *1 Tbsp*	n/a	70	25	3	2	n/a	0	11	n/a	10	<1	0	0	0	0
Hershey's Chips															
butterscotch — *1 Tbsp*	n/a	80	35	4	4	0	10	10	0	9	<1	0	0	2	0
chocolate, semi-sweet, reduced-fat — *1 Tbsp*	n/a	60	20	3.5	3.5	0	0	10	0	9	<1	0	0	0	0
mint — *1 Tbsp*	n/a	80	35	4	2.5	0	0	10	0	8	1	0	0	0	2
raspberry — *1 Tbsp*	n/a	80	35	4	2.5	n/a	0	10	0	8	<1	0	0	0	2
vanilla — *1 Tbsp*	n/a	80	35	4	3	n/a	30	9	n/a	9	1	0	0	2	0
M&M's Baking Bits															
chocolate, milk — *1 Tbsp*	n/a	70	30	3.5	2	5	10	10	0	9	1	0	0	0	0
chocolate, semi-sweet — *1 Tbsp*	n/a	70	35	3.5	2	0	0	9	1	8	1	0	0	0	2
Nestlé Crunch Baking Pieces — *1 ½ Tbsp*	n/a	70	30	3	2	0	25	10	0	8	<1	0	0	0	0
Nestlé Morsels															
butterscotch — *1 Tbsp*	n/a	80	35	4	3.5	0	15	9	0	9	0	0	0	0	0
chocolate, milk — *1 Tbsp*	n/a	70	40	4	2.5	<5	0	9	0	8	<1	0	0	0	0
chocolate, mint — *1 Tbsp*	n/a	70	35	4	2	0	0	9	2	7	0	0	0	0	0
chocolate, semi-sweet — *1 Tbsp*	n/a	70	40	4	2	0	0	9	2	7	0	0	0	0	0
Reese's															
Bits for Baking — *1 Tbsp*	n/a	70	25	3	1.5	n/a	40	10	n/a	9	<1	0	0	0	0
peanut butter chips — *1 Tbsp*	n/a	80	35	4	4	n/a	35	7	n/a	6	3	0	0	2	0
Skor English Toffee Bits for Baking — *1 Tbsp*	n/a	70	40	4.5	2.5	10	60	7	n/a	7	0	0	0	0	0

Candy: Chocolate

	Weight g	Calories	Calories from fat	Total fat g	Sat. fat g	Cholesterol mg	Sodium mg	Carbohydrates g	Dietary fiber g	Sugars g	Protein g	Vitamin A % DV	Vitamin C % DV	Calcium % DV	Iron % DV
Almond Joy — *1 bar*	50	240	120	13	8	0	70	29	2	22	2	0	0	2	2
Baby Ruth 75th Anniversary — *1 bar*	59	280	120	13	7	0	130	36	1	27	4	0	0	2	0
Buncha Cruncha — *1 bag*	40	200	90	10	6	10	60	26	<1	20	2	0	0	4	0
Butterfinger — *1 bar*	59	280	100	11	6	0	120	41	1	29	4	0	0	0	2
Butterfinger BB's — *1 bag*	48	230	90	10	7	0	90	34	1	32	2	0	0	0	2
Cadbury's															
Caramello — *1 bar*	45	220	90	10	6	10	60	29	<1	22	3	0	0	8	2
Krisp Milk — *9 pieces*	142	200	90	10	10	10	80	25	<1	19	3	0	0	8	2
mint chocolate — *5 pieces*	142	190	70	8	5	<5	5	27	1	22	2	0	0	0	2
roast almond — *9 pieces*	142	220	120	13	7	10	80	21	1	18	4	0	0	10	2
Dove															
chocolate, dark — *1 bar*	36.9	200	110	12	7	5	0	22	2	19	2	<2	<2	<2	4
chocolate, milk — *1 bar*	36.9	200	110	12	7	5	25	22	1	21	2	2	<2	6	<2
5th Avenue — *1 bar*	57	280	110	12	5	<5	95	38	1	26	5	0	0	4	4
Goobers — *1 bag*	39	210	120	13	5	<5	20	19	3	16	5	0	0	4	2
Hershey's															
Cookies 'n' Creme white chocolate bar — *1 bar*	43	230	120	13	7	5	85	24	0	21	4	0	0	10	0
Cookies 'n' Creme white chocolate nuggets — *4 pieces*	40	200	100	11	6	5	75	22	0	19	4	0	0	10	0
Cookies 'n' Mint chocolate bar — *1 bar*	44	230	110	12	6	10	80	27	1	21	3	0	0	8	4
Cookies 'n' Mint milk chocolate nuggets — *4 pieces*	40	200	90	10	5	5	70	24	1	19	3	0	0	6	4
milk chocolate bar — *1 bar*	44	230	120	13	9	10	40	25	1	22	3	0	0	8	2
milk chocolate bar w/ almonds — *1 bar*	41	230	130	14	7	5	35	20	1	18	5	0	0	8	4
milk chocolate nuggets — *4 pieces*	40	210	110	12	8	10	35	23	1	20	3	0	0	8	2

	Weight g	Calories	Calories from fat	Total fat g	Sat. fat g	Cholesterol mg	Sodium mg	Carbohydrates g	Dietary fiber g	Sugars g	Protein g	Vitamin A % DV	Vitamin C % DV	Calcium % DV	Iron % DV
milk chocolate w/ almond nuggets — *4 pieces*	40	210	120	13	6	5	30	20	1	16	4	0	0	8	2
Miniatures — *5 pieces*	397	230	120	13	7	5	30	25	1	22	3	0	0	4	2
Special Dark — *1 bar*	41	230	120	13	8	0	0	25	2	19	2	0	0	0	6
Hershey's Golden Collection															
Almond — *1 bar*	79	450	270	30	13	10	50	36	3	30	10	0	0	15	8
macadamia chocolate bar — *1 bar*	68	380	220	24	11	15	60	35	2	28	6	0	0	15	2
Solitaires — *1 pouch*	79	450	260	29	12	10	45	37	3	29	9	0	0	15	10
Hershey's Hugs															
plain — *8 pieces*	368	200	100	11	7	10	30	n/a	0	22	3	0	0	8	0
w/ almonds — *9 pieces*	368	230	130	14	7	10	30	22	<1	21	3	0	0	8	0
Hershey's Kisses															
plain — *8 kisses*	397	210	110	12	8	10	35	23	1	20	3	0	0	8	2
w/ almonds — *8 kisses*	397	210	120	13	7	5	25	19	1	17	4	0	0	8	4
Hershey's Sweet Escapes															
Chocolate Toffee Crisp — *l bar*	40	190	70	8	5	<5	90	27	<1	22	3	0	0	6	2
Triple Chocolate Wafer Bar — *1 bar*	40	160	45	5	2.5	n/a	55	27	n/a	24	1	n/a	n/a	2	2
Hershey's Symphony															
plain — *1 bar*	43	230	130	14	9	10	40	24	<1	21	3	0	0	10	2
w/ almonds & toffee chips — *1 bar*	43	240	140	15	8	10	60	22	1	19	4	0	0	8	2
Kit Kat — *1 bar*	43	220	110	12	8	5	35	26	<1	18	3	0	0	4	0
Krackel — *1 bar*	41	220	110	12	7	10	55	25	1	21	3	0	0	6	2
Kudos — *1 bar*	27.8	120	40	4.5	2.5	5	80	19	1	11	2	10	10	20	10
M&M's															
almond — *1 bag*	37.1	200	100	11	3k5	5	15	21	2	18	3	<2	<2	4	2

Foods, Brand Name

	Weight g	Calories	Calories from fat	Total fat g	Sat. fat g	Cholesterol mg	Sodium mg	Carbohydrates g	Dietary fiber g	Sugars g	Protein g	Vitamin A % DV	Vitamin C % DV	Calcium % DV	Iron % DV
peanut — *1 bag*	49	250	120	13	5	5	25	30	2	25	5	<2	<2	4	2
peanut butter — *1 bag*	46	240	120	13	8	5	95	27	2	22	5	<2	<2	4	2
plain — *1 bag*	48	240	90	10	6	5	30	34	1	31	2	<2	<2	4	2
Mars Almond Bar — *1 bar*	50	240	110	12	4	5	80	31	1	26	3	<2	<2	6	2
Milky Way															
lite — *1 bar*	45	170	50	5	3	5	80	34	0	24	1	<2	<2	2	<2
regular — *1 bar*	61	280	100	11	5	5	100	43	1	37	2	<2	<2	6	<2
Mounds — *1 bar*	54	250	120	13	11	0	80	31	3	21	2	0	0	0	6
Mr. Goodbar — *1 bar*	50	270	150	17	7	5	20	25	2	21	5	0	0	4	4
Nestlé															
Chunky — *1 bar*	40	210	100	11	6	5	20	24	1	21	3	0	0	4	2
Crunch — *1 bar*	44	230	100	12	7	10	65	29	<1	24	2	0	0	4	0
milk chocolate — *1 bar*	41	220	110	13	7	10	30	23	2	21	4	0	0	8	0
Nutrageous — *1 bar*	45	240	140	15	4	0	80	22	4	18	5	0	0	2	2
Oh Henry! — *1 pkg*	51	230	80	9	4	<5	125	32	2	30	6	0	0	4	0
100 Grand — *1 bar*	43	200	70	8	5	10	75	30	<1	27	2	0	0	4	0
Raisinets — *1 bag*	45	200	70	8	4	<5	15	31	2	28	2	0	0	4	2
Reese's Peanut Butter Cups															
crunchy — *2 cups*	45	250	140	16	6	<5	75	21	2	16	6	0	0	4	2
regular — *2 cups*	45	240	130	14	6	<5	150	24	1	19	5	0	0	2	2
Rolo Caramels in Milk Chocolate — *1 pkg*	54	220	100	11	6	10	95	28	0	26	3	0	0	8	0
Skor — *1 bar*	40	220	120	13	9	20	110	23	1	21	2	0	0	4	0
Snickers — *1 bar*	59	280	130	14	5	19	159	35	1	28	5	<2	<2	4	2
Sno Caps — *1 box*	65	300	110	13	8	0	0	48	3	38	2	0	0	0	6

	Weight g	Calories	Calories from fat	Total fat g	Sat. fat g	Cholesterol mg	Sodium mg	Carbohydrates g	Dietary fiber g	Sugars g	Protein g	Vitamin A % DV	Vitamin C % DV	Calcium % DV	Iron % DV
3 Musketeers — *1 bar*	60	260	70	8	4.5	5	110	46	1	40	2	<2	<2	2	2
Turtles — *2 pieces*	n/a	160	80	9	3	<5	30	20	1	13	2	0	0	4	0
Whatchamacallit — *1 bar*	48	250	120	13	10	5	125	29	1	19	4	n/a	n/a	4	0
York Peppermint Patty — *1 bar*	43	150	25	3	2	n/a	10	34	n/a	27	<1	n/a	n/a	n/a	2

Candy: Sweets

	Weight g	Calories	Calories from fat	Total fat g	Sat. fat g	Cholesterol mg	Sodium mg	Carbohydrates g	Dietary fiber g	Sugars g	Protein g	Vitamin A % DV	Vitamin C % DV	Calcium % DV	Iron % DV
Amazin' Fruit Gummy Bears — *1 bag*	54	180	0	0	0	0	60	41	0	25	3	0	0	0	0
Hershey's Tastetations															
butterscotch or caramel — *3 pieces*	198	60	15	1.2	1	<5	75	11	n/a	9	0	0	0	0	0
chocolate — *3 pieces*	198	60	10	1	0.5	<5	35	12	n/a	11	0	0	0	0	0
peppermint — *3 pieces*	198	60	0	0	0	0	0	14	n/a	14	0	0	0	0	0
Kraft															
Butter Mints — *7 pieces*	15	60	0	0	0	0	35	14	0	14	0	0	0	0	0
caramels — *5 pieces*	41	170	30	3	1	<5	110	32	0	27	2	0	0	8	0
Fudgies — *5 pieces*	41	180	45	5	2.5	0	90	32	0	27	1	0	0	2	2
party mints — *7 pieces*	15	60	0	0	0	0	35	14	0	14	0	0	0	0	0
peanut brittle — *5 pieces*	38	170	40	5	1	0	310	29	1	21	3	0	0	0	0
Lifesavers															
assorted — *4 candies*	10	40	0	0	0	0	0	10	0	8	0	0	0	0	0
butter rum — *4 candies*	10	38	0	0	0	0	47	9	0	9	0	0	0	0	0
Gummi Savers, five-flavor — *11 candies*	39	130	0	0	0	0	0	30	0	20	2	0	0	0	0
Nibs															
cherry — *22 pieces*	170	140	10	1	n/a	n/a	85	31	n/a	17	1	0	0	0	0
licorice — *22 pieces*	170	140	10	1	n/a	n/a	220	31	n/a	16	1	0	0	0	0
Reese's Pieces — *1 bag*	46	230	90	10	8	0	75	28	1	24	6	0	0	4	2

	Weight *g*	Calories	Calories from fat	Total fat *g*	Sat. fat *g*	Cholesterol *mg*	Sodium *mg*	Carbohydrates *g*	Dietary fiber *g*	Sugars *g*	Protein *g*	Vitamin A *% DV*	Vitamin C *% DV*	Calcium *% DV*	Iron *% DV*
Skittles — *1 bag*	61.5	250	25	3	1	0	10	55	0	47	0	<2	50	<2	<2
Twizzlers															
cherry — *4 pieces*	142	150	10	1	0	n/a	125	33	n/a	18	1	n/a	n/a	n/a	n/a
chocolate — *5 pieces*	113	140	10	1	0.5	n/a	160	31	n/a	15	1	n/a	n/a	n/a	n/a
licorice — *4 pieces*	198	140	5	0.5	0	n/a	230	33	n/a	15	1	n/a	n/a	n/a	2
Pull 'n' Peel Cherry — *1 piece*	n/a	110	10	1	0	n/a	85	23	1	17	1	n/a	n/a	n/a	2
strawberry — *4 pieces*	142	140	5	0.5	0	n/a	105	33	n/a	15	1	n/a	n/a	n/a	n/a

Cereal: Hot

	Weight *g*	Calories	Calories from fat	Total fat *g*	Sat. fat *g*	Cholesterol *mg*	Sodium *mg*	Carbohydrates *g*	Dietary fiber *g*	Sugars *g*	Protein *g*	Vitamin A *% DV*	Vitamin C *% DV*	Calcium *% DV*	Iron *% DV*
Cream of Wheat (Nabisco) — *1 cup*	n/a	120	0	0	0	0	90	25	1	0	3	0	0	10	50
H-O Cream Farina — *1 cup*	n/a	120	0	0	0	0	0	26	1	0	3	0	0	0	6
100% Wheat Hot Cereal (Ralston) — *½ cup*	42	150	10	1	n/a	n/a	0	31	5	n/a	5	0	0	0	8
Quaker Instant Oatmeal															
low-sodium (unprepared) — *1 packet*	28	100	20	2	0	0	80	19	3	0	4	25	2	20	70
raisin, date & walnut (unprepared) — *1 packet*	37	130	20	2.5	0.5	0	240	27	3	12	3	20	0	15	30
Strawberries 'N Stuff (unprepared) — *1 packet*	40	150	20	2	0.5	0	170	31	3	13	3	25	0	15	30
Quaker Quick N' Hearty Instant Oatmeal															
apple spice (unprepared) — *1 packet*	45	170	20	2	0.5	0	280	35	3	15	8	20	0	10	20
brown sugar cinnamon — *1 packet*	42	200	20	2	0.5	0	325	37	3	18	8	25	2	25	20
honey bran (unprepared) — *1 packet*		150	20	2	0.5	0	250	30	3	12	4	20	0	10	20
regular (unprepared) — *1 packet*		110	20	2	0.5	0	150	19	2	1	4	20	0	10	45
Wheat Hearts (General Mills) — *¼ cup*	36	130	10	1	0	0	0	26	2	1	5	0	0	0	60

Cereal: Ready-to-eat

	Weight *g*	Calories	Calories from fat	Total fat *g*	Sat. fat *g*	Cholesterol *mg*	Sodium *mg*	Carbohydrates *g*	Dietary fiber *g*	Sugars *g*	Protein *g*	Vitamin A *% DV*	Vitamin C *% DV*	Calcium *% DV*	Iron *% DV*
All-Bran (Kellogg's) — *½ cup*	31	80	10	1	0	0	280	23	10	6	4	15	25	10	25
All-Bran, Extra Fiber (Kellogg's) — *½ cup*	26	50	10	0.5	0	0	110	20	13	0	3	15	25	10	25

	Weight g	Calories	Calories from fat	Total fat g	Sat. fat g	Cholesterol mg	Sodium mg	Carbohydrates g	Dietary fiber g	Sugars g	Protein g	Vitamin A % DV	Vitamin C % DV	Calcium % DV	Iron % DV
Alpha-Bits (Post) — *1 cup*	32	130	5	1	0	0	210	27	1	13	3	25	0	0	15
Amaranth Flakes (Health Valley) — *¾ cup*	n/a	100	0	0	0	0	35	24	4	4	3	2	0	0	4
Apple Cinnamon Squares (Kellogg's) — *¾ cup*	55	180	10	1	0	0	20	44	5	12	4	0	0	2	90
Apple Jacks (Kellogg's) — *1 cup*	33	120	0	0	0	0	150	30	1	16	2	15	25	0	25
Apple Raisin Crisp (Kellogg's) — *1 cup*	53	180	0	0	0	0	360	45	4	15	3	15	0	0	10
Apple Zaps (Quaker) — *1 cup*	30	118	9	1	<1	0	132	27	<1	14	1	20	20	0	25
Banana Nut Crunch (Post) — *1 cup*	59	250	50	6	1	0	200	43	4	11	5	25	0	2	10
Basic 4 (General Mills) — *1 cup*	55	210	30	3	0	0	330	42	3	13	4	25	25	25	25
Berry Berry (General Mills) — *¾ cup*	30	120	10	1.5	0	0	180	26	0	9	1	15	25	4	25
Betty Crocker Cereals (General Mills)															
dutch apple — *1 cup*	55	220	20	2	0	0	310	46	1	17	4	15	25	4	25
streusel — *¾ cup*	30	120	10	1.5	0	0	180	25	1	8	4	15	25	2	25
Blue Corn Bran Flakes (Health Valley) — *¾ cup*	n/a	100	0	0	n/a	0	10	24	4	4	3	2	0	0	4
Blueberry Squares (Kellogg's) — *¾ cup*	54	180	10	1	0	0	20	43	5	11	4	0	0	0	90
Body Buddies Natural Fruit (General Mills) — *1 cup*	30	120	10	1	0	0	290	26	0	6	2	15	25	4	45
Boo Berry (General Mills) — *1 cup*	30	120	5	0.5	0	0	210	27	0	14	1	0	25	2	25
Bran Buds (Kellogg's) — *⅓ cup*	30	80	5	0.5	0	0	200	24	12	8	3	15	25	2	25
Bran Cereal w/ Apples & Cinnamon (Health Valley) — *¾ cup*	n/a	160	0	0	n/a	0	10	41	7	10	5	2	0	0	10
Bran Cereal w/ Honey (Health Valley) — *¾ cup*	n/a	160	0	0	n/a	0	10	40	6	10	5	2	0	0	10
Bran Flakes (Post) — *⅔ cup*	28	90	5	0.5	0	0	210	22	6	5	3	25	0	0	45
Bran'Nola Original (Post) — *½ cup*	53	200	25	3	0.5	0	240	43	5	15	4	25	0	0	25
Bran-O's (Health Valley)															
apple cinnamon — *¾ cup*	n/a	100	0	0	n/a	0	90	23	3	4	3	2	0	0	6
regular — *½ cup*	n/a	100	0	0	n/a	0	90	23	3	5	3	2	0	0	4

	Weight g	Calories	Calories from fat	Total fat g	Sat. fat g	Cholesterol mg	Sodium mg	Carbohydrates g	Dietary fiber g	Sugars g	Protein g	Vitamin A % DV	Vitamin C % DV	Calcium % DV	Iron % DV
Cap'n Crunch (Quaker Oat)															
original — *¾ cup*	27	110	15	1.5	0.5	0	210	23	1	12	1	0	0	0	25
peanut butter — *¾ cup*	27	112	18	2	<1	0	204	22	<1	9	2	0	0	0	25
w/ Crunch Berries — *¾ cup*	26	100	15	1.5	0.5	0	190	22	1	11	1	0	0	0	25
Cheerios (General Mills)															
apple cinnamon — *¾ cup*	30	120	15	2	0	0	160	25	1	13	2	15	25	2	25
frosted — *1 cup*	30	120	10	1	0	0	210	25	1	13	2	15	25	2	25
honey nut — *1 cup*	30	120	10	1.5	0	0	270	24	2	11	3	15	25	0	25
multi-grain — *1 cup*	30	110	10	1	0	0	240	24	3	6	3	15	25	4	45
original — *1 cup*	30	110	15	2	0	0	280	23	3	1	3	25	25	4	45
Cinnamon Oat Squares (Quaker) — *1 cup*	60	230	25	2.5	0.5	0	260	48	5	13	7	10	10	4	80
Cinnamon Toast Crunch (General Mills) — *¾ cup*	30	130	30	3.5	0.5	0	210	24	1	10	1	15	25	4	25
Cocoa Blasts (Quaker) — *1 cup*	33	129	9	1	<1	0	133	29	<1	16	1	22	22	0	27
Cocoa Krispies (Kellogg's) — *¾ cup*	31	120	10	1	0.5	0	210	27	0	13	2	15	25	0	10
Cocoa Pebbles (Post) — *¾ cup*	29	120	10	1	1	0	160	25	<1	13	1	25	0	0	10
Cocoa Puffs (General Mills) — *1 cup*	30	120	10	1	0	0	190	27	0	14	1	0	25	2	25
Common Sense Oat Bran Flakes (Kellogg's) — *¾ cup*	30	110	10	1	0	0	270	23	4	6	4	15	0	0	45
Complete Bran Flakes (Kellogg's) — *¾ cup*	29	90	5	0.5	0	0	230	24	5	5	3	25	25	0	45
Corn Flakes (Kellogg's) — *1 cup*	28	100	0	0	0	0	300	24	1	2	2	15	25	0	45
Corn Pops (Kellogg's) — *1 cup*	31	120	0	0	0	0	120	28	0	14	1	15	25	0	10
Corn Quakes (Quaker) — *¾ cup*	30	121	18	2	<1	0	218	25	<1	11	1	22	20	1	25
Count Chocula (General Mills) — *1 cup*	30	120	10	1	0	0	190	26	0	14	1	0	25	2	25
Country Corn Flakes (General Mills) — *1 cup*	30	120	5	0.5	0	0	290	26	0	2	2	15	25	4	45
Cracklin' Oat Bran (Kellogg's) — *¾ cup*	49	190	50	6	1.5	0	170	36	6	15	4	15	25	2	10

	Weight *g*	Calories	Calories from fat	Total fat *g*	Sat. fat *g*	Cholesterol *mg*	Sodium *mg*	Carbohydrates *g*	Dietary fiber *g*	Sugars *g*	Protein *g*	Vitamin A *% DV*	Vitamin C *% DV*	Calcium *% DV*	Iron *% DV*
Crispix (Kellogg's) — *1 cup*	29	110	0	0	0	0	240	25	1	3	2	15	25	0	10
Crunchy Bran (Quaker) — *¾ cup*	27	90	<9	<1	<1	0	253	23	5	6	2	0	0	2	47
Fiber 7 Flakes (Health Valley) — *¾ cup*	n/a	100	0	0	0	0	15	24	4	4	3	2	0	0	4
Fiber One (General Mills) — *½ cup*	30	60	10	1	0	0	125	24	13	0	2	0	15	4	25
Frankenberry (General Mills) — *1 cup*	30	120	5	1	0	0	210	27	0	14	1	0	25	2	25
French Toast Crunch (General Mills) — *¾ cup*	30	120	15	1.5	0	0	170	26	0	12	1	15	25	6	25
Frosted Bran (Kellogg's) — *¾ cup*	30	100	0	0	0	0	200	26	3	10	2	15	25	0	25
Frosted Flakers (Quaker) — *¾ cup*	31	116	<9	<1	<1	0	281	28	1	12	1	26	26	0	26
Frosted Flakes (Kellogg's) — *¾ cup*	31	120	0	0	0	0	200	28	0	13	1	15	25	0	25
Frosted Krispies (Kellogg's) — *¾ cup*	26	100	0	0	0	0	190	24	0	10	1	15	25	0	10
Frosted Mini-Wheats (Kellogg's) — *1 cup*	51	170	10	1	0	0	0	41	5	10	5	0	0	0	80
Frosted Wheat Bites (Nabisco) — *1 cup*	52	190	10	1	0	0	10	44	5	12	4	0	0	2	10
Fruit & Fibre (Post)															
dates, raisins & walnuts — *1 cup*	60	210	25	3	0.5	0	260	46	6	18	4	30	0	2	35
peaches, raisins & almonds — *1 cup*	60	210	25	3	0.5	0	270	46	6	15	4	30	0	2	30
Fruit Loops (Kellogg's) — *1 cup*	32	120	10	1	0.5	0	150	28	1	15	2	15	25	0	25
Fruity Mashmallow Krispies (Kellogg's) — *¾ cup*	28	110	0	0	0	0	170	25	0	13	1	15	25	0	10
Fruity Pebbles (Post) — *¾ cup*	27	110	10	1	0.5	0	150	24	0	12	1	25	0	0	10
Golden Crisp (Post) — *¾ cup*	27	110	0	0	0	0	40	25	0	15	1	25	0	0	10
Golden Flax (Health Valley) — *½ cup dry*	n/a	190	27	3	n/a	0	30	38	6	8	6	2	0	6	8
Golden Grahams (General Mills) — *¾ cup*	30	120	10	1	0	0	280	25	1	11	1	15	25	0	25
Granola O's (Health Valley) — *¾ cup*	n/a	120	0	0	n/a	0	90	26	3	3	3	2	0	0	4
Granola, Low-Fat (Kellogg's) — *½ cup*	49	190	25	3	0.5	0	120	39	3	12	4	15	0	2	10
Grape Nuts (Post) — *½ cup*	58	200	10	1	0	0	350	47	5	7	6	25	0	2	45

	Weight *g*	Calories	Calories from fat	Total fat *g*	Sat. fat *g*	Cholesterol *mg*	Sodium *mg*	Carbohydrates *g*	Dietary fiber *g*	Sugars *g*	Protein *g*	Vitamin A *% DV*	Vitamin C *% DV*	Calcium *% DV*	Iron *% DV*
Great Grains (Post)															
crunchy pecan — *2/3 cup*	53	220	60	6	1	0	150	38	4	8	5	25	0	2	15
raisins, dates & pecans — *2/3 cup*	54	210	45	5	0.5	0	150	39	4	13	4	30	0	2	20
Healthy Choice (Kellogg's)															
almond crunch w/ raisins — *1 cup*	58	210	20	2	0	0	300	50	5	12	5	10	0	2	35
golden multi-grain flakes — *3/4 cup*	31	110	0	0	0	0	180	26	3	6	3	10	0	0	35
multi-grain flakes — *1 cup*	30	100	0	0	0	0	210	25	3	6	3	10	0	0	35
multi-grain raisins & almonds — *1 1/4 cups*	55	200	20	2	0	0	240	45	4	16	4	10	0	2	35
multi-grain squares — *1 1/4 cups*	55	190	10	1	0	0	0	45	6	8	5	10	0	0	35
toasted brown sugar squares — *1 cup*	54	190	10	1	0	0	0	44	5	9	5	10	0	0	35
Healthy Fiber Flakes (Health Valley) — *3/4 cup*	n/a	100	0	0	0	0	10	23	4	3	3	2	0	0	4
Heartland Granola, Low-Fat (Pillsbury) — *1/2 cup*	53	210	25	3	1	0	50	40	3	19	5	20	0	2	10
original — *1/2 cup*	64	300	100	11	1.5	0	160	41	4	18	9	0	0	4	15
raisin — *1/2 cup*	64	290	90	10	1.5	0	140	42	4	21	8	0	0	4	15
Honey Bunches of Oats (Post) — *3/4 cup*	30	120	15	1.5	0.5	0	190	25	1	6	2	25	0	0	15
Honey Clusters & Flakes (Health Valley) — *3/4 cup*	n/a	130	0	0	0	0	35	31	4	4	3	2	0	0	2
Honey Nut Clusters (General Mills) — *1 cup*	55	210	20	2.5	0	0	270	46	3	16	4	0	15	4	25
Honey Sweetened Puffed Corn (Health Valley) — *1 cup*	n/a	80	0	0	0	0	0	28	2	3	2	0	0	0	2
Honeycomb (Post) — *1 2/3 cups*	29	110	0	0	0	0	190	26	<1	11	2	25	0	0	15
Just Right (Kellogg's)															
fruit & nut — *1 cup*	60	210	15	1.5	0	0	290	48	3	15	4	25	0	0	90
w/ crunchy nuggets — *1 cup*	56	210	15	1.5	0	0	320	47	3	12	4	25	0	0	90
Kaboom (General Mills) — *1 1/4 cups*	30	120	10	1.5	0	0	280	24	1	6	3	15	25	4	45
King Vitamin (Quaker) — *1 1/2 cups*	31	120	9	1	<1	0	260	26	1	6	2	21	70	0	17

	Weight g	Calories	Calories from fat	Total fat g	Sat. fat g	Cholesterol mg	Sodium mg	Carbohydrates g	Dietary fiber g	Sugars g	Protein g	Vitamin A % DV	Vitamin C % DV	Calcium % DV	Iron % DV
Kix (General Mills) — *1 ⅓ cups*	30	120	5	0.5	0	0	270	26	1	3	2	25	25	4	45
Life Cereal (Quaker Oat)															
cinnamon — *¾ cup*	32	120	10	1	0	0	140	26	2	10	3	<2	<2	8	25
original — *¾ cup*	32	120	15	1.5	0	0	170	25	2	6	3	<2	<2	8	45
Lucky Charms (General Mills) — *1 cup*	30	120	10	1	0	0	210	25	1	13	2	15	25	2	25
Marshmallow Safari (Quaker) — *¾ cup*	30	119	18	2	<1	0	192	25	1	14	2	20	20	3	25
Müeslix (Kellogg's)															
apple & almond crunch — *¾ cup*	53	200	45	5	1	0	260	39	5	9	5	15	0	4	25
raisin & almond crunch w/ dates — *⅔ cup*	55	200	25	3	0	0	160	40	4	17	4	4	0	2	25
Nature Valley Cereal (General Mills)															
100% Natural Oat Cinnamon & Raisin — *¾ cup*	55	240	70	8	1	0	90	38	3	14	5	0	0	4	6
100% Natural Oat Fruit & Nut — *⅔ cup*	55	250	100	11	2	0	75	34	3	13	6	0	0	4	8
low-fat fruit granola — *⅔ cup*	55	210	25	2.5	0	0	210	44	3	19	4	0	0	2	8
98% Fat-Free Granola (Health Valley) — *⅔ cup*	n/a	180	9	1	0	0	90	43	6	10	5	2	4	4	8
Nut & Honey Crunch (Kellogg's) — *1 ¼ cups*	55	220	20	2.5	0.5	0	370	46	1	18	4	15	25	0	25
Nutri-Grain (Kellogg's)															
almond raisin — *1 ¼ cups*	49	180	25	3	0	0	170	38	4	7	4	0	0	15	8
golden wheat — *¾ cup*	30	100	5	1	0	0	225	24	4	0	3	0	25	0	6
Oat Bran (Quaker) — *½ cup*	40	150	25	3	0.5	0	0	25	6	1	7	0	0	2	15
Oat Bran Flakes (Health Valley) — *¾ cup*	n/a	100	0	0	0	0	15	24	4	4	3	2	0	0	4
Oat Bran Flakes w/ Raisins (Health Valley) — *¾ cup*	n/a	110	0	0	0	0	15	26	4	6	3	2	0	0	4
Oat Squares (Quaker) — *1 cup*	56	220	25	3	0.5	0	260	44	4	9	7	10	10	4	80
Oatmeal Crisp (General Mills)															
almond — *1 cup*	55	220	45	5	0.5	0	250	42	4	15	6	0	15	2	25

	Weight *g*	Calories	Calories from fat	Total fat *g*	Sat. fat *g*	Cholesterol *mg*	Sodium *mg*	Carbohydrates *g*	Dietary fiber *g*	Sugars *g*	Protein *g*	Vitamin A *% DV*	Vitamin C *% DV*	Calcium *% DV*	Iron *% DV*
apple cinnamon — *1 cup*	55	210	20	2	0	0	280	46	4	19	4	0	15	2	25
raisin — *1 cup*	55	210	25	2.5	0	0	210	44	3	19	4	15	0	2	25
Oh!s (Quaker)															
Fruitangy — *1 cup*	31	121	9	1	<1	0	160	27	<1	13	2	21	70	0	17
Honey Graham — *¾ cup*	27	112	18	2	<1	0	178	23	<1	11	1	20	20	<2	20
100% Natural Granola (Quaker)															
low-fat, w/ raisins — *⅔ cup*	55	213	27	3	<1	<1	145	44	3	18	5	0	0	3	8
oats & honey — *½ cup*	48	219	81	9	4	<1	20	31	3	13	5	0	0	6	7
oats, honey & raisins — *½ cup*	51	225	81	9	4	<1	19	34	3	16	5	0	0	6	7
100% Bran (Nabisco) — *⅓ cup*	29	80	5	0.5	0	0	120	23	8	7	4	25	0	2	45
Pop-Tarts Crunch, Frosted Strawberry (Kellogg's) — *1 cup*	33	130	10	1	0	0	125	29	0	17	1	15	25	0	25
Post Toasties — *1 cup*	28	100	0	0	0	0	270	24	1	2	2	25	0	0	2
Product 19 (Kellogg's) — *1 cup*	30	100	0	0	0	0	280	25	1	4	2	15	100	0	100
Quisp (Quaker) — *1 cup*	27	109	9	1	<1	0	194	23	<1	12	1	0	0	0	26
Raisin Bran (Kellogg's) — *1 cup*	61	200	15	1.5	0	0	390	47	8	18	6	15	0	4	25
Raisin Bran (Post) — *1 cup*	59	190	10	1	0	0	300	46	8	20	4	35	0	2	35
Raisin Bran Flakes (Health Valley) — *1 ¼ cups*	n/a	190	0	0	0	0	90	47	6	13	5	2	0	0	6
Raisin Nut Bran (General Mills) — *¾ cup*	55	200	35	4	0.5	0	250	41	5	16	4	0	0	6	25
Real Oat Bran (Health Valley) — *½ cup*	n/a	200	27	3	n/a	0	90	34	5	9	6	2	0	0	4
Reese's Peanut Butter Puffs (General Mills) — *¾ cup*	30	130	25	3	0.5	0	210	23	0	12	2	15	25	2	25
Rice Krispies (Kellogg's)															
apple cinnamon — *¾ cup*	29	110	0	0	0	0	220	26	0	11	1	15	25	0	10
original — *1 ¼ cups*	33	120	0	0	0	0	350	29	0	3	2	15	25	0	10
Rice Krispies Treats (Kellogg's) — *¾ cup*	30	120	15	1.5	0	0	190	26	0	9	1	15	25	0	10

	Weight g	Calories	Calories from fat	Total fat g	Sat. fat g	Cholesterol mg	Sodium mg	Carbohydrates g	Dietary fiber g	Sugars g	Protein g	Vitamin A % DV	Vitamin C % DV	Calcium % DV	Iron % DV
S'Mores Grahams (General Mills) — *¾ cup*	30	120	10	1	0	0	220	26	0	13	1	15	25	0	25
Shredded Wheat (Nabisco)															
'N Bran — *1 ¼ cups*	59	200	5	1	0	0	0	47	8	1	7	0	0	2	15
original — *2 biscuits*	46	160	5	0.5	0	0	0	38	5	0	5	0	0	2	8
Spoon Size — *1 cup*	49	170	5	0.5	0	0	0	41	5	0	5	0	0	2	8
Smacks (Kellogg's) — *¾ cup*	27	100	5	0.5	0	0	50	24	1	15	2	15	25	0	10
Special K (Kellogg's) — *1 cup*	31	110	0	0	0	0	250	22	1	3	6	15	25	0	45
Sun Country Granola															
raisin & date — *½ cup*	60	262	72	8	1	0	15	43	4	18	6	0	0	5	14
w/ almonds — *½ cup*	57	266	81	9	1	0	19	38	3	12	7	0	0	5	13
Sun Crunchers (General Mills) — *1 cup*	55	220	30	3	0	0	370	45	2	16	5	15	25	8	25
Sun Flakes — *¾ cup*	27	110	10	1	0	0	210	23	<1	0	2	20	20	0	8
Sweet Puffs (Quaker) — *1 cup*	34	133	<9	<1	<1	0	80	30	1	16	2	0	0	0	4
Team Flakes (Nabisco) — *1 ¼ cups*	57	220	0	0	0	0	360	49	1	10	4	25	25	0	45
Toasted Oatmeal Honey Nut Cereal (Quaker) — *1 cup*	49	200	40	4.5	1	0	180	37	3	12	5	10	25	4	45
Toasted Wheat Bran (Kretschmer) — *¼ cup*	16	32	<9	<1	<1	0	<1	10	7	<1	3	0	0	1	12
Total (General Mills)															
corn flakes — *1 ⅓ cups*	30	110	5	0.5	0	0	210	25	0	3	2	25	100	20	100
raisin bran — *1 cup*	55	180	10	1	0	0	240	43	5	19	4	25	0	20	100
whole grain — *¾ cup*	30	110	10	1	0	0	200	24	3	5	3	25	100	25	100
Triples (General Mills) — *1 cup*	30	120	10	1	0	0	190	25	0	6	2	25	25	4	45
Trix (General Mills) — *1 cup*	30	120	15	1.5	0	0	200	26	0	13	1	15	25	2	25
Wheaties (General Mills)															
Crispy Wheaties 'n Raisins — *1 cup*	55	190	10	1	0	0	270	44	4	20	4	25	0	4	25

	Weight g	Calories	Calories from fat	Total fat g	Sat. fat g	Cholesterol mg	Sodium mg	Carbohydrates g	Dietary fiber g	Sugars g	Protein g	Vitamin A % DV	Vitamin C % DV	Calcium % DV	Iron % DV
Honey Frosted — *¾ cup*	30	110	0	0	0	0	200	27	0	12	1	15	25	2	25
original — *1 cup*	30	110	10	1	0	0	220	24	3	4	3	25	25	0	45
Whole Wheat Natural Cereal (Quaker) — *½ cup*	40	134	0	<1	<1	0	1	30	4	<1	5	0	0	1	7

Cheese & Cheese Products

	Weight g	Calories	Calories from fat	Total fat g	Sat. fat g	Cholesterol mg	Sodium mg	Carbohydrates g	Dietary fiber g	Sugars g	Protein g	Vitamin A % DV	Vitamin C % DV	Calcium % DV	Iron % DV
Borden American-Style Process Cheese															
nonfat — *1 slice*	21	30	0	0	0	0	310	2	0	1	5	4	0	15	0
Premium — *1 slice*	21	80	60	7	4	20	320	1	0	0	4	2	0	10	0
Singles — *1 slice*	19	70	45	5	3	15	260	2	0	1	3	4	0	10	0
Singles, light — *1 slice*	21	45	25	2.5	1.5	10	300	1	0	<1	5	2	0	15	0
The Big! American Cheese (white or yellow) — *1 slice*	24	80	50	6	4	20	310	2	0	1	4	6	0	10	0
The Big! Nacho Cheese — *1 slice*	24	80	50	6	3.5	20	340	2	0	1	4	4	0	10	0
Cheez Whiz Zap-A-Pack															
process cheese sauce — *2 Tbsp*	33	90	70	8	5	20	580	3	0	3	3	6	0	10	0
process cheese sauce, w/ mild salsa — *2 Tbsp*	33	90	70	8	5	25	580	3	0	3	3	8	0	10	0
Cracker Barrel															
cheddar, sharp, ⅓ less fat — *1 oz*	28	80	45	5	3	20	220	<1	0	0	9	6	0	25	0
cheddar, sharp, cold pack — *2 Tbsp*	31	100	70	8	5	25	290	4	0	3	5	6	0	15	0
Harvest Moon															
american, imitation, shredded — *¼ cup*	36	120	80	9	2	0	500	3	0	2	6	4	0	25	0
mozzarella, imitation, part-skim, shredded — *¼ cup*	36	110	80	8	1.5	0	430	1	0	0	8	0	0	30	0
slices, american-style — *1 slice*	19	70	50	6	4	20	320	0	0	0	4	4	0	10	0
spread, american-flavor — *¾ oz*	21	60	40	4.5	3	15	300	2	0	2	3	4	0	10	0
Healthy Choice															
cheddar, swiss, or american — *1 slice*	21	30	0	0	0	<5	290	2	<1	0	5	10	0	15	0

	Weight g	Calories	Calories from fat	Total fat g	Sat. fat g	Cholesterol mg	Sodium mg	Carbohydrates g	Dietary fiber g	Sugars g	Protein g	Vitamin A % DV	Vitamin C % DV	Calcium % DV	Iron % DV
cheese loaf, process — *1 oz*	30	35	0	0	0	<5	390	3	<1	0	8	15	0	20	0
mozzarella string cheese — *1 stick*	30	45	0	0	0	2.5	200	1	0	0	9	6	0	25	0
Kraft															
american cheese food, grated — *1 Tbsp*	5	25	10	1.5	1	<5	135	1	0	1	1	0	0	4	0
cheddar, fat-free, shredded — *¼ cup*	29	45	0	0	0	<5	220	1	0	0	10	8	0	25	0
cheddar, natural, ⅓ less fat — *1 oz*	28	80	45	5	3.5	20	220	0	0	0	9	6	0	25	0
cheese spread w/ bacon — *2 Tbsp*	32	90	70	8	5	25	570	<1	0	0	5	10	0	15	0
cheese spread, olive & pimento — *2 Tbsp*	32	70	60	6	4	20	220	3	0	2	2	6	0	2	0
cheese spread, pimento — *2 Tbsp*	32	80	60	6	4	20	170	3	0	2	2	6	0	2	0
house italian, grated, ⅓ less fat — *2 tsp*	6	25	10	1	0.5	<5	115	1	0	0	2	0	0	8	0
jack, ⅓ less fat — *1 oz*	28	80	45	5	3.5	20	220	0	0	0	9	6	0	25	0
process cheese spread, jalapeño pepper — *1 oz*	28	80	60	6	4	20	470	2	0	2	5	10	0	15	0
Kraft Deluxe															
american — *1 slice*	21	80	60	7	4	20	340	<1	0	0	4	4	0	10	0
pimento — *1 slice*	28	100	70	8	6	25	430	<1	0	0	6	6	0	15	0
swiss — *1 slice*	28	90	60	7	5	25	420	<1	0	0	7	6	0	20	0
Kraft Healthy Favorites Mozzarella (fat-free shredded) — *¼ cup*	30	50	0	0	0	<5	280	2	<1	0	9	6	0	25	0
Kraft Singles															
mexican w/ jalapeño peppers — *¾ oz*	21	70	45	5	3.5	15	330	2	0	1	4	6	0	10	0
swiss — *¾ oz*	21	70	45	5	3.5	15	320	1	0	1	4	4	0	15	0
w/ garlic — *1 oz*	28	90	60	7	5	20	370	2	0	2	5	6	0	15	0
w/ pimento — *1 slice*	21	70	45	5	3.5	15	290	2	0	<1	4	6	0	10	0
white american style — *1 slice*	21	70	45	5	3.5	15	290	2	0	1	4	4	0	10	0
yellow american style — *1 slice*	21	70	45	5	3.5	15	290	2	0	1	4	6	0	10	0

	Weight *g*	Calories	Calories from fat	Total fat *g*	Sat. fat *g*	Cholesterol *mg*	Sodium *mg*	Carbohydrates *g*	Dietary fiber *g*	Sugars *g*	Protein *g*	Vitamin A *% DV*	Vitamin C *% DV*	Calcium *% DV*	Iron *% DV*
Lite Line (low-fat)															
american-style (white or yellow) — *1 slice*	19	30	10	1	1	<5	260	1	0	1	4	4	0	15	0
american-style, sharp — *1 slice*	19	30	10	1	1	<5	260	1	0	1	4	4	0	15	0
swiss-flavor — *1 slice*	19	30	10	1	1	<5	260	1	0	1	4	4	0	15	0
Mohawk Valley Process Cheese Spread, Limburger — *2 Tbsp*	32	80	60	7	4.5	20	500	0	0	0	4	6	0	15	0
Old English															
process cheese slices, american — *1 oz*	28	100	80	9	6	30	460	<1	0	0	6	6	0	15	0
process cheese spread, sharp — *2 Tbsp*	32	90	70	8	5	25	520	<1	0	0	5	10	0	15	0
Philadelphia Brand Cream Cheese															
fat-free (brick) — *1 oz*	28	25	0	0	0	<5	135	2	0	1	4	10	0	8	0
light (soft) — *2 Tbsp*	32	70	50	5	3.5	15	150	2	0	2	3	8	0	4	0
neufchâtel — *1 oz*	28	70	60	6	4	20	120	<1	0	<1	3	4	0	2	0
regular — *1 oz*	28	100	90	10	6	30	90	<1	0	<1	2	6	0	0	0
Philadelphia Brand Cream Cheese, Soft															
w/ chives — *1 oz*	28	90	80	9	6	30	150	<1	0	<1	2	6	0	0	0
w/ herb & garlic — *2 Tbsp*	31	110	90	10	7	30	180	2	0	<1	2	8	0	2	0
w/ olive & pimento — *2 Tbsp*	31	170	80	9	6	30	100	2	0	<1	2	8	0	2	0
w/ smoked salmon — *2 Tbsp*	31	100	80	9	6	30	200	1	0	<1	2	4	0	2	0
w/ strawberries — *2 Tbsp*	32	100	80	9	6	30	65	5	0	3	1	6	0	2	0
Polly-O Mozzarella															
fat-free — *1 oz*	28	35	0	0	0	<5	220	<1	0	<1	7	4	0	15	0
fat-free, shredded — *¼ cup*	34	45	0	0	0	<5	270	1	<1	<1	10	6	0	20	0
light — *1 oz*	28	60	25	2.5	2	10	230	<1	0	<1	7	6	0	15	0
lite, shredded — *¼ cup*	31	60	25	3	2	15	220	1	0	<1	8	6	0	15	0

	Weight g	Calories	Calories from fat	Total fat g	Sat. fat g	Cholesterol mg	Sodium mg	Carbohydrates g	Dietary fiber g	Sugars g	Protein g	Vitamin A % DV	Vitamin C % DV	Calcium % DV	Iron % DV
part-skim, low-moisture, shredded — *¼ cup*	28	80	45	5	4	15	200	1	<1	<1	8	4	0	20	0
Polly-O Ricotta															
fat-free — *¼ cup*	64	50	0	0	0	<5	80	2	0	2	10	4	0	30	0
light — *¼ cup*	64	70	25	3	2	10	80	3	0	2	8	8	0	25	0
Squeez-A-Snak Cheese Spread — *2 Tbsp*	32	90	70	8	5	25	440	<1	0	0	5	6	0	15	0
Temp-Tee Whipped Cream Cheese — *3 Tbsp*	33	110	90	10	7	30	115	1	0	1	3	8	0	2	0
Velveeta															
shredded — *¼ cup*	36	130	80	9	6	30	500	3	0	3	8	15	0	20	0
slices — *1 slice*	21	60	40	4.5	3	15	300	2	0	1	4	4	0	10	0
spread — *1 oz*	28	80	50	6	4	20	420	3	0	2	5	6	0	15	0
spread, italiana — *1 oz*	28	80	60	6	4	20	430	2	0	2	5	4	0	10	0
w/ jalapeño — *2 Tbsp*	33	90	70	8	5	25	530	2	0	1	5	6	0	15	0
Weight Watchers															
cheddar, natural, sharp (yellow) — *1 oz*	28	80	45	5	3	15	180	1	0	0	8	6	0	20	0
cheddar, sharp, slices, fat-free — *2 slices*	21	30	0	0	0	0	320	3	0	2	5	6	0	15	0
italian topping, grated, fat-free — *1 Tbsp*	n/a	20	0	0	0	0	60	2	0	1	2	0	0	2	0
slices, american-style — *2 slices*	21	30	0	0	0	0	160	3	0	2	5	6	0	15	0
swiss, slices, fat-free — *2 slices*	21	30	0	0	0	0	320	2	0	2	5	6	0	15	0

Chicken, Frozen

	Weight g	Calories	Calories from fat	Total fat g	Sat. fat g	Cholesterol mg	Sodium mg	Carbohydrates g	Dietary fiber g	Sugars g	Protein g	Vitamin A % DV	Vitamin C % DV	Calcium % DV	Iron % DV
Banquet Bone-In Chicken															
fried chicken (Our Original) — *3 oz*	85	270	160	18	5	65	620	13	1	1	14	0	6	8	4
fried chicken, breasts (Our Original) — *1 piece*	n/a	410	240	26	13	85	600	18	4	2	23	0	8	6	4
fried chicken, country — *3 oz*	85	270	160	18	5	65	620	13	1	1	14	0	6	8	4
fried chicken, drums & thighs — *3 oz*	85	260	160	18	5	65	540	10	2	1	15	0	8	2	2

	Weight g	Calories	Calories from fat	Total fat g	Sat. fat g	Cholesterol mg	Sodium mg	Carbohydrates g	Dietary fiber g	Sugars g	Protein g	Vitamin A % DV	Vitamin C % DV	Calcium % DV	Iron % DV
fried chicken, hot 'n spicy — *3 oz*	85	260	160	18	5	65	590	13	1	1	14	0	6	8	4
fried chicken, skinless — *3 oz*	85	210	120	13	3	55	480	7	2	1	18	0	10	2	2
fried chicken, skinless, honey BBQ — *3 oz*	85	210	120	13	3	55	480	7	2	1	18	0	10	2	2
fried chicken, skinless, lemon pepper — *3 oz*	85	210	120	13	3	55	560	7	2	1	18	0	10	2	2
fried chicken, southern — *3 oz*	85	270	160	18	5	65	590	13	1	1	14	0	6	8	4
wings, hot 'n spicy — *4 pieces*	n/a	230	140	16	5	85	280	5	1	0	15	0	6	2	4
Banquet Boneless Chicken															
breast patties, fat-free — *1 patty*	n/a	100	0	0	0	20	350	15	1	0	9	0	0	0	2
breast tenders (Our Original) — *3 pieces*	n/a	240	140	15	3.5	30	480	15	<1	1	12	0	2	0	4
breast tenders, fat-free — *3 pieces*	n/a	130	0	0	0	30	480	20	2	0	13	0	0	0	4
breast tenders, southern — *3 tenders*	n/a	260	140	16	4	15	460	16	1	1	12	0	2	0	4
chicken & cheddar chunks — *4 pieces*	n/a	280	180	19	6	25	560	13	1	2	12	0	0	8	4
Micro Nuggets w/ BBQ Sauce — *6 pieces w/ sauce*	127	340	180	20	4	45	840	22	2	0	16	0	4	2	10
Micro Nuggets w/ sweet & sour sauce — *6 pieces w/ sauce*	127	320	160	18	4	45	670	25	2	0	16	0	2	2	10
nuggets (Our Original) — *6 pieces*	n/a	240	130	15	3	35	540	12	1	2	14	0	0	0	6
patties, original — *1 patty*	n/a	180	100	11	2.5	25	360	10	1	2	10	0	0	0	4
patties, southern — *1 patty*	n/a	170	90	10	2	20	430	10	1	1	10	0	2	0	4
Butterball Chicken Requests, Crispy Baked Breasts															
italian-style herb — *1 piece*	n/a	180	60	6	2	40	610	14	1	0	17	0	2	0	4
lemon pepper — *1 piece*	n/a	180	60	6	2	45	380	14	2	0	16	0	2	0	4
original — *1 piece*	n/a	180	60	6	2	45	450	14	2	0	18	0	2	0	4
parmesan — *1 piece*	n/a	180	60	7	3	45	520	12	1	0	18	0	2	6	2
southwestern — *1 piece*	n/a	170	50	6	2	35	590	13	2	0	17	2	2	0	4

	Weight g	Calories	Calories from fat	Total fat g	Sat. fat g	Cholesterol mg	Sodium mg	Carbohydrates g	Dietary fiber g	Sugars g	Protein g	Vitamin A % DV	Vitamin C % DV	Calcium % DV	Iron % DV
Country Skillet Chicken															
chicken chunks — *5 pieces*	n/a	270	150	16	3	20	720	18	1	2	12	0	0	2	8
chicken chunks, southern fried — *5 pieces*	n/a	250	140	15	3	20	550	16	1	4	12	0	0	2	8
fried chicken — *3 oz*	n/a	270	160	18	5	65	620	13	1	1	14	0	6	8	4
nuggets — *10 pieces*	n/a	280	160	17	4	25	610	16	1	2	14	0	0	2	8
patties — *1 patty*	n/a	190	100	11	2.5	20	490	12	1	3	9	0	0	0	6
patties, southern fried — *1 patty*	n/a	190	110	12	2.5	20	440	12	1	3	9	0	2	0	6
Empire Kosher Chicken															
breast, battered & breaded — *8 oz*	85	170	70	8	2	45	440	8	<1	0	21	0	0	2	0
chicken stix, battered & breaded — *4 stix*	88	200	90	10	2	5	280	14	1	1	13	0	0	0	0
drum & thigh — *8 oz*	85	240	140	16	4	80	260	7	2	0	16	0	0	0	2
fried chicken (assorted pieces) — *8 oz*	84	200	110	12	8	75	240	8	0	0	15	0	0	0	4
nuggets, battered & breaded — *5 nuggets*	85	180	80	9	1.5	15	370	12	1	<1	13	0	0	0	0
Tyson Boxed Wings & Drumsticks															
drumsticks, hot-barbecue-style — *1 piece*	59	90	40	4.5	1	70	260	2	0	1	12	2	6	0	0
wings, barbecue-style — *4 pieces*	96	220	130	15	4	130	160	2	0	2	20	0	0	2	0
wings, hot — *4 pieces*	96	220	130	15	3.5	110	560	1	0	0	20	6	6	2	6
wings, teriyaki-style — *4 pieces*	96	190	110	12	3	120	210	2	2	1	21	2	4	2	0
Tyson Breaded Boneless Chicken															
breast fillets, southern fried — *2 fillets*	85	170	60	7	1	30	440	13	1	0	13	0	4	2	2
Chick'n Chunks — *6 chunks*	84	280	180	20	5	50	490	14	2	0	11	2	0	0	4
patties, Chick'n w/ Cheddar — *1 patty*	73	220	130	14	4	40	270	12	0	1	11	0	0	6	2
patties, Thick'n Crispy — *1 patty*	73	200	120	14	3	40	320	10	1	1	10	0	0	2	6

	Weight g	Calories	Calories from fat	Total fat g	Sat. fat g	Cholesterol mg	Sodium mg	Carbohydrates g	Dietary fiber g	Sugars g	Protein g	Vitamin A % DV	Vitamin C % DV	Calcium % DV	Iron % DV
Tyson Stuffed Chicken Entrées															
chicken cordon bleu — *1 breast*	170	320	120	13	3.5	75	1370	20	0	0	31	0	0	15	4
chicken divan — *1 breast*	170	290	100	11	2.5	65	1140	21	<1	1	27	6	20	8	6
chicken kiev — *1 breast*	170	460	280	31	15	120	1270	19	0	0	25	20	0	4	4

Chips & Pretzels

	Weight g	Calories	Calories from fat	Total fat g	Sat. fat g	Cholesterol mg	Sodium mg	Carbohydrates g	Dietary fiber g	Sugars g	Protein g	Vitamin A % DV	Vitamin C % DV	Calcium % DV	Iron % DV
Bugles															
nacho — *1 ⅓ cups*	30	160	80	9	7	0	300	18	<1	2	2	0	0	0	0
original — *1 ⅓ cups*	30	150	60	7	6	0	340	20	<1	1	1	0	0	0	0
ranch — *1 ⅓ cups*	30	160	80	9	8	0	310	18	<1	2	2	0	0	0	0
sour cream & onion — *1 ⅓ cups*	30	160	80	9	8	0	260	18	0	2	2	0	0	0	0
Bugles, Baked															
cheddar cheese — *1 ½ cups*	30	130	30	3.5	0.5	0	430	23	0	2	2	0	0	0	0
original — *1 ½ cups*	30	130	30	3.5	0.5	0	350	23	0	2	2	0	0	0	0
Cape Cod Potato Chips															
golden russet — *1 oz*	28	140	70	7	1.5	0	150	17	1	<1	2	0	8	0	2
mesquite BBQ — *1 oz*	28	150	70	8	2	0	160	17	1	<1	2	0	10	0	2
no-salt — *1 oz*	28	150	90	10	2.5	0	0	14	<1	<1	2	0	15	0	2
reduced-fat — *1 oz*	28	130	50	6	0.5	0	110	18	1	<1	2	0	10	0	2
regular — *1 oz*	28	150	70	8	2	0	110	17	1	<1	2	0	10	0	2
sea salt & vinegar — *1 oz*	28	150	70	8	2	0	130	17	1	<1	2	0	10	0	2
sour cream & chive — *1 oz*	28	150	80	9	2	0	160	15	1	<1	2	0	10	0	2
Cheetos															
Cheesy Checkers — *12 chips*	28	150	90	10	2.5	<5	350	15	<1	1	2	n/a	n/a	n/a	n/a
crunchy — *21 chips*	28	150	80	9	2	0	300	16	<1	<1	2	n/a	n/a	n/a	n/a

Foods, Brand Name

	Weight *g*	Calories	Calories from fat	Total fat *g*	Sat. fat *g*	Cholesterol *mg*	Sodium *mg*	Carbohydrates *g*	Dietary fiber *g*	Sugars *g*	Protein *g*	Vitamin A *% DV*	Vitamin C *% DV*	Calcium *% DV*	Iron *% DV*
curls — *15 chips*	28	150	80	9	2.5	0	280	16	1	1	2	n/a	n/a	n/a	n/a
Flamin' Hot — *21 chips*	28	160	90	9	2	0	240	16	<1	1	2	n/a	n/a	n/a	n/a
Puffed Balls — *38 chips*	28	160	90	10	2.5	<5	370	13	<1	1	2	n/a	n/a	n/a	n/a
Puffs — *29 chips*	28	160	90	10	2.5	0	370	15	<1	<1	2	n/a	n/a	n/a	n/a
Combos Snacks															
cheddar cheese — *1 bag*	48	250	120	13	3	5	510	28	1	3	5	n/a	n/a	6	2
cheddar cheese pretzel — *1 bag*	51	240	80	9	1.5	5	560	34	1	8	5	n/a	n/a	10	2
nacho cheese pretzel — *1 bag*	48	230	70	8	1.5	0	580	34	1	8	5	n/a	n/a	8	2
Doritos															
Chester's Cheese — *11 chips*	28	140	60	7	1.5	0	160	18	1	1	2	n/a	n/a	n/a	n/a
Cooler Ranch — *15 chips*	28	140	60	7	1	0	160	18	1	<1	2	n/a	n/a	n/a	n/a
Cooler Ranch, reduced-fat — *13 chips*	28	130	45	5	1	0	200	1	1	1	2	n/a	n/a	n/a	n/a
Dunkers — *6 chips*	28	140	50	6	1	0	80	19	1	0	2	n/a	n/a	n/a	n/a
Flamin Hot — *15 chips*	28	140	70	8	1	0	270	17	1	2	2	n/a	n/a	n/a	n/a
Nacho Cheesier — *15 chips*	28	140	60	7	1	0	170	18	1	2	2	n/a	n/a	n/a	n/a
Nacho Cheesier, reduced-fat — *13 chips*	28	130	45	5	1	0	210	19	1	2	3	n/a	n/a	n/a	n/a
Pizza Cravers — *12 chips*	28	140	60	7	1.5	0	170	18	1	1	2	n/a	n/a	n/a	n/a
Taco Bell Taco Supreme — *15 chips*	28	140	70	7	1.5	0	200	18	1	1	2	n/a	n/a	n/a	n/a
toasted corn — *18 chips*	28	140	60	6	1	0	65	19	1	0	2	n/a	n/a	n/a	n/a
Fritos															
BBQ — *29 chips*	28	150	80	9	1.5	0	310	16	1	<1	2	n/a	n/a	n/a	n/a
chili cheese — *29 chips*	28	160	90	10	1.5	0	260	15	1	<1	2	n/a	n/a	n/a	n/a
king size — *12 chips*	28	160	90	10	1.5	0	150	15	1	0	2	n/a	n/a	n/a	n/a
original — *32 chips*	1	160	90	10	1.5	0	170	15	1	0	2	n/a	n/a	n/a	n/a

	Weight g	Calories	Calories from fat	Total fat g	Sat. fat g	Cholesterol mg	Sodium mg	Carbohydrates g	Dietary fiber g	Sugars g	Protein g	Vitamin A % DV	Vitamin C % DV	Calcium % DV	Iron % DV
Scoops — *10 chips*	28	150	80	9	1.5	0	135	16	1	0	2	n/a	n/a	n/a	n/a
Texas Grill Honey BBQ — *15 chips*	28	150	80	9	1.5	0	250	16	1	1	2	n/a	n/a	n/a	n/a
Texas Grill Sizzlin Fajita — *14 chips*	28	150	80	9	1.5	0	200	16	1	<1	2	n/a	n/a	n/a	n/a
Wild n' Mild — *28 chips*	28	160	90	10	1.5	0	170	15	1	<1	2	n/a	n/a	n/a	n/a
Funyuns — *13 chips*	28	140	60	7	1.5	0	250	18	<1	1	2	n/a	n/a	n/a	n/a
Health Valley Low-Fat Potato Puffs															
cheddar cheese — *1 ½ cup*	n/a	110	27	3	n/a	5	260	21	1	1	2	2	10	4	2
garlic w/ cheese — *1 ½ cup*	n/a	110	27	3	n/a	0	260	21	1	1	2	2	10	4	2
Zesty Ranch — *1 ½ cup*	n/a	110	23	3	n/a	0	260	21	1	1	2	2	10	4	2
Health Valley Snacks, Cheddar Lites — *1 ¾ cups*	n/a	120	27	3	n/a	5	170	21	1	1	3	10	0	4	2
Lay's Potato Chips															
Flamin' Hot — *17 chips*	28	150	90	10	2.5	0	180	15	1	2	1	n/a	n/a	n/a	n/a
hickory bbq — *15 chips*	28	150	90	10	2	0	220	15	1	<1	1	n/a	n/a	n/a	n/a
KC Masterpiece BBQ — *15 chips*	28	150	90	9	2.5	0	270	15	1	0	2	n/a	n/a	n/a	n/a
onion & garlic — *19 chips*	28	150	80	9	2.5	0	200	16	1	1	2	n/a	n/a	n/a	n/a
original — *18 chips*	28	150	90	10	2.5	0	180	15	1	0	2	n/a	n/a	n/a	n/a
salsa & cheese — *16 chips*	28	160	80	9	2.5	0	180	19	1	1	2	n/a	n/a	n/a	n/a
salt & vinegar — *19 chips*	28	160	90	10	2.5	0	340	15	1	1	2	n/a	n/a	n/a	n/a
sour cream & onion — *22 chips*	28	160	90	9	2.5	0	180	15	1	1	2	n/a	n/a	n/a	n/a
unsalted — *18 chips*	28	150	90	10	2.5	0	120	15	1	0	2	n/a	n/a	n/a	n/a
Wavy, Hidden Valley Ranch — *11 chips*	28	160	100	11	3	0	150	14	1	0	2	n/a	n/a	n/a	n/a
Wavy, Original — *11 chips*	28	160	90	10	2.5	0	120	15	1	0	2	n/a	n/a	n/a	n/a
Lay's Potato Crisps, Baked															
original — *12 chips*	28	110	15	1.5	0	0	150	23	2	1	2	n/a	n/a	n/a	n/a

	Weight g	Calories	Calories from fat	Total fat g	Sat. fat g	Cholesterol mg	Sodium mg	Carbohydrates g	Dietary fiber g	Sugars g	Protein g	Vitamin A % DV	Vitamin C % DV	Calcium % DV	Iron % DV
sour cream & onion — *12 chips*	28	110	15	1.5	3	0	170	23	1	3	2	n/a	n/a	n/a	n/a
Munchos															
BBQ — *16 chips*	28	160	90	10	2	0	250	15	1	2	1	n/a	n/a	n/a	n/a
regular — *16 chips*	28	150	90	10	2.5	0	270	18	1	0	1	n/a	n/a	n/a	n/a
Pepperidge Farm Bagel Chips															
onion multigrain — *1 oz*	n/a	120	35	3.5	0	0	200	19	1	1	3	0	0	0	6
three cheese — *1 oz*	n/a	140	60	7	1	5	240	16	<1	2	4	0	0	4	8
toasted onion & garlic — *1 oz*	n/a	110	40	4.5	1	0	280	18	2	1	3	0	0	0	8
Pepperidge Farm Snack Mix															
extra nutty — *½ cup*	36	180	80	9	1.5	25	330	20	2	2	5	0	0	4	4
Goldfish, original — *½ cup*	36	170	70	8	1.5	5	360	21	2	3	5	0	0	4	10
Goldfish, Zesty Cheddar — *½ cup*	36	180	90	10	1.5	<5	390	19	1	3	1	0	0	2	4
honey mustard & onion — *½ cup*	36	180	90	10	1.5	<5	390	19	1	3	4	0	0	2	4
lightly seasoned — *½ cup*	36	170	70	8	1	<5	400	22	1	3	4	0	0	2	6
Pringles Potato Crisps															
original — *approx 14 chips*	28	160	90	11	2.5	0	170	n/a	n/a	n/a	2	<2	6	<2	<2
sour cream n' onion — *approx 14 chips*	28	160	90	10	2.5	0.8	135	15	n/a	n/a	2	<2	6	<2	<2
Pringles Ridges Potato Crisps															
cheddar & sour cream — *approx 12 chips*	28	150	90	10	2.5	0	200	n/a	n/a	n/a	1	<2	6	<2	<2
original — *approx 12 chips*	28	150	90	10	2.5	0	150	n/a	n/a	n/a	1	<2	6	<2	<2
Pringles Right Potato Crisps															
BBQ — *approx 16 chips*	28	140	60	7	2	0	160	n/a	n/a	n/a	2	<2	6	<2	<2
original — *approx 16 chips*	28	140	60	7	2	0	135	n/a	n/a	n/a	1	<2	6	<2	<2
sour cream n' onion, ranch — *approx 16 chips*	28	140	60	7	2	0	120	n/a	n/a	n/a	2	<2	6	<2	<2

	Weight g	Calories	Calories from fat	Total fat g	Sat. fat g	Cholesterol mg	Sodium mg	Carbohydrates g	Dietary fiber g	Sugars g	Protein g	Vitamin A % DV	Vitamin C % DV	Calcium % DV	Iron % DV
Pringles Rippled Original Potato Crisps — *approx 10 chips*	28	160	100	11	3	0	150	15	n/a	n/a	2	<2	6	<2	<2
Rold Gold Pretzels															
bavarian — *3 pretzels*	28	110	15	2	0.5	0	440	21	1	1	3	n/a	n/a	n/a	n/a
hard sourdough, fat-free — *1 pretzel*	28	110	10	1	0	0	370	23	1	1	2	n/a	n/a	n/a	n/a
rods — *3 pretzels*	28	110	10	1.5	0.5	0	370	22	1	1	3	n/a	n/a	n/a	n/a
sticks, fat-free — *48 pretzels*	28	110	0	0	0	0	530	23	1	1	3	n/a	n/a	n/a	n/a
thins — *10 pretzels*	28	110	10	1	0	0	510	22	1	1	3	n/a	n/a	n/a	n/a
thins, fat-free — *12 pretzels*	28	110	0	0	0	0	520	23	1	<1	2	n/a	n/a	n/a	n/a
tiny twists, fat-free — *18 pretzels*	28	100	0	0	0	0	420	23	1	<1	3	n/a	n/a	n/a	n/a
Ruffles Potato Chips															
cheddar & sour cream — *13 chips*	28	160	90	10	2.5	0	230	15	1	0	1	n/a	n/a	n/a	n/a
french onion — *11 chips*	28	150	90	10	3	0	180	15	1	1	2	n/a	n/a	n/a	n/a
golden dijon — *12 chips*	28	150	80	9	2.5	0	190	16	1	<1	1	n/a	n/a	n/a	n/a
KC Masterpiece Mesquite BBQ — *15 chips*	28	150	90	9	3	0	120	15	1	2	1	n/a	n/a	n/a	n/a
original — *12 chips*	28	150	90	10	3	0	125	14	1	0	2	n/a	n/a	n/a	n/a
ranch — *13 chips*	28	150	80	9	2.5	0	280	15	1	1	2	n/a	n/a	n/a	n/a
regular, reduced-fat — *16 chips*	28	140	60	6.7	1	0	130	18	1	0	2	n/a	n/a	n/a	n/a
sour cream & onion, reduced-fat — *14 chips*	28	130	50	6	1	0	200	18	1	<1	3	n/a	n/a	n/a	n/a
Santitas Tortilla Chips															
100% white corn — *6 chips*	28	140	60	6	1	0	75	19	1	<1	2	n/a	n/a	n/a	n/a
restaurant-style chips — *7 chips*	28	140	60	6	1	0	75	19	1	<1	2	n/a	n/a	n/a	n/a
restaurant-style strips — *12 chips*	28	140	60	6	1	0	40	19	1	0	2	n/a	n/a	n/a	n/a
Sun Chips															
french onion — *13 chips*	28	140	60	7	1	0	115	18	2	2	2	n/a	n/a	n/a	n/a

	Weight g	Calories	Calories from fat	Total fat g	Sat. fat g	Cholesterol mg	Sodium mg	Carbohydrates g	Dietary fiber g	Sugars g	Protein g	Vitamin A % DV	Vitamin C % DV	Calcium % DV	Iron % DV
Harvest Cheddar — *13 chips*	28	140	60	7	1	0	180	18	2	2	2	n/a	n/a	n/a	n/a
original — *14 chips*	28	140	60	7	1	0	160	18	2	2	2	n/a	n/a	n/a	n/a
Tostitos															
bite-size — *24 chips*	28	140	70	8	1	0	110	17	1	0	2	n/a	n/a	n/a	n/a
crispy rounds — *13 chips*	28	150	70	8	1	0	85	17	1	0	2	n/a	n/a	n/a	n/a
Lime n' Chile — *6 chips*	28	150	70	7	1	0	180	17	1	1	2	n/a	n/a	n/a	n/a
restaurant-style — *6 chips*	28	130	50	6	1	0	80	19	1	0	2	n/a	n/a	n/a	n/a
restaurant-style, unsalted — *6 chips*	28	140	70	8	1	0	10	18	1	0	2	n/a	n/a	n/a	n/a
Santa Fe Gold — *7 chips*	28	140	50	6	1	0	80	19	1	0	2	n/a	n/a	n/a	n/a
Tostitos, Baked															
Cool Ranch — *11 chips*	28	120	30	3	0	3	170	21	1	0	2	n/a	n/a	n/a	n/a
original — *9 chips*	140	110	5	1	0	0	200	24	2	0	2	n/a	n/a	n/a	n/a
unsalted — *13 chips*	28	110	10	1	0	0	0	24	1	0	2	n/a	n/a	n/a	n/a
Utz Potato Chips — *20 chips*	28	150	80	9	2	0	95	14	1	<1	2	<2	10	<2	2
Weight Watchers															
barbecue-flavored curls — *1 bag*	14	60	15	1.5	0	0	110	11	1	0	1	0	0	0	0
cheese curls — *1 bag*	14	70	25	2.5	1	0	85	10	0	0	1	0	0	0	0
pretzel nuggets, oat bran — *1 bag*	43	170	25	2.5	0	0	250	33	3	0	4	0	0	0	4

Condiments: Barbecue & Steak Sauces

	Weight g	Calories	Calories from fat	Total fat g	Sat. fat g	Cholesterol mg	Sodium mg	Carbohydrates g	Dietary fiber g	Sugars g	Protein g	Vitamin A % DV	Vitamin C % DV	Calcium % DV	Iron % DV
A.1. Steak Sauce, Original — *1 Tbsp*	17	15	0	0	n/a	n/a	250	3	n/a	2	0	n/a	n/a	n/a	n/a
Heinz 57															
barbecue sauce — *2 Tbsp*	34	50	0	0	0	0	380	12	1	8	0	0	0	0	0
hickory smoke sauce — *1 Tbsp*	17	15	0	0	0	0	200	4	0	3	0	0	0	0	0
original — *1 Tbsp*	17	15	0	0	0	0	220	4	0	3	0	0	0	0	0

	Weight *g*	Calories	Calories from fat	Total fat *g*	Sat. fat *g*	Cholesterol *mg*	Sodium *mg*	Carbohydrates *g*	Dietary fiber *g*	Sugars *g*	Protein *g*	Vitamin A *% DV*	Vitamin C *% DV*	Calcium *% DV*	Iron *% DV*
Heinz Thick & Rich Barbecue Sauce															
buffalo wing — *2 Tbsp*	34	15	0	0	0	0	750	4	1	2	0	6	0	0	0
cajun-style — *2 Tbsp*	34	35	0	0	0	0	480	9	1	7	0	2	0	0	0
chunky — *2 Tbsp*	34	35	0	0	0	0	480	9	0	6	0	2	0	0	0
hawaiian — *2 Tbsp*	34	50	0	0	0	0	260	12	1	10	0	8	2	0	0
hickory smoke — *2 Tbsp*	34	35	0	0	0	0	480	9	0	6	0	0	0	0	0
honey, mesquite smoke — *2 Tbsp*	34	35	0	0	0	0	480	9	0	7	0	0	0	0	0
old fashioned — *2 Tbsp*	34	40	0	0	0	0	440	10	0	8	0	0	4	0	0
original — *2 Tbsp*	34	35	0	0	0	0	510	9	0	6	0	2	0	0	0
Heinz Traditional Steak Sauce — *1 Tbsp*	15	10	0	0	0	0	190	2	0	2	0	10	0	0	0
K.C. Masterpiece Barbecue Sauce															
bold — *2 Tbsp*	n/a	60	0	0	0	0	240	12	n/a	n/a	<1	n/a	n/a	n/a	n/a
hickory — *2 Tbsp*	n/a	60	0	0	0	0	220	13	n/a	n/a	0	n/a	n/a	n/a	n/a
honey dijon — *2 Tbsp*	n/a	50	9	1	0	0	570	10	n/a	n/a	0	n/a	n/a	n/a	n/a
honey teriyaki — *2 Tbsp*	n/a	60	9	1	0	0	720	13	n/a	n/a	<1	n/a	n/a	n/a	n/a
mesquite — *2 Tbsp*	n/a	60	0	0	0	0	210	13	n/a	n/a	0	n/a	n/a	n/a	n/a
original — *2 Tbsp*	n/a	60	0	0	0	0	210	13	n/a	n/a	0	n/a	n/a	n/a	n/a
original, no salt — *2 Tbsp*	n/a	60	0	0	0	0	40	13	n/a	n/a	0	n/a	n/a	n/a	n/a
spicy — *2 Tbsp*	n/a	60	0	0	0	0	200	13	n/a	n/a	0	n/a	n/a	n/a	n/a
Kraft Barbecue Sauce															
Char-Grill — *2 Tbsp*	33	60	5	1	0	0	440	12	0	10	0	0	0	0	4
garlic — *2 Tbsp*	33	40	0	0	0	0	420	9	0	7	0	4	0	0	0
hickory smoke — *2 Tbsp*	33	40	0	0	0	0	440	10	0	8	0	4	0	0	0
hickory smoke, hot — *2 Tbsp*	33	40	0	0	0	0	360	9	0	7	0	4	0	0	0

	Weight g	Calories	Calories from fat	Total fat g	Sat. fat g	Cholesterol mg	Sodium mg	Carbohydrates g	Dietary fiber g	Sugars g	Protein g	Vitamin A % DV	Vitamin C % DV	Calcium % DV	Iron % DV
kansas city-style — *2 Tbsp*	33	45	0	0	0	0	280	11	21	8	0	0	0	0	4
original, extra-rich — *2 Tbsp*	33	50	0	0	0	0	360	12	0	9	0	4	0	0	0
Kraft Thick 'N Spicy Barbecue Sauce															
hickory smoke — *2 Tbsp*	34	50	0	0	0	0	440	12	0	10	0	6	0	0	2
honey — *2 Tbsp*	34	60	0	0	0	0	350	13	0	11	0	4	0	0	2
kansas city-style — *2 Tbsp*	34	60	0	0	0	0	280	13	<1	11	0	0	0	2	2
original — *2 Tbsp*	34	50	0	0	0	0	440	12	0	10	0	4	0	0	2

Condiments: Gravy & Sauces

	Weight g	Calories	Calories from fat	Total fat g	Sat. fat g	Cholesterol mg	Sodium mg	Carbohydrates g	Dietary fiber g	Sugars g	Protein g	Vitamin A % DV	Vitamin C % DV	Calcium % DV	Iron % DV
Chi-Chi's															
enchilada sauce — *¼ cup*	60	30	15	1.5	0.5	0	210	3	0	0	0	10	0	0	0
taco sauce — *1 Tbsp*	15	10	0	0	0	0	75	1	0	1	0	0	0	0	0
Chicken Tonight Sauce															
chicken cacciatore — *½ cup*	126	70	15	1.5	0	0	480	11	2	7	2	10	6	0	4
country french chicken — *½ cup*	122	120	90	10	1.5	15	860	6	1	2	<1	10	0	0	0
creamy mushroom chicken — *½ cup*	121	80	50	6	1	10	750	5	1	1	<1	0	8	0	0
light honey mustard — *½ cup*	124	60	5	0.5	0	0	420	13	3	8	1	35	2	5	5
sweet & sour chicken — *½ cup*	130	120	0	0	0	0	340	29	1	23	<1	4	15	0	2
Del Monte															
seafood cocktail sauce — *¼ cup*	78	100	0	0	0	0	910	24	0	22	1	20	4	0	0
sloppy joe sauce, hickory — *¼ cup*	69	70	0	0	0	0	700	18	0	15	1	25	2	0	6
sloppy joe sauce, original — *¼ cup*	67	70	0	0	0	0	680	16	0	13	1	25	2	0	6
Heinz															
chili sauce — *1 Tbsp*	17	15	0	0	0	0	230	4	0	3	0	15	4	0	0
horseradish sauce — *1 tsp*	5	25	25	2.5	0	0	35	1	0	0	0	0	0	0	0

	Weight g	Calories	Calories from fat	Total fat g	Sat. fat g	Cholesterol mg	Sodium mg	Carbohydrates g	Dietary fiber g	Sugars g	Protein g	Vitamin A % DV	Vitamin C % DV	Calcium % DV	Iron % DV
Savory Sauce — *1 Tbsp*	17	20	0	0	0	0	220	5	0	5	0	0	0	0	0
tartar sauce — *2 Tbsp*	30	140	130	14	2	5	250	4	0	3	0	0	0	0	0
Heinz Fat-Free Gravy															
beef — *¼ cup*	60	10	0	0	0	0	350	3	0	0	1	0	0	0	0
chicken — *¼ cup*	60	15	0	0	0	0	330	3	0	0	1	0	0	0	0
mushroom — *¼ cup*	60	10	0	0	0	0	300	3	0	0	0	0	0	0	0
turkey — *¼ cup*	60	15	0	0	0	0	310	3	0	0	1	0	0	0	0
Heinz Homestyle Gravy															
beef — *¼ cup*	60	25	10	1	0	0	350	2	0	0	2	0	0	0	0
Bistro-Style Au Jus — *¼ cup*	60	15	0	0.5	0	0	350	2	0	0	1	0	0	0	0
Blue Ribbon Country Gravy — *¼ cup*	60	25	10	1	0	0	240	4	1	0	0	0	0	0	0
chicken — *¼ cup*	60	25	10	1	0	0	360	3	0	0	1	0	0	0	0
pork — *¼ cup*	60	25	10	1	0	0	340	3	0	0	1	0	0	0	0
rich mushroom — *¼ cup*	60	20	5	0.5	0	0	370	3	0	0	1	0	0	0	0
turkey — *¼ cup*	60	30	15	1.5	0	0	370	3	0	0	1	0	0	0	0
zesty onion — *¼ cup*	60	25	10	1	0	0	350	3	0	0	1	0	0	0	0
Hormel Not-So-Sloppy-Joe Sauce — *¼ cup*	64	70	0	0	0	0	720	15	1	3	1	2	2	2	2
House of Tsang Stir Fry Sauce															
Bangkok Padang — *1 Tbsp*	n/a	45	20	2.5	0.5	0	240	4	0	3	1	0	0	0	0
classic — *1 Tbsp*	n/a	25	5	1	0	0	570	4	0	3	0	0	0	0	0
Korean Teriyaki — *1 Tbsp*	n/a	30	5	.5	0	0	430	6	0	4	0	0	0	0	0
Saigon Sizzle — *1 Tbsp*	n/a	40	5	1	0	0	350	8	0	6	0	0	0	0	0
Kraft															
sweet 'n sour sauce — *2 tsp*	37	80	5	0.5	0	0	180	19	0	16	0	0	0	0	0

	Weight g	Calories	Calories from fat	Total fat g	Sat. fat g	Cholesterol mg	Sodium mg	Carbohydrates g	Dietary fiber g	Sugars g	Protein g	Vitamin A % DV	Vitamin C % DV	Calcium % DV	Iron % DV
tartar sauce, nonfat — *2 tsp*	32	25	0	0	0	0	210	5	<1	3	0	0	0	0	0
La Choy															
dim sum sauce — *1 Tbsp*	18	10	0	0	0	0	230	2	0	1	<1	0	0	0	0
stir-fry sauce & marinade — *1 Tbsp*	19	25	<1	<1	0	0	672	5	0	5	<1	0	3	0	0
teriyaki sauce — *1 Tbsp*	18	16	<1	<1	0	0	941	3	0	3	<1	0	0	0	0
McIlhenny Tabasco Sauce															
hot pepper — *1 tsp*	5	0	0	0	n/a	n/a	30	0	n/a	n/a	0	4	n/a	n/a	n/a
jalapeño — *1 tsp*	3	0	0	0	0	0	70	0	0	0	0	n/a	n/a	n/a	n/a
Ocean Spray															
cranberry sauce, jellied — *¼ cup*	n/a	110	0	0	n/a	n/a	35	27	1	26	0	n/a	n/a	n/a	n/a
cranberry sauce, whole berry — *¼ cup*	n/a	110	0	0	n/a	n/a	10	28	1	27	0	n/a	n/a	n/a	n/a
Pillsbury Gravy Mix															
brown — *2 tsp*	n/a	15	0	0	0	0	270	3	0	<1	0	0	0	0	0
chicken-style — *2 tsp*	n/a	20	0	0	0	0	260	4	0	2	<1	0	0	2	0
Homestyle — *2 tsp*	n/a	15	0	0	0	0	270	3	0	<1	0	0	0	0	0
Ragu Pizza Quick															
100% natural pizza sauce — *¼ cup*	63	30	5	1	0	0	270	4	1	3	1	10	10	0	2
chunky mushroom, garlic & basil — *¼ cup*	63	40	15	1.5	0	0	340	6	1	4	1	8	8	0	2
chunky tomato sauce — *¼ cup*	64	50	15	1.5	0	0	300	7	1	5	1	15	2	2	4
pepperoni-flavored sauce — *¼ cup*	63	60	35	2	1	<5	420	5	1	3	1	8	8	0	2
traditional sauce — *¼ cup*	63	40	15	1.5	0	0	340	5	1	3	1	8	8	0	2

Condiments: Ketchup

	Weight g	Calories	Calories from fat	Total fat g	Sat. fat g	Cholesterol mg	Sodium mg	Carbohydrates g	Dietary fiber g	Sugars g	Protein g	Vitamin A % DV	Vitamin C % DV	Calcium % DV	Iron % DV
Del Monte — *1 Tbsp*	17	15	0	0	0	0	190	4	0	4	0	2	2	0	0
Smucker's Ketchup — *1 Tbsp*	17	25	0	0	0	0	110	7	0	6	0	0	0	0	0

Condiments: Mayonnaise

	Weight g	Calories	Calories from fat	Total fat g	Sat. fat g	Cholesterol mg	Sodium mg	Carbohydrates g	Dietary fiber g	Sugars g	Protein g	Vitamin A % DV	Vitamin C % DV	Calcium % DV	Iron % DV
Kraft, Light Mayonnaise Dressing — *1 Tbsp*	15	50	45	5	1	0	110	1	0	0	0	0	0	0	0
Miracle Whip Free Nonfat Dressing — *1 Tbsp*	16	15	0	0	0	0	120	3	0	2	0	0	0	0	0
Miracle Whip Light — *1 Tbsp*	15	40	30	3	0	0	120	3	0	2	0	0	0	0	0
Mrs. Filbert's Mayonnaise															
light — *1 Tbsp*	15	30	25	3	0	0	130	1	0	0	0	0	0	0	0
regular — *1 Tbsp*	15	100	100	12	2	10	80	0	0	0	0	0	0	0	0
Weight Watchers Mayonnaise															
fat-free dressing — *1 Tbsp*	n/a	10	0	0	0	0	105	3	0	2	0	0	0	0	0
light — *1 Tbsp*	n/a	25	15	2	0	5	130	1	0	1	0	0	0	0	0
light, low-sodium — *1 Tbsp*	n/a	25	20	2	0	5	40	1	0	0	0	0	0	0	0

Condiments: Mustard

	Weight g	Calories	Calories from fat	Total fat g	Sat. fat g	Cholesterol mg	Sodium mg	Carbohydrates g	Dietary fiber g	Sugars g	Protein g	Vitamin A % DV	Vitamin C % DV	Calcium % DV	Iron % DV
Gulden's Spicy Brown Mustard — *1 tsp*	5	5	0	0	0	0	50	0	0	0	0	0	0	0	0
Kraft, Horseradish Mustard — *1 tsp*	5	0	0	0	0	0	55	0	0	0	0	0	0	0	0

Condiments: Other

	Weight g	Calories	Calories from fat	Total fat g	Sat. fat g	Cholesterol mg	Sodium mg	Carbohydrates g	Dietary fiber g	Sugars g	Protein g	Vitamin A % DV	Vitamin C % DV	Calcium % DV	Iron % DV
Heinz Relish															
dill relish — *1 Tbsp*	15	0	0	0	0	0	220	0	0	0	0	0	0	0	0
hamburger relish — *1 Tbsp*	15	10	0	0	0	0	180	3	0	2	0	2	0	0	0
hot dog relish, squeezeable — *1 Tbsp*	15	15	0	0	0	0	105	4	0	3	0	0	0	0	0
india relish — *1 Tbsp*	15	20	0	0	0	0	100	5	0	3	0	0	0	0	0
piccalilli relish — *1 Tbsp*	15	15	0	0	0	0	75	4	0	3	0	0	0	0	0
sweet relish, squeezable — *1 Tbsp*	15	15	0	0	0	0	90	4	0	3	0	0	0	0	0
Imperial Seasoning Spreads															
garlic & herb — *1 Tbsp*	14	90	90	10	2	0	110	0	0	0	0	10	0	0	0

	Weight g	Calories	Calories from fat	Total fat g	Sat. fat g	Cholesterol mg	Sodium mg	Carbohydrates g	Dietary fiber g	Sugars g	Protein g	Vitamin A % DV	Vitamin C % DV	Calcium % DV	Iron % DV
parmesan & herb — *1 Tbsp*	14	90	90	10	2	0	110	0	0	0	0	10	0	0	0
Kraft															
cream-style horseradish — *1 tsp*	5	0	0	0	0	0	50	0	0	0	0	0	2	0	0
Sandwich Spread & Burger Sauce — *1 tsp*	15	50	45	5	0.5	<5	100	3	0	3	0	0	0	0	0

Cookies: Doughs & Mixes

	Weight g	Calories	Calories from fat	Total fat g	Sat. fat g	Cholesterol mg	Sodium mg	Carbohydrates g	Dietary fiber g	Sugars g	Protein g	Vitamin A % DV	Vitamin C % DV	Calcium % DV	Iron % DV
Betty Crocker Brownie Mix															
caramel — *1/18 of recipe*	n/a	190	80	9	1.5	25	150	27	0	19	2	0	0	0	4
chocolate chip — *1/18 of recipe*	n/a	200	90	10	3	25	100	26	0	19	2	0	0	0	4
cookies & cream — *1/18 of recipe*	n/a	200	90	10	2	25	115	27	0	19	2	0	0	0	2
dark chocolate fudge — *1/18 of recipe*	n/a	190	80	8	2	25	120	27	1	19	2	0	0	0	8
frosted — *1/18 of recipe*	n/a	230	90	10	2.5	25	140	33	1	24	2	0	0	0	6
fudge — *1/18 of recipe*	n/a	200	80	9	2	25	125	28	1	19	2	0	0	0	4
german chocolate — *1/18 of recipe*	n/a	220	80	9	2.5	25	130	33	1	24	2	0	0	0	4
hot fudge — *1/18 of recipe*	n/a	190	80	9	2.5	25	130	25	0	18	2	0	0	0	4
original — *1/18 of recipe*	n/a	200	80	9	2	25	120	29	1	21	2	0	0	0	4
Reese's peanut butter candy pieces — *1/18 of recipe*	n/a	210	90	10	3	25	100	27	0	19	2	0	0	0	4
walnut — *1/18 of recipe*	n/a	200	100	11	2	25	105	24	1	16	2	0	0	0	4
white chocolate swirl — *1/18 of recipe*	n/a	210	90	10	3	25	115	28	0	20	2	0	0	2	4
Betty Crocker Classic Dessert Date Bar Mix — *1/12 of recipe*	n/a	160	60	7	2	0	90	23	1	14	1	0	0	0	2
Betty Crocker Supreme Dessert Bar Mix															
caramel oatmeal — *1/20 of recipe*	n/a	180	70	8	2	0	115	24	<1	12	2	0	0	0	4
chocolate chunk — *1/20 of recipe*	n/a	180	80	9	2.5	10	160	24	0	16	2	0	0	0	4
chocolate peanut butter — *1/20 of recipe*	n/a	170	70	7	2	10	180	23	1	10	3	0	0	0	2
easy layer — *1/20 of recipe*	n/a	170	70	8	4	0	130	24	0	15	1	2	0	2	2

	Weight g	Calories	Calories from fat	Total fat g	Sat. fat g	Cholesterol mg	Sodium mg	Carbohydrates g	Dietary fiber g	Sugars g	Protein g	Vitamin A % DV	Vitamin C % DV	Calcium % DV	Iron % DV
M&M's cookie bars — *1/20 of recipe*	n/a	170	70	8	2.5	10	160	24	0	16	1	0	0	0	2
raspberry — *1/20 of recipe*	n/a	170	50	6	1.5	0	160	26	0	13	2	0	0	0	2
strawberry swirl cheese cake — *1/24 of recipe*	n/a	180	90	10	2.5	20	110	20	0	10	2	4	0	0	0
Sunkist Lemon — *1/24 of recipe*	n/a	140	35	4	1	35	85	23	0	16	2	0	0	0	0
Pillsbury Deluxe Bar Mix															
apple streusel — *1/24 of recipe*	n/a	150	50	6	1.5	0	55	23	<1	13	1	0	0	0	4
Chips Ahoy — *1/20 of recipe*	n/a	150	45	5	2	10	125	25	<1	16	2	2	0	0	8
fudge swirl cookie — *1/20 of recipe*	n/a	180	70	8	1.5	10	110	25	<1	16	1	0	0	0	4
lemon cheesecake — *1/24 of recipe*	n/a	190	90	10	3	25	105	22	0	13	2	6	0	2	4
M&M's — *1/18 of recipe*	n/a	170	50	6	2	10	140	27	<1	17	2	2	0	0	6
Nutter Butter — *1/18 of recipe*	n/a	180	60	7	1.5	15	170	26	0	15	3	2	0	0	6
Oreo — *1/18 of recipe*	n/a	180	60	7	1.5	10	160	26	<1	16	2	0	0	0	4
Pillsbury Deluxe Brownie Mix															
chocolate deluxe — *1/20 of recipe*	n/a	180	60	7	1.5	10	110	28	<1	19	2	0	0	0	6
fudge — *1/20 of recipe*	n/a	180	70	8	1.5	10	90	25	1	16	2	0	0	0	6
Thick 'n Fudgy cheesecake swirl — *1/16 of recipe*	n/a	170	80	9	2.5	30	90	21	<1	15	2	0	0	0	4
Thick 'n Fudgy double chocolate — *1/16 of recipe*	n/a	150	50	6	1	15	95	23	<1	15	1	0	0	0	4
Thick 'n Fudgy walnut — *1/12 of recipe*	n/a	190	90	10	1.5	20	100	24	1	15	2	0	0	0	6
Pillsbury Refrigerated Cookies															
chocolate chip — *2 cookies*	28	130	40	6	2	<5	85	17	<1	12	1	0	0	0	4
chocolate chip w/ walnuts — *2 cookies*	28	140	60	7	2	<5	90	17	<1	10	1	0	0	0	4
chocolate chip, reduced-fat — *2 cookies*	28	110	35	4	1.5	<5	80	18	<1	11	1	0	0	0	4
chocolate chunk — *2 cookies*	28	130	50	6	2	<5	90	18	<1	11	1	0	0	0	4
Heath — *2 cookies*	28	140	60	7	2	5	105	17	0	10	1	0	0	0	0

	Weight g	Calories	Calories from fat	Total fat g	Sat. fat g	Cholesterol mg	Sodium mg	Carbohydrates g	Dietary fiber g	Sugars g	Protein g	Vitamin A % DV	Vitamin C % DV	Calcium % DV	Iron % DV
holiday varieties — *2 cookies*	28	130	60	7	2	<5	100	16	0	7	1	0	0	0	0
M&M's — *2 cookies*	28	130	50	6	2	<5	80	18	<1	12	1	0	0	0	4
oatmeal chocolate chip — *2 cookies*	28	130	50	6	2	<5	95	17	<1	10	1	0	0	0	4
peanut butter — *2 cookies*	28	110	45	5	1	<5	135	15	0	9	2	0	0	0	2
Reese's — *2 cookies*	28	130	50	6	2.5	<5	105	15	<1	10	3	0	0	0	4
sugar — *2 cookies*	32	130	45	5	1.5	<5	125	19	0	10	1	0	0	0	4
SnackWell's Cookie Mix															
devil's food — *1/12 of recipe*	n/a	140	25	2.5	0.5	0	105	28	<1	20	2	0	0	0	8
fudge — *1/12 of recipe*	n/a	150	25	2.5	0.5	0	115	29	1	20	2	0	0	0	8
SnackWell's Reduced-Fat Refrigerated Cookies															
chocolate chip — *2 cookies*	28	110	25	3	1.5	<5	85	19	<1	12	1	0	0	0	4
chocolate fudge — *2 cookies*	28	90	15	1.5	0	<5	95	18	<1	10	1	0	0	0	6
Sweet Rewards Supreme Brownie Mix, Reduced-Fat — *1 prepared*	n/a	150	40	4	1	20	110	27	0	19	2	0	0	0	6

Cookies: Ready-to-eat

	Weight g	Calories	Calories from fat	Total fat g	Sat. fat g	Cholesterol mg	Sodium mg	Carbohydrates g	Dietary fiber g	Sugars g	Protein g	Vitamin A % DV	Vitamin C % DV	Calcium % DV	Iron % DV
Barnum's Animals (Nabisco) — *12 crackers*	31	140	35	4	0.5	0	160	23	1	8	2	0	0	0	6
Chips Ahoy! (Nabisco) — *3 cookies*	32	160	70	8	2.5	0	105	21	1	10	2	0	0	0	4
Chips Deluxe (Keebler)															
bite-size — *8 cookies*	32	160	80	9	3	<5	110	20	<1	10	2	0	0	0	4
Chocolate Lovers — *1 cookie*	17	90	40	5	2.5	10	75	11	<1	6	<1	2	0	0	2
Rainbow — *1 cookie*	16	80	35	4	2	<5	45	10	<1	5	1	0	0	0	2
Rainbow, bite-size — *7 cookies*	29	140	60	7	2.5	<5	95	19	<1	9	2	0	0	0	4
regular — *1 cookie*	15	80	40	4.5	1.5	0	60	9	0	4	1	0	0	0	2
25% reduced-fat — *1 cookie*	15	70	30	3	1	0	70	11	0	0	1	0	0	0	2
Chocolate Wafers, 30% Reduced-Fat (Keebler) — *8 cookies*	31	130	30	3.5	0.5	0	170	25	0	11	1	0	0	0	6

	Weight g	Calories	Calories from fat	Total fat g	Sat. fat g	Cholesterol mg	Sodium mg	Carbohydrates g	Dietary fiber g	Sugars g	Protein g	Vitamin A % DV	Vitamin C % DV	Calcium % DV	Iron % DV
Danish Wedding Cookies (Keebler) — *4 cookies*	27	120	45	5	2	0	80	20	<1	11	1	0	0	0	2
Dunkaroos (Betty Crocker)															
chocolate chip w/ chocolate frosting — *1 tray*	28	120	40	4.5	1	0	85	20	<1	13	1	0	0	0	0
cinnamon graham w/ vanilla frosting — *1 tray*	28	130	40	4.5	1	0	65	21	0	14	1	0	0	0	2
cookies & creme — *1 tray*	28	130	40	4.5	1	0	110	20	0	14	1	0	0	0	2
E. L. Fudge (Keebler)															
butter-flavored w/ fudge creme filling — *3 cookies*	34	170	70	8	2	<5	105	24	<1	11	2	0	0	0	6
chocolate w/ vanilla creme filling — *3 cookies*	35	170	70	8	2	0	125	23	1	14	2	0	0	0	6
fudge w/ fudge creme filling — *3 cookies*	34	160	60	7	2	0	100	23	1	11	2	0	0	0	6
Elfin Delights (Keebler)															
chocolate w/ vanilla creme, 50% reduced-fat — *2 cookies*	25	110	25	2.5	0.5	0	120	19	<1	8	1	0	0	0	4
chocolate w/ fudge creme, 50% reduced-fat — *2 cookies*	25	110	25	2.5	0.5	0	100	19	<1	10	1	0	0	0	4
creme, 50% reduced-fat — *2 cookies*	25	110	25	2.5	0.5	0	90	19	0	10	1	0	0	0	4
devil's food, fat-free — *1 cookie*	21	70	0	0	0	0	110	14	<1	9	1	0	0	0	4
devil's food, w/ vanilla creme, fat-free — *1 cookie*	21	70	0	0	0	0	100	14	0	9	1	0	0	0	2
Entenmann's															
chocolate chip — *3 cookies*	30	140	60	7	2	10	90	20	<1	11	1	0	0	0	0
chocolate chip peanut butter — *3 cookies*	30	140	60	7	3	15	110	17	<1	8	3	0	0	0	0
milk chocolate chunk — *2 cookies*	30	150	70	8	3.5	15	90	19	<1	12	2	0	0	2	4
oatmeal raisin, fat-free — *2 cookies*	24	80	0	0	0	0	120	18	<1	11	1	0	0	0	0
Famous Amos															
chocolate chip — *4 cookies*	28	130	60	7	2	0	105	19	1	11	1	4	0	0	4
oatmeal raisin — *4 cookies*	28	130	45	5	1	<5	150	20	1	10	2	4	0	2	4
Famous Chocolate Wafers (Nabisco) — *5 cookies*	32	140	35	4	1.5	<5	230	24	1	10	2	0	0	0	6

Foods, Brand Name

	Weight g	Calories	Calories from fat	Total fat g	Sat. fat g	Cholesterol mg	Sodium mg	Carbohydrates g	Dietary fiber g	Sugars g	Protein g	Vitamin A % DV	Vitamin C % DV	Calcium % DV	Iron % DV
Fudge Shoppe (Keebler)															
Deluxe Grahams — *3 cookies*	28	140	60	7	4.5	0	105	19	<1	10	1	0	0	0	4
Deluxe Grahams, reduced-fat — *3 cookies*	26	120	45	5	2	0	130	19	0	11	1	0	0	2	4
Fudge 'N Caramel — *2 cookies*	24	120	50	6	4	<5	55	16	<1	12	<1	0	0	0	2
Fudge Sticks — *3 cookies*	29	150	70	8	4.5	0	55	20	<1	15	1	0	0	0	2
Fudge Stripes — *3 cookies*	32	160	70	8	4.5	0	140	21	<1	10	1	0	0	0	4
Fudge Stripes, reduced-fat — *3 cookies*	31	150	45	5	2.5	0	180	23	0	13	1	0	0	0	6
Fudge Truffles — *3 cookies*	35	180	90	10	5	0	105	22	<1	14	1	0	0	2	4
Grasshopper — *4 cookies*	30	150	60	7	5	0	70	20	<1	12	1	0	0	0	4
P.B. Fudgebutters — *2 cookies*	24	130	70	7	4	<5	90	14	<1	9	2	0	0	0	2
S'mores — *3 cookies*	32	150	60	7	4.5	0	90	21	<1	12	1	0	0	2	4
Ginger Snaps, Old Fashioned, Nabisco — *4 cookies*	28	120	25	2.5	0.5	0	210	22	<1	10	1	0	0	2	6
Golden Vanilla Wafers (Keebler) — *8 cookies*	31	150	6	7	2	0	120	20	<1	9	1	0	0	0	2
Graham Selects (Keebler)															
cinnamon crisp, low-fat — *8 crackers*	28	110	10	1.5	0.5	0	190	24	1	9	2	0	0	0	6
french vanilla, low-fat — *8 crackers*	28	110	15	1.5	0.5	0	90	24	<1	9	2	0	0	0	4
old fashioned — *8 crackers*	29	130	30	3	1	0	135	23	<1	7	2	0	0	0	4
old fashioned, honey — *8 crackers*	31	150	50	6	1.5	0	140	21	1	6	2	0	0	0	4
Grandma's															
Cookie Bits, fudge — *9 cookies*	n/a	170	70	8	2	0	230	24	1	2	2	n/a	n/a	n/a	n/a
Cookie Bits, peanut butter — *9 cookies*	n/a	150	60	6	1.5	0	135	21	1	9	3	n/a	n/a	n/a	n/a
Cookie Bits, vanilla — *9 cookies*	n/a	150	60	7	1.5	<5	80	21	<1	10	2	n/a	n/a	n/a	n/a
fudge sandwich — *1 pkg*	n/a	240	70	7	2	0	270	41	1	21	2	n/a	n/a	n/a	n/a
peanut butter sandwich — *5 cookies*	n/a	210	80	9	2	0	190	29	1	13	4	n/a	n/a	n/a	n/a

	Weight g	Calories	Calories from fat	Total fat g	Sat. fat g	Cholesterol mg	Sodium mg	Carbohydrates g	Dietary fiber g	Sugars g	Protein g	Vitamin A % DV	Vitamin C % DV	Calcium % DV	Iron % DV
Rich N' Chewy — *1 pkg*	n/a	270	100	11	4	10	135	38	1	22	3	n/a	n/a	n/a	n/a
vanilla sandwich — *1 pkg*	n/a	240	60	7	1.5	0	220	43	<1	23	3	n/a	n/a	n/a	n/a
Grandma's Big Cookies															
chocolate chip — *1 cookie*	39	190	80	9	2.5	<5	130	25	1	11	2	n/a	n/a	n/a	n/a
fudge chocolate chip — *1 cookie*	39	170	60	6	2	<5	160	27	1	11	2	n/a	n/a	n/a	n/a
nutty fudge — *1 cookie*	40	190	70	8	1.5	<5	150	25	1	14	3	n/a	n/a	n/a	n/a
oatmeal apple spice — *1 cookie*	39	170	50	6	1.5	<5	220	26	2	9	2	n/a	n/a	n/a	n/a
old time molasses — *1 cookie*	39	160	35	4	1.5	<5	230	29	<1	12	2	n/a	n/a	n/a	n/a
peanut butter — *1 cookie*	39	190	80	9	2	<5	180	22	1	10	4	n/a	n/a	n/a	n/a
peanut butter chocolate chip — *1 cookie*	39	190	90	10	3	<5	170	23	1	13	4	n/a	n/a	n/a	n/a
Grandma's Value Line															
fudge sandwich — *3 cookies*	n/a	180	50	5	1.5	0	200	31	<1	15	2	n/a	n/a	n/a	n/a
fudge sandwich wafer — *4 cookies*	n/a	160	60	6	1.5	0	50	25	1	15	2	n/a	n/a	n/a	n/a
fudge vanilla sandwich — *3 cookies*	n/a	150	40	4	1	0	160	25	1	12	2	n/a	n/a	n/a	n/a
strawberry sandwich wafer — *4 cookies*	n/a	160	45	5	1	0	45	26	<1	17	1	n/a	n/a	n/a	n/a
vanilla sandwich — *3 cookies*	n/a	180	45	5	1.5	0	160	32	<1	17	2	n/a	n/a	n/a	n/a
vanilla sandwich wafer — *4 cookies*	n/a	160	45	5	1.5	0	50	26	<1	16	1	n/a	n/a	n/a	n/a
Health Valley															
Amaranth Graham, oat bran — *8 crackers*	n/a	100	0	0	0	0	30	23	3	5	4	2	0	2	4
Amaranth Graham, original — *6 crackers*	n/a	120	27	3	0	0	80	22	3	5	4	0	0	4	4
Double-Chocolate-Flavored Healthy Chips — *3 cookies*	n/a	100	0	n/a	0	0	40	24	4	10	3	2	2	2	6
Healthy Biscotti, amaretto or chocolate — *2 cookies*	n/a	120	27	3	0	0	50	23	3	7	3	2	0	0	4
Healthy Chips, original or old fashioned — *3 cookies*	n/a	100	0	0	0	0	40	24	4	10	3	2	2	2	6
Healthy Chocolate — *2 cookies*	n/a	70	0	0	0	0	25	17	3	10	2	2	2	2	6

	Weight *g*	Calories	Calories from fat	Total fat *g*	Sat. fat *g*	Cholesterol *mg*	Sodium *mg*	Carbohydrates *g*	Dietary fiber *g*	Sugars *g*	Protein *g*	Vitamin A *% DV*	Vitamin C *% DV*	Calcium *% DV*	Iron *% DV*
jumbo, raspberry, or apple raisin — *1 cookie*	n/a	80	0	0	0	0	35	19	3	9	2	2	2	2	6
raisin oatmeal — *3 cookies*	n/a	100	0	0	0	0	50	24	3	11	2	2	4	2	4
Raspberry Fruit Center — *1 cookie*	n/a	70	0	0	0	0	20	18	2	9	2	10	2	2	4
Honey Maid Graham Crackers (Nabisco)															
chocolate — *8 crackers*	28	120	25	3	0.5	0	180	22	<1	8	2	0	0	0	6
honey — *8 crackers*	28	120	25	3	0.5	0	180	22	1	7	2	0	0	0	6
Hydrox Creme Filled Chocolate Cookies (Sunshine) — *3 cookies*	31	150	60	7	2	0	125	21	1	11	2	0	0	0	6
Iced Animal Cookies (Keebler) — *6 cookies*	32	140	40	4.5	2	0	130	24	<1	9	2	0	0	0	4
Keebler Classic Collection															
chocolate fudge creme sandwich — *1 cookie*	17	80	30	3.5	1	0	75	12	0	6	1	0	0	0	2
french vanilla creme sandwich — *1 cookie*	17	80	30	3.5	1	0	65	12	0	6	1	0	0	0	2
oatmeal — *2 cookies*	30	150	70	8	4	25	150	18	<1	8	2	4	0	0	4
peanut butter — *2 cookies*	30	150	80	9	4	25	150	18	<1	10	2	4	0	0	4
sugar — *2 cookies*	30	150	70	8	4	25	150	18	<1	8	2	4	0	0	4
Krisp Kreem Sugar Wafers (Keebler) — *5 pieces*	27	140	60	7	1.5	0	50	19	0	13	1	0	0	0	2
Lorna Doone Shortbread Cookies (Nabisco) — *4 cookies*	29	140	60	7	1	5	130	19	<1	6	2	0	0	0	6
Newtons, Nabisco															
cranberry, fat-free — *2 cookies*	29	70	0	0	0	0	90	21	<1	8	2	0	0	0	2
fig — *2 cookies*	31	110	20	2.5	1	0	120	20	1	13	1	0	0	0	4
Nilla Wafers (Nabisco) — *8 wafers*	32	140	40	5	1	5	105	24	0	12	2	0	0	2	4
Nutter Butter Peanut Butter Sandwich Cookies (Nabisco) — *2 cookies*	28	130	50	6	1	<5	110	19	1	8	2	0	0	0	4
Oreo (Nabisco)															
reduced-fat — *3 cookies*	32	130	30	3.5	1	0	210	25	1	13	2	0	0	0	6
regular — *3 cookies*	33	160	60	7	1.5	0	220	23	1	13	2	0	0	0	4

	Weight g	Calories	Calories from fat	Total fat g	Sat. fat g	Cholesterol mg	Sodium mg	Carbohydrates g	Dietary fiber g	Sugars g	Protein g	Vitamin A % DV	Vitamin C % DV	Calcium % DV	Iron % DV
Pecan Sandies (Keebler)															
bite-size — *8 cookies*	32	170	90	10	2	<5	110	18	<1	7	2	0	0	0	4
simply sandies — *1 cookie*	15	80	40	4.5	2	10	75	9	0	3	1	2	0	0	2
w/ crunchy pecan pieces — *1 cookie*	16	80	45	5	1	<5	75	9	<1	3	<1	0	0	0	2
w/ crunchy pecan pieces, 25% reduced-fat — *1 cookie*	15	70	30	3	0.5	0	50	10	0	3	1	0	0	0	0
w/ praline creme — *2 cookies*	29	160	100	11	2	5	70	16	0	8	1	0	0	0	2
Pepperidge Farm American Collection															
Beacon Hill — *1 cookie*	26	130	60	7	2	5	100	16	<1	8	2	0	0	0	4
Charleston — *1 cookie*	26	130	60	7	2.5	20	110	16	<1	9	1	0	0	0	2
Chesapeake — *1 cookie*	26	140	70	8	1.5	10	100	15	<1	7	2	0	0	0	4
Nantucket — *1 cookie*	26	130	60	7	3	10	75	16	<1	8	1	0	0	0	2
Santa Fe — *1 cookie*	26	120	40	4.5	1	<5	110	18	<1	7	2	0	0	0	2
Sausalito — *1 cookie*	26	140	7	7	2	10	110	16	<1	8	2	0	0	0	2
Tahoe — *1 cookie*	26	130	70	7	3	15	110	16	<1	7	2	0	0	2	2
Pepperidge Farm Distinctive Cookies															
Bordeaux — *4 cookies*	28	130	50	5	2.5	10	95	20	<1	12	2	0	0	0	2
Brussels — *3 cookies*	31	150	60	7	3	5	80	20	1	11	2	0	0	0	4
Brussels Mint — *3 cookies*	37	190	90	10	3.5	0	100	22	1	13	2	0	0	0	4
Butter Chessman — *3 cookies*	26	120	45	5	3	20	80	18	<1	5	2	0	0	0	2
Chantilly Hazlenut Raspberry — *1 cookie*	17	80	30	3	0.5	5	50	12	<1	7	<1	0	0	0	2
Chocolate Laced Pirouette — *5 cookies*	34	180	90	10	2.5	5	90	20	<1	13	2	0	0	0	4
Dessert Favorites — *3 cookies*	34	170	80	9	3	5	90	21	1	11	2	0	0	0	4
Geneva — *3 cookies*	31	160	80	9	3.5	0	95	19	1	8	2	0	0	0	6
Lido — *1 cookie*	17	90	40	4.5	1.5	5	45	11	0	5	<1	0	0	0	4

	Weight g	Calories	Calories from fat	Total fat g	Sat. fat g	Cholesterol mg	Sodium mg	Carbohydrates g	Dietary fiber g	Sugars g	Protein g	Vitamin A % DV	Vitamin C % DV	Calcium % DV	Iron % DV
Linzer Raspberry Filled — *1 cookie*	23	100	35	4	1	5	65	15	<1	10	1	0	0	0	2
Party Favorites — *3 cookies*	31	170	80	8	3	10	90	21	1	10	2	0	0	0	4
Personal Favorites — *4 cookies*	34	170	80	9	3	10	90	21	<1	10	2	0	0	0	4
Toy Chest Butter Assortment — *3 cookies*	26	120	45	5	3	20	80	18	<1	5	2	0	0	0	2
Pepperidge Farm Distinctive Cookies, Milano															
double chocolate — *2 cookies*	28	150	70	8	3	10	70	17	<1	10	2	0	0	0	4
hazelnut — *2 cookies*	26	130	70	7	2	5	65	15	1	7	2	0	0	0	4
mint — *2 cookies*	26	140	70	8	3.5	<5	70	16	<1	9	1	0	0	0	4
original — *3 cookies*	34	180	90	10	3.5	10	80	21	<1	11	2	0	0	0	6
Pepperidge Farm Fruit Cookies															
apricot raspberry — *3 cookies*	31	140	50	6	2	5	110	22	<1	10	2	0	0	0	2
cherry cobbler — *1 cookie*	17	70	25	2.5	1	<5	45	11	0	5	<1	0	0	2	2
peach tart — *2 cookies*	31	120	25	3	1	0	115	23	<1	11	1	0	6	0	4
strawberry — *3 cookies*	31	140	50	6	2	5	110	22	<1	10	5	0	0	0	2
Pepperidge Farm International Collection															
Biarritz — *6 cookies*	31	160	70	8	4	0	50	21	<1	11	1	0	0	0	2
Deli Chocolate Dark Chocolate — *2 cookies*	26	110	35	4	2	0	50	19	0	9	1	0	0	0	2
Highland Shortbread — *2 cookies*	28	140	70	7	5	17	<1	5	2	11	25	0	0	0	0
Selection De Choix — *5 cookies*	28	150	60	7	4	5	60	19	0	8	1	0	0	0	2
Pepperidge Farm International Collection, Esprit															
Blanc — *1 cookie*	17	80	40	4.5	2.5	10	50	10	0	3	1	0	0	0	0
Noir — *1 cookie*	17	90	45	5	3.5	10	50	10	0	3	1	0	0	0	0
Pepperidge Farm Old Fashioned Cookies															
brownie chocolate nut — *3 cookies*	31	160	80	9	3	15	115	18	2	9	2	0	0	0	4

	Weight g	Calories	Calories from fat	Total fat g	Sat. fat g	Cholesterol mg	Sodium mg	Carbohydrates g	Dietary fiber g	Sugars g	Protein g	Vitamin A % DV	Vitamin C % DV	Calcium % DV	Iron % DV
chocolate chip — *3 cookies*	28	140	60	7	2.5	10	65	18	<1	9	2	0	0	0	6
gingerman — *4 cookies*	28	120	35	3.5	1	10	95	21	<1	11	2	0	0	0	4
hazelnut — *3 cookies*	31	160	70	8	2	0	135	21	<1	6	2	0	0	0	4
irish oatmeal — *3 cookies*	28	130	50	6	1.5	<5	70	19	2	7	2	0	0	0	2
lemon nut crunch — *3 cookies*	31	170	80	9	2	15	60	18	2	7	2	0	0	0	0
oatmeal raisin — *3 cookies*	34	160	60	6	1.5	10	150	23	1	12	2	0	0	0	6
pecan shortbread — *2 cookies*	26	140	80	9	2.5	<5	85	14	1	4	1	0	0	0	2
shortbread — *2 cookies*	26	140	70	7	2.5	10	105	16	<1	5	2	0	0	0	2
sugar — *3 cookies*	31	140	60	6	1.5	15	90	20	<1	10	2	0	0	0	4
Pepperidge Farm Soft Baked															
caramel pecan — *1 cookie*	26	130	60	7	1.5	20	55	16	<1	8	2	0	0	0	2
chocolate chocolate walnut — *1 cookie*	26	130	50	6	2	5	45	16	1	9	2	0	0	0	4
chocolate chunk — *1 cookie*	26	130	50	6	2.5	10	35	16	2	9	1	0	0	0	4
milk chocolate macadamia — *1 cookie*	26	130	60	6	2.5	10	55	16	1	9	1	0	0	0	4
oatmeal raisin — *1 cookie*	26	110	40	4	1	15	60	17	1	9	1	0	0	0	2
Pepperidge Farm Tiny Goldfish Cookies															
chocolate — *19 pieces*	30	140	45	5	1.5	10	85	22	2	8	2	0	0	0	4
chocolate chunk — *19 pieces*	30	150	60	7	2.5	20	50	21	1	6	2	0	0	0	4
graham goldfish — *19 pieces*	30	150	70	7	2.5	15	150	20	2	7	2	0	0	0	4
vanilla — *19 pieces*	30	150	60	7	2.5	20	50	21	1	6	2	0	0	0	4
SnackWell's															
chocolate chip, bite size — *13 cookies*	29	130	35	3.5	1.5	0	180	22	1	10	2	0	0	0	4
creme sandwich — *2 cookies*	26	110	20	2.5	0.5	0	100	21	<1	10	1	0	0	2	2
Social Tea Biscuits (Nabisco) — *6 cookies*	28	120	30	4	0.5	5	105	20	<1	7	2	0	0	0	8

	Weight g	Calories	Calories from fat	Total fat g	Sat. fat g	Cholesterol mg	Sodium mg	Carbohydrates g	Dietary fiber g	Sugars g	Protein g	Vitamin A % DV	Vitamin C % DV	Calcium % DV	Iron % DV
Soft Batch (Keebler)															
chocolate chip — *1 cookie*	16	80	35	3.5	1	0	70	10	<1	6	<1	0	0	0	2
oatmeal raisin — *1 cookie*	16	70	30	3	1	0	65	10	<1	6	<1	0	0	0	0
Stella D'oro Breakfast Treats — *1 treat*	23	100	30	3	1	10	80	16	<1	7	1	0	0	0	4
Sweet Spots (Keebler) — *1 pkg*	n/a	120	50	6	3	<5	80	17	<1	9	1	0	0	0	4
Teddy Grahams (Nabisco)															
chocolate — *25 pieces*	30	140	40	5	1	0	150	22	1	9	2	0	0	0	4
honey — *25 pieces*	30	140	40	4	1	0	150	22	1	8	2	0	0	0	4
Twix Cookie Bars (M&M/Mars) — *2 bars*	57	280	130	14	5	5	115	37	1	27	3	0	0	4	2
Vienna Fingers Sandwich Cookies (Sunshine) — *2 cookies*	29	140	50	6	1.5	0	105	21	<1	8	2	<2	<2	<2	4
Weight Watchers															
brownie (frozen), chocolate-frosted — *1 brownie*	35	100	20	2.5	1	0	135	22	3	18	2	0	2	0	4
brownie (frozen), peanut butter fudge — *1 brownie*	35	110	20	2.5	0.5	0	140	21	3	16	2	0	0	2	6
chocolate chip cookies — *2 cookies*	30	140	45	5	2	0	90	22	1	15	2	0	0	2	4
chocolate sandwich — *2 cookies*	30	140	35	3.5	1	0	160	23	1	16	2	0	0	0	6
fruit-filled fig — *1 bar*	20	70	0	0	0	0	50	16	0	9	1	0	0	2	2
oatmeal raisin — *2 cookies*	30	120	15	2	0	0	90	22	1	13	2	0	0	2	2
	Crackers														
American Vintage Wine Biscuits — *5 crackers*	28	140	60	7	1	0	190	17	<1	5	2	0	0	2	4
Better Cheddars (Nabisco) — *22 crackers*	30	150	70	8	2	<5	290	17	<1	<1	4	2	0	4	6
Cheez-It Snack Crackers (Sunshine) — *27 crackers*	30	160	80	8	2	0	240	16	<1	<1	4	<2	<2	4	6
Club Partners (Keebler)															
50% reduced-sodium — *4 crackers*	14	70	25	3	1	0	80	9	<1	1	1	0	0	0	2
original — *4 crackers*	14	70	25	3	1	0	160	9	<1	1	1	0	0	0	0

	Weight g	Calories	Calories from fat	Total fat g	Sat. fat g	Cholesterol mg	Sodium mg	Carbohydrates g	Dietary fiber g	Sugars g	Protein g	Vitamin A % DV	Vitamin C % DV	Calcium % DV	Iron % DV
33% reduced-fat — *5 crackers*	16	70	20	2	0	0	200	12	0	2	1	0	0	0	2
Cracker Paks (Keebler)															
cheese & peanut butter — *1 pkg*	n/a	190	80	9	2	<5	420	22	<1	4	6	0	0	0	4
club & cheddar — *1 pkg*	n/a	190	100	11	2.5	10	320	20	<1	4	3	0	0	4	4
toast & peanut butter — *1 pkg*	n/a	190	80	9	2	0	300	23	1	5	5	0	0	0	4
Town House & cheddar — *1 pkg*	n/a	200	120	13	2.5	10	300	19	<1	4	3	0	0	4	4
Frito-Lay Crackers															
bacon cheddar — *1 pkg*	n/a	200	90	10	3	<5	380	24	1	3	3	n/a	n/a	n/a	n/a
cheddar — *1 pkg*	n/a	220	90	10	2.5	<5	530	27	1	<1	5	n/a	n/a	n/a	n/a
cheese/peanut butter — *1 pkg*	n/a	200	90	10	2	0	400	22	1	3	6	n/a	n/a	n/a	n/a
Golden Toast cheddar — *1 pkg*	n/a	230	120	13	4	5	510	25	1	4	3	n/a	n/a	n/a	n/a
Golden Toast cream cheese & chive — *1 pkg*	n/a	240	130	14	3	<5	490	25	1	4	3	n/a	n/a	n/a	n/a
jalapeño cheddar — *1 pkg*	n/a	200	90	10	2.5	<5	470	24	1	3	4	n/a	n/a	n/a	n/a
toast peanut butter — *1 pkg*	n/a	190	80	9	1.5	0	380	23	1	4	5	n/a	n/a	n/a	n/a
wheat cheese — *1 pkg*	n/a	200	90	9	2	<5	430	24	1	6	4	n/a	n/a	n/a	n/a
Handi-Snacks															
Cheez'n Breadsticks — *1 pkg*	32	130	60	7	4	15	340	11	0	3	4	8	0	8	0
Cheez'n Crackers — *1 pkg*	31	130	70	8	4.5	15	340	10	0	2	4	6	0	8	2
Cheez'n Pretzels — *1 pkg*	30	110	60	6	4	15	420	11	<1	2	4	6	0	8	0
Peanut Butter'n Crackers — *1 pkg*	31	180	100	12	3	0	150	12	1	3	5	0	0	0	4
Peanut Butter'n Grahamsticks — *1 pkg*	32	170	90	10	2.5	0	130	14	1	4	5	0	0	0	4
Health Valley															
healthy pizza crackers — *6 crackers*	n/a	50	0	0	0	0	140	11	2	1	2	10	2	0	2
low-fat crackers — *6 crackers*	n/a	60	5	1.5	0	0	90	10	2	1	2	2	2	2	2

	Weight *g*	Calories	Calories from fat	Total fat *g*	Sat. fat *g*	Cholesterol *mg*	Sodium *mg*	Carbohydrates *g*	Dietary fiber *g*	Sugars *g*	Protein *g*	Vitamin A *% DV*	Vitamin C *% DV*	Calcium *% DV*	Iron *% DV*
original rice bran — *6 crackers*	n/a	110	0	3	0	0	70	19	3	4	3	2	2	2	4
Health Valley Whole-Wheat															
cheese-flavor — *5 crackers*	n/a	50	0	0	0	0	100	11	2	1	2	10	0	2	2
herb, onion — *5 crackers*	n/a	50	0	0	0	0	80	11	2	1	2	10	0	2	2
plain — *5 crackers*	n/a	50	0	0	0	0	80	11	2	1	2	10	0	2	2
vegetable — *5 crackers*	n/a	50	0	0	0	0	80	11	2	1	2	10	2	2	2
vegetable, no salt — *5 crackers*	n/a	50	0	0	0	0	15	11	2	1	2	10	2	0	2
Munch'ems (Keebler)															
cheddar, 55% reduced-fat — *30 crackers*	30	130	35	4	1	0	330	21	<1	2	3	0	0	2	4
chili cheese, 33% reduced-fat — *28 crackers*	31	130	35	4	2	0	470	23	1	4	2	0	0	0	2
original — *30 crackers*	30	130	45	5	1	0	350	20	<1	1	3	0	0	0	4
original, 55% reduced-fat — *35 crackers*	30	130	35	4	0.5	0	450	21	<1	1	2	0	0	2	4
ranch, 55% reduced-fat — *33 crackers*	29	130	35	4	0.5	0	310	21	<1	2	3	0	0	2	4
salsa, 55% reduced-fat — *28 crackers*	31	130	35	4	1	0	260	23	1	3	2	0	0	0	2
sour cream & onion, 55% reduced-fat — *33 crackers*	30	130	30	3.5	0.5	0	390	22	0	2	2	0	0	0	2
Oysterettes (Nabisco) — *19 crackers*	15	60	20	2.5	0.5	0	150	10	<1	0	1	0	0	0	4
Pepperidge Farm Distinctive Crackers															
butter-flavored thins — *4 crackers*	14	70	25	3	1	10	95	10	0	1	1	0	0	0	4
cracked wheat — *2 crackers*	14	70	25	2.5	1	0	150	9	<1	0	1	0	0	0	0
hearty wheat — *3 crackers*	17	80	30	3.5	0	0	100	10	1	2	2	0	0	0	4
Quartet cracker assortment — *3 crackers*	14	60	20	2.5	0	<5	80	9	0.5	<1	1	0	0	0	4
sesame — *3 crackers*	14	70	25	2.5	0	0	95	9	2	0	1	0	0	0	4
three-cracker assortment — *3 crackers*	14	60	25	2.5	0.5	0	90	9	0	0	1	0	0	0	0

	Weight g	Calories	Calories from fat	Total fat g	Sat. fat g	Cholesterol mg	Sodium mg	Carbohydrates g	Dietary fiber g	Sugars g	Protein g	Vitamin A % DV	Vitamin C % DV	Calcium % DV	Iron % DV
Pepperidge Farm International Collection															
cracked pepper water biscuit — *5 crackers*	14	60	10	1	0.5	<5	90	12	<1	0	2	0	0	0	2
original water biscuit — *5 crackers*	14	60	10	1	0.5	<5	100	11	<1	0	2	0	0	0	0
Pepperidge Farm Tiny Goldfish Crackers															
cheddar cheese — *55 pieces*	31	140	50	6	1.5	10	200	19	<1	0	4	0	0	2	8
cheddar cheese, reduced-sodium — *60 pieces*	31	150	60	6	1.5	10	140	18	<1	0	3	0	0	4	4
original — *55 pieces*	31	140	60	6	2	0	230	19	<1	0	3	0	0	0	6
pizza — *55 pieces*	31	140	60	6	1.5	0	160	19	1	<1	3	0	0	0	8
pretzel — *45 pieces*	31	120	25	2.5	0.5	0	430	22	<1	<1	3	0	0	0	10
Ritz Air Crisps (Nabisco) — *1 pkg*	57	270	80	9	1.5	0	460	42	1	5	3	0	0	8	10
Ritz Crackers (Nabisco) — *5 crackers*	16	80	35	4	0.5	0	135	10	<1	1	1	0	0	2	4
Royal Lunch Milk Crackers (Nabisco) — *1 cracker*	11	50	15	2	0	0	65	8	0	<1	<1	0	0	2	2
SnackWell's															
classic golden — *6 crackers*	14	60	10	1	0	0	140	11	0	2	1	0	0	2	4
wheat — *5 crackers*	15	60	0	0	0	0	170	12	1	2	2	0	2	0	4
Sociables Flavor Crisps (Nabisco) — *7 crackers*	15	80	35	4	0.5	0	150	9	<1	<1	1	0	0	2	4
Toasteds Complements (Keebler)															
Buttercrisp — *9 crackers*	29	140	60	7	1.5	<5	280	19	<1	2	2	0	0	0	4
onion — *9 crackers*	29	140	50	6	1	0	310	19	<1	3	2	0	0	0	4
sesame — *9 crackers*	29	140	60	6	1	0	320	19	<1	1	3	0	0	0	6
sesame, reduced-fat — *10 crackers*	29	120	30	3	0.5	0	310	21	2	2	3	0	0	2	6
wheat — *9 crackers*	29	140	60	6	1.5	0	270	19	<1	3	2	0	0	0	4
wheat, reduced-fat — *10 crackers*	29	120	30	3	1	0	300	22	1	2	3	0	0	0	4

	Weight *g*	Calories	Calories from fat	Total fat *g*	Sat. fat *g*	Cholesterol *mg*	Sodium *mg*	Carbohydrates *g*	Dietary fiber *g*	Sugars *g*	Protein *g*	Vitamin A *% DV*	Vitamin C *% DV*	Calcium *% DV*	Iron *% DV*
Town House Classic (Keebler)															
original — *5 crackers*	16	80	40	4.5	1	0	150	9	<1	1	1	0	0	0	2
original, 50% reduced-sodium — *5 crackers*	16	80	40	4.5	1	0	75	10	<1	1	1	0	0	0	2
reduced-fat — *6 crackers*	15	70	20	2	0.5	0	180	11	<1	2	1	0	0	0	2
wheat crackers — *5 crackers*	16	80	40	4	1	0	140	10	<1	1	1	0	0	0	2
Triscuit (Nabisco) — *7 crackers*	31	140	45	5	1	0	170	21	4	0	3	0	0	0	8
Uneeda Biscuit, Unsalted Tops (Nabisco) — *2 crackers*	15	60	15	1.5	0	0	110	11	<1	0	1	0	0	0	4
Wheat Thins, Multi-Grain (Nabisco) — *17 crackers*	30	130	35	4	0.5	0	290	21	2	4	2	0	0	4	8
Wheatables Wheat Snack Crackers (Keebler)															
french onion, 30% reduced-fat — *27 crackers*	30	130	35	4	1	0	320	21	<1	2	3	0	2	2	2
original — *26 crackers*	30	150	60	7	2	0	320	18	1	2	3	0	0	0	6
original, 30% reduced-fat, 50% reduced-sodium — *29 crackers*	30	130	40	4.5	1	0	160	21	<1	2	3	0	2	0	2
original, 50% reduced-fat — *29 crackers*	30	130	30	3.5	1	0	320	21	1	3	3	0	0	0	6
ranch, 30% reduced-fat — *29 crackers*	30	130	35	4	1	0	340	21	1	2	3	0	4	2	4
white cheddar-flavor, 30% reduced-fat — *27 crackers*	30	130	35	4	1	0	330	21	<1	2	3	0	2	2	2
Wheatsworth Stone Ground Wheat Crackers (Nabisco) — *5 crackers*	16	80	30	3.5	0.5	0	170	10	1	1	2	0	0	0	4
Zesta Saltine Crackers (Keebler)															
50% reduced-sodium — *5 crackers*	15	60	20	2	0.5	0	95	11	<1	0	1	0	0	0	2
fat-free — *5 crackers*	14	50	0	0	0	0	90	11	<1	0	1	0	0	0	2
original — *5 crackers*	15	60	20	2	0.5	0	190	10	<1	0	1	0	0	0	2
soup & oyster — *42 crackers*	15	70	25	2.5	1	0	160	10	<1	0	1	0	0	0	2
unsalted tops — *5 crackers*	15	70	20	2	0.5	0	190	10	<1	0	1	0	0	0	2

Dessert Toppings: Icings & Frostings

	Weight g	Calories	Calories from fat	Total fat g	Sat. fat g	Cholesterol mg	Sodium mg	Carbohydrates g	Dietary fiber g	Sugars g	Protein g	Vitamin A % DV	Vitamin C % DV	Calcium % DV	Iron % DV
Betty Crocker Creamy Deluxe															
butter cream — *2 Tbsp*	n/a	150	50	6	1.5	0	70	25	0	24	0	0	0	0	0
butter pecan — *2 Tbsp*	n/a	150	50	6	1.5	0	45	25	0	23	0	0	0	0	0
caramel chocolate chip — *2 Tbsp*	n/a	140	50	6	1.5	0	55	21	0	19	0	0	0	0	0
cherry — *2 Tbsp*	n/a	140	45	5	1.5	0	40	24	0	23	0	0	0	0	0
chocolate — *2 Tbsp*	n/a	150	50	6	1.5	0	45	23	0	21	0	0	0	0	2
chocolate chip — *2 Tbsp*	n/a	160	60	6	2.5	0	25	25	0	24	0	0	0	0	0
chocolate chip cookie dough — *2 Tbsp*	n/a	160	50	6	1.5	0	25	25	0	24	0	0	0	0	0
chocolate chocolate chip — *2 Tbsp*	n/a	150	60	7	2.5	0	45	23	0	20	<1	0	0	0	2
chocolate fudge — *2 Tbsp*	n/a	140	40	4.5	1	0	50	24	0	22	<1	2	0	0	2
chocolate swiss almond — *2 Tbsp*	n/a	150	45	5	1	0	50	25	0	24	0	0	0	0	0
chocolate w/ dinosaurs — *2 Tbsp*	n/a	150	50	5	1.5	0	45	24	0	21	0	0	0	0	2
coconut pecan — *2 Tbsp*	n/a	150	80	8	3.5	0	55	18	0	16	<1	0	0	0	0
cream cheese — *2 Tbsp*	n/a	140	45	5	1.5	0	65	24	0	22	0	0	0	0	0
creamy vanilla — *2 Tbsp*	n/a	130	40	4	1	0	35	24	0	20	0	2	0	0	0
dark chocolate — *2 Tbsp*	n/a	150	50	6	1.5	0	50	22	0	19	1	0	0	0	4
french vanilla — *2 Tbsp*	n/a	140	45	5	1.5	0	20	24	0	23	0	0	0	0	0
lemon — *2 Tbsp*	n/a	140	45	5	1.5	0	65	24	0	22	0	0	0	0	0
milk chocolate — *2 Tbsp*	n/a	150	50	6	1.5	0	45	24	0	21	0	0	0	0	0
rainbow chip — *2 Tbsp*	n/a	160	60	6	3	0	25	25	0	23	0	0	0	0	0
sour cream chocolate — *2 Tbsp*	n/a	150	50	6	1.5	0	85	23	0	21	<1	0	0	0	2
sour cream white — *2 Tbsp*	n/a	150	50	6	1.5	0	45	25	0	24	0	0	0	0	0
strawberry cream cheese — *2 Tbsp*	n/a	150	50	6	1.5	0	70	26	0	25	0	0	0	0	0

	Weight g	Calories	Calories from fat	Total fat g	Sat. fat g	Cholesterol mg	Sodium mg	Carbohydrates g	Dietary fiber g	Sugars g	Protein g	Vitamin A % DV	Vitamin C % DV	Calcium % DV	Iron % DV
vanilla — *2 Tbsp*	n/a	140	45	5	1	0	35	24	0	23	0	0	0	0	0
vanilla w/ bears — *2 Tbsp*	n/a	140	45	5	1	0	35	24	0	23	0	0	0	0	0
white chocolate — *2 Tbsp*	n/a	140	45	5	1.5	0	45	24	0	23	0	0	0	0	0
Betty Crocker Creamy Deluxe Light															
chocolate — *2 Tbsp*	n/a	120	10	1	0.5	0	50	27	0	25	<1	0	0	0	2
milk chocolate — *2 Tbsp*	n/a	120	5	0.5	0.5	0	55	27	0	25	<1	0	0	0	0
vanilla — *2 Tbsp*	n/a	120	5	0.5	0.5	0	25	28	0	24	0	0	0	0	0
Betty Crocker Fluffy Frosting Mix, White — *6 Tbsp*	n/a	100	0	0	0	0	60	24	0	23	<1	0	0	0	0
Betty Crocker Whipped Deluxe															
cream cheese — *2 Tbsp*	n/a	110	45	5	1.5	0	45	16	0	14	0	0	0	0	0
lemon — *2 Tbsp*	n/a	110	45	5	1.5	0	45	16	0	14	0	0	0	0	0
strawberry — *2 Tbsp*	n/a	110	45	5	1.5	0	25	16	0	15	0	0	0	0	0
vanilla cream — *2 Tbsp*	n/a	110	45	5	1.5	0	25	16	0	15	0	0	0	0	0
Pillsbury Creamy Supreme															
banana creme — *2 Tbsp*	34	150	50	6	1.5	0	70	23	0	21	0	0	0	0	0
caramel pecan — *2 Tbsp*	35	150	70	8	2	0	65	19	0	16	0	0	0	0	0
chocolate — *2 Tbsp*	35	140	50	6	1.5	0	80	21	0	18	0	0	0	0	4
chocolate mocha — *2 Tbsp*	34	140	50	6	1.5	0	60	22	0	19	0	0	0	0	0
coconut pecan — *2 Tbsp*	35	160	90	10	4	0	60	17	<1	14	0	0	0	0	0
cream cheese — *2 Tbsp*	35	150	50	6	1.5	0	70	24	0	22	0	0	0	0	0
dark chocolate — *2 Tbsp*	34	130	50	6	1.5	0	45	20	0	17	0	0	0	0	4
french vanilla — *2 Tbsp*	38	150	50	6	1.5	0	80	25	0	23	0	0	0	0	0
Funfetti pink vanilla — *2 Tbsp*	35	150	50	6	1.5	0	70	24	0	22	0	0	0	0	0
lemon creme — *2 Tbsp*	35	150	50	6	1.5	0	75	24	0	21	0	0	0	0	0

	Weight g	Calories	Calories from fat	Total fat g	Sat. fat g	Cholesterol mg	Sodium mg	Carbohydrates g	Dietary fiber g	Sugars g	Protein g	Vitamin A % DV	Vitamin C % DV	Calcium % DV	Iron % DV
milk chocolate — *2 Tbsp*	35	140	50	6	1.5	0	60	21	<1	18	0	0	0	0	0
Oreo — *2 Tbsp*	34	150	50	6	1.5	0	75	23	0	20	0	0	0	0	0
strawberry creme — *2 Tbsp*	35	150	50	6	1.5	0	75	24	0	21	0	0	0	0	0
swirl milk chocolate w/ fudge glaze — *2 Tbsp*	35	140	50	6	1.5	0	60	22	<1	18	0	0	0	0	4
vanilla — *2 Tbsp*	34	150	50	6	1.5	0	70	23	0	21	0	0	0	0	0
Snackwell's Ready-to-Spread															
chocolate fudge — *2 Tbsp*	32	120	25	3	1	0	65	22	0	20	0	0	0	0	2
milk chocolate — *2 Tbsp*	32	120	25	3	1	0	80	22	<1	20	0	0	0	0	2
vanilla — *2 Tbsp*	33	130	25	3	0.5	0	65	25	0	22	0	0	0	0	0
Sweet Rewards Reduced-Fat															
chocolate — *1 Tbsp*	36	130	25	2.5	1	0	65	26	0	22	0	0	0	0	2
milk chocolate — *1 Tbsp*	36	130	25	2.5	1	0	45	26	0	23	0	0	0	0	2
vanilla — *1 Tbsp*	34	130	20	2	1	0	30	26	0	24	0	0	0	0	0

Dessert Toppings: Whipped Toppings

	Weight g	Calories	Calories from fat	Total fat g	Sat. fat g	Cholesterol mg	Sodium mg	Carbohydrates g	Dietary fiber g	Sugars g	Protein g	Vitamin A % DV	Vitamin C % DV	Calcium % DV	Iron % DV
Cool Whip															
extra-creamy — *2 Tbsp*	9	30	20	2	2	0	5	2	0	2	0	0	0	0	0
Lite — *2 Tbsp*	8	20	10	1	1	0	0	2	0	1	0	0	0	0	0
regular — *2 Tbsp*	9	25	15	1.5	1.5	0	0	2	0	1	0	0	0	0	0
Dream Whip Mix — *2 Tbsp*	3	15	5	0.5	0.5	0	0	2	0	2	0	0	0	0	0
Kraft															
real cream — *2 Tbsp*	7	20	15	1.5	1	5	0	1	0	1	0	0	0	0	0
whipped topping — *2 Tbsp*	7	20	15	1.5	1	0	0	1	0	1	0	0	0	0	0

Dessert Toppings: Other

	Weight *g*	Calories	Calories from fat	Total fat *g*	Sat. fat *g*	Cholesterol *mg*	Sodium *mg*	Carbohydrates *g*	Dietary fiber *g*	Sugars *g*	Protein *g*	Vitamin A *% DV*	Vitamin C *% DV*	Calcium *% DV*	Iron *% DV*
Dove Chocolate Topping															
chocolate, dark — *2 Tbsp*	n/a	140	45	5	1.5	0	80	22	5	15	<1	0	0	0	6
chocolate, milk — *2 Tbsp*	n/a	130	35	4	1.5	0	75	21	4	17	2	0	0	8	6
Hershey's Syrup															
chocolate — *2 Tbsp*	680	100	0	0	0	0	25	24	0	21	1	0	0	0	2
chocolate malt — *2 Tbsp*	623	100	0	0	0	0	55	25	0	21	<1	0	0	0	0
chocolate, Special Dark — *2 Tbsp*	453	110	0	0	0	0	35	27	0	22	<1	0	0	0	2
Kraft															
butterscotch-flavored — *2 Tbsp*	41	130	15	1.5	1	<5	150	28	0	18	<1	4	0	0	0
caramel — *2 Tbsp*	41	120	0	0	0	0	90	28	0	19	2	0	0	6	0
hot fudge — *2 Tbsp*	41	140	40	4	2	0	100	24	<1	17	1	0	0	4	2
pineapple — *2 Tbsp*	40	110	0	0	0	0	15	28	0	19	0	0	8	0	0
strawberry — *2 Tbsp*	41	110	0	0	0	0	15	29	0	22	0	0	6	0	0
Marshmallow Fluff — *2 Tbsp*	18	60	0	0	0	0	10	15	0	9	0	n/a	n/a	n/a	n/a
Smucker's															
butterscotch & caramel topping, fat-free — *2 Tbsp*	41	130	0	0	0	0	110	31	n/a	21	0	0	0	2	0
fruit dip, caramel, fat-free — *2 Tbsp*	n/a	130	0	0	0	0	85	30	0	22	1	0	0	4	0
fruit dip, chocolate, fat-free — *2 Tbsp*	n/a	130	5	0	0	0	75	31	<1	19	2	0	0	4	0
fruit syrup, light — *¼ cup*	n/a	130	0	0	0	0	0	33	0	33	0	0	0	0	0
fruit syrup, natural — *¼ cup*	n/a	210	0	0	0	0	0	52	0	52	0	0	0	0	0
hot fudge, light — *2 Tbsp*	39	90	0	0	0	0	90	23	2	15	2	0	0	4	5
Magic Shell — *2 Tbsp*	34	220	150	16	6	0	25	16	0	16	1	0	0	0	7
peanut butter caramel — *2 Tbsp*	41	150	40	4.5	0.5	0	125	24	<1	16	3	0	0	2	0

	Weight *g*	Calories	Calories from fat	Total fat *g*	Sat. fat *g*	Cholesterol *mg*	Sodium *mg*	Carbohydrates *g*	Dietary fiber *g*	Sugars *g*	Protein *g*	Vitamin A *% DV*	Vitamin C *% DV*	Calcium *% DV*	Iron *% DV*
pecans in syrup — *2 Tbsp*	40	190	100	11	1	0	0	22	0	14	1	0	0	1	2
pineapple — *2 Tbsp*	40	110	0	0	0	0	0	28	0	28	0	0	0	0	0
Special Recipe Butterscotch Caramel — *2 Tbsp*	42	130	10	1	0.5	5	70	30	<1	28	1	0	0	4	0
Special Recipe Hot Fudge — *2 Tbsp*	38	140	35	4	1	0	70	22	<1	16	2	0	0	6	4
walnuts in syrup — *2 Tbsp*	40	190	90	10	1	0	0	23	0	15	2	0	0	1	2

Dips

	Weight *g*	Calories	Calories from fat	Total fat *g*	Sat. fat *g*	Cholesterol *mg*	Sodium *mg*	Carbohydrates *g*	Dietary fiber *g*	Sugars *g*	Protein *g*	Vitamin A *% DV*	Vitamin C *% DV*	Calcium *% DV*	Iron *% DV*
Breakstone's Sour Cream Dip															
jalapeño cheddar — *2 Tbsp*	31	60	35	4	3	15	170	2	0	1	1	2	0	4	0
toasted onion — *2 Tbsp*	31	50	35	4	3	20	180	2	0	1	1	2	0	2	0
Chi-Chi's Fiesta Dip															
bean — *2 Tbsp*	27	35	15	1.5	0.5	0	140	4	1	0	1	0	0	0	2
cheese — *2 Tbsp*	26	40	20	3	1	10	270	3	0	1	1	0	0	2	0
Frito-Lay															
french onion — *2 Tbsp*	33	60	45	5	3	15	230	4	0	1	1	n/a	n/a	n/a	n/a
Fritos bean dip — *2 Tbsp*	35	40	10	1	0.5	0	140	6	0	0	2	n/a	n/a	n/a	n/a
Fritos jalapeño bean dip — *2 Tbsp*	35	35	10	1	0	0	220	5	2	0	2	n/a	n/a	n/a	n/a
jalapeño & cheddar cheese — *2 Tbsp*	34	50	30	3	1	5	280	3	0	<1	2	n/a	n/a	n/a	n/a
mild cheddar cheese — *2 Tbsp*	34	50	30	3	1	5	240	4	0	<1	2	n/a	n/a	n/a	n/a
Fritos Chili Cheese Dip — *2 Tbsp*	34	45	30	3	1	<5	310	3	0	1	1	n/a	n/a	n/a	n/a
Hidden Valley Ranch Party Dip Mixes															
fiesta — *2 Tbsp*	n/a	70	54	6	n/a	15	260	2	n/a	n/a	<1	n/a	n/a	n/a	n/a
french onion — *2 Tbsp*	n/a	70	54	6	n/a	15	160	2	n/a	n/a	<1	n/a	n/a	n/a	n/a
garden vegetable — *2 Tbsp*	n/a	70	54	6	n/a	15	150	2	n/a	n/a	<1	n/a	n/a	n/a	n/a
original — *2 Tbsp*	n/a	70	54	6	n/a	15	230	2	n/a	n/a	<1	n/a	n/a	n/a	n/a

	Weight *g*	Calories	Calories from fat	Total fat *g*	Sat. fat *g*	Cholesterol *mg*	Sodium *mg*	Carbohydrates *g*	Dietary fiber *g*	Sugars *g*	Protein *g*	Vitamin A *% DV*	Vitamin C *% DV*	Calcium *% DV*	Iron *% DV*
original, reduced-calorie — *2 Tbsp*	n/a	40	27	3	n/a	10	240	2	n/a	n/a	<1	n/a	n/a	n/a	n/a
Knudsen Sour Cream Dip															
french onion — *2 Tbsp*	31	50	35	4	3	20	160	2	0	1	1	2	0	2	0
nacho cheese — *2 Tbsp*	31	60	35	4	3	15	200	3	0	2	2	2	0	4	0
bacon & onion — *2 Tbsp*	31	60	45	5	3	20	170	2	0	1	1	2	0	2	0
Kraft															
avocado — *2 Tbsp*	32	60	40	4	3	0	240	4	0	<1	1	0	0	0	0
bacon & horseradish — *2 Tbsp*	31	60	45	5	3	0	220	3	0	<1	1	0	0	0	0
bacon & horseradish, premium — *2 Tbsp*	31	50	40	5	3	15	200	2	0	<1	1	2	2	0	0
blue cheese, premium — *2 Tbsp*	31	45	35	4	2.5	10	200	2	0	<1	1	2	0	4	0
creamy cucumber, premium — *2 Tbsp*	31	50	40	4	3	15	140	2	0	1	<1	2	0	2	0
creamy onion, premium — *2 Tbsp*	31	45	35	4	2.5	10	160	2	0	<1	<1	2	0	2	0
french onion — *2 Tbsp*	31	60	40	4	3	0	230	4	0	<1	1	0	0	0	0
french onion, premium — *2 Tbsp*	31	50	35	4	2.5	10	160	2	0	<1	<1	2	0	2	0
green onion — *2 Tbsp*	31	60	40	4	3	0	190	4	0	<1	1	0	0	0	0
jalapeño — *2 Tbsp*	31	60	40	4	3	0	260	3	0	<1	1	0	0	0	0
jalapeño cheese, premium — *2 Tbsp*	32	60	45	5	3	15	250	1	0	0	2	4	0	6	0
nacho cheese, premium — *2 Tbsp*	32	60	45	5	3	15	270	2	0	<1	2	4	0	8	0
ranch — *2 Tbsp*	31	60	40	4	3	0	210	3	0	<1	1	0	0	0	0
Land O'Lakes No-Fat															
french onion — *2 Tbsp*	n/a	30	0	0	0	<5	320	5	n/a	n/a	1	4	0	4	0
ranch — *2 Tbsp*	n/a	30	0	0	0	<5	180	6	n/a	n/a	1	4	0	4	0
Lay's Sour Cream & Onion Dip, Low Fat — *2 Tbsp*	35	40	10	1	0	<5	230	6	<1	<1	1	n/a	n/a	n/a	n/a
Old El Paso Dips, Black Bean — *2 Tbsp*	30	20	0	0	0	0	150	4	1	0	1	0	0	0	2

	Weight g	Calories	Calories from fat	Total fat g	Sat. fat g	Cholesterol mg	Sodium mg	Carbohydrates g	Dietary fiber g	Sugars g	Protein g	Vitamin A % DV	Vitamin C % DV	Calcium % DV	Iron % DV
Ruffles Dip															
french onion — *2 Tbsp*	33	70	50	5	1	0	240	4	1	<1	1	n/a	n/a	n/a	n/a
french onion, low-fat — *2 Tbsp*	34	40	10	1	0	0	230	6	<1	<1	2	n/a	n/a	n/a	n/a
ranch — *2 Tbsp*	33	70	50	6	1	0	300	4	0	0	1	n/a	n/a	n/a	n/a
ranch, low-fat — *2 Tbsp*	34	40	10	1	0	0	230	6	<1	<1	2	n/a	n/a	n/a	n/a

Egg Rolls, Frozen

	Weight g	Calories	Calories from fat	Total fat g	Sat. fat g	Cholesterol mg	Sodium mg	Carbohydrates g	Dietary fiber g	Sugars g	Protein g	Vitamin A % DV	Vitamin C % DV	Calcium % DV	Iron % DV
Chun King Egg Rolls															
mini, chicken — *5 egg rolls*	n/a	170	50	6	1.5	10	570	22	2	2	6	15	0	2	6
mini, pork & shrimp — *12 egg rolls*	205	420	150	16	4	25	500	56	6	3	11	4	10	4	6
mini, shrimp — *5 egg rolls*	n/a	160	30	3.5	1	5	580	26	3	2	6	15	0	2	6
restaurant-style, chicken — *1 egg roll*	85	170	50	5	2.5	10	450	25	4	4	7	20	2	2	6
restaurant-style, pork — *1 egg roll*	85	170	50	6	1.5	5	390	23	3	6	6	8	0	2	8
restaurant-style, shrimp — *1 egg roll*	85	150	35	4	0.5	10	420	24	3	6	6	4	0	4	8
Empire Kosher Miniature Egg Rolls — *6 egg rolls*	138	280	70	8	1.5	0	740	43	4	6	9	15	0	4	15
La Choy Egg Rolls															
mini, chicken — *6 egg rolls*	n/a	180	50	5	1.5	10	550	26	3	2	7	15	2	2	6
mini, chinese-style vegetables w/ lobster — *14 egg rolls*	n/a	410	100	11	2.5	0	690	65	9	6	13	2	6	4	10
mini, pork & shrimp — *14 egg rolls*	205	430	110	12	3	15	890	65	7	10	15	4	0	4	15
mini, shrimp — *6 egg rolls*	n/a	170	30	3.5	1	5	530	28	2	2	6	15	0	2	6
restaurant-style, chicken — *1 egg roll*	n/a	170	50	5	2.5	10	450	25	4	4	7	20	2	2	6
restaurant-style, pork — *1 egg roll*	85	170	50	6	1.5	5	390	23	3	6	6	8	0	2	8
restaurant-style, shrimp — *1 egg roll*	n/a	150	35	4	0.5	10	420	24	3	6	6	4	0	4	8
restaurant-style, sweet & sour chicken — *1 egg roll*	n/a	180	40	4	1	5	300	29	3	10	6	2	4	2	8
La Choy Spring Rolls, Battered Chicken — *4 pieces*	126	270	110	13	4	10	670	37	4	4	7	0	0	0	0

Fast Foods: Burger King

	Weight g	Calories	Calories from fat	Total fat g	Sat. fat g	Cholesterol mg	Sodium mg	Carbohydrates g	Dietary fiber g	Sugars g	Protein g	Vitamin A % DV	Vitamin C % DV	Calcium % DV	Iron % DV
Apple Pie — *1 order*	113	300	140	15	3	0	230	39	2	22	3	0	10	0	8
Biscuit															
w/ bacon, egg & cheese — *1 sandwich*	171	510	280	31	10	225	1530	39	1	3	19	8	0	15	15
w/ sausage — *1 sandwich*	151	590	360	40	13	45	1390	41	1	2	16	0	0	6	20
BK Big Fish Sandwich — *1 sandwich*	225	700	370	41	6	90	980	56	3	4	26	2	2	6	15
BK Broiler Chicken Sandwich — *1 sandwich*	248	550	260	29	6	80	480	41	2	4	30	6	10	6	30
Cheeseburger															
double — *1 burger*	210	600	320	36	17	135	1060	28	1	5	41	8	0	20	25
double, w/ bacon — *1 burger*	218	640	350	39	18	145	1240	28	1	5	44	8	0	20	25
regular — *1 burger*	138	380	170	19	9	65	770	28	1	5	23	6	0	10	15
Chicken Sandwich — *1 sandwich*	229	710	390	43	9	60	1400	54	2	4	26	0	0	10	20
Chicken Tenders — *8 pieces*	117	310	150	17	4	50	710	19	3	0	21	2	0	0	6
Croissan'wich w/ Sausage Egg & Cheese — *1 sandwich*	176	600	410	46	16	260	1140	25	1	3	22	8	0	15	20
Dipping Sauce															
A.M. express dip — *1 serving*	28	80	0	0	0	0	20	21	0	14	0	n/a	n/a	n/a	n/a
barbecue — *1 serving*	28	35	0	0	0	0	400	9	0	7	0	n/a	n/a	n/a	n/a
honey — *1 serving*	28	90	0	0	0	0	10	23	0	23	0	n/a	n/a	n/a	n/a
ranch — *1 serving*	28	170	160	17	3	0	200	2	0	1	0	n/a	n/a	n/a	n/a
sweet & sour — *1 serving*	28	45	0	0	0	0	50	11	0	10	0	n/a	n/a	n/a	n/a
French Fries, Medium — *1 order*	116	370	180	20	5	0	240	43	3	0	5	0	6	0	6
French Toast Sticks — *1 order*	141	500	240	27	7	0	490	60	1	11	4	0	0	6	15
Hamburger — *1 burger*	126	330	140	15	6	55	530	28	1	4	20	2	0	4	15
Hash Browns — *1 order*	71	220	110	12	3	0	320	25	2	0	2	10	8	0	2

	Weight g	Calories	Calories from fat	Total fat g	Sat. fat g	Cholesterol mg	Sodium mg	Carbohydrates g	Dietary fiber g	Sugars g	Protein g	Vitamin A % DV	Vitamin C % DV	Calcium % DV	Iron % DV
Onion Rings — *1 order*	124	310	130	14	2	0	810	41	6	6	4	0	0	10	8
Salad															
chicken, broiled — *1 salad*	302	200	90	10	4	60	110	7	3	4	21	100	25	15	20
garden — *1 salad*	215	100	45	5	3	15	110	7	3	4	6	110	50	15	6
side — *1 salad*	133	60	25	3	2	5	55	4	2	2	3	50	20	8	4
Shake															
chocolate — *1 medium*	284	320	60	7	4	20	230	54	3	48	9	6	0	20	10
strawberry — *1 medium*	341	420	50	6	4	20	260	83	1	78	9	6	6	30	0
vanilla — *1 medium*	284	300	50	6	4	20	230	53	1	47	9	6	6	30	0
Whopper															
double — *1 burger*	351	870	500	56	19	170	940	45	3	8	46	10	15	8	40
double w/ cheese — *1 burger*	375	960	570	63	24	195	1420	46	3	8	52	15	15	25	40
junior — *1 burger*	164	420	220	24	8	60	530	29	2	5	21	4	8	6	20
junior w/ cheese — *1 burger*	177	460	250	28	10	75	770	29	2	5	23	8	8	15	20
regular — *1 burger*	270	640	350	39	11	90	870	45	3	8	27	10	15	8	25
regular w/ cheese — *1 burger*	294	730	410	46	16	115	1350	46	3	8	33	15	15	25	25

Fast Foods: Domino's Pizza

	Weight g	Calories	Calories from fat	Total fat g	Sat. fat g	Cholesterol mg	Sodium mg	Carbohydrates g	Dietary fiber g	Sugars g	Protein g	Vitamin A % DV	Vitamin C % DV	Calcium % DV	Iron % DV
Deep Dish Pizza (12-inch)															
cheese — *¼ pizza*	205	560	210	23.8	9	31	1184	63.2	3.2	4.3	26.2	15	5	45	26
italian sausage & mushroom — *¼ pizza*	236	618	250	28.2	10.8	43	1356	65.5	3.7	4.6	26.2	16	6	46	29
pepperoni — *¼ pizza*	218	622	260	29.4	11.2	44.5	1383	63.4	3.2	4.4	26.2	16	5	46	28
veggie — *¼ pizza*	236	576	220	24.7	9.2	31.5	1233	65	3.7	4.5	24	16	22	46	28
Hand-Tossed Pizza (12-inch)															
cheese — *¼ pizza*	147	344	90	9.5	4.4	19.1	980	50	2.4	1	14.8	9	4	28	22

	Weight g	Calories	Calories from fat	Total fat g	Sat. fat g	Cholesterol mg	Sodium mg	Carbohydrates g	Dietary fiber g	Sugars g	Protein g	Vitamin A % DV	Vitamin C % DV	Calcium % DV	Iron % DV
ham — *¼ pizza*	161	362	90	10.2	4.6	26.1	1143	50.3	2.4	1.2	17.2	9	4	28	23
italian sausage & mushroom — *¼ pizza*	176	402	120	13.9	6.1	30.5	1151	52.2	2.9	1.3	17.5	10	5	29	25
pepperoni — *¼ pizza*	159	406	140	15.1	6.6	32.1	1179	50.2	2.5	1	17.5	9	5	28	24
veggie — *¼ pizza*	176	360	90	10.4	4.5	19.1	1028	51.7	3	1.2	15.9	10	21	29	24
Thin Crust Pizza (12-inch)															
cheese — *¼ pizza*	141	364	140	15.5	6.3	25.5	1012	40.1	1.9	2.2	16.1	11	6	42	8
ham — *¼ pizza*	159	388	150	16.5	6.6	34.8	1229	40.5	1.9	2.5	19.3	11	6	42	9
italian sausage & mushroom — *¼ pizza*	179	442	190	21.4	8.6	40.7	1240	43.1	2.5	2.6	19.8	12	7	43	12
pepperoni — *¼ pizza*	157	447	210	23	9.2	42.8	1277	40.4	2	2.3	19.7	12	6	43	1
veggie — *¼ pizza*	179	386	150	16.7	6.5	25.5	1076	42.5	2.6	2.5	16.7	12	28	43	12

Fast Foods: Jack in the Box

	Weight g	Calories	Calories from fat	Total fat g	Sat. fat g	Cholesterol mg	Sodium mg	Carbohydrates g	Dietary fiber g	Sugars g	Protein g	Vitamin A % DV	Vitamin C % DV	Calcium % DV	Iron % DV
Apple Turnover — *1 order*	110	350	170	19	4	0	460	48	0	13	3	0	15	0	10
Bacon & Cheddar Potato Wedges — *1 order*	265	800	520	58	16	55	1470	49	4	2	20	10	20	35	10
Breakfast Jack — *1 sandwich*	121	300	110	12	5	185	890	30	0	5	18	8	15	20	15
Burger, ¼ pound — *1 burger*	172	510	240	27	10	65	1080	39	0	8	26	6	0	15	20
Cheeseburger															
double — *1 burger*	152	450	220	24	12	75	970	35	0	6	24	10	25	0	20
single — *1 burger*	110	320	130	15	6	35	670	32	0	5	16	6	2	15	15
Chicken Caesar Sandwich — *1 sandwich*	237	520	230	26	6	55	1050	44	4	5	27	8	4	25	15
Chicken Fajita Pita — *1 sandwich*	189	290	70	8	3	35	700	29	3	<1	24	10	10	25	15
Chicken Sandwich — *1 sandwich*	160	400	160	18	4	45	1290	38	0	<1	20	4	0	15	10
Chicken Strips — *6 pieces*	177	450	180	20	5	80	1100	28	0	<1	39	0	0	0	6
Chicken Supreme — *1 sandwich*	245	620	320	36	11	75	1520	48	0	5	25	10	4	20	15

	Weight g	Calories	Calories from fat	Total fat g	Sat. fat g	Cholesterol mg	Sodium mg	Carbohydrates g	Dietary fiber g	Sugars g	Protein g	Vitamin A % DV	Vitamin C % DV	Calcium % DV	Iron % DV
Chicken Teriyaki Bowl — *1 order*	440	580	10	1.5	<1	30	1220	115	6	20	28	110	15	10	10
Dipping Sauce															
barbeque — *1 packet*	28	45	0	0	0	0	300	11	0	7	1	0	0	0	0
buttermilk house — *1 packet*	25	130	110	13	5	10	240	3	<1	<1	<1	0	2	0	<2
sweet & sour — *1 packet*	28	40	0	0	0	0	160	11	0	10	<1	0	0	0	0
Egg Rolls — *5 pieces*	285	750	370	41	12	50	1640	92	7	10	5	0	10	15	20
French Fries, Regular — *1 order*	109	350	150	17	4	0	190	45	4	0	4	0	40	0	6
Fries, Seasoned Curly — *1 order*	109	360	180	20	5	0	1070	39	4	0	5	0	8	2	8
Garden Chicken Salad — *1 salad*	253	200	80	9	4	65	420	8	3	4	23	70	20	20	4
Grilled Chicken Fillet — *1 sandwich*	211	430	170	19	5	65	1070	36	0	7	29	6	10	15	35
Grilled Sourdough Burger — *1 burger*	223	670	390	43	16	110	1180	39	0	4	32	15	10	20	25
Hamburger — *1 burger*	97	280	100	11	4	25	470	31	0	5	13	2	2	10	15
Hash Browns — *1 order*	57	160	100	11	2.5	0	310	14	1	0	1	0	10	0	2
Jalapeños, Stuffed — *10 pieces*	195	600	350	39	16	75	2320	41	4	4	22	20	20	50	4
Jumbo Jack															
w/ cheese — *1 burger*	254	650	360	40	14	90	1150	42	0	6	31	10	10	25	25
regular — *1 burger*	229	560	290	32	10	65	740	41	0	6	26	4	10	10	25
Milkshake															
chocolate — *regular*	310	630	240	27	16	85	330	85	<1	67	11	15	0	35	2
strawberry — *regular*	299	640	250	28	15	85	300	85	0	67	10	15	0	35	0
vanilla — *regular*	306	610	280	31	18	95	320	73	0	12	12	15	0	40	0
Onion Rings — *1 order*	103	380	210	23	6	0	450	38	0	4	5	0	4	2	10
Pancake Platter — *1 order*	160	400	110	12	3	30	980	59	3	12	13	0	0	8	10
Sausage Croissant — *1 croissant*	182	670	430	48	19	250	940	39	2	4	21	20	2	15	20

	Weight g	Calories	Calories from fat	Total fat g	Sat. fat g	Cholesterol mg	Sodium mg	Carbohydrates g	Dietary fiber g	Sugars g	Protein g	Vitamin A % DV	Vitamin C % DV	Calcium % DV	Iron % DV
Scrambled Egg Pocket — *1 order*	183	430	190	21	8	355	1060	31	0	<1	29	20	0	20	20
Side Salad — *1 salad*	110	70	40	4	2.5	10	80	3	2	1	4	25	0	10	2
Sourdough Breakfast Sandwich — *1 sandwich*	147	380	180	20	7	235	1120	31	0	2	21	15	15	25	20
Spicy Crispy Chicken Sandwich — *1 sandwich*	224	560	240	27	5	50	1020	55	0	5		4	8	10	15
Supreme Croissant — *1 croissant*	172	570	330	36	15	245	1240	39	2	4	21	15	20	10	20
Taco															
Monster — *1 taco*	130	283	150	17	6	30	760	22	3	1	12	0	3	15	10
regular — *1 taco*	78	190	100	11	4	20	410	15	2	0	7	0	0	10	6
Ultimate Breakfast Sandwich — *1 sandwich*	242	620	320	35	11	455	1800	39	<1	4	36	15	15	25	25
Ultimate Cheeseburger — *1 burger*	278	1030	710	79	26	205	1200	30	0	6	50	10	2	30	35

Fast Foods: Kenny Rogers Roasters

	Weight g	Calories	Calories from fat	Total fat g	Sat. fat g	Cholesterol mg	Sodium mg	Carbohydrates g	Dietary fiber g	Sugars g	Protein g	Vitamin A % DV	Vitamin C % DV	Calcium % DV	Iron % DV
Chicken Noodle Soup — *1 bowl*	283	91	16	2	0.3	22	931	12	n/a	n/a	7	n/a	n/a	n/a	n/a
Chicken Pot Pie — *1 pot pie*	340	708	297	33	10.5	69.3	1500	77.6	0.4	n/a	25.5	n/a	n/a	n/a	n/a
Pita															
BBQ chicken — *1 sandwich*	207	401	64	7	1	112	1307	51	n/a	n/a	32.6	n/a	n/a	n/a	n/a
chicken caesar — *1 sandwich*	261	606	321	34.8	3	122	829	34	0.8	n/a	36.1	n/a	n/a	n/a	n/a
roasted chicken — *1 sandwich*	306	685	322	35	3	159	1620	42	0.1	n/a	47	n/a	n/a	n/a	n/a
Salad															
chicken caesar — *1 salad*	266	285	77	8.7	3	122	704	18	1.47	n/a	34	n/a	n/a	n/a	n/a
roasted chicken — *1 salad*	479	292	88	10.3	2.4	218	573	18.5	6.4	n/a	34.3	n/a	n/a	n/a	n/a
Turkey Sandwich — *1 sandwich*	261	385	108	12	2	87.7	923	30	0.7	n/a	38.7	n/a	n/a	n/a	n/a

Fast Foods: KFC

	Weight g	Calories	Calories from fat	Total fat g	Sat. fat g	Cholesterol mg	Sodium mg	Carbohydrates g	Dietary fiber g	Sugars g	Protein g	Vitamin A % DV	Vitamin C % DV	Calcium % DV	Iron % DV
BBQ Flavored Chicken Sandwich — *1 sandwich*	150	256	74	8	1	57	782	28	2	18	17	<2	6	6	23
Chicken Pot Pie, Chunky — *1 pot pie*	368	770	378	42	13	70	2160	69	5	8	29	80	2	10	10

	Weight g	Calories	Calories from fat	Total fat g	Sat. fat g	Cholesterol mg	Sodium mg	Carbohydrates g	Dietary fiber g	Sugars g	Protein g	Vitamin A % DV	Vitamin C % DV	Calcium % DV	Iron % DV
Colonel's Crispy Strips (Chicken) — *3 strips*	92	261	142	15.8	3.7	40	658	10	3	0	19	<2	<2	<2	3
Cornbread — *1 piece*	57	228	117	13	2	42	194	25	1	10	3	n/a	n/a	6	4
Extra Tasty Crispy Chicken															
breast — *1 piece*	167	470	250	28	7	80	930	25	1	0	31	<2	<2	4	6
drumstick — *1 piece*	68	190	100	11	3	60	260	8	<1	0	13	<2	<2	<2	4
thigh — *1 piece*	119	370	220	25	6	70	540	18	2	0	19	<2	<2	2	4
whole wing — *1 piece*	54	200	120	13	4	45	290	10	<1	0	10	<2	<2	<2	2
Garden Rice — *1 serving*	125	120	10	1.5	0	0	890	23	1	2	3	10	15	2	n/a
Hot & Spicy Chicken															
breast — *1 piece*	184	530	310	35	8	119	1119	23	2	0	32	<2	<2	4	6
drumstick — *1 piece*	65	190	100	11	3	50	300	10	<1	9	13	<2	<2	<2	4
thigh — *1 piece*	108	370	240	27	7	90	570	13	1	0	18	<2	<2	<2	6
whole wing — *1 piece*	54	210	130	15	4	50	340	9	<1	0	10	<2	<2	4	2
Hot Wings — *6 pieces*	136	471	297	33	8	150	1230	18	2	0	27	0	0	4	8
Kentucky Chicken Nuggets — *6 pieces*	96	284	162	18	4	66	865	15	<1	0	16	<2	<2	2	4
Macaroni & Cheese — *1 serving*	153	180	70	8	3	10	860	21	2	2	7	20	<2	15	<2
Mashed Potatoes w/ Gravy — *1 serving*	136	120	50	6	1	<1	440	17	2	0	1	<2	<2	<2	<2
Mean Greens — *1 serving*	153	70	30	3	1	10	650	11	5	1	4	60	10	20	10
Original Recipe Chicken															
breast — *1 piece*	153	400	220	24	6	135	1116	16	1	0	29	0	0	4	6
chicken sandwich — *1 sandwich*	207	497	201	22.3	4.8	52	1213	45.5	3	2	28.6	<2	<2	10	15
drumstick — *1 piece*	62	140	80	9	2	75	422	4	0	0	13	0	0	0	4
thigh — *1 piece*	123	250	160	18	4.5	95	747	6	1	0	16	0	0	2	4
whole wing — *1 piece*	45	140	90	10	2.5	55	414	5	0	0	9	0	0	0	2

	Weight g	Calories	Calories from fat	Total fat g	Sat. fat g	Cholesterol mg	Sodium mg	Carbohydrates g	Dietary fiber g	Sugars g	Protein g	Vitamin A % DV	Vitamin C % DV	Calcium % DV	Iron % DV
Potato Wedges — *1 serving*	136	280	120	13	4	5	750	28	5	1	5	<2	2	2	n/a
Red Beans & Rice — *1 serving*	128	130	30	3	1	5	360	3	2	5	5	<2	<2	2	4
Tender Roast Chicken															
breast w/ skin — *1 piece*	139	251	97	10.8	3	151	830	1	0	<1	37	<2	<2	<2	<2
breast w/o skin — *1 piece*	119	169	39	4.3	1.2	112	797	1	0	0	31.4	<2	<2	<2	<2
drumstick w/ skin — *1 piece*	54	97	39	4.3	1.2	85	271	<1	0	<1	14.5	<2	<2	<2	<2
drumstick w/o skin — *1 piece*	34	67	22	2.4	0.7	63	259	<1	0	0	11	<2	<2	<2	<2
thigh w/ skin — *1 piece*	91	207	126	12	3.8	120	504	<2	0	<1	18.4	<2	<2	<2	<2
thigh w/o skin — *1 piece*	59	106	50	5.5	1.7	84	312	<1	0	<1	12.9	<2	<2	<2	<2
wing w/ skin — *1 piece*	51	121	69	7.7	2.1	74	331	1	0	<1	12.2	<2	<2	<2	<2

Fast Foods: McDonald's

	Weight g	Calories	Calories from fat	Total fat g	Sat. fat g	Cholesterol mg	Sodium mg	Carbohydrates g	Dietary fiber g	Sugars g	Protein g	Vitamin A % DV	Vitamin C % DV	Calcium % DV	Iron % DV
Apple Pie, Baked — *1 order*	77	260	120	13	3.5	0	200	34	<1	13	3	<2	40	2	6
Arch Deluxe															
regular — *1 sandwich*	247	570	280	31	11	90	1110	43	4	9	29	10	10	8	25
w/ bacon — *1 sandwich*	255	610	310	34	12	100	1250	43	4	9	33	10	10	8	25
Bacon, Egg & Cheese Biscuit — *1 sandwich*	142	440	230	26	8	235	1310	33	1	4	17	10	<2	10	15
Big Mac — *1 sandwich*	215	530	250	28	10	80	880	47	3	8	25	6	4	20	25
Biscuit — *1 biscuit*	76	260	120	13	3	0	840	32	1	2	4	<2	<2	6	10
Breakfast Burrito — *1 order*	117	320	180	20	7	195	600	23	1	2	13	10	15	8	10
Cheeseburger — *1 burger*	120	320	130	14	6	45	770	35	2	7	15	6	4	15	15
Chicken McNuggets — *6 pieces*	106	290	150	17	3.5	60	510	15	0	0	18	<2	<2	2	6
Crispy Deluxe Chicken Sandwich — *1 sandwich*	232	530	230	26	4	60	1140	47	4	6	27	6	8	6	15
Danish															
apple — *1 danish*	105	360	140	16	5	40	290	51	1	29	5	10	<2	8	6

	Weight *g*	Calories	Calories from fat	Total fat *g*	Sat. fat *g*	Cholesterol *mg*	Sodium *mg*	Carbohydrates *g*	Dietary fiber *g*	Sugars *g*	Protein *g*	Vitamin A *% DV*	Vitamin C *% DV*	Calcium *% DV*	Iron *% DV*
cheese — *1 danish*	105	410	200	22	8	70	340	47	0	26	7	15	<2	8	6
Dipping Sauce															
barbecue — *1 pkg*	28	45	0	0	0	0	250	10	0	10	0	<2	6	<2	<2
honey — *1 pkg*	14	45	0	0	0	0	0	12	0	11	0	<2	<2	<2	<2
sweet 'n sour — *1 pkg*	28	50	0	0	0	0	140	11	0	10	0	6	<2	<2	<2
Egg McMuffin — *1 sandwich*	137	290	110	12	4.5	235	710	27	1	3	17	10	2	15	15
English Muffin — *1 muffin*	55	140	20	2	0	0	210	25	1	1	4	<2	<2	10	8
Fish Filet Deluxe Sandwich — *1 sandwich*	236	510	180	20	4.5	50	1120	59	5	6	24	6	4	8	15
French Fries — *1 large*	147	450	200	22	4	0	290	57	5	0	6	<2	30	2	6
Grilled Deluxe Chicken Sandwich — *1 sandwich*	213	330	50	6	1	50	970	42	4	6	27	4	8	6	15
Hamburger — *1 sandwich*	106	270	90	10	3.5	30	530	34	2	7	12	2	4	15	15
Hash Browns — *1 order*	53	130	70	8	1.5	0	330	14	1	0	1	<2	4	<2	2
Hotcakes (Plain) — *1 order*	150	310	60	7	1.5	15	610	53	2	11	9	<2	<2	10	15
Milkshake															
chocolate, low-fat — *1 small*	n/a	340	50	5	3.5	25	270	62	1	56	12	4	4	40	4
strawberry, low-fat — *1 small*	n/a	340	45	5	3.5	25	200	61	0	57	12	4	10	35	4
vanilla, low-fat — *1 small*	n/a	340	50	5	3.5	25	270	60	0	56	12	4	4	35	2
Muffin, Low-Fat Apple Bran — *1 muffin*	114	300	30	3	0.5	0	380	61	3	32	6	<2	<2	10	8
Quarter Pounder															
regular — *1 sandwich*	172	430	190	21	8	70	730	37	2	8	23	2	4	15	25
w/ cheese — *1 sandwich*	200	530	270	30	13	95	1200	38	2	9	28	10	4	15	25
Salad															
garden — *1 salad*	177	35	0	0	0	0	20	7	2	3	2	120	40	4	4
Grilled Chicken Deluxe — *1 salad*	213	110	10	1	0	45	240	5	2	2	21	110	25	4	8

	Weight g	Calories	Calories from fat	Total fat g	Sat. fat g	Cholesterol mg	Sodium mg	Carbohydrates g	Dietary fiber g	Sugars g	Protein g	Vitamin A % DV	Vitamin C % DV	Calcium % DV	Iron % DV
Sausage McMuffin, w/ Egg — *1 sandwich*	163	440	250	28	10	255	810	27	1	3	19	10	<2	15	15
Shake															
chocolate, low-fat — *1 small*	n/a	340	50	5	3.5	25	270	62	1	56	12	4	4	40	4
strawberry, low-fat — *1 small*	n/a	340	45	5	3.5	25	200	61	0	57	12	4	10	35	4
vanilla, low-fat — *1 small*	n/a	340	50	5	3.5	25	270	60	0	56	12	4	4	35	2
Sundae															
hot caramel, low-fat ice cream — *1 order*	182	300	30	3	2	5	210	62	<1	45	7	10	2	20	<2
strawberry, low-fat ice cream — *1 order*	178	240	10	1	0.5	5	130	51	<1	44	6	10	2	20	2
Eggs, Scrambled — *1 order*	102	160	100	11	3.5	425	170	1	0	1	13	10	<2	4	6

Fast Foods: Pizza Hut

	Weight g	Calories	Calories from fat	Total fat g	Sat. fat g	Cholesterol mg	Sodium mg	Carbohydrates g	Dietary fiber g	Sugars g	Protein g	Vitamin A % DV	Vitamin C % DV	Calcium % DV	Iron % DV
Bigfoot Pizza, Pepperoni, Mushroom & Italian Sausage — *1 slice*	90	214	72	8	4	21	665	25	2	n/a	11	7	n/a	11	9
Hand Tossed Pizza (medium)															
cheese — *1 slice*	108	235	63	7	4	25	621	29	2	n/a	13	10	n/a	14	8
italian sausage — *1 slice*	116	267	99	11	5	31	737	29	2	n/a	13	9	n/a	10	9
Meat Lover's — *1 slice*	130	314	99	11	6	38	958	29	2	n/a	17	9	n/a	11	12
pepperoni — *1 slice*	104	238	72	8	4	24	689	29	2	n/a	12	9	n/a	10	9
Pepperoni Lover's — *1 slice*	123	306	126	14	6	40	897	30	2	n/a	16	12	n/a	15	8
Super Supreme — *1 slice*	143	296	117	13	5	34	946	30	3	n/a	16	10	n/a	12	12
Supreme — *1 slice*	136	284	108	12	5	30	884	30	3	n/a	16	10	n/a	12	12
Veggie Lover's — *1 slice*	133	216	54	6	3	17	632	30	3	n/a	11	9	n/a	11	10
Pan Pizza (medium)															
cheese — *1 slice*	108	261	99	11	5	25	501	28	2	n/a	12	11	n/a	14	8
italian sausage — *1 slice*	116	293	135	15	5	31	617	27	2	n/a	12	9	n/a	11	9
Meat Lover's — *1 slice*	130	340	162	18	7	38	838	28	2	n/a	16	9	n/a	11	12

	Weight g	Calories	Calories from fat	Total fat g	Sat. fat g	Cholesterol mg	Sodium mg	Carbohydrates g	Dietary fiber g	Sugars g	Protein g	Vitamin A % DV	Vitamin C % DV	Calcium % DV	Iron % DV
pepperoni — *1 slice*	104	265	108	12	4	24	569	28	2	n/a	11	10	n/a	10	9
Pepperoni Lover's — *1 slice*	123	332	153	17	7	40	777	28	2	n/a	15	12	n/a	15	10
Super Supreme — *1 slice*	143	323	153	17	6	34	826	28	3	n/a	15	10	n/a	12	12
Supreme — *1 slice*	136	311	135	15	6	30	764	28	3	n/a	15	10	n/a	12	13
Veggie Lover's — *1 slice*	132.9	243	90	10	3	17	512	29	3	n/a	10	10	n/a	11	10
Thin 'N Crispy Pizza (medium)															
cheese — *1 slice*	87	205	72	8	4	25	534	21	2	n/a	11	11	n/a	15	6
italian sausage — *1 slice*	94	236	108	12	5	31	650	21	2	n/a	11	9	n/a	11	7
Meat Lover's — *1 slice*	110	288	117	13	6	39	892	21	2	n/a	15	10	n/a	11	9
pepperoni — *1 slice*	84	215	90	10	4	25	627	21	1	n/a	11	10	n/a	10	6
Pepperoni Lover's — *1 slice*	105	289	144	16	7	42	862	22	2	n/a	15	13	n/a	15	7
Super Supreme — *1 slice*	124	270	126	14	6	35	880	22	2	n/a	14	10	n/a	12	9
Supreme — *1 slice*	116	257	117	13	5	31	795	21	2	n/a	14	10	n/a	12	10
Veggie Lover's — *1 slice*	117	186	63	7	3	17	545	22	2	n/a	9	10	n/a	11	7

Fast Foods: Subway

	Weight g	Calories	Calories from fat	Total fat g	Sat. fat g	Cholesterol mg	Sodium mg	Carbohydrates g	Dietary fiber g	Sugars g	Protein g	Vitamin A % DV	Vitamin C % DV	Calcium % DV	Iron % DV
Chicken Breast (Roasted) Sub — *6" sub*	n/a	348	54	6	n/a	48	978	47	n/a	n/a	27	n/a	n/a	n/a	n/a
Cookie															
oatmeal raisin — *1 cookie*	n/a	200	72	8	n/a	15	160	29	n/a	n/a	3	n/a	n/a	n/a	n/a
peanut butter — *1 cookie*	n/a	220	108	12	n/a	0	180	26	n/a	n/a	3	n/a	n/a	n/a	n/a
Meatball Sub — *6" sub*	n/a	419	144	16	n/a	33	1046	51	n/a	n/a	19	n/a	n/a	n/a	n/a
Pizza Sub — *6" sub*	n/a	464	198	22	n/a	50	1621	48	n/a	n/a	19	n/a	n/a	n/a	n/a
Roast Beef															
deli-style sandwich — *1 sandwich*	n/a	245	36	4	n/a	13	638	38	n/a	n/a	13	n/a	n/a	n/a	n/a
sub — *6" sub*	n/a	303	45	5	n/a	20	939	45	n/a	n/a	20	n/a	n/a	n/a	n/a

	Weight *g*	Calories	Calories from fat	Total fat *g*	Sat. fat *g*	Cholesterol *mg*	Sodium *mg*	Carbohydrates *g*	Dietary fiber *g*	Sugars *g*	Protein *g*	Vitamin A *% DV*	Vitamin C *% DV*	Calcium *% DV*	Iron *% DV*
Salad (w/o dressing)															
chicken breast, roasted — *1 salad*	n/a	162	36	4	n/a	48	693	13	n/a	n/a	20	n/a	n/a	n/a	n/a
pizza — *1 salad*	n/a	277	180	20	n/a	50	1336	13	n/a	n/a	12	n/a	n/a	n/a	n/a
subway club — *1 salad*	n/a	126	27	3	n/a	26	1067	12	n/a	n/a	14	n/a	n/a	n/a	n/a
subway seafood & crab — *1 salad*	n/a	244	153	17	n/a	34	575	10	n/a	n/a	13	n/a	n/a	n/a	n/a
tuna — *1 salad*	n/a	356	270	30	n/a	36	601	10	n/a	n/a	12	n/a	n/a	n/a	n/a
turkey breast — *1 salad*	n/a	102	18	2	n/a	19	1117	12	n/a	n/a	11	n/a	n/a	n/a	n/a
veggie delite — *1 salad*	n/a	51	9	1	n/a	0	308	10	n/a	n/a	2	n/a	n/a	n/a	n/a
Subway Club Sub — *6″ sub*	n/a	312	45	5	n/a	26	1352	46	n/a	n/a	21	n/a	n/a	n/a	n/a
Subway Melt — *6″ sub*	n/a	382	108	12	n/a	42	1746	46	n/a	n/a	23	n/a	n/a	n/a	n/a
Subway Seafood & Crab Sub															
regular — *6″ sub*	n/a	430	171	19	n/a	34	860	44	n/a	n/a	20	n/a	n/a	n/a	n/a
w/ light mayonnaise — *6″ sub*	n/a	347	90	10	n/a	32	884	45	n/a	n/a	20	n/a	n/a	n/a	n/a
Tuna															
deli-style sandwich — *1 sandwich*	n/a	354	162	18	n/a	18	557	37	n/a	n/a	11	n/a	n/a	n/a	n/a
sub — *6″ sub*	n/a	542	288	32	n/a	36	886	44	n/a	n/a	19	n/a	n/a	n/a	n/a
sub (w/ light mayonnaise) — *6″ sub*	n/a	391	135	15	n/a	32	940	46	n/a	n/a	19	n/a	n/a	n/a	n/a
Turkey Breast Sub — *6″ sub*	n/a	289	36	4	n/a	19	1403	46	n/a	n/a	18	n/a	n/a	n/a	n/a

Fast Foods: Wendy's

	Weight *g*	Calories	Calories from fat	Total fat *g*	Sat. fat *g*	Cholesterol *mg*	Sodium *mg*	Carbohydrates *g*	Dietary fiber *g*	Sugars *g*	Protein *g*	Vitamin A *% DV*	Vitamin C *% DV*	Calcium *% DV*	Iron *% DV*
Big Bacon Classic — *1 burger*	287	610	290	33	13	105	1510	45	3	11	36	15	25	25	35
Cheeseburger Deluxe, Junior — *1 burger*	179	360	150	16	6	45	840	36	3	9	18	10	10	15	20
Chicken Club Sandwich — *1 sandwich*	220	500	200	23	5	70	1090	44	2	7	32	4	15	10	20
Chicken Nuggets — *6 pieces*	94	280	180	20	5	50	600	12	0	n/a	14	0	0	2	4
Chili — *8 oz*	227	210	60	7	2.5	30	800	21	5	5	15	8	6	8	15

	Weight g	Calories	Calories from fat	Total fat g	Sat. fat g	Cholesterol mg	Sodium mg	Carbohydrates g	Dietary fiber g	Sugars g	Protein g	Vitamin A % DV	Vitamin C % DV	Calcium % DV	Iron % DV
Cookie, Chocolate Chip — *1 cookie*	57	270	100	11	8	15	150	38	3	23	4	0	0	6	4
Dipping Sauce															
barbecue sauce — *1 packet*	28	50	0	0	0	0	100	11	n/a	n/a	1	6	0	0	4
sweet mustard — *1 packet*	28	50	10	1	0	0	140	9	n/a	n/a	1	0	0	0	0
French Fries, Medium — *1 order*	130	380	170	19	4	0	120	47	5	0	5	0	10	2	6
Frosty Dairy Dessert — *16 oz*	324	460	120	13	7	55	260	76	4	63	12	10	0	40	6
Grilled Chicken Sandwich — *1 sandwich*	189	310	70	8	1.5	65	780	35	2	8	27	4	10	10	15
Hamburger, Junior — *1 burger*	117	270	90	10	3	30	560	34	2	7	15	2	2	10	20
Hamburger, Kids' Meal — *1 burger*	111	270	90	10	3	30	560	33	2	7	15	2	0	10	20
Potato, Baked															
w/ chili & cheese — *1 potato*	439	620	220	24	9	40	780	83	9	7	20	20	60	35	30
w/ sour cream & chives — *1 potato*	314	380	60	6	4	15	40	74	8	6	8	30	80	8	25
Salad (w/o dressing)															
chicken, grilled — *1 salad*	338	200	70	8	1.5	50	690	10	4	5	25	110	60	20	10
deluxe garden — *1 salad*	271	110	50	6	1	0	320	10	4	5	7	110	60	20	8
side — *1 salad*	155	60	25	3	0.5	0	160	5	2	2	4	50	30	10	4
Single (hamburger)															
plain — *1 burger*	133	360	140	16	6	65	460	31	2	5	25	0	0	10	25
w/ everything — *1 burger*	219	420	180	20	7	70	810	37	3	9	26	6	10	10	30
Taco Salad — *1 salad*	510	590	270	30	11	65	1230	53	10	8	29	35	40	40	25

Fish, Canned

	Weight g	Calories	Calories from fat	Total fat g	Sat. fat g	Cholesterol mg	Sodium mg	Carbohydrates g	Dietary fiber g	Sugars g	Protein g	Vitamin A % DV	Vitamin C % DV	Calcium % DV	Iron % DV
Bumble Bee Salmon															
keta, w/ liquid — *3 ¾ oz*	n/a	150	63	7	1.5	70	460	0	0	0	21	0	0	15	4
pink, w/ liquid — *3 ¾ oz*	n/a	160	72	8	2	70	460	0	n/a	n/a	21	0	0	15	4

	Weight g	Calories	Calories from fat	Total fat g	Sat. fat g	Cholesterol mg	Sodium mg	Carbohydrates g	Dietary fiber g	Sugars g	Protein g	Vitamin A % DV	Vitamin C % DV	Calcium % DV	Iron % DV
red, w/ liquid — *3 ¾ oz*	n/a	190	99	11	2.5	70	460	0	n/a	n/a	22	4	0	15	2
Bumble Bee Salmon, pink, skinless & boneless drained — *2 oz*	n/a	70	18	2	0	40	220	0	0	0	21	0	0	0	2
Bumble Bee Tuna															
chunk light, in oil, drained — *2 oz*	n/a	110	50	6	1	30	250	0	0	0	13	0	0	0	2
chunk light, in water, drained — *2 oz*	n/a	60	5	0.5	0	30	250	0	0	0	14	0	0	0	2
chunk white, diet, in water, drained — *2 oz*	n/a	70	10	1	0	25	35	0	0	0	14	0	0	0	0
chunk white, in oil, drained — *2 oz*	n/a	100	45	5	1	25	250	0	0	0	13	0	0	0	0
chunk white, in water, drained — *2 oz*	n/a	60	10	1	0	25	250	0	0	0	13	0	0	0	0
solid white, in oil, drained — *2 oz*	n/a	90	30	3	0.5	25	250	0	0	0	14	0	0	0	0
solid white, in water, drained — *2 oz*	n/a	70	10	1	0	25	250	0	0	0	15	0	0	0	0
StarKist Charlie's Lunch Kit															
chunk light, in spring water — *1 kit*	n/a	230	80	9	1.5	40	730	17	1	4	20	0	0	0	8
chunk white, in spring water — *1 kit*	n/a	230	80	9	1.5	35	730	17	1	4	20	0	4	8	4
StarKist Tuna Salad — *1 kit*	n/a	190	60	6	2.5	5	420	25	2	11	9	0	0	4	8

Frozen Bars & Pops

	Weight g	Calories	Calories from fat	Total fat g	Sat. fat g	Cholesterol mg	Sodium mg	Carbohydrates g	Dietary fiber g	Sugars g	Protein g	Vitamin A % DV	Vitamin C % DV	Calcium % DV	Iron % DV
Ben & Jerry's Peace Pop															
cherry garcia, yogurt — *1 bar*	97	260	130	14	9	15	70	31	2	25	5	2	6	6	0
chocolate cookie dough — *1 bar*	97	420	230	25	14	55	130	44	0	34	5	15	0	10	6
vanilla — *1 bar*	97	330	210	23	16	75	55	29	1	28	4	10	0	10	4
vanilla w/ Heath Toffee Crunch — *1 bar*	97	330	200	22	14	65	105	33	0	32	4	10	0	10	4
Ben & Jerry's Vanilla Brownie Bar — *1 bar*	112	330	150	17	8	60	170	43	2	39	4	8	0	8	6
Breyers															
almond bar — *1 bar*	n/a	300	200	22	11	50	65	28	n/a	26	n/a	n/a	n/a	n/a	n/a
vanilla bar — *1 bar*	n/a	300	170	19	11	50	55	27	n/a	25	n/a	n/a	n/a	n/a	n/a

	Weight *g*	Calories	Calories from fat	Total fat *g*	Sat. fat *g*	Cholesterol *mg*	Sodium *mg*	Carbohydrates *g*	Dietary fiber *g*	Sugars *g*	Protein *g*	Vitamin A *% DV*	Vitamin C *% DV*	Calcium *% DV*	Iron *% DV*
Breyers Cone, Butter Pecan — *1 cone*	n/a	300	150	17	7	45	200	31	n/a	21	n/a	n/a	n/a	n/a	n/a
DoveBar															
almond — *1 bar*	100	350	220	24	14	40	140	29	1	27	6	8	0	15	2
vanilla w/ dark chocolate — *1 bar*	98	330	200	21	14	35	40	32	0	30	4	6	0	10	4
vanilla w/ milk chocolate — *1 bar*	97	330	190	21	15	40	55	31	0	30	4	8	0	15	0
Good Humor Cones															
American Glory Cone — *1 cone*	n/a	230	70	8	4.5	5	135	36	n/a	20	n/a	n/a	n/a	n/a	n/a
King Cone — *1 cone*	n/a	300	90	10	6	20	110	48	n/a	25	n/a	n/a	n/a	n/a	n/a
Premium Cone — *1 cone*	n/a	290	120	14	7	20	85	33	n/a	22	n/a	n/a	n/a	n/a	n/a
Good Humor Sandwiches															
American Glory Sandwich — *1 sandwich*	n/a	190	70	8	4	15	120	28	n/a	22	n/a	n/a	n/a	n/a	n/a
Choco Taco — *1 sandwich*	n/a	310	150	17	10	20	100	37	n/a	27	n/a	n/a	n/a	n/a	n/a
Giant Neapolitan Sandwich — *1 sandwich*	n/a	260	90	10	7	20	150	39	n/a	26	n/a	n/a	n/a	n/a	n/a
Giant Vanilla Sandwich — *1 sandwich*	n/a	240	90	10	6	20	160	35	n/a	22	n/a	n/a	n/a	n/a	n/a
Good Humor Single Serve															
Candy Center Crunch Bar — *1 bar (3.75 fl oz)*	n/a	280	190	21	17	15	75	21	n/a	20	n/a	n/a	n/a	n/a	n/a
Chocolate Eclair Bar — *1 bar (3.75 fl oz)*	n/a	220	90	10	7	10	80	28	n/a	22	n/a	n/a	n/a	n/a	n/a
Premium Ice Cream Bar — *1 bar (3.75 fl oz)*	n/a	220	120	13	9	20	40	14	n/a	18	n/a	n/a	n/a	n/a	n/a
Reese's Nutrageous Ice Cream Bar — *1 bar (2 fl oz)*	n/a	240	130	15	7	10	75	22	n/a	15	n/a	n/a	n/a	n/a	n/a
Toasted Almond Bar — *1 bar (3.75 fl oz)*	n/a	230	100	11	4	15	30	31	n/a	27	n/a	n/a	n/a	n/a	n/a
Häagen-Dazs Ice Cream Bar															
chocolate & dark chocolate — *1 bar*	112	400	240	27	18	85	90	33	3	29	5	8	0	10	10
coffee & almond crunch — *1 bar*	106	360	230	26	15	100	85	27	1	25	5	10	0	15	4
vanilla & almonds — *1 bar*	106	370	240	27	14	90	80	26	1	24	6	10	0	15	4

	Weight *g*	Calories	Calories from fat	Total fat *g*	Sat. fat *g*	Cholesterol *mg*	Sodium *mg*	Carbohydrates *g*	Dietary fiber *g*	Sugars *g*	Protein *g*	Vitamin A *% DV*	Vitamin C *% DV*	Calcium *% DV*	Iron *% DV*
vanilla & dark chocolate — *1 bar*	112	390	240	27	18	85	65	33	2	29	5	10	0	10	10
vanilla & milk chocolate — *1 bar*	100	330	220	24	14	90	75	24	<1	24	5	10	0	15	4
Häagen-Dazs Ice Cream Sandwich															
vanilla — *1 sandwich*	80	260	120	13	8	65	125	32	0	19	4	6	0	8	4
vanilla & chocolate — *1 sandwich*	80	260	120	13	8	65	120	31	1	19	4	6	0	8	6
Häagen-Dazs Sorbet 'n Yogurt Bars															
banana strawberry — *1 bar*	71	80	0	0	0	0	15	20	0	14	2	0	6	6	0
chocolate & cherry — *1 bar*	71	100	0	0	0	0	40	21	<1	13	3	0	0	6	2
raspberry & vanilla — *1 bar*	71	90	0	0	0	0	15	20	0	14	20	0	0	6	0
Häagen-Dazs Sorbet Bars															
chocolate — *1 bar*	76	80	0	0	0	0	50	20	1	15	2	0	0	0	4
wild berry — *1 bar*	76	90	0	0	0	0	5	22	<1	17	0	0	4	0	0
Klondike Bars															
almond bar — *1 bar (5 fl oz)*	n/a	310	190	21	14	25	90	26	n/a	19	n/a	n/a	n/a	n/a	n/a
Big Bear Sandwich, fat-free — *1 bar (4 fl oz)*	n/a	190	0	0	0	0	115	33	n/a	15	n/a	n/a	n/a	n/a	n/a
caramel crunch bar — *1 bar (5 fl oz)*	n/a	300	170	18	13	30	95	31	n/a	30	n/a	n/a	n/a	n/a	n/a
chocolate/chocolate bar — *1 bar (5 fl oz)*	n/a	280	180	20	14	20	60	22	n/a	17	n/a	n/a	n/a	n/a	n/a
Krispy Bar — *1 bar (5 fl oz)*	n/a	300	180	20	13	25	85	28	n/a	22	n/a	n/a	n/a	n/a	n/a
original bar — *1 bar (5 fl oz)*	n/a	290	180	20	14	15	65	24	n/a	24	n/a	n/a	n/a	n/a	n/a
Sundae Kone — *1 bar (4.6 fl oz)*	n/a	310	150	17	7	20	100	34	n/a	21	n/a	n/a	n/a	n/a	n/a
vanilla bar, reduced-fat, no-sugar-added — *1 bar (4 fl oz)*	n/a	190	90	10	7	5	65	19	n/a	6	n/a	n/a	n/a	n/a	n/a
Milky Way															
vanilla w/ dark chocolate — *1 bar*	69	220	110	13	10	15	60	23	0	21	3	4	0	6	0
vanilla w/ dark chocolate, reduced-fat — *1 bar*	48	140	60	7	3	5	50	19	0	19	2	2	0	6	0

	Weight g	Calories	Calories from fat	Total fat g	Sat. fat g	Cholesterol mg	Sodium mg	Carbohydrates g	Dietary fiber g	Sugars g	Protein g	Vitamin A % DV	Vitamin C % DV	Calcium % DV	Iron % DV
Sealtest Popsicle															
Big Stick (Cherry/Pineapple) — *1 bar (3.5 fl oz)*	n/a	50	0	0	0	0	5	12	n/a	10	n/a	n/a	n/a	n/a	n/a
Creamsicle Bar — *1 bar (2.7 fl oz)*	n/a	110	25	3	2	10	30	20	n/a	15	n/a	n/a	n/a	n/a	n/a
Creamsicle Orange Pops — *1 bar (1.75 fl oz)*	n/a	70	15	2	1	<5	15	13	n/a	12	n/a	n/a	n/a	n/a	n/a
Fudgsicle Bar — *1 bar (2.7 fl oz)*	n/a	90	5	1	0.5	5	55	17	n/a	14	n/a	n/a	n/a	n/a	n/a
Fudgsicle Pops — *1 bar (1.75 fl oz)*	n/a	120	10	1	0	5	75	24	n/a	20	n/a	n/a	n/a	n/a	n/a
Fudgsicle Variety Pops — *1 bar (1.75 fl oz)*	n/a	60	5	1	0.5	<5	40	12	n/a	10	n/a	n/a	n/a	n/a	n/a
Ice Cream Bar — *1 bar (3 fl oz)*	n/a	160	100	11	9	15	35	15	n/a	15	n/a	n/a	n/a	n/a	n/a
Ice Cream Sandwich — *1 bar (3.5 fl oz)*	n/a	190	70	8	4	15	120	28	n/a	22	n/a	n/a	n/a	n/a	n/a
Pop Ups Rainbow — *1 bar (2.75 fl oz)*	n/a	90	10	1	0	<5	15	19	n/a	15	n/a	n/a	n/a	n/a	n/a
Rainbow Pop — *1 bar (3.5 fl oz)*	n/a	90	0	0	0	0	0	22	n/a	21	n/a	n/a	n/a	n/a	n/a
Sherbet Big Stick — *1 bar (3.5 fl oz)*	n/a	110	10	1	0.5	5	20	24	n/a	19	n/a	n/a	n/a	n/a	n/a
Squeeze-Ups — *1 bar (3.7 fl oz)*	n/a	90	0	0	0	0	0	22	n/a	17	n/a	n/a	n/a	n/a	n/a
Super Twin — *1 bar (2.5 fl oz)*	n/a	70	0	0	0	0	5	16	n/a	13	n/a	n/a	n/a	n/a	n/a
Supersicle Double-Fudge — *1 bar (4.5 fl oz)*	n/a	150	10	2	1	10	95	29	n/a	28	n/a	n/a	n/a	n/a	n/a
Supersicle Sour Tower — *1 bar (4.5 fl oz)*	n/a	80	0	0	0	0	0	20	n/a	14	n/a	n/a	n/a	n/a	n/a
Sealtest Col. Crunch															
Chocolate Eclair — *1 bar (3 fl oz)*	n/a	160	60	7	4	10	60	21	n/a	15	n/a	n/a	n/a	n/a	n/a
Strawberry Shortcake — *1 bar (3 fl oz)*	n/a	170	70	8	6	10	45	22	n/a	15	n/a	n/a	n/a	n/a	n/a
Popsicle "Smart Eating"															
Fudgsicle, fat-free — *1 bar (1.75 fl oz)*	n/a	60	0	0	0	0	50	13	n/a	10	n/a	n/a	n/a	n/a	n/a
Fudgsicle, sugar-free — *1 bar (1.75 fl oz)*	n/a	40	5	0.5	0	<5	35	8	n/a	0	n/a	n/a	n/a	n/a	n/a
Popsicle, all natural — *1 bar (1.75 fl oz)*	n/a	50	0	0	0	0	0	12	n/a	9	n/a	n/a	n/a	n/a	n/a
Tropical, sugar-free — *1 bar (1.75 fl oz)*	n/a	15	0	0	0	0	0	3	n/a	0	n/a	n/a	n/a	n/a	n/a

	Weight g	Calories	Calories from fat	Total fat g	Sat. fat g	Cholesterol mg	Sodium mg	Carbohydrates g	Dietary fiber g	Sugars g	Protein g	Vitamin A % DV	Vitamin C % DV	Calcium % DV	Iron % DV
Snickers, Frozen — *1 bar*	52	200	110	13	8	15	55	19	0	19	4	4	0	6	0
3 Musketeers, Vanilla — *1 bar*	63	190	100	11	8	20	40	21	0	21	2	6	0	8	2
Weight Watchers															
chocolate dip — *1 bar*	n/a	100	50	6	3	5	15	11	0	6	2	2	0	8	0
chocolate mousse bar — *1 bar*	n/a	40	5	1	0.5	5	20	9	1	3	2	4	0	8	0
vanilla sandwich bars — *1 bar*	n/a	150	25	3	1	5	150	28	1	14	3	4	0	15	4

Frozen Entrées & Meals

	Weight g	Calories	Calories from fat	Total fat g	Sat. fat g	Cholesterol mg	Sodium mg	Carbohydrates g	Dietary fiber g	Sugars g	Protein g	Vitamin A % DV	Vitamin C % DV	Calcium % DV	Iron % DV
Banquet Extra Helping Dinners															
chicken fried beef steak — *1 meal*	528	800	400	44	14	55	2050	73	6	14	29	0	0	25	15
chicken parmigiana — *1 meal*	538	650	300	33	8	65	1770	64	9	9	24	4	180	15	15
fried chicken — *1 meal*	538	790	350	39	9	110	1820	72	8	14	37	0	0	15	10
fried chicken, all white meat — *1 meal*	538	820	370	41	9	95	1890	72	8	13	40	0	0	15	10
fried chicken, southern — *1 meal*	489	750	330	37	9	120	2140	67	9	14	38	0	0	15	15
meat loaf — *1 meal*	538	650	340	38	16	85	2100	49	10	13	29	90	170	10	20
salisbury steak — *1 meal*	538	740	410	46	19	75	1860	52	11	3	31	2	10	10	20
turkey & gravy w/ dressing — *1 meal*	533	560	180	20	5	75	1910	63	7	26	32	0	0	10	20
Banquet Family-Size Entrées															
beef patties w/ onion gravy — *1 patty w/ gravy*	n/a	180	130	14	6	20	630	7	2	5	8	0	0	2	6
beef patties, charbroiled, w/ mushroom gravy — *1 patty w/ gravy*	n/a	180	120	13	6	25	640	7	2	0	15	0	0	2	6
beef stew, hearty — *1 cup*	n/a	160	35	4	2	25	1120	17	4	3	14	10	15	2	8
beef, sliced, w/ brown gravy — *2 slices w/ gravy*	n/a	100	30	3	1.5	40	850	7	<1	2	13	0	0	0	10
chicken & dumplings, country-style — *1 cup*	n/a	290	120	14	5	40	1270	30	2	2	12	0	0	4	8
chicken parmigiana patties w/ tomato sauce — *1 patty w/ sauce*	n/a	240	120	13	5	20	690	18	2	4	11	4	60	10	6
egg noodles w/ beef & brown gravy — *1 cup*	n/a	140	30	4	2	35	1120	16	2	1	11	0	2	2	8

	Weight *g*	Calories	Calories from fat	Total fat *g*	Sat. fat *g*	Cholesterol *mg*	Sodium *mg*	Carbohydrates *g*	Dietary fiber *g*	Sugars *g*	Protein *g*	Vitamin A *% DV*	Vitamin C *% DV*	Calcium *% DV*	Iron *% DV*
lasagna w/ meat sauce — *1 cup*	n/a	230	70	8	4	35	530	29	3	<1	12	2	100	15	8
macaroni & cheese — *1 cup*	n/a	210	40	5	2	10	1290	33	4	7	8	2	0	10	6
meatloaf w/ savory gravy — *1 patty w/ gravy*	n/a	160	90	10	4.5	35	620	8	1	<1	10	0	0	0	6
salisbury steak w/ brown gravy — *1 patty w/ gravy*	n/a	200	120	14	6	25	610	7	2	0	12	0	0	2	6
turkey, sliced, w/ homestyle gravy — *2 slices w/ gravy*	n/a	120	70	8	3	35	670	5	1	1	8	0	0	0	4
veal parmigiana patties w/ tomato sauce — *1 patty w/ sauce*	n/a	230	120	14	4	20	740	19	2	2	9	4	90	4	4
Banquet Meal															
BBQ-style chicken — *1 meal*	237	320	110	12	2.5	60	800	36	3	15	18	6	10	6	10
beef enchilada — *1 meal*	312	380	110	12	5	15	1330	54	10	7	15	15	0	15	15
beef enchilada & tamale combo — *1 meal*	312	400	120	13	5	15	1520	56	10	7	14	15	0	15	15
beef patty w/ country-style vegetables — *1 meal*	269	300	180	20	8	35	1060	21	3	2	11	6	6	4	10
beef, sliced — *1 meal*	255	240	60	7	3	70	660	19	4	12	26	4	10	4	20
cheese enchilada — *1 meal*	312	340	60	6	2.5	15	1500	56	9	7	15	15	6	20	15
chicken & dumplings w/ gravy — *1 meal*	283	260	70	8	2.5	35	780	35	3	16	13	40	0	4	6
chicken chow mein w/ egg rolls — *1 meal*	255	210	60	7	2	30	850	28	3	3	9	10	15	2	4
chicken enchilada — *1 meal*	312	360	90	10	3	20	1580	54	9	7	15	15	0	15	15
chicken fried beef steak — *1 meal*	283	400	180	20	6	30	1180	39	4	9	15	2	0	10	10
chicken nugget — *1 meal*	191	410	190	21	5	45	650	38	4	11	18	0	10	2	10
chicken parmigiana — *1 meal*	269	290	130	15	4	50	900	27	3	3	14	6	100	6	10
chicken pasta primavera — *1 meal*	269	300	110	12	5	25	840	36	6	9	11	50	20	6	10
chimichanga — *1 meal*	269	470	210	23	7	15	1180	56	9	9	13	8	10	6	15
enchilada combo meal — *1 meal*	312	350	80	9	3.5	35	1640	53	10	3	15	15	0	20	15
fettuccine alfredo — *1 meal*	269	330	150	16	7	25	850	36	4	5	11	4	30	15	6
fried chicken (Our Original) — *1 meal*	269	470	240	27	9	105	980	35	6	1	21	0	8	8	6

	Weight g	Calories	Calories from fat	Total fat g	Sat. fat g	Cholesterol mg	Sodium mg	Carbohydrates g	Dietary fiber g	Sugars g	Protein g	Vitamin A % DV	Vitamin C % DV	Calcium % DV	Iron % DV
fried chicken, southern-style — *1 meal*	249	520	280	31	7	100	1410	32	4	1	26	0	10	6	10
fried chicken, white meat — *1 meal*	249	470	250	28	11	100	1100	33	6	2	22	0	8	4	8
lasagna w/ meat sauce — *1 meal*	269	260	70	8	2	10	820	35	6	10	12	15	100	15	10
macaroni & cheese — *1 meal*	269	320	100	11	3.5	20	970	43	4	6	12	25	40	15	8
meat loaf — *1 meal*	269	280	140	16	6	80	1020	22	3	3	13	4	10	4	10
oriental-style chicken w/ egg rolls — *1 meal*	255	260	80	9	2.5	40	610	34	4	16	12	25	30	4	6
pasta w/ italian sausage & peppers — *1 meal*	269	300	110	12	3.5	10	760	39	6	9	10	10	100	6	10
pork cutlet meal — *1 meal*	292	410	220	24	7	25	1060	39	4	21	11	4	15	8	8
pork riblet, boneless — *1 meal*	283	400	170	19	8	40	1070	39	7	18	18	8	4	10	10
salisbury steak — *1 meal*	269	340	170	19	7	60	1040	28	4	4	15	0	4	0	10
turkey (Mostly White Meat) — *1 meal*	263	290	90	10	2.5	55	1060	34	5	7	17	2	10	4	10
veal parmigiana — *1 meal*	255	320	130	14	5	25	960	35	7	14	13	6	45	6	10
western-style beef patty — *1 meal*	269	350	180	20	9	30	1400	28	5	4	14	0	4	4	10
white cheddar & broccoli — *1 meal*	269	320	100	11	4	15	810	43	5	4	11	20	100	15	10
Chi-Chi's Frozen Dinner															
baja enchilada — *1 dinner*	437	570	160	18	7	50	1510	74	9	8	27	25	2	20	20
beef burro — *1 dinner*	428	570	150	17	6	50	1540	73	9	8	26	25	4	25	20
beef chimichanga — *1 dinner*	428	610	210	23	6	50	1540	73	9	8	26	25	4	25	20
chicken burro — *1 dinner*	428	530	130	14	5	55	1710	75	9	8	26	10	4	20	20
chicken chimichanga — *1 dinner*	428	590	190	21	5	55	1710	85	9	8	26	10	4	20	20
chicken enchilada suprema — *1 dinner*	422	590	180	20	9	70	1830	78	9	9	24	15	4	20	20
Empire Kosher Blintzes															
blueberry — *2 blintzes*	124	190	35	7	1	10	260	36	2	12	5	0	8	0	8
cheese — *2 blintzes*	124	200	50	6	2	20	310	29	3	8	11	0	2	4	8

	Weight g	Calories	Calories from fat	Total fat g	Sat. fat g	Cholesterol mg	Sodium mg	Carbohydrates g	Dietary fiber g	Sugars g	Protein g	Vitamin A % DV	Vitamin C % DV	Calcium % DV	Iron % DV
cherry — *2 blintzes*	124	200	35	4	1	10	280	38	3	10	5	0	4	0	6
potato — *2 blintzes*	124	190	50	8	1.5	10	590	32	3	0	8	0	2	2	8
Empire Kosher Express Meal															
chicken fajita — *1 fajita*	106	130	20	2.5	0	10	450	15	2	3	8	8	32	6	8
chicken pasta — *1 cup*	160	140	20	2	0.5	15	400	17	2	3	10	35	30	2	6
chicken stir-fry — *1 cup*	145	160	20	2.5	0.5	20	500	20	2	5	12	45	5	2	8
Empire Kosher Pierogies															
potato cheese — *5.3 oz*	150	247	36	4	1	60	233	44	0.7	13	7	3	0	8	3
potato onion — *5.3 oz*	150	243	36	4	1	48	280	47	0.7	12	5	3	0	0	13
Healthy Choice Meal															
beef & peppers cantonese — *1 meal*	326	270	50	6	2.5	55	480	32	5	4	22	30	60	4	10
beef broccoli beijing — *1 meal*	340	300	40	4.5	1.5	25	420	45	6	11	21	60	60	4	15
beef stroganoff — *1 meal*	312	310	50	6	2.5	60	440	44	3	19	21	15	0	4	10
beef tips, traditional — *1 meal*	320	260	50	6	3	40	390	32	6	18	20	60	70	2	10
cacciatore chicken — *1 meal*	354	250	25	2.5	0.5	25	550	36	6	4	21	4	20	4	10
chicken broccoli alfredo — *1 meal*	326	300	50	6	2.5	40	530	38	4	0	25	4	45	15	10
chicken cantonese — *1 meal*	306	260	20	2	1	40	430	35	4	6	25	100	20	6	10
chicken dijon — *1 meal*	312	270	50	5	2	40	470	33	6	6	23	90	30	8	8
chicken enchilada suprema — *1 meal*	320	270	35	4	2	20	560	45	6	2	14	20	50	10	6
chicken francesca — *1 meal*	354	330	60	6	2.5	30	600	46	5	0	23	2	25	10	10
chicken parmigiana — *1 meal*	326	300	35	4	2	35	490	47	5	13	20	70	30	10	8
chicken picante — *1 meal*	306	260	50	6	2.5	45	550	30	4	3	21	15	50	10	10
chicken teriyaki — *1 meal*	312	230	25	3	1.5	45	580	32	4	8	19	20	60	2	6
chicken, roasted — *1 meal*	312	220	30	3	1	35	470	27	6	9	23	90	25	2	8

	Weight g	Calories	Calories from fat	Total fat g	Sat. fat g	Cholesterol mg	Sodium mg	Carbohydrates g	Dietary fiber g	Sugars g	Protein g	Vitamin A % DV	Vitamin C % DV	Calcium % DV	Iron % DV
country breaded chicken — *1 meal*	292	360	80	9	2	45	480	53	5	20	18	10	0	6	8
country herb chicken — *1 meal*	346	310	35	4	1.5	45	540	49	4	21	20	50	0	4	10
ginger chicken hunan — *1 meal*	357	350	20	2.5	0.5	25	430	59	5	11	24	15	0	6	15
herb baked fish — *1 meal*	309	340	60	7	1.5	35	480	54	5	11	16	60	0	4	4
lemon pepper fish — *1 meal*	303	290	45	5	1	25	360	47	7	20	14	10	50	2	6
meatloaf, traditional — *1 meal*	340	320	45	5	2.5	35	460	52	6	17	15	15	90	4	10
mesquite beef w/ barbecue sauce — *1 meal*	312	310	70	8	2.5	40	490	38	6	14	21	50	30	8	20
mesquite chicken barbecue — *1 meal*	297	270	20	2.5	1	60	490	44	6	13	19	50	15	4	10
pasta shells marinara — *1 meal*	340	380	50	6	3.5	25	390	55	5	10	25	10	0	40	10
pork patty, grilled glazed — *1 meal*	272	280	35	4	1.5	20	380	46	6	28	16	45	50	4	10
salisbury steak, traditional — *1 meal*	326	320	60	6	3	45	470	48	7	20	18	30	100	4	10
sesame chicken shanghai — *1 meal*	340	310	25	2.5	0	25	550	47	7	0	23	35	30	4	10
shrimp & vegetables Maria — *1 meal*	354	270	25	3	1	35	540	46	5	<1	15	10	35	4	15
shrimp marinara — *1 meal*	297	220	5	0.5	0	50	220	44	5	27	10	6	45	6	10
southwestern grilled chicken — *1 meal*	290	200	25	3	1.5	40	450	23	4	1	21	15	70	4	6
steak patty, charbroiled — *1 meal*	312	280	50	6	3	25	550	41	7	4	16	50	10	2	10
sweet & sour chicken — *1 meal*	312	330	45	5	1.5	45	210	53	5	30	20	40	50	4	6
yankee pot roast — *1 meal*	312	280	50	5	2	45	460	38	5	20	19	60	70	4	10
Healthy Choice, Beef															
beef macaroni — *1 meal*	241	210	20	2	0.5	15	450	34	5	9	14	10	90	4	15
beef pepper steak oriental — *1 meal*	269	250	35	4	2	35	470	34	3	0	19	4	15	2	6
beef tips français — *1 meal*	269	280	40	5	1.5	30	520	40	4	1	20	0	0	2	10
grilled peppercorn steak patty — *1 meal*	255	220	60	6	2.5	30	470	26	5	1	16	4	45	6	10
lasagna roma — *1 meal*	382	390	45	5	2	15	580	60	9	11	26	10	10	15	20

	Weight g	Calories	Calories from fat	Total fat g	Sat. fat g	Cholesterol mg	Sodium mg	Carbohydrates g	Dietary fiber g	Sugars g	Protein g	Vitamin A % DV	Vitamin C % DV	Calcium % DV	Iron % DV
spaghetti & sauce w/ seasoned beef — *1 meal*	283	260	25	3	1	15	470	43	5	7	14	10	25	4	20
swedish meatballs — *1 meal*	258	280	50	9	2.5	60	590	35	4	4	22	0	0	10	15
Healthy Choice, Chicken															
chicken & vegetable marsala — *1 meal*	326	230	15	1.5	0.5	30	440	32	3	1	22	10	6	6	10
chicken con queso burrito — *1 meal*	300	360	25	3	1	15	590	66	8	11	16	30	25	10	15
chicken enchilada suiza — *1 meal*	283	270	40	4	2	25	440	43	5	4	14	6	4	15	6
chicken fettuccine alfredo — *1 meal*	241	260	40	4.5	2	40	410	35	3	3	22	0	0	10	8
chicken imperial — *1 meal*	255	230	40	4	1	50	470	31	3	2	17	15	15	2	8
country-glazed chicken — *1 meal*	241	210	20	2	0	30	480	30	3	<1	17	0	0	2	2
fiesta chicken fajitas — *1 meal*	198	260	35	4	1	30	410	36	5	6	21	15	60	2	10
garlic chicken milano — *1 meal*	269	240	40	4	2	35	510	34	3	4	18	10	30	10	6
grilled chicken sonoma — *1 meal*	255	240	25	2.5	0.5	40	540	34	6	2	19	60	40	4	10
grilled chicken w/ mashed potatoes — *1 meal*	227	170	30	3.5	1.5	40	600	18	3	0	18	4	8	0	4
honey mustard chicken — *1 meal*	269	260	20	2	0	30	550	40	4	4	21	30	0	2	2
mandarin chicken — *1 meal*	283	280	20	2.5	0	35	520	44	4	9	20	30	25	2	4
sesame chicken — *1 meal*	278	240	25	3	0.5	30	600	38	3	9	16	35	20	2	4
Healthy Choice, Meatless															
cheddar broccoli potatoes — *1 meal*	297	310	40	5	2	15	550	53	8	8	13	6	45	20	10
cheese ravioli parmigiana — *1 meal*	255	260	45	5	2.5	20	290	44	6	14	11	15	0	15	10
fettuccine alfredo — *1 meal*	227	250	45	5	2	15	480	39	3	4	11	0	0	15	8
garden potato casserole — *1 meal*	263	210	45	5	1.5	10	520	30	6	5	11	25	35	10	4
macaroni & cheese — *1 meal*	255	290	45	5	2	15	580	45	4	13	15	0	0	30	6
manicotti w/ three cheeses — *1 meal*	312	260	40	4.5	2	25	450	40	5	7	16	15	0	35	10
penne w/ tomato sauce — *1 meal*	227	230	45	5	1	10	490	36	5	3	9	10	0	4	10

	Weight g	Calories	Calories from fat	Total fat g	Sat. fat g	Cholesterol mg	Sodium mg	Carbohydrates g	Dietary fiber g	Sugars g	Protein g	Vitamin A % DV	Vitamin C % DV	Calcium % DV	Iron % DV
vegetable pasta italiano — *1 meal*	283	240	15	1.5	0.5	5	480	48	6	8	9	10	4	6	15
zucchini lasagna — *1 meal*	382	330	15	1.5	1	10	310	58	11	11	20	25	0	20	15
Healthy Choice, Turkey															
breast of turkey, traditional — *1 meal*	297	280	25	3	1	45	460	40	7	20	22	8	100	2	8
Country Inn roast turkey — *1 meal*	283	250	30	4	1	30	530	29	6	3	26	30	0	4	10
country-roast turkey w/ mushrooms — *1 meal*	241	220	35	4	1	25	440	28	3	0	19	15	0	2	4
Hormel Quick Meal															
beef burrito — *1 burrito*	113	300	120	13	6	40	550	37	3	4	9	2	0	2	8
beef, barbecue — *1 meal*	122	360	140	16	6	55	560	39	2	10	15	0	0	2	10
cheese burrito — *1 burrito*	113	250	50	6	2	30	640	41	4	5	9	0	0	6	8
chicken, grilled — *1*	13	300	80	9	3	60	640	36	2	6	20	0	0	4	10
fish fillet — *1*	147	400	140	16	4	75	850	48	2	6	15	2	0	8	6
pork, barbecue — *1*	122	350	130	15	6	60	580	39	2	10	15	0	0	2	10
red chili burrito — *1 burrito*	113	280	100	11	4.5	35	560	37	3	4	9	2	0	2	8
Hormel Tamales															
beef, hot-spicy — *3 tamales*	213	280	190	21	8	35	1010	20	3	1	6	15	0	2	4
beef, jumbo — *3 tamales*	198	270	180	20	8	35	940	18	3	1	5	10	0	2	4
chicken — *3 tamales*	213	210	90	11	4	50	1020	22	2	2	6	0	2	4	4
Kid Cuisine															
Big League Hamburger Pizza — *1 meal*	235	400	100	11	3.5	25	530	61	6	28	14	4	10	10	10
Buckaroo Beef Patty Sandwich w/ Cheese — *1 meal*	241	410	130	15	5	15	540	58	4	27	12	2	0	15	10
Circus Show Corn Dog — *1 meal*	249	450	140	15	4.5	20	750	70	5	46	8	0	20	8	10
Cosmic Chicken Nuggets — *1 meal*	258	440	150	16	4.5	30	1070	54	5	12	18	0	0	10	10
Funtastic Fish Sticks — *1 meal*	234	370	110	12	2.5	15	550	55	4	21	11	0	0	6	8

	Weight g	Calories	Calories from fat	Total fat g	Sat. fat g	Cholesterol mg	Sodium mg	Carbohydrates g	Dietary fiber g	Sugars g	Protein g	Vitamin A % DV	Vitamin C % DV	Calcium % DV	Iron % DV
High Flying Fried Chicken — *1 meal*	286	440	170	19	4.5	40	940	49	5	12	18	0	0	8	8
Magical Macaroni & Cheese — *1 meal*	300	410	110	13	5	15	840	63	5	27	10	10	0	10	6
Pirate Pizza w/ Cheese — *1 meal*	227	430	100	11	3	20	440	71	5	34	12	2	0	15	10
Raptor Ravoli w/ Cheese — *1 meal*	278	310	50	5	2	1.5	730	59	5	30	7	10	0	4	6
Rip-Roaring Macaroni & Beef — *1 meal*	272	370	90	9	4	30	900	58	5	23	12	2	0	10	8
La Choy Frozen															
chicken chow mein — *1 cup*	221	133	28	3	1	5	857	19	1	6	8	0	13	3	0
chicken pot stickers — *8 pieces*	141	240	90	11	3	40	670	24	2	2	12	0	0	0	0
chicken shu mai — *7 pieces*	140	210	100	11	3	55	560	12	1	2	16	0	0	0	0
vegetable chow mein — *1 cup*	255	108	21	2	0.4	0	1135	20	5	3	2	0	10	4	0
Marie Callender's Meal															
angel hair pasta w/ sausage & breadstick — *½ meal*	227	460	140	16	4.5	10	740	60	5	9	18	15	0	10	20
beef stroganoff & noodles — *1 cup*	184	440	250	27	11	40	780	23	3	4	24	2	10	2	8
breaded shrimp over angel hair pasta — *1 cup*	212	300	110	12	2	30	470	37	3	5	11	2	15	8	10
Callender's Deluxe Pasta — *1 cup*	184	450	250	27	12	80	680	35	4	1	15	4	0	15	10
chicken & dumplings — *1 cup*	198	260	110	12	5	90	1030	22	3	8	17	50	0	6	8
chicken cordon bleu — *1 dinner*	368	590	230	25	8	55	1920	58	7	0	33	45	60	25	15
chicken fried beef steak & gravy — *1 dinner*	425	650	280	31	10	50	2260	69	7	9	23	15	40	15	15
chicken marsala — *1 dinner*	397	450	150	17	7	70	1260	42	6	5	33	8	55	6	15
chicken parmigiana, baked — *1 dinner*	453	620	250	27	8	50	730	63	9	9	31	20	15	2	20
chili & cornbread — *½ meal*	227	350	120	13	6	30	1380	45	5	13	14	0	6	6	6
country fried chicken & gravy — *1 dinner*	453	610	240	27	8	55	1680	67	6	9	25	6	15	2	2
country fried pork chop — *1 dinner*	425	550	240	27	9	65	2240	50	9	16	26	100	15	15	15
escalloped noodles & chicken — *1 cup*	184	270	140	16	6	20	670	22	1	2	10	6	4	4	4

	Weight g	Calories	Calories from fat	Total fat g	Sat. fat g	Cholesterol mg	Sodium mg	Carbohydrates g	Dietary fiber g	Sugars g	Protein g	Vitamin A % DV	Vitamin C % DV	Calcium % DV	Iron % DV
extra cheese lasagna — *1 cup*	212	330	140	16	8	32	770	32	4	8	25	6	2	20	4
fettucini alfredo & garlic bread — *1 cup*	198	460	240	27	10	45	590	39	2	2	15	15	4	15	10
fettucini primavera w/ tortellini — *½ meal*	198	310	170	19	8	50	380	25	2	2	10	6	25	8	4
fettucini w/ broccoli & chicken — *1 cup*	184	410	220	24	10	45	550	32	4	0	18	6	15	15	8
grilled chicken in mushroom sauce — *1 dinner*	397	480	140	15	6	65	1030	54	7	0	33	10	90	8	15
ham steak (baked) w/ macaroni & cheese — *1 dinner*	397	450	80	9	4	60	2200	63	6	32	29	70	50	4	6
herb roasted chicken & mashed potatoes — *1 dinner*	397	670	380	31	15	205	2100	32	7	7	43	15	100	10	10
lasagna primavera — *1 cup*	184	260	110	12	5	90	1030	22	3	8	17	50	0	6	8
lasagna w/ meat sauce — *1 cup*	212	370	170	18	9	35	740	34	4	8	17	10	6	30	15
macaroni & beef — *1 meal*	397	590	160	18	5	30	1230	80	9	16	28	30	0	15	30
meatloaf & gravy w/ mashed potatoes — *1 dinner*	397	540	270	30	11	80	1230	44	7	9	23	4	8	4	6
old fashioned pot roast & gravy — *1 cup*	212	250	60	6	2.5	45	790	31	3	5	17	35	2	2	10
pasta primavera w/ chicken — *1 cup*	198	340	180	20	8	40	520	27	3	3	12	60	35	10	10
pasta w/ beef & broccoli — *1 dinner*	425	570	140	15	4	70	1160	73	6	32	35	8	25	4	25
rigatoni parmigiana w/ soft breadstick — *1 cup*	212	300	130	14	6	25	650	32	3	7	12	0	0	25	6
sirloin salisbury steak & gravy — *1 dinner*	397	550	220	25	11	85	1680	51	6	14	30	30	20	25	20
spaghetti & meat sauce w/ garlic bread — *1 cup*	n/a	260	90	10	3	5	570	32	3	5	11	2	6	6	6
spaghetti marinara w/ cheese garlic bread — *1 cup*	227	270	90	10	3	10	540	35	3	5	10	6	25	8	6
sweet & sour chicken — *1 dinner*	397	530	80	9	2	35	700	86	7	36	25	100	45	6	15
turkey w/ gravy & dressing — *1 dinner*	397	530	150	17	7	85	2030	51	2	4	33	8	90	10	20
Marie Callender's Meal, Family-Size															
chicken & dumplings — *1 cup*	297	310	140	15	7	80	1190	25	3	4	17	35	4	6	8
chicken fried steak w/ mashed potatoes — *1 cup*	340	480	210	23	8	75	1960	46	4	2	21	0	0	10	15
country fried chicken w/ gravy & mashed potatoes — *1 cup*	340	520	200	22	6	70	1550	57	5	3	21	0	0	10	6

	Weight g	Calories	Calories from fat	Total fat g	Sat. fat g	Cholesterol mg	Sodium mg	Carbohydrates g	Dietary fiber g	Sugars g	Protein g	Vitamin A % DV	Vitamin C % DV	Calcium % DV	Iron % DV
Morton Dinners															
beef patty, charbroiled, w/ gravy — *1 meal*	255	290	140	16	7	25	1210	26	6	3	11	0	4	4	10
chicken nuggets — *1 meal*	198	320	150	17	4	30	460	30	3	12	13	40	4	4	8
chicken patty, breaded — *1 meal*	193	280	140	15	3	20	840	24	4	12	11	60	0	4	6
chili gravy w/ beef enchilada & tamale — *1 meal*	283	260	70	7	3	5	1000	40	8	3	8	10	10	8	10
fried chicken — *1 meal*	255	420	220	25	8	85	1000	30	4	4	20	45	15	6	6
macaroni & cheese — *½ meal*	227	230	35	4	2	5	1000	40	3	<1	9	10	0	10	8
meat loaf w/ tomato sauce — *1 meal*	255	250	110	13	4	20	1110	24	5	17	9	50	0	4	8
salisbury steak w/ gravy — *1 meal*	255	210	80	9	4	20	950	23	3	7	9	40	4	4	8
spaghetti w/ meat sauce — *1 meal*	241	170	25	3	1	<5	600	30	4	13	6	50	0	2	10
turkey w/ dressing & gravy — *1 meal*	255	230	70	8	3	35	1090	27	5	5	14	50	0	4	10
veal parmigiana w/ tomato sauce — *1 meal*	248	280	120	13	4	20	950	30	4	8	9	45	30	4	10
Old El Paso Frozen Burrito															
bean & cheese — *1 burrito*	141	300	80	9	4.5	15	840	44	3	3	12	4	8	15	15
beef & bean, medium — *1 burrito*	141	320	90	10	4	15	800	46	3	4	12	0	0	6	20
beef & bean, hot — *1 burrito*	141	320	90	10	4	15	850	45	3	4	12	0	4	6	20
beef & bean, mild — *1 burrito*	141	320	80	9	3	15	690	48	4	4	12	0	0	6	20
Old El Paso Frozen Chimichanga															
beef — *1 chimichanga*	127	360	180	20	5	10	470	37	3	0	9	0	0	4	20
chicken — *1 chimichanga*	127	340	140	16	4	20	540	39	2	0	11	0	0	6	10
Old El Paso Frozen Pizza Burrito															
cheese — *1 burrito*	99	240	80	9	4	20	430	27	0	3	13	0	0	25	10
pepperoni — *1 burrito*	99	260	90	10	5	20	510	31	0	3	12	0	0	15	15
sausage — *1 burrito*	99	250	80	9	4	15	420	32	0	2	11	0	0	15	10

	Weight g	Calories	Calories from fat	Total fat g	Sat. fat g	Cholesterol mg	Sodium mg	Carbohydrates g	Dietary fiber g	Sugars g	Protein g	Vitamin A % DV	Vitamin C % DV	Calcium % DV	Iron % DV
Patio Britos															
beef & bean — *10 britos*	170	420	170	19	7	20	800	51	7	2	11	10	4	4	8
chicken & cheese, spicy — *10 britos*	170	400	150	16	4	25	640	52	3	2	13	0	0	10	10
nacho beef — *10 britos*	170	410	170	18	18	20	1050	48	5	3	13	2	2	6	8
nacho cheese — *10 britos*	170	360	110	13	4	15	500	52	3	8	10	0	4	15	6
Patio Burritos															
bean & cheese — *1 burrito*	142	270	50	5	2.55	5	530	46	7	2	9	4	6	6	6
beef & bean w/ green chili — *1 burrito*	142	270	60	7	3.5	10	870	42	4	3	10	0	2	2	4
beef & bean w/ red chili peppers — *1 burrito*	142	270	60	6	2	10	850	42	6	4	11	8	6	2	15
beef & bean, medium — *1 burrito*	142	280	60	7	3	15	860	45	7	5	10	6	2	0	0
beef & bean, red chili — *1 burrito*	142	260	45	5	2	10	640	42	7	3	11	4	8	2	10
chicken — *1 burrito*	142	260	35	4	1.5	15	740	44	3	5	12	0	2	6	4
Patio Dinners															
beef enchilada — *1 meal*	340	350	90	10	4	15	1700	52	9	2	12	10	6	15	10
cheese enchilada — *1 meal*	340	350	70	8	3	15	1570	52	10	7	13	10	8	20	10
chicken enchilada — *1 meal*	340	380	80	9	3	25	1470	58	9	8	14	6	0	20	15
fiesta — *1 meal*	340	340	80	9	4	15	1760	51	11	5	13	8	6	15	10
mexican-style — *1 meal*	377	430	130	15	6	20	1840	59	13	3	15	10	10	10	15
Ranchera — *1 meal*	368	410	130	15	6	25	2400	55	14	1	13	10	10	10	15
Salisbury Con Queso — *1 meal*	312	390	180	20	11	40	1570	33	10	7	18	6	6	10	15
Pepperidge Farms Frozen Meal Kits															
beef stroganoff — *1 filled*	159	420	260	29	12	40	500	27	5	1	13	0	0	8	4
chicken á la king — *1 filled*	159	400	230	26	10	35	560	28	5	2	11	15	15	10	4
hors d'oeuvre — *7 filled*	144	470	250	28	8	15	520	41	7	2	11	0	0	15	2

	Weight g	Calories	Calories from fat	Total fat g	Sat. fat g	Cholesterol mg	Sodium mg	Carbohydrates g	Dietary fiber g	Sugars g	Protein g	Vitamin A % DV	Vitamin C % DV	Calcium % DV	Iron % DV
shrimp newburg — *1 filled*	159	340	180	20	7	60	670	31	4	3	8	6	6	15	4
Tyson Chicken Dinners															
BBQ — *1 meal*	308	360	90	10	2.5	30	590	49	6	17	18	10	8	4	6
blackened chicken — *1 meal*	252	260	35	4	1	30	370	38	4	5	17	6	10	6	6
chicken kiev — *1 meal*	259	440	230	25	11	85	680	36	2	4	18	140	15	4	0
grilled italian-style w/ herb glaze — *1 meal*	252	190	35	3.5	1.5	30	440	19	3	3	21	50	4	8	6
honey BBQ — *1 meal*	350	430	140	16	3.5	35	520	53	5	7	20	15	2	6	10
marinara — *1 meal*	252	180	45	5	1.5	30	520	19	4	6	15	70	2	4	6
parmigiana — *1 meal*	306	290	100	11	2.5	20	680	31	4	7	17	60	40	10	6
primavera — *1 meal*	385	390	70	8	2.5	45	790	52	6	4	29	10	50	15	6
Tyson Meal Kits															
beef fajita — *1 fajita*	102	130	20	2	1	15	300	18	2	3	9	30	30	2	6
beef stir-fry — *1 ¼ cups*	169	180	20	2	0.5	20	660	30	2	11	11	25	15	2	0
chicken breast fajita — *1 fajita*	107	120	15	1.5	0.5	15	410	18	2	3	8	15	30	2	6
chicken fried rice — *1 ⅓ cups*	185	200	20	2	0.5	20	670	34	2	9	11	15	6	2	6
chicken stir-fry — *1 ¼ cups*	169	180	20	2	0.5	20	720	31	2	10	10	25	20	2	0
Weight Watchers															
baked potato, broccoli & cheese — *1 potato*	283	250	60	7	2	10	590	35	6	3	12	20	15	25	8
chicken cordon bleu — *1 entrée*	255	230	40	4.5	1.5	20	650	31	2	3	15	20	8	15	15
chicken enchiladas suiza — *1 entrée*	255	270	80	9	4.5	40	540	33	4	8	14	4	4	25	6
fettucini alfredo w/ broccoli — *1 entrée*	241	230	50	6	3	20	450	34	3	8	10	6	2	25	8
garden lasagna — *1 entrée*	312	270	60	7	3.5	30	540	36	5	4	14	50	15	35	15
lasagna alfredo — *1 entrée*	255	300	70	7	4	25	650	45	2	3	15	4	10	25	10
lasagna w/ meat sauce — *1 entrée*	290	270	60	7	3	35	570	38	6	6	14	30	4	40	15

	Weight g	Calories	Calories from fat	Total fat g	Sat. fat g	Cholesterol mg	Sodium mg	Carbohydrates g	Dietary fiber g	Sugars g	Protein g	Vitamin A % DV	Vitamin C % DV	Calcium % DV	Iron % DV
penne pasta w/ sun-dried tomatoes — *1 entrée*	283	290	80	9	3	15	560	41	4	2	12	10	25	20	10
spaghetti w/ meat sauce — *1 entrée*	283	290	50	6	2	15	560	41	4	8	17	10	15	0	15
swedish meatballs — *1 entrée*	255	300	90	10	4	50	510	33	2	3	19	6	4	10	20
turkey breast, stuffed — *1 entrée*	255	230	45	5	1	15	680	28	6	7	17	45	10	8	10
Weight Watchers International Selections															
bowtie pasta & mushrooms marsala — *1 entrée*	273	280	80	9	3.5	10	560	36	5	3	13	2	4	20	6
pasta & spinach romano — *1 entrée*	295	240	70	8	3.5	5	510	32	4	10	11	30	15	25	8
pasta w/ tomato basil sauce — *1 entrée*	272	260	80	9	3.5	10	360	33	5	3	12	4	6	20	10
pilaf florentine — *1 entrée*	287	290	60	7	2	5	550	47	6	3	9	25	15	15	10
risotto w/ cheese & mushrooms — *1 entrée*	283	290	80	8	4	20	540	44	4	5	11	25	15	20	4
spicy penne pasta & ricotta — *1 entrée*	289	280	50	6	2	5	370	45	5	5	12	6	6	15	20
vegetables & rice, hunan style — *1 entrée*	293	250	60	7	2	5	630	39	8	6	7	15	15	6	6
Weight Watchers Smart Ones															
angel hair pasta — *1 entrée*	255	170	15	2	0	0	520	29	4	5	8	10	15	10	15
chicken chow mein — *1 entrée*	255	200	15	2	0.5	25	570	34	3	5	12	20	8	2	4
honey mustard chicken — *1 entrée*	241	200	15	2	0.5	30	370	37	3	10	11	10	15	4	6
lasagna w/ meat sauce — *1 entrée*	255	240	20	2	0.5	10	520	43	4	5	13	10	8	15	10
macaroni & cheese — *1 entrée*	255	220	15	2	0.5	5	640	42	4	5	9	6	0	10	8
ravioli florentine — *1 entrée*	241	220	15	2	0.5	5	490	43	4	5	9	40	15	10	10
shrimp marinara — *1 entrée*	255	190	15	2	0.5	40	470	35	4	6	9	15	10	10	10
vegetables & chicken, spicy szechuan-style — *1 entrée*	255	220	15	2	0.5	10	730	39	3	1	11	15	4	15	10

Frozen Entrées & Meals: Pot Pies

	Weight g	Calories	Calories from fat	Total fat g	Sat. fat g	Cholesterol mg	Sodium mg	Carbohydrates g	Dietary fiber g	Sugars g	Protein g	Vitamin A % DV	Vitamin C % DV	Calcium % DV	Iron % DV
Banquet Family-Size Entrées, Chicken Pie, Hearty — *1 cup*	n/a	480	260	29	11	35	1010	39	6	14	14	15	0	4	8
Banquet Pot Pie															
beef — *1 pie*	198	330	140	15	7	25	1000	38	3	2	9	15	0	2	6
chicken — *1 pie*	198	350	160	18	7	40	950	36	3	2	10	20	0	2	6
macaroni & cheese — *1 pie*	184	200	30	3	1.5	10	600	35	2	2	7	0	0	10	6
turkey — *1 pie*	198	370	180	20	8	45	850	38	3	3	10	15	0	4	6
vegetable cheese — *1 pie*	198	390	160	18	8	15	1000	49	3	2	8	25	0	8	6
Empire Kosher Pot Pie															
chicken — *1 pot pie*	n/a	440	190	21	8	30	960	41	11	<1	23	20	0	2	15
turkey — *1 pot pie*	n/a	470	210	23	5	25	820	45	11	2	21	15	0	4	30
Marie Callender's Pot Pie															
chicken — *1 pot pie*	283	680	400	44	9	30	920	54	3	5	13	2	4	4	10
chicken & broccoli — *1 pot pie*	283	780	440	48	16	20	1030	88	3	13	18	4	4	8	20
chicken au gratin — *1 pot pie*	283	720	430	48	13	25	1040	53	4	5	19	4	4	15	15
turkey — *1 pot pie*	283	710	420	46	10	20	770	57	4	5	17	2	4	4	10
yankee — *1 pot pie*	283	690	400	44	10	25	1390	57	3	4	16	2	8	4	10
Morton Pot Pie															
vegetable pie w/ beef — *1 pot pie*	198	320	150	17	8	15	1380	34	2	2	7	10	0	2	6
vegetable pie w/ chicken — *1 pot pie*	198	320	160	18	7	25	1020	32	3	2	8	10	0	4	6
vegetable pie w/ turkey — *1 pot pie*	198	300	160	18	9	25	1060	29	2	2	8	10	0	4	6
Mrs. Paterson's Aussie Pie															
chicken — *1 pie*	156	460	220	25	8	90	770	45	2	3	12	20	0	2	8
chicken, low-fat — *1 pie*	156	380	150	17	6	35	930	44	1	3	13	10	0	2	8

	Weight g	Calories	Calories from fat	Total fat g	Sat. fat g	Cholesterol mg	Sodium mg	Carbohydrates g	Dietary fiber g	Sugars g	Protein g	Vitamin A % DV	Vitamin C % DV	Calcium % DV	Iron % DV
philly steak — *1 pie*	156	480	250	27	9	85	940	41	1	3	18	15	0	25	10
Tyson Pot Pie															
chicken — *1 pie*	252	550	310	35	8	20	740	46	1	2	15	25	2	4	15
chicken, broccoli & cheese — *1 pie*	252	580	310	35	9	25	1150	48	2	2	18	4	6	2	15
chicken, broccoli & cheese reduced-fat — *1 pie*	252	470	210	23	7	30	1030	51	3	5	16	4	15	8	15
chicken, Meat Lover's Recipe — *1 pie*	252	600	350	39	8	25	790	48	1	2	16	0	0	4	15
chicken, reduced-fat — *1 pie*	255	470	210	23	6	35	750	50	3	4	15	25	2	8	15
turkey — *1 pie*	252	550	300	33	8	20	780	49	4	6	15	10	0	4	6

Frozen Entrées & Meals: Sandwiches

	Weight g	Calories	Calories from fat	Total fat g	Sat. fat g	Cholesterol mg	Sodium mg	Carbohydrates g	Dietary fiber g	Sugars g	Protein g	Vitamin A % DV	Vitamin C % DV	Calcium % DV	Iron % DV
Banquet Hot Sandwich Toppers															
creamed chipped beef — *1 bag*	113	100	35	3	1.5	25	700	8	0	1	9	0	0	8	4
gravy & sailsbury steak — *1 bag*	142	220	140	16	7	25	790	8	2	1	9	0	2	2	6
gravy & sliced beef — *1 bag*	113	70	20	2	1	25	440	5	0	<1	8	0	0	0	6
gravy & sliced turkey — *1 bag*	142	140	80	9	4	30	670	6	0	0	8	0	0	2	2
Green Giant Harvest Burgers															
original — *1 patty*	90	140	35	4	1.5	0	370	8	5	<1	18	0	0	8	15
southwestern — *1 patty*	90	140	35	4	1.5	0	370	9	5	1	16	0	0	8	15
Healthy Choice Meals to Go, Hearty Handfuls															
chicken & broccoli — *1 meal*	173	320	50	5	1.5	20	580	51	5	6	17	4	20	10	15
chicken & mushrooms — *1 meal*	173	300	35	4	1.5	20	560	49	4	6	17	2	8	10	15
garlic chicken — *1 meal*	173	330	45	5	1.5	25	600	53	6	3	20	25	6	10	20
philly beef steak — *1 meal*	173	290	45	5	1.5	15	550	47	5	6	16	0	10	10	20
roast beef — *1 meal*	173	310	45	4.5	1.5	15	550	52	5	11	14	15	6	6	15
turkey & vegetables — *1 meal*	173	310	35	4.5	1.5	20	560	51	5	10	18	40	15	15	15

	Weight g	Calories	Calories from fat	Total fat g	Sat. fat g	Cholesterol mg	Sodium mg	Carbohydrates g	Dietary fiber g	Sugars g	Protein g	Vitamin A % DV	Vitamin C % DV	Calcium % DV	Iron % DV
Hormel Quick Meal															
bacon cheeseburger — *1 burger*	142	420	200	22	6	80	740	34	1	5	23	0	0	8	10
cheeseburger — *1 burger*	136	400	180	20	9	80	580	35	2	6	21	2	0	8	10
chicken sandwich, breaded — *1 burger*	122	340	110	12	3	60	480	42	1	6	14	0	0	4	6
corn dog — *1 dog*	78	220	100	11	3	45	520	25	1	8	6	0	6	2	4
corn dog, mini — *5 mini dogs*	79	250	140	15	5	50	570	23	1	7	6	0	6	2	4
hamburger — *1 burger*	122	350	150	16	6	45	400	34	1	6	17	0	0	2	10
Sara Lee Croissants															
chicken & broccoli — *1 croissant*	106	280	120	13	3.5	30	430	30	2	0	11	2	0	6	10
ham & swiss — *1 croissant*	106	300	140	16	4.5	45	570	27	2	1	12	2	2	15	8
original — *1 croissant*	43	170	70	8	3	<5	200	20	1	0	4	4	<2	2	6
petite — *2 croissants*	57	230	100	11	4	<5	260	26	1	0	6	4	0	4	8
Totino's Big & Hearty Stuffed Sandwich															
Chicken Fajita Grande — *1 sandwich*	135	270	90	10	4	20	950	35	2	5	11	0	10	8	15
Mega Meat Pizza — *1 sandwich*	135	330	140	15	6	25	720	35	2	5	14	0	0	20	15
Packed w/ Pepperoni Pizza — *1 sandwich*	135	350	150	17	7	30	740	34	1	5	15	0	0	20	15
Piled High Ham & Cheese — *1 sandwich*	135	310	130	14	6	35	1020	32	1	3	15	0	0	15	10
Weight Watchers Classic Omelet Sandwich — *1 sandwich*	109	220	50	6	2.5	20	410	26	2	1	15	4	2	20	10
Weight Watchers Sausage Biscuit — *1 biscuit*	85	230	100	11	3.5	25	660	20	2	1	11	0	0	2	6

Fruit Snacks

	Weight g	Calories	Calories from fat	Total fat g	Sat. fat g	Cholesterol mg	Sodium mg	Carbohydrates g	Dietary fiber g	Sugars g	Protein g	Vitamin A % DV	Vitamin C % DV	Calcium % DV	Iron % DV
Del Monte Snack Fruit Cup															
mixed fruit in fruit juices — *4 oz*	113	50	0	0	0	0	10	13	<1	12	0	2	4	0	2
mixed fruit in heavy syrup — *4 oz*	113	80	0	0	0	0	10	20	<1	19	0	2	4	0	2
mixed fruit, lite, in extra-light syrup — *4 oz*	113	50	0	0	0	0	10	13	<1	12	0	2	4	0	2

	Weight *g*	Calories	Calories from fat	Total fat *g*	Sat. fat *g*	Cholesterol *mg*	Sodium *mg*	Carbohydrates *g*	Dietary fiber *g*	Sugars *g*	Protein *g*	Vitamin A *% DV*	Vitamin C *% DV*	Calcium *% DV*	Iron *% DV*
peaches, diced, in pear & peach juices — *4 oz*	113	50	0	0	0	0	10	13	<1	12	0	4	6	0	2
peaches, diced, in heavy syrup — *4 oz*	113	80	0	0	0	0	10	20	<1	19	0	4	6	0	2
peaches, lite, diced, in extra-light syrup — *4 oz*	113	50	0	0	0	0	10	13	<1	12	0	4	6	0	2
pears in extra light syrup — *4 oz*	113	50	0	0	0	0	10	13	<1	12	0	0	4	0	0
pears, diced, in heavy syrup — *4 oz*	113	80	0	0	0	0	10	20	<1	19	0	0	4	0	0
pineapple tidbits in pineapple juice — *4 oz*	113	50	0	0	0	0	10	15	<1	13	0	0	15	0	2
Fruit by the Foot															
cherry, grape, or watermelon — *1 roll*	21	80	10	1.5	0.5	0	45	17	0	10	0	0	25	0	0
Color By the Foot Rainbow Punch — *1 roll*	21	80	10	1.5	0.5	0	45	17	0	9	0	0	25	0	0
Fruit Roll-Ups, Pouch															
cherry — *1 roll*	14	50	5	0.5	0	0	55	12	0	5	0	0	25	0	0
Crazy Colors — *1 roll*	14	50	5	0.5	0	0	55	12	0	5	0	0	25	0	0
grape — *1 roll*	14	50	5	0.5	0	0	50	12	0	5	0	0	0	0	0
Hot Colors — *1 roll*	14	50	5	0.5	0	0	55	12	0	5	0	0	25	0	0
Peel 'n Build — *1 roll*	14	50	5	0.5	0	0	55	12	0	5	0	0	25	0	0
raspberry — *1 roll*	14	50	5	0.5	0	0	55	12	0	5	0	0	0	0	0
Secret Pictures — *1 roll*	14	50	5	0.5	0	0	55	12	0	5	0	0	25	0	0
strawberry — *1 roll*	14	50	5	0.5	0	0	55	12	0	5	0	0	25	0	0
Webslinger Blue — *1 roll*	14	50	5	0.5	0	0	50	12	0	5	0	0	0	0	0
Fruit String Thing — *1 pouch*	21	80	10	1	0	0	45	17	0	9	0	0	25	0	0
Fun Snacks															
Bugs Bunny & Friends — *1 pouch*	26	90	10	1	0	0	20	21	0	12	0	0	25	0	0
Kid Cash — *1 pouch*	26	90	10	1	0	0	25	21	0	12	0	0	0	0	0
Rollerblade — *1 pouch*	25	90	10	1	0	0	30	21	0	13	0	0	0	0	0

	Weight g	Calories	Calories from fat	Total fat g	Sat. fat g	Cholesterol mg	Sodium mg	Carbohydrates g	Dietary fiber g	Sugars g	Protein g	Vitamin A % DV	Vitamin C % DV	Calcium % DV	Iron % DV
Shark Bite — *1 pouch*	25	90	10	1	0	0	20	21	0	12	0	0	25	0	0
Tazmanian Devil — *1 pouch*	26	90	10	1	0	0	20	21	0	12	0	0	25	0	0
X men — *1 pouch*	25	90	10	1	0	0	25	21	0	12	0	0	0	0	0
Weight Watchers															
apple chips — *1 bag*	21	70	0	0	0	0	125	18	3	13	0	0	0	0	0
fruit snack-apple & cinnamon — *1 pouch*	14	50	0	0	0	0	125	13	2	9	0	0	0	0	0

Granola & Snack Bars

	Weight g	Calories	Calories from fat	Total fat g	Sat. fat g	Cholesterol mg	Sodium mg	Carbohydrates g	Dietary fiber g	Sugars g	Protein g	Vitamin A % DV	Vitamin C % DV	Calcium % DV	Iron % DV
Carnation Breakfast Bars															
chocolate chip, chewy — *1 bar*	35	150	50	6	2	0	80	24	0	11	2	25	25	50	25
granola, chocolate chunk — *1 bar*	35	130	25	2.5	1	0	40	26	0.5	12	2	25	25	50	25
granola, honey & oats — *1 bar*	35	130	25	2.5	0.5	0	45	26	0.5	11	2	25	25	50	25
peanut butter chocolate chip, chewy — *1 bar*	35	150	50	5	1.5	0	85	22	<1	10	3	25	25	50	25
Figurines Diet Bars															
chocolate — *2 bars*	43	220	100	11	2.5	<5	110	24	1	15	5	20	25	15	25
chocolate caramel — *2 bars*	43	220	100	11	2.5	<5	130	24	1	14	5	20	25	15	25
chocolate peanut butter — *2 bars*	43	220	100	11	3	<5	110	23	2	13	5	20	25	15	25
s'mores — *2 bars*	43	220	100	11	2.5	<5	115	25	0	16	4	20	25	15	25
vanilla — *2 bars*	43	220	100	11	2.5	<5	115	25	0	15	4	20	25	15	25
Grandma's Fat-Free Cereal Bar															
apple — *1 bar*	48	160	0	0	0	0	135	38	1	26	1	n/a	n/a	n/a	n/a
blueberry — *1 bar*	48	160	0	0	0	0	125	39	1	23	1	n/a	n/a	n/a	n/a
raspberry — *1 bar*	48	160	0	0	0	0	135	39	1	25	1	n/a	n/a	n/a	n/a
strawberry — *1 bar*	48	160	0	0	0	0	140	39	1	24	1	n/a	n/a	n/a	n/a

Foods, Brand Name

	Weight g	Calories	Calories from fat	Total fat g	Sat. fat g	Cholesterol mg	Sodium mg	Carbohydrates g	Dietary fiber g	Sugars g	Protein g	Vitamin A % DV	Vitamin C % DV	Calcium % DV	Iron % DV
Grandma's Snack Bars															
fudge chocolate chip — *1 bar*	43	190	60	7	2.5	10	160	29	1	14	2	n/a	n/a	n/a	n/a
granola, soft — *1 bar*	43	180	50	6	1.5	15	260	29	2	12	3	n/a	n/a	n/a	n/a
oatmeal apple spice — *1 bar*	43	170	50	5	1.5	10	270	28	1	12	2	n/a	n/a	n/a	n/a
peanut butter chocolate chip — *1 bar*	43	210	90	10	3	10	150	24	1	15	4	n/a	n/a	n/a	n/a
Granola Dipps, Chocolate Chip (Quaker) — *1 bar*	35	164	63	7	4	2	91	24	1	15	2	0	0	3	3
Health Valley															
Bakes — *1 bar*	n/a	70	0	0	0	0	30	19	2	11	2	2	4	0	4
Breakfast Bakes — *1 bar*	n/a	110	0	0	0	0	25	26	3	13	2	2	2	4	4
brownie bar w/ fudge filling — *1 bar*	n/a	110	0	0	0	0	30	26	4	17	3	2	2	2	10
cereal — *1 bar*	n/a	110	0	0	0	0	25	26	3	13	2	2	4	2	4
cheesecake — *1 bar*	n/a	160	14	1.5	n/a	0	30	34	3	17	3	2	2	2	4
chocolate-flavor — *1 bar*	n/a	150	0	0	0	0	30	35	3	18	3	2	2	2	4
energy bar — *1 bar*	n/a	180	14	1.5	n/a	0	10	40	4	12	3	10	2	2	6
granola — *1 bar*	n/a	140	0	0	0	0	5	35	3	14	2	2	2	2	6
oat bran fruit — *1 bar*	n/a	160	9	1	n/a	0	10	34	2	18	3	10	0	0	8
Health Valley Fruit Bars															
apple — *1 bar*	n/a	140	0	0	0	0	0	35	3	13	3	10	0	0	10
apricot — *1 bar*	n/a	140	0	0	0	0	5	35	4	12	3	10	0	0	6
date — *1 bar*	n/a	140	0	0	0	0	5	34	3	12	3	10	0	0	4
raisin — *1 bar*	n/a	140	0	0	0	0	5	35	3	17	2	10	0	0	6
Health Valley Healthy Crisp Rice Bars															
apple raisin — *1 bar*	n/a	110	0	0	0	0	5	26	1	15	1	10	10	2	2
orange date — *1 bar*	n/a	110	0	0	0	0	5	26	1	15	1	10	4	2	2

	Weight g	Calories	Calories from fat	Total fat g	Sat. fat g	Cholesterol mg	Sodium mg	Carbohydrates g	Dietary fiber g	Sugars g	Protein g	Vitamin A % DV	Vitamin C % DV	Calcium % DV	Iron % DV
tropical fruit — *1 bar*	n/a	110	0	0	0	0	5	26	1	15	1	10	0	2	2
Nature Valley Low-Fat Chewy Granola Bars															
apple brown sugar — *1 bar*	28	110	15	2	0	0	65	21	1	8	2	0	0	0	2
chocolate chip — *1 bar*	28	110	20	2	0.5	0	80	21	1	7	2	0	0	0	2
honey nut — *1 bar*	28	110	15	2	0	0	65	21	1	8	2	0	0	0	2
oatmeal raisin — *1 bar*	28	110	15	2	0	0	65	22	2	7	2	0	0	0	2
orchard blend — *1 bar*	28	110	20	2	0	0	65	22	1	8	2	0	0	0	2
triple berry — *1 bar*	28	110	20	2	0	0	65	21	1	7	2	0	0	0	2
Nature Valley Reduced-Fat Granola Bars															
cinnamon — *2 bars*	47	200	60	6	1	0	170	35	3	14	4	0	0	0	6
oats 'n honey — *2 bars*	47	200	60	6	1	0	170	35	3	14	4	0	0	0	6
peanut butter — *2 bars*	47	200	60	6	1	0	170	33	2	13	5	0	0	0	6
Nestlé Snack Bars															
chocolate brownie, chewy — *1 bar*	n/a	120	35	4	2	<5	45	23	3	13	2	15	15	15	15
chocolate chip, chewy — *1 bar*	n/a	120	35	4	2	<5	40	23	3	10	2	15	15	15	15
chocolate peanut butter, chewy — *1 bar*	n/a	120	35	4	2	<5	35	23	3	12	2	15	15	15	15
Nestlé Snack Bars, Low-Fat															
apple cinnamon spice — *1 bar*	n/a	120	20	2	0.5	0	100	24	3	8	2	15	15	15	15
oatmeal raisin almond — *1 bar*	n/a	120	20	2	0.5	0	100	23	3	10	2	15	15	15	15
Nutri-Grain Cereal Bars — *1 bar*	37	140	25	3	0.5	0	60	27	1	12	2	10	0	0	10
PowerBar															
apple-cinnamon — *1 bar*	65	230	25	2.5	0.5	0	90	45	3	14	10	0	100	30	35
banana — *1 bar*	65	230	20	2	0.5	0	90	45	3	20	9	0	100	30	35
chocolate — *1 bar*	65	230	15	2.0	0.5	0	90	45	3	14	10	0	100	30	35

	Weight *g*	Calories	Calories from fat	Total fat *g*	Sat. fat *g*	Cholesterol *mg*	Sodium *mg*	Carbohydrates *g*	Dietary fiber *g*	Sugars *g*	Protein *g*	Vitamin A *% DV*	Vitamin C *% DV*	Calcium *% DV*	Iron *% DV*
Malt-Nut — *1 bar*	65	230	25	2.5	0.5	0	90	45	3	18	10	0	100	30	35
mocha — *1 bar*	65	230	25	2.5	1.0	0	90	45	3	17	10	0	100	30	35
oatmeal raisin — *1 bar*	65	230	25	2.5	0.5	0	120	45	3	20	10	0	100	30	35
peanut butter — *1 bar*	65	230	25	2.5	0.5	0	110	45	3	20	10	0	100	30	35
wild berry — *1 bar*	65	230	25	2.5	0.5	0	90	45	3	14	10	0	100	30	35
Quaker Chewy Granola Bars															
apple berry — *1 bar*	28	109	18	2	<1	<1	79	22	1	10	1	0	0	<1	3
chocolate chip — *1 bar*	28	120	36	4	2	<1	68	21	1	9	2	0	0	<1	3
chocolate mint, low-fat — *1 bar*	28	112	18	2	1	<1	80	22	1	10	2	0	0	<1	4
oatmeal cookie, low-fat — *1 bar*	28	111	18	2	<1	<1	105	22	<1	10	1	0	0	<1	3
peanut butter & chocolate chip — *1 bar*	28	122	45	5	1	<1	104	19	1	8	3	0	0	1	3
Quaker Chewy Granola Bars, Low-Fat															
chocolate chunk or s'mores — *1 bar*	28	110	18	2	n/a	0	105	22	n/a	n/a	2	n/a	n/a	n/a	n/a
oatmeal cookie — *1 bar*	28	110	18	2	n/a	0	22	1	n/a	n/a	3	n/a	n/a	n/a	n/a
Rice Krispies Cereal Bars (Kellogg's)															
chewy granola bar w/ chocolate chips — *1 bar*	28	120	35	4	1.5	0	60	20	1	8	1	10	0	0	10
Treats, squares — *1 bar*	22	90	20	2	0	0	75	18	0	11	1	4	0	0	2
Sweet Rewards Fat-Free Snack Bars															
blueberry w/ drizzle — *1 bar*	37	120	0	0	0	0	80	29	<1	19	1	0	0	0	4
double fudge supreme — *1 bar*	32	110	0	0	0	0	90	25	1	15	2	0	0	2	6
homestyle brownie — *1 bar*	32	100	0	0	0	0	120	24	1	16	2	0	0	0	6
raspberry — *1 bar*	37	120	0	0	0	0	80	29	<1	19	1	0	0	0	4
strawberry w/ drizzle — *1 bar*	37	120	0	0	0	0	80	29	<1	19	1	0	0	0	4
Weight Watchers Apple Raisin Bars — *1 bar*	21	70	20	2	0.5	0	60	14	2	4	1	0	0	0	0

Hot Dogs

	Weight g	Calories	Calories from fat	Total fat g	Sat. fat g	Cholesterol mg	Sodium mg	Carbohydrates g	Dietary fiber g	Sugars g	Protein g	Vitamin A % DV	Vitamin C % DV	Calcium % DV	Iron % DV
Empire Kosher Franks															
chicken — *1 frank*	57	100	65	7	2	70	465	1	0	0	8	0	0	4	8
turkey — *1 frank*	57	90	55	6	1.5	35	410	<1	0	0	9	0	0	4	4
Healthy Choice Franks															
beef — *1 frank*	50	60	15	1.5	0.5	15	430	5	0	2	7	0	4	0	2
deli beef, low-fat — *1 frank*	75	100	25	3	1	35	480	7	0	2	11	0	8	2	2
Jumbo Bunsize — *1 frank*	50	60	15	1.5	0.5	20	430	6	0	2	6	0	6	4	2
low-fat — *1 frank*	40	45	10	1	0.5	15	350	5	0	1	5	0	4	2	2
Hebrew National Beef Franks															
97% fat-free — *1 frank*	n/a	45	15	1.5	0.5	15	390	2	n/a	n/a	6	n/a	n/a	n/a	n/a
original — *1 frank*	48	150	120	14	5	30	370	1	0	0	6	0	0	0	3
reduced-fat — *1 frank*	48	120	90	10	4	25	350	1	0	0	8	0	0	0	4
Hormel Light & Lean 100 Beef Franks — *1 frank*	50	45	0	0	0	10	590	5	0	2	6	0	10	0	0
Hormel Wranglers Franks															
beef, smoked — *1 frank*	56	170	130	15	6	40	530	1	0	1	7	0	15	0	4
cheese — *1 frank*	56	170	130	15	7	40	550	1	0	1	7	0	15	4	2
Louis Rich Franks & Wieners															
beef franks — *1 link*	57	70	25	3	1	30	500	3	0	1	7	0	0	0	4
cheese franks (made w/ turkey & chicken) — *1 link*	45	90	60	6	2.5	40	480	2	0	<1	6	0	0	10	6
franks (made w/ turkey & chicken) — *1 link*	43	80	50	6	2	40	490	2	0	<1	5	0	0	6	6
wieners (made w/ turkey, chicken, & beef) — *1 link*	57	70	25	3	1	30	500	3	0	1	7	0	0	0	4
Mr Turkey Cheese Franks — *3 ½ oz*	100	248	189	21	7	85	1202	4	<1	2	12	<1	17	16	24

	Weight g	Calories	Calories from fat	Total fat g	Sat. fat g	Cholesterol mg	Sodium mg	Carbohydrates g	Dietary fiber g	Sugars g	Protein g	Vitamin A % DV	Vitamin C % DV	Calcium % DV	Iron % DV
Oscar Mayer Big and Juicy Wieners and Franks															
beef franks, deli-style — *1 link*	76	230	190	22	10	50	680	1	0	0	9	0	0	0	8
Smokie Links Wieners — *1 link*	76	220	180	19	7	50	770	1	0	<1	10	0	0	0	6
wieners, hot 'n spicy — *1 link*	76	220	180	20	8	45	750	1	0	<1	10	0	0	0	6
Oscar Mayer Free															
beef, fat-free — *1 link*	50	35	0	0	0	20	480	2	0	2	7	0	0	0	6
hot dogs, fat-free — *1 link*	50	40	0	0	0	15	490	2	0	1	7	0	0	0	2
Oscar Mayer Wieners and Franks															
beef franks, light — *1 link*	57	110	80	8	3.5	30	620	2	0	1	6	0	0	0	4
cheese — *1 link*	45	140	120	13	5	35	530	1	0	<1	5	0	0	8	4
little wieners, hot & spicy — *6 links*	57	170	140	16	6	40	580	1	0	1	7	0	0	0	4
wieners, light — *1 link*	57	110	80	9	3	35	590	2	0	1	7	0	0	2	4

Ice Cream

	Weight g	Calories	Calories from fat	Total fat g	Sat. fat g	Cholesterol mg	Sodium mg	Carbohydrates g	Dietary fiber g	Sugars g	Protein g	Vitamin A % DV	Vitamin C % DV	Calcium % DV	Iron % DV
Ben & Jerry's															
butter pecan — *½ cup*	n/a	310	220	25	11	85	125	20	1	20	5	15	0	10	6
Cherry Garcia — *½ cup*	n/a	240	140	16	9	75	55	25	0	24	3	10	0	8	4
chocolate chip cookie dough — *½ cup*	n/a	270	140	15	8	75	85	30	0	25	5	15	0	8	4
chocolate fudge brownie — *½ cup*	n/a	260	110	13	7	50	80	32	2	28	4	10	0	8	8
Chubby Hubby — *½ cup*	n/a	350	210	23	11	75	160	31	2	26	8	15	2	10	4
Chunky Monkey — *½ cup*	n/a	280	170	18	10	70	50	29	1	28	4	10	20	10	6
coffee w/ Heath Toffee Crunch — *½ cup*	n/a	280	170	19	10	80	120	28	0	28	4	15	0	10	2
Coffee, Coffee BuzzBuzzBuzz! — *½ cup*	n/a	290	170	19	14	75	70	27	<1	25	4	10	0	10	4
Cool Britannia — *½ cup*	n/a	260	140	15	10	75	70	29	0	26	3	10	10	10	2
mint chocolate cookie — *½ cup*	n/a	260	160	17	10	80	120	27	1	23	4	15	0	10	4

	Weight g	Calories	Calories from fat	Total fat g	Sat. fat g	Cholesterol mg	Sodium mg	Carbohydrates g	Dietary fiber g	Sugars g	Protein g	Vitamin A % DV	Vitamin C % DV	Calcium % DV	Iron % DV
New York Super Fudge Chunk — *½ cup*	n/a	290	180	20	10	45	45	28	2	25	4	10	0	8	6
Peanut Butter Cup — *½ cup*	n/a	370	240	26	12	75	140	30	2	27	8	10	0	15	4
Rainforest Crunch — *½ cup*	n/a	300	200	23	11	85	140	24	0	22	5	15	0	10	4
vanilla carmel fudge swirl — *½ cup*	n/a	280	150	17	10	95	75	33	1	30	4	15	2	10	2
vanilla w/ Heath Toffee Crunch — *½ cup*	n/a	280	170	19	11	80	115	28	0	28	3	10	0	10	2
Vanilla/World's Best — *½ cup*	n/a	230	150	17	10	95	55	21	0	21	4	15	0	15	2
Wavy Gravy — *½ cup*	n/a	330	210	24	10	80	95	29	2	26	6	15	2	15	6
Breyers All Natural															
chocolate — *½ cup*	n/a	160	80	8	6	30	30	19	n/a	17	n/a	n/a	n/a	n/a	n/a
chocolate chip cookie dough — *½ cup*	n/a	170	80	9	5	25	65	20	n/a	17	n/a	n/a	n/a	n/a	n/a
coffee — *½ cup*	n/a	150	70	8	5	35	45	15	n/a	15	n/a	n/a	n/a	n/a	n/a
cookies in cream — *½ cup*	n/a	170	80	9	6	30	55	19	n/a	17	n/a	n/a	n/a	n/a	n/a
deluxe rocky road — *½ cup*	n/a	190	80	9	5	25	30	24	n/a	21	n/a	n/a	n/a	n/a	n/a
french vanilla — *½ cup*	n/a	170	90	10	6	105	45	15	n/a	15	n/a	n/a	n/a	n/a	n/a
mint chocolate chip — *½ cup*	n/a	170	90	10	6	35	40	18	n/a	17	n/a	n/a	n/a	n/a	n/a
strawberry — *½ cup*	n/a	130	60	6	4	25	35	15	n/a	15	n/a	n/a	n/a	n/a	n/a
Take Two Vanilla/Orange Sherbet — *½ cup*	n/a	140	45	5	3	25	35	21	n/a	17	n/a	n/a	n/a	n/a	n/a
toffee bar crunch — *½ cup*	n/a	170	80	9	4	30	60	18	n/a	17	n/a	n/a	n/a	n/a	n/a
vanilla — *½ cup*	n/a	150	80	8	6	35	45	15	n/a	15	n/a	n/a	n/a	n/a	n/a
vanilla/chocolate/strawberry — *½ cup*	n/a	150	70	8	5	30	35	16	n/a	16	n/a	n/a	n/a	n/a	n/a
Breyers Blends															
Hershey's Chocolate w/ Almonds — *½ cup*	n/a	190	70	8	4.5	25	20	23	n/a	18	n/a	n/a	n/a	n/a	n/a
Reese's NutRageous Candy Bars — *½ cup*	n/a	200	90	10	5	25	70	22	n/a	19	n/a	n/a	n/a	n/a	n/a
Reese's Peanut Butter Cups — *½ cup*	n/a	210	100	11	5	20	100	24	n/a	20	n/a	n/a	n/a	n/a	n/a

	Weight g	Calories	Calories from fat	Total fat g	Sat. fat g	Cholesterol mg	Sodium mg	Carbohydrates g	Dietary fiber g	Sugars g	Protein g	Vitamin A % DV	Vitamin C % DV	Calcium % DV	Iron % DV
Sara Lee Fudge Brownies — *½ cup*	n/a	190	80	9	5	25	70	23	n/a	19	n/a	n/a	n/a	n/a	n/a
Breyers Fat-Free															
caramel praline crunch — *½ cup*	n/a	120	0	0	0	5	70	27	n/a	19	n/a	n/a	n/a	n/a	n/a
chocolate — *½ cup*	n/a	90	0	0	0	<5	45	20	n/a	13	n/a	n/a	n/a	n/a	n/a
mint cookies in cream — *½ cup*	n/a	100	0	0	0	<5	70	22	n/a	16	n/a	n/a	n/a	n/a	n/a
vanilla — *½ cup*	n/a	100	0	0	0	<5	50	21	n/a	14	n/a	n/a	n/a	n/a	n/a
vanilla/chocolate/strawberry — *½ cup*	n/a	90	0	0	0	<5	40	19	n/a	15	n/a	n/a	n/a	n/a	n/a
Breyers Light (Low-Fat)															
chocolate chip cookie dough — *½ cup*	n/a	110	10	1	0	5	45	22	n/a	16	n/a	n/a	n/a	n/a	n/a
french vanilla — *½ cup*	n/a	90	15	1.5	0	30	45	17	n/a	5	n/a	n/a	n/a	n/a	n/a
mint chocolate chip — *½ cup*	n/a	110	15	2	1	<5	45	21	n/a	17	n/a	n/a	n/a	n/a	n/a
rocky road — *½ cup*	n/a	120	15	2	1	0	40	23	n/a	7	n/a	n/a	n/a	n/a	n/a
vanilla — *½ cup*	n/a	130	40	4	3	35	55	18	n/a	15	n/a	n/a	n/a	n/a	n/a
Breyers No-Sugar-Added Light															
mint chocolate chip — *½ cup*	n/a	100	45	5	3	20	40	13	n/a	5	n/a	n/a	n/a	n/a	n/a
praline pecan — *½ cup*	n/a	110	35	4	2	20	45	18	n/a	4	n/a	n/a	n/a	n/a	n/a
vanilla — *½ cup*	n/a	80	35	4	2.5	20	35	11	n/a	5	n/a	n/a	n/a	n/a	n/a
vanilla fudge twirl — *½ cup*	n/a	90	35	3.5	2.5	20	40	14	n/a	5	n/a	n/a	n/a	n/a	n/a
vanilla/chocolate/strawberry — *½ cup*	n/a	90	35	4	2.5	20	35	11	n/a	5	n/a	n/a	n/a	n/a	n/a
Breyers Viennetta															
cappuccino — *1 slice*	68	190	100	11	7	40	35	19	n/a	16	n/a	n/a	n/a	n/a	n/a
chocolate — *1 slice*	68	190	100	12	8	25	40	18	n/a	15	n/a	n/a	n/a	n/a	n/a
vanilla or mint — *1 slice*	68	190	100	11	7	40	40	19	n/a	16	n/a	n/a	n/a	n/a	n/a

	Weight g	Calories	Calories from fat	Total fat g	Sat. fat g	Cholesterol mg	Sodium mg	Carbohydrates g	Dietary fiber g	Sugars g	Protein g	Vitamin A % DV	Vitamin C % DV	Calcium % DV	Iron % DV
Häagen-Dazs															
butter pecan — *½ cup*	106	320	220	24	11	105	140	20	<1	19	5	10	0	15	2
chocolate — *½ cup*	106	270	160	18	11	115	75	22	1	21	5	10	0	15	6
chocolate chocolate chip — *½ cup*	102	300	180	20	12	100	70	26	2	24	5	10	0	10	8
coffee — *½ cup*	106	270	160	18	11	120	85	21	0	21	5	10	0	15	0
coffee chip — *½ cup*	102	290	170	19	12	100	75	25	<1	23	5	10	0	15	4
cookies & cream — *½ cup*	102	270	150	17	11	110	115	23	0	20	5	10	0	15	4
deep chocolate peanut butter — *½ cup*	106	370	230	25	11	85	100	27	4	22	8	8	0	10	8
macadamia brittle — *½ cup*	106	300	180	20	11	110	120	25	0	23	4	10	0	15	0
rum raisin — *½ cup*	106	270	150	17	10	110	75	22	0	21	4	10	0	10	0
strawberry — *½ cup*	106	250	140	16	10	95	80	23	<1	21	4	10	15	15	0
swiss chocolate almond — *½ cup*	102	300	180	20	11	100	65	23	2	20	6	10	0	10	8
vanilla — *½ cup*	106	270	160	18	11	120	85	21	0	21	5	10	0	15	0
vanilla chocolate chip — *½ cup*	102	290	170	19	12	100	75	24	<1	23	5	10	0	10	4
vanilla fudge — *½ cup*	106	280	160	18	11	105	105	25	0	25	5	10	0	15	2
vanilla swiss almond — *½ cup*	106	310	190	21	11	105	80	23	1	21	6	10	0	15	4
Healthy Choice															
Bananas Foster — *½ cup*	n/a	110	15	1.5	1	5	60	21	1	20	3	4	15	10	0
black forest — *½ cup*	n/a	120	20	2	1	5	50	23	1	16	3	4	0	10	4
butter pecan crunch — *½ cup*	n/a	120	20	2	1	<5	60	22	1	21	3	4	0	10	0
cappuccino chocolate chunk — *½ cup*	n/a	120	20	2	1	10	60	22	1	14	3	4	2	10	0
cappuccino mocha fudge — *½ cup*	n/a	120	20	2	1	<5	50	23	1	19	3	4	0	10	2
cherry chocolate chunk — *½ cup*	n/a	110	20	2	1	<5	55	19	<1	19	3	4	0	10	0
chocolate fudge mousse — *½ cup*	n/a	120	20	2	1	<5	50	21	1	20	3	4	0	10	0

	Weight *g*	Calories	Calories from fat	Total fat *g*	Sat. fat *g*	Cholesterol *mg*	Sodium *mg*	Carbohydrates *g*	Dietary fiber *g*	Sugars *g*	Protein *g*	Vitamin A *% DV*	Vitamin C *% DV*	Calcium *% DV*	Iron *% DV*
Cookie Creme de Mint — *½ cup*	n/a	130	20	2	1	<5	60	24	<1	20	3	4	0	10	0
cookies 'n cream — *½ cup*	n/a	120	20	2	1	<5	90	21	<1	19	3	4	0	10	0
fudge brownie — *½ cup*	n/a	120	20	2	1	5	55	22	<2	15	3	4	0	10	0
fudge brownie á la mode — *½ cup*	n/a	120	20	2	1	5	55	22	<2	15	3	4	0	10	0
mint chocolate chip — *½ cup*	n/a	120	20	2	1	<5	50	21	<1	20	3	4	0	10	0
praline & caramel — *½ cup*	n/a	130	20	2	0.5	<5	70	25	<1	24	3	4	0	10	0
praline caramel cluster — *½ cup*	n/a	130	20	2	0.5	<5	70	25	<1	24	3	4	0	10	0
rocky road — *½ cup*	n/a	140	20	2	1	<5	60	28	2	19	3	4	0	10	0
strawberry shortcake — *½ cup*	n/a	120	20	2	1	<5	50	23	<1	22	3	4	4	8	0
triple chocolate chunk — *½ cup*	n/a	110	20	2	1	<5	60	21	1	18	3	4	0	10	2
Turtle Fudge Cake — *½ cup*	n/a	130	20	2	1	<5	60	25	2	23	3	4	0	10	4
vanilla — *½ cup*	n/a	100	20	2	1	5	50	18	1	17	3	6	0	10	0
Sealtest															
butter pecan — *½ cup*	n/a	160	80	9	5	30	115	16	n/a	12	n/a	n/a	n/a	n/a	n/a
chocolate chip cookie dough — *½ cup*	n/a	160	80	8	4	25	70	20	n/a	19	n/a	n/a	n/a	n/a	n/a
fudge royal — *½ cup*	n/a	150	60	7	4	25	55	19	n/a	14	n/a	n/a	n/a	n/a	n/a
Heavenly Hash — *½ cup*	n/a	150	60	7	4	25	50	20	n/a	14	n/a	n/a	n/a	n/a	n/a
vanilla — *½ cup*	n/a	140	60	7	5	30	55	16	n/a	13	n/a	n/a	n/a	n/a	n/a
vanilla chocolate strawberry — *½ cup*	n/a	140	50	6	4	25	50	18	n/a	14	n/a	n/a	n/a	n/a	n/a
Sealtest Ice Cream Cups															
chocolate — *4 fl oz*	n/a	140	60	7	4	25	50	19	n/a	15	n/a	n/a	n/a	n/a	n/a
vanilla — *4 fl oz*	n/a	140	60	7	5	30	55	16	n/a	13	n/a	n/a	n/a	n/a	n/a
vanilla, fat-free — *4 fl oz*	n/a	100	0	0	0	0	40	22	n/a	12	n/a	n/a	n/a	n/a	n/a
vanilla, no-sugar-added — *4 fl oz*	n/a	90	40	4.5	2	20	45	12	n/a	4	n/a	n/a	n/a	n/a	n/a

Luncheon Meats

	Weight g	Calories	Calories from fat	Total fat g	Sat. fat g	Cholesterol mg	Sodium mg	Carbohydrates g	Dietary fiber g	Sugars g	Protein g	Vitamin A % DV	Vitamin C % DV	Calcium % DV	Iron % DV
Bil Mar Deli Perfect															
turkey ham, smoked, sliced — *2 oz*	56	62	27	3	<1	37	653	<1	<1	1	9	0	18	0	8
turkey pastrami, dark — *2 oz*	56	70	27	3	<1	38	609	2	<1	1	9	<1	16	<1	27
turkey pastrami, sliced — *2 oz*	56	64	0	<1	<1	28	513	2	<1	<1	12	<1	9	<1	4
turkey roll, white, cooked — *2 oz*	56	80	45	5	1	28	422	<1	<1	<1	9	<1	n/a	<1	4
Bil Mar Signature Turkey Breast															
fat-free — *2 oz*	56	54	<9	<1	<1	17	486	1	<1	0	11	0	2	<1	3
natural smoked — *2 oz*	56	65	18	2	<1	30	507	<1	0	<1	12	<1	<1	<1	5
peppered, skinless — *2 oz*	56	48	<9	<1	<1	17	459	2	<1	<1	10	0	2	<1	4
reduced-sodium — *2 oz*	56	50	<9	<1	<1	13	344	1	0	0	10	<1	<1	<1	<1
Bil Mar Turkey Products															
turkey bologna — *2 oz*	56	133	99	11	3	49	744	2	<1	2	7	0	12	7	9
turkey salami — *2 oz*	56	97	63	7	2	42	470	2	0	2	8	0	0	2	9
Goya Luncheon Meat — *2 oz*	56	180	145	16	6	0	590	1	0	1	8	0	25	0	0
Hebrew National Deli Meats															
beef bologna, lean — *2 oz*	56	90	50	6	2	25	430	0	0	0	8	0	0	0	6
beef salami, lean — *2 oz*	56	90	50	6	2	30	340	1	0	0	9	0	0	2	10
oven roasted turkey breast — *2 oz*	56	50	5	0.5	0	25	450	0	n/a	n/a	11	n/a	n/a	0	0
turkey pastrami — *2 oz*	56	60	20	2.5	0.5	45	560	0	n/a	n/a	10	n/a	n/a	0	4
turkey, smoked — *2 oz*	56	60	10	0.5	0	25	330	1	n/a	n/a	12	n/a	n/a	0	2
Hormel Black Label Chopped Ham — *2 oz*	56	140	110	12	4.5	35	720	2	0	2	7	0	2	0	2
Hormel Deli Cooked Ham — *2 oz*	56	60	20	2.5	1	20	640	0	0	0	10	0	0	0	0

	Weight g	Calories	Calories from fat	Total fat g	Sat. fat g	Cholesterol mg	Sodium mg	Carbohydrates g	Dietary fiber g	Sugars g	Protein g	Vitamin A % DV	Vitamin C % DV	Calcium % DV	Iron % DV
Louis Rich Cold Cuts															
chicken breast, deluxe oven-roasted — *1 slice*	28	30	5	0.5	0	15	330	1	0	0	5	0	0	0	0
turkey bologna — *1 slice*	28	50	30	3.5	1	20	270	1	0	0	3	0	0	4	2
turkey ham — *1 slice*	28	30	10	1	0	20	300	0	0	0	5	0	0	0	2
turkey ham, deli-thin brand — *4 slices*	52	60	15	1.5	0.5	35	580	1	0	<1	9	0	0	0	2
turkey ham, honey-cured — *1 slice*	28	30	5	1	0	20	290	1	0	<1	5	0	0	0	2
turkey pastrami — *1 slice*	28	30	10	1	0	20	320	0	0	0	5	0	0	0	2
turkey salami cotto — *1 slice*	28	40	25	2.5	1	25	290	0	0	0	5	0	0	0	2
turkey salami, cooked — *1 slice*	28	40	25	2.5	1	20	280	0	0	0	4	0	0	0	0
Louis Rich Fat-Free, Skinless Breast of Turkey															
barbecued — *2 oz*	56	60	0	0	0	25	600	2	0	1	12	0	0	0	4
hickory smoked — *2 oz*	56	50	0	0	0	25	720	1	0	0	11	0	0	0	4
oven-roasted — *2 oz*	56	50	0	0	0	20	660	1	0	0	11	0	0	0	4
rotisserie-flavor — *2 oz*	56	50	0	0	0	20	670	1	0	1	11	0	0	0	4
Louis Rich Fat-Free, Turkey Breast Slices															
hickory-smoked — *1 slice*	56	50	0	0	0	25	720	1	0	0	11	0	0	0	4
honey-roasted — *1 slice*	56	60	0	0	0	20	660	3	0	2	11	0	0	0	4
oven-roasted — *1 slice*	56	50	0	0	0	20	660	1	0	0	11	0	0	0	4
Louis Rich Turkey Chunk Meats															
turkey breast & white turkey, oven roasted — *2 oz*	56	60	10	1	0.5	20	630	2	0	<1	9	0	0	0	4
turkey ham — *2 oz*	56	70	25	3	1	35	610	1	0	<1	10	0	0	0	4
turkey pastrami — *2 oz*	56	60	20	2	1	35	590	1	0	0	11	0	0	0	4
turkey salami, cooked — *2 oz*	56	100	70	8	3	45	500	1	0	0	8	0	0	6	4

	Weight *g*	Calories	Calories from fat	Total fat *g*	Sat. fat *g*	Cholesterol *mg*	Sodium *mg*	Carbohydrates *g*	Dietary fiber *g*	Sugars *g*	Protein *g*	Vitamin A *% DV*	Vitamin C *% DV*	Calcium *% DV*	Iron *% DV*
Mr Turkey Poultry Products															
breakfast turkey ham, smoked — *3 ½ oz*	100	110	45	5	1	66	1166	1	<1	2	16	0	32	<1	13
chicken breast, rotisserie-smoked — *3 ½ oz*	100	99	0	<1	<1	45	1260	8	1	4	16	<1	11	<1	5
deli honey breast, fat-free — *3 ½ oz*	100	89	9	1	<1	31	1128	6	<1	2	14	<1	11	<1	4
honey-cured ham, deli slices — *3 ½ oz*	100	120	36	4	1	76	1064	3.5	<1	3	18	0	11	<1	12
turkey bologna, slices — *3 ½ oz*	100	237	180	20	6	87	1328	4	<1	3	12	<1	22	12	17
turkey breast, rotisserie-smoked — *3 ½ oz*	100	92	<9	<1	<1	40	1268	7.5	1	4	14	<1	22	<1	6
turkey ham — *3 ½ oz*	100	119	45	5	1	84	1312	1.5	<1	1		1	30	0	7
turkey ham, cooked — *3 ½ oz*	100	119	45	5	1	84	1312	1.5	<1	1	18	1	30	<1	7
turkey ham, smoked — *3 ½ oz*	100	124	54	6	2	76	1190	1.5	<1	1	17	<1	27	1	21
turkey ham, smoked, slices — *3 ½ oz*	100	117	45	5	2	70	1134	1.5	0	1	16	0	0	<1	13
turkey pastrami, deli slices — *3 ½ oz*	100	125	36	4	1	76	914	4	<1	2	18	0	27	1	19
turkey pastrami, hardwood-smoked — *3 ½ oz*	100	125	36	4	1	76	914	4	<1	2	18	0	27	1	19
turkey salami, slices — *3 ½ oz*	100	174	108	12	4	75	840	3	0	3	14	0	0	3	16
white turkey, smoked — *3 ½ oz*	100	118	45	5	2	55	1250	3	<1	1	15.5	0	17	<2	12
Oscar Mayer Deluxe Lunchables															
chicken/turkey — *5.1 oz*	145	390	210	23	11	70	1830	25	<1	8	21	8	0	20	10
turkey ham — *5.1 oz*	145	370	190	21	10	65	1940	25	<1	8	21	8	0	30	10
Oscar Mayer Free (fat-free)															
bologna — *1 slice*	28	20	0	0	0	5	280	2	0	<1	4	0	0	0	0
chicken breast, oven-roasted — *4 slices*	52	45	0	0	0	25	650	1	0	<1	10	0	0	0	4
ham, baked — *3 slices*	47	35	0	0	0	15	520	1	0	1	7	0	0	0	2
ham, honey — *3 slices*	47	35	0	0	0	15	580	2	0	1	7	0	0	0	2
ham, smoked — *3 slices*	47	35	0	0	0	15	550	1	0	<1	7	0	0	0	2

	Weight *g*	Calories	Calories from fat	Total fat *g*	Sat. fat *g*	Cholesterol *mg*	Sodium *mg*	Carbohydrates *g*	Dietary fiber *g*	Sugars *g*	Protein *g*	Vitamin A *% DV*	Vitamin C *% DV*	Calcium *% DV*	Iron *% DV*
turkey breast, oven-roasted — *4 slices*	52	40	0	0	0	15	670	2	0	<1	8	0	0	0	4
turkey breast, smoked — *4 slices*	52	40	0	0	0	15	570	2	0	<1	8	0	0	0	2
Oscar Mayer Fun Pack Lunchables (w/ Drink)															
bologna (w/ wild cherry) — *1 pkg*	318	530	250	28	14	60	1180	60	1	46	13	8	0	20	8
ham (w/ fruit punch) — *1 pkg*	318	440	180	20	9	50	1270	54	1	40	15	8	0	20	8
pizza, mozzarella (w/ fruit punch) — *1 pkg*	347	450	140	15	9	30	740	61	2	35	17	8	8	35	15
pizza, pepperoni (w/ orange) — *1 pkg*	347	450	140	16	8	35	850	62	2	36	16	8	8	25	15
turkey (w/ Pacific Cooler) — *1 pkg*	318	450	180	20	10	50	1340	54	1	39	16	6	0	20	8
turkey (w/ Surfer Cooler) — *1 pkg*	318	430	140	15	8	45	1250	61	0	46	13	6	15	15	8
Oscar Mayer Low-Fat Lunchables (w/ drink)															
ham (w/ fruit punch) — *1 pkg*	359	350	90	10	4.5	35	1150	50	0	38	17	6	0	35	6
ham (w/ Surfer Cooler) — *1 pkg*	374	390	100	11	5	35	1350	58	<1	41	17	15	0	30	8
turkey (w/ Pacific Cooler) — *1 pkg*	359	360	80	9	4.5	30	1190	56	<1	42	15	10	0	25	8
Oscar Mayer Lunchables															
bologna w/ american — *4 ½ oz*	128	470	320	35	17	90	1670	22	<1	5	17	8	0	30	10
ham w/ cheddar — *4 ½ oz*	128	360	200	22	11	75	1750	21	<1	5	20	10	0	25	8
ham w/ swiss — *4 ½ oz*	128	340	180	20	10	70	1780	20	<1	4	21	8	0	35	8
pizza w/ 2 cheeses — *4 ½ oz*	128	300	110	13	7	30	710	29	2	3	17	10	10	35	10
pizza, pepperoni w/ mozzarella — *4 ½ oz*	128	330	140	15	7	35	850	32	2	4	17	8	10	25	8
salami w/ american — *4 ½ oz*	128	430	270	30	15	80	1610	21	<1	5	18	10	0	25	10
turkey w/ cheddar — *4 ½ oz*	128	350	180	20	11	70	1760	22	1	5	20	10	0	25	10
turkey w/ monterey jack — *4 ½ oz*	128	350	190	21	11	75	1690	20	1	5	20	8	0	25	10
Oscar Mayer Meats, Ham, Lower-Sodium — *3 slices*	63	70	20	2.5	1	30	520	2	0	1	10	0	0	0	4

	Weight g	Calories	Calories from fat	Total fat g	Sat. fat g	Cholesterol mg	Sodium mg	Carbohydrates g	Dietary fiber g	Sugars g	Protein g	Vitamin A % DV	Vitamin C % DV	Calcium % DV	Iron % DV
Oscar Mayer Spreads															
Braunschweiger, liver sausage — *2 oz*	56	190	150	17	6	90	630	1	0	<1	8	190	8	0	30
sandwich spread — *2 oz*	56	130	90	10	4	25	460	8	0	4	4	0	0	0	2
Sara Lee Poultry Products															
turkey breast pastrami — *2 oz*	56	64	<9	<1	<1	29	514	2	<1	<1	12	n/a	n/a	n/a	n/a
turkey breast, honey-cured, sliced — *2 oz*	56	60	<9	<1	<1	20	552	2	0	1	12	n/a	n/a	n/a	n/a
turkey ham, black forest honey — *2 oz*	56	71	27	3	1	39	662	2	0	2	10	<1	n/a	n/a	n/a
turkey ham, deli, honey-cured — *2 oz*	56	71	27	3	1	39	662	2	0	2	10	n/a	n/a	n/a	n/a
Spam															
lite — *2 oz*	56	110	70	8	3	45	560	0	0	0	9	0	30	0	4
regular — *2 oz*	56	170	140	16	6	40	750	0	0	0	7	0	0	0	2
Underwood Spreads															
chunky chicken — *¼ cup*	55	120	70	8	2.5	40	390	2	0	<1	9	0	0	0	4
chunky turkey — *¼ cup*	55	110	60	7	2	40	420	2	0	0	9	0	0	0	2
deviled ham — *¼ cup*	55	160	130	14	4.5	45	440	0	0	0	8	0	0	0	6
honey ham — *¼ cup*	56	190	140	16	6	45	380	3	0	3	8	0	0	0	4
liverwurst — *¼ cup*	56	170	130	14	5	65	380	3	1	1	7	150	4	0	25
roast beef — *¼ cup*	57	140	100	11	4.5	45	390	0	0	0	9	0	0	0	8

Main Courses Mixes

	Weight g	Calories	Calories from fat	Total fat g	Sat. fat g	Cholesterol mg	Sodium mg	Carbohydrates g	Dietary fiber g	Sugars g	Protein g	Vitamin A % DV	Vitamin C % DV	Calcium % DV	Iron % DV
Bil Mar Turkey Meatloaf Mix — *3 ½ oz*	100	151	54	7	2	80	748	8	3	0	14	n/a	5	14	9
Dinty Moore American Classics Entrées															
beef stew — *1 bowl*	283	250	100	11	5	45	1170	22	2	3	15	30	2	2	10
chicken & noodles — *1 bowl*	283	270	70	8	4	80	1140	28	2	30	22	15	0	6	8
chicken w/ potatoes — *1 bowl*	283	240	40	4	1.5	35	1240	25	2	2	20	0	0	4	4

	Weight *g*	Calories	Calories from fat	Total fat *g*	Sat. fat *g*	Cholesterol *mg*	Sodium *mg*	Carbohydrates *g*	Dietary fiber *g*	Sugars *g*	Protein *g*	Vitamin A *% DV*	Vitamin C *% DV*	Calcium *% DV*	Iron *% DV*
pot roast — *1 bowl*	283	200	25	3	1	45	730	19	2	3	21	20	2	2	15
roast beef w/ potatoes — *1 bowl*	283	240	45	5	2	45	870	24	2	3	24	0	0	4	15
salisbury steak — *1 bowl*	283	300	120	13	6	60	1060	24	3	2	22	0	4	20	15
turkey & dressing — *1 bowl*	283	290	70	8	2.5	45	1120	32	3	5	22	0	0	4	6
Hamburger Helper															
beef pasta — *1 cup*	n/a	270	90	10	4	50	910	26	<1	2	20	0	0	4	10
beef romanoff — *1 cup*	n/a	290	100	11	4	50	930	28	<1	4	20	0	0	6	10
beef stew — *1 cup*	n/a	250	90	10	3.5	50	750	26	2	3	18	10	0	2	10
beef taco — *1 cup*	n/a	310	100	11	4	50	920	30	1	3	20	10	0	4	15
beef teriyaki — *1 cup*	n/a	290	90	10	3.5	50	990	34	2	5	18	10	0	6	15
cheddar 'n bacon — *1 cup*	n/a	350	140	16	6	65	890	28	<1	5	24	2	0	10	10
cheddar melt — *1 cup*	n/a	310	100	12	4.5	55	900	31	<1	4	20	0	0	8	10
cheddar primavera, reduced-sodium — *1 cup*	n/a	320	120	14	5	60	650	27	1	5	21	10	0	10	10
cheeseburger macaroni — *1 cup*	n/a	360	140	16	6	65	1000	31	<1	6	23	0	0	10	15
cheesy italian — *1 cup*	n/a	330	120	14	5	60	920	29	<1	6	22	6	0	10	15
cheesy shells — *1 cup*	n/a	340	130	14	5	60	850	30	<1	5	22	2	0	10	10
chili macaroni — *1 cup*	n/a	290	90	10	4	55	870	30	<1	4	19	20	0	2	15
fettuccini alfredo — *1 cup*	n/a	310	120	13	5	55	850	26	1	5	20	0	0	8	10
hamburger stew — *1 cup*	n/a	250	90	10	4	55	920	22	3	3	19	20	0	2	10
italian herb — *1 cup*	n/a	270	90	10	3.5	50	650	29	2	6	19	10	0	2	15
italian rigatoni — *1 cup*	n/a	180	90	10	4	50	870	29	1	6	19	6	0	2	15
lasagne — *1 cup*	n/a	280	90	10	4	50	950	30	0	7	19	0	0	2	15
meat loaf — *1 cup*	n/a	280	130	15	6	110	600	11	0	3	25	0	0	4	15
mushroom & wild rice — *1 cup*	n/a	310	110	12	4.5	55	880	30	2	4	20	2	0	10	15

	Weight *g*	Calories	Calories from fat	Total fat *g*	Sat. fat *g*	Cholesterol *mg*	Sodium *mg*	Carbohydrates *g*	Dietary fiber *g*	Sugars *g*	Protein *g*	Vitamin A *% DV*	Vitamin C *% DV*	Calcium *% DV*	Iron *% DV*
nacho cheese — *1 cup*	n/a	320	120	13	5	55	930	30	<1	5	22	0	0	10	10
pizza pasta w/ cheese topping — *1 cup*	n/a	290	90	10	4	50	700	31	1	5	19	6	0	4	10
Pizzabake — *1 serving*	n/a	270	90	10	3.5	45	720	28	<1	4	17	4	0	4	15
potato stroganoff — *1 cup*	n/a	270	100	12	4.5	55	870	25	2	2	18	0	0	6	10
potatoes au gratin — *1 cup*	n/a	290	120	14	5	55	820	24	2	5	18	2	0	6	10
rice oriental — *1 cup*	n/a	310	90	10	4	55	1050	35	0	4	19	0	0	0	10
salisbury — *1 cup*	n/a	270	90	10	4	50	790	26	<1	2	19	6	0	4	10
southwestern beef — *1 cup*	n/a	300	90	10	4	50	650	32	2	6	21	10	0	2	15
spaghetti — *1 cup*	n/a	300	100	11	4	55	940	29	<1	6	21	10	0	2	15
stroganoff — *1 cup*	n/a	320	110	13	5	55	830	30	0	7	21	2	0	10	15
swedish meatballs — *1 cup*	n/a	300	130	14	5	55	780	24	<1	2	19	8	0	2	10
three cheese — *1 cup*	n/a	340	130	15	5	55	830	32	<1	5	21	2	0	8	10
zesty italian — *1 cup*	n/a	320	100	11	4	55	890	34	<1	8	21	6	0	2	15
zesty mexican — *1 cup*	n/a	300	100	11	4	50	730	32	1	5	19	15	0	6	15
Old El Paso Dinner Kit															
burrito — *1 burrito*	n/a	280	60	7	3	65	830	37	3	1	16	2	0	6	15
fajita — *2 fajitas*	n/a	330	60	7	2	45	910	47	2	6	20	2	40	10	15
One Skillet Mexican, nacho-cheese-flavor — *2 tacos*	n/a	490	170	19	7	65	1470	55	2	5	24	10	6	10	20
One Skillet Mexican, salsa-flavor — *2 tacos*	n/a	460	140	16	5	55	1390	57	3	5	23	20	25	4	20
One Skillet Mexican, taco-flavor — *2 tacos*	n/a	440	140	16	5	55	1170	53	2	2	22	10	6	2	20
soft taco — *2 tacos*	n/a	380	100	11	4.5	65	1340	46	3	3	25	2	0	10	20
taco — *2 tacos*	n/a	270	120	13	4.5	60	910	21	4	3	18	2	0	10	10
Skillet Chicken Helper — *1 cup*	n/a	270	90	9	2	110	810	30	1	1	18	6	0	6	4

	Weight *g*	Calories	Calories from fat	Total fat *g*	Sat. fat *g*	Cholesterol *mg*	Sodium *mg*	Carbohydrates *g*	Dietary fiber *g*	Sugars *g*	Protein *g*	Vitamin A *% DV*	Vitamin C *% DV*	Calcium *% DV*	Iron *% DV*
Tuna Helper															
au gratin — *1 cup*	n/a	310	110	12	3	20	930	36	1	5	14	8	0	10	8
cheesy pasta — *1 cup*	n/a	280	100	11	3	20	890	32	<1	5	14	8	0	10	8
creamy broccoli — *1 cup*	n/a	310	110	12	3	20	880	35	1	6	14	8	0	8	8
creamy pasta — *1 cup*	n/a	300	120	13	3.5	20	910	31	1	4	14	10	0	8	8
fettuccine alfredo — *1 cup*	n/a	310	120	14	3.5	15	950	32	1	6	14	8	0	8	8
garden cheddar — *1 cup*	n/a	310	110	12	3	20	1040	35	1	5	16	10	0	10	8
pasta salad — *⅔ cup*	n/a	380	240	27	3	10	730	26	1	4	10	2	0	2	8
tetrazzini — *1 cup*	n/a	310	110	12	3	20	1010	33	1	3	17	8	0	6	10
tuna pot pie — *1 cup*	n/a	440	220	24	7	110	1080	40	1	9	18	25	0	15	10
tuna romanoff — *1 cup*	n/a	280	70	8	1.5	20	800	38	1	3	15	4	0	4	8

Muffins & Quick Breads: Mixes

	Weight *g*	Calories	Calories from fat	Total fat *g*	Sat. fat *g*	Cholesterol *mg*	Sodium *mg*	Carbohydrates *g*	Dietary fiber *g*	Sugars *g*	Protein *g*	Vitamin A *% DV*	Vitamin C *% DV*	Calcium *% DV*	Iron *% DV*
Aunt Jemima Easy Corn Bread — *⅓ cup unprepared*	37	147	36	4	1	0	448	26	1	6	2	0	0	0	7
Betty Crocker Muffin															
banana nut — *1 muffin*	n/a	150	45	5	1	20	200	24	0	12	2	0	0	0	4
cinnamon streusel — *1 muffin*	n/a	170	70	7	1.5	20	180	22	0	11	3	0	0	4	4
lemon poppyseed — *1 muffin*	n/a	190	60	7	1.5	20	220	30	0	15	2	0	0	2	4
Twice the Blueberry — *1 muffin*	n/a	140	35	4	1	20	180	25	0	13	2	0	0	0	4
Betty Crocker Fat-Free Muffin															
apple/cinnamon — *1 muffin*	n/a	120	0	0	0	0	200	26	0	14	2	n/a	n/a	n/a	n/a
blueberry — *1 muffin*	n/a	120	0	0	0	0	200	27	0	15	2	0	0	0	2
Corn Muffin, Jiffy — *1 muffin*	n/a	180	50	4	1.5	0	320	28	1	8	2	0	0	6	6
Flako Corn Muffin — *⅓ cup*	41	163	36	4	<1	0	383	29	1	8	3	0	0	2	2

	Weight g	Calories	Calories from fat	Total fat g	Sat. fat g	Cholesterol mg	Sodium mg	Carbohydrates g	Dietary fiber g	Sugars g	Protein g	Vitamin A % DV	Vitamin C % DV	Calcium % DV	Iron % DV
Pillsbury Quick Bread															
apple/cinnamon — *1/12 recipe*	n/a	180	50	6	1	20	170	30	1	17	2	0	0	2	6
banana — *1/12 recipe*	n/a	170	50	6	1	35	200	26	<1	14	3	0	0	0	6
blueberry — *1/12 recipe*	n/a	180	50	6	1	20	160	29	<1	16	2	0	0	2	6
carrot — *1/16 recipe*	n/a	140	45	5	1	25	150	22	<1	12	2	15	0	2	6
cinnamon swirl — *1/12 recipe*	n/a	220	80	9	2	35	170	32	0	20	2	0	0	4	8
cranberry — *1/12 recipe*	n/a	160	35	4	1	20	160	30	<1	16	2	0	0	0	6
date — *1/12 recipe*	n/a	180	35	4	1	20	160	32	1	18	3	0	0	0	6
lemon poppy seed — *1/12 recipe*	n/a	180	60	7	1.5	20	160	27	<1	13	3	0	0	4	6
nut — *1/12 recipe*	n/a	170	50	6	1	20	190	27	1	15	3	0	0	2	6
pumpkin — *1/12 recipe*	n/a	170	50	6	1	35	200	27	<1	14	3	4	0	2	6
SnackWell's Muffin															
apple/cinnamon — *1/6 recipe*	n/a	180	45	5	1.5	5	190	31	<1	18	3	0	0	6	6
blueberry — *1 muffin*	n/a	120	0	0	0	0	170	28	<1	16	2	0	0	6	4
blueberry, low-fat — *1/5 recipe*	n/a	160	20	2	1	0	210	34	<1	21	2	9	9	6	6
chocolate chip — *1/6 recipe*	n/a	190	50	6	2.5	5	190	31	<1	18	3	0	0	6	8
strawberry — *1/6 recipe*	n/a	180	45	5	1.5	5	190	31	0	18	3	0	0	6	6
Sweet Rewards, Fat-Free															
apple/cinnamon — *1 muffin*	n/a	120	0	0	0	0	200	28	0	16	2	0	0	0	4
wild blueberry — *1 muffin*	n/a	120	0	0	0	0	200	27	0	15	2	0	0	0	2

Muffins: Ready-to-eat

	Weight g	Calories	Calories from fat	Total fat g	Sat. fat g	Cholesterol mg	Sodium mg	Carbohydrates g	Dietary fiber g	Sugars g	Protein g	Vitamin A % DV	Vitamin C % DV	Calcium % DV	Iron % DV
Arnold															
Bran' Nola — *1 muffin*	66	130	15	1.5	0	0	160	29	3	5	6	0	0	6	10
raisin — *1 muffin*	66	150	10	1	0	0	160	32	1	10	5	0	0	6	8

	Weight *g*	Calories	Calories from fat	Total fat *g*	Sat. fat *g*	Cholesterol *mg*	Sodium *mg*	Carbohydrates *g*	Dietary fiber *g*	Sugars *g*	Protein *g*	Vitamin A *% DV*	Vitamin C *% DV*	Calcium *% DV*	Iron *% DV*
sourdough — *1 muffin*	57	120	10	1	0	0	200	25	1	2	4	0	0	6	8
Entenmann's															
chocolate chip — *1 muffin*	57	250	120	14	4.5	50	220	28	>1	15	3	4	0	2	2
chocolate chocolate chip — *1 muffin*	57	220	100	11	3.5	50	220	29	1	18	3	2	0	0	4
corn — *1 muffin*	57	200	70	8	1.5	25	340	28	0	11	3	0	0	2	0
Orowheat															
blueberry — *1 muffin*	66	170	15	1.5	0	0	200	33	1	7	5	0	0	2	8
Healthnut — *1 muffin*	66	170	30	3	0	0	220	30	2	3	6	0	0	8	10
honey wheat — *1 muffin*	66	150	10	1	0	0	200	31	3	3	6	0	0	2	8
Master's Best Raisins, Dates & Pecans — *1 muffin*	71	200	30	3	0	0	210	37	3	13	6	0	0	6	10
Oatnut Bran — *1 muffin*	66	160	25	3	0	0	230	30	2	5	5	0	0	4	10
Pepperidge Farm Wholesome Choice (frozen)															
apple oatmeal — *1 muffin*	59	160	35	3.5	0.5	0	190	28	3	11	4	0	0	2	10
blueberry — *1 muffin*	54	140	20	2.5	0	0	190	27	2	11	3	0	0	0	4
bran w/ raisins — *1 muffin*	59	150	20	2.5	0.5	0	260	30	4	10	4	0	2	4	10
corn — *1 muffin*	54	150	25	3	0	0	190	28	3	11	4	0	0	2	10
Sara Lee Hearty Muffins															
blueberry, frozen — *1 muffin*	64	220	100	11	2	15	170	27	<1	12	3	<2	0	2	4
corn — *1 muffin*	64	260	130	14	3	25	220	30	1	14	3	<2	0	2	4
Weight Watchers (frozen)															
banana, fat-free — *1 muffin*	71	170	0	0	0	0	310	41	3	17	3	0	0	8	2
blueberry, fat-free — *1 muffin*	71	160	0	0	0	0	290	38	2	15	3	0	0	6	4
chocolate chip — *1 muffin*	71	190	20	2	1	0	350	39	4	14	3	0	0	8	10
Harvest Honey Bran, fat-free — *1 muffin*	71	160	0	0	0	0	240	36	3	18	3	0	0	8	4

	Weight g	Calories	Calories from fat	Total fat g	Sat. fat g	Cholesterol mg	Sodium mg	Carbohydrates g	Dietary fiber g	Sugars g	Protein g	Vitamin A % DV	Vitamin C % DV	Calcium % DV	Iron % DV
Pancake & Waffle Mixes															
Aunt Jemima (unprepared)															
buckwheat — *¼ cup*	34	106	<9	<1	<1	0	490	24	4	1	4	0	0	15	11
buttermilk — *¼ cup*	34	115	<9	<1	<1	2	437	24	1	2	3	0	0	13	10
original — *⅓ cup*	47	161	<9	<1	<1	0	645	35	1	5	5	0	0	<2	11
whole-wheat — *¼ cup*	38	124	<9	<1	<1	0	523	26	3	4	5	0	0	16	18
Aunt Jemima Complete (unprepared)															
buttermilk — *⅓ cup*	45	162	18	2	<1	9	409	32	1	5	5	0	0	19	12
buttermilk, reduced-calorie pancake mix — *⅓ cup*	43	136	9	1	<1	15	572	29	5	4	7	0	0	32	19
regular — *⅓ cup*	46	167	18	2	<1	15	405	34	1	7	5	0	0	22	13
Betty Crocker Complete Pancake Mix, Buttermilk — *3 pancakes*	n/a	200	25	2.5	0.5	10	540	39	1	7	5	0	0	10	8
Betty Crocker Pancake Mix, Original — *3 pancakes*	n/a	200	25	3	1	10	540	39	1	9	6	0	0	10	10
Bisquick Shake 'N Pour															
blueberry — *3 pancakes*	n/a	220	40	4	1	0	640	40	1	8	6	0	0	8	10
buttermilk — *3 pancakes*	n/a	200	30	3	1	0	680	38	1	6	7	0	0	8	10
original — *3 pancakes*	n/a	210	30	4	1	0	710	39	<1	9	5	0	0	8	8
Hungry Jack Complete (unprepared)															
buttermilk — *⅓ cup*	46	160	15	1.5	0	<5	560	32	<1	7	4	0	0	15	10
Extra-Lights — *⅓ cup*	44	150	20	2	0.5	0	600	30	<1	5	4	0	0	10	10
Hungry Jack Pancake Mix (unprepared)															
buttermilk — *⅓ cup*	46	160	15	1.5	0	0	650	33	<1	5	4	0	0	4	10
Extra-Lights — *⅓ cup*	45	160	15	1.5	0	0	590	33	<1	4	3	0	0	15	10
original — *⅓ cup*	44	150	15	1.5	0	0	640	32	<1	4	3	0	0	2	10
Hungry Jack Pancake Mix, Potato — *3-inch pancake*	n/a	90	15	1.5	0	50	380	16	1	<1	3	0	0	10	4

Foods, Brand Name

Pasta & Noodle Products

	Weight g	Calories	Calories from fat	Total fat g	Sat. fat g	Cholesterol mg	Sodium mg	Carbohydrates g	Dietary fiber g	Sugars g	Protein g	Vitamin A % DV	Vitamin C % DV	Calcium % DV	Iron % DV
Chef Boyardee Pasta Dishes															
ABC's & 123's in tomato & cheese sauce — *1 cup*	255	200	0	0	0	0	950	45	3	10	6	4	0	2	10
ABC's & 123's w/ meatballs in tomato sauce — *1 cup*	245	280	80	9	4	25	930	39	3	10	9	10	0	0	10
beef ravioli in tomato & meat sauce — *1 cup*	254	230	45	5	2	15	1120	38	3	7	9	15	2	0	15
cheese ravioli in tomato sauce — *1 cup*	251	210	0	0	0	<5	860	44	4	9	7	10	2	4	20
cheese ravioli w/ beef, in tomato sauce — *1 cup*	246	220	30	3	1.5	15	1110	38	4	6	9	6	2	2	15
cheese tortellini in hearty tomato sauce — *1 cup*	258	230	10	1	0	15	770	46	4	12	9	10	0	8	10
lasagna w/ chunky tomato & meat sauce — *1 cup*	249	270	70	8	3	20	680	41	3	10	10	8	4	4	10
meat tortellini in hearty tomato & meat sauce — *1 cup*	258	260	30	3.5	1.5	30	810	48	4	12	10	10	4	4	10
spaghetti & meat balls in tomato sauce — *1 cup*	240	250	90	10	4	25	950	32	3	7	9	6	0	0	10
Di Giorno Stuffed Pastas															
cheese ravioli, italian herb — *1 cup*	107	350	120	13	8	45	610	44	2	2	15	0	4	15	8
cheese tortellini — *¾ cup*	81	260	60	6	3.5	30	230	37	1	2	12	2	0	20	6
ravioli, w/ italian sausage — *¾ cup*	103	340	110	12	5	50	630	41	2	3	16	4	0	15	8
Di Giorno Light Varieties															
ravioli, cheese & garlic — *1 cup*	104	270	20	2	1	5	580	45	1	3	17	8	0	20	8
ravioli, tomato & cheese — *1 cup*	104	280	25	3	1.5	10	490	49	2	4	14	8	0	15	10
Hormel Kid's Kitchen Microwave Meals															
Cheezy Mac & beef — *1 cup*	213	260	60	7	3	30	910	33	1	7	15	8	2	10	8
macaroni & cheese — *1 cup*	213	260	100	11	6	35	690	30	1	3	11	6	0	10	4
macaroni, beefy — *1 cup*	213	190	50	6	2.5	30	790	23	2	4	11	15	0	4	8
noodle rings & franks — *1 cup*	213	150	35	4	1.5	30	1110	17	1	1	10	0	0	4	4
ravioli, mini — *1 cup*	213	240	60	7	3	20	950	34	1	6	10	10	2	4	8

	Weight g	Calories	Calories from fat	Total fat g	Sat. fat g	Cholesterol mg	Sodium mg	Carbohydrates g	Dietary fiber g	Sugars g	Protein g	Vitamin A % DV	Vitamin C % DV	Calcium % DV	Iron % DV
spaghetti & meatballs — *1 cup*	213	220	60	7	4	25	950	28	1	10	11	10	0	6	6
spaghetti rings — *1 cup*	213	190	15	2	1.5	10	920	34	2	12	8	10	2	8	6
spaghetti rings & franks — *1 cup*	213	240	80	9	3.5	25	810	32	0	11	9	8	4	8	4
spaghetti rings & meatballs — *1 cup*	213	250	60	7	3	20	1200	35	3	12	11	8	2	6	8
Hormel Microcup Meal															
lasagna — *1 cup*	213	250	120	14	7	25	950	24	1	6	8	6	0	4	6
macaroni & cheese — *1 cup*	213	260	100	11	6	35	690	30	1	3	11	6	0	10	4
noodles & chicken — *1 cup*	213	200	80	9	2.5	40	1140	21	1	2	8	10	0	2	4
ravioli w/ tomato sauce — *1 cup*	213	220	50	56	2	15	840	34	2	12	8	4	4	6	6
spaghetti & meatballs — *1 cup*	213	220	60	7	4	25	930	28	1	10	11	10	0	6	8
Kraft															
egg noodle dinner, cheddar cheese — *1 cup*	229	430	190	21	6	70	780	46	1	8	12	20	0	15	15
spaghetti dinner, mild american — *1 cup*	230	270	40	4.5	1	<5	690	48	3	5	9	15	15	4	15
spaghetti dinner, tangy italian — *1 cup*	226	270	40	4.5	1	<5	780	46	3	4	10	15	15	8	15
spaghetti dinner, w/ meat sauce — *1 cup*	235	330	100	11	4	15	830	46	3	8	12	10	2	10	20
Kraft Macaroni & Cheese Dinner															
deluxe original — *1 cup*	175	320	90	10	6	25	730	44	1	4	14	10	0	20	15
dinosaurs, spirals, or teddy bears, — *1 cup*	193	390	150	17	4.5	10	770	48	1	8	12	15	0	15	15
original — *1 cup*	196	390	150	17	4	10	730	48	1	8	11	15	0	10	15
Kraft Pasta Salad															
classic ranch w/ bacon — *¾ cup*	135	360	210	23	4	15	500	30	2	3	7	6	0	2	10
creamy caesar — *¾ cup*	137	350	200	22	4	15	650	30	2	5	7	2	2	6	10
garden primavera — *¾ cup*	142	280	110	12	2.5	<5	730	34	2	4	8	4	2	8	10
light italian — *¾ cup*	142	190	20	2	1	<5	660	34	2	5	8	4	2	8	10

	Weight g	Calories	Calories from fat	Total fat g	Sat. fat g	Cholesterol mg	Sodium mg	Carbohydrates g	Dietary fiber g	Sugars g	Protein g	Vitamin A % DV	Vitamin C % DV	Calcium % DV	Iron % DV
parmesan peppercorn — *¾ cup*	140	360	220	25	4.5	20	610	28	2	3	8	6	0	8	10
La Choy Crispy Wide Chow Mein Noodles — *½ cup*	28	140	56	6	1	0	209	17	2	0	4	0	0	0	0
Lipton Noodles & Sauce															
beef — *1 cup*	n/a	280	90	9.5	2	60	910	43	2	2	8	6	0	0	15
butter — *1 cup*	n/a	310	130	14	5.5	70	870	41	2	4	8	8	0	0	15
chicken — *1 cup*	n/a	290	100	10.5	3	65	830	42	2	2	8	10	0	0	15
chicken broccoli — *1 cup*	n/a	310	100	11	3.5	70	840	44	2	4	11	8	6	8	15
chicken tetrazzini — *1 cup*	n/a	300	110	11.5	4	70	950	41	2	4	10	10	0	8	15
parmesan — *1 cup*	n/a	330	140	15	6	75	850	40	2	5	12	10	4	15	15
sour cream & chives — *1 cup*	n/a	310	130	14	5.5	70	870	41	2	4	8	8	2	2	15
stroganoff — *1 cup*	n/a	300	100	11	4	70	950	40	2	5	11	10	0	8	15
Lipton Pasta & Sauce															
bow tie chicken primavera — *1 cup*	n/a	290	90	10	3.5	10	820	43	2	6	9	20	2	10	10
bow tie italian cheese — *1 cup*	n/a	300	110	11.5	4.5	15	900	41	<1	4	10	8	0	15	8
butter & herb — *1 cup*	n/a	270	90	9.5	2.5	5	830	40	2	3	7	6	0	0	8
cheddar broccoli — *1 cup*	n/a	340	100	10.5	3.5	15	970	49	1	6	11	10	6	15	10
chicken broccoli — *1 cup*	n/a	260	60	8	1	0	810	43	2	2	8	6	6	2	10
chicken stir-fry — *1 cup*	n/a	270	70	8	1	0	900	43	2	3	8	15	2	2	10
creamy mushroom — *1 cup*	n/a	320	100	10.5	4	15	870	46	0	4	10	8	0	10	10
garlic & butter — *1 cup*	n/a	260	80	9	2	5	850	40	2	3	7	6	0	2	10
mild cheddar cheese — *1 cup*	n/a	290	90	10	3.5	10	930	41	<1	4	10	8	0	15	8
parmesan — *1 cup*	n/a	280	90	11	3	10	960	41	2	3	8	8	0	6	10
rotini primavera — *1 cup*	n/a	320	110	11.5	4.5	15	980	45	2	4	10	15	6	10	10
spanish — *1 cup*	n/a	280	70	8	1	0	900	47	2	2	6	10	8	2	15

	Weight g	Calories	Calories from fat	Total fat g	Sat. fat g	Cholesterol mg	Sodium mg	Carbohydrates g	Dietary fiber g	Sugars g	Protein g	Vitamin A % DV	Vitamin C % DV	Calcium % DV	Iron % DV
three-cheese rotini — *1 cup*	n/a	320	110	12	5	15	970	44	<1	5	11	8	0	15	10
Pasta Roni (unprepared)															
angel hair w/ lemon & butter — *2 ½ oz*	70	253	27	3	1	1	842	48	2	5	9	11	<2	6	11
angel hair w/ parmesan cheese — *2 oz*	56	212	41	4.5	1	<1	756	37	2	4	7	3	1	6	8
broccoli — *2 oz*	56	202	27	3	<1	<1	751	36	2	3	7	4	20	3	8
broccoli & mushroom — *2 ½ oz*	70	258	45	5	1	<1	884	47	2	4	9	3	2	7	11
broccoli au gratin — *2 oz*	56	205	27	3	1	1	780	37	2	4	7	3	2	7	11
chicken — *2 oz*	56	203	27	3	<1	<1	883	38	2	2	8	0	0	<2	8
corkscrews w/ creamy garlic sauce — *2 oz*	56	212	36	4	1	1	762	37	2	5	7	8	0	8	8
fettuccine w/ alfredo sauce — *2 ½ oz*	70	273	63	7	2	2	913	45	2	4	9	6	0	5	10
linguine w/ chicken & broccoli sauce — *2 ½ oz*	70	251	27	3	<1	<1	780	48	3	2	10	<2	4	4	12
mild cheddar — *2 oz*	56	207	36	4	1	1	803	37	2	4	7	0	0	7	8
oriental stir-fry — *2 oz*	56	195	18	2	<1	0	891	38	2	3	7	4	<2	2	9
parmesano — *2 ½ oz*	70	256	36	4	1	2	780	46	2	4	10	5	<2	8	10
penne w/ herb & butter sauce — *2 oz*	56	199	27	3	<1	<1	630	38	2	3	7	11	<2	5	8
rigatoni w/ white cheddar & broccoli sauce — *2 oz*	56	214	45	5	2	4	672	36	2	4	7	2	3	8	8
romanoff — *2 ½ oz*	70	273	63	7	2	5	910	45	2	6	9	1	0	5	9
shells & white cheddar — *2 ½ oz*	70	270	54	6	2	7	892	45	2	6	9	<2	0	10	9
stroganoff — *2 ½ oz*	70	272	63	7	2	2	914	44	2	5	9	0	0	7	9
vermicelli w/ garlic & olive oil sauce — *2 ½ oz*	70	254	36	4	<1	<1	876	48	2	3	9	4	0	<2	10
Velveeta															
rotini & cheese, broccoli — *1 cup*	205	400	140	16	10	45	1240	46	2	3	18	15	4	30	15
shells & cheese, bacon — *1 cup*	195	360	120	14	8	40	1140	43	1	4	17	10	0	25	15
shells & cheese, original — *1 cup*	188	360	120	13	8	40	1030	44	1	4	16	10	0	25	15

Pasta Sauces

	Weight g	Calories	Calories from fat	Total fat g	Sat. fat g	Cholesterol mg	Sodium mg	Carbohydrates g	Dietary fiber g	Sugars g	Protein g	Vitamin A % DV	Vitamin C % DV	Calcium % DV	Iron % DV
Classico															
beef & pork — ½ *cup*	124	90	45	5	1	10	610	7	2	5	3	2	6	2	2
four cheese — ½ *cup*	124	70	35	4	1	<5	480	7	1	4	2	10	10	6	2
mushrooms & ripe olives — ½ *cup*	124	50	10	1	0.5	0	490	8	2	5	2	8	4	4	2
onion & garlic — ½ *cup*	124	80	35	4	0.5	0	410	9	2	5	2	8	10	2	4
spicy red pepper — ½ *cup*	124	60	20	2.5	0.5	0	270	6	2	6	2	6	10	6	2
sun-dried tomato — ½ *cup*	124	80	40	4.5	1	0	430	8	2	4	2	10	15	0	4
sweet peppers & onions — ½ *cup*	124	70	35	4	0.5	0	380	8	3	5	1	10	8	2	2
tomato & basil — ½ *cup*	124	60	15	1.5	0	0	430	9	2	6	2	8	15	4	2
tomato & pesto — ½ *cup*	124	110	50	6	1.5	<5	450	10	2	4	1	10	10	6	4
Contadina Pasta Ready															
tomatoes — ½ *cup*	n/a	40	15	2	n/a	n/a	620	5	1	5	1	6	10	4	2
tomatoes primavera — ½ *cup*	n/a	50	15	1.5	n/a	n/a	600	8	1	5	1	15	15	6	4
tomatoes w/ mushrooms — ½ *cup*	n/a	50	15	1.5	n/a	n/a	640	9	1	5	1	10	15	6	4
tomatoes w/ olives — ½ *cup*	n/a	60	30	3	0.5	n/a	640	8	1	5	1	10	15	8	4
tomatoes w/ three cheeses — ½ *cup*	n/a	70	35	4	n/a	<5	650	8	<1	5	1	10	15	10	4
tomatoes w/crushed red pepper — ½ *cup*	n/a	60	30	3	0.5	n/a	690	8	1	4	1	10	15	8	6
Del Monte Chunky Spaghetti Sauce															
garden style — ½ *cup*	124	60	10	1	0	0	510	11	<1	9	2	15	4	4	6
garlic & herb — ½ *cup*	124	60	10	1.5	0	0	490	11	<1	9	2	10	4	4	4
italian herb — ½ *cup*	124	60	10	1	0	0	520	12	<1	8	2	10	4	4	6
tomato basil — ½ *cup*	124	60	10	1	0	0	480	11	<1	8	2	10	4	4	4

	Weight *g*	Calories	Calories from fat	Total fat *g*	Sat. fat *g*	Cholesterol *mg*	Sodium *mg*	Carbohydrates *g*	Dietary fiber *g*	Sugars *g*	Protein *g*	Vitamin A *% DV*	Vitamin C *% DV*	Calcium *% DV*	Iron *% DV*
Del Monte D'Italia															
classic marinara — *½ cup*	124	50	10	1.5	0	0	510	9	<1	7	2	15	4	8	10
four cheese — *½ cup*	124	60	15	2	0	0	370	8	<1	6	2	15	4	8	10
spicy red pepper — *½ cup*	124	50	15	1.5	0	0	510	9	<1	7	2	15	4	8	10
tomato & basil — *½ cup*	124	50	15	1.5	0	0	390	9	<1	7	2	15	4	8	10
Del Monte Spaghetti Sauce															
traditional — *½ cup*	125	60	10	1	0	0	500	14	3	9	2	25	4	4	8
w/ garlic & onion — *½ cup*	125	60	10	1	0	0	460	13	2	7	2	20	4	4	8
w/ green peppers & mushrooms — *½ cup*	125	60	10	1	0	0	390	12	3	7	2	15	4	4	8
w/ meat — *½ cup*	125	70	15	2	0	<5	510	13	3	7	3	10	4	4	8
w/ mushrooms — *½ cup*	125	70	10	1	0	0	520	15	2	10	2	15	4	2	6
Di Giorno															
alfredo — *¼ cup*	62	230	200	22	10	45	550	2	0	2	4	8	0	10	0
four cheese — *¼ cup*	63	200	170	19	11	45	410	2	0	2	5	15	0	15	0
marinara — *½ cup*	128	100	40	4.5	1	<5	530	12	3	7	3	10	0	4	4
meat, traditional — *½ cup*	128	120	50	6	2	15	610	12	3	7	6	10	0	8	6
olive oil & garlic w/ grated cheeses — *¼ cup*	60	370	320	36	8	20	540	3	0	<1	9	2	0	30	0
pesto — *¼ cup*	62	320	280	31	7	15	500	3	0	0	8	15	0	25	2
plum tomato & mushroom — *½ cup*	126	70	0	0	0	0	310	15	2	9	2	10	2	2	4
Di Giorno Light Varieties															
alfredo, reduced-fat — *¼ cup*	69	170	90	10	6	30	600	16	0	3	5	8	0	15	0
chunky tomato w/ basil — *½ cup*	127	70	0	0	0	0	290	16	2	10	2	15	0	2	4
Five Brother's															
alfredo w/ mushrooms — *¼ cup*	61	80	60	6	4	20	460	3	0	1	2	8	0	6	0

	Weight g	Calories	Calories from fat	Total fat g	Sat. fat g	Cholesterol mg	Sodium mg	Carbohydrates g	Dietary fiber g	Sugars g	Protein g	Vitamin A % DV	Vitamin C % DV	Calcium % DV	Iron % DV
garden vegetable primavera — *½ cup*	125	70	20	2	0	0	490	11	3	8	2	30	20	8	6
marinara w/ burgundy wine — *½ cup*	125	80	25	3	0.5	0	480	12	3	10	2	25	25	6	6
mediterranean tomato & olive — *½ cup*	127	80	35	4	0.5	0	530	9	3	8	2	15	15	8	6
romano w/ garlic — *½ cup*	127	90	35	4	1	n/a	570	10	3	9	3	15	10	10	6
summer tomato basil — *½ cup*	125	60	15	1.5	0	0	470	10	3	8	2	20	25	6	6
tomato alfredo — *½ cup*	128	150	70	8	4.5	25	680	13	3	11	5	20	8	15	6
Healthy Choice															
garlic & herbs — *½ cup*	126	50	0	0	0	0	390	10	2	7	2	8	10	4	6
garlic & onions — *½ cup*	125	40	0	0	0	0	390	9	2	7	2	6	10	4	6
italian-style vegetables — *½ cup*	125	40	0	0	0	0	390	9	2	7	2	10	8	4	4
mushroom — *½ cup*	126	50	0	0	0	0	390	11	2	8	2	6	10	4	6
super chunky mushrooms — *½ cup*	125	40	0	0	0	0	390	9	2	8	2	4	10	4	6
super chunky mushrooms & sweet peppers — *½ cup*	125	45	0	0	0	0	390	9	2	6	2	4	10	4	6
super chunky tomato, mushroom & garlic — *½ cup*	126	45	0	0	0	0	390	10	2	8	2	10	10	4	4
super chunky vegetable primavera — *½ cup*	124	45	0	0	0	0	390	9	2	7	2	15	8	4	4
traditional — *½ cup*	126	50	0	0	0	0	390	11	2	8	2	6	10	4	6
Newman's Own															
Bombolina — *½ cup*	127	100	40	4	0.5	0	590	15	5	9	1	15	0	4	4
Diavolo — *½ cup*	125	70	25	3	0	0	510	10	3	4	0	15	0	6	10
Say Cheese — *½ cup*	127	80	25	3	1	<5	560	9	3	6	3	15	0	6	8
Sockarooni — *½ cup*	125	60	15	2	0	0	590	9	3	7	2	15	0	6	10
spaghetti sauce — *½ cup*	125	60	15	2	0	0	590	9	3	7	2	15	0	6	10
spaghetti sauce w/ mushrooms — *½ cup*	125	60	15	2	0	0	590	9	3	7	2	15	0	6	10

	Weight *g*	Calories	Calories from fat	Total fat *g*	Sat. fat *g*	Cholesterol *mg*	Sodium *mg*	Carbohydrates *g*	Dietary fiber *g*	Sugars *g*	Protein *g*	Vitamin A *% DV*	Vitamin C *% DV*	Calcium *% DV*	Iron *% DV*
Prego Extra Chunky															
garden combination — *½ cup*	n/a	90	10	1	0.5	0	480	16	3	12	2	25	50	2	4
garlic & cheese — *½ cup*	n/a	120	20	2	0.5	0	570	22	3	15	3	40	15	6	6
garlic supreme — *½ cup*	n/a	130	25	3	0.5	0	570	23	3	15	3	20	8	6	8
mushroom & diced onion — *½ cup*	n/a	110	25	3	1	0	500	18	3	11	2	15	15	4	4
mushroom & diced tomato — *½ cup*	n/a	110	35	3	1	0	510	19	3	8	2	25	15	2	6
mushroom & green pepper — *½ cup*	n/a	120	40	4.5	0.5	5	430	18	6	11	2	20	6	6	6
mushroom supreme — *½ cup*	n/a	130	40	4.5	0.5	5	490	21	3	13	3	20	10	4	8
mushroom w/extra spice — *½ cup*	n/a	120	35	4	0	0	510	19	3	12	2	30	15	4	4
sausage & pepper — *½ cup*	n/a	180	80	9	2.5	10	570	22	3	12	4	20	35	6	8
tomato supreme — *½ cup*	n/a	120	25	3	0.5	0	580	20	3	14	2	20	15	6	6
tomato, onion & garlic — *½ cup*	n/a	110	30	3.5	1	0	480	19	3	13	2	15	25	4	4
vegetable supreme — *½ cup*	n/a	90	30	3	0.5	5	490	15	3	10	2	25	4	4	4
Zesty Basil — *½ cup*	n/a	110	15	1.5	0.5	0	510	22	3	15	2	30	15	6	2
Zesty Oregano — *½ cup*	n/a	130	30	3	0.5	0	540	25	3	16	2	45	15	4	6
Prego Sauces															
diced onion & garlic — *½ cup*	n/a	110	45	3	0.5	0	420	19	3	12	2	25	35	4	6
marinara — *½ cup*	n/a	110	50	6	1.5	0	670	12	3	8	2	20	30	4	4
mushroom parmesan — *½ cup*	n/a	120	30	3.5	1	10	570	19	3	12	3	20	15	8	6
three cheese — *½ cup*	n/a	100	20	2	1	5	460	18	3	14	3	15	25	6	4
tomato & basil — *½ cup*	n/a	110	30	3	0.5	0	420	19	3	12	2	25	35	4	6
tomato parmesan — *½ cup*	n/a	120	25	3	1	5	570	19	3	13	3	20	15	8	6
traditional — *½ cup*	n/a	140	40	4.5	1.5	0	610	23	2	15	2	20	15	4	8
traditional w/mushrooms — *½ cup*	n/a	150	45	5	1.5	0	670	23	3	14	2	25	25	4	6

	Weight g	Calories	Calories from fat	Total fat g	Sat. fat g	Cholesterol mg	Sodium mg	Carbohydrates g	Dietary fiber g	Sugars g	Protein g	Vitamin A % DV	Vitamin C % DV	Calcium % DV	Iron % DV
traditional, no-salt-added — ½ *cup*	n/a	110	50	6	1.5	0	25	11	3	7	2	25	6	4	6
Progresso															
chunky mushroom — ½ *cup*	124	80	25	3	0	0	360	11	2	5	2	8	4	2	6
creamy clam — ½ *cup*	120	110	50	6	1.5	10	440	8	0	0	5	0	0	0	4
lobster — ½ *cup*	123	100	60	7	1	5	430	6	2	3	3	6	0	2	6
marinara — ½ *cup*	123	80	40	4.5	0.5	<5	480	8	2	5	2	10	0	2	4
meat flavor — ½ *cup*	124	100	40	4.5	1	5	610	12	3	9	4	6	0	4	6
pizza — ¼ *cup*	63	35	10	1	0	0	140	5	1	2	1	8	10	2	4
red clam — ½ *cup*	125	80	25	3	0.5	5	620	8	1	5	6	4	0	2	4
spaghetti — ½ *cup*	124	100	40	4.5	1	<5	620	12	2	8	3	10	4	2	6
white clam — ½ *cup*	124	130	80	7	1.5	15	310	1	0	0	10	0	4	2	2
Progresso, Authentic															
alfredo — ½ *cup*	124	300	250	28	13	70	810	5	2	1	8	15	0	25	0
marinara — ½ *cup*	124	90	45	5	1.5	<5	440	9	5	5	3	15	0	8	6
white clam — ½ *cup*	124	90	60	7	1.5	10	470	2	0	0	5	0	2	0	4
Ragu Chunky Garden Style															
mushroom & green pepper — ½ *cup*	128	110	30	3.5	0.5	0	570	18	3	12	2	20	4	4	8
mushroom & onion — ½ *cup*	128	120	30	3.5	0.5	0	560	19	3	13	2	20	4	4	8
sweet bell pepper & onion — ½ *cup*	128	110	30	3.5	0.5	0	570	19	2	13	2	25	10	4	4
tomato, garlic & onion — ½ *cup*	128	120	30	3.5	0.5	0	550	19	3	13	2	20	6	6	8
tomato, spinach & cheese — ½ *cup*	128	120	30	3.5	1	0	550	18	3	13	2	25	4	6	6
vegetable primavera — ½ *cup*	128	110	30	3.5	0.5	0	480	17	4	10	2	35	10	4	6
Ragu Hearty															
herb w/ red wine — ½ *cup*	129	100	25	3	0	0	550	16	3	12	2	15	8	4	6

	Weight g	Calories	Calories from fat	Total fat g	Sat. fat g	Cholesterol mg	Sodium mg	Carbohydrates g	Dietary fiber g	Sugars g	Protein g	Vitamin A % DV	Vitamin C % DV	Calcium % DV	Iron % DV
parmesan — *½ cup*	129	120	30	3.5	1	<5	570	18	3	13	4	25	15	8	6
roasted garlic — *½ cup*	129	120	25	3	0	0	570	21	3	15	2	15	8	6	6
sauteed beef — *½ cup*	129	120	35	4	1	<5	530	18	3	13	3	20	15	4	8
sauteed onion & mushroom — *½ cup*	129	110	30	3.5	0.5	0	540	17	3	12	2	20	6	4	6
seven-herb tomato — *½ cup*	129	110	25	3	0.5	0	580	18	3	12	3	20	4	4	8
spicy red pepper — *½ cup*	129	110	15	1.5	0	0	510	21	3	14	2	25	15	4	8
Ragu Light															
chunky garden combination — *½ cup*	126	50	0	0	0	0	390	11	3	9	2	20	8	2	8
chunky mushroom — *½ cup*	126	50	0	0	0	0	390	11	2	8	3	20	4	2	8
tomato & basil — *½ cup*	126	50	0	0	0	0	390	11	2	9	2	20	6	2	8
tomato & basil, no sugar added — *½ cup*	125	60	15	1.5	0	0	390	9	3	5	3	20	4	4	8
Ragu Old-World Style															
marinara — *½ cup*	125	80	40	4.5	1	0	820	9	3	7	2	20	2	4	6
meat-flavored — *½ cup*	125	80	30	3.5	1	<5	820	9	3	7	2	20	2	4	6
traditional or mushroom — *½ cup*	125	80	25	3	0.5	0	820	10	3	7	2	20	2	4	6
Ragu															
alfredo — *¼ cup*	61	110	90	10	6	40	430	3	0	1	2	10	0	6	0
Pasta Toss, herbs & olive oil — *½ cup*	125	120	70	8	1	0	900	11	2	8	2	15	10	8	6
traditional italian cooking sauce — *½ cup*	124	60	20	2	0	0	550	8	3	5	2	20	0	6	8
Weight Watchers Pasta Sauce w/ Mushrooms — *½ cup*	n/a	60	0	0	0	0	420	11	4	6	2	10	25	0	6

Pastries

	Weight g	Calories	Calories from fat	Total fat g	Sat. fat g	Cholesterol mg	Sodium mg	Carbohydrates g	Dietary fiber g	Sugars g	Protein g	Vitamin A % DV	Vitamin C % DV	Calcium % DV	Iron % DV
Entenmann's Doughnuts															
caramel rich frosted — *1 donut*	60	280	160	18	5	10	220	30	<1	19	3	0	0	6	6
glazed — *1 donut*	60	260	120	14	3	15	250	32	<1	19	3	0	0	6	2

	Weight g	Calories	Calories from fat	Total fat g	Sat. fat g	Cholesterol mg	Sodium mg	Carbohydrates g	Dietary fiber g	Sugars g	Protein g	Vitamin A % DV	Vitamin C % DV	Calcium % DV	Iron % DV
glazed popems — *4 pieces*	51	210	90	10	2.5	15	190	29	<1	19	2	0	0	6	2
red glazed donuts, 50% less fat — *1 donut*	64	220	50	6	1.5	15	270	40	<1	28	2	0	0	10	4
Entenmann's Hot Cross Buns — *1 bun*	66	230	70	7	2	20	170	38	2	20	4	0	4	4	2
Morton Honey Buns (frozen) — *1 bun*	258	250	90	10	2.5	0	160	35	2	16	3	0	0	0	8
Pepperidge Farm Cinnamon Roll (frozen) — *1 roll*	64	250	100	12	2.5	15	220	33	2	15	4	0	0	4	8
Pepperidge Farm Danish (frozen)															
apple — *1 danish*	65	210	80	9	2.5	15	190	29	2	15	4	0	0	4	6
cheese — *1 danish*	65	230	100	11	3.5	55	230	25	1	8	6	0	0	6	8
Pepperidge Farm Pastries (frozen)															
apple dumplings — *1 dumpling*	85	290	100	11	2.5	0	160	44	3	6	3	0	4	4	6
apple turnover w/ vanilla icing — *1 turnover*	96	330	130	14	3	0	190	53	2	10	4	0	0	4	8
apple turnovers — *1 turnover*	91	330	130	14	3	0	180	48	6	5	4	0	0	4	8
cherry turnovers — *1 turnover*	89	320	120	13	3	0	190	46	6	6	4	0	4	0	8
milk chocolate clouds — *2 pastries*	121	580	340	38	15	55	400	54	3	25	6	0	0	6	20
raspberry turnovers w/ vanilla icing — *1 turnover*	96	360	130	14	3	0	190	53	3	10	4	0	4	0	8
Pillsbury Sweet Rolls (refrigerated)															
apple cinnamon rolls w/ icing — *1 roll*	44	150	50	6	1.5	0	320	23	<1	10	2	0	0	0	4
caramel — *1 roll*	49	170	60	7	1.5	0	330	24	<1	10	2	0	0	0	6
cinnamon raisin rolls w/ icing — *1 roll*	49	170	50	6	1.5	0	320	26	<1	12	2	0	0	0	6
cinnamon rolls w/ icing — *1 roll*	44	150	50	6	1.5	0	340	23	0	10	2	0	0	0	4
cinnamon rolls w/ icing, reduced-fat — *1 roll*	44	140	35	4	1	0	340	24	0	9	2	0	0	0	4
orange sweet rolls w/ icing — *1 roll*	49	170	60	7	1.5	0	330	25	<1	10	2	0	0	0	6
Pillsbury Turnovers (refrigerated)															
apple — *2 turnovers*	113	350	150	17	3.5	0	650	46	1	23	4	0	0	0	8

	Weight g	Calories	Calories from fat	Total fat g	Sat. fat g	Cholesterol mg	Sodium mg	Carbohydrates g	Dietary fiber g	Sugars g	Protein g	Vitamin A % DV	Vitamin C % DV	Calcium % DV	Iron % DV
cherry — *2 turnovers*	113	360	150	17	3.5	0	640	48	<1	25	4	4	0	0	8
Sara Lee Deluxe Cinnamon Rolls (frozen) — *1 roll w/ icing*	76	370	140	15	9	40	300	53	1	30	5	6	0	2	6
Weight Watchers Cinnamon Rolls, glazed (frozen) — *1 roll*	59	200	45	5	1.5	5	200	33	2	10	4	0	0	4	4

Pie Crusts

	Weight g	Calories	Calories from fat	Total fat g	Sat. fat g	Cholesterol mg	Sodium mg	Carbohydrates g	Dietary fiber g	Sugars g	Protein g	Vitamin A % DV	Vitamin C % DV	Calcium % DV	Iron % DV
Betty Crocker Pie Crust Mix — *⅛ of 9" crust*	n/a	110	70	8	2	0	150	9	0	0	1	0	0	0	2
Flako Pie Crust Mix — *¼ cup (unprepared)*	25	128	72	8	3	7	170	13	<1	<1	2	0	0	0	0
Mrs. Smith's Shells															
9 ⅝-inch crust — *⅛ crust*	28	120	60	6	1	0	110	14	0	1	1	n/a	n/a	n/a	n/a
9-inch, deep — *⅛ crust*	27	110	60	7	1.5	0	105	12	0	1	1	n/a	n/a	n/a	n/a
9-inch, reduced-fat — *⅛ crust*	27	100	50	5	1	0	95	13	0	1	1	n/a	n/a	n/a	n/a
9-inch, shallow — *⅛ crust*	18	70	40	4	1	0	70	8	0	1	1	n/a	n/a	n/a	n/a
Pet-Ritz Pie Crust															
⅝-inch extra large — *⅛ crust*	27	110	50	6	2.5	5	95	14	0	2	1	0	0	0	0
9-inch — *⅛ crust*	18	80	35	4	1.5	<5	65	9	0	1	<1	0	0	0	0
deep-dish — *⅛ crust*	21	90	45	5	2	<5	80	11	0	0	1	0	0	0	0
savory, 9-inch — *⅛ crust*	19	80	40	4.5	1	0	70	10	0	0	1	0	0	0	0
savory, deep-dish — *⅛ crust*	21	90	45	5	1	0	80	11	0	0	1	0	0	0	0
Pillsbury All Ready Pie Crust — *⅛ crust*	27	120	60	7	3	5	100	13	0	<1	<1	0	0	0	0

Pies & Cobblers

	Weight g	Calories	Calories from fat	Total fat g	Sat. fat g	Cholesterol mg	Sodium mg	Carbohydrates g	Dietary fiber g	Sugars g	Protein g	Vitamin A % DV	Vitamin C % DV	Calcium % DV	Iron % DV
Banquet Cream Pies															
banana — *⅓ pie*	n/a	350	190	21	5	<5	290	39	<1	28	3	0	0	4	2
chocolate — *⅓ pie*	n/a	360	180	20	5	<5	240	43	3	33	3	0	0	4	6
coconut — *⅓ pie*	n/a	350	180	20	6	<5	250	39	2	30	3	0	0	4	2
lemon — *⅓ pie*	n/a	360	180	20	5	<5	240	43	2	31	3	0	0	4	2

	Weight *g*	Calories	Calories from fat	Total fat *g*	Sat. fat *g*	Cholesterol *mg*	Sodium *mg*	Carbohydrates *g*	Dietary fiber *g*	Sugars *g*	Protein *g*	Vitamin A *% DV*	Vitamin C *% DV*	Calcium *% DV*	Iron *% DV*
Banquet Fruit Pies															
apple — *1/5 pie*	n/a	300	120	13	6	5	370	41	2	22	3	0	0	0	6
cherry — *1/5 pie*	n/a	290	120	14	6	5	310	39	2	14	3	4	0	0	2
peach — *1/5 pie*	n/a	260	110	12	5	5	340	36	2	17	3	0	10	0	2
Entenmann's Homestyle Apple Pie — *1/6 pie*	123	300	130	14	4	0	310	43	2	17	2	0	0	0	0
Marie Callender's Cobblers (frozen)															
apple — *1/4 cobbler*	120	350	160	18	4	0	170	45	2	26	2	2	70	0	8
berry — *1/4 cobbler*	120	390	170	19	5	<5	170	41	1	29	3	0	6	2	10
blueberry — *1/4 cobbler*	120	340	160	18	4	0	220	42	2	17	3	0	2	0	6
cherry — *1/4 cobbler*	120	390	170	19	5	<5	100	50	0	28	3	0	8	0	6
peach — *1/4 cobbler*	120	370	160	18	3	0	170	47	0	24	3	0	6	0	6
Mrs. Smith's 8-Inch Pies (frozen)															
apple — *1/6 pie*	123	270	100	11	2	0	300	41	1	18	2	n/a	n/a	n/a	n/a
apple, reduced-fat — *1/6 pie*	123	250	70	8	1.5	0	290	43	1	18	2	n/a	n/a	n/a	n/a
apple, reduced-fat, no-sugar-added — *1/6 pie*	123	210	70	8	1.5	0	290	32	2	6	2	n/a	n/a	n/a	n/a
banana cream — *1/4 pie*	108	280	130	14	4	0	170	37	1	25	2	n/a	n/a	n/a	n/a
berry — *1/6 pie*	123	280	100	11	2	0	340	44	0	21	2	n/a	n/a	n/a	n/a
boston cream — *1/8 pie*	69	170	50	5	1.5	25	140	29	0	19	2	n/a	n/a	n/a	n/a
cherry — *1/6 pie*	123	270	100	11	2	0	320	41	1	19	2	n/a	n/a	n/a	n/a
cherry, reduced-fat — *1/6 pie*	123	250	70	8	1.5	0	310	44	1	19	2	n/a	n/a	n/a	n/a
cherry, reduced-fat, no-sugar-added — *1/6 pie*	123	220	70	8	1.5	0	310	35	1	5	3	n/a	n/a	n/a	n/a
hearty pumpkin — *1/5 pie*	147	280	90	10	3	60	350	46	2	26	5	n/a	n/a	n/a	n/a
key lime — *1/5 pie*	125	380	130	14	5	15	240	58	0	45	5	n/a	n/a	n/a	n/a
peach — *1/6 pie*	123	260	100	11	2	0	310	38	1	17	2	n/a	n/a	n/a	n/a

	Weight *g*	Calories	Calories from fat	Total fat *g*	Sat. fat *g*	Cholesterol *mg*	Sodium *mg*	Carbohydrates *g*	Dietary fiber *g*	Sugars *g*	Protein *g*	Vitamin A *% DV*	Vitamin C *% DV*	Calcium *% DV*	Iron *% DV*
pecan — *⅙ pie*	136	520	210	23	4	70	450	73	1	45	5	n/a	n/a	n/a	n/a
Sara Lee Homestyle Pie															
apple — *⅛ pie*	131	340	140	16	3.5	0	310	46	1	26	3	<2	2	<2	6
apple, reduced-fat — *⅙ pie*	128	290	70	8	1.5	<5	400	51	2	16	4	<2	0	2	10
blueberry — *⅛ pie*	131	360	130	15	3.5	0	340	54	2	26	3	<2	4	<2	6
cherry — *⅛ pie*	131	330	130	15	3.5	0	290	46	2	27	3	8	<2	<2	6
chocolate cream pie — *⅕ pie*	136	500	280	32	16	<5	440	49	2	35	4	<2	0	4	10
coconut cream — *⅕ pie*	136	480	280	31	14	0	430	47	2	35	4	<2	0	4	6
dutch apple — *⅛ pie*	131	350	130	15	3	0	320	53	2	30	3	<2	2	<2	8
lemon meringue — *⅙ pie*	142	350	100	11	2.5	0	460	59	5	42	2	<2	0	<2	8
mince, 9-inch — *⅛ pie*	131	390	160	17	4	0	450	56	3	30	3	<2	4	2	8
peach — *⅛ pie*	131	330	120	13	3	0	250	50	2	30	3	4	35	<2	8
pecan, 9-inch — *⅛ pie*	121	520	220	24	4.5	45	480	70	3	28	5	<2	<2	2	6
pumpkin, 9-inch — *⅛ pie*	131	260	100	11	2.5	30	460	37	2	18	4	15	0	6	8
raspberry — *⅛ pie*	131	380	170	19	4.5	<5	330	48	2	20	3	<2	8	<2	8
Weight Watchers Frozen Desserts Mississippi Mud Pie — *1 pie*	69	160	45	5	1.5	5	120	24	0	13	4	2	0	8	4

Pizza, Frozen

	Weight *g*	Calories	Calories from fat	Total fat *g*	Sat. fat *g*	Cholesterol *mg*	Sodium *mg*	Carbohydrates *g*	Dietary fiber *g*	Sugars *g*	Protein *g*	Vitamin A *% DV*	Vitamin C *% DV*	Calcium *% DV*	Iron *% DV*
Empire Kosher															
bagel pizza — *1 bagel*	83	100	30	3	1.5	10	170	14	1	1	5	4	8	10	6
english muffin pizza — *1 muffin*	57	130	45	5	2.5	15	390	15	1	2	7	4	2	20	4
three cheese pizza — *4 oz*	112	220	35	4	2	10	240	37	1	1	9	6	8	8	15
Healthy Choice Meals to Go															
pepperoni — *1 pizza*	170	340	45	5	1.5	20	510	49	6	5	24	6	0	30	30
sausage — *1 pizza*	170	300	25	3	1	25	500	48	5	5	21	4	0	15	15

	Weight g	Calories	Calories from fat	Total fat g	Sat. fat g	Cholesterol mg	Sodium mg	Carbohydrates g	Dietary fiber g	Sugars g	Protein g	Vitamin A % DV	Vitamin C % DV	Calcium % DV	Iron % DV
supreme — *1 pizza*	181	310	25	3	1	20	500	51	6	5	21	8	0	15	20
vegetable — *1 pizza*	170	270	20	2.5	1	10	370	45	5	5	17	4	0	30	15
Healthy Choice Meals to Go French Bread Pizza, Cheese — *1 pizza*	170	320	25	3	1	5	410	51	7	4	22	4	0	40	25
Jeno's Crisp 'N Tasty Pizza															
canadian-style bacon — *1 pizza*	195	430	160	18	3.5	10	1150	49	2	6	17	0	0	20	8
cheese — *1 pizza*	195	450	170	19	6	20	870	51	2	6	19	0	0	35	8
combination — *1 pizza*	198	520	250	28	7	25	1120	49	3	5	17	0	0	20	8
hamburger — *1 pizza*	206	500	230	25	6	25	1090	49	3	5	19	0	0	20	10
pepperoni — *1 pizza*	192	500	230	26	6	25	1170	49	2	5	17	0	0	20	8
sausage — *1 pizza*	198	510	240	27	6	20	1070	49	3	5	17	0	0	20	8
supreme — *1 pizza*	204	520	250	28	7	25	1120	49	3	5	17	0	0	20	8
three meat — *1 pizza*	198	500	230	26	6	25	1180	48	2	5	18	0	0	20	8
Jeno's Pizza, Microwave For One															
cheese — *1 pizza*	104	240	100	11	3.5	15	530	25	1	3	10	0	0	20	10
combination — *1 pizza*	119	310	160	18	4.5	15	720	25	1	3	11	0	0	15	10
pepperoni — *1 pizza*	113	280	140	16	3.5	15	710	25	1	3	10	0	0	15	10
sausage — *1 pizza*	116	280	140	16	4	10	650	25	1	3	10	0	0	15	10
Pappalo's Deep Dish Pizza															
four meat — *1⁄5 pizza*	128	330	120	13	5	25	690	37	2	3	15	0	0	15	15
pepperoni — *1⁄5 pizza*	126	340	130	14	6	30	700	37	2	3	16	0	0	20	15
sausage — *1⁄5 pizza*	129	330	130	14	6	25	640	37	2	3	15	0	0	20	15
sausage & pepperoni — *1⁄5 pizza*	129	340	130	14	6	25	670	37	2	3	16	0	0	20	15
supreme — *1⁄5 pizza*	139	350	140	15	6	30	700	38	2	3	16	0	0	20	15
three cheese — *1⁄4 pizza*	150	370	110	12	6	25	660	46	2	3	19	0	0	30	15

	Weight g	Calories	Calories from fat	Total fat g	Sat. fat g	Cholesterol mg	Sodium mg	Carbohydrates g	Dietary fiber g	Sugars g	Protein g	Vitamin A % DV	Vitamin C % DV	Calcium % DV	Iron % DV
Pappalo's Pizza For One															
pepperoni — *1 pizza*	199	520	230	25	10	55	1190	48	3	4	26	0	0	35	20
sausage & pepperoni — *1 pizza*	204	530	240	27	12	50	1130	48	3	4	24	0	0	35	20
supreme — *1 pizza*	215	520	230	26	12	50	1140	48	3	4	24	0	0	35	20
three cheese — *1 pizza*	204	500	180	20	10	45	960	50	3	4	19	0	0	50	15
Pappalo's Pizzeria Style Crust (12 inch)															
four meat — *¼ pizza*	143	380	140	16	7	35	840	40	1	2	18	0	0	25	15
pepperoni — *¼ pizza*	140	390	150	17	7	35	820	40	1	1	19	0	0	30	15
sausage — *¼ pizza*	144	380	150	17	8	30	760	40	1	2	17	0	0	25	15
sausage & pepperoni — *¼ pizza*	145	390	160	18	8	35	810	40	1	1	17	0	0	25	15
supreme — *¼ pizza*	155	390	150	17	8	35	810	41	2	2	17	0	0	25	15
three cheese — *¼ pizza*	135	340	110	12	6	30	640	40	1	2	18	0	0	35	15
Pepperidge Farm Croissant Crust Pizza															
cheese — *1 pizza*	125	390	180	20	7	90	770	39	6	11	12	6	4	20	10
deluxe — *1 pizza*	144	450	240	27	10	85	910	40	7	12	14	4	2	20	15
pepperoni — *1 pizza*	130	420	200	23	9	90	810	39	5	8	15	6	6	15	10
Tombstone Double Top															
pepperoni w/ double cheese — *⅙ pizza*	129	350	180	20	10	45	850	25	2	5	19	10	10	35	6
sausage & pepperoni w/ double cheese — *⅙ pizza*	135	360	180	20	10	45	800	25	2	5	20	10	10	40	6
sausage w/ double cheese — *⅙ pizza*	135	350	170	19	10	40	740	25	2	5	20	10	10	40	8
Tombstone For One															
cheese & pepperoni — *1 pizza*	198	580	320	35	15	50	1170	41	3	8	25	20	15	40	10
extra cheese — *1 pizza*	198	540	270	30	14	45	910	41	3	8	27	25	15	60	8
italian sausage — *1 pizza*	201	560	300	33	14	55	1130	40	3	7	25	20	10	40	10

	Weight g	Calories	Calories from fat	Total fat g	Sat. fat g	Cholesterol mg	Sodium mg	Carbohydrates g	Dietary fiber g	Sugars g	Protein g	Vitamin A % DV	Vitamin C % DV	Calcium % DV	Iron % DV
sausage & pepperoni — *1 pizza*	200	590	330	37	15	55	1200	40	3	8	25	20	15	40	10
supreme — *1 pizza*	215	570	310	34	14	50	1130	41	3	8	24	25	25	40	10
Tombstone For One, ½ Less Fat															
cheese — *1 pizza*	184	360	90	10	4.5	15	920	45	3	8	23	15	6	35	6
pepperoni — *1 pizza*	192	400	120	13	5	35	1040	45	4	8	26	20	4	30	10
supreme — *1 pizza*	219	400	110	13	5	35	1090	45	4	9	27	25	4	30	10
vegetable — *1 pizza*	206	360	90	10	4	15	730	46	5	8	22	30	6	30	10
Tombstone Light															
supreme — *⅕ pizza*	138	270	80	9	3.5	20	710	30	2	7	25	20	10	40	10
vegetable — *⅕ pizza*	131	240	60	7	2.5	10	500	31	3	7	25	20	10	40	10
Tombstone original (12 inch)															
cheese & hamburger — *⅕ pizza*	125	320	150	16	8	30	660	29	2	5	15	10	10	25	8
cheese & pepperoni — *⅕ pizza*	125	340	160	18	8	35	750	29	2	5	15	10	10	25	6
cheese & sausage — *⅕ pizza*	125	320	150	16	8	30	650	29	2	5	15	10	10	25	8
deluxe — *⅕ pizza*	134	320	140	16	7	30	640	29	2	5	15	10	15	25	8
extra cheese — *¼ pizza*	145	370	150	17	9	30	680	36	2	6	18	15	15	35	6
sausage & pepperoni — *⅕ pizza*	125	340	160	18	8	35	740	29	2	5	16	10	10	25	8
Tombstone original (9 inch)															
cheese & pepperoni — *⅓ pizza*	118	340	170	19	8	30	740	28	2	4	15	10	10	20	6
cheese & sausage — *⅓ pizza*	118	310	140	16	7	30	610	28	2	5	14	10	10	20	6
deluxe — *⅓ pizza*	129	320	150	16	7	30	620	28	2	5	15	15	15	20	6
extra cheese — *½ pizza*	160	420	170	19	9	30	730	42	3	7	20	15	15	35	8
pepperoni & sausage — *⅓ pizza*	125	360	190	21	9	35	820	28	2	5	16	10	10	20	8

	Weight g	Calories	Calories from fat	Total fat g	Sat. fat g	Cholesterol mg	Sodium mg	Carbohydrates g	Dietary fiber g	Sugars g	Protein g	Vitamin A % DV	Vitamin C % DV	Calcium % DV	Iron % DV
Tombstone Special Order (12 inch)															
four cheese — *1/5 pizza*	149	400	170	19	10	40	760	37	2	6	20	15	10	40	6
pepperoni — *1/6 pizza*	128	360	170	19	9	40	790	31	2	5	16	10	10	25	6
super supreme — *1/6 pizza*	138	350	160	18	9	40	800	31	2	5	17	15	15	25	6
three sausage — *1/6 pizza*	131	340	150	17	8	35	740	31	2	5	16	10	10	25	6
Tombstone Special Order (9 inch)															
pepperoni — *1/3 pizza*	144	400	190	21	10	45	880	35	2	5	19	15	10	30	8
super supreme — *1/3 pizza*	156	400	180	21	10	45	900	36	2	6	19	15	15	30	8
three sausage — *1/3 pizza*	147	390	170	19	9	40	830	35	2	6	19	15	10	30	8
Tombstone Thin Crust															
italian-style, four meat combo — *1/4 pizza*	146	410	230	25	12	50	940	25	2	5	20	15	10	35	8
italian-style, italian sausage — *1/4 pizza*	146	400	220	24	11	50	880	25	2	5	19	15	8	35	6
italian-style, pepperoni — *1/4 pizza*	142	420	240	27	13	55	950	25	2	5	20	15	8	35	8
italian-style, supreme — *1/4 pizza*	151	400	220	24	11	45	880	26	2	5	18	20	10	30	8
italian-style, three cheese — *1/4 pizza*	138	380	200	22	12	45	730	25	2	5	20	20	8	45	4
mexican-style, supreme taco — *1/4 pizza*	145	380	210	23	11	50	850	26	2	5	16	25	15	25	8
Totino's Microwave Pizza For One															
cheese — *1 pizza*	104	240	100	11	3.5	15	530	25	1	3	10	0	0	20	10
combination — *1 pizza*	119	310	160	18	4.5	15	720	25	1	3	11	0	0	15	10
pepperoni — *1 pizza*	113	280	140	16	3.5	15	710	25	1	3	10	0	0	15	10
sausage — *1 pizza*	116	280	140	16	4	10	650	25	1	3	10	0	0	15	10
supreme — *1 pizza*	121	290	150	17	4	15	680	25	2	3	10	0	0	15	10
Totino's Party Pizza															
bacon burger — *1/2 pizza*	149	380	190	21	5	15	870	33	2	4	15	0	0	20	10

	Weight *g*	Calories	Calories from fat	Total fat *g*	Sat. fat *g*	Cholesterol *mg*	Sodium *mg*	Carbohydrates *g*	Dietary fiber *g*	Sugars *g*	Protein *g*	Vitamin A *% DV*	Vitamin C *% DV*	Calcium *% DV*	Iron *% DV*
canadian-style bacon — *½ pizza*	147	320	140	15	2.5	10	900	33	2	4	14	0	0	25	10
cheese — *½ pizza*	139	320	130	14	5	20	630	33	2	4	15	0	0	30	10
combination — *½ pizza*	152	390	190	21	4.5	20	910	34	2	4	15	0	0	25	10
hamburger — *½ pizza*	155	370	180	20	4.5	15	850	33	2	4	15	0	0	25	10
pepperoni — *½ pizza*	145	380	190	21	5	20	920	33	2	4	14	0	0	25	10
sausage — *½ pizza*	153	380	180	20	4.5	15	870	34	2	4	15	0	0	25	10
supreme — *½ pizza*	155	380	180	20	4.5	20	890	34	2	4	15	0	0	25	10
three meat — *½ pizza*	149	360	170	19	4	15	910	33	2	4	15	0	0	25	10
zesty italiano — *½ pizza*	152	390	190	21	4.5	20	900	35	2	4	15	0	0	25	10
zesty mexican-style — *½ pizza*	155	370	170	19	4.5	15	750	34	2	3	15	0	0	25	10
Totino's Party Pizza, Family Size															
cheese — *⅓ pizza*	160	360	140	16	6	20	720	38	2	5	16	0	0	30	10
combination — *¼ pizza*	125	300	140	16	3.5	15	740	28	1	3	12	0	0	20	10
pepperoni — *⅓ pizza*	160	410	200	22	5	20	1000	37	2	4	15	0	0	25	10
sausage — *¼ pizza*	128	300	140	16	3.5	10	720	28	2	3	15	0	0	20	10
Totino's Pizza Rolls															
combination — *6 rolls*	85	220	100	11	3	25	410	22	1	2	8	0	0	6	4
hamburger & cheese — *6 rolls*	85	200	80	9	2.5	20	400	22	1	3	6	0	0	6	6
pepperoni & cheese — *6 rolls*	85	230	110	12	3	25	470	22	1	3	8	0	0	6	6
sausage & cheese — *6 rolls*	85	210	90	10	2.5	20	320	22	1	3	8	0	0	6	6
sausage & mushrooms — *6 rolls*	85	200	80	9	2	15	410	23	1	3	7	0	0	6	6
spicy italian-style — *6 rolls*	85	220	100	11	3	25	410	22	1	2	8	0	0	6	8
supreme — *6 rolls*	85	210	80	9	2	20	290	23	1	3	8	0	0	6	4
three cheese — *6 rolls*	85	200	70	8	3	20	330	24	1	4	8	0	0	15	4

	Weight g	Calories	Calories from fat	Total fat g	Sat. fat g	Cholesterol mg	Sodium mg	Carbohydrates g	Dietary fiber g	Sugars g	Protein g	Vitamin A % DV	Vitamin C % DV	Calcium % DV	Iron % DV
three meat — *6 rolls*	85	210	90	10	2.5	20	380	22	1	3	8	0	0	6	4
Totino's Select Pizza															
sausage & pepperoni — *1/3 pizza*	142	360	170	19	7	30	780	30	2	3	17	0	0	25	10
supreme — *1/3 pizza*	156	360	170	19	7	35	810	31	2	4	17	0	0	25	10
three cheese — *1/3 pizza*	126	300	130	14	6	20	610	30	1	4	14	0	0	30	10
two cheese & canadian-style bacon — *1/3 pizza*	138	310	130	14	5	30	770	30	1	4	16	0	0	25	10
two cheese & pepperoni — *1/3 pizza*	136	360	180	20	7	35	810	30	1	3	16	0	0	25	10
two cheese & sausage — *1/3 pizza*	143	360	170	19	7	30	760	31	2	3	17	0	0	25	10
Weight Watchers Pizza															
deluxe combo — *1 entrée*	186	380	100	11	3.5	40	550	47	6	4	23	15	8	50	20
extra cheese — *1 entrée*	163	390	100	12	4	35	590	49	6	3	23	8	10	70	10
pepperoni — *1 entrée*	158	390	100	12	4	45	650	46	4	3	23	8	8	45	10

Popcorn: Microwave

	Weight g	Calories	Calories from fat	Total fat g	Sat. fat g	Cholesterol mg	Sodium mg	Carbohydrates g	Dietary fiber g	Sugars g	Protein g	Vitamin A % DV	Vitamin C % DV	Calcium % DV	Iron % DV
Newman's Own															
butter-flavored — *3 1/2 cups*	30	170	100	11	2	0	180	16	3	0	2	0	0	0	4
butter-flavored, light — *3 1/2 cups*	30	110	30	3	1	0	90	20	3	0	2	0	0	0	4
natural-flavored — *3 1/2 cups*	30	170	100	11	2	0	180	16	3	0	2	0	0	0	4
Pop-Secret															
butter — *1 cup*	7	35	20	2.5	0.5	0	50	4	<1	0	<1	0	0	0	0
butter, 94% fat-free — *1 cup*	5	20	0	0	0	0	40	4	<1	0	<1	0	0	0	0
butter, jumbo pop — *1 cup*	7	40	25	2.5	0.5	0	55	4	<1	0	<1	0	0	0	0
butter, jumbo pop, movie theatre — *1 cup*	7	40	25	2.5	0.5	0	55	4	<1	0	<1	0	0	0	0
butter, light — *1 cup*	5	25	10	1	0	0	35	4	<1	0	<1	0	0	0	0
butter, movie theatre — *1 cup*	7	40	25	3	0.5	0	55	3	<1	0	<1	0	0	0	0

	Weight g	Calories	Calories from fat	Total fat g	Sat. fat g	Cholesterol mg	Sodium mg	Carbohydrates g	Dietary fiber g	Sugars g	Protein g	Vitamin A % DV	Vitamin C % DV	Calcium % DV	Iron % DV
butter, movie theatre, light — *1 cup*	5	25	10	1	0	0	45	4	<1	0	<1	0	0	0	0
cheddar cheese — *1 cup*	6	30	20	2	0.5	0	45	3	<1	0	<1	0	0	0	0
nacho cheese — *1 cup*	6	30	20	2	0.5	0	50	3	<1	0	<1	0	0	0	0
natural — *1 cup*	7	35	20	2.5	0.5	0	65	4	<1	0	<1	0	0	0	0
natural, 94% fat-free — *1 cup*	5	20	0	0	0	0	40	4	<1	0	<1	0	0	0	0
natural, light — *1 cup*	5	25	10	1	0	0	45	4	<1	0	<1	0	0	0	0
real butter — *1 cup*	7	35	25	2.5	0.5	0	60	4	<1	0	<1	0	0	0	0

Popcorn: Ready-to-eat

	Weight g	Calories	Calories from fat	Total fat g	Sat. fat g	Cholesterol mg	Sodium mg	Carbohydrates g	Dietary fiber g	Sugars g	Protein g	Vitamin A % DV	Vitamin C % DV	Calcium % DV	Iron % DV
Cape Cod, White Cheddar Cheese — *2 ⅓ cups*	30	170	110	12	2.5	8	270	13	2	2	4	2	0	6	2
Cracker Jack															
butter toffee — *⅔ cup*	28	130	45	5	1.5	5	150	21	1	15	1	4	0	0	0
butter toffee, fat-free — *1 cup*	28	110	0	0	0	0	95	26	<1	17	<1	0	2	0	0
nutty deluxe — *½ cup*	28	130	50	6	2	5	135	19	<1	13	1	4	0	0	0
original — *⅔ cup*	28	120	20	2.5	0.5	0	90	23	1	15	2	0	0	2	2
original, fat-free — *1 cup*	28	110	0	0	0	0	85	26	<1	15	<1	0	0	0	2
Crunch 'N Munch															
butter toffee w/ peanuts — *⅔ cup*	31	140	35	4	1	5	160	24	<1	17	2	0	0	0	0
caramel w/ peanuts — *⅔ cup*	32	140	30	3.5	1	10	105	25	1	15	2	0	0	0	0
toffee, fat-free — *¾ cup*	28	110	0	0	0	0	190	26	<1	15	<1	0	0	0	0
Healthy Choice															
butter-flavor — *1 cup*	38	20	0	0	0	0	35	5	<1	n/a	n/a	0	n/a	n/a	0
natural-flavor — *1 cup*	38	20	0	0	0	0	35	5	<1	n/a	<1	0	n/a	n/a	0
Weight Watchers															
caramel — *1 bag*	26	100	10	1	0	0	45	22	1	11	1	0	0	0	4

	Weight g	Calories	Calories from fat	Total fat g	Sat. fat g	Cholesterol mg	Sodium mg	Carbohydrates g	Dietary fiber g	Sugars g	Protein g	Vitamin A % DV	Vitamin C % DV	Calcium % DV	Iron % DV
white cheddar cheese — *1 bag*	19	90	35	4	1	0	125	12	2	0	2	0	0	0	2

Potato Mixes

	Weight g	Calories	Calories from fat	Total fat g	Sat. fat g	Cholesterol mg	Sodium mg	Carbohydrates g	Dietary fiber g	Sugars g	Protein g	Vitamin A % DV	Vitamin C % DV	Calcium % DV	Iron % DV
Betty Crocker Potato Mix, Potato Buds															
cheddar cheese — *⅔ cup*	n/a	190	90	10	2	<5	580	23	1	2	3	6	0	4	2
original — *⅔ cup*	n/a	160	70	8	1.5	<5	460	19	1	2	3	6	0	2	2
sour cream 'n chive — *⅔ cup*	n/a	190	100	11	2.5	<5	560	23	1	2	3	6	0	4	2
Betty Crocker Potato Shakers															
cheddar, zesty — *⅔ cup*	n/a	140	45	5	1	<5	490	22	2	2	3	0	0	2	4
garlic — *⅔ cup*	n/a	130	35	4	0.5	0	460	23	2	1	3	2	0	0	4
original — *⅔ cup*	n/a	140	35	4	0.5	<5	560	23	2	2	3	2	0	2	6
parmesan & herb — *⅔ cup*	n/a	140	40	4	0.5	<5	490	23	2	2	3	0	0	2	4
Betty Crocker Specialty Potatoes															
au gratin — *½ cup*	n/a	130	30	3	1	<5	580	22	1	3	3	0	0	2	0
au gratin, broccoli — *½ cup*	n/a	110	25	2.5	0.5	<5	510	21	2	2	3	2	0	4	2
butter & herb — *½ cup*	n/a	160	70	8	2.5	5	510	20	1	2	3	6	0	6	2
cheddar & Bac'os — *½ cup*	n/a	120	25	3	1	<5	630	21	1	2	3	0	0	4	0
cheddar & sour cream — *½ cup*	n/a	130	25	3	1	5	580	25	1	3	3	0	0	6	2
cheddar cheese — *½ cup*	n/a	120	20	2.5	1	<5	600	21	1	2	3	2	0	6	2
cheddar, smoky — *½ cup*	n/a	120	20	2.5	1	<5	570	22	1	2	3	0	0	8	2
cheesy scalloped — *½ cup*	n/a	120	25	3	1	<5	520	20	1	3	3	2	0	6	2
hash brown — *½ cup*	n/a	200	70	8	1.5	0	590	31	2	0	3	6	0	2	4
julienne — *½ cup*	n/a	110	25	2.5	1	5	600	20	1	4	3	2	0	6	0
mashed — *½ cup*	n/a	160	70	8	2.5	10	440	19	1	2	3	6	0	6	2
ranch — *½ cup*	n/a	130	20	2	1	<5	600	25	1	3	3	2	0	6	0

	Weight g	Calories	Calories from fat	Total fat g	Sat. fat g	Cholesterol mg	Sodium mg	Carbohydrates g	Dietary fiber g	Sugars g	Protein g	Vitamin A % DV	Vitamin C % DV	Calcium % DV	Iron % DV
scalloped — *½ cup*	n/a	130	30	3	1	<5	600	23	1	3	3	2	0	6	2
scalloped & ham — *½ cup*	n/a	120	25	3	1	<5	540	21	1	2	3	2	0	4	2
sour cream & chives — *½ cup*	n/a	120	25	3	1	5	530	22	1	3	3	2	0	6	2
three cheese — *½ cup*	n/a	120	25	2.5	0.5	<5	580	23	1	2	3	0	0	4	0
white cheddar — *½ cup*	n/a	120	25	3	1	<5	540	22	1	3	3	0	0	4	0
Betty Crocker Twice-Baked Potatoes (prepared) — *⅔ cup*	n/a	210	100	11	3	85	610	22	1	6	6	8	0	8	4
Hungry Jack Mashed Potatoes															
butter-flavored — *½ cup*	n/a	150	60	7	1.5	<5	350	19	1	2	3	6	0	6	2
flakes — *½ cup*	n/a	160	60	7	1.5	<5	240	20	1	2	3	6	0	6	2
garlic-flavored — *½ cup*	n/a	150	60	7	1.5	<5	360	19	1	2	3	6	0	6	2
parsley-butter-flavored — *½ cup*	n/a	150	60	7	1.5	<5	380	19	1	2	3	6	0	6	2
sour cream & chives — *½ cup*	n/a	150	60	7	2	<5	380	19	1	2	3	6	0	6	2
Hungry Jack Potato Casserole															
cheddar & bacon — *⅛ serving*	n/a	150	40	4.5	2.5	10	540	24	2	3	3	4	2	8	2
creamy scalloped — *⅛ serving*	n/a	150	45	5	2.5	10	460	24	2	3	3	4	2	6	2
scalloped cheesy — *⅛ serving*	n/a	150	45	5	2.5	10	570	24	1	3	3	4	2	6	2
sour cream & chives — *⅛ serving*	n/a	160	50	6	3.5	15	510	23	1	3	3	6	4	6	2
Pillsbury Idaho Mashed Potatoes															
flakes — *½ cup*	n/a	150	50	6	1.5	<5	240	1	1	2	3	6	0	6	2
granules — *½ cup*	n/a	160	60	7	1.5	<5	300	22	2	2	3	6	0	6	2

Puddings & Gelatin

	Weight g	Calories	Calories from fat	Total fat g	Sat. fat g	Cholesterol mg	Sodium mg	Carbohydrates g	Dietary fiber g	Sugars g	Protein g	Vitamin A % DV	Vitamin C % DV	Calcium % DV	Iron % DV
Betty Crocker Creamy Chilled Dessert Mix															
banana cream — *⅑ of recipe*	n/a	250	90	11	3	50	430	35	0	22	4	8	0	10	0
Chocolate French Silk — *⅛ of recipe*	n/a	270	100	11	4	5	250	39	1	26	5	6	0	8	8

	Weight g	Calories	Calories from fat	Total fat g	Sat. fat g	Cholesterol mg	Sodium mg	Carbohydrates g	Dietary fiber g	Sugars g	Protein g	Vitamin A % DV	Vitamin C % DV	Calcium % DV	Iron % DV
coconut cream — *⅛ of recipe*	n/a	290	120	13	6	60	480	38	1	24	5	8	0	10	0
cookies & cream — *⅙ of recipe*	n/a	380	150	16	4	5	420	53	0	34	5	8	0	10	2
Sunkist lemon supreme — *1/9 of recipe*	n/a	320	110	13	3.5	30	140	52	0	38	2	4	0	0	0
Jell-O Brand Cook & Serve Pudding & Pie Filling															
banana cream — *½ cup*	n/a	140	20	2.5	1.5	10	240	26	0	21	4	4	0	15	0
butterscotch — *½ cup*	n/a	160	20	2.5	1.5	10	190	30	0	25	4	4	0	15	0
chocolate — *½ cup*	n/a	150	25	2.5	1.5	10	170	28	<1	21	5	4	0	15	4
vanilla — *½ cup*	n/a	140	20	2.5	1.5	10	200	26	0	21	4	4	0	15	0
Jell-O Brand Gelatin															
apricot, black cherry, or blackberry — *½ cup prepared*	n/a	80	0	0	0	0	50	19	0	19	2	0	0	0	0
cherry or cranberry — *½ cup prepared*	n/a	80	0	0	0	0	70	19	0	19	2	0	0	0	0
grape, mango, or tropical punch — *½ cup prepared*	n/a	80	0	0	0	0	45	19	0	19	2	0	0	0	0
lemon or wild strawberry — *½ cup prepared*	n/a	80	0	0	0	0	75	19	0	19	2	0	0	0	0
Jell-O Brand Gelatin Snacks — *1 snack*	99	80	0	0	0	0	45	18	0	18	1	0	0	0	0
Jell-O Brand Gelatin Sugar-Free Low-Calorie															
Berry Blue or lime — *½ cup*	n/a	10	0	0	0	0	60	0	0	0	1	0	0	0	0
cherry — *½ cup*	n/a	10	0	0	0	0	70	0	0	0	1	0	0	0	0
grape, hawaiian pineapple, or mixed fruit — *½ cup*	n/a	10	0	0	0	0	50	0	0	0	1	0	0	0	0
raspberry, strawberry, or watermelon — *½ cup*	n/a	10	0	0	0	0	55	0	0	0	1	0	0	0	0
Jell-O Brand Instant Pudding & Pie Filling															
banana cream — *½ cup*	n/a	150	20	2.5	1.5	10	410	29	0	24	4	4	0	15	0
butter pecan — *½ cup*	n/a	160	25	3	1.5	10	410	29	0	24	4	4	0	15	0
butterscotch — *½ cup*	n/a	150	20	2.5	1.5	10	450	29	0	24	4	4	0	15	0
chocolate — *½ cup*	n/a	160	25	2.5	1.5	10	470	31	<1	25	4	4	0	15	2

	Weight g	Calories	Calories from fat	Total fat g	Sat. fat g	Cholesterol mg	Sodium mg	Carbohydrates g	Dietary fiber g	Sugars g	Protein g	Vitamin A % DV	Vitamin C % DV	Calcium % DV	Iron % DV
french vanilla — *½ cup*	n/a	150	20	2.5	1.5	10	410	29	0	24	4	4	0	15	0
Jell-O Brand Pudding Snacks															
chocolate — *1 serving*	113	160	45	5	2	0	190	28	0	23	3	2	0	10	6
chocolate/vanilla swirl — *1 serving*	113	160	45	5	2	0	180	27	0	22	3	2	0	10	4
vanilla — *1 serving*	113	160	50	5	2	0	170	25	0	21	3	2	0	10	0
Jell-O Brand Pudding, Fat-Free, Sugar-Free, Reduced-Calorie															
butterscotch, instant — *½ cup*	n/a	70	0	0	0	0	400	12	0	6	4	4	0	15	0
chocolate, instant — *½ cup*	n/a	80	0	0	0	0	390	14	<1	6	5	4	0	15	4
vanilla, instant — *½ cup*	n/a	70	0	0	0	0	400	12	0	6	4	4	0	15	0
Jell-O Brand Pudding, Sugar-Free, Reduced-Calorie															
chocolate — *½ cup*	n/a	90	25	2.5	1.5	10	170	12	<1	6	5	4	0	15	6
vanilla — *½ cup*	n/a	80	20	2.5	1.5	10	170	11	0	6	4	6	0	15	0
Kraft Handi-Snacks — *1 snack*	99	80	0	0	0	0	40	20	0	20	0	0	0	0	0
My-T-Fine Pudding															
chocolate fudge — *½ cup*	22	150	25	0	0	0	140	21	1	13	<1	6	15	2	2
tapioca vanilla — *½ cup*	21	140	20	0	0	0	160	20	0	13	0	6	15	2	0
Royal Pudding															
butterscotch, instant — *½ cup*	24	150	20	0	0	0	380	22	0	18	0	6	15	2	0
chocolate, instant — *½ cup*	27	160	25	0	0	0	390	24	<1	19	0	6	15	2	2
tapioca vanilla — *½ cup*	21	140	20	0	0	0	60	20	<1	14	<1	6	15	2	0
vanilla, cook & serve — *½ cup*	19	130	20	0	0	0	160	18	0	14	0	6	15	2	0

Rice Cakes

	Weight g	Calories	Calories from fat	Total fat g	Sat. fat g	Cholesterol mg	Sodium mg	Carbohydrates g	Dietary fiber g	Sugars g	Protein g	Vitamin A % DV	Vitamin C % DV	Calcium % DV	Iron % DV
Quaker 100% Popcorn Minicakes															
butter — *6 minicakes*	14	48	0	<1	<1	0	142	11	2	<1	2	0	0	0	2

	Weight g	Calories	Calories from fat	Total fat g	Sat. fat g	Cholesterol mg	Sodium mg	Carbohydrates g	Dietary fiber g	Sugars g	Protein g	Vitamin A % DV	Vitamin C % DV	Calcium % DV	Iron % DV
caramel — *5 minicakes*	15	54	4	<1	<1	<1	70	12	1	4	1	0	0	0	0
cheddar cheese — *6 minicakes*	15	54	8	<1	<1	<1	192	11	2	<1	2	0	0	<1	2
Quaker Corn Cakes															
caramel-flavored — *1 cake*	13	50	<2	<1	<1	0	28	12	<1	4	<1	0	0	0	0
strawberry crunch — *1 cake*	13	49	<2	<1	<1	0	3	11	<1	4	<1	3	0	0	0
Quaker Corn Grain Cakes															
monterey jack — *1 cake*	10	38	3	<1	<1	<1	82	8	<1	<1	<1	0	0	<1	<1
white cheddar, mild — *1 cake*	10	38	3	<1	<1	<1	89	8	<1	<1	<1	0	0	<1	<1
Quaker Mini Rice Cakes															
apple cinnamon — *5 minicakes*	14	54	3	<1	<1	0	<1	12	<1	4	<1	0	0	0	1
caramel corn — *5 minicakes*	14	53	2	<1	<1	0	25	12	<1	3	<1	0	0	0	<1
chocolate crunch — *5 minicakes*	14	54	3	<1	<1	0	10	12	<1	3	1	0	0	0	2
white cheddar — *6 minicakes*	14	53	3	<1	<1	<1	120	11	<1	<1	1	0	0	1	1
Quaker Popcorn Cakes, Caramel — *1 cake*	13	47	<3	<1	<1	0	25	11	1	4	1	0	0	0	1
Quaker Rice Cakes															
banana nut — *1 cake*	13	50	2	<1	<1	0	44	11	<1	5	<1	0	0	0	0
chocolate crunch — *1 cake*	13	50	<3	<1	<1	0	12	11	<1	4	<1	0	0	0	2

Rice Mixes

	Weight g	Calories	Calories from fat	Total fat g	Sat. fat g	Cholesterol mg	Sodium mg	Carbohydrates g	Dietary fiber g	Sugars g	Protein g	Vitamin A % DV	Vitamin C % DV	Calcium % DV	Iron % DV
Carolina Rice Mixes															
black beans & rice — *1 cup*	n/a	200	5	1.5	0	0	850	39	6	1	8	0	0	8	15
red beans & rice — *1 cup*	n/a	190	9	1	0	0	790	40	6	1	6	10	10	4	15
saffron yellow rice — *1 cup*	n/a	190	0	0	0	0	970	43	<1	1	4	0	6	4	10
Goya Rice Mix															
mexican — *¾ cup cooked*	n/a	160	0	0	0	0	325	37	0	1	3	0	0	0	6

	Weight *g*	Calories	Calories from fat	Total fat *g*	Sat. fat *g*	Cholesterol *mg*	Sodium *mg*	Carbohydrates *g*	Dietary fiber *g*	Sugars *g*	Protein *g*	Vitamin A *% DV*	Vitamin C *% DV*	Calcium *% DV*	Iron *% DV*
yellow — *¾ cup cooked*	n/a	170	0	0	0	0	546	37	1	0	4	0	0	0	6
Lipton Rice & Sauce															
beef-flavor — *1 cup*	n/a	280	70	8	1	0	1010	48	1	1	5	6	0	2	15
cajun-style — *1 cup*	n/a	280	70	7	1	0	910	48	1	0	6	10	6	2	15
cajun-style w/ beans — *1 cup*	n/a	310	70	8	1	0	530	53	6	1	10	10	2	2	20
cheddar broccoli — *1 cup*	n/a	280	80	9	2.5	5	1010	46	1	1	7	8	8	4	10
chicken broccoli — *1 cup*	n/a	280	80	9	2	0	910	46	2	1	7	10	10	4	15
chicken flavor — *1 cup*	n/a	280	80	9	2	5	960	46	<1	1	7	6	0	2	15
mushroom — *1 cup*	n/a	270	70	8	1	0	960	46	<1	1	6	4	0	2	15
original recipe — *1 cup*	n/a	280	70	8	1	0	940	49	2	2	7	15	4	4	15
pilaf — *1 cup*	n/a	270	70	8	1	0	930	45	1	1	6	4	0	2	15
Rice Medley — *1 cup*	n/a	270	70	9	1.5	5	870	44	2	1	7	10	2	2	15
risotto, chicken & parmesan — *1 cup*	n/a	270	80	9	1.5	0	830	44	<1	0	6	6	0	2	15
scampi-style — *1 cup*	n/a	270	80	9	2	5	910	44	<1	1	6	6	0	2	15
Lipton Seasoned Rice															
oriental stir-fry — *1 cup*	n/a	270	70	7.5	1	0	860	47	1	2	5	15	4	0	15
salsa-style — *1 cup*	n/a	220	70	7	1	0	540	37	2	1	4	8	6	0	10
Mahatma Rice Mixes															
broccoli & cheese — *1 cup*	n/a	200	5	1.5	0.5	5	620	41	2	1	5	2	4	8	8
chicken — *1 cup*	n/a	190	5	0.5	0	0	970	41	1	1	5	0	0	2	10
gumbo — *1 cup*	n/a	160	25	2.5	0.5	0	720	31	1	2	3	2	2	2	10
long grain & wild — *1 cup*	n/a	190	0	0.5	0	0	710	41	2	0	5	0	0	2	10
pilaf — *1 cup*	n/a	190	0	0	0	0	820	43	<1	0	5	0	0	0	10
red beans & rice — *1 cup*	n/a	190	5	1	0	0	790	40	6	1	6	10	10	4	15

	Weight g	Calories	Calories from fat	Total fat g	Sat. fat g	Cholesterol mg	Sodium mg	Carbohydrates g	Dietary fiber g	Sugars g	Protein g	Vitamin A % DV	Vitamin C % DV	Calcium % DV	Iron % DV
Rice-A-Roni															
beef — *1 cup*	n/a	238	0	<1	<1	0	1068	52	2	3	7	5	0	2	11
beef & mushroom — *1 cup*	n/a	240	9	1	<1	<1	1148	51	2	3	7	5	6	5	12
beef flavor, ⅓ less salt — *1 cup*	n/a	242	9	1	<1	0	707	52	2	3	7	3	0	<2	11
broccoli au gratin — *1 cup*	70	269	54	6	2	4	819	47	2	4	7	3	4	7	11
broccoli au gratin, ⅓ less salt — *1 cup*	70	257	36	4	1	3	514	50	2	3	7	3	4	5	11
chicken — *1 cup*	70	240	9	1	<1	<1	981	52	2	2	7	0	1	2	11
chicken w/ mushrooms — *1 cup*	n/a	241	18	2	<1	<1	1329	50	2	2	7	0	1	2	12
chicken, ⅓ less salt — *1 cup*	n/a	244	9	1	<1	<1	644	53	1	2	7	0	1	2	11
fried rice — *1 cup*	n/a	240	18	2	<1	0	1425	51	2	5	6	0	<2	3	11
herb & butter — *1 cup*	n/a	242	9	1	<1	3	1074	53	1	2	6	8	3	5	11
pilaf — *1 cup*	n/a	240	9	1	<1	<1	1085	52	1	1	7	0	0	<2	11
risotto — *1 cup*	n/a	238	9	1	<1	<1	1442	51	2	2	6	0	0	2	11
spanish — *1 cup*	n/a	189	0	<1	<1	<1	938	41	2	1	5	5	16	3	9
stroganoff — *1 cup*	n/a	261	45	5	1	2	916	49	1	3	7	0	1	7	9
white cheddar w/ herbs — *1 cup*	n/a	263	45	5	2	6	878	48	1	4	8	3	7	3	10
yellow — *1 cup*	70	234	0	<1	<1	0	1111	54	1	<1	5	0	4	<2	11
Success Rice Mixes															
beef-flavored — *1 cup*	n/a	190	5	0.5	0	0	920	43	2	2	5	0	15	4	10
broccoli & cheese — *1 cup*	n/a	210	40	4.5	3	25	840	40	1	4	4	2	6	6	8
brown & wild — *1 cup*	n/a	190	10	1	0	0	830	40	3	1	6	8	0	2	6
classic chicken — *1 cup*	n/a	150	5	1	0	0	720	32	1	0	4	2	4	2	6
red beans & rice — *1 cup*	n/a	300	60	0.5	0	0	920	51	8	1	7	10	8	4	15

	Weight *g*	Calories	Calories from fat	Total fat *g*	Sat. fat *g*	Cholesterol *mg*	Sodium *mg*	Carbohydrates *g*	Dietary fiber *g*	Sugars *g*	Protein *g*	Vitamin A *% DV*	Vitamin C *% DV*	Calcium *% DV*	Iron *% DV*
Uncle Ben's															
brown & wild-mushroom-flavor — *2/3 cup*	n/a	140	10	1	0	0	460	31	2	1	5	0	4	2	4
long grain & wild, fast-cook — *1 cup*	n/a	200	10	1	0	5	850	42	1	0	6	0	2	4	10
long grain & wild, garden-vegetable blend — *3/4 cup*	n/a	200	15	1.5	0	0	750	41	1	2	6	20	2	2	8
long grain & wild, original — *1 cup*	n/a	190	5	0.5	0	0	630	42	1	1	6	0	4	2	10
Uncle Ben's Country Inn Recipes															
broccoli & white cheddar — *1 cup*	n/a	270	45	5	3	5	580	48	2	3	8	2	4	8	10
broccoli rice au gratin — *1 cup*	n/a	260	35	4	2	5	740	49	2	4	8	2	10	10	10
chicken stock rice — *1 cup*	n/a	260	25	3	1	5	560	50	1	1	9	0	2	4	10
chicken w/ wild rice — *1 cup*	n/a	200	10	1	0	0	570	42	1	1	6	0	0	2	8
creamy mushroom & wild rice — *1 cup*	n/a	250	25	2.5	1.5	5	700	50	1	7	8	0	0	8	10
green bean almondine — *1 cup*	n/a	260	35	4	1.5	5	550	50	2	2	8	0	4	6	10
herbed-rice au gratin — *1 cup*	n/a	260	30	3.5	1.5	5	770	51	2	5	7	0	0	8	10
homestyle chicken & vegetable — *1 cup*	n/a	270	60	6	3	15	590	47	2	2	8	2	0	4	10
tomato & herb — *1 cup*	n/a	240	10	1	0	0	900	52	1	4	6	10	30	4	10
vegetable pilaf — *1 cup*	n/a	200	10	1	0	0	610	43	1	3	5	0	6	2	8
Uncle Ben's Specialty Blends															
multigrain blend — *1 cup*	n/a	160	10	1	0	0	0	35	1	0	4	0	0	0	2
pilaf — *1 cup*	n/a	170	0	0.5	0	0	0	36	1	0	5	0	0	2	8
rice trio — *1 cup*	n/a	160	10	1	0	0	0	35	1	0	4	0	0	0	4
wild blend — *1 cup*	n/a	160	0	0.5	0	0	0	36	1	0	4	0	0	2	6

Salad Dressings

	Weight *g*	Calories	Calories from fat	Total fat *g*	Sat. fat *g*	Cholesterol *mg*	Sodium *mg*	Carbohydrates *g*	Dietary fiber *g*	Sugars *g*	Protein *g*	Vitamin A *% DV*	Vitamin C *% DV*	Calcium *% DV*	Iron *% DV*
Betty Crocker Suddenly Salad (mix)															
caesar — *3/4 cup*	n/a	220	80	9	1.5	0	580	30	1	4	5	0	0	2	8

	Weight g	Calories	Calories from fat	Total fat g	Sat. fat g	Cholesterol mg	Sodium mg	Carbohydrates g	Dietary fiber g	Sugars g	Protein g	Vitamin A % DV	Vitamin C % DV	Calcium % DV	Iron % DV
classic pasta — *¾ cup*	n/a	220	60	7	1	0	830	34	1	3	5	0	0	0	8
garden italian, 98% fat-free — *¾ cup*	n/a	140	10	1	0	0	540	29	2	4	5	15	0	2	8
ranch & bacon — *¾ cup*	n/a	320	170	19	3	15	490	31	1	3	7	15	0	2	8
Hidden Valley Ranch (mix)															
bacon — *2 Tbsp*	n/a	120	108	12	n/a	10	220	2	0	n/a	1	n/a	n/a	n/a	n/a
blue cheese — *2 Tbsp*	n/a	120	108	12	n/a	10	200	2	0	n/a	<1	n/a	n/a	n/a	n/a
honey dijon — *2 Tbsp*	n/a	120	108	12	n/a	10	210	4	0	n/a	<1	n/a	n/a	n/a	n/a
original, buttermilk — *2 Tbsp*	n/a	110	99	11	n/a	10	240	1	0	n/a	<1	n/a	n/a	n/a	n/a
original, low-fat — *2 Tbsp*	n/a	30	9	1	n/a	0	240	4	0	n/a	1	n/a	n/a	n/a	n/a
original, milk — *2 Tbsp*	n/a	120	108	12	n/a	10	210	2	0	n/a	<1	n/a	n/a	n/a	n/a
original, reduced-calorie — *2 Tbsp*	n/a	70	54	6	n/a	5	240	2	0	n/a	1	n/a	n/a	n/a	n/a
Hidden Valley Ranch, Reduced-Calorie															
ranch, italian — *2 Tbsp*	n/a	50	45	5	n/a	0	240	3	0	n/a	0	n/a	n/a	n/a	n/a
ranch, original — *2 Tbsp*	n/a	80	63	7	n/a	0	270	2	0	n/a	0	n/a	n/a	n/a	n/a
Hidden Valley Ranch, Low-Fat															
blue cheese — *2 Tbsp*	n/a	20	0	0	n/a	0	270	4	0	n/a	0	n/a	n/a	n/a	n/a
coleslaw — *2 Tbsp*	n/a	35	0	0	n/a	0	200	9	0	n/a	0	n/a	n/a	n/a	n/a
french — *2 Tbsp*	n/a	35	9	1	<1	0	210	7	0	n/a	0	n/a	n/a	n/a	n/a
honey dijon — *2 Tbsp*	n/a	35	0	n/a	n/a	0	270	7	0	n/a	1	n/a	n/a	n/a	n/a
italian parmesan — *2 Tbsp*	n/a	20	0	0	n/a	0	240	4	0	n/a	0	n/a	n/a	n/a	n/a
original — *2 Tbsp*	n/a	40	27	3	n/a	0	270	5	0	n/a	0	n/a	n/a	n/a	n/a
parmesan, creamy — *2 Tbsp*	n/a	30	0	0	n/a	0	250	5	0	n/a	1	n/a	n/a	n/a	n/a
thousand island — *2 Tbsp*	n/a	35	9	1	n/a	0	240	6	0	n/a	0	n/a	n/a	n/a	n/a

	Weight *g*	Calories	Calories from fat	Total fat *g*	Sat. fat *g*	Cholesterol *mg*	Sodium *mg*	Carbohydrates *g*	Dietary fiber *g*	Sugars *g*	Protein *g*	Vitamin A *% DV*	Vitamin C *% DV*	Calcium *% DV*	Iron *% DV*
Kraft															
bacon & tomato — *2 Tbsp*	30	140	130	14	2.5	<5	260	2	0	2	<1	0	0	0	0
caesar — *2 Tbsp*	30	130	120	13	2.5	<5	370	2	0	1	<1	0	0	2	0
coleslaw — *2 Tbsp*	32	150	110	12	2	25	420	8	0	8	0	0	0	0	0
french — *2 Tbsp*	31	120	100	12	2	0	260	4	0	4	0	10	0	0	0
garlic, creamy — *2 Tbsp*	30	110	100	11	2	0	350	2	0	2	0	0	0	0	0
honey dijon — *2 Tbsp*	31	150	130	15	2	0	200	4	0	3	0	0	0	0	0
house italian — *2 Tbsp*	30	120	110	12	2	<5	240	3	0	2	0	0	0	0	0
italian, creamy — *2 Tbsp*	30	110	100	11	4	0	230	3	0	2	0	0	0	0	0
italian, oil-free, fat-free — *2 Tbsp*	31	5	0	0	0	0	450	2	0	1	0	0	0	0	0
Presto Italian — *2 Tbsp*	30	140	130	15	2.5	0	290	2	0	2	0	0	0	0	0
ranch — *2 Tbsp*	29	170	162	18	3	5	270	2	0	1	0	0	0	0	0
ranch, buttermilk — *2 Tbsp*	29	150	140	16	3	<5	230	2	0	2	0	0	0	0	0
ranch, caesar — *2 Tbsp*	29	140	130	15	2.5	10	300	1	0	0	<1	0	0	2	0
ranch, cucumber — *2 Tbsp*	30	150	140	15	2.5	0	220	2	0	2	0	0	0	0	0
ranch, peppercorn — *2 Tbsp*	29	170	160	18	3	10	340	1	0	1	<1	0	0	2	0
ranch, sour cream & onion — *2 Tbsp*	29	170	160	18	3	10	240	1	0	1	0	0	0	0	0
russian — *2 Tbsp*	33	130	90	10	1.5	0	280	10	0	9	0	8	0	0	0
thousand island — *2 Tbsp*	31	110	90	10	1.5	10	310	5	0	5	0	0	0	0	0
Zesty Italian — *2 Tbsp*	30	110	100	11	1.5	0	530	2	0	2	0	0	0	0	0
Kraft Deliciously Right (reduced-calorie)															
bacon & tomato — *2 Tbsp*	31	60	45	5	1	<5	300	3	0	3	<1	0	0	0	0
caesar — *2 Tbsp*	31	60	50	5	1	<5	560	2	0	2	<1	0	0	2	0
french — *2 Tbsp*	32	50	30	3	0.5	0	260	6	0	5	0	10	0	0	0

	Weight g	Calories	Calories from fat	Total fat g	Sat. fat g	Cholesterol mg	Sodium mg	Carbohydrates g	Dietary fiber g	Sugars g	Protein g	Vitamin A % DV	Vitamin C % DV	Calcium % DV	Iron % DV
italian — *2 Tbsp*	31	70	60	7	1	0	240	3	0	2	0	0	0	0	0
italian, creamy — *2 Tbsp*	31	50	40	5	1	0	250	3	0	2	0	0	0	0	0
ranch — *2 Tbsp*	30	110	100	11	2	10	310	2	0	1	0	0	0	0	0
ranch, cucumber — *2 Tbsp*	31	60	45	5	1	0	450	2	0	2	0	0	0	0	0
thousand island — *2 Tbsp*	32	70	40	4	1	5	320	8	0	5	0	0	0	0	0
Kraft Free (fat-free)															
blue-cheese-flavor — *2 Tbsp*	35	50	0	0	0	0	340	12	1	3	1	0	0	0	0
Catalina — *2 Tbsp*	35	45	0	0	0	0	360	11	<1	7	0	10	0	0	0
french-style — *2 Tbsp*	35	50	0	0	0	0	300	12	<1	5	0	10	0	0	0
honey dijon — *2 Tbsp*	35	50	0	0	0	0	330	11	1	5	<1	0	0	0	2
italian — *2 Tbsp*	31	10	0	0	0	0	290	2	0	2	0	0	0	0	0
ranch — *2 Tbsp*	35	50	0	0	0	0	310	11	<1	2	<1	0	0	0	0
ranch, peppercorn — *2 Tbsp*	35	50	0	0	0	0	360	11	1	2	<1	0	0	0	0
red wine vinegar — *2 Tbsp*	32	15	0	0	0	0	400	3	0	3	0	0	0	0	0
thousand island — *2 Tbsp*	35	45	0	0	0	0	300	11	1	6	0	0	0	0	0
Newman's Own															
balsamic — *2 Tbsp*	30	90	80	9	1	0	350	3	0	1	0	0	0	0	0
caesar — *2 Tbsp*	31	150	140	16	1.5	<5	450	1	0	1	1	0	0	0	0
italian, light — *2 Tbsp*	31	20	5	0.5	0	0	380	3	0	2	0	0	0	0	0
olive oil & vinegar — *2 Tbsp*	27	150	150	16	2.5	0	150	1	0	1	0	0	0	0	0
ranch — *2 Tbsp*	29	180	170	19	3	5	170	2	0	1	1	0	0	0	0
Seven Seas															
blue cheese, chunky — *2 Tbsp*	33	90	70	7	4	10	470	5	0	3	1	0	0	2	0
caesar, creamy — *2 Tbsp*	29	140	130	15	2.5	10	300	1	0	0	<1	0	0	2	0

	Weight g	Calories	Calories from fat	Total fat g	Sat. fat g	Cholesterol mg	Sodium mg	Carbohydrates g	Dietary fiber g	Sugars g	Protein g	Vitamin A % DV	Vitamin C % DV	Calcium % DV	Iron % DV
green goddess — *2 Tbsp*	29	120	110	13	2	0	260	1	0	1	0	0	0	0	0
herbs & spices — *2 Tbsp*	30	120	110	12	2	0	320	1	0	1	0	0	0	0	0
italian, creamy — *2 Tbsp*	30	110	110	12	2	0	510	2	0	2	0	0	0	0	0
ranch — *2 Tbsp*	29	150	140	16	2.5	5	250	2	0	1	0	0	0	0	0
red wine vinegar & oil — *2 Tbsp*	31	110	100	11	2	0	510	2	0	2	0	0	0	0	0
two cheese italian — *2 Tbsp*	31	70	60	7	1	0	240	3	0	2	0	0	0	0	0
Seven Seas (reduced-calorie)															
creamy italian — *2 Tbsp*	31	60	45	5	1	0	490	2	0	2	0	0	0	0	0
italian w/ olive oil — *2 Tbsp*	31	50	40	5	1	0	450	2	0	2	0	0	0	0	0
ranch — *2 Tbsp*	31	100	80	9	1.5	0	320	5	0	1	0	0	0	0	0
red wine vinegar & oil — *2 Tbsp*	31	60	45	5	1	0	310	2	0	2	0	0	0	0	0
Viva italian — *2 Tbsp*	31	45	35	4	1	0	390	2	0	2	0	0	0	0	0
Seven Seas Free (fat-free)															
italian — *2 Tbsp*	32	10	0	0	0	0	480	2	0	2	0	0	0	0	0
ranch — *2 Tbsp*	35	50	0	0	0	0	330	12	1	3	<1	0	0	2	0
red wine vinegar — *2 Tbsp*	32	15	0	0	0	0	400	3	0	2	0	0	0	0	0
Seven Seas Viva															
caesar — *2 Tbsp*	31	120	110	12	2	0	500	2	0	2	<1	0	0	2	0
italian — *2 Tbsp*	30	110	100	11	1.5	0	580	2	0	2	0	0	0	0	0
russian — *2 Tbsp*	30	150	140	16	2.5	0	230	3	0	2	0	0	0	0	0
Weight Watchers Salad Celebrations															
caesar, fat-free — *2 Tbsp*	n/a	10	0	0	0	0	390	1	0	1	0	0	0	0	0
french-style — *2 Tbsp*	n/a	40	0	0	0	0	200	9	0	6	0	0	0	0	0
honey dijon, fat-free — *2 Tbsp*	n/a	45	0	0	0	0	150	11	0	5	0	0	0	0	0

	Weight g	Calories	Calories from fat	Total fat g	Sat. fat g	Cholesterol mg	Sodium mg	Carbohydrates g	Dietary fiber g	Sugars g	Protein g	Vitamin A % DV	Vitamin C % DV	Calcium % DV	Iron % DV
italian, creamy, fat-free — *2 Tbsp*	n/a	30	0	0	0	0	360	7	0	2	0	0	0	0	0
italian, fat-free — *2 Tbsp*	n/a	10	0	0	0	0	360	2	0	1	0	0	0	0	0
thousand island — *2 Tbsp*	n/a	45	15	1.5	0	10	190	8	0	5	0	4	0	0	0
Wishbone															
blue cheese, chunky — *2 Tbsp*	n/a	170	150	17	2.5	0	290	3	0	1	0	0	0	0	0
caesar — *2 Tbsp*	n/a	110	90	10	1.5	5	300	2	0	2	1	0	0	0	0
Classic House Italian — *2 Tbsp*	n/a	140	130	14	2	5	360	2	0	1	0	0	0	0	0
Classic Olive Oil Italian — *2 Tbsp*	n/a	60	45	5	0.5	0	350	4	0	3	0	0	0	0	0
creamy caesar — *2 Tbsp*	n/a	180	170	18	2.5	10	290	1	0	1	1	0	0	2	0
italian — *2 Tbsp*	n/a	80	70	8	1	0	490	3	0	2	0	0	0	0	0
italian, creamy — *2 Tbsp*	n/a	110	90	10	1.5	0	240	4	0	2	1	0	0	0	0
ranch — *2 Tbsp*	n/a	160	150	17	2.5	10	200	1	0	1	0	0	0	0	0
red wine vinaigrette — *2 Tbsp*	n/a	80	45	5	0.5	0	230	9	0	8	0	0	0	0	0
Robusto Italian — *2 Tbsp*	n/a	90	70	8	1	0	550	4	0	3	0	0	0	0	0
russian — *2 Tbsp*	n/a	110	50	6	1	0	350	15	0	7	0	0	0	0	0
thousand island — *2 Tbsp*	n/a	140	110	12	1.5	10	340	7	0	6	0	0	0	0	0
Wishbone Fat-Free															
blue cheese, chunky — *2 Tbsp*	n/a	35	0	0	0	0	290	7	<1	1	0	0	0	2	0
caesar — *2 Tbsp*	n/a	25	0	0	0	0	320	5	0	2	1	2	0	2	0
french-style, deluxe — *2 Tbsp*	n/a	30	0	0	0	0	230	7	<1	6	0	6	0	0	0
honey dijon — *2 Tbsp*	n/a	45	0	0	0	0	270	10	0	9	1	0	0	0	0
italian — *2 Tbsp*	n/a	10	0	0	0	0	280	2	0	1	0	0	0	0	0
italian, creamy — *2 Tbsp*	n/a	35	0	0	0	0	250	9	<1	3	0	0	0	0	0
ranch — *2 Tbsp*	n/a	40	0	0	0	0	280	9	<1	2	0	0	0	0	0

	Weight g	Calories	Calories from fat	Total fat g	Sat. fat g	Cholesterol mg	Sodium mg	Carbohydrates g	Dietary fiber g	Sugars g	Protein g	Vitamin A % DV	Vitamin C % DV	Calcium % DV	Iron % DV
red wine vinaigrette — *2 Tbsp*	n/a	35	0	0	0	0	230	7	0	6	0	0	0	0	0
thousand island — *2 Tbsp*	n/a	35	0	0	0	0	290	9	<1	6	0	0	0	0	0
Wishbone Lite															
blue cheese, chunky — *2 Tbsp*	n/a	70	50	6	1	0	400	3	0	1	1	0	0	0	0
french — *2 Tbsp*	n/a	50	20	2	0	5	240	8	0	7	0	0	0	0	0
italian — *2 Tbsp*	n/a	15	5	0.5	0	0	500	2	0	1	0	0	0	0	0
ranch — *2 Tbsp*	n/a	100	80	8	1	5	300	5	0	1	0	0	0	0	0
thousand island — *2 Tbsp*	n/a	80	45	5	0.5	10	270	8	0	6	0	0	0	0	0

Salsa

	Weight g	Calories	Calories from fat	Total fat g	Sat. fat g	Cholesterol mg	Sodium mg	Carbohydrates g	Dietary fiber g	Sugars g	Protein g	Vitamin A % DV	Vitamin C % DV	Calcium % DV	Iron % DV
Chi-Chi's															
con queso — *2 Tbsp*	32	90	60	7	3	15	480	4	0	3	3	0	0	8	0
hot — *2 Tbsp*	30	10	0	0	0	0	160	2	0	1	0	0	0	0	0
medium — *2 Tbsp*	30	10	0	0	0	0	140	1	0	1	0	0	0	0	0
mild — *2 Tbsp*	30	10	0	0	0	0	140	2	0	1	0	0	0	0	0
picante, hot — *2 Tbsp*	30	10	0	0	0	0	270	2	0	2	0	0	0	0	0
picante, mild — *2 Tbsp*	30	10	0	0	0	0	210	2	0	2	0	0	0	0	0
picante, medium — *2 Tbsp*	30	10	1	1	1	1	200	2	0	2	0	0	0	0	0
verde, medium or mild — *2 Tbsp*	33	15	0	0	0	0	180	3	0	2	0	0	4	0	0
Chi-Chi's Pico de Gallo — *2 Tbsp*	34	10	0	0	0	0	170	2	0	2	0	2	4	0	0
Old El Paso Dips															
Cheese 'N Salsa, low-fat, medium — *2 Tbsp*	29	30	15	1.5	1	<5	240	3	0	0	<1	0	0	2	0
Cheese 'N Salsa, mild or medium — *2 Tbsp*	29	40	25	3	1	<5	300	3	0	0	<1	0	0	2	0
chunky salsa, mild or medium — *2 Tbsp*	30	15	0	0	0	0	230	3	<1	2	1	2	0	0	0
jalapeño — *2 Tbsp*	29	30	10	1	0	<5	125	4	2	0	1	0	0	0	2

	Weight g	Calories	Calories from fat	Total fat g	Sat. fat g	Cholesterol mg	Sodium mg	Carbohydrates g	Dietary fiber g	Sugars g	Protein g	Vitamin A % DV	Vitamin C % DV	Calcium % DV	Iron % DV
Pace															
Thick & Chunky salsa — *2 Tbsp*	n/a	10	0	0	0	0	220	3	0	2	0	0	8	0	0
picante sauce — *2 Tbsp*	n/a	10	0	0	0	0	220	2	0	1	0	4	0	0	0
Tostitos Dip															
con queso — *2 Tbsp*	34	40	20	2	0.5	<5	650	5	<1	0	1	n/a	n/a	n/a	n/a
con queso, low-fat — *2 Tbsp*	35	40	14	1.5	1	<5	280	5	<1	<1	1	n/a	n/a	n/a	n/a
medium or hot — *2 Tbsp*	33	15	0	0	0	0	230	3	1	1	<1	n/a	n/a	n/a	n/a
mild — *2 Tbsp*	33	15	0	0	0	0	230	3	1	1	<1	n/a	n/a	n/a	n/a

Sorbet & Sherbet

	Weight g	Calories	Calories from fat	Total fat g	Sat. fat g	Cholesterol mg	Sodium mg	Carbohydrates g	Dietary fiber g	Sugars g	Protein g	Vitamin A % DV	Vitamin C % DV	Calcium % DV	Iron % DV
Ben & Jerry's Sorbet															
cranberry orange — *½ cup*	n/a	130	0	0	0	0	10	32	0	32	0	0	15	2	0
devil's food chocolate — *½ cup*	n/a	160	18	2	1	0	60	36	<1	33	2	0	0	4	6
Doonesberry — *½ cup*	n/a	130	0	0	0	0	15	33	<1	33	0	0	4	0	0
piña colada — *½ cup*	n/a	140	0	0	0	0	15	34	<1	32	0	0	8	0	0
Purple Passion — *½ cup*	n/a	120	0	0	0	0	15	33	0	31	0	0	6	0	0
strawberry kiwi — *½ cup*	n/a	130	0	0	0	0	20	33	<1	32	0	0	20	0	0
Breyers Sherbet															
orange — *½ cup*	n/a	120	10	1	0.5	<5	25	26	n/a	19	n/a	n/a	n/a	n/a	n/a
rainbow or tropical — *½ cup*	n/a	120	10	1	0	<5	25	26	n/a	19	n/a	n/a	n/a	n/a	n/a
raspberry — *½ cup*	n/a	120	10	1	0.5	<5	25	27	n/a	20	n/a	n/a	n/a	n/a	n/a
Häagen-Dazs Sorbet															
banana/strawberry — *½ cup*	113	140	0	0	0	0	5	34	<1	28	<1	0	15	0	0
chocolate — *½ cup*	113	130	0	0	0	0	80	30	2	22	2	0	0	0	6
mango — *½ cup*	113	120	0	0	0	0	0	30	<1	27	0	30	20	0	0

	Weight g	Calories	Calories from fat	Total fat g	Sat. fat g	Cholesterol mg	Sodium mg	Carbohydrates g	Dietary fiber g	Sugars g	Protein g	Vitamin A % DV	Vitamin C % DV	Calcium % DV	Iron % DV
orchard peach — *½ cup*	113	140	0	0	0	0	0	35	<1	31	<1	4	8	0	0
raspberry — *½ cup*	113	120	0	0	0	0	5	29	1	26	0	0	0	0	0
strawberry — *½ cup*	113	130	0	0	0	0	0	33	1	30	0	0	25	0	0
zesty lemon — *½ cup*	113	120	0	0	0	0	0	31	<1	28	0	0	6	0	0
Häagen-Dazs Sorbet & Cream, Orange — *½ cup*	106	190	80	9	5	60	45	24	0	23	2	6	15	8	0
Sealtest Cups, Orange Sherbet — *4 fl oz*	n/a	130	10	1	1	5	25	28	n/a	20	n/a	n/a	n/a	n/a	n/a

Soups, Chili & Stews

	Weight g	Calories	Calories from fat	Total fat g	Sat. fat g	Cholesterol mg	Sodium mg	Carbohydrates g	Dietary fiber g	Sugars g	Protein g	Vitamin A % DV	Vitamin C % DV	Calcium % DV	Iron % DV
Campbell's Low-Sodium															
chicken broth — *10 ½ oz*	n/a	40	20	2	1	5	140	2	0	1	4	0	0	2	0
chicken noodle — *7 ¼ oz*	n/a	80	25	3	1	15	90	10	1	1	4	20	0	2	4
chunky vegetable beef — *10 ¾ oz*	n/a	160	40	4.5	1.5	80	95	19	4	6	13	90	20	6	10
cream of mushroom — *10 ½ oz*	n/a	200	130	14	4	20	65	18	3	5	3	0	0	6	6
split pea — *10 ¾ oz*	n/a	240	35	4	3	5	50	38	5	6	12	25	0	4	10
tomato soup — *10 ½ oz*	n/a	170	50	6	2.5	10	60	28	2	17	4	25	60	4	8
Campbell's Baked Ramen Noodle Soups															
beef-flavor — *1 pkg*	n/a	210	10	1	0	0	980	44	2	3	6	6	0	2	10
chicken-flavor — *1 pkg*	n/a	210	10	1	0	0	1150	43	2	3	6	8	0	2	10
oriental-flavor — *1 pkg*	n/a	220	15	1.5	0.5	0	1300	45	2	3	6	6	0	4	10
Campbell's Broth, Chicken, low-sodium — *1 cup*	n/a	40	20	2	5	5	140	2	0	1	4	0	0	2	0
Campbell's Condensed (unprepared)															
bean w/ bacon — *½ cup*	n/a	180	45	5	2	<5	890	25	7	4	8	10	0	8	10
beef broth, double-rich, double-strength — *½ cup*	n/a	15	0	0	0	<5	900	1	0	0	3	0	0	2	0
beef noodle — *½ cup*	n/a	70	25	2.5	1	15	920	8	1	1	5	2	0	2	6
beef w/ vegetables & barley — *½ cup*	n/a	80	20	2	1	15	920	11	2	1	5	25	2	4	2

	Weight *g*	Calories	Calories from fat	Total fat *g*	Sat. fat *g*	Cholesterol *mg*	Sodium *mg*	Carbohydrates *g*	Dietary fiber *g*	Sugars *g*	Protein *g*	Vitamin A *% DV*	Vitamin C *% DV*	Calcium *% DV*	Iron *% DV*
beefy mushroom — *½ cup*	n/a	70	25	3	1	10	1000	6	1	1	5	0	0	4	0
black bean — *½ cup*	n/a	120	20	2	0.5	0	1030	19	5	4	6	4	0	4	10
broccoli cheese — *½ cup*	n/a	110	60	7	3	10	860	9	2	2	3	30	2	4	2
california-style vegetable — *½ cup*	n/a	60	10	1	0	0	850	10	2	2	3	20	50	2	2
cheddar cheese — *½ cup*	n/a	90	35	4	3	15	950	10	1	2	4	20	0	10	0
chicken & stars — *½ cup*	n/a	70	20	2	0.5	<1	1010	9	1	1	3	15	2	2	4
chicken alphabet w/ vegetables — *½ cup*	n/a	80	20	2	1	10	880	11	1	1	4	15	0	2	4
chicken broth — *½ cup*	n/a	30	20	2	0.5	<5	770	2	0	1	2	0	0	0	0
chicken dumplings — *½ cup*	n/a	80	25	3	1	25	1050	10	2	1	4	8	0	2	2
chicken gumbo — *½ cup*	n/a	60	15	1.5	0.5	10	990	9	1	1	2	4	0	2	2
chicken mushroom — *½ cup*	n/a	130	80	9	2.5	15	1000	9	1	1	3	15	0	2	2
chicken noodle — *½ cup*	n/a	70	20	2	1	15	980	9	1	1	3	6	0	2	4
chicken Noodle O's — *½ cup*	n/a	80	25	3	1	15	980	10	1	1	4	20	2	2	6
chicken rice — *½ cup*	n/a	70	25	2.5	1	<5	940	9	0	0	3	8	0	0	2
chicken vegetable — *½ cup*	n/a	80	20	2	0.5	10	940	12	2	4	3	50	0	2	4
chicken vegetable, southwestern-style — *½ cup*	n/a	110	15	1.5	0.5	10	900	18	4	4	7	10	40	4	6
chicken w/ white & wild rice — *½ cup*	n/a	70	20	2	0.5	10	900	9	1	1	3	8	25	2	2
chili beef & bean soup — *½ cup*	n/a	170	45	5	2.5	15	910	24	4	4	7	15	2	10	4
consomme beef soup — *½ cup*	n/a	25	0	0	0	5	820	2	0	2	4	0	0	2	0
cream of asparagus — *½ cup*	n/a	90	30	3.5	1	5	860	11	1	3	3	2	4	4	2
cream of broccoli — *½ cup*	n/a	100	50	6	2.5	<5	770	9	1	2	2	6	4	2	2
cream of celery — *½ cup*	n/a	110	60	7	2.5	<5	900	9	1	1	2	6	0	2	2
cream of chicken — *½ cup*	n/a	130	70	8	3	10	890	11	1	1	3	10	0	2	2
cream of chicken & broccoli — *½ cup*	n/a	120	70	8	2.5	15	860	9	1	2	4	15	2	2	2

	Weight *g*	Calories	Calories from fat	Total fat *g*	Sat. fat *g*	Cholesterol *mg*	Sodium *mg*	Carbohydrates *g*	Dietary fiber *g*	Sugars *g*	Protein *g*	Vitamin A *% DV*	Vitamin C *% DV*	Calcium *% DV*	Iron *% DV*
cream of mexican pepper — *½ cup*	n/a	110	60	7	2	<5	860	10	2	1	2	0	2	2	2
cream of mushroom — *½ cup*	n/a	110	60	7	2.5	<5	870	9	1	1	2	0	0	2	2
cream of onion — *½ cup*	n/a	110	50	6	1.5	20	910	13	1	4	2	6	0	2	4
cream of potato — *½ cup*	n/a	90	25	3	1.5	10	890	14	1	2	2	0	0	2	4
cream of shrimp — *½ cup*	n/a	100	60	7	2	20	890	8	1	1	2	0	0	2	2
creamy chicken noodle — *½ cup*	n/a	130	60	7	2	15	880	12	2	2	5	25	0	2	4
curly chicken noodle — *½ cup*	n/a	80	25	2.5	1	15	840	12	1	1	3	15	0	2	6
double noodle in chicken broth — *½ cup*	n/a	100	25	2.5	1	15	810	15	2	1	4	30	0	2	6
fiesta tomato — *½ cup*	n/a	70	0	0	0	0	860	16	1	8	1	8	10	10	4
french onion — *½ cup*	n/a	70	25	2.5	0	<5	980	10	1	5	2	0	4	2	2
golden corn — *½ cup*	n/a	120	30	3.5	1	<5	730	20	2	7	2	10	0	2	2
golden mushroom — *½ cup*	n/a	80	25	3	1	5	930	10	1	1	2	15	0	2	0
green pea — *½ cup*	n/a	180	25	3	1	5	890	29	5	6	9	4	0	8	2
hearty vegetable w/ pasta — *½ cup*	n/a	90	10	1	0	0	830	18	2	8	2	45	0	2	4
homestyle chicken noodle — *½ cup*	n/a	70	25	2.5	1.5	20	970	9	1	1	4	15	2	2	4
italian tomato w/ basil & oregano — *½ cup*	n/a	100	5	0.5	0	0	820	23	2	16	2	15	30	4	6
manhattan-style clam chowder — *½ cup*	n/a	60	5	0.5	0	<5	910	12	2	2	2	30	6	2	4
minestrone — *½ cup*	n/a	100	20	2	0.5	0	960	16	4	3	5	20	2	4	6
nacho cheese soup/dip — *½ cup*	n/a	140	80	8	4	15	810	11	2	2	5	25	2	10	2
new england clam chowder — *½ cup*	n/a	100	25	2.5	1	<5	980	15	1	1	4	0	2	2	6
noodles & ground beef — *½ cup*	n/a	100	35	4	2	25	900	11	2	1	5	20	0	2	6
oyster stew — *½ cup*	n/a	90	50	6	3.5	20	940	6	0	1	2	0	6	10	2
pepperpot — *½ cup*	n/a	100	45	5	2	15	1020	9	1	1	4	20	2	2	4
scotch broth — *½ cup*	n/a	80	25	3	1.5	10	870	9	1	1	4	40	0	4	2

	Weight g	Calories	Calories from fat	Total fat g	Sat. fat g	Cholesterol mg	Sodium mg	Carbohydrates g	Dietary fiber g	Sugars g	Protein g	Vitamin A % DV	Vitamin C % DV	Calcium % DV	Iron % DV
split pea w/ham — *½ cup*	n/a	180	30	3.5	2	<5	860	28	5	4	10	10	0	2	10
tomato — *½ cup*	n/a	100	20	2	0	0	730	18	2	10	2	10	30	2	4
tomato bisque — *½ cup*	n/a	130	25	3	1.5	5	900	24	2	15	2	10	25	4	4
tomato rice, old fashioned — *½ cup*	n/a	120	20	2	0.5	5	790	23	1	11		8	10	2	2
turkey noodle — *½ cup*	n/a	80	25	2.5	1	15	970	10	1	1	4	10	0	2	4
turkey vegetable — *½ cup*	n/a	80	25	2.5	1	10	840	11	2	2	3	50	0	2	4
vegetable beef — *½ cup*	n/a	80	20	2	1	10	810	10	2	2	5	40	0	2	4
vegetable soup — *½ cup*	n/a	80	15	1.5	0.5	<5	920	14	2	7	3	30	2	2	4
vegetable, old fashioned — *½ cup*	n/a	70	25	2.5	0.5	<5	950	10	2	2	2	50	0	2	4
vegetarian vegetable — *½ cup*	n/a	70	10	1	0	0	770	14	2	6	2	35	4	2	4
won ton — *½ cup*	n/a	45	10	1	0	15	940	5	1	1	4	2	0	2	2
Campbell's Condensed, 98% fat-free (unprepared)															
cream of broccoli — *½ cup*	n/a	80	25	3	1	<5	730	12	1	3	2	4	10	4	2
cream of broccoli cheese — *½ cup*	n/a	80	25	3	1.5	10	850	11	1	2	3	30	6	6	0
cream of celery — *½ cup*	n/a	70	25	3	1	<5	850	9	1	1	2	2	0	4	2
cream of chicken — *½ cup*	n/a	80	25	3	1.5	10	830	10	0	0	3	8	0	2	2
cream of mushroom — *½ cup*	n/a	70	25	3	1	<5	830	9	0	1	1	0	0	2	0
Campbell's Home Cookin' Soups															
bean & ham — *1 cup*	n/a	180	15	1.5	0.5	5	720	33	9	8	9	30	4	8	15
chicken rice — *1 cup*	n/a	110	15	1.5	0.5	15	910	17	2	4	6	50	4	2	4
chicken vegetable — *1 cup*	n/a	130	35	3.5	1	10	820	20	3	6	6	80	2	4	6
chicken w/ egg noodles — *1 cup*	n/a	100	30	3.5	1	15	980	11	1	4	7	60	0	4	4
country mushroom & rice — *1 cup*	n/a	80	5	0.5	0	0	820	16	2	2	3	50	4	4	2
country vegetable — *1 cup*	n/a	110	10	1	0	5	760	19	2	7	3	90	2	4	6

	Weight *g*	Calories	Calories from fat	Total fat *g*	Sat. fat *g*	Cholesterol *mg*	Sodium *mg*	Carbohydrates *g*	Dietary fiber *g*	Sugars *g*	Protein *g*	Vitamin A *% DV*	Vitamin C *% DV*	Calcium *% DV*	Iron *% DV*
cream of chicken — *1 cup*	n/a	210	160	18	6	15	1170	8	2	1	3	0	4	2	4
cream of mushroom — *1 cup*	n/a	170	120	13	4	15	970	9	3	1	3	0	0	0	0
lentil, savory — *1 cup*	n/a	130	5	0.5	0.5	0	860	24	5	3	7	40	0	4	20
minestrone — *1 cup*	n/a	120	20	2	1	5	990	19	3	5	4	70	2	6	6
new england clam chowder — *1 cup*	n/a	200	120	13	5	5	950	16	1	2	5	0	2	4	10
potato w/roasted garlic — *1 cup*	n/a	180	80	9	2.5	5	800	21	2	2	3	0	4	2	4
salsa bean — *1 cup*	n/a	160	10	1	0	0	730	31	7	12	7	10	10	8	10
split pea w/ ham — *1 cup*	n/a	170	15	1.5	0.5	5	880	30	6	6	10	40	4	4	10
tuscany minestrone — *1 cup*	n/a	160	60	7	1.5	5	880	21	5	4	5	60	4	8	15
vegetable beef — *1 cup*	n/a	120	20	2	1	5	1010	18	3	6	7	70	0	4	6
vegetable, Harborside — *1 cup*	n/a	80	15	1.5	1	5	770	13	2	4	3	40	8	4	6
vegetable, italian — *1 cup*	n/a	100	35	4	1.5	5	860	14	2	6	3	120	4	6	4
vegetable, southwestern — *1 cup*	n/a	130	25	2.5	0.5	0	750	24	4	4	3	90	4	6	6
Campbell's Microwave Soups															
bean w/ bacon — *10 ½ oz*	n/a	280	50	6	2	15	1300	40	11	8	14	35	10	10	20
chicken noodle — *1 container*	n/a	130	35	4	1	25	1320	18	2	4	7	50	0	4	8
chicken rice — *10 ½ oz*	n/a	120	25	2.5	1	10	1130	20	2	4	5	50	0	4	2
vegetable beef — *1 container*	n/a	140	5	0.5	0	10	1240	26	5	4	9	50	2	8	8
Campbell's Quality Soup & Recipe Mix (unprepared)															
chicken noodle — *3 Tbsp*	n/a	90	15	1.5	0.5	10	660	15	0	3	4	0	0	0	4
double noodle chicken — *1 package*	n/a	170	20	2	1	30	740	32	1	4	7	0	0	2	8
onion — *1 Tbsp*	n/a	20	0	0	0	0	530	5	0	3	0	0	0	0	0
w/ real chicken broth — *3 Tbsp*	n/a	100	10	1.5	0.5	10	740	17	1	2	3	0	0	0	4

	Weight g	Calories	Calories from fat	Total fat g	Sat. fat g	Cholesterol mg	Sodium mg	Carbohydrates g	Dietary fiber g	Sugars g	Protein g	Vitamin A % DV	Vitamin C % DV	Calcium % DV	Iron % DV
Campbell's Ramen Noodle Soups (unprepared)															
beef-flavor, oriental — *½ block*	n/a	170	60	6	4	0	750	26	1	2	3	0	0	0	6
chicken-flavor — *1 pkg*	n/a	290	100	11	3	0	1120	41	2	3	6	2	0	2	10
pork-flavor — *½ block*	n/a	170	50	6	4	0	850	26	1	2	4	0	0	0	6
Campbell's Sanwa Ramen Noodle (unprepared)															
chicken-flavor — *½ block*	n/a	170	50	6	4	0	730	26	1	2	3	0	0	0	8
chicken-flavor, spicy, oriental — *½ block*	n/a	170	50	6	4	0	740	26	1	2	3	0	0	0	6
oriental-flavor — *½ block*	n/a	170	50	6	4	0	780	26	1	2	3	0	0	0	6
shrimp-flavor — *½ block*	n/a	170	50	6	4	0	740	26	1	2	3	0	0	0	6
Campbell's Soups in Glass Jars															
chicken pasta — *1 cup*	n/a	90	10	1	0	5	850	14	1	2	6	50	2	4	6
cream of mushroom — *1 cup*	n/a	260	210	23	5	15	1130	10	1	0	0	0	2	2	2
garden vegetable & pasta — *1 cup*	n/a	110	5	0.5	0.5	5	720	21	2	7	4	70	4	6	6
minestrone — *1 cup*	n/a	120	10	1	0.5	0	1150	23	4	5	5	60	0	6	8
tomato vegetable — *1 cup*	n/a	80	5	0.5	0.5	0	1000	14	2	2	4	50	6	4	4
Chunky Soups (Campbell's)															
bean'n ham soup, hearty — *1 cup*	n/a	190	20	2	1	10	880	29	10	4	14	50	10	8	15
beef pasta — *1 cup*	n/a	150	25	3	1	20	970	18	2	5	13	60	2	4	10
beef w/ country vegetables soup — *1 cup*	n/a	160	35	4	1	25	900	18	3	4	13	150	2	4	10
chicken & pasta w/ mushrooms soup — *1 cup*	n/a	120	30	3.5	1.5	25	930	10	1	1	12	15	2	2	4
chicken broccoli cheese soup — *1 cup*	n/a	200	110	12	5	25	1120	14	1	1	9	20	0	4	2
chicken corn chowder — *1 cup*	n/a	250	140	15	7	25	870	18	3	4	10	80	4	2	4
chicken mushroom chowder — *1 cup*	n/a	210	110	12	4	10	970	15	3	1	10	0	8	2	8
chicken vegetable soup — *1 cup*	n/a	130	30	3	1.5	20	950	12	3	2	9	100	0	4	6

	Weight g	Calories	Calories from fat	Total fat g	Sat. fat g	Cholesterol mg	Sodium mg	Carbohydrates g	Dietary fiber g	Sugars g	Protein g	Vitamin A % DV	Vitamin C % DV	Calcium % DV	Iron % DV
chicken w/vegetable, hearty — *1 cup*	n/a	90	20	2	0.5	10	800	12	2	2	6	30	0	2	4
chili beef soup w/ beans — *11 oz*	n/a	300	60	7	2	20	1080	38	9	4	21	30	15	8	25
classic chicken noodle — *1 cup*	n/a	130	35	3	1	20	1050	16	2	3	9	50	4	4	6
manhattan clam chowder — *1 cup*	n/a	130	35	4	1	5	900	20	3	3	6	80	15	4	10
minestrone — *1 cup*	n/a	140	45	5	1.5	5	800	22	2	4	5	90	8	8	10
new england clam chowder soup — *1 cup*	n/a	240	135	15	5	10	980	21	2	1	7	0	0	4	8
pepper steak soup — *1 cup*	n/a	140	25	2.5	1	20	830	18	3	4	11	50	8	4	10
potato ham chowder — *1 cup*	n/a	220	130	14	8	20	840	16	3	1	6	0	0	2	6
savory chicken rice soup — *1 cup*	n/a	140	30	3	1	25	840	18	2	2	9	80	2	4	4
sirloin burger w/ vegetables — *1 cup*	n/a	190	80	9	3.5	20	930	20	4	3	11	90	0	4	10
spicy chicken vegetable — *1 cup*	n/a	90	10	1	0	10	870	13	3	2	7	35	6	2	10
split pea n' ham — *1 cup*	n/a	190	25	3	1	20	1120	27	3	5	14	80	10	4	10
steak 'n potato — *1 cup*	n/a	160	35	4	1	20	890	20	3	1	12	0	6	2	8
tortellini w/ chicken & vegetables — *1 cup*	n/a	110	15	1.5	0.5	10	910	18	2	3	6	35	0	6	6
vegetable — *1 cup*	n/a	130	30	3	1	0	870	22	4	5	3	80	4	6	8
vegetable beef, old fashioned — *1 cup*	n/a	150	45	5	1.5	15	870	17	3	3	10	90	6	4	10
vegetable w/ pasta, hearty — *1 cup*	n/a	130	25	3	0.5	0	1080	21	3	6	4	0	2	8	10
College Inn Broth															
beef, lower-sodium — *1 cup*	n/a	20	0	0	n/a	0	620	0	n/a	n/a	4	n/a	n/a	n/a	n/a
chicken — *1 cup*	n/a	25	15	1.5	0.5	<5	1050	1	n/a	1	1	n/a	n/a	n/a	n/a
chicken, lower-sodium — *1 cup*	n/a	25	15	1.5	0.5	<5	640	1	n/a	1	1	n/a	n/a	n/a	n/a
Dinty Moore Stew															
beef — *1 cup*	236	230	120	14	7	10	950	16	2	3	11	23	0	2	6
chicken — *1 cup*	241	220	100	11	3	40	980	16	2	3	12	40	2	2	4

	Weight g	Calories	Calories from fat	Total fat g	Sat. fat g	Cholesterol mg	Sodium mg	Carbohydrates g	Dietary fiber g	Sugars g	Protein g	Vitamin A % DV	Vitamin C % DV	Calcium % DV	Iron % DV
meatball stew — *1 cup*	240	270	140	16	7	35	1110	18	3	3	13	15	0	2	10
turkey — *1 cup*	241	140	25	3	1	15	850	19	2	3	10	15	6	2	2
Health Valley															
beef broth — *1 cup*	n/a	20	0	0	0	0	160	0	0	2	5	0	0	0	0
black bean & vegetable — *1 cup*	n/a	110	0	0	0	0	280	24	12	8	11	200	15	4	20
broccoli carotene soup — *1 cup*	n/a	70	0	0	0	0	240	16	7	12	6	500	15	4	20
chicken broth — *1 cup*	n/a	45	13.5	0	0	25	250	0	0	0	7	0	0	0	0
chicken broth, fat-free — *1 cup*	n/a	30	0	0	0	0	170	0	0	0	7	0	0	0	0
chicken broth, no salt added — *1 cup*	n/a	35	13.5	0	0	0	75	0	0	0	8	0	2	0	0
country corn & vegetable — *1 cup*	n/a	70	0	0	0	0	135	17	7	8	5	200	10	4	10
five-bean vegetable — *1 cup*	n/a	140	0	0	0	0	250	32	13	9	10	200	20	8	30
garden vegetable — *1 cup*	n/a	80	0	0	0	0	250	17	4	8	6	200	25	4	10
italian minestrone — *1 cup*	n/a	80	0	0	0	0	210	21	11	6	8	200	8	4	20
italian, plus carotene — *1 cup*	n/a	80	0	0	0	0	240	19	6	5	7	500	10	4	20
lentil & carrots — *1 cup*	n/a	90	0	0	0	0	220	25	14	7	10	200	4	6	30
split pea & carrots — *1 cup*	n/a	110	0	0	0	0	230	17	4	7	8	200	15	4	15
tomato vegetable — *1 cup*	n/a	80	0	0	0	0	240	17	5	9	6	200	15	4	30
vegetable barley — *1 cup*	n/a	90	0	0	0	0	210	19	4	4	6	200	25	4	15
vegetable power carotene — *1 cup*	n/a	70	0	0	0	0	240	17	6	7	5	500	10	4	20
Health Valley Chili															
fajita, burrito, or enchilada flavor — *½ cup*	n/a	80	0	0	0	0	160	15	7	4	7	100	20	2	10
vegetarian lentil, mild — *½ cup*	n/a	80	0	0	0	0	100	14	6	3	7	100	10	2	15
vegetarian lentil, mild, no salt — *½ cup*	n/a	80	0	0	0	0	50	14	6	3	7	100	10	2	15
vegetarian w/ black beans, mild or spicy — *½ cup*	n/a	80	0	0	0	0	160	15	7	4	7	100	20	2	10

	Weight g	Calories	Calories from fat	Total fat g	Sat. fat g	Cholesterol mg	Sodium mg	Carbohydrates g	Dietary fiber g	Sugars g	Protein g	Vitamin A % DV	Vitamin C % DV	Calcium % DV	Iron % DV
vegetarian, mild or spicy — *½ cup*	n/a	80	0	0	0	0	100	15	7	4	7	100	15	2	15
vegetarian, mild, no salt — *½ cup*	n/a	80	0	0	0	0	35	15	6	4	7	100	15	2	15
vegetarian, spicy, no salt — *½ cup*	n/a	80	0	0	0	0	35	15	7	4	7	100	15	2	15
Health Valley Chili in a Cup — *¾ cup*	n/a	120	9	1	n/a	0	290	21	6	3	10	10	6	6	10
Health Valley Organic															
black bean — *1 cup*	n/a	110	0	0	0	0	290	28	10	14	8	200	40	4	20
black bean, no salt — *1 cup*	n/a	110	0	0	0	0	45	28	10	14	8	200	40	4	20
lentil — *1 cup*	n/a	90	0	0	0	0	240	20	9	7	9	200	6	4	20
lentil, no salt — *1 cup*	n/a	90	0	0	0	0	40	20	9	7	9	200	6	4	20
minestrone — *1 cup*	n/a	90	0	0	0	0	190	23	10	6	8	200	15	4	10
minestrone, no salt — *1 cup*	n/a	90	0	0	0	0	115	23	10	6	8	200	15	4	10
mushroom barley — *1 cup*	n/a	60	0	0	0	0	220	15	8	5	5	200	12	2	8
mushroom barley, no salt — *1 cup*	n/a	60	0	0	0	0	95	15	8	5	5	200	12	2	8
potato leek — *1 cup*	n/a	70	0	0	0	0	230	15	3	5	4	100	0	2	6
potato leek, no salt — *1 cup*	n/a	70	0	0	0	0	35	15	3	5	4	100	0	2	6
split pea — *1 cup*	n/a	110	0	0	0	0	160	23	8	5	10	200	2	2	10
split pea, no salt — *1 cup*	n/a	110	0	0	0	0	115	23	8	5	10	200	2	2	10
tomato — *1 cup*	n/a	90	0	0	0	0	250	22	4	20	4	200	20	2	12
tomato, no salt — *1 cup*	n/a	90	0	0	0	0	25	22	4	20	4	200	20	2	12
vegetable — *1 cup*	n/a	80	0	0	0	0	230	18	6	10	5	200	8	4	20
vegetable, no salt — *1 cup*	n/a	80	0	0	0	0	80	18	6	10	5	200	8	4	20
Health Valley Pasta Soup															
cacciatore — *1 cup*	n/a	100	0	0	0	0	290	20	4	6	4	100	20	6	4
fagioli — *1 cup*	n/a	100	0	0	0	0	290	25	4	5	6	100	20	6	15

	Weight g	Calories	Calories from fat	Total fat g	Sat. fat g	Cholesterol mg	Sodium mg	Carbohydrates g	Dietary fiber g	Sugars g	Protein g	Vitamin A % DV	Vitamin C % DV	Calcium % DV	Iron % DV
primavera — *1 cup*	n/a	110	0	0	0	0	290	23	3	5	3	100	20	4	15
rotini & vegetable — *1 cup*	n/a	100	0	0	0	0	290	20	4	4	4	100	20	6	15
Healthy Choice															
bean & ham — *1 cup*	249	170	10	1.5	0	<5	480	31	7	3	9	6	10	8	8
beef & potato — *1 cup*	243	120	10	1	0.5	5	450	16	0	3	11	15	10	<2	4
broccoli cheese — *1 cup*	238	120	15	2	1	<5	480	22	2	1	4	15	2	6	2
chicken alfredo — *1 cup*	236	130	20	2.5	1	10	480	17	2	3	12	0	15	6	4
chicken corn chowder — *1 cup*	252	180	30	3	1	10	470	30	2	2	8	8	15	2	4
chicken noodle — *1 cup*	250	140	25	3	1	10	400	20	<1	0	9	15	20	4	6
chicken w/ pasta — *1 cup*	246	120	25	2.5	1	5	470	17	<1	0	8	15	8	4	4
chicken w/ rice — *1 cup*	240	110	25	3	1	5	430	15	<1	0	7	15	10	2	2
chili, beef — *1 cup*	258	170	15	1.5	0.5	10	380	30	5	5	14	10	15	8	15
country vegetable — *1 cup*	246	100	5	0.5	0	0	430	23	2	1	4	30	15	4	6
cream of chicken w/ vegetables — *1 cup*	254	130	20	2	1	10	480	21	1	0	7	6	<2	10	2
cream of mushroom — *1 cup*	250	80	10	1	0.5	0	450	14	<1	0	4	0	0	10	0
garden vegetable — *1 cup*	246	120	10	1	0	0	400	26	3	0	5	35	15	4	8
hearty chicken — *1 cup*	249	130	25	2.5	1	20	460	20	1	0	8	30	20	4	4
lentil — *1 cup*	247	150	10	1	0.5	0	420	29	5	1	9	35	20	4	15
minestrone — *1 cup*	245	110	10	1	0	0	390	23	3	3	6	35	15	8	8
new england clam chowder — *1 cup*	251	120	10	1.5	1	10	480	23	2	3	6	<2	2	4	<2
split pea w/ ham — *1 cup*	250	160	20	2	1	10	400	25	2	3	11	20	10	4	10
tomato garden — *1 cup*	244	110	15	1.5	0.5	0	420	21	3	7	5	35	10	8	8
turkey w/ white & wild rice — *1 cup*	240	90	20	2.5	1	0	360	13	1	0	6	15	15	4	<2
vegetable beef — *1 cup*	252	130	10	1	0	<5	420	22	2	0	10	15	20	4	8

	Weight g	Calories	Calories from fat	Total fat g	Sat. fat g	Cholesterol mg	Sodium mg	Carbohydrates g	Dietary fiber g	Sugars g	Protein g	Vitamin A % DV	Vitamin C % DV	Calcium % DV	Iron % DV
Healthy Choice Condensed (unprepared)															
broccoli cheddar — *½ cup*	124	90	15	2	1	5	480	15	2	<1	3	6	6	10	0
celery — *½ cup*	122	70	20	2	1	<5	480	14	3	2	<1	0	0	0	0
chicken — *½ cup*	123	90	25	3	1	<5	480	13	3	<1	2	4	0	0	0
garlic — *½ cup*	124	60	10	1	0	0	480	13	3	0	<1	0	0	0	0
mushroom — *½ cup*	123	60	5	0.5	0	0	480	13	3	0	<1	0	0	0	0
tomato — *½ cup*	127	80	10	1	0	0	480	18	3	11	2	2	6	10	4
Healthy Request Condensed (unprepared)															
bean w/bacon — *½ cup*	n/a	150	20	2	1	5	480	26	7	6	7	10	0	6	10
chicken noodle — *½ cup*	n/a	70	20	2	0.5	15	480	9	0	1	3	10	0	0	4
chicken vegetable — *½ cup*	n/a	80	20	2	0.5	5	480	12	1	4	3	40	2	2	2
chicken w/ rice — *½ cup*	n/a	60	25	2.5	1	15	480	10	<1	<1	2	20	20	0	0
cream of broccoli — *½ cup*	n/a	70	20	2	1	5	480	9	1	3	2	10	6	2	0
cream of celery — *½ cup*	n/a	70	20	2	0.5	5	480	11	1	3	2	0	0	15	0
cream of chicken — *½ cup*	n/a	70	20	2	1	15	480	12	0	2	2	10	0	0	0
cream of chicken & broccoli — *½ cup*	n/a	80	25	2.5	1	5	480	10	1	2	3	10	6	2	0
cream of mushroom — *½ cup*	n/a	70	25	2.5	1	10	480	10	0	2	1	0	0	10	0
hearty vegetable & pasta — *½ cup*	n/a	90	10	1	0	5	480	16	2	4	3	60	4	2	4
minestrone — *½ cup*	n/a	90	10	1	0.5	0	480	17	2	2	4	45	0	2	6
tomato — *½ cup*	n/a	90	15	1.5	0.5	0	460	18	1	11	1	8	40	0	2
vegetable — *½ cup*	n/a	90	10	1	0	5	480	16	2	5	3	40	0	2	4
vegetable beef — *½ cup*	n/a	80	20	2	1	5	480	11	2	2	5	40	2	2	4
Healthy Request Creative Chef Condensed (unprepared)															
cream of potato — *½ cup*	n/a	80	20	2	1	<5	480	14	1	2	2	0	6	10	2

	Weight g	Calories	Calories from fat	Total fat g	Sat. fat g	Cholesterol mg	Sodium mg	Carbohydrates g	Dietary fiber g	Sugars g	Protein g	Vitamin A % DV	Vitamin C % DV	Calcium % DV	Iron % DV
cream of roasted chicken — *½ cup*	n/a	80	25	2.5	1	5	480	12	0	1	2	10	0	2	2
creamy broccoli — *½ cup*	n/a	70	20	2	1	5	480	11	1	2	3	40	10	4	0
tomato w/ herbs — *½ cup*	n/a	100	10	1	0	0	480	20	2	12	2	10	40	2	4
Healthy Request Ready to Serve															
chicken broth — *1 cup*	n/a	20	0	0	0	0	450	1	0	1	3	0	15	0	0
chicken noodle — *1 cup*	n/a	160	30	3	1	20	480	25	2	3	9	40	0	4	10
chicken rice — *1 cup*	n/a	100	20	2	0.5	40	480	15	1	2	6	35	0	2	2
chicken vegetable — *1 cup*	n/a	120	20	2	0.5	20	480	18	2	3	7	90	0	2	4
minestone — *1 cup*	n/a	120	20	2	0.5	<5	480	24	3	5	4	90	6	0	6
new england clam chowder — *1 cup*	n/a	120	30	3	0.5	15	480	17	1	2	5	0	0	10	8
southwest veg w/ black bean — *1 cup*	n/a	140	10	1	0.5	0	480	28	5	10	5	10	6	6	8
split pea w/ham — *1 cup*	n/a	170	20	2	0.5	15	480	28	4	6	9	40	2	2	10
tomato vegetable w/ pasta — *1 cup*	n/a	120	20	2	0.5	5	480	22	3	9	4	90	8	6	6
turkey veg. w/wild rice — *1 cup*	n/a	120	25	2.5	1	15	480	17	2	3	7	120	4	4	4
vegetable — *1 cup*	n/a	100	10	1	0	0	470	20	2	6	3	100	0	4	6
vegetable beef — *1 cup*	n/a	140	25	2.5	1	20	480	20	3	4	9	100	4	4	6
zesty penne pasta — *1 cup*	n/a	90	5	0.5	0	5	470	17	2	5	4	45	100	4	4
Hormel Chili															
chunky w/ beans — *1 cup*	247	330	140	16	6	60	1040	30	8	3	17	15	0	4	15
hot — *1 cup*	236	410	270	30	13	75	950	16	3	3	19	25	0	4	10
hot w/ beans — *1 cup*	247	340	150	17	7	60	1200	30	9	3	18	15	0	4	15
regular — *1 cup*	236	410	270	30	13	75	950	16	3	3	19	25	0	4	10
turkey — *1 cup*	236	190	25	3	1	75	1250	17	3	4	24	25	0	4	15
turkey w/ beans — *1 cup*	247	200	25	3	1	50	1210	25	5	3	18	25	0	8	15

	Weight *g*	Calories	Calories from fat	Total fat *g*	Sat. fat *g*	Cholesterol *mg*	Sodium *mg*	Carbohydrates *g*	Dietary fiber *g*	Sugars *g*	Protein *g*	Vitamin A *% DV*	Vitamin C *% DV*	Calcium *% DV*	Iron *% DV*
vegetarian — *1 cup*	247	200	0	0	0	0	830	38	9	6	12	25	0	6	15
vegetarian w/ beans — *1 cup*	247	340	150	17	7	60	1200	30	9	3	18	15	0	4	15
Hormel Microcup Meal															
beef stew — *1 cup*	213	190	90	10	4	35	990	15	2	3	11	10	2	2	6
chili — *1 cup*	209	290	150	17	8	65	910	15	3	3	18	20	0	4	10
chili mac — *1 cup*	213	200	80	9	4	25	980	17	2	3	11	15	0	0	10
chili, hot, w/ beans — *1 cup*	209	250	100	11	5	50	980	23	6	2	15	10	0	4	15
chili w/ beans — *1 cup*	209	250	100	11	5	50	990	24	6	2	14	10	0	4	15
Pritikin Fat-Free Vegetable Broth — *1 cup*	237	20	0	0	0	0	250	3	0	1	2	10	0	0	0
Progresso															
bean & ham — *1 cup*	238	160	20	2	0.5	10	870	25	8	2	10	30	0	8	15
beef barley — *1 cup*	242	130	35	4	1.5	25	780	13	3	0	10	30	0	4	10
beef minestrone — *1 cup*	241	140	35	4	1.5	25	850	14	3	0	12	40	4	4	15
beef noodle — *1 cup*	241	140	30	3.5	1.5	30	950	15	1	2	13	15	0	2	10
black bean — *1 cup*	242	170	15	1.5	0	<5	730	30	10	0	8	4	0	6	20
chicken barley — *1 cup*	241	100	20	2	0.5	15	770	13	3	0	8	35	0	2	8
chicken broth — *1 cup*	233	15	5	0.5	0	5	860	1	0	0	2	0	0	0	0
chicken minestrone — *1 cup*	239	100	15	1.5	0	10	740	14	2	2	8	20	4	2	6
chicken noodle — *1 cup*	238	80	15	1.5	0.5	25	750	7	1	1	9	20	0	0	4
chicken rice w/ vegetables — *1 cup*	238	100	25	3	1	20	800	11	<1	0	6	25	0	2	4
chicken vegetable — *1 cup*	240	100	20	2	0	10	600	13	3	2	7	20	0	2	4
cream of mushroom — *1 cup*	238	130	70	8	3.5	20	920	12	1	0	3	0	0	2	4
escarole in chicken broth — *1 cup*	232	25	10	1	0	<5	980	2	0	0	2	15	0	2	4
homestyle chicken w/ vegetables — *1 cup*	240	80	20	2	0.5	30	750	9	1	0	7	35	0	0	6

	Weight g	Calories	Calories from fat	Total fat g	Sat. fat g	Cholesterol mg	Sodium mg	Carbohydrates g	Dietary fiber g	Sugars g	Protein g	Vitamin A % DV	Vitamin C % DV	Calcium % DV	Iron % DV
lentil — *1 cup*	241	140	20	2	0	0	750	22	7	0	9	15	0	4	20
manhattan clam chowder — *1 cup*	239	110	20	2	0	10	710	11	3	3	12	45	6	4	10
minestrone — *1 cup*	240	120	20	2	0	0	960	21	5	4	5	40	0	4	8
minestrone parmesan — *1 cup*	237	100	25	2.5	0.5	0	700	16	3	3	3	35	2	4	6
new england clam chowder — *1 cup*	240	200	90	10	2.5	15	1050	21	2	3	6	2	6	6	10
split pea w/ ham — *1 cup*	243	150	35	4	1.5	15	830	20	5	1	9	25	4	4	10
tomato vegetable — *1 cup*	241	90	20	2	0	0	990	15	4	8	3	30	2	2	10
tortellini in chicken broth — *1 cup*	236	70	20	2	0.5	5	750	10	2	1	4	60	0	4	10
vegetable — *1 cup*	238	90	20	2	0.5	<5	850	15	3	4	4	70	2	4	8
Progresso Pasta Soup															
broccoli & shells — *1 cup*	243	80	10	1	0	<5	780	13	3	2	5	25	0	2	8
chicken & rotini — *1 cup*	238	90	20	2	0.5	25	920	8	0	0	9	45	6	0	4
lentil & shells — *1 cup*	243	130	15	1.5	0	0	850	23	5	2	7	6	0	2	15
minestrone & shells — *1 cup*	240	110	15	1.5	0	0	770	20	4	3	5	40	8	2	6
penne in chicken broth — *1 cup*	238	90	10	1	0	<5	860	14	2	2	5	8	0	0	2
spicy chicken & penne — *1 cup*	241	110	25	3	1	20	770	14	4	4	7	20	0	2	6
tomato & rotini — *1 cup*	242	130	15	1.5	0	<5	820	23	4	7	5	20	0	2	10
tomato tortellini — *1 cup*	239	120	45	5	1.5	10	910	13	2	5	5	30	2	6	10
vegetable & rotini — *1 cup*	239	110	10	1	0	0	720	20	3	2	4	60	0	4	8
Progresso, 99% Fat-Free															
beef barley — *1 cup*	241	140	20	2	1	20	470	20	3	1	11	45	6	2	10
beef vegetable — *1 cup*	241	160	20	2	0.5	10	870	24	3	4	11	30	8	0	8
chicken noodle — *1 cup*	237	90	15	1.5	0	20	620	12	1	2	7	20	0	0	4
chicken rice w/ vegetables — *1 cup*	239	90	15	1.5	0	15	460	13	<1	0	6	35	0	2	6

	Weight g	Calories	Calories from fat	Total fat g	Sat. fat g	Cholesterol mg	Sodium mg	Carbohydrates g	Dietary fiber g	Sugars g	Protein g	Vitamin A % DV	Vitamin C % DV	Calcium % DV	Iron % DV
creamy mushroom chicken — *1 cup*	237	90	20	2	0.5	10	840	12	1	2	7	10	4	0	2
lentil — *1 cup*	242	130	15	1.5	0	0	440	20	6	0	8	20	0	4	15
minestrone — *1 cup*	241	130	15	1.5	0	0	710	23	4	3	7	20	0	4	8
new england clam chowder — *1 cup*	244	130	20	2	0	5	700	22	2	3	5	0	4	2	6
split pea — *1 cup*	253	170	15	1.5	0	0	620	29	5	5	10	15	0	0	6
tomato garden vegetable — *1 cup*	245	100	15	1.5	0	0	660	19	2	7	3	25	8	2	6
vegetable — *1 cup*	238	80	15	1.5	0	5	470	13	1	2	4	60	2	4	8
white cheddar potato — *1 cup*	244	140	25	2.5	1.5	5	930	26	2	2	4	10	10	4	4
Swanson Broth															
chicken, clear — *1 cup*	n/a	30	20	2	0.5	0	1000	1	0	0	2	0	0	0	0
chicken, Natural Goodness, clear — *1 cup*	n/a	15	10	0	0	0	560	1	0	1	3	0	0	0	0
clear — *1 cup*	n/a	20	10	1	0.5	0	820	1	0	1	2	0	0	0	2
vegetable — *1 cup*	n/a	20	15	1	0	0	1000	3	0	3	2	4	0	0	0
Weight Watchers Minestrone — *1 can*	297	130	20	2	0.5	5	760	23	6	7	5	60	2	10	10

Soups, Chili & Stews: Dry

	Weight g	Calories	Calories from fat	Total fat g	Sat. fat g	Cholesterol mg	Sodium mg	Carbohydrates g	Dietary fiber g	Sugars g	Protein g	Vitamin A % DV	Vitamin C % DV	Calcium % DV	Iron % DV
Dinty Moore Microwave Cups															
beef stew — *1 cup*	213	190	90	10	4	30	870	15	2	2	11	30	0	2	6
chicken & dumplings — *1 cup*	213	200	50	6	2	35	890	21	1	1	15	0	0	2	6
chicken stew — *1 cup*	213	180	70	8	2	30	920	18	2	2	10	40	8	2	2
corned beef hash — *1 cup*	213	350	200	22	9	60	850	19	2	1	19	0	0	2	10
hearty burger stew — *1 cup*	213	240	120	13	5	40	930	19	3	5	12	35	0	6	8
meatball stew — *1 cup*	213	250	130	15	7	30	990	16	2	3	12	15	0	2	8
turkey stew — *1 cup*	213	130	25	2.5	1	10	760	16	2	3	9	10	6	2	2

	Weight g	Calories	Calories from fat	Total fat g	Sat. fat g	Cholesterol mg	Sodium mg	Carbohydrates g	Dietary fiber g	Sugars g	Protein g	Vitamin A % DV	Vitamin C % DV	Calcium % DV	Iron % DV
Health Valley Soup Mix (unprepared)															
black bean w/ couscous, spciy — *⅓ cup*	n/a	130	0	0	0	0	190	29	5	3	6	10	6	4	10
black bean w/ rice, zesty — *⅓ cup*	n/a	100	0	0	0	0	190	22	4	2	5	10	6	4	10
chicken-flavored noodles w/ vegetables — *⅓ cup*	n/a	110	0	0	0	0	190	24	3	1	3	10	10	2	8
corn chowder w/ tomatoes — *¼ cup*	n/a	100	0	0	0	0	190	21	3	1	4	10	15	2	8
health pasta soups — *½ cup*	n/a	100	0	0	0	0	190	20	1	1	5	10	10	4	6
lentil w/ couscous — *⅓ cup*	n/a	130	0	0	0	0	190	28	5	1	7	10	8	4	10
pasta italiano — *½ cup*	n/a	140	0	0	0	0	190	31	3	1	5	10	20	2	8
potato w/ broccoli, creamy — *⅓ cup*	n/a	70	0	0	0	0	190	17	3	2	4	10	20	6	4
split pea w/ carrots — *½ cup*	n/a	130	0	0	0	0	190	22	2	2	8	25	10	4	8
Herb-Ox Bouillon Cubes															
chicken — *1 cube*	4	10	0	0	0	0	890	<1	0	0	<1	0	0	0	0
vegetable — *1 cube*	4	5	0	0	0	0	960	<1	0	0	0	0	0	0	0
Herb-Ox Instant Bouillon Powder															
beef — *1 tsp*	4.5	10	0	0	0	0	860	1	0	0	<1	0	0	0	0
chicken — *1 tsp*	4	10	0	0	0	0	890	<1	0	0	<1	0	0	0	0
Hormel Micro Cup Soup															
bean & ham soup — *1 cup*	213	190	35	4	1	15	680	29	7	2	9	8	2	2	8
beef vegetable — *1 cup*	213	90	5	1	0	10	790	15	1	3	6	50	0	2	4
broccoli cheese w/ ham — *1 cup*	213	170	120	13	5	60	700	10	1	2	4	6	15	6	2
chicken & rice — *1 cup*	213	110	25	3	1	15	950	17	1	3	5	35	2	2	2
chicken noodle — *1 cup*	213	13	2	<2	<2	4	101	2	<2	<2	1	1	<2	<2	1
new england clam chowder — *1 cup*	213	130	40	5	2.5	25	820	16	1	0	5	0	0	2	2
potato cheese w/ ham — *1 cup*	213	190	120	13	5	60	730	16	1	2	4	2	0	6	0

	Weight *g*	Calories	Calories from fat	Total fat *g*	Sat. fat *g*	Cholesterol *mg*	Sodium *mg*	Carbohydrates *g*	Dietary fiber *g*	Sugars *g*	Protein *g*	Vitamin A *% DV*	Vitamin C *% DV*	Calcium *% DV*	Iron *% DV*
Knorr Soup Mix (unprepared)															
chicken-flavor noodle — *3 Tbsp*	25	90	15	1.5	0.5	15	770	16	0	1	5	0	0	0	2
leek — *2 Tbsp*	17	70	25	3	1	<5	730	9	0	2	2	0	2	0	2
tomato with basil — *3 Tbsp*	22	80	20	2	0.5	0	970	14	0	5	2	25	90	4	4
Lipton Cup-a-Soup (unprepared)															
chicken broth — *1 pkg*	6	20	0	0	0	0	440	3	0	0	1	0	0	0	0
chicken broth w/ pasta — *1 pkg*	13	45	0	0	0	0	450	8	0	0	2	0	0	0	2
chicken noodle — *1 pkg*	13	50	10	1	0	10	540	8	0	0	2	0	0	0	2
chicken noodle, hearty — *1 pkg*	16	60	10	1	0	15	590	10	0	0	3	0	0	0	2
chicken vegetable, creamy — *1 pkg*	19	80	40	4	1.5	0	590	10	<1	3	2	0	0	0	0
chicken-vegetable-flavor — *1 pkg*	14	50	10	1	0	10	520	10	0	1	1	0	0	0	2
cream of chicken — *1 pkg*	17	70	20	2	0	0	640	12	<1	3	<1	0	0	0	0
green pea — *1 pkg*	21	80	10	1	0	0	520	12	3	1	4	0	0	0	0
mushroom, creamy — *1 pkg*	15	60	20	2	0	0	610	10	0	2	1	0	0	0	0
spring vegetable — *1 pkg*	13	45	10	1	0	10	500	8	<1	1	2	0	0	0	2
tomato — *1 pkg*	26	90	10	1	0	0	510	20	<1	6	2	4	6	8	0
Lipton Recipe Secrets (unprepared)															
beefy onion — *1 Tbsp*	8	25	5	0.5	0	0	610	5	0	0	0	0	0	0	0
italian herb w/ tomato — *2 Tbsp*	12	40	5	0.5	0	0	510	9	0	3	<1	2	4	0	2
onion — *1 Tbsp*	7	20	0	0	0	0	610	4	0	0	0	0	0	0	0
onion mushroom — *2 Tbsp*	10	30	5	1	0	0	630	6	0	0	<1	0	0	0	0
vegetable — *1 ⅔ Tbsp*	10	30	0	0	0	0	600	7	1	2	<1	4	4	0	0
Lipton Soup Secrets															
chicken noodle w/ white chicken meat — *3 Tbsp*	20	80	15	2	0.5	15	650	12	0	1	3	0	0	0	4

	Weight g	Calories	Calories from fat	Total fat g	Sat. fat g	Cholesterol mg	Sodium mg	Carbohydrates g	Dietary fiber g	Sugars g	Protein g	Vitamin A % DV	Vitamin C % DV	Calcium % DV	Iron % DV
extra-noodle w/ chicken broth — *3 Tbsp*	23	90	15	1.5	0.5	25	680	15	<1	1	3	0	0	0	4
noodle soup w/ chicken broth — *2 Tbsp*	16	60	15	2	0.5	15	710	9	0	1	2	0	0	0	2
spiral pasta w/ chicken broth — *3 Tbsp*	18	60	10	1	0	0	660	12	0	1	2	0	0	0	2
Lipton Soup Secrets Kettle-Style (unprepared)															
chicken 'n onion — *¼ cup*	34	120	10	1	0	5	730	24	1	1	4	0	2	2	4
chicken w/ pasta & beans — *¼ cup*	30	110	10	1.5	0	5	700	19	3	1	5	10	0	2	6
country chicken w/ pasta & herbs — *¼ cup*	27	100	15	1.5	0	5	740	18	1	1	4	10	0	2	4
lentil, homestyle — *¼ cup*	36	130	10	1	0	0	750	22	5	1	7	10	0	0	10
minestrone — *¼ cup*	31	110	10	1	0	0	750	21	3	4	4	10	4	2	6
Uncle Ben's Soup Mix (unprepared)															
black bean & rice — *1.5 oz*	42	150	10	1.5	0	0	430	28	6	2	7	0	0	4	8
broccoli cheese & rice — *1.5 oz*	42	160	25	3	1.5	5	870	26	1	4	7	2	2	15	4
Weight Watchers Instant Broth (unprepared)															
beef — *1 packet*	5	10	0	0	0	0	800	2	0	2	0	0	0	0	2
chicken — *1 packet*	5	10	0	0	0	0	830	2	0	2	0	0	0	0	0
Wyler's Bouillon															
cubes, beef or chicken flavor — *1 cube*	3.5	5	0	0	0	0	900	1	0	0	0	0	0	0	0
cubes, beef-flavor, reduced-sodium — *1 cube*	3.5	5	0	0	0	0	600	1	0	0	0	0	0	0	0
cubes, chicken-flavor, reduced-sodium — *1 cube*	3.5	5	0	0	0	0	600	1	0	0	0	0	0	0	0
instant, beef- or chicken-flavor — *1 tsp*	3.5	5	0	0	0	0	900	1	0	0	0	0	0	0	0
instant, beef-flavor, reduced-sodium — *1 tsp*	3.5	5	0	0	0	0	600	1	0	0	0	0	0	0	0
instant, chicken-flavor, reduced-sodium — *1 tsp*	3.5	5	0	0	0	0	600	1	0	0	0	0	0	0	0

Stuffing Mixes, Bread Crumbs & Croutons

	Weight *g*	Calories	Calories from fat	Total fat *g*	Sat. fat *g*	Cholesterol *mg*	Sodium *mg*	Carbohydrates *g*	Dietary fiber *g*	Sugars *g*	Protein *g*	Vitamin A *% DV*	Vitamin C *% DV*	Calcium *% DV*	Iron *% DV*
4C Bread Crumbs															
flavored — *⅓ cup*	30	110	15	1.5	0.5	0	630	20	2	2	5	0	0	10	6
plain — *⅓ cup*	30	110	10	1	0	0	230	22	2	2	4	0	0	8	6
Arnold Bread Crumbs															
italian — *½ oz*	14	50	0	<1	0	0	200	8	<1	n/a	2	0	0	0	2
plain — *½ oz*	14	50	0	<1	0	0	80	8	<1	n/a	2	0	0	0	4
Arnold Crispy Croutons															
cheese garlic — *3 Tbsp*	7	30	10	1	0	0	50	5	0	0	1	0	0	0	2
fine herb or seasoned — *2 Tbsp*	7	30	10	1	0	0	60	5	0	0	1	0	0	0	2
italian — *2 Tbsp*	7	30	10	1	0	0	65	4	0	0	1	0	0	0	2
onion & garlic — *2 Tbsp*	7	30	10	1	0	0	80	5	0	0	1	0	0	0	2
Arnold Stuffing															
cornbread — *2 cups*	67	250	35	4	1	0	800	49	2	3	9	0	0	4	15
sage & onion — *2 cups*	67	240	30	3	0.5	0	960	48	4	3	9	0	0	4	15
seasoned — *2 cups*	67	250	30	3	0.5	0	820	49	2	3	9	0	0	4	15
unspiced — *2 cups*	67	250	25	3	0.5	0	460	50	2	3	9	0	0	2	15
Brownberry Classic Croutons															
seasoned — *2 Tbsp*	7	30	10	1	0	0	70	4	0	0	<1	0	0	0	2
toasted — *2 Tbsp*	7	30	10	1	0	0	45	5	0	0	<1	0	0	0	2
Croutettes Stuffing Mix — *1 cup*	35	120	0	0	0	0	460	25	0	0	5	0	0	4	10
Hidden Valley Ranch Salad Crispins															
cheddar/onion or sour cream-herb — *1 Tbsp*	n/a	35	9	1	n/a	0	115	4	0	n/a	<1	0	0	0	0
italian parmesan — *1 Tbsp*	n/a	35	9	1	n/a	0	95	4	0	n/a	<1	0	0	0	0

	Weight g	Calories	Calories from fat	Total fat g	Sat. fat g	Cholesterol mg	Sodium mg	Carbohydrates g	Dietary fiber g	Sugars g	Protein g	Vitamin A % DV	Vitamin C % DV	Calcium % DV	Iron % DV
ranch — *1 Tbsp*	n/a	35	9	1	n/a	0	125	4	n/a	n/a	<1	n/a	n/a	n/a	n/a
Kelloggs Corn Flake Crumbs — *2 Tbsp*	11	40	0	0	0	0	120	9	0	1	1	0	8	0	15
Orowheat Traditional Stuffing															
cornbread — *2 cups*	67	250	35	3.5	0.5	0	800	51	2	4	8	0	0	2	15
herb seasoned — *1 cup*	55	200	25	2.5	0.5	0	630	41	3	4	7	4	0	4	20
Pepperidge Farm Croutons															
caesar homestyle — *6 croutons*	7	35	15	1.5	0	0	90	4	0	0	1	0	0	0	0
cracked pepper & parmesan — *6 croutons*	9	35	15	1.5	0	0	90	4	0	0	1	0	0	0	0
ranch — *9 croutons*	7	35	15	1.5	0.5	<5	65	4	0	<1	1	0	0	4	0
seasoned — *9 croutons*	7	35	10	1.5	0	0	85	4	0	0	1	0	0	0	0
Pepperidge Farm Distinctive Stuffing															
classic chicken — *½ cup*	34	130	15	1.5	0	0	490	24	3	3	5	0	10	4	10
country garden & herb — *½ cup*	34	150	10	5	1	0	360	22	2	4	4	0	0	4	10
honey pecan cornbread — *½ cup*	34	140	45	5	0.5	0	400	23	<1	5	3	15	6	2	6
wild rice & mushroom — *⅔ cup*	37	170	50	6	1.5	0	410	22	2	2	5	0	10	4	10
Pepperidge Farm Stuffing															
cornbread — *¾ cup*	43	170	20	2	0	0	480	33	2	2	4	0	0	4	10
herb seasoned — *¾ cup*	43	170	15	1.5	0	0	600	33	3	2	5	0	0	4	10
Progresso Bread Crumbs															
garlic & herb — *¼ cup*	28	100	15	1.5	0	0	530	18	1	1	4	0	0	4	8
italian-style — *¼ cup*	28	110	15	1.5	0	0	430	20	1	1	4	0	0	4	8
lemon-herb — *¼ cup*	27	100	10	1	0	0	480	20	2	2	3	0	0	4	4
parmesan — *¼ cup*	28	100	15	1.5	0	0	870	17	1	1	4	0	0	4	8
plain — *¼ cup*	28	110	15	1.5	0	0	210	19	1	1	4	0	0	4	8

	Weight g	Calories	Calories from fat	Total fat g	Sat. fat g	Cholesterol mg	Sodium mg	Carbohydrates g	Dietary fiber g	Sugars g	Protein g	Vitamin A % DV	Vitamin C % DV	Calcium % DV	Iron % DV
tomato basil — *¼ cup*	28	120	15	1.5	0	0	750	22	2	3	4	0	0	8	8
Rice-A-Roni Stuffing (unprepared)															
chicken w/ rice — *1oz*	28	101	9	1	<1	1	416	20	1	2	4	0	2	6	8
cornbread w/ rice — *1 oz*	28	101	0	<1	<1	<1	556	21	<1	2	3	0	0	2	8
herb & butter — *1 oz*	28	101	9	1	<1	1	401	20	1	2	3.5	6	3	6	8
wild rice — *1 oz*	28	102	9	1	<1	1	486	20	1	2	3	0	4	2	6

Turkey, Frozen

	Weight g	Calories	Calories from fat	Total fat g	Sat. fat g	Cholesterol mg	Sodium mg	Carbohydrates g	Dietary fiber g	Sugars g	Protein g	Vitamin A % DV	Vitamin C % DV	Calcium % DV	Iron % DV
Empire Kosher Turkey Patties, Battered & Breaded — *1 patty*	85	200	90	10	2	5	280	14	1	1	13	0	0	0	0
Louis Rich Breaded Turkey															
turkey nuggets — *4 nuggets*	92	260	150	16	3	35	640	15	0	0	13	0	0	0	4
turkey patties — *1 patty*	85	220	120	13	2.5	35	530	13	0	0	12	0	0	0	4
turkey sticks — *3 sticks*	85	230	130	15	3	35	580	12	0	0	12	0	0	0	4

Vegetable Products, Frozen

	Weight g	Calories	Calories from fat	Total fat g	Sat. fat g	Cholesterol mg	Sodium mg	Carbohydrates g	Dietary fiber g	Sugars g	Protein g	Vitamin A % DV	Vitamin C % DV	Calcium % DV	Iron % DV
Birds Eye International Recipe															
austrian-brand vegetables — *½ cup*	127	110	50	6	3	15	370	9	2	3	5	6	10	60	2
italian-style vegetables — *1 cup*	151	140	80	9	3.5	15	380	13	3	3	3	20	6	60	6
Birds Eye Pasta Secrets, Zesty Garlic — *1 cup*	n/a	240	90	10	2.5	5	310	31	2	6	7	35	25	15	6
Birds Eye Side Orders, Italian-Style Vegetables in Garlic Basil Sauce — *1 cup*	165	150	90	10	3	15	380	12	3	3	3	10	30	4	6
Empire Kosher															
french fried potatoes, crinkle cut — *17 pieces*	85	120	25	3	0	0	45	21	2	1	2	0	8	0	2
potato panckes/latkes — *1 latke*	58	80	20	2	1.5	0	200	15	8	0	1	0	0	0	8
zucchini, breaded — *7 pieces*	83	100	5	0.5	0	0	280	18	1	4	5	4	0	0	0
Green Giant															
broccoli in cheese-flavored sauce — *⅔ cup*	112	70	25	2.5	1	<5	520	9	2	5	3	20	70	6	4

	Weight g	Calories	Calories from fat	Total fat g	Sat. fat g	Cholesterol mg	Sodium mg	Carbohydrates g	Dietary fiber g	Sugars g	Protein g	Vitamin A % DV	Vitamin C % DV	Calcium % DV	Iron % DV
broccoli, cauliflower & carrots in cheese-flavored sauce — *2/3 cup*	122	80	25	2.5	1.5	<5	560	11	2	5	3	60	25	6	2
cauliflower in cheese-flavored sauce — *1/2 cup*	99	60	25	2.5	0.5	<5	510	8	2	4	2	20	30	6	0
corn, cream-style — *1/2 cup*	118	110	10	1	0	0	330	23	2	6	2	0	4	0	0
spinach, creamed — *1/2 cup*	109	80	25	3	1.5	0	520	10	2	4	4	30	25	10	4
Green Giant Create A Meal															
alfredo, creamy — *1 1/4 cup*	n/a	380	110	12	4.5	75	990	33	4	9	34	45	40	25	15
broccoli stir-fry — *1 1/3 cup*	n/a	290	120	13	3	60	1160	16	4	7	27	15	90	6	25
cheddar, creamy — *1 1/2 cup*	n/a	290	90	10	6	45	1470	29	4	8	20	60	60	20	10
cheese & herb primavera — *1 1/4 cup*	n/a	330	100	11	3.5	65	920	27	4	3	30	15	50	15	15
chicken noodle, creamy — *1 1/4 cup*	n/a	350	100	11	4.5	65	970	34	3	8	28	60	8	15	15
garlic herb — *1 1/4 cup*	n/a	340	130	14	6	145	670	30	4	4	24	50	40	15	25
hearty vegetable stew — *1 1/4 cup*	n/a	280	80	9	2	55	1000	25	3	5	23	60	25	4	20
lemon herb — *1 1/2 cup*	n/a	360	100	11	3.5	65	830	37	3	12	28	10	40	10	15
lo mein stir-fry — *1 1/4 cup*	n/a	320	60	7	1.5	60	980	35	4	9	30	30	30	6	10
mushrooms & wine — *1 1/4 cup*	n/a	390	140	16	6	75	910	31	4	5	28	40	10	4	25
sweet & sour stir-fry — *1 1/4 cup*	n/a	290	60	7	1	60	460	29	5	16	27	90	30	8	10
szechuan stir-fry — *1 1/4 cup*	n/a	340	140	15	3.5	60	1280	22	5	10	28	80	60	6	20
teriyaki stir-fry — *1 1/4 cup*	n/a	240	50	6	1	55	940	18	4	10	27	15	70	6	8
vegetable almond stir-fry — *1 1/3 cup*	n/a	320	100	11	1.5	65	1190	22	6	9	32	110	15	8	10
Green Giant Pasta Accents															
alfredo — *2 cups*	160	210	70	8	2.5	15	480	25	4	5	9	6	20	15	8
creamy cheddar — *2 1/3 cups*	190	250	70	8	3	15	700	36	5	6	9	80	10	15	8
florentine — *2 cups*	206	310	80	9	3	20	910	44	5	5	13	120	8	30	10
garden herb seasoning — *2 cups*	195	230	60	7	4	15	750	32	7	4	9	35	15	8	8

	Weight *g*	Calories	Calories from fat	Total fat *g*	Sat. fat *g*	Cholesterol *mg*	Sodium *mg*	Carbohydrates *g*	Dietary fiber *g*	Sugars *g*	Protein *g*	Vitamin A *% DV*	Vitamin C *% DV*	Calcium *% DV*	Iron *% DV*
garlic seasoning — *2 cups*	188	260	90	10	5	15	650	36	5	5	7	50	8	6	8
oriental-style — *1 cup*	n/a	270	90	10	4	20	600	37	4	7	8	60	40	8	10
primavera — *2 ¼ cups*	200	320	110	12	5	20	500	40	7	5	13	15	25	15	15
white cheddar sauce — *1 ¾ cups*	181	300	110	12	3.5	20	570	38	4	7	10	10	10	20	10
Lynden Farms Potatoes															
hash brown patties — *1 patty*	n/a	110	70	8	2.5	10	340	19	2	0	1	0	4	0	2
spuds w/ skins, 5/16 inch — *3 oz*	n/a	130	40	5	1.5	<5	60	20	2	0	2	0	4	0	4
taters — *9 taters*	n/a	150	60	7	2.5	5	300	20	2	0	2	0	15	0	2
Ore-Ida Onion Rings, Classic — *4 pieces*	86	220	110	12	2	0	510	26	2	<1	4	0	0	0	0
Ore-Ida Potatoes															
cheddar browns — *1 patty*	87	80	15	2	1	5	370	14	1	<1	3	0	6	4	4
Crispy Crunchies — *approx 12 fries*	85	160	70	8	1.5	0	310	20	2	<1	2	0	2	0	2
fast fries — *approx 23 fries*	85	150	60	6	1	0	330	20	2	<1	2	0	2	0	2
fast fries, ranch-flavor — *approx 22 fries*	85	150	60	7	1.5	0	430	21	1	<1	2	0	6	0	4
french fries, deep fries — *approx 22 fries*	85	160	70	7	1.5	0	20	22	2	<1	2	0	10	0	0
fries, golden — *approx 15 fries*	85	120	35	3.5	0.5	0	20	20	1	<1	2	0	0	0	0
homestyle potato wedges w/ skin — *approx 7 wedges*	85	110	30	3	0.5	0	15	19	2	<1	2	0	0	0	2
mashed potatoes — *⅔ cup*	69	90	20	2.5	0	<5	150	16	1	<1	2	4	8	0	0
Ore-Ida Potatoes, Frozen															
potatoes o'brien — *¾ cup*	89	60	0	0	0	0	20	15	2	<1	1	0	10	0	0
southern-style hash browns — *¾ cup*	87	80	0	0	0	0	30	17	2	<1	2	0	2	0	0
tater tots — *9 pieces*	85	160	70	8	1.5	0	300	21	2	<1	2	0	0	0	0
topped baked potato, broccoli & cheese — *½ baker*	159	150	35	4	2	10	410	25	2	5	6	8	25	10	6
twice-baked potato, butter flavor — *1 baker*	141	200	80	8	1.5	0	360	26	5	<1	4	6	10	4	4

	Weight g	Calories	Calories from fat	Total fat g	Sat. fat g	Cholesterol mg	Sodium mg	Carbohydrates g	Dietary fiber g	Sugars g	Protein g	Vitamin A % DV	Vitamin C % DV	Calcium % DV	Iron % DV
twice-baked potato, cheddar cheese — *1 baker*	141	190	70	8	2	<5	450	26	3	1	5	0	4	4	4
twice-baked potato, sour cream & chives — *1 baker*	141	190	60	7	1.5	0	360	27	3	<1	4	0	4	4	6

Waffles, Frozen

	Weight g	Calories	Calories from fat	Total fat g	Sat. fat g	Cholesterol mg	Sodium mg	Carbohydrates g	Dietary fiber g	Sugars g	Protein g	Vitamin A % DV	Vitamin C % DV	Calcium % DV	Iron % DV
Eggo															
blueberry — *2 waffles*	78	220	70	8	1.5	20	450	33	0	7	5	20	0	4	20
buttermilk — *2 waffles*	78	220	70	8	1.5	25	480	30	0	3	5	20	0	4	20
homestyle — *2 waffles*	78	220	70	8	1.5	25	470	30	0	3	5	20	0	4	20
Nut & Honey — *2 waffles*	78	240	90	10	2	25	480	32	0	7	6	20	2	4	20
Special K — *2 waffles*	58	140	0	0	0	0	250	29	0	5	6	20	0	4	20
Pillsbury Downyflake															
apple/cinnamon — *2 waffles*	71	190	50	6	1.5	0	490	30	<1	6	3	20	0	0	20
blueberry — *2 waffles*	71	190	50	6	1.5	0	490	30	<1	7	3	20	0	0	20
buttermilk — *2 waffles*	68	170	50	6	1.5	0	480	26	<1	3	3	20	0	2	20
Homestyle — *2 waffles*	68	170	50	6	1.5	0	490	26	<1	3	3	20	0	0	20
Homestyle, low-fat — *2 waffles*	71	170	20	2	0.5	0	340	34	2	3	4	20	0	0	20

Yogurt

	Weight g	Calories	Calories from fat	Total fat g	Sat. fat g	Cholesterol mg	Sodium mg	Carbohydrates g	Dietary fiber g	Sugars g	Protein g	Vitamin A % DV	Vitamin C % DV	Calcium % DV	Iron % DV
Breyers, low-fat, 1% milkfat															
blueberry — *8 oz*	227	250	25	2.5	1.5	15	110	48	0	48	8	0	0	30	0
mixed berry — *8 oz*	227	250	25	2.5	1.5	15	110	48	0	46	8	0	0	30	0
peach — *8 oz*	227	250	25	2.5	1.5	15	110	48	0	47	8	0	0	30	0
pineapple — *8 oz*	227	250	25	2.5	1.5	15	110	49	0	48	8	0	0	30	0
strawberry — *8 oz*	227	250	25	2.5	1.5	15	110	47	0	46	8	0	2	30	0
Breyers, low-fat, 1.5% milkfat															
coffee — *8 oz*	227	220	25	3	2	20	135	38	0	37	10	2	0	35	0

	Weight *g*	Calories	Calories from fat	Total fat *g*	Sat. fat *g*	Cholesterol *mg*	Sodium *mg*	Carbohydrates *g*	Dietary fiber *g*	Sugars *g*	Protein *g*	Vitamin A *% DV*	Vitamin C *% DV*	Calcium *% DV*	Iron *% DV*
creamy lemon — *8 oz*	227	220	25	3	2	20	140	38	0	37	10	2	0	35	0
plain — *8 oz*	227	130	30	3	2	20	150	15	0	15	11	2	0	40	0
vanilla — *8 oz*	227	220	25	3	2	20	135	38	0	38	10	2	0	35	0
Colombo Fat-Free															
banana/strawberry — *8 oz*	227	220	0	0	0	5	120	45	0	41	8	0	0	25	0
cappuccino, french roast, lemon, or vanilla — *8 oz*	227	170	0	0	0	5	140	32	0	29	9	0	0	30	0
fruited flavors — *8 oz*	227	220	0	0	0	5	120	41	0	36	8	0	0	25	0
Colombo Light (all flavors) — *8 oz*	227	100	0	0	0	<5	110	16	0	10	7	0	0	25	0
Dannon Chunky Fruit w/ Fruit Juice (nonfat)															
apple cinnamon — *6 oz*	170	160	0	0	0	5	100	33	0	29	7	0	4	20	0
blueberry — *6 oz*	170	160	0	0	0	5	110	32	0	29	7	0	4	20	0
cherry vanilla — *6 oz*	170	160	0	0	0	5	100	31	0	28	7	0	8	20	0
peach — *6 oz*	170	160	0	0	0	5	100	33	0	29	7	0	4	20	0
strawberry — *6 oz*	170	160	0	0	0	5	105	32	0	28	7	0	20	20	0
strawberry banana — *6 oz*	170	160	0	0	0	5	105	32	0	28	7	0	20	20	0
Dannon Double Delights Low-Fat w/ Choc. Topping, Choc.-Dipped — *6 oz*	170	210	10	1	0.5	10	150	45	0	41	8	0	0	25	4
Dannon Fruit on the Bottom (low-fat)															
apple cinnamon — *8 oz*	227	240	25	3	1.5	15	140	46	1	45	9	2	4	35	0
blueberry — *8 oz*	227	240	25	3	1.5	15	140	46	1	44	9	2	8	35	0
boysenberry — *8 oz*	227	240	25	3	1.5	15	150	45	1	42	9	2	6	35	0
cherry — *8 oz*	227	240	25	3	1.5	15	135	46	1	44	9	4	10	35	0
mixed berries — *8 oz*	227	240	25	3	1.5	15	150	45	1	43	9	2	10	35	0
orange — *8 oz*	227	240	25	3	1.5	15	135	45	0	44	9	2	25	35	0
peach — *8 oz*	227	240	25	3	1.5	15	140	45	1	44	9	2	4	35	0

	Weight *g*	Calories	Calories from fat	Total fat *g*	Sat. fat *g*	Cholesterol *mg*	Sodium *mg*	Carbohydrates *g*	Dietary fiber *g*	Sugars *g*	Protein *g*	Vitamin A *% DV*	Vitamin C *% DV*	Calcium *% DV*	Iron *% DV*
raspberry — *8 oz*	227	240	25	3	1.5	15	150	45	1	43	9	2	10	35	0
strawberry — *8 oz*	227	240	25	3	1.5	15	135	46	1	44	9	2	20	35	0
strawberry-banana — *8 oz*	227	240	25	3	1.5	15	140	43	1	40	9	2	25	35	0
Dannon Light 'n Crunchy (nonfat)															
caramel apple crunch — *8 oz*	227	140	0	0	0	5	160	26	0	14	8	0	0	25	4
chocolate eclair or chocolate cheesecake — *6 oz*	227	220	10	1	0.5	10	150	45	0	42	8	0	0	25	4
lemon blueberry cobbler — *8 oz*	227	140	0	0	0	5	135	25	0	17	8	0	0	25	4
mint chocolate chip — *8 oz*	227	140	0	0	0	5	150	27	0	14	8	0	0	25	4
mocha cappuccino — *8 oz*	227	140	0	0	0	5	150	26	0	14	8	0	0	25	4
raspberry w/ granola — *8 oz*	227	140	0	0	0	5	120	26	2	13	9	0	4	25	4
vanilla chocolate crunch — *8 oz*	227	130	0	0	0	5	140	23	0	13	8	0	0	25	4
Dannon Light (nonfat)															
banana cream pie, creme caramel, or tangerine chiffon — *8 oz*	227	100	0	0	0	5	120	15	0	9	8	0	0	25	0
blueberry — *8oz.*	227	100	0	0	0	5	115	18	0	12	8	0	0	25	0
capuccino — *8 oz*	227	100	0	0	0	5	120	16	0	9	8	0	0	25	0
cherry vanilla — *8 oz.*	227	100	0	0	0	5	115	18	0	11	8	0	0	25	0
coconut cream pie — *8 oz*	227	100	0	0	0	5	120	16	0	9	8	0	0	25	0
lemon chiffon — *8 oz*	227	100	0	0	0	5	120	15	0	9	8	0	0	25	0
mint chocolate cream pie — *8 oz*	227	100	0	0	0	5	120	17	0	9	8	0	0	25	0
peach — *8 oz*	227	100	0	0	0	5	120	16	0	11	8	0	0	25	0
raspberry — *8 oz*	227	100	0	0	0	5	115	17	0	10	8	0	8	25	0
strawberry — *8 oz*	227	100	0	0	0	5	115	17	0	10	8	0	20	25	0
strawberry/kiwi — *8 oz*	227	100	0	0	0	5	120	16	0	10	8	0	15	25	0
strawberry/banana — *8 oz*	227	100	0	0	0	5	120	17	0	11	8	0	6	25	0

	Weight g	Calories	Calories from fat	Total fat g	Sat. fat g	Cholesterol mg	Sodium mg	Carbohydrates g	Dietary fiber g	Sugars g	Protein g	Vitamin A % DV	Vitamin C % DV	Calcium % DV	Iron % DV
vanilla — *8 oz*	227	100	0	0	0	5	120	15	0	9	8	0	0	25	0
Dannon Low-Fat															
lemon or cranberry-raspberry — *8 oz*	227	210	30	3	2	15	160	36	0	35	10	4	4	40	0
plain — *8 oz*	227	140	30	4	2	20	150	16	0	16	12	4	4	35	0
vanilla or coffee — *8 oz*	227	210	30	3	2	15	160	36	0	34	10	4	4	40	0
Dannon Nonfat, Plain — *8 oz*	227	110	0	0	0	5	150	16	0	16	12	0	4	35	0
Knudsen Cal 70 (nonfat)															
blueberry — *6 oz*	170	70	0	0	0	5	80	12	0	8	7	0	0	20	0
peach — *6 oz*	170	70	0	0	0	5	80	11	<1	9	7	0	0	20	0
strawberry — *6 oz*	170	70	0	0	0	5	85	11	0	8	7	0	0	20	0
strawberry banana — *6 oz*	170	70	0	0	0	5	85	11	0	8	7	0	0	20	0
vanilla — *6 oz*	170	70	0	0	0	5	80	11	0	8	7	0	0	20	0
Knudsen Free (nonfat)															
mixed berry — *6 oz*	170	170	0	0	0	5	105	33	0	29	8	0	0	25	0
red raspberry — *6 oz*	170	160	0	0	0	5	105	31	0	28	8	0	0	25	0
strawberry — *6 oz*	170	160	0	0	0	5	105	32	0	30	8	0	0	25	0
vanilla — *6 oz*	170	170	0	0	0	5	100	32	0	29	8	0	0	25	0
Light n' Lively Free (nonfat)															
blueberry — *6 oz*	170	190	0	0	0	5	105	38	0	33	8	0	0	30	0
mixed berry — *6 oz*	170	170	0	0	0	5	105	34	0	31	8	0	0	25	0
strawberry — *6 oz*	170	180	0	0	0	5	105	36	0	33	8	0	0	30	0
vanilla — *6 oz*	170	160	0	0	0	5	105	32	0	29	8	0	0	25	0
Light n' Lively Free 50 Calories															
blueberry or red raspberry — *4.4 oz*	125	50	0	0	0	<5	60	8	0	6	5	0	0	15	0

	Weight g	Calories	Calories from fat	Total fat g	Sat. fat g	Cholesterol mg	Sodium mg	Carbohydrates g	Dietary fiber g	Sugars g	Protein g	Vitamin A % DV	Vitamin C % DV	Calcium % DV	Iron % DV
strawberry banana — *4.4 oz*	125	50	0	0	0	<5	60	8	0	6	5	0	0	15	0
Light n' Lively Free 70 Calories															
blueberry — *6 oz*	170	70	0	0	0	<5	80	11	0	8	7	0	0	20	0
lemon — *6 oz*	170	70	0	0	0	<5	120	12	0	8	7	0	0	20	0
red raspberry — *6 oz*	170	70	0	0	0	<5	80	11	0	8	7	0	0	20	0
strawberry — *6 oz*	170	70	0	0	0	<5	85	11	0	8	7	0	0	20	0
strawberry banana — *6 oz*	170	70	0	0	0	<5	85	11	0	8	7	0	0	20	0
Light n' Lively Kidpack (low-fat)															
berry blue — *4.4 oz*	125	150	10	1	0.5	10	65	30	0	26	5	0	0	15	0
grape — *4.4 oz*	125	130	10	1	1	10	65	24	0	21	5	0	0	15	0
tropical punch — *4.4 oz*	125	140	10	1	0.5	10	65	27	0	24	5	0	0	15	0
wild stawberry — *4.4 oz*	125	140	10	1	0.5	10	65	28	0	25	5	0	0	15	0
Weight Watchers, Nonfat															
blueberries 'n creme — *1 cup*	227	90	0	0	0	5	140	14	3	9	8	0	0	25	0
cappuccino — *1 cup*	227	90	0	0	0	5	140	14	0	7	8	0	0	25	0
lemon chiffon — *1 cup*	227	90	0	0	0	5	140	14	1	7	8	0	0	25	0
plain — *1 cup*	227	90	0	0	0	5	150	14	0	8	8	0	0	30	0
strawberry — *1 cup*	227	90	0	0	0	5	140	14	2	7	8	0	0	25	0
vanilla — *1 cup*	227	90	0	0	0	5	140	14	0	7	8	0	0	25	0
Yoplait Crunch 'n Yogurt Light															
cherry cheesecake w/ graham crunch — *7 oz*	199	130	15	1.5	0	<5	115	23	0	13	7	0	0	25	0
lemon creme — *7 oz*	199	140	20	2	0	<5	135	22	0	12	7	0	0	25	0
strawberry yogurt w/ granola — *7 oz*	199	140	15	1.5	0	<5	115	25	2	13	8	0	0	25	0
vanilla yogurt w/ chocolate crunchies — *7 oz*	199	140	20	2	0	<5	150	22	0	13	8	0	0	20	0

	Weight g	Calories	Calories from fat	Total fat g	Sat. fat g	Cholesterol mg	Sodium mg	Carbohydrates g	Dietary fiber g	Sugars g	Protein g	Vitamin A % DV	Vitamin C % DV	Calcium % DV	Iron % DV
Yoplait Custard-Style															
all fruit flavors — *6 oz*	170	190	30	3	2	15	100	32	0	30	8	0	0	20	0
vanilla — *6 oz*	170	190	30	3	2	15	95	32	0	29	8	0	0	20	0
Yoplait Light															
banana cream pie, caramel apple, lemon cream pie, or key lime pie — *6 oz*	170	90	0	0	0	5	95	16	0	10	6	0	0	20	0
cherry vanilla custard, peach custard, vanilla custard — *6 oz*	170	90	0	0	0	<5	95	15	0	9	6	0	0	20	0
fruit flavors — *6 oz*	170	90	0	0	0	5	75	16	0	10	5	0	0	20	0
Yoplait Original															
99% fat-free (all fruit flavors except coconut) — *6 oz*	170	180	15	1.5	1	10	125	33	0	30	7	0	0	20	0
café au lait — *6 oz*	170	170	15	2	1	10	90	31	0	28	8	0	0	20	0
coconut cream pie — *6 oz*	170	200	25	3	2	19	125	35	0	31	7	0	0	20	0
Yoplait Original Non Fat															
plain — *8 oz*	227	130	0	0	0	10	170	19	0	14	13	0	0	45	0
vanilla — *8 oz*	227	200	0	0	0	5	160	40	0	32	10	0	0	35	0
Yoplait Trix Yogurt, All Fruit Flavors — *6 oz*	170	160	15	2	1	5	95	28	0	24	7	0	0	20	0
Yoplait, Fat-Free Fruit-on-the-Bottom, All Fruit Flavors — *6 oz*	170	160	0	0	0	<5	95	34	0	30	7	0	0	20	0

Yogurt: Frozen

	Weight g	Calories	Calories from fat	Total fat g	Sat. fat g	Cholesterol mg	Sodium mg	Carbohydrates g	Dietary fiber g	Sugars g	Protein g	Vitamin A % DV	Vitamin C % DV	Calcium % DV	Iron % DV
Ben & Jerry's															
black raspberry swirl, no fat — *½ cup*	n/a	140	0	0	0	0	55	32	0	28	3	2	6	10	0
cappuccino, no fat — *½ cup*	n/a	140	0	0	0	0	85	32	0	23	3	2	0	10	0
Cherry Garcia — *½ cup*	n/a	170	25	3	2	5	70	30	0	29	3	4	0	10	2
chocolate chip cookie dough — *½ cup*	n/a	210	35	3.5	2.5	10	110	39	<1	30	5	4	0	15	4
chocolate fudge brownie — *½ cup*	n/a	180	20	2	1	5	115	34	2	32	6	2	0	10	8
chocolate fudge, no fat — *½ cup*	n/a	140	0	0	0	0	55	31	1	27	4	2	0	10	0

	Weight *g*	Calories	Calories from fat	Total fat *g*	Sat. fat *g*	Cholesterol *mg*	Sodium *mg*	Carbohydrates *g*	Dietary fiber *g*	Sugars *g*	Protein *g*	Vitamin A *% DV*	Vitamin C *% DV*	Calcium *% DV*	Iron *% DV*
chocolate, no fat — *½ cup*	n/a	130	0	0	0	0	50	29	1	24	3	2	0	10	0
coffee almond fudge — *½ cup*	n/a	200	45	5	1	5	75	30	1	28	5	4	0	10	4
coffee fudge, no fat — *½ cup*	n/a	140	0	0	0	0	55	31	<1	27	4	2	0	10	0
vanilla fudge swirl, no fat — *½ cup*	n/a	150	0	0	0	5	80	32	0	24	3	2	0	10	2
vanilla w/ Heath Toffee Crunch — *½ cup*	n/a	190	50	6	2.5	10	115	32	0	32	3	4	0	10	0
Breyers Cup, Chocolate Chip — *1 serving*	n/a	230	45	5	4	15	125	38	n/a	32	n/a	n/a	n/a	n/a	n/a
Breyers Fat-Free															
cappuccino — *½ cup*	n/a	100	0	0	0	0	45	22	n/a	16	n/a	n/a	n/a	n/a	n/a
caramel praline crunch — *½ cup*	n/a	120	0	0	0	0	70	27	n/a	19	n/a	n/a	n/a	n/a	n/a
chocolate — *½ cup*	n/a	100	0	0	0	0	40	23	n/a	17	n/a	n/a	n/a	n/a	n/a
cookies in cream — *½ cup*	n/a	110	0	0	0	<5	80	25	n/a	15	n/a	n/a	n/a	n/a	n/a
vanilla — *½ cup*	n/a	100	0	0	0	<5	50	21	n/a	14	n/a	n/a	n/a	n/a	n/a
vanilla/chocolate/strawberry — *½ cup*	n/a	100	0	0	0	0	40	22	n/a	15	n/a	n/a	n/a	n/a	n/a
Breyers Low-Fat															
chocolate — *½ cup*	n/a	130	25	2.5	2	10	40	24	n/a	17	n/a	n/a	n/a	n/a	n/a
chocolate chip cookie dough — *½ cup*	n/a	150	25	3	2	10	40	27	n/a	19	n/a	n/a	n/a	n/a	n/a
french vanilla — *½ cup*	n/a	110	15	1.5	1	35	45	21	n/a	5	n/a	n/a	n/a	n/a	n/a
mint chocolate chip — *½ cup*	n/a	140	25	3	1.5	5	40	26	n/a	21	n/a	n/a	n/a	n/a	n/a
strawberry — *½ cup*	n/a	120	20	2.5	1.5	10	35	23	n/a	18	n/a	n/a	n/a	n/a	n/a
Toffee Bar Crunch — *½ cup*	n/a	140	25	3	1.5	10	50	26	n/a	17	n/a	n/a	n/a	n/a	n/a
vanilla — *½ cup*	n/a	130	25	2.5	1.5	10	45	23	n/a	18	n/a	n/a	n/a	n/a	n/a
Colombo Cooler, All Flavors — *½ cup*	n/a	60	0	0	0	10	170	19	0	14	13	0	0	10	0
Colombo Low-Fat															
chocolate, Old World — *½ cup*	n/a	110	15	2	1	10	65	22	1	17	3	0	0	10	0

	Weight *g*	Calories	Calories from fat	Total fat *g*	Sat. fat *g*	Cholesterol *mg*	Sodium *mg*	Carbohydrates *g*	Dietary fiber *g*	Sugars *g*	Protein *g*	Vitamin A *% DV*	Vitamin C *% DV*	Calcium *% DV*	Iron *% DV*
peanut butter — *½ cup*	n/a	120	25	2.5	0.5	<5	75	20	0	16	4	0	0	10	0
vanilla/fruit flavors — *½ cup*	n/a	110	15	1.5	1	10	55	21	0	16	3	0	0	10	0
Colombo Nonfat															
butter nut toffee & butter pecan — *½ cup*	n/a	100	0	0	0	<5	140	20	0	16	3	0	0	10	0
german chocolate fudge — *½ cup*	n/a	110	0	0	0	<5	60	23	1	16	4	0	0	10	0
vanilla — *½ cup*	n/a	100	0	0	0	<5	60	22	0	17	3	0	0	10	0
Colombo Slender Sensations															
chocolate — *½ cup*	n/a	70	0	0	0	<5	70	11	0	8	4	0	0	10	0
vanilla/fruit flavors — *½ cup*	n/a	60	0	0	0	<5	60	11	0	8	4	0	0	10	0
Dannon Fat-Free															
blueberry pie — *4 oz*	113	100	0	0	0	0	55	21	0	16	3	2	0	10	0
capuccino — *4 oz*	113	100	0	0	0	0	55	20	0	16	3	2	0	10	0
chocolate — *4 oz*	113	100	0	0	0	0	50	22	1	19	3	0	0	10	0
strawberry or vanilla — *4 oz*	113	100	0	0	0	0	60	20	0	16	3	2	0	10	0
Dannon Light 'n Crunchy															
banana cream pie — *½ cup*	79	110	10	1	0	0	65	23	0	11	3	0	0	10	0
caramel toffee crunch — *½ cup*	79	110	10	1	0.5	0	75	26	0	13	3	0	0	10	0
mocha chocolate chunk — *½ cup*	79	110	10	1	1	0	60	23	0	9	4	0	0	10	0
peanut chocolate crunch — *½ cup*	79	110	10	1	0.5	0	65	24	0	11	4	0	0	10	0
rocky road — *½ cup*	79	110	5	0.5	0	0	60	27	<1	12	3	0	0	10	0
triple chocolate frozen yogurt — *½ cup*	79	110	10	1	1	0	60	25	<1	11	4	0	0	10	2
vanilla streusel — *½ cup*	79	110	10	1	0.5	0	80	25	0	11	3	0	0	10	0
Häagen-Dazs															
cherry vanilla — *½ cup*	93	140	0	0	0	<5	40	30	0	19	6	2	2	15	0

Foods, Brand Name

	Weight *g*	Calories	Calories from fat	Total fat *g*	Sat. fat *g*	Cholesterol *mg*	Sodium *mg*	Carbohydrates *g*	Dietary fiber *g*	Sugars *g*	Protein *g*	Vitamin A *% DV*	Vitamin C *% DV*	Calcium *% DV*	Iron *% DV*
chocolate — ½ *cup*	93	140	0	0	0	<5	45	28	<1	17	6	0	0	20	4
coffee — ½ *cup*	93	140	0	0	0	<5	45	29	0	17	6	0	0	20	0
vanilla — ½ *cup*	93	140	0	0	0	<5	45	29	0	17	6	0	0	20	0
vanilla fudge — ½ *cup*	93	160	0	0	0	<5	100	34	0	22	6	0	0	15	0
vanilla raspberry swirl — ½ *cup*	96	130	0	0	0	<5	30	28	0	19	4	0	0	10	0

Index

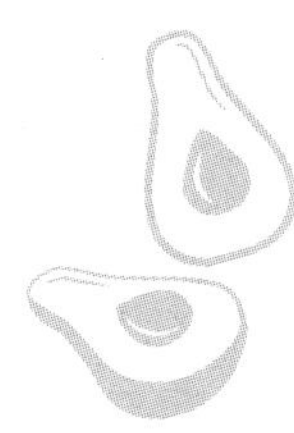

A

B

Index

Index

Index

C

Index

(*Chicken, continued*)

Index

Index

Index

D

Index

E

F

Index

G

H

I

J

K

L

Index

Index

M

Index

Index

Index

N

Index

O

P

Index

Index

Q

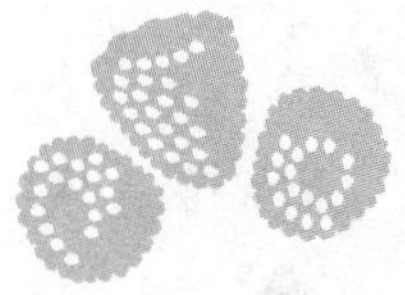

R

Index

S

T

Index

Index

U

V

Index

W

Y

Z

THE UNIVERSITY OF CALIFORNIA
LET THERE BE LIGHT
1868